Microsoft

Microsoft Copilot Studio Step by Step: Customizing Copilot and creating agents

Lisa Crosbie

Microsoft Copilot Studio Step by Step
Published with the authorization of Microsoft Corporation by:
Pearson Education, Inc.

ISBN-13: 978-0-13-549150-8
ISBN-10: 0-13-549150-9

Library of Congress Control Number: On File

4 2026

Trademarks
Microsoft and the trademarks listed at http://www.microsoft.com on the
"Trademarks" webpage are trademarks of the Microsoft group of companies.
All other marks are property of their respective owners.

Warning and Disclaimer
Every effort has been made to make this book as complete and as accurate as
possible, but no warranty or fitness is implied. The information provided is on
an "as is" basis. The author, the publisher, and Microsoft Corporation shall have
neither liability nor responsibility to any person or entity with respect to any loss
or damages arising from the information contained in this book or from the use of
the programs accompanying it.

Cover Credit: BonkersArt/stock.adobe.com

Editor-in-Chief
Julie Phifer

Portfolio Manager
Loretta Yates

Acquisitions Editor
Shourav Bose

Development Editor
Songlin Qiu

Managing Editor
Sandra Schroeder

Production Editor
Mary Roth

Copy Editor
Jill Hobbs

Technical Editor
Thomas Palathra

Indexer
Timothy Wright

Proofreader
Donna E. Mulder

Cover Designer
Chuti Prasertsith

Compositor
codeMantra

Contents

2   Designing effective agents 29

6   Grounding agents in knowledge................................169

7 Authoring topics **233**

8   Extending agents with tools **317**

9   Designing multi-agent orchestration **391**

10 Publishing and authenticating agents 413

11 Monitoring agent performance 441

12 Working with voice and customer engagement systems 465

13 Extending Copilot Studio agents with Azure AI 493

Foreword

We are living through a remarkable moment in the history of work. True intelligence, once limited to humans, is now able available on demand as a service with artificial intelligence (AI). Across industries, AI is matching or even surpassing human performance in key areas, signaling a fundamental shift in how work gets done.

This transformation is not just about work being done more efficiently or at greater scale, it is about truly reimagining how work itself flows and the role of people in it. Leaders are rethinking operating models. Individuals are learning new tools and experimenting with new ways to create. It is a top-down and bottom-up movement that is reshaping work culture as much as it is changing technology.

For most of the digital era, people have navigated through various applications and browser tabs to get to the digital spaces where they do work. Workflow and data silos between apps required constant context switching to stay productive. These patterns were designed for a different age, one that required humans to know where the work was and how to get there. The next era is different. Now, work comes to you. Intelligent systems bring together context, collaboration, actions, and tasks in one unified experience. They meet you where you are, anticipate your needs, and help you stay in flow.

Platforms like **Copilot Studio** are central to this shift. They enable professional makers and IT administrators to create AI-powered solutions, including agents and agentic workflows, that shift more of a company's work and operations into the digital layer. Soon, most of the functions and operations of a company will be managed via these intelligent agents. This is a revolution in how companies become more productive, with leaders driving top-down transformation across the enterprise and employees building and engaging with agents across all their workflows from the bottom up.

Thriving in this new environment requires new skills. Everyone must learn to delegate to AI agents effectively, defining objectives and constraints clearly so the agent can act with purpose and get the feedback and iterations it needs to succeed. This is a new skill for many people. We also need to become great at building evaluations, to regularly measure that agents are reasoning correctly and delivering reliable results. And we must learn how to tune and improve these systems over time, so that performance grows with experience. Organizations that continue to prioritize and reward traditional skills over emerging ones will lose momentum. Those that invest in these new capabilities will gain a lasting advantage, combining human judgment with machine intelligence to achieve more than either could alone.

Across industries, three clear patterns of AI adoption are emerging. Enabling you to build these types of agents is what Copilot Studio is all about.

- The first is real-time collaboration, where people and intelligent agents work together in the flow of daily productivity. These agents respond in seconds, expanding human capability and freeing us to focus on creativity and judgment.

- The second is delegation. Instead of completing every step ourselves, we assign meaningful tasks to agents that can plan, execute, ask questions, and return with results for review.

- The third pattern is trigger-based automation, where agents operate independently within trusted guardrails such as budgets, service levels, or customer satisfaction thresholds. These autonomous systems only seek human input when they encounter exceptions. In these moments, the person who designed the system becomes the one who fixes it.

Each of these patterns unlocks new layers of productivity, especially in the autonomous stage where efficiency gains are steep. But the transition requires intention. Teams must often slow down to speed up, taking the time to change their habits and learn to do their work in new, AI-first ways by building and using agents. The pace of AI-first work is more iterative, collaborative, and dynamic than what came before, requiring teams to meet more frequently. The pace and rhythm of collaboration is changing.

In this fast-moving landscape, there is a growing knowledge gap. Many people are eager to build with AI but lack the conceptual foundation to do so confidently. They know what these tools can do but not why they work the way they do or how to design with them effectively. *That is why this book matters.* Lisa Crosbie has written a guide that bridges that gap. It provides enduring principles that stay relevant even as technology evolves. It explains the reasoning behind each capability in Copilot Studio, not just the steps to use it. It gives readers a structured path from curiosity to mastery. Lisa's work will help low-code makers and IT professionals develop the design mindset and skills required to succeed in this new era of work.

What is covered in these pages will be critical for those responsible for guiding their company's operations and technology adoption. They are essential for participating

in the future economy and shaping an AI-first workplace, and the learnings apply across platforms. As work becomes more intelligent and personalized, the ability to design, evaluate, and collaborate with agents will define digital fluency itself.
We are entering a world where people and intelligent systems work side by side, each learning from the other.

This book is a guide to that future. I'm excited that you have picked it up and I hope that you find it useful on your journey to building agents with AI. Here's to the future!

Dan Lewis
Corporate Vice President
Microsoft Copilot Studio

Acknowledgments

Writing a book on cutting-edge technology could be seen as a ridiculous undertaking, especially when layered on top of full-time work, travel, family life, and everything else that fills the days. This book has been a passion project from the start, and there is nothing like an audacious goal and a deadline on the calendar to make things happen.

My sincere thanks to the wonderful publishing and editorial team at Pearson who made all this possible. It was a pleasure to work again with Loretta Yates and Shourav Bose, who guided me through all the decisions and processes, and Songlin Qiu, whose eye for detail and consistency is truly admirable. To the wonderful production, project management, and editorial team—Mary Roth, Jayaprakash P ("JP"), and Jill Hobbs, thank you for the final polish and for bringing everything together so smoothly.

I'm grateful for the encouragement of my family, friends, and colleagues, who have patiently listened to me talk about nothing but writing this book for months. I'm looking forward to getting back to other topics soon!

I could not have done this without the incredible support of my husband, David Barnes, who keeps our life in working order while I travel the world speaking at conferences and spend weekends creating content. Thank you for understanding and supporting what drives me. With love to my mum, who has always believed in me, and to my incredibly smart and beautiful ("super-duper awesome") daughters Steph and Bridge—your brilliance and creativity will take you wherever you want to go.

This book is dedicated to my dad, Jeff Crosbie, who introduced me to technology back when the Commodore 64 was cutting edge, coding from magazine articles and spending hours playing text-based adventure games together. Your love of technology and reading will always be with me, and is captured in this book.

Finally, this book is for the incredible community of people who show up every day with curious minds to learn, share, and push boundaries with their innovative and creative thinking. You build solutions that change the way your organizations work. I hope this book is a worthwhile contribution to your learning journey.

About the author

Lisa Crosbie is a globally recognized thought leader in Microsoft Copilot Studio, AI-powered productivity, and low-code development. A six-time Microsoft Most Valuable Professional (MVP), YouTuber, published author, and international speaker, Lisa is known for making complex technology accessible, engaging, and actionable. Her popular YouTube channel has reached millions of viewers around the world with tutorials that help people learn Microsoft 365 Copilot, Copilot Studio, and the Power Platform.

Passionate about empowering beginners, Lisa focuses on breaking down barriers to technology adoption and helping people take their first steps with confidence. She shares her knowledge with the global community, inspiring others to explore, experiment, and understand what's possible with AI and low-code solutions. In her work with enterprises and her collaborations with Microsoft product teams, Lisa stays at the cutting edge of technology, translating new advancements into practical applications that solve real-world challenges and transform the way organizations work.

Introduction

Microsoft Copilot Studio is an agent-building platform that enables low-code makers to build agents that transform business processes. It allows you to design agents for internal scenarios, extending Microsoft 365 Copilot to provide employees with a natural language chat experience for accessing information and performing tasks by interacting with other line-of-business systems. You can also use Copilot Studio to build externally facing agents to enable and scale customer self-service, or to create autonomous agents that use AI to reimagine business process automation. Copilot Studio is part of Microsoft's Power Platform and includes built-in controls for governance, management, data security, and responsible AI.

In this book, you'll learn how to build agents with Copilot Studio, explore practical use cases, and gain a deep understanding of when, why, and how to apply this technology to solve real-world problems in your organization.

Who this book is for

Microsoft Copilot Studio Step by Step is for anyone who is interested in building AI-powered agents using low code—whether you're a business user, a low-code maker, or a professional developer. If you're already familiar with Power Platform and want to expand your skills, this book builds on your existing knowledge, guiding you through the concepts and hands-on steps needed to become an agent builder. If you're new to Power Platform, it serves as your introduction to becoming a low-code maker, with links provided for deeper learning about the broader platform capabilities.

This book is also suitable for solution architects, consultants, and IT professionals who are exploring how Copilot Studio can be used to improve internal processes or deliver customer-facing agent solutions. No prior experience with AI or coding is required, but familiarity with Microsoft 365, Power Platform, or business process automation will help you get the most out of the content.

The *Step by Step* approach

This book is divided into four parts.

- **Part 1** outlines the core concepts of Microsoft Copilot Studio, agent terminology and architecture, and the principles of effective agent design.

- **Part 2** covers in detail the practical skills you need to build agents. Dedicated chapters cover different types of agents (e.g., the Copilot Studio lite experience for business users, autonomous agents, and multi-agent orchestration) as well as each of the main building blocks for building agents in Copilot Studio (i.e., knowledge, topics, and tools). These chapters can also serve as an ongoing reference as you practice and develop your skills with this platform.

- **Part 3** demonstrates how to publish your agent to internal or external channels and monitor its performance.

- **Part 4** explores the extensibility of Copilot Studio agents, showing how they work with voice and customer engagement systems and how you can bring your own data and models to Copilot Studio from Azure AI. The chapters in this part are designed for readers who already have experience in these technologies and want to learn how to expand their solutions with Copilot Studio agents.

At the end of each chapter, you will find a series of practice tasks that you can complete on your own by using the skills taught in the chapter. At the end of the book, Appendices A and B provide two full-length practice tasks, which take you through building an internal agent and an external-facing agent, bringing together all the skills you have learned throughout the book.

Features and conventions

This book is designed to lead you step by step through all the tasks you're likely to need as a low-code maker building agents with Copilot Studio. The topics are structured in a logical order to build your knowledge and skills in an incremental manner. To some extent, the later chapters depend on knowledge from the earlier chapters, so the content is best consumed in sequence.

The following features of this book will help you locate specific information:

- **Detailed table of contents** Browse the listing of the topics, sections, and sidebars within each chapter.

- **Chapter thumb tabs and running heads** Identify the pages of each chapter by the thumb tabs on the book pages' open fore edge. Find a specific chapter by number or title by looking at the running heads at the top of even-numbered (verso) pages.

- **Topic-specific running heads** Within a chapter, quickly locate the topic you want by looking at the running heads at the top of odd-numbered (recto) pages.

- **Practice tasks page tabs** Easily locate the practice tasks at the end of each chapter by looking for the full-page stripe on the book's fore edge.

- **Detailed index** Look up coverage of specific tasks and features in the index at the back of the book.

You can save time when reading this book by understanding how the *Step by Step* series provides procedural instructions and auxiliary information and identifies on-screen and physical elements that you interact with. The following table lists the content formatting conventions used in this book.

Convention	Meaning
TIP	This reader aid provides a helpful hint or shortcut to simplify a task.
IMPORTANT	This reader aid alerts you to a common problem or provides information necessary to successfully complete a procedure.
SEE ALSO	This reader aid directs you to more information about a topic in this book or elsewhere.
1. Numbered steps 2. 3.	Numbered steps guide you through generic procedures in each topic and hands-on practice tasks at the end of each chapter.
■ Bulleted lists	Bulleted lists indicate single-step procedures and sets of multiple alternative procedures.

Convention	Meaning
Interface objects	In procedures and practice tasks, semibold black text indicates on-screen elements that you should select (click or tap).
User input	Light semibold formatting identifies specific information that you should enter when completing procedures or practice tasks.
Ctrl+P	A plus sign between two keys indicates that you must select those keys at the same time. For example, "press **Ctrl+P**" directs you to hold down the **Ctrl** key while you press the **P** key.
Emphasis and *URLs*	In expository text, italic formatting identifies web addresses and words or phrases we want to emphasize.

Download the practice files

Before you can complete the examples and practice tasks in this book, you need to download the book's practice files to your computer. These practice files, and other resources, can be downloaded from the following page:

MicrosoftPressStore.com/copilotstudio/downloads

> ⚠ **IMPORTANT** Copilot Studio is a paid subscription, which is not available from this website. You can work through the examples and practice tasks in this book using a free trial, but to publish agents for production use you will need to pay for message consumption.

The following table lists the practice files for this book.

Chapter	File
Chapter 7: Authoring topics	AdaptiveCardJSON.json

Important note about changes to Copilot Studio

Generative AI tools are evolving rapidly, and Copilot Studio is a core investment area for Microsoft, with frequent updates and new features being added on a regular basis. The content and examples in this book are designed to focus on the principles of "why to" as well as "how to." So, even if the user interface changes slightly from the screenshots shown in this book, you will still be able to follow along and apply what you've learned.

We will do our best to keep this content up-to-date in subsequent editions of the book. Throughout the book, you will find links to Microsoft's official documentation, where you can check for the latest changes and updates relevant to each section. You can also find full-length tutorials and feature updates on my YouTube channel at *www.youtube.com/lisacrosbie.*

Errata, updates, and support

We've made every effort to ensure the accuracy of this book and its companion content. Any errors that have been reported since this book was published are listed at:

MicrosoftPressStore.com/copilotstudio/errata

If you discover an error that is not already listed, please submit it to us at the same page.

For additional book support and information, please visit *MicrosoftPressStore.com/support.*

Please note that product support for Microsoft software and hardware is not offered through the previous addresses. For help with Microsoft software or hardware, visit *support.microsoft.com.*

Understanding Copilot Studio and agents

Practice files

No practice files are necessary to complete the practice tasks in this chapter.

Microsoft Copilot Studio is a low-code platform for building AI-powered agents. You can use it to build stand-alone agents to transform business processes, extend Microsoft 365 Copilot with new skills and connections, or build custom agent solutions. Agents can be internal facing, designed to improve employee experience, or external facing, to enable customer self-service at scale.

With Copilot Studio, you can build a range of agents—from simple retrieval agents that can answer questions based on your business data, to fully autonomous agents that can reason, make decisions, and carry out tasks independently. You can also build multi-agent systems where agents specialize in one specific process or domain and hand off tasks to other specialized agents as needed.

In this chapter, you will learn what agents are and what they can do. You will also learn about the capabilities of Copilot Studio and see how it fits within Microsoft's broader agent-building toolset. Along the way, you will sign up for a trial environment for hands-on learning, build your first agent using a natural language

In this chapter

- Get started with Copilot Studio
- Understand the capabilities of Copilot Studio
- Explore use cases for Copilot Studio agents

conversational interface, and learn how to identify and assess the value of use cases for Copilot Studio agents.

Get started with Copilot Studio

Copilot Studio is a full end-to-end Software-as-a-Service (SaaS) platform with no infrastructure to deploy or maintain, and no models to train. When you build an agent in Copilot Studio, it is instantly live and ready to use. Copilot Studio is built on Microsoft's Responsible AI platform, so it includes built-in controls for management, governance, regulatory compliance, and data security.

Copilot Studio is a low-code toolset that allows makers to create agents with a graphical interface. The low-code SaaS platform empowers developers at any level to build, publish, and improve agents rapidly, and enables effective collaboration with subject-matter experts, who can use natural language to respond immediately to changing market and customer needs. Copilot Studio also allows for a hybrid approach of low-code and pro-code development. Professional developers can use the Visual Studio Code extension to edit Copilot Studio agents from within Visual Studio Code instead of using the low-code user interface (UI). Developers can also take advantage of the integration between Copilot Studio and Azure AI Foundry to build custom or highly tuned models and make them available for low-code makers to use.

While these pro-code capabilities are available, the primary experience – and the focus of this book – is the low-code interface, designed to enable makers to build and publish agents without writing code.

What is an agent?

An agent is an AI-powered assistant that works on your behalf to retrieve information, perform tasks, interact with users, and achieve business goals based on its under-standing of context, instructions, and available knowledge and tools. It can be a chat-based agent where the user interacts directly, or an autonomous agent that runs a business process independently, interacting with a human in the loop where needed. Unlike traditional automation, which follows fixed, deterministic workflows, agents use large language models and generative AI to interpret intent and business goals. They reason over the knowledge and tools provided to create a plan and follow the best course of action at runtime. This allows them to handle more complex processes where reasoning or decisions are involved, which can't be automated using deterministic "if this, then that" rules.

Information work is expected to move from employees using AI assistants, to teams of humans working alongside agents that act as digital colleagues, to humans setting the direction for agents that act autonomously to execute business processes and workflows. As agents become an everyday tool used for productivity and process automation, learning how to build and use these agents will become a critical skill for information workers.

Sign up for a Copilot Studio free trial

To get started with Copilot Studio, and to follow along with the practical exercises in this book, sign up for a free trial. You will need a Microsoft work, school, or developer account to sign up for the trial and use Copilot Studio.

> ⚠ **IMPORTANT** In some organizations, work accounts are restricted from signing up for trials or connecting to other Microsoft services. If your work account does not allow the required access, you can start by signing up for the Microsoft 365 Developer Program (eligibility requirements apply) (https://developer.microsoft.com/en-us/microsoft-365/dev-program) or for a Microsoft 365 Business trial at aka.ms/office365signup. You can then use that account to sign up for the Copilot Studio trial following the steps in this section. To follow along with all the exercises in this book, it is recommended that you have a Microsoft 365 business account or trial that includes SharePoint and Outlook.

> ⚠ **IMPORTANT** Microsoft 365 Copilot is available only with a paid license; there is no free trial available. Some exercises in this book will show how to use the lite experience of Copilot Studio, and how to use Copilot Studio to extend Microsoft 365 Copilot. You will be able to follow along with these exercises only if you have a paid Microsoft 365 Copilot license.

To sign up for a Copilot Studio trial

1. Navigate to https://copilotstudio.microsoft.com.

2. Sign in with your work, school, or developer account.

3. Select your country/region and then select **Start free trial.**

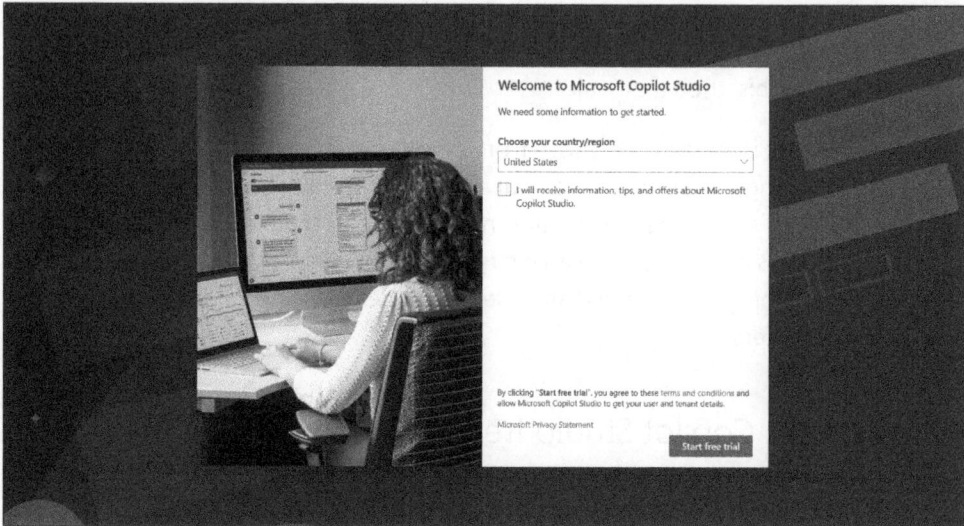

Select your country/region and then select "Start free trial."

4. You will be redirected to a welcome screen where you can select **Next** to view the carousel of welcome messages or select **Skip** to go to the Copilot Studio home page.

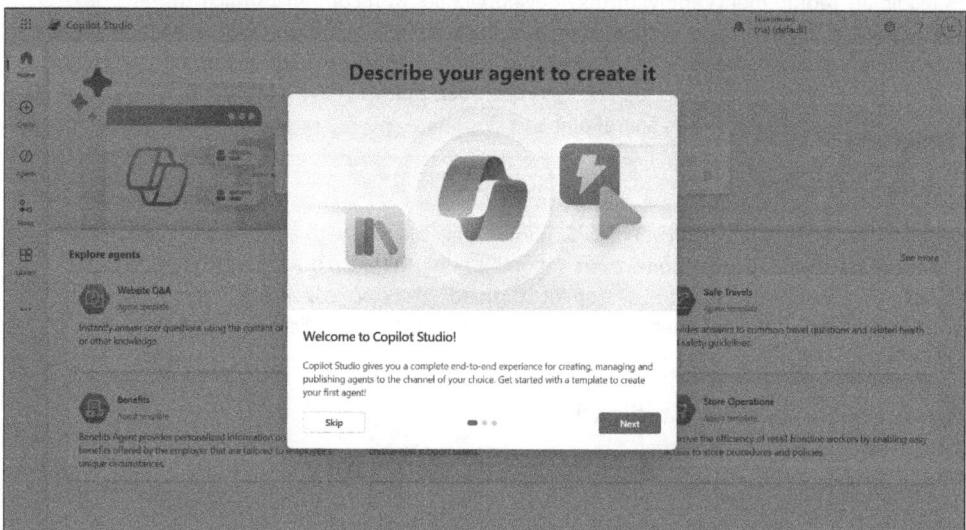

Scroll through the welcome messages or skip to the main Copilot Studio home page.

5. You are now on the home page for Copilot Studio. Bookmark this site for future use.

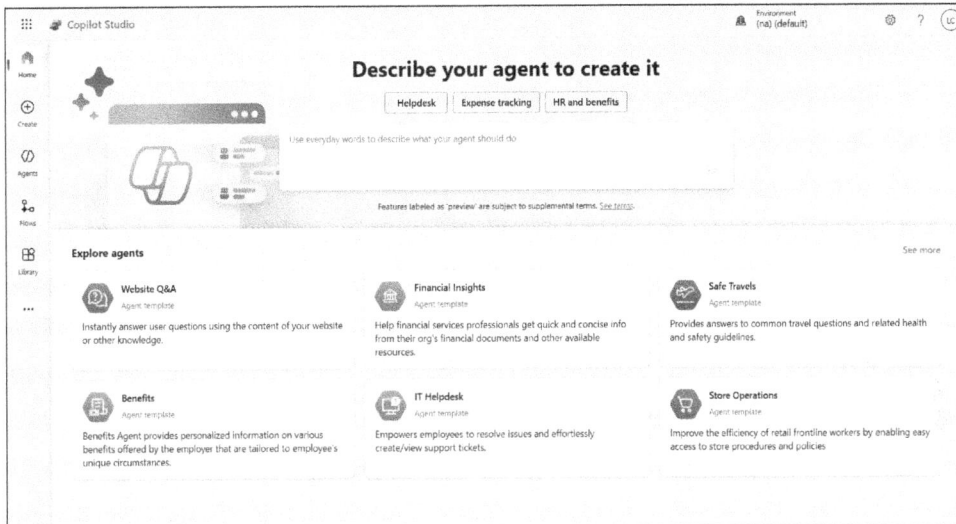

Bookmark the Copilot Studio home page.

Create an agent in Copilot Studio by describing it

Copilot Studio offers three ways to get started with creating an agent:

1. Describe the agent you want to create using a natural language prompt.

2. Start with a template.

3. Start with the low-code configuration experience.

In this section, you will create a basic agent connected to a website by describing it in natural language.

To create an agent by describing it

1. Write a sentence in the prompt area to describe the purpose of the agent you want to create, such as **Help answer customer questions about Microsoft Surface devices**. Click or tap on the icon in the prompt area to send your prompt.

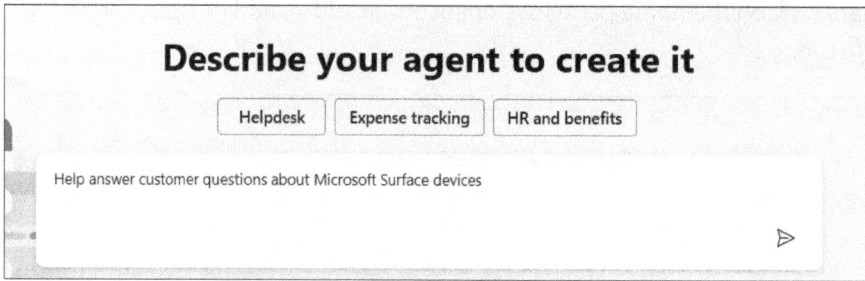

Use natural language to describe the agent you want to create.

2. You will be redirected to a Copilot conversational experience to continue building your agent. On the main part of the screen, you will find the chat interface with Copilot that helps you build your agent. On the right side of the screen is the output of the conversation that will be used to build the agent description and instructions. Note as you continue to refine the agent by chatting with Copilot, the output to be used to build the agent will be updated.

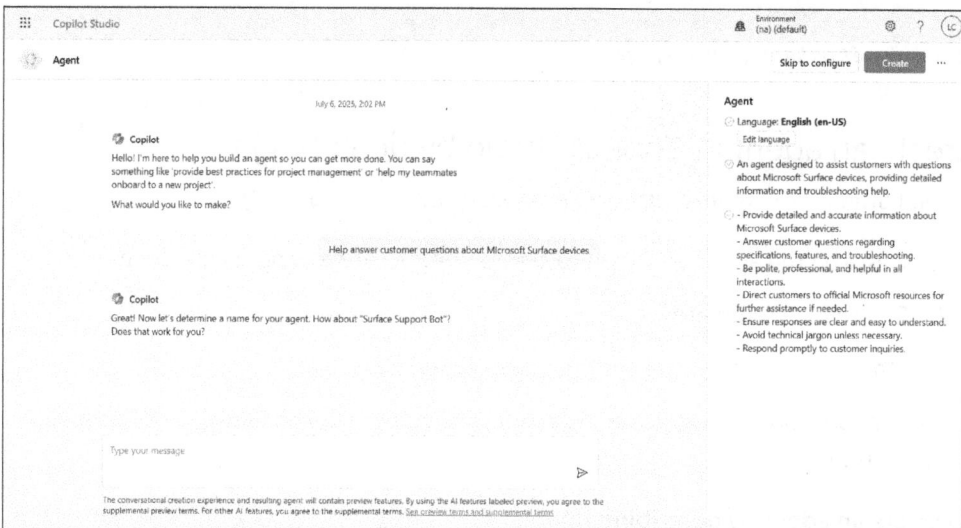

Use the conversational experience with Copilot to create your agent.

3. Enter a new name (the maximum length for the agent name is 30 characters) or confirm the suggested name in the chat. When you have renamed or confirmed the name of your agent, the agent name in the output panel on the right of the screen will be updated to reflect the new name.

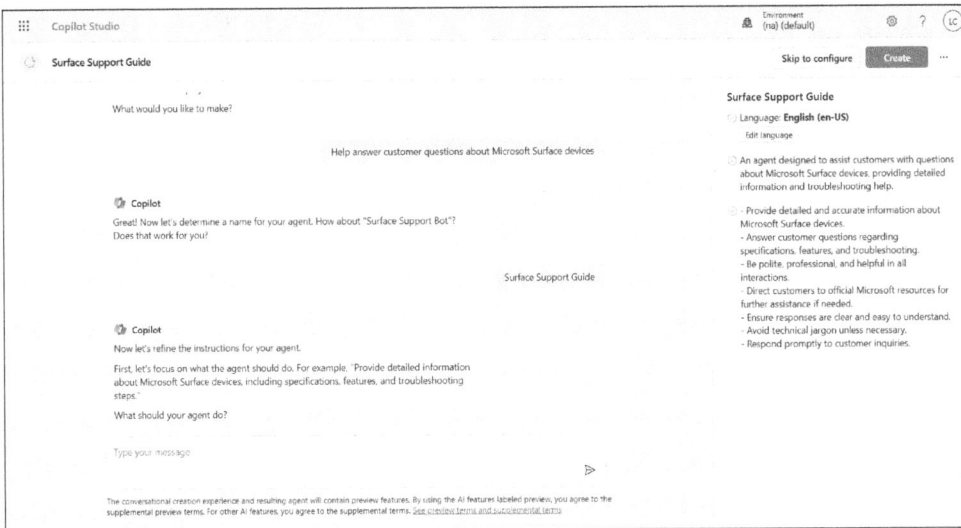

As you use the conversation with Copilot to build your agent, the output on the right will be automatically updated.

4. Copilot will now prompt you to refine the instructions by providing specific information about what the agent should do, such as the main tasks or goals. Enter the following into the chat: **Provide information about the latest Surface models and help customers compare and find the right option for their needs.**

5. Copilot now prompts you to add any publicly available data sources for the agent. This is where you can add a website that the agent will use as a knowledge source to provide answers. Enter the following URL: **https://www.microsoft.com/en-us/surface**

> ✓ **TIP** You can use a URL only up to 2 levels deep.

6. Copilot will add the knowledge source and then ask whether you have any more modifications you want to make to the agent. At this stage, you can provide additional information such as the tone or type of language you want the agent to use. Enter the following into the chat: **Maintain a friendly and enthusiastic tone, always happy to help the customer with any questions. Your answers should be accurate and clear to non-technical customers.** Note the change to the output in the right-side pane.

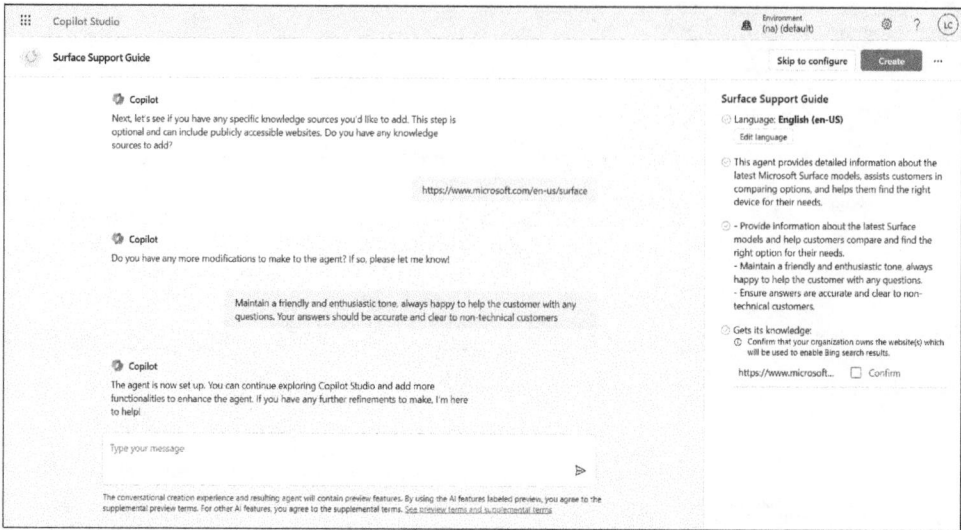

The agent is now set up and ready to create.

7. Select the **Create** button at the top right of the screen to create the agent.

8. Wait for your agent to be created. When it is ready, you will be redirected to the main agent configuration screen, displaying the **Name**, **Description**, **General Instructions**, and **Knowledge** you created for the agent during the conversational experience, with a **test** pane on the right of the screen.

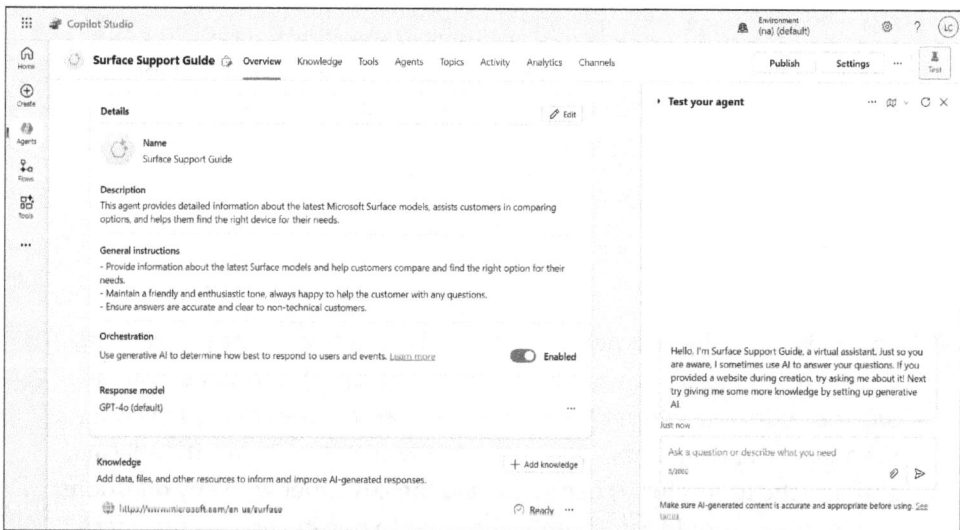

Your agent is ready to test.

9. Test your agent by entering a prompt in the test pane: **How does the Surface Pro compare to the Surface Laptop?**

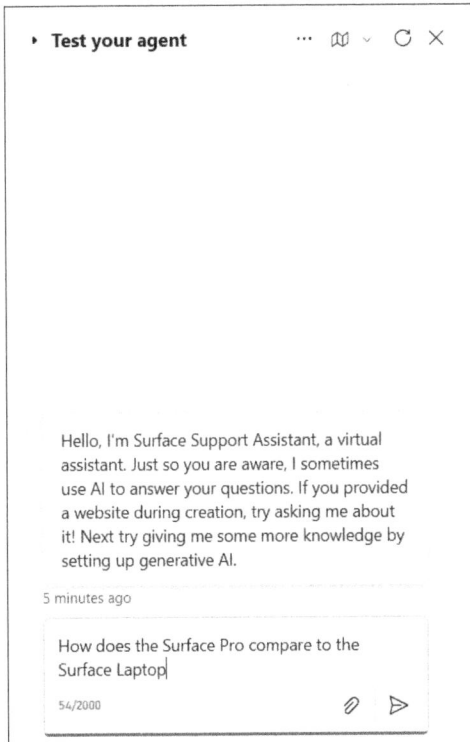

Enter a prompt to test your agent.

10. The agent will search the knowledge source to find the answer and then generate a response. You will see that the **activity map** replaces the configuration experience on the main part of the screen while you are testing the agent. This activity map shows the knowledge sources searched and the knowledge source used to generate the output and confirms when the session is complete. The agent responds with an AI-generated answer based on the knowledge source.

11. Select the **Home** icon at the top of the left navigation rail to return to the Copilot Studio home page.

12. Your agent will now be listed in the **Recent** section of the home page. You can select it from that list to open it again and continue editing.

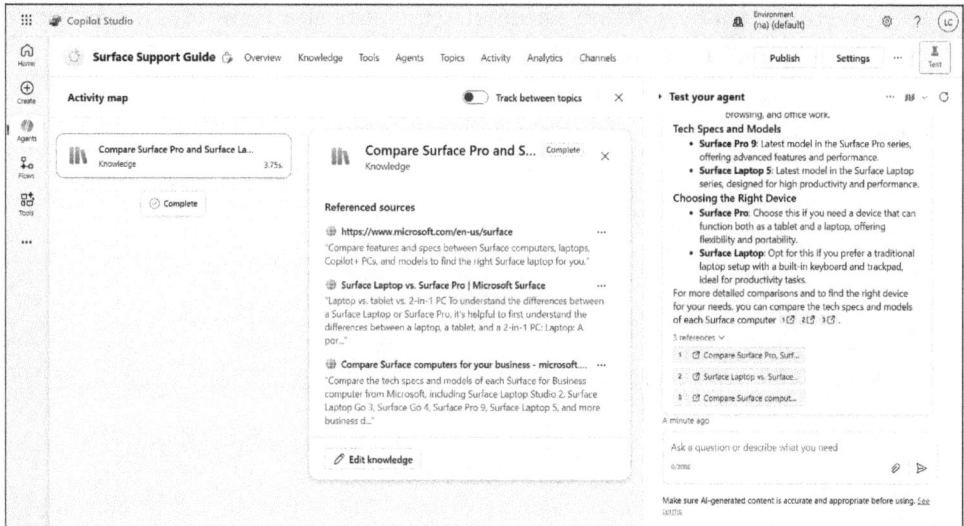

Your agent is ready to test.

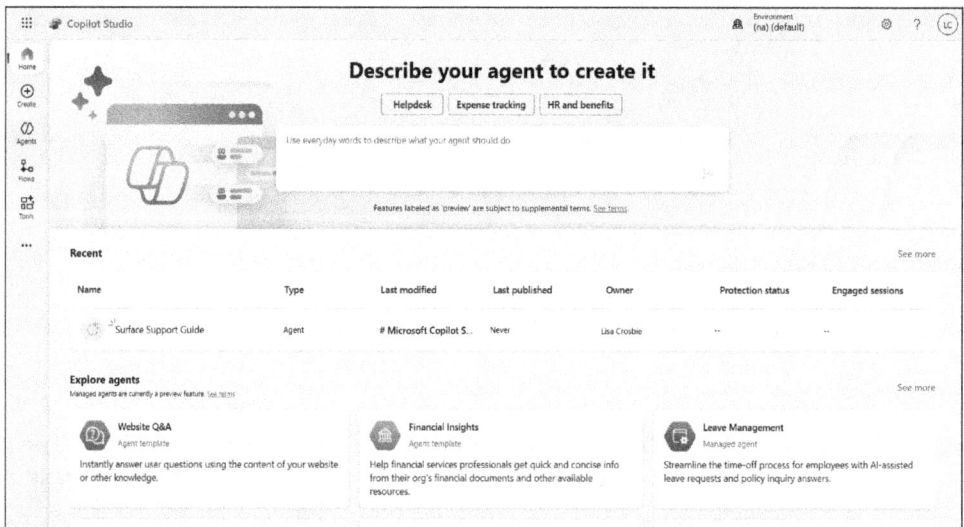

Your agent appears in the Recent list of agents.

This conversational building experience allows the user to get started quickly and easily by creating a basic agent using natural language. Experienced makers will usually skip this step and go straight to the main low-code configuration experience to build agents.

> 🔍 **SEE ALSO** You will learn about the full navigation of the Copilot Studio home page and how to create agents using templates and the low-code configuration experience in Chapter 4: Building agents in Copilot Studio.

Understand the capabilities of Copilot Studio

Microsoft has different agent-building tools that can be used depending on the use case, the skill of the maker or developer, and the amount of customization and control required. In this section, you will learn about the different tools available for creating agents, and the role Copilot Studio plays in each of these scenarios.

Microsoft's agent-building toolset

The Microsoft agent-building toolset caters to different levels of user experience:

- Agents for business productivity, which can be built by information workers using the lite experience of Copilot Studio available in the Microsoft 365 Copilot app

- Agents for business process transformation, which can be built by low-code makers using Copilot Studio

- Custom agent solutions, which can be built by professional developers using Azure AI Foundry and other tools including the Microsoft 365 Agents Toolkit and SDK

Copilot Studio sits at the heart of this toolset. It is the core platform for building enterprise-grade agents that can transform business processes.

Agents for business productivity

Agents for business productivity are the agents that information workers use in their everyday work to make them more productive. These agents can help with tasks like writing emails and reports, brainstorming ideas, and answering questions about products, projects, or policies. Business users can create their own agents in the Microsoft 365 Copilot app using the lite experience of Copilot Studio. This natural language, no-code configuration experience enables information workers to quickly and easily extend their Microsoft 365 Copilot Chat experience and share agents with their colleagues.

The lite version of Copilot Studio is embedded in Microsoft 365 Copilot, providing a simplified, limited experience for building agents for yourself or for a small team in your organization. You can direct your agent's behavior, tone, and scope with natural language instructions, and add limited knowledge sources and tools. These agents can only be published and used in Microsoft 365 Copilot Chat.

> **SEE ALSO** Agents built in the free version of Microsoft 365 Copilot Chat have further limitations on the knowledge sources and tools that can be used without needing either a Microsoft 365 Copilot license or pay-as-you-go consumption billing. See the section "Understand and calculate agent costs" in Chapter 2 for more information.

> **SEE ALSO** You will learn how to use the lite experience of Copilot Studio in Chapter 3: Building agents with the lite experience of Copilot Studio.

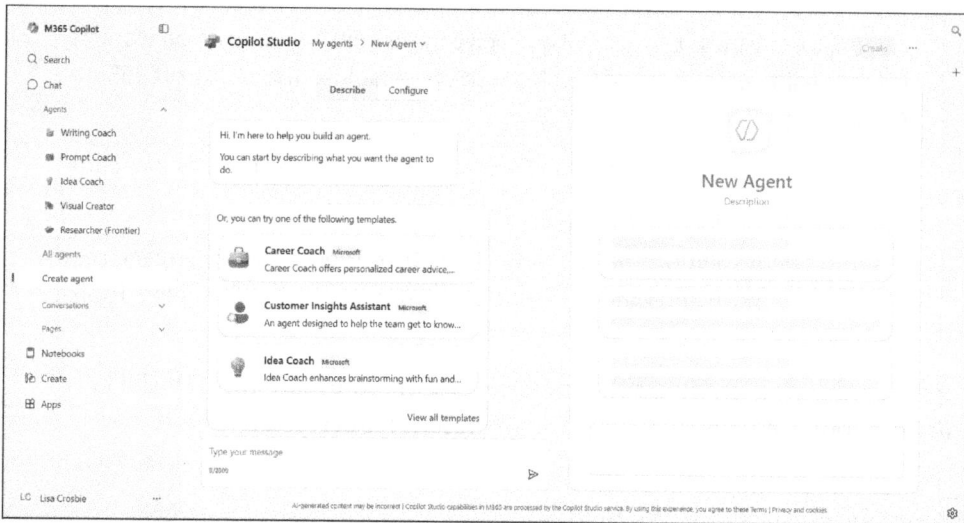

The lite experience of Copilot Studio in Microsoft 365 Copilot Chat.

Microsoft 365 Copilot can also be extended with the full set of options for grounding agents in knowledge, adding tools, and using other capabilities. To do so, you can build an agent in the full Copilot Studio experience and publish it to Microsoft 365 Copilot as a channel.

Agents for business process transformation

Copilot Studio is the tool used to extend Microsoft 365 Copilot, or to build stand-alone internal- or external-facing agents. These agents can be used to support internal sales, service, human resources (HR), and supply chain processes, or they can act as self-service agents on a website or app for customers or suppliers.

Building agents with Copilot Studio requires a maker or developer skill set, as well as the ability to design effective conversational AI experiences. Agents built in Copilot Studio can range from simple agents for answering questions or handling tasks, to complex multi-agent systems that operate independently, reason, make decisions, and orchestrate business processes. Copilot Studio agents can be grounded in multiple enterprise knowledge sources, connected to a range of tools, and published across different channels.

The full capabilities of Copilot Studio and use of the low-code experience to build agents are the focus of this book.

Custom agent solutions

In some cases, a business problem may need a fully customized, code-first solution. Microsoft provides a rich set of tools for professional developers that integrates with Copilot Studio, so that you can work with capabilities beyond the limited ones available in the low-code toolset.

Azure AI Foundry is where you can build, test, and deploy custom AI models and agent solutions. This platform offers thousands of models and gives you full control over the training, orchestration, grounding, reasoning, and integration of your agents. Copilot Studio is integrated with Azure AI Foundry, so you can leverage the data and models you have built there to expand your Copilot Studio agent to include custom, fine-tuned, or industry-specific models. Azure AI Foundry gives you complete control over all components of your agent solution. As such, its use requires a higher level of technical skill compared to Copilot Studio. It is mostly used by professional developers, engineers, and data scientists, who can use this platform to fine-tune a model and make it available to the low-code maker.

Professional developers working with the Microsoft 365 Agents SDK can use this toolset to extend or integrate with Copilot Studio agents. They can use it to extend a Copilot Studio agent using skills, or to connect to a Copilot Studio agent from their code to get access to all the capabilities and functionality in Copilot Studio.

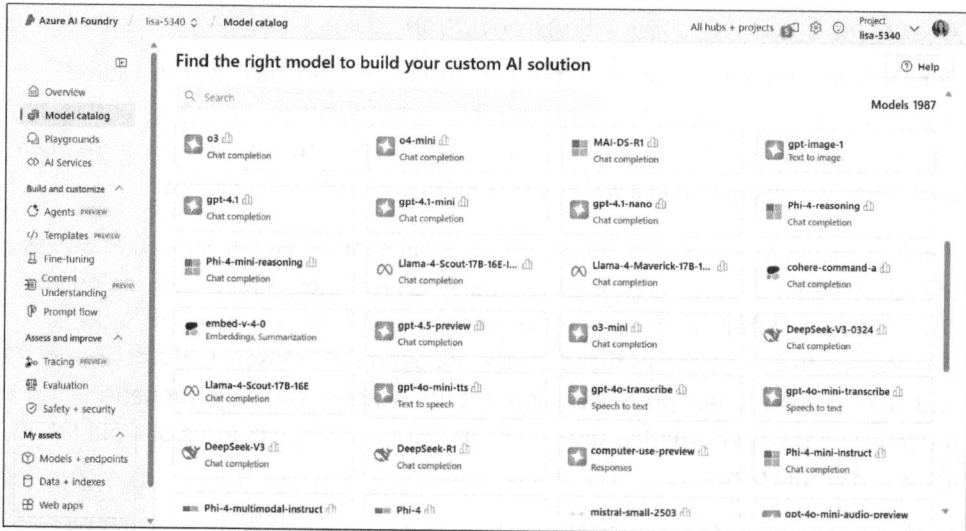

The model catalog in Azure AI Foundry.

Microsoft has strategically designed its AI agent-building tools to work together. As a result, makers and developers can work together to build solutions using the tools they are skilled to use, bringing together the capabilities they need.

Key components of agent architecture

The agent architecture of Copilot Studio consists of five key components: experience, knowledge, tools, orchestrator, and models. In this section, you will learn the key terminology, and see how these components work together to determine how the agent behaves, what information it uses, and what actions it can take.

Experience

Experience determines how a user interacts with an agent, or whether it is triggered by an event to run autonomously in the background without direct interaction with a user. In Copilot Studio, user experiences are channels where the agent can be published, such as Microsoft 365 Copilot, Microsoft Teams, websites, apps, social media, and other chat channels. Setting your agent up with an event trigger to run autonomously means you can also create an experience that doesn't have a user interface or channel.

> 🔍 **SEE ALSO** Experience is covered in detail in Chapter 5: Building autonomous agents and Chapter 10: Publishing and authenticating agents.

Knowledge

Knowledge is the information the agent has access to and that it can use to respond to questions or to complete tasks. When knowledge is added to an agent, we refer to this as "grounding." Grounding is an important component in building an agent that operates in the context of your business. Grounding an agent in business knowledge means you are providing your agent with accurate and relevant information, substantially reducing the risk of hallucination compared with an agent that answers only using a large language model.

> 🔍 **SEE ALSO** Knowledge is covered in detail in Chapter 6: Grounding agents in knowledge.

Tools

Tools are the components an agent uses to do things, or to take action. A wide variety of tools are available in Copilot Studio to enable your agent to connect to Microsoft and third-party systems and to complete tasks by running flows or calling APIs.

> 🔍 **SEE ALSO** Tools are covered in detail in Chapter 8: Extending agents with tools.

Orchestrator

The orchestrator is the agent's decision-making control center: It determines what the agent does and when. It decides when to call a knowledge source or when to use a tool, by reasoning over the user request or business goal (in the case of an autonomous agent) and the components it has available, to create and execute a plan.

> 🔍 **SEE ALSO** Orchestration is covered in detail in Chapter 2: Designing effective agents.

Models

Models refer to large language models (LLMs) that understand user input, reason over instructions, and generate responses. The orchestrator and the model work together, with the orchestrator telling the model what to do and when. Copilot Studio provides a choice of managed models, or you can extend it to bring in custom models from Azure AI Foundry.

> **SEE ALSO** Models are covered in more detail in Chapter 13: Extending Copilot Studio agents with Azure AI.

Core capabilities of Copilot Studio

Copilot Studio provides a comprehensive platform for building, deploying, managing, monitoring, and improving AI-powered agents for your business needs using these architectural components. With Copilot Studio, you can:

- Create agents using natural language, low-code, or pro-code tools.

  - Build an agent by describing what you want it to do, configuring the agent with a low-code visual authoring tool, or editing it using Visual Studio Code.

  - Trigger agents using chat, events (such as a form submission, when an email arrives, or when a row is updated in a database), or API calls.

  - Design structured topics and dialogs to guide and control conversational logic for business-critical scenarios.

- Ground agents in enterprise knowledge.

  - Connect an agent to enterprise knowledge from documents, websites, Microsoft 365 sources, structured databases, and third-party systems, to search and reason over that knowledge to provide generative answers.

  - Choose and fine-tune the models you use for your retrieval-augmented generation (RAG) pipeline—an architecture designed to enhance LLMs by allowing them to access and incorporate external, up-to-date, or domain-specific information not present in their original training data.

- Enable agents to do more with tools.

  - Build structured agent flows that define deterministic logic for multi-step tasks.

- Enable agents to take actions such as reading, updating, or creating rows in your line-of-business systems using connectors or REST APIs.

- Connect with existing knowledge servers and data sources using the Model Context Protocol, an open standard designed to standardize how artificial intelligence (AI) models connect to, access, and interact with external data sources, tools, and services.

- Add a computer use tool that enables your agent to interact with any system using UI automation.

- Create your own prompts that can generate responses using the context of the conversation, variables, instructions, and knowledge.

- Create agents that can use reasoning and act autonomously.

  - Create autonomous agents with deep reasoning capabilities that can perform analysis and chain-of-thought thinking to handle complex tasks.

- Design multi-agent systems.

  - Build a multi-agent system in which agents can call and hand off to other agents specific tasks, knowledge, or parts of the process.

- Publish agents across multiple channels.

  - Publish agents to internal and external channels including Microsoft 365 Copilot, Microsoft Teams, websites, apps, social media, and chat applications.

  - Build a voice-enabled IVR (Interactive Voice Response) agent that can interact with customers in natural language to answer questions or route calls.

  - Configure handoff to customer engagement hubs including Dynamics 365 Customer Service, ServiceNow, and Salesforce.

- Monitor and improve agent performance.

  - Analyze agent interactions and quality of responses, and monitor return on investment (ROI) and consumption.

  - Use the built-in analytics to identify opportunities to fine-tune and improve agent performance.

- Integrate with Azure AI Foundry.
  - Extend agent capabilities with Azure AI Foundry by integrating knowledge from Azure AI search or by using custom AI models tailored to your specific use case.

SEE ALSO Copilot Studio is a major investment area for Microsoft, and new capabilities are being added on a regular basis. To keep up with the latest features and features planned for upcoming releases, refer to the "What's new in Copilot Studio" page on Microsoft Learn: https://learn.microsoft.com/en-us/microsoft-copilot-studio/whats-new.

Explore use cases for Copilot Studio agents

Before you start designing or building an agent, it's important to understand how to identify business problems that can be effectively solved with agents. This section explores some sample use cases for Copilot Studio agents, including the business value, impact, and thought processes behind them. The goal is to help you understand the ways that agents can transform processes and add value in your organization.

Start by looking for the everyday friction points that slow employees down, such as repetitive helpdesk questions, swivel chair tasks, or searching for policy or product information. Consider parts of your customer experience or processes where customers drop off, such as abandoned forms, website traffic patterns, or low-value/high-volume queries that come into the call center.

Agents can respond to user questions, run autonomously based on triggers, retrieve information, and take actions. As you identify business problems that could be solved with agents, consider the following questions to help evaluate each use case:

- What knowledge does the agent need? How well organized or curated is that knowledge? Generative AI isn't a magic solution to a mess of inconsistent and poorly organized knowledge.
- What actions can it take and when (e.g., sending emails, writing summaries, reading or updating information in your line-of-business systems)? Which data or systems will it need to access to perform those actions?
- Which parts of the process need to be structured with step-by-step flows, and which parts could be handled by an agent reasoning and making decisions?

1

■ Is the business problem best solved using a chat experience, or could it run as an autonomous background process?

The most important thing to remember is that you should always start with a business problem you are trying to solve, rather than thinking about how to use AI. Consider the business impact an agent could have, the key performance indicators (KPIs) it could influence, and the ROI for building an agent.

Here are some examples of use cases for agents you can build in Copilot Studio, framed using this thought process.

Internal agents (for employees)

The use cases that are most commonly identified first involve internal agents that make it easy for employees to find information about products, policies, systems, or projects, thereby reducing the time they spend searching for documents or answers. These use cases are often found in internal service departments such as HR or IT, where staff spend a lot of time answering a high volume of routine questions. These agents are often published in Microsoft 365 Copilot Chat or Microsoft Teams, but can also be published on internal-facing websites or in apps used by employees.

Here are some examples.

IT Helpdesk Agent

Business challenge: The IT support team is overwhelmed by tickets for common issues like password resets, Wi-Fi and network issues, email access, permission requests, and onboarding tasks. Responding to these frequent, routine tasks takes time, frustrating employees who expect immediate help, and reducing the capacity of the IT staff to focus on system improvements and innovative projects.

How an agent can help: The IT Helpdesk Agent can act as a virtual assistant embedded in Microsoft 365 Copilot or Teams that helps employees find answers to their questions and resolve common issues. This agent draws on procedures and knowledge that are maintained by the IT department, ensuring that its information is always accurate and up-to-date. It can chat with the employees to understand more complex problems, gather all the required information, and raise tickets in the IT service management (ITSM) system when needed. The employee experience is streamlined so that employees don't need to switch to another system to fill out a form or send an email when they need help.

Areas of impact:

- Employee experience and productivity are improved with access to instant, accurate, and up-to-date answers to common questions, and the ability to raise tickets without switching systems.

- IT team productivity is improved with a substantial reduction in routine requests, and all issues are consistently and accurately logged in the ITSM system rather than coming in through multiple channels.

- The reduced workload frees the IT team members to focus on innovation and strategic projects that help drive business goals.

Onboarding Agent

Business challenge: New employees often face a slow and disjointed onboarding experience. They may have trouble finding resources, learning procedures, and completing onboarding tasks, and they may not know who to contact for help. This can lead to frustration, distract from their focus on the core responsibilities of their new role, and add to the workload of the IT and HR staff, who must spend time responding to frequent and repetitive questions about policies, equipment, training, and tools. Overall, onboarding can be a poor experience for new employees at an important time—when they are first joining the company.

How an agent can help: An agent can act as a digital guide for the employee from day 1, welcoming them and guiding them through the onboarding process. It can answer questions, provide links to help them find essential resources, and prompt them through onboarding tasks and mandatory training. It can tailor guidance and responses based on the employee's role, department, or location.

In a multi-agent system, the onboarding agent could hand off to the IT Helpdesk Agent to handle IT-specific questions and requests.

Areas of impact:

- Faster ramp-up allows new employees to become productive sooner.

- Consistent and smooth onboarding for all new employees contributes to better first impressions and improves employee engagement and retention.

- The reduction in support work for IT and HR staff frees up their time to focus on higher-value strategic work.

Customer Support Assistant

Business challenge: Customer service agents in banking face the challenge of having to navigate complex procedures while ensuring strict compliance when responding to customer inquiries. Answering questions often requires knowing where to find the right procedure or policy across thousands of documents, which can in turn lead to long wait times for the customer, even for routine questions. Such delays can result in long call times, abandoned calls, lost business, and low customer satisfaction.

How an agent can help: An agent can serve as an additional (virtual) member of the customer service team, helping the customer service representatives find the right information and follow the correct procedures. This kind of agent is connected to the internal policy documents, procedure manuals, and product information, and is designed with conversational dialog flows that ensure compliance in responses.

In an industry like banking, a multi-agent system can be designed where each agent is a specialist in one area of banking, such as personal loans or business banking. With this approach, each agent has its own knowledge and tools based on the role it needs to fulfill, and hands off to the other agents as needed.

Areas of impact:

- There is a reduced risk of incorrect or noncompliant responses, especially when training new staff.

- Employee confidence, satisfaction, and productivity all improve.

- Faster and more accurate responses, reduced call times, and lower call abandonment rates all improve customer satisfaction.

- The contact center capacity is freed up to be able to handle more calls and help drive business growth through better service delivery.

Access Request Coordinator (Autonomous Agent)

Business challenge: When employees start in new roles or join projects, they often need access to specific systems, documents, and data. When these access requests are handled manually, they can involve multiple people needing to provide approvals. That can result in delays of up to several days before the employee can get started on the role or project. This slows down productivity for the employees and the managers involved.

How an agent can help: The Access Request Coordinator is an autonomous agent triggered by a form submission or by an update in a project management system when an employee is added as a resource to a new project. The agent automatically checks for any required training, initiates workflows to request approvals from managers or data owners, and follows up until it has all the required approvals. It then raises a ticket for the IT department to provide the required access. The process is streamlined and does not require any manual intervention.

Areas of impact:

- The agent standardizes and automates the request and approval process, including reminders for outstanding approvals, resulting in operational efficiencies.

- The agent maintains a record of requests, approvals, and fulfillment for auditing and security.

- The agent reduces manual work and bottlenecks, providing employees with the required access more quickly, allowing projects to kick off sooner.

External agents (for customers or suppliers)

Although internal use cases are where most organizations start with agents, it is also important to consider where agents can help in customer-facing scenarios. The highest-value use cases for agents are those that can enable customer or supplier self-service at scale, thereby reducing costs or employee workload, or augmenting your team to drive business growth. Website chat experiences that answer questions are a good starting point, but it is worth challenging yourself to think beyond that use case to other ways that agents can transform business processes.

Travel Booking Assistant

Business challenge: Customers visiting a travel company's website struggle to find the information they need about destinations, pricing, travel packages, and booking policies. Navigating the site and collecting all the information they need to put together their holiday package can be confusing, resulting in many customers abandoning the online booking process. Customers visit the site from all over the world, and the call center can't scale to operate 24/7 and in multiple languages.

How an agent can help: An agent embedded on the website can act as a digital travel concierge, answering questions and guiding customers through package options, making recommendations, helping them compare prices and options, and taking action on their behalf to make a booking. It can support multiple languages and time zones, scaling the global reach of the service. It can handle cancellations and booking changes by reasoning over the internal policy documents, and can escalate the engagement to a human representative when needed.

This booking assistant could hand off to another agent after the booking is made, to proactively monitor for changes to flights or weather issues, and update the customer in real time.

Areas of impact:

- Increase in sales by helping customers find the information they need and make a booking without needing to speak to someone in the call center

- Improved customer experience and access to an expanded market through 24/7 multilingual support

- Reduced call center volume and costs

Legal Services Assistant

Business challenge: When potential clients reach out to a law firm through their website, they often don't know which legal service they need or who they need to speak to. Their inquiries may be submitted via a generic web form, and administrative staff must then spend time manually reviewing and routing requests, adding to their workload and impacting the firm's ability to respond to new clients.

How an agent can help: An agent embedded on the website can act as a smart intake and routing assistant. It can engage with potential clients in natural language to understand their legal needs, urgency, and background details. It can identify the right area of law and expertise needed, summarize the request, and automatically email the details to the right lawyer or team, ensuring a fast and accurate handoff.

Areas of impact:

- Improved client experience, leaving a professional impression on prospective clients from their first engagement

- Reduced response time and faster intake for new clients, which means the business can handle more urgent and sensitive legal matters

- Operational efficiencies and reduced administrative load for the business

Insurance Claims Agent

Business challenge: Filing a health insurance claim can be a confusing and time-consuming experience for customers, who usually don't know whether their claim is eligible, how to submit it, or which documentation is needed. This can lead to incomplete or incorrect claims, delays in processing, and high call volumes to the call center from customers asking questions about how to submit a claim or following up on the status of an existing claim.

How an agent can help: An agent can guide customers step by step through the claims process, asking relevant questions to determine eligibility, gather the required information, and explain the process and the documentation required in clear language. It can be integrated into the back-end claims system so that it can authenticate the user and then check on the status of an existing claim to provide an update. The agent is available 24/7, allowing the customer to get the information they need at a time convenient for them, thereby improving accessibility and reducing wait times.

In a business that handles multiple types of insurance, a multi-agent system could have agents specializing in each area. These agents can orchestrate the handoff to the agent with the right expertise.

Areas of impact:

- The agent simplifies the claims process, resulting in faster claim submissions.
- Status updates are handled by self-service, improving the customer experience and reducing call volume to the contact center.
- The reduced error rate minimizes frustration and double-handling, resulting in operational efficiencies and cost savings.

Retail Exchange Assistant (Autonomous Agent)

Business challenge: Returns and exchanges are a common source of friction in retail scenarios. Customers are often confused about return policies, shipping labels, or whether they have the option to get an exchange instead of a refund. This results in high call volumes, slow resolution times, and lost revenue for retailers that might otherwise retain some sales with an exchange.

How an agent can help: An autonomous agent can manage the entire return and exchange process without human intervention (or with a human in the loop to authorize the final decision before it is sent to the customer). It can use policy and order history knowledge to validate the customer's request, issue a return label, and offer an exchange when that option is available, suggesting the same item in a different size or color. It can automatically communicate with the customer via their preferred channel (e.g., email, WhatsApp, or Facebook Messenger) and provide updates throughout the process. It can also update the data in the back-end system.

Areas of impact:

- Improves the customer experience with a fast and convenient return or exchange process with proactive communication

- Helps increase revenue by offering and encouraging exchanges rather than refunds

- Reduces overhead for an area of the business that usually results in loss of revenue, by automating decision making and system updates

> **SEE ALSO** You can explore a range of real-world customer stories by searching for **Copilot Studio** at www.microsoft.com/en-us/customers/search.

Success metrics

In addition to considering the business problems and areas of impact when looking for agent use cases, it is important to understand and define what success means for your agent by connecting it to key departmental or business goals or KPIs. This will help you demonstrate the ROI and business value for your agent.

For most agents, success metrics will fall into one or more of the following categories:

- Increasing revenue
  - 10% higher average booking value via travel assistant upsell options
  - $1 million revenue increase from converting returns to exchanges
  - 20% increase in legal consultation bookings
- Reducing costs
  - 35% of support queries resolved by the agent without human escalation
  - Freed up 1 FTE (full-time equivalent) worth of effort in IT through automation
  - 20% fewer unqualified leads that need follow-up

- Improving customer experience

  - CSAT score increased from 3.5 to 4.5

  - First-call resolution time decreased from 30 minutes to 5 minutes

  - Claim status inquiries resolved in less than 2 minutes, on average

- Improving employee experience

  - Administrative workload reduced by 35%

  - IT resolution accuracy improved by 20%

  - HR feedback shows 90% of new hires felt supported by onboarding agent

These examples demonstrate that agents can support and improve a range of business metrics, leading to greater satisfaction, operational efficiencies, and growth. Although the focus of agents and automation is often cost reduction, it is important to think more broadly about the benefits this technology can bring to your organization. Cost reduction does not necessarily have to mean reducing the number of jobs. Consider how agents can help augment what you do, free up time for more innovative and strategic work that can drive new business, or help with employee retention.

The future of work involves humans and agents collaborating and working together. Think about how agents can help you to "hire" whole new teams of digital colleagues.

Skills review

In this chapter, you learned how to:

- Sign up for a Copilot Studio trial and create an agent grounded in website knowledge by describing it in natural language.

- Understand the key components of agent architecture, and the core capabilities for agent building in Copilot Studio.

- Explore real use cases for Copilot Studio, using a framework to determine the business value, impacts, and success metrics in each case.

Practice tasks

No practice files are necessary to complete the practice tasks in this chapter.

Get started with Copilot Studio

Navigate to the Copilot Studio home page in your browser (https://copilotstudio. microsoft.com) and then complete the following tasks:

1. For this exercise, you can use your organization's website, or the website of a local public or government service in your area. Describe the agent you want to build using natural language. Think of a use case that makes sense for your chosen organization, such as answering customer questions about products or services.

2. Confirm the suggested name for your agent or suggest a different name.

3. Describe any specific tasks or information you want your agent to provide, or the tone of voice it should use.

4. Enter the URL of your chosen organization's website (up to 2 levels deep).

5. Select **Continue**.

6. Wait for your agent to be created, and then ask a question related to the information on the website by entering a prompt in the test pane.

7. Notice that the activity map shows the knowledge source used and the agent provides a response.

Understand the capabilities of Copilot Studio

Use the agent that you created in the first exercise, which is connected to a single public website, as a knowledge source and consider how it can be extended. Answer the following questions:

1. Who is the user of this agent? What problem are they trying to solve?

2. What other knowledge sources could the agent use to help the user with this problem?

3. What actions could it take on behalf of the user?

4. What channels could you publish this agent to? Will it be on a public-facing website, or are there other channels where the user could interact with it?

5. Could the problem be solved in a different way, with an agent that can act autonomously in the background?

Explore use cases for Copilot Studio agents

Review the examples provided in this chapter and think about the challenges you face in your business where employees or customers have trouble finding the information or answers they need. Complete the following tasks:

1. Think of one internal business problem where employees spend a lot of time finding the information they need for a project, product information, policies, or procedures.

2. Describe the agent use case using the following structure:

   - Business challenge

   - How an agent can help

   - Areas of impact

   - Success metrics

3. Think of one business problem that affects customers, where they struggle to get information or service after hours or where the only way to transact or resolve a problem is by phone.

4. Describe the agent use case using the following structure:

   - Business challenge

   - How an agent can help

   - Areas of impact

   - Success metrics

Designing effective agents

2

Practice files

No practice files are necessary to complete the practice tasks in this chapter.

Before you start building an agent, it is important to understand the principles of agent design and some key decisions you need to make about the behavior of your agents. These design decisions will affect the performance, capability, and cost of your agent, and will set you up for success in solving your business problem effectively.

In this chapter, you will work through the design and thought process that covers what your agent is for, how it behaves, and what it will cost to run. You will learn how to choose whether to extend Microsoft 365 Copilot or build a stand-alone agent. You will also see how to determine the right type of agent for your use case, designing an agent either as a chat interaction, an autonomous agent that works independently, or a system of multiple agents that hand off to each other for specific parts of the process. Copilot Studio offers both classic and generative orchestration options, and you will learn how they work, their strengths and limitations, and the types of scenarios that are best suited to each. You'll learn about designing the agent's core capabilities, planning for knowledge,

In this chapter

- Choose the type of agent
- Select the agent's orchestration model
- Design the agent's capabilities
- Understand and calculate agent costs

tools, logic, and fallback. Finally, you'll discover how each of these design choices affects the cost of running your agent so that you can optimize and calculate costs against your use case.

Choose the type of agent

The first decision you need to make is what kind of agent you are building. In this section, you will learn how to choose the right type of agent for your scenario.

Extend Microsoft 365 Copilot or build a stand-alone agent

Copilot Studio can be used either to extend Microsoft 365 Copilot or to build stand-alone agents for internal or external use. Here are the key considerations for deciding when to extend or when to build.

Extend Microsoft 365 Copilot when:

- Your users have Microsoft 365 Copilot licenses, or they work in the Microsoft 365 Copilot Chat experience in their daily work, and your scenario fits well with that user experience.

- You want a customized version of the Microsoft 365 Copilot chat experience tailored to your specific business needs or use case.

- You want Microsoft 365 Copilot to integrate with and reason over more of your enterprise data sources or domain knowledge.

- You want Microsoft 365 Copilot to be able to handle specific tasks, workflows, or business processes that are connected to your line-of-business systems beyond Microsoft 365 products.

> ✅ **TIP** The agent store has prebuilt agents that extend Microsoft 365 Copilot and are ready to deploy and use immediately. These are good examples of the kinds of agents that you can build yourself and that are connected to other systems.

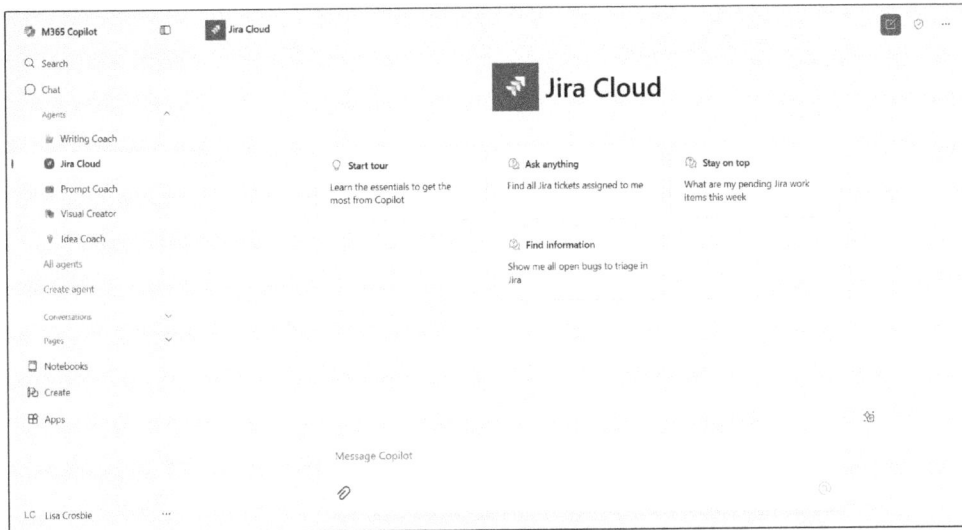

The Jira Cloud agent is an example of extending Microsoft 365 Copilot to connect with line-of-business systems outside of Microsoft 365.

Build a stand-alone agent when:

- You are building an agent for an external-facing scenario, such as customer or supplier self-service.

- Your agent is for internal use, but your users do not have Microsoft 365 Copilot licenses, or they do not use the free Microsoft 365 Copilot Chat experience in their daily work.

- You want flexibility to publish to an internal channel or surface outside of the Microsoft 365 Copilot Chat experience, or to publish to multiple internal channels. This could include your company's business applications, mobile apps, or internal websites or web apps.

- You want more control over the agent branding or user experience.

- You want more control and choice with regard to the language models, orchestration, fine-tuning of knowledge sources, instructions, or responses.

- Your use case is best served by a multi-agent system.

> **IMPORTANT** Internal agents can be extensions of Microsoft 365 Copilot, or they can be stand-alone agents published to an internal channel. If your use case is for external customers or suppliers, you will build a stand-alone agent. Extending Microsoft 365 Copilot is suitable only for internal-facing agents.

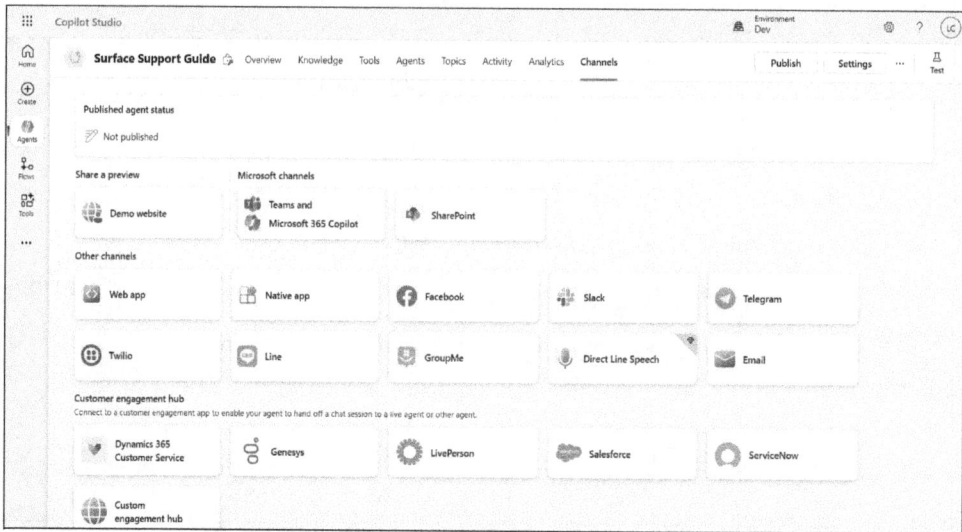

When you build a stand-alone agent in Copilot Studio, you can publish it to a wide range of channels.

> ✅ **TIP** With Copilot Studio you can build an agent and publish it on multiple channels. So, if you design an agent that can be used both internally and externally, you can build it once and publish it in different ways. An agent can start as internal and expand to external once it has been tested and proven as an internal agent. This is a common pattern with the development of customer self-service agents, where the first iteration may be an internal agent supporting the customer service representatives as they look for information, and then be refined or expanded to become a customer-facing external agent on the website or other customer channels.

Conversational agents

Conversational agents are what we are most familiar with in our experience as consumers chatting with a "bot" on a website, using consumer AI tools such as ChatGPT, or using Microsoft 365 Copilot at work. A conversational agent interacts with the user in a chat interface, using natural language to answer questions, guide processes, or complete tasks.

You should use a conversational agent when your scenario is typically user-initiated, or where the user will drive the interaction on demand to ask questions or get help. Consider the users' behavior and the channels they use in the scenario. Is there a natural fit for a digital assistant on a chat channel or other channels (e.g., Microsoft 365 Copilot, Microsoft Teams, website, app, or Facebook Messenger) where the users will find it easy and natural to interact with the agent?

2

Agents that are primarily designed for information retrieval are usually conversational agents. Conversational agents can also perform tasks as part of the chat interaction—for example, asking the customer for details, retrieving their transaction from a line-of-business system, updating the status, and providing confirmation or results back to the user. Conversational agents are a useful "front door" to knowledge or internal systems that can save the user from switching contexts and applications.

> **SEE ALSO** Designing an effective conversational agent requires understanding and planning the scope, tone, behavior, and dialog. You will learn more about this topic in the section "Design the agent's capabilities" later in this chapter.

Autonomous agents

While we are most familiar with conversational agents, they are not the only type of agent you can build with Copilot Studio to solve your business problem. Agents can also be triggered by events—such as a form submission, an incoming email, or a new row added to a database—and run autonomously in the background, without any chat experience involved.

Autonomous agents open up new scenarios for business process and workflow automation that were not previously possible. Notably, they require a different kind of thinking than designing a conversational agent. Autonomous agents can do more than traditional "if this, then that" workflow automation. When you design an autonomous agent, you define the trigger that initiates it, and provide it with the knowledge, tools, and instructions it needs. Instead of following predefined branching logic, the autonomous agent reasons over the knowledge and tools using generative AI to determine the best course of action, operating independently and interacting with a human only if or when needed.

Unlike workflow automation, which relies on a fixed logic path, autonomous agents make decisions dynamically, using the context to decide which actions to take and when. Autonomous agents can still invoke deterministic flows for parts of the process that need to remain fixed and structured (e.g., retrieve an order record from a database, get the value of the transaction, or apply branching logic to determine the next step based on the value of the transaction), and then return to using generative AI for other answers and actions.

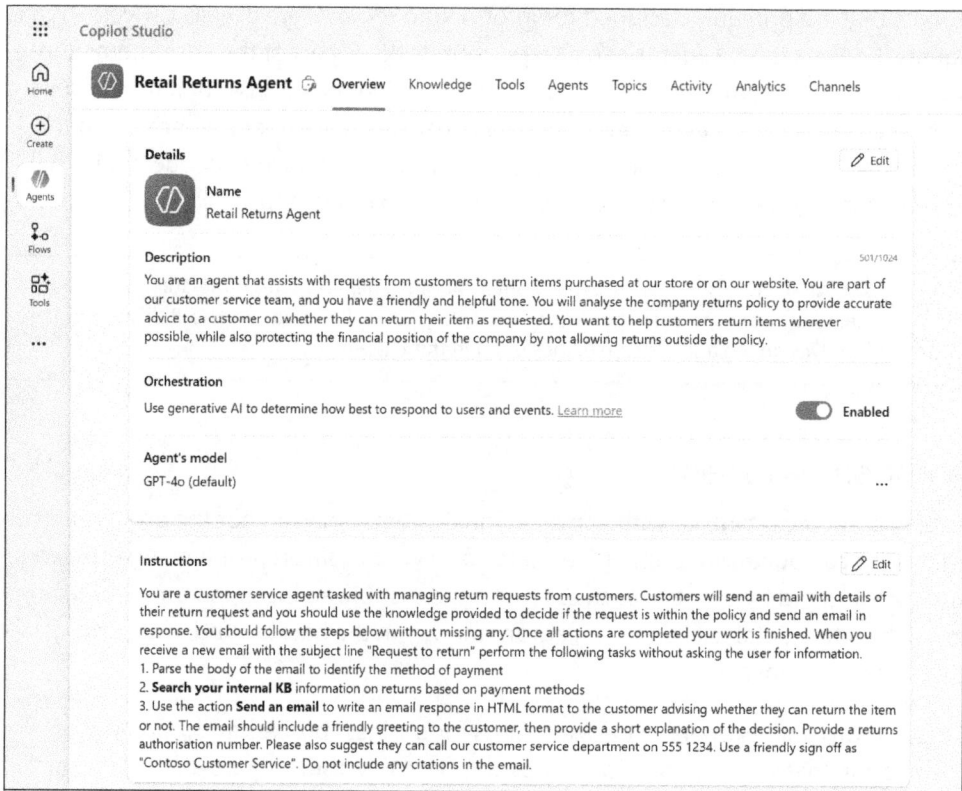

An autonomous agent uses generative AI to reason over instructions, knowledge, and tools at runtime to automate a process.

Think about the business processes that you have not been able to automate in the past because they require human reasoning or decision making. These are likely use cases for autonomous agents, which can use advanced reasoning models to make decisions and perform complex tasks.

> ⚠️ **IMPORTANT** Autonomous agents use generative orchestration; you can't design an autonomous agent using classic orchestration. Orchestration is covered in detail in the next section.

> 🔍 **SEE ALSO** You will learn more about autonomous agents in Chapter 5: Building autonomous agents.

Multi-agent systems

When designing your agent, you need to consider whether your scenario is best handled by a single agent or by a system of agents. In a multi-agent system, each agent has separate knowledge, tools, and responsibilities, and the various agents have the ability to hand off or work with each other.

Single agents work best when you are designing an agent that will work within a clearly defined business domain or source of knowledge. If your agent design requires more than four or five sources of knowledge or tools, then you can likely achieve better performance by building multiple agents that can hand off to each other. For instance, in a banking scenario, you may develop separate specialist agents for each product or service, such as personal loans, mortgages, and business banking. Each agent has knowledge sources and tools specific to that one domain or task and can call or hand off to the other agents when needed.

In Copilot Studio, you can build a multi-agent system by designing a single agent with "child" agents inside it. Alternatively, you can connect your agent to other existing agents.

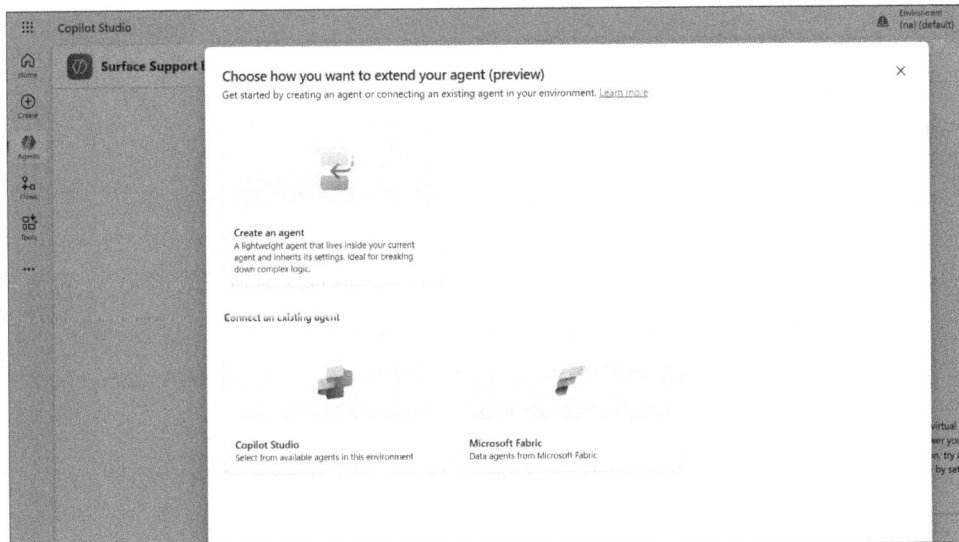

In Copilot Studio, you can connect your agents to other agents in a multi-agent design.

> **SEE ALSO** You will learn how to build these kinds of agents in Chapter 9: Designing multi-agent orchestration.

Select the agent's orchestration model

The orchestration layer controls how the agent decides which knowledge sources and tools to use, and when. When you are building an agent in Copilot Studio, you can use either generative orchestration or classic (deterministic) orchestration. This design choice affects the capability, performance, and cost of your agent, so it is important to understand how each option works, as well as the benefits and limitations of each.

The following concepts are important in understanding how orchestration models work:

- An *intent* represents the goal or purpose behind the user input. It answers the question, "What does the user want to do?" Intents are used by the agent to understand the user's request and trigger the right answer or action.

- An *entity* is a specific piece of information that can be extracted from an unstructured user input. It represents a known data type or category—such as a date, location, or product name—that the agent needs to complete a task.

> **TIP** This is a different meaning and use of the word *entity* than the way this term is used in building database schema, where the word *entity* refers to a data table.

- Entities are used in *slot filling,* which is the process of the agent collecting all the information it requires before it can act.

Consider the following example: A retailer has an agent on its website that can answer user questions about products and assist with returns. To process a return, the agent needs to know the product, size, purchase location, and condition. A customer visits the website and enters the following information into the chat:

"Hi, I'd like to return the AS49 waterproof jacket I bought from the Chicago store. It's a men's size L and it still has the tags on."

The orchestration model would identify the following intent and entities from this input:

- Intent: Product return

- Entities:

  - Product name: AS49 waterproof jacket

  - Purchase location: Chicago store

- Size: Men's L

- Condition: Tags on

The way in which your agent determines the intent, identifies the entities, and performs the slot filling will differ depending on whether you are using generative or classic orchestration.

Generative orchestration

When you create a new agent in Copilot Studio, it will be configured to use generative orchestration by default. Generative orchestration uses generative AI to reason over the instructions, knowledge, and tools in the agent to determine what to do next.

Generative orchestration works with intents by using a large language model to decide what to do based on the user input. It reasons, "Given this user input, what is the best action or response to take?" It can generate an answer from knowledge, trigger a topic, call a tool, or ask a clarifying question to get more information from the user if the input is ambiguous. It can chain together multiple topics, tools, and knowledge, and provide a consolidated answer based on the combined outputs of all these things. It can also handle vague or complex inputs that include multiple intents, because it doesn't rely on matching against a strict set of examples.

Generative orchestration handles entity extraction and slot filling by using the LLM and reasoning to understand which information is needed and whether it has already been provided. It looks at the meaning of the user input in context and extracts relevant information based on the task it needs to execute. It can reason to extract entities without needing structured entity labels or definitions. It can also automatically ask follow-up questions to prompt the user for the additional information it needs. When you build an agent that uses generative orchestration, you don't need to build conversational flows that specifically ask for each piece of information in turn.

Generative orchestration is more "clever" and powerful than classic orchestration. However, it is less predictable than a classic orchestration model, where you manually train and classify intents. It also has a higher consumption cost than using classic orchestration.

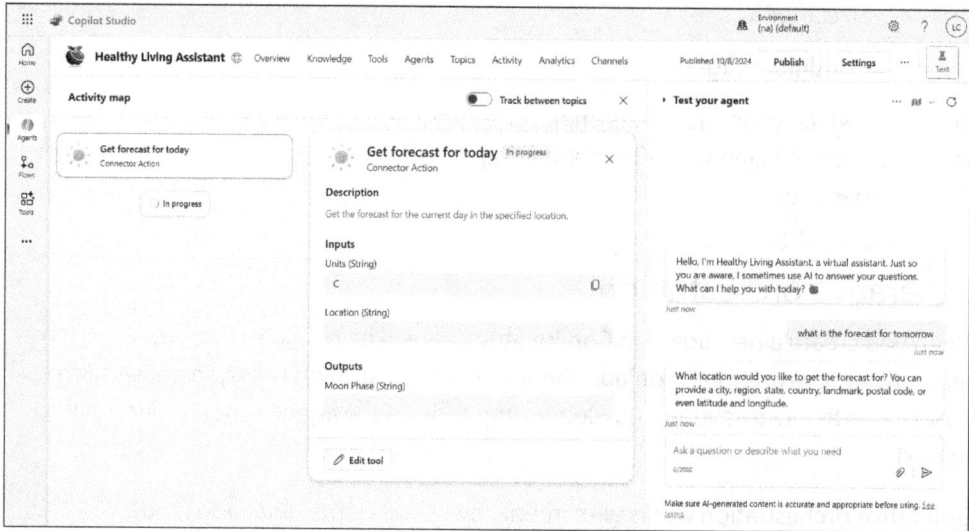

With generative orchestration, the agent calls a tool and automatically generates questions to ask for the information it needs to complete the task.

> 🔍 **SEE ALSO** Refer to the section "Understand and calculate agent costs" later in this chapter for more details on calculating the cost of generative orchestration.

If you plan to use generative orchestration, it is important to write meaningful instructions as well as clear descriptions for every trigger, knowledge source, and tool you add to your agent. Generative orchestration uses these descriptions to understand the purpose of each tool or component, and to reason over them to decide what to use.

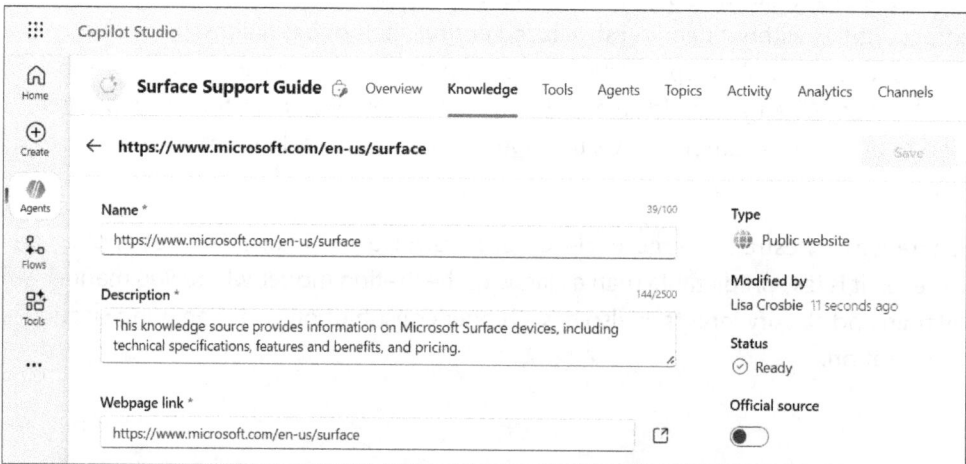

The description for the knowledge source helps the orchestrator understand when to use this knowledge.

> ⚠️ **IMPORTANT** The quality of your descriptions will have a substantial impact on the performance of generative orchestration for your agent. If you add triggers, knowledge, or tools and leave the description as the default suggestion, or leave it blank, that will affect the performance of your agent.

Classic orchestration

You can choose to build your agent in Copilot Studio with classic orchestration, which uses a natural language understanding (NLU) model to orchestrate the agent. Classic orchestration is less sophisticated than generative orchestration and has some limitations, which we will explore in this section. However, it is more predictable, controllable, and cost-effective, and it can be a good choice for the right use case.

Classic orchestration uses an NLU model to identify intents by classifying the user input into predefined categories. Unlike the generative orchestration model, which begins by reasoning over the best course of action to take, classic orchestration starts by determining which intent the user input matches.

When you build your agent using classic orchestration, you set up intents using topics—specifically, by providing 5–10 trigger phrases that the NLU uses to under-stand the intent for each topic. When the orchestration model receives the user input, it will classify the intent and match it to the most suitable topic.

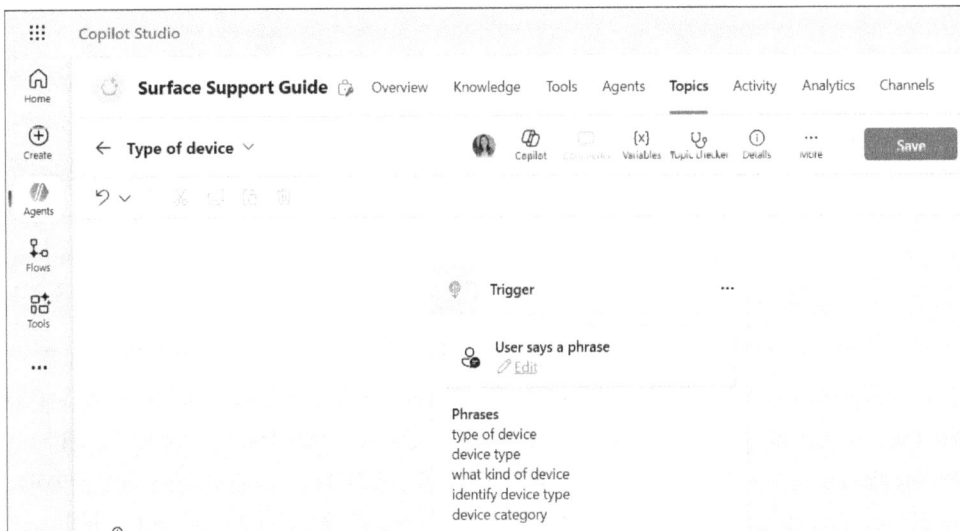

A topic in classic orchestration is triggered when the user asks about the type of device, based on a series of trigger phrases.

If the model doesn't find a suitable topic match (or if you haven't authored any topics in the agent), then it will use Conversational boosting—the fallback topic—to answer the question. If you have added a knowledge source to your agent (as you did for the quick agent you built in Chapter 1), it will use that knowledge source to generate an answer using generative AI. With classic orchestration, generative AI is used to reason over knowledge to provide answers, but not to determine the course of action taken by the agent itself.

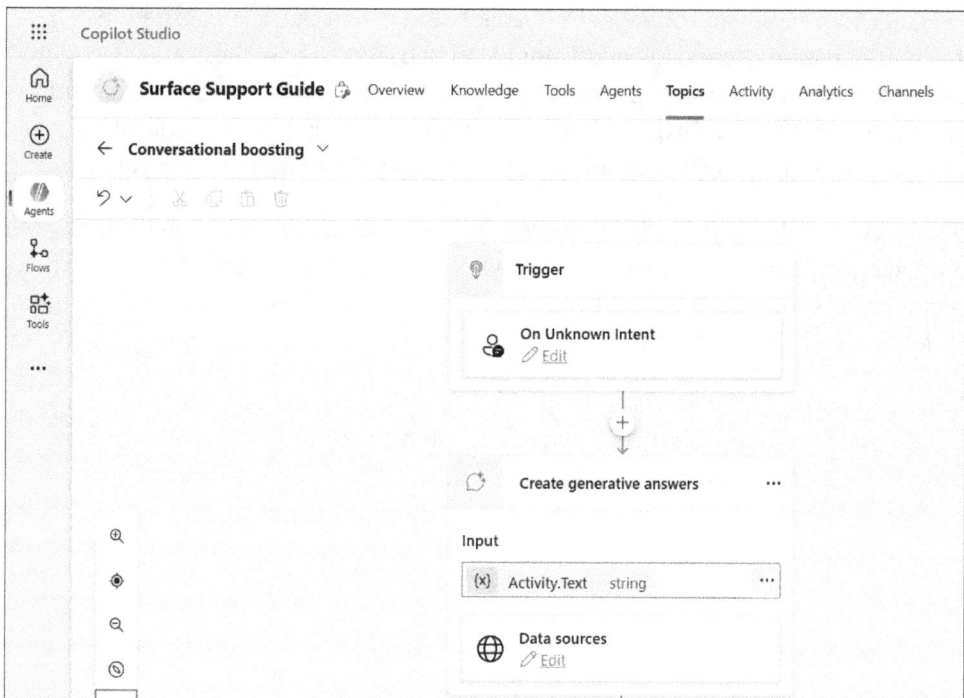

The system-generated Conversational boosting topic is triggered by an unknown intent to use generative answers to respond.

> **SEE ALSO** You will learn about other design options for fallback and escalation in the section "Design the agent's capabilities" later in this chapter.

Intent classification when you are using classic orchestration is more controlled than when you are using generative orchestration, because you are training the NLU with the trigger phrases you configure for each topic. If you design your agent using classic orchestration, you will need to carefully map out the intents so that they are disambiguated. You will also need to understand the likely user inputs and author trigger phrases that match the anticipated user intents.

Classic orchestration extracts entities from the user input based on the defined list of entities to which it has access. Copilot Studio provides out-of-the-box entities for commonly used pieces of information, such as age, location, and color. In addition, you can configure your own custom entities for things specific to your industry or business, such as product name, size, and condition, as shown in the earlier example.

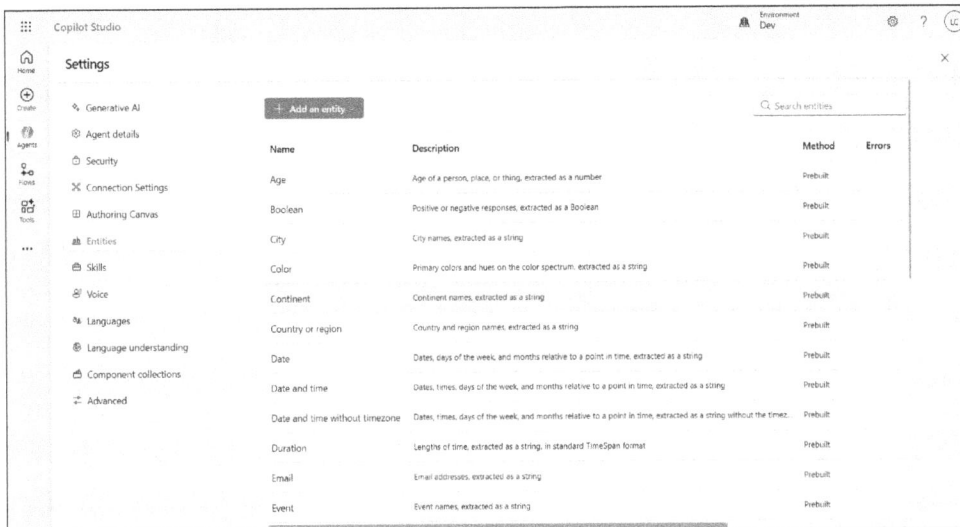

Copilot Studio comes with prebuilt entities for common entities like Age, City, Color, Country, and Date.

> **SEE ALSO** You will learn more about authoring topics and creating and working with entities in Chapter 7: Authoring topics.

If you design your agent using classic orchestration, you should understand and consider the limitations of this model, and factor these into your design and configurations:

- An agent designed with classic orchestration can detect only one intent per user input. Returning to the earlier example, suppose the user asked, "I want to return the AS49 waterproof jacket I bought from the Chicago store and what are the opening hours of that store." The agent would not be able to detect and handle both intents (initiate return, ask about opening hours).

- If the user input includes multiple instances of an entity, this model won't be able to disambiguate them. For example, if the user states, "I want to return the AS49 waterproof jacket and the HL23 hiking boots," two products are mentioned.

- The only customization you can do when working with the out-of-the-box NLU model is to configure topics (by providing a few sample trigger phrases) and to configure custom entities. The agent will learn to match those phrases in the topics or extract entities from user input using the general-purpose NLU model. You can't control or customize the actual underlying AI model.

> ✓ **TIP** If you want to customize the NLU model, you can swap the out-of-the-box NLU model with a custom Azure model, as described in the next section on Azure CLU integration.

- You need to author question nodes in topics to prompt the user for any required information. This kind of model will not automatically identify or prompt the user for missing entities.

- You need to author message nodes in topics to respond to the user after they have provided information.

- If you want your agent to use tools to take actions, you need to set up a topic to explicitly call that tool after the intent has been detected and that topic triggered.

- You cannot build an autonomous agent using classic orchestration.

> ⚠ **IMPORTANT** If you are using generative answers over a knowledge source, as we did in the example in Chapter 1, the response will appear to handle both intents. That's because generative answers can respond, even though only the first intent is truly recognized. If you have a workflow or automation dependent on the second intent, it will not be triggered or executed.

Generative orchestration is the default option for new agents created in Copilot Studio. If you want to switch to classic orchestration, you can make the change with a simple toggle switch.

To switch to classic orchestration

1. Open your agent and find the Orchestration section. You will see that the option for using generative AI to determine how best to respond to users and events is set to **Enabled**.

2. Switch this toggle to **Disabled**. Copilot will take a moment to process and save the change.

3. When this process is finished, the changes will be saved, and the generative orchestration toggle will be set to **Disabled**.

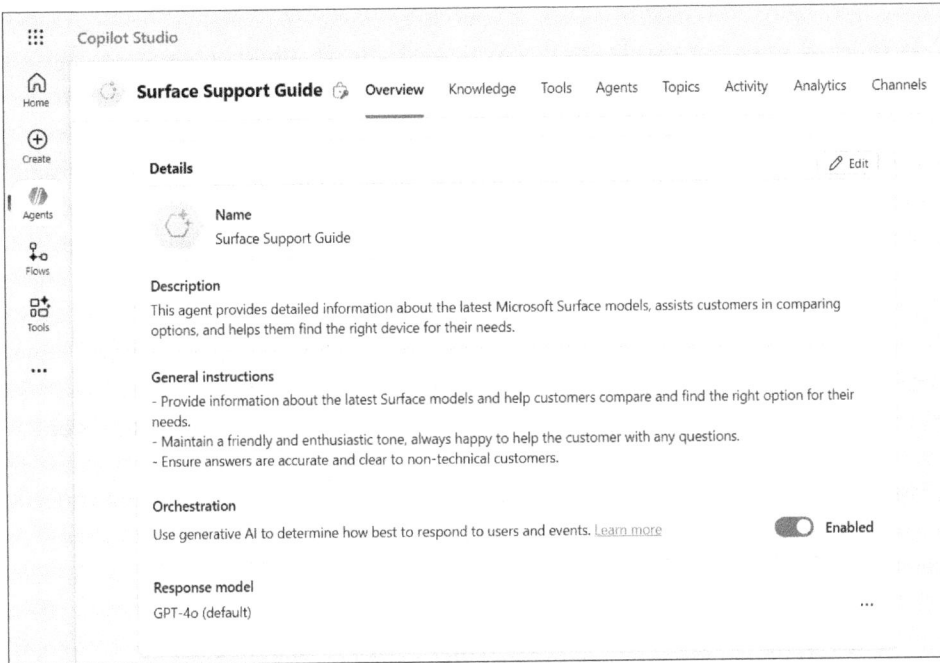

The generative orchestration setting is enabled by default.

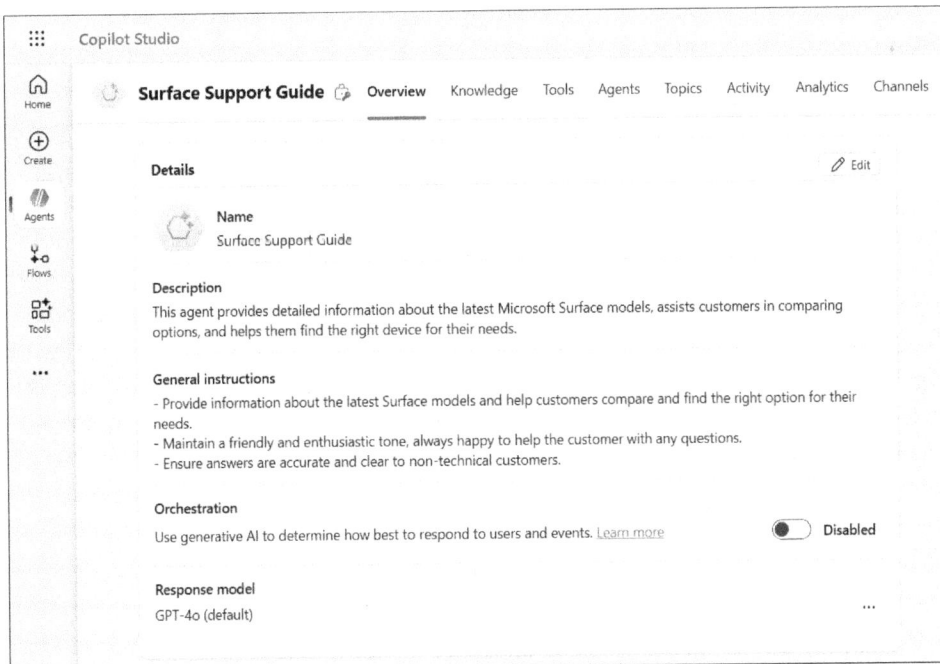

The orchestration mode is set to classic when the orchestration toggle is switched to Disabled.

Consider using classic orchestration when your agent use case is relatively straightforward, or when you are working with explicitly designed processes, such as password resets, leave requests, address updates, or policy checks. It is the ideal choice for scenarios where you need full control and predictability, whether for compliance or for validation. It is also a more cost-effective solution than generative orchestration.

Azure CLU integration

If you want to build and train your own language model and use that in Copilot Studio instead of the one provided, you can switch to a custom conversational language understanding (CLU) model built in Azure. Building your own CLU model allows you to define exactly how intents work and which entities to extract, and to train the model with as many examples as you want. You can include domain- or industry-specific vocabulary, complex phrases, and synonyms. You can also create entity lists or custom extraction rules.

> **SEE ALSO** Conversational language understanding is one of the custom features offered by Azure AI Language. If you want to learn how to build your own CLU model in Azure, refer to the Microsoft product documentation: https://learn.microsoft.com/en-us/azure/ai-services/language-service/conversational-language-understanding/overview.

The custom CLU model will improve how well intents and entities are recognized, but it still has the limitation that it will detect only one intent per user input. Unlike the NLU model, it can support multiple values for a single entity. You can train the entity recognizer to extract both values separately, so it could handle our earlier example where the user asked to return two different products in one input.

To integrate a CLU model with a Copilot Studio agent, you must have a fully trained CLU model that includes intents for the system topics and any custom topics you have authored in your Copilot Studio agent. You will map the CLU intents to those topics. The entities you have built in your Azure CLU will be imported into Copilot Studio and can be used alongside the prebuilt, out-of-the-box entities.

> **SEE ALSO** To learn more about how to set up and integrate a CLU model with your Copilot Studio agent, refer to the Microsoft documentation: https://learn.microsoft.com/en-us/microsoft-copilot-studio/advanced-clu-get-started.

2

Using a CLU model is a good choice when you have the skills to develop a custom model in Azure for a complex, domain-specific, or industry-specific language, or when the intents sound so similar that the built-in NLU model cannot understand them well enough. It will provide more precise and accurate responses, particularly for specialized language, and it is a good option for improving intent and entity recognition in languages other than English. However, you need to invest the time and effort in scaling, managing, and monitoring your CLU model, and must also pay the associated consumption costs in Azure.

Design the agent's capabilities

Once you've defined the type of agent that works best for your scenario and selected an orchestration model, the next stage is defining what the agent is responsible for and what it will need to complete the job you are assigning it. In this section, you will learn about designing these core capabilities of your agent.

When designing the agent's capabilities, you should consider the agent's purpose and scope, the brand voice, and the knowledge and tools the agent needs to access. You must also decide how to structure the responses using a balance of deterministic logic, topics, and generative answers, and how to plan for fallback and escalation.

Define the agent's scope and purpose

Every design decision should be informed by a clear, user-centric understanding of the agent's purpose and the business problem you are solving. Revisit the work you did in Chapter 1 to document the business problem, impact, and success metrics, and keep these top of mind as you design your agent.

Start by collaborating with users and internal stakeholders to identify the most common questions, tasks, and challenges they face. Support this discovery process with any available data or reports, such as FAQ documents, reports on the most frequently raised tickets, customer complaints, employee onboarding feedback, or website analytics. Consult with customer service representatives, HR or IT staff, or any frontline worker who interacts with the users of your agent to understand their experience and insights.

Earlier in this chapter you learned how orchestration models work with intents. Understanding the underlying human intent of your users is even more important.

Give the agent your brand voice

Your external agent is a representative of your brand, and you should think of it as a virtual customer-facing team member when you design it. Designing your agent so that it reflects the tone and personality of your brand voice can build trust with your customers and align the agent's actions with the rest of your external-facing communication. Doing so will help the users feel as if they are interacting with your organization rather than a generic AI chatbot.

Consider the tone (formal, friendly, direct, playful), style (concise, empathetic, detailed), vocabulary (specific industry terminology or abbreviations), and the emotional context of the user. The "personality" of an agent for a fashion retailer and an agent for an insurance company can and should feel very different.

Identify the knowledge sources and tools your agent needs

Once the agent's purpose is clearly defined, you will be able to identify the knowledge and actions it will need to take to fulfill that purpose effectively. As part of this step, you will need to determine the data sources and tools your agent will use to answer questions and complete tasks.

Start by assessing what knowledge your agent will need to find information and generate answers. Will it use internal documents, SharePoint libraries, public websites, structured data, or connections with your enterprise systems? Do you already have data indexed in Azure AI that you want to use? If you are using unstructured knowledge sources (particularly SharePoint document libraries), consider whether they are well organized and curated to be able to provide consistent and accurate answers. Generative AI doesn't provide a magic solution to inconsistent, conflicting, or duplicate information. You will find your agent performs much better when it is working with knowledge that is backed by a good content management strategy.

2

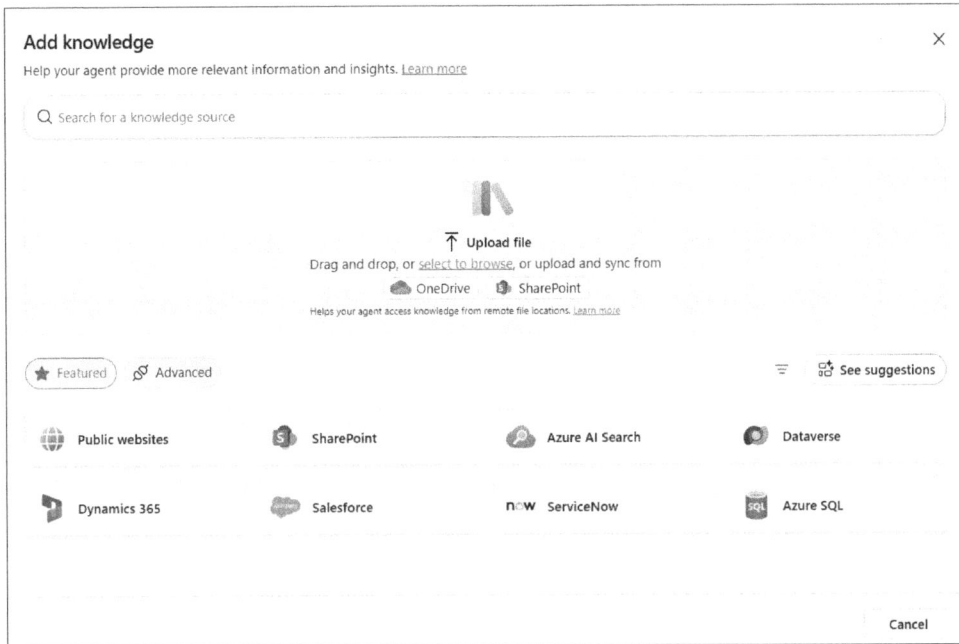

You can add a range of knowledge sources to your agent, including public websites and SharePoint, Dataverse, and enterprise data sources.

> **SEE ALSO** You will learn about working with knowledge in detail in Chapter 6: Grounding agents in knowledge.

Next, define the actions your agent will perform, and the tools it will need to do so. Which business processes does it support or automate? Will it only retrieve data from business systems, or will it also write back to databases, initiate workflows, create content, or send notifications? For each task or action, consider which tools, connectors, integration, and authentication will be required.

Copilot Studio provides a range of tools that you can use for your agent, including prompts, agent flows, custom connectors, REST APIs, the computer use tool, and the Model Context Protocol.

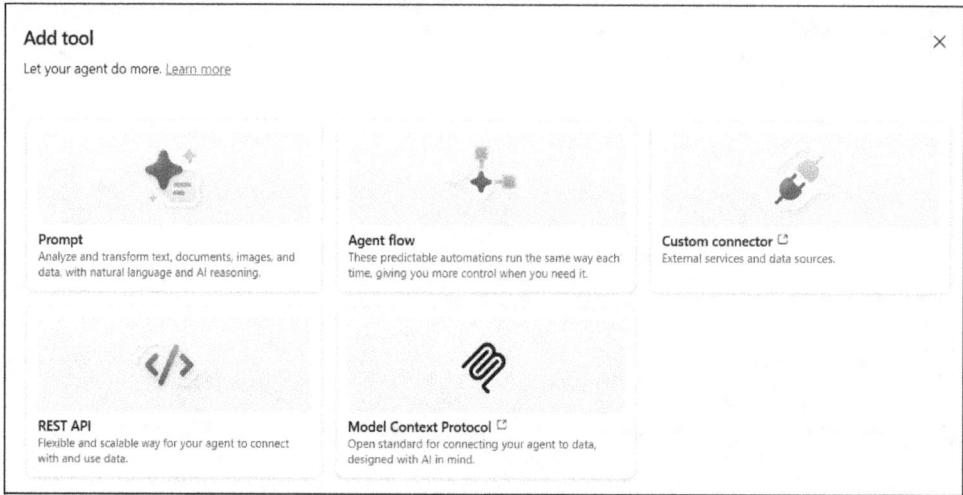

In Copilot Studio, you can add a wide range of tools to extend your agent.

> **SEE ALSO** Tools are covered in detail in Chapter 8: Extending agents with tools.

> **TIP** Your agent should be designed for a specific business domain with a role to perform. Don't overload one agent with too many knowledge sources and tools, which puts it at risk of being unreliable. If your scenario involves multiple business functions and diverse knowledge or tasks, consider designing a multi-agent system with clear handoffs between agents.

Define the logic strategy

Defining the logic strategy for your agent involves defining which tasks or parts of the process should be handled by generative AI and which should be handled by deterministic logic. Copilot Studio allows you to blend both to create effective and reliable agents.

Generative AI has enabled us to create more comprehensive and powerful conversational AI experiences than were possible in the past. Before it became available, building a traditional chatbot meant designing and authoring topics for every intent you wanted the chatbot to handle, leaving a long tail of user experiences where the chatbot just couldn't help or had to escalate to a human agent. With generative AI, we can design agents that are grounded in trusted knowledge and have tools to perform actions. These agents can handle more powerful and natural conversations without the need to perform a lot of manual authoring.

However, generative AI can sometimes be unpredictable and risky. Your agent scenario most likely includes critical business processes or information where you need reliable, repeatable tasks run in a specific sequence. Striking the right balance between generative and deterministic logic is key in designing an effective agent.

Generative AI is very powerful for tasks like answering questions, summarizing information, or providing helpful explanations, especially when the user input is unpredictable. However, it can be less effective in scenarios where precision, order, or compliance is critical. In all but the most basic retrieval agents, you should not rely entirely on generative answers, especially in high-risk or high-value scenarios.

Deterministic logic plays an essential role in agent design, because it allows you to build in structured, rule-based flows that can work alongside generative AI. Deterministic agent flows are the right choice for processes that follow strict business rules, or that require a series of specific steps to be executed in a defined order, such as compliance checks, approvals, payments, and password resets.

Understanding when to use generative AI and when to use deterministic logic will result in an agent that can handle a wide range of conversations and user intent, while also providing consistent and trustworthy answers where needed.

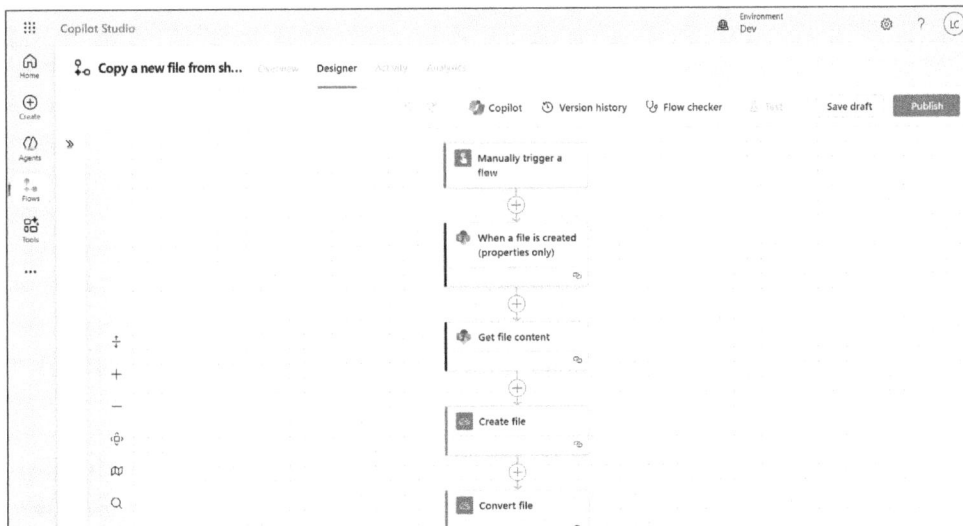

Use an agent flow in Copilot Studio to define a series of sequential steps in a task or process.

Identify topics

In addition to using deterministic logic for tasks and process automation, Copilot Studio allows you to design deterministic dialog flows, or topics, that you can use to control business-critical parts of the conversation where you don't want to rely on generative AI to respond. In Copilot Studio, topics are the core building blocks of an agent that defines the conversational dialog using messages, questions, variables, and branching logic.

Topics are how you can create consistent, predictable responses in the agent conversation. For instance, suppose that when you are building your IT Helpdesk Agent, you discover that users frequently ask, "How do I create a Teams channel?" Your organizational policy is that users cannot create channels on their own, and you have a link to a form for requesting a new channel. Rather than relying on generative answers to find this information, you could author a topic that provides the right information every time along with the link to the request form.

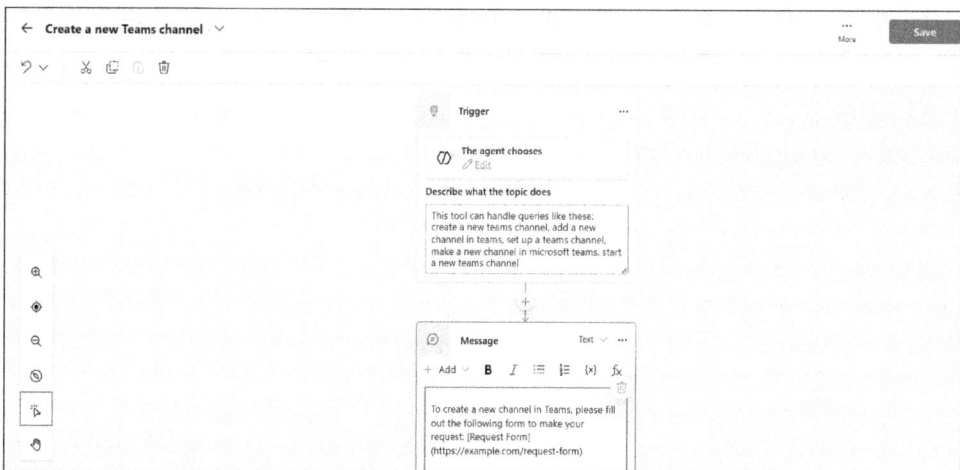

A topic is used to control the response to critical parts of the conversation.

Topics can be triggered by the user input, or by being called from another topic or tool in the agent. Topics can be complex, with branching logic and variables, or they can be just a simple intent and response.

To decide which topics you should build for your agent, start with a few of the most frequently asked questions or tasks that have the highest impact on your success metrics. Look for issues that generate the highest volume of calls, queries, or unnecessary manual work in your business scenario. Think about these tasks from the user's point of view, reviewing the sources you've used in defining the agent's purpose and scope.

Keep your topic structure manageable and modular. Don't try to cover every interaction or answer with a topic. Copilot Studio has a limit of 1000 topics, but if you are hitting that limit you are likely creating an overly complex design that will be hard to manage and maintain. Use knowledge sources and generative answers to handle the long tail of less frequently asked questions, and consider creating knowledge sources or using FAQ documents specifically for this purpose. Remember, you can also consider a multi-agent handoff design rather than including everything in a single agent.

As you design topics, look for opportunities to create reusable topics that can work like subroutines to simplify the overall conversational design. These can be small, simple topics with inputs and outputs that are called by other topics. Reusable topics can help with tasks like collecting customer information, capturing feedback, and confirming an action. You can pass variables or context from one topic to another.

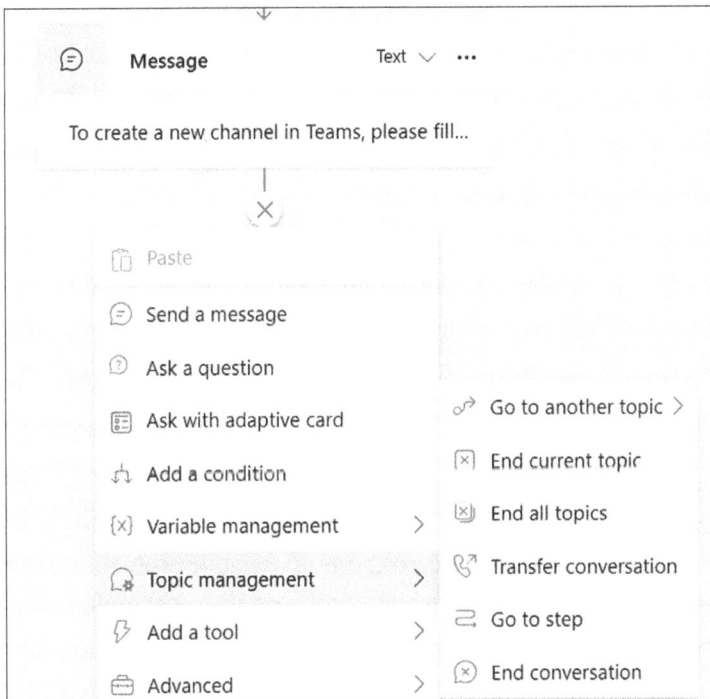

You can design a point in the conversation where you redirect the dialog to another topic.

To avoid confusion during runtime, make sure your topics are well defined and distinct from each other, avoiding overlap in the intents, trigger phrases, and descriptions. When mapping out your topics, if you identify intents that are likely to overlap, consider using disambiguation topics. A disambiguation topic is used when multiple topics could be triggered by the user input; it prompts the user to clarify their intent. For example, suppose the user asks, "I need help with leave." You could create a disambiguation topic that asks whether the user wants to check their leave balance, apply for leave, or understand the leave policy. From there, you can redirect the agent to the appropriate topic.

You can combine deterministic topics with generative answers inside the dialog flow to help focus generative AI on a specific knowledge source. For instance, you can handle the intent "return an item" by building a topic that collects the information required and then uses generative answers within that topic to reason over the return policy to provide the appropriate response.

As noted in Chapter 1, Copilot Studio is a low-code SaaS tool that allows you to quickly and easily iterate and republish your agent without needing a full development cycle. You should review the performance of your agent over time, and identify topics that are ambiguous as well as frequent questions from the users that could be better handled by a topic. Use of agents is a process of continuous iteration and review. Involve the business users and customer service representatives who are subject-matter experts to refine the topic language and descriptions, and to identify new or trending intents that should be added as new topics.

> **SEE ALSO** You will learn how to build topics and conversational paths in Chapter 7: Authoring topics.

Plan for fallback and escalation

No matter how well you design your agent, there will undoubtedly be situations where it doesn't understand the intent or can't find an answer, either because the answer isn't in the knowledge sources or because the user is asking for something out of scope for the agent's purpose. Planning for fallback and escalation is therefore an important part of the design process.

In Chapter 1, you created a very basic agent that was connected to a public website and was immediately able to answer questions. This capability was enabled by the system's Conversational boosting topic, which acts as a fallback to generate answers from knowledge.

In most agent designs, you will use both topics and generative answers as described in the previous section. At runtime, the agent will first check whether the user intent matches any of the authored topics. It will then use those topics to provide answers and perform actions where it finds a match.

You can design the fallback behavior to handle cases where your agent doesn't find a match in the authored topics, using the following capabilities in Copilot Studio:

- You can enable general knowledge or web search to allow your agent to use the large language model or to search all public websites to generate an answer.

> **SEE ALSO** Enabling general knowledge and web search are covered in Chapter 6: Grounding agents in knowledge.

- You can use the **Conversational boosting** system topic for generative answers. This topic will act as the first fallback for unrecognized intent, automatically applying reasoning across all the knowledge sources you have added to your agent and providing a response.

- If generative answers still can't answer the user query, the agent will trigger the system's **Fallback** topic. By default, this topic prompts the user for clarification, and if necessary, responds with a message stating that it can't help. You can configure the message, tone, and behavior of the fallback topic to match your scenario.

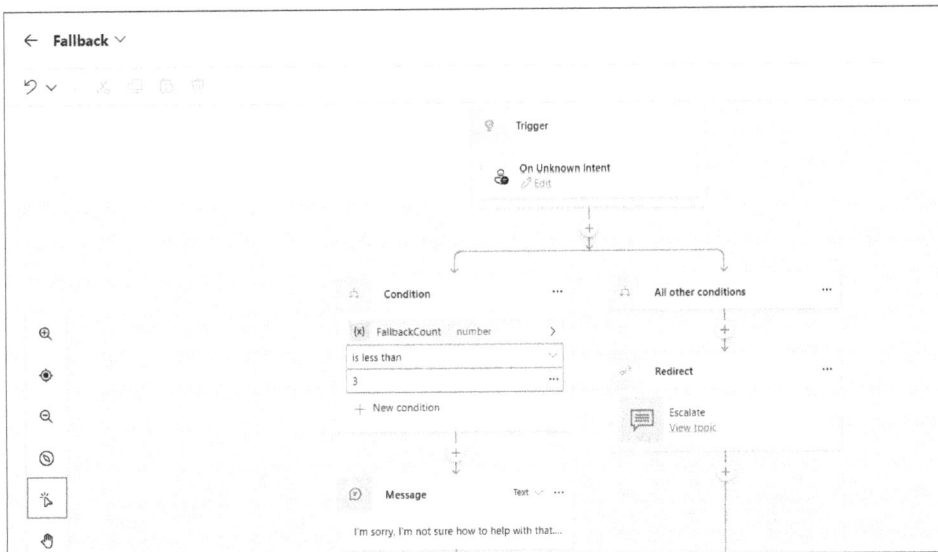

The system's Fallback topic sends a message to the user or redirects to the Escalate topic when the intent can't be determined.

- If the user's request still isn't resolved, you can configure the fallback to behave or escalate in the following ways:

  - End the conversation with a helpful message

  - Integrate with an external system by calling another generative AI model using a custom connector

  - Hand off to a live agent using a customer engagement application

- You can also use fallback behavior in your topic design by adding generative answers inside the topic and directing the user to a different topic or escalation option if that fails to provide a useful response.

> ✓ **TIP** Remember to monitor the fallback patterns after you have published your agent, with the aim of identifying gaps in topic coverage or additional agent use cases where users are asking questions that fall outside the scope of the agent.

Ultimately, all these capabilities are geared toward setting your agent up for success, solving the business problem you defined, and providing a reliable and user-friendly experience.

Understand and calculate agent costs

When designing your agent, it is important to understand and be able to calculate the cost of running the agent in production. In this section, you will learn the principles of how licensing and consumption costs work in Copilot Studio.

> ⚠ **IMPORTANT** This section covers the principles of licensing and consumption costs rather than the specific values. All licensing is subject to change. For the most up-to-date licensing information and billing rates, refer to https://learn.microsoft.com/en-us/ microsoft-copilot-studio/billing-licensing and download the latest Power Platform licensing guide at http://aka.ms/powerplatformlicensingguide.

The cost of running your agent in Copilot Studio is calculated using the currency of "messages." Everything the agent does—such as responding to a user question, retrieving information from a knowledge source, or performing an action using a tool—consumes messages. These messages are metered at runtime.

2

Messages are consumed at different rates depending on what the agent is doing. The main factors that affect the consumption of messages and the cost of your agent are as follows:

- The capability being invoked

- The orchestration model used

- Tenant graph grounding, the channel, and the user license

The capability being invoked

The number of messages consumed depends on the amount of computing effort required for the capability being invoked. The more an agent grounds, reasons, or calls other AI tools, the more messages the interaction consumes. Using topics (classic answers) for predictable FAQs and reserving the higher-cost AI capabilities for the parts of the process that genuinely need them can help you manage these costs effectively.

- The lightest capability is when the agent uses "classic answers"—that is, static, authored responses in topics. In such a case, the agent doesn't need to use any AI or intelligence to produce this response to a user input. Classic answers are available only when using classic orchestration, but using topics with generative orchestration can still reduce message consumption compared with using generative answers for everything.

- Generative answers—where the agent is grounded in knowledge such as a website, document, or enterprise system—require the agent to use the large language model to generate a dynamic response. These answers consume more messages than using topics or classic answers.

- Specialized tools that extend the agent's capabilities—such as AI Builder prompts, code execution, document processing, and reasoning—consume the most messages because they run dedicated models.

> ⚠️ **IMPORTANT** Copilot Studio messages are consumed by any of the services or models you can select from within Copilot Studio. If you extend your Copilot Studio agent with custom models or indexing from Azure AI Foundry, the costs for those services are metered separately in Azure, in addition to the Copilot Studio message consumption.

The orchestration model used

As described earlier in this chapter, you can use either classic or generative orchestration for your agent. Classic orchestration uses lower-cost topics for classic answers. Generative orchestration uses the more powerful AI capabilities that are metered at a higher rate. Using classic orchestration for agents that handle narrow or predictive scenarios will prevent unnecessary costs here. Use the generative orchestration capabilities for agents with a high value and return on investment.

When you build an agent that uses generative orchestration, there is additional message consumption by the orchestrator as it reasons about what it should do and when. This is separate from (and in addition to) the consumption cost for the actual action or answer provided by the agent described previously.

For instance, if the agent reasons over a grounded knowledge source to find an answer, there is a consumption charge for the generative answer. If the agent also uses generative orchestration to decide which knowledge source to use, there is an extra consumption charge for that reasoning step.

> ⚠️ **IMPORTANT** Each interaction with an agent can utilize multiple message consumption rates simultaneously.

Tenant graph grounding, the channel, and the user license

When you have at least one Microsoft 365 Copilot license in your tenant, you have access to an additional premium feature that improves the way your agent searches in SharePoint and Microsoft 365 data sources. Deploying Microsoft 365 Copilot activates semantic search on the tenant. In Copilot Studio, this is referred to as "tenant graph grounding with semantic search." This option is enabled by default in the settings of your agent if you have a Microsoft 365 Copilot license in the tenant.

Search
Tenant graph grounding with semantic search 💎 Premium   On 🔘
Can provide improved search performance for Microsoft 365 Copilot tenants. Availability varies by data source. Learn more

Tenant graph grounding with semantic search will be enabled for your agent if you have a Microsoft 365 Copilot license in the tenant.

> ⚠ **IMPORTANT** This option is available only if you have at least one Microsoft 365 Copilot license in the same tenant. Without this option, you can still ground your agent on Microsoft 365 files and SharePoint, but it will not use this more advanced and effective search capability.

This feature is primarily used in Copilot Studio for extending Microsoft 365 Copilot. However, you need to be aware of and careful about consumption costs if you are building an agent for users who do not have that license, or if you are publishing an agent using this capability outside a Microsoft 365 surface. A Microsoft 365 Copilot license includes tenant graph grounding with semantic search *for that licensed user when the agent is published in a Microsoft 365 surface (e.g., Microsoft 365 Copilot, Teams, SharePoint).*

If you build an agent grounded on SharePoint or any Microsoft 365 data source with this setting enabled, and then publish it in any of the following ways, you will incur additional message consumption costs based on usage:

- Microsoft 365 Copilot Chat, Teams, and SharePoint for users who do not have a Microsoft 365 Copilot license

- An internal channel that is not a Microsoft 365 surface (e.g., an intranet or custom app), even if the user has a Microsoft 365 Copilot license

- A channel for external users

The message consumption rate for this feature is relatively high and will add up quickly if you build an agent that is used very frequently. Weigh the cost of a Microsoft 365 Copilot license for the users who will work with the agent (this license includes these costs as well as a wealth of other features) against these consumption costs for an individual agent.

Purchasing message packs for your agent

There are two main ways to license Copilot Studio:

- Prepaid packs of messages, billed by month for the tenant. This is the better option when your consumption is high and relatively regular or predictable. You stack prepaid packs to get the volume of messages you need. Messages expire at the end of the month, and do not roll over.

■ Post-paid "pay as you go" billing, where you pay for what you consume each month. The rate per message is higher than for the prepaid packs, but this option will be more cost-effective for agents with unpredictable, irregular, or seasonal usage.

Check the latest licensing guidelines from Microsoft for accurate and up-to-date cost and consumption calculations.

Using the Copilot Studio agent usage estimator

Microsoft provides an estimator to help you calculate the likely message consumption of your Copilot Studio agent. You can use this tool to estimate the costs and understand the impacts on message consumption of the different decisions you make in your agent design.

> ⚠ **IMPORTANT** This is a message consumption estimator only, not a pricing calculator.

You can access and use the Copilot Studio agent usage estimator online at https://microsoft.github.io/copilot-studio-estimator/.

Use the Copilot Studio agent usage estimator to understand and estimate message consumption for your agent.

Skills review

In this chapter, you learned how to:

- Choose between building a stand-alone agent or extending Microsoft 365 Copilot, and align your use case to a conversational agent, autonomous agent, or multi-agent system.

- Select the right orchestration model for your agent.

- Design your agent's core capabilities, planning for scope, tools, knowledge, logic, topics, and fallback.

- Understand how messages are used to calculate consumption costs for your agent.

Practice tasks

No practice files are necessary to complete the practice tasks in this chapter.

Choose the type of agent

Review the agent use case you developed in Chapter 1 and consider the following questions to decide which type of agent you should build.

1. What is the best user experience for this agent? Could this be an autonomous agent that acts in the background, or is it a conversational agent with which the user interacts directly?

2. How broad and varied is the domain knowledge or process that your agent needs to cover? Could it be more effective as an agent with multiple child agents handling specific parts of the process, or can a single agent handle everything required?

Select the agent's orchestration model

Navigate to the Surface Support Guide agent you built in the first chapter and complete the following tasks.

1. In the test pane, ask the question: **What is the difference between a 12-inch and 13-inch Surface Pro?**

2. Review the answer given and the activity map on the left side of the screen, which shows how the agent reasoned over the input and which knowledge source it used to generate the response.

3. Select **Overview** from the top menu to return to the agent configuration screen.

4. Switch the generative orchestration toggle to **Disabled** and wait a couple of minutes for confirmation that the change has been saved. Your agent is now using classic orchestration.

5. Refresh the test pane.

6. Ask the same question in the test pane: **What is the difference between a 12-inch and 13-inch Surface Pro?**

7. Review the difference in the quality of the answer compared with the generative orchestration mode. Note that you don't see the activity map in this mode.

8. Switch the generative orchestration back to **Enabled**.

Design the agent's capabilities

Navigate to the Surface Support Guide you built in Chapter 1 and perform the following tasks.

1. Review the description of the agent. It describes the tone of voice of the agent as "friendly and enthusiastic."

2. Refer to the Microsoft brand voice guidelines here: https://learn.microsoft.com/en-us/style-guide/brand-voice-above-all-simple-human.

3. Copy the section that describes the "three voice principles"—warm and relaxed, crisp and clear, and ready to lend a hand.

4. Go back to your agent and select the **Edit** button at the top of the Details section on the main configuration page.

5. Replace the section of the description that describes the tone of voice with the Microsoft voice principles copied in the previous steps.

6. Select the Save button to save the changes to the description.

7. Refresh the test pane and ask the question: **What is the difference between a 12-inch and 13-inch Surface Pro?**

8. Compare the tone of the response with the one you got at the beginning of the previous exercise. What differences do you notice?

Understand and calculate agent costs

Consider the Surface Support Guide agent you built in Chapter 1, which uses generative orchestration and web-grounded answers connected to the Microsoft Surface website.

1. Download the latest Power Platform licensing guide from http://aka.ms/powerplatformlicensingguide.

2. Go to the section in the document for Microsoft Copilot Studio. Your agent is using generative orchestration. Review the billing rates for web-grounded

answers and agent actions (AI-led orchestration). Imagine your agent gets 1000 single-turn question and answer interactions each day.

3. Calculate the message consumption for 1000 web-grounded answers.

4. Calculate the AI-led orchestration message consumption for 1000 agent actions.

5. Add these numbers together. This is the total estimated number of messages your agent will consume for this scenario.

6. Visit the Copilot Studio agent usage estimator at https://microsoft.github.io/copilot-studio-estimator/.

7. Enter an estimate for the number of users and the number of times per month your users will interact with the agent, and review the estimated message consumption.

8. Make some changes and review the changes to the estimate.

Building agents with the lite experience of Copilot Studio

3

Practice files

No practice files are necessary to complete the practice tasks in this chapter.

In this chapter

- Describe and configure an agent
- Build an agent from a template
- Share and manage agents

> ⚠ **IMPORTANT** This chapter describes the full functionality available with the lite experience of Copilot Studio when used with a paid Microsoft 365 Copilot license. There is also a more limited version of this experience available with the free version of Microsoft 365 Copilot Chat. The Practice tasks at the end of the chapter can all be completed using the Copilot Studio trial account set up in Chapter 1, together with the free version of Microsoft 365 Copilot Chat.

The lite experience of Copilot Studio is a no-code tool that makers and business users can use to build declarative agents, extending Microsoft 365 Copilot to fit their own business scenarios. It can be used to create simple agents with instructions and starter prompts that can act as a coach or learning tool on a subject. It can also be used to create agents grounded in your business data to support users in their everyday work in a specific domain or business process. The agents you build in the lite experience of Copilot Studio take on the same look and feel as the main Microsoft 365 Copilot Chat user interface, with an icon, name, and starter prompts. Users can switch between the main Copilot Chat and these agents, or they can "@ mention" these agents from the main chat experience to focus the chat on the specific topic or knowledge handled by an agent.

The lite experience of Copilot Studio is embedded in the Microsoft 365 Copilot app. Its interface is designed to guide the user through the steps of building the agent by describing it with natural language. It has a limited set of configuration capabilities to extend the agent with knowledge, connectors, and capabilities. The overall configuration experience is designed to be simple and intuitive, enabling business users to build agents with no code.

> **TIP** If you want to build agents for Microsoft 365 Copilot that have more capability than what the lite experience of Copilot Studio allows, you can build agents using the full Copilot Studio experience, using the skills in the rest of this book, and publish those agents to Microsoft 365 Copilot as a channel.

> **SEE ALSO** The lite experience of Copilot Studio is one of the tools available for building declarative agents. For other tools and use cases, refer to: https://learn. microsoft.com/en-us/microsoft-365-copilot/extensibility/declarative-agent-tool-comparison.

In this chapter, you will learn about the capabilities of the lite experience of Copilot Studio, as well as how to use it to describe, configure, edit, share, and manage agents in Microsoft 365 Copilot.

Describe and configure an agent

In this section, you will learn how to build an agent by describing it, how to configure an agent that is grounded in knowledge, and how to edit existing agents to make changes. You access the lite experience of Copilot Studio via the Microsoft 365 Copilot app.

> ⚠️ **IMPORTANT** The lite experience of Copilot Studio is available in both the free version of Microsoft 365 Copilot Chat and the paid licensed version of Microsoft 365 Copilot. The capabilities available to you will depend on your license. For full details, refer to https://learn.microsoft.com/en-us/microsoft-365-copilot/extensibility/prerequisites#agent-capabilities-for-microsoft-365-users.

3

Create an agent by describing it

Let's start with a simple agent that can help you improve the tone of your emails. This agent uses instructions and starter prompts to act as an expert in writing professional and friendly emails. It helps the user with correct grammar, spelling, and appropriate wording for different types of emails.

To create an agent with the lite experience of Copilot Studio

1. Navigate to Microsoft 365 Copilot Chat: https://m365.cloud.microsoft/chat.

2. Select **Create agent** from the left navigation menu. This will launch the lite experience of Copilot Studio.

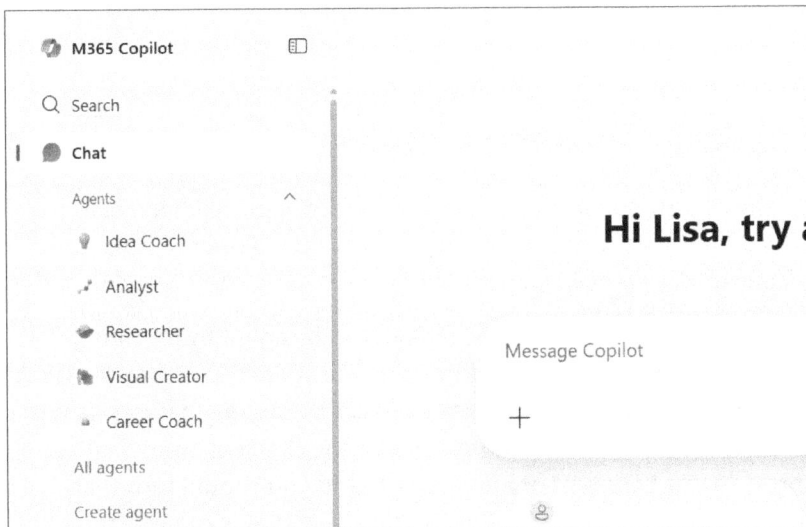

Select Create agent on the left navigation menu in the Microsoft 365 Copilot app.

3. Start by entering a description in the prompt area with a high-level description of what you want your agent to do. For example: **Help me draft emails using a professional and friendly tone, with correct grammar and spelling**.

> 🔍 **SEE ALSO** You can also create an agent from a template. This process is covered in the next section of this chapter.

4. Copilot will use your description to suggest a name and a set of starter prompts. These appear in the preview area and will be updated as you continue to describe and configure your agent.

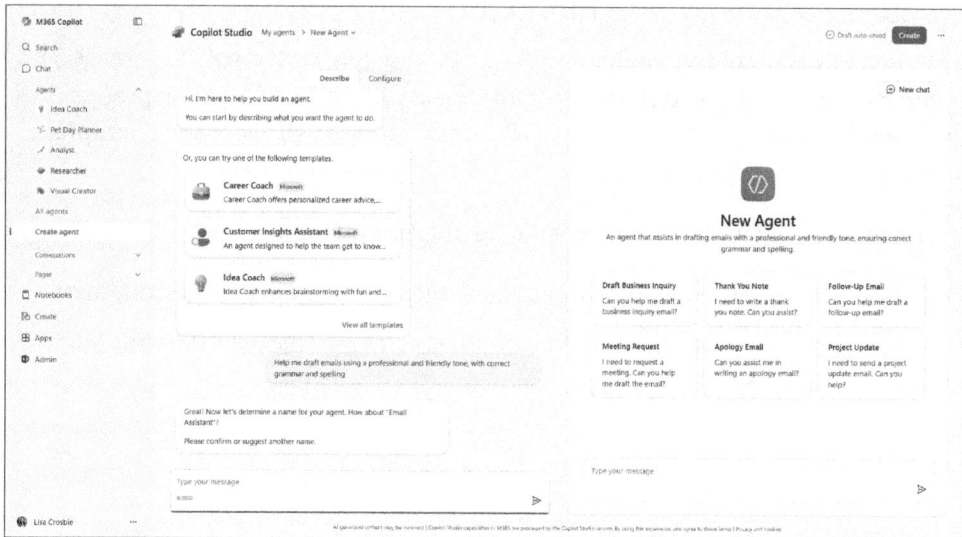

You can view a preview of your agent as you describe or configure it.

5. Respond in the chat by either confirming that you are happy with the name or suggesting a different name. Note that the preview on the right will change to show the name of the agent when you confirm it.

6. You will then be asked to refine the instructions for the agent by providing more details on the specific tasks or information the agent should handle. Think about general guidelines, directions, tone, and restrictions on how you want the agent to behave. Enter these instructions into the chat. For example: **The user will provide draft content or bullet points and you should turn that into professionally written emails. Always use a tone that is suitable for a corporate context. Emails may be internal to other staff, or client-facing communications. You will also offer suggestions to improve drafts the user shares.**

> ✓ **TIP** You can use Copilot Chat to get ideas or help with writing effective instructions.

7. Next, you will be asked if there are any specific guidelines or constraints for the agent. Enter the details into the chat. For example: **You should not help with writing personal emails. You should ensure that the tone is warm and relaxed, as well as professional. Please write using clear language**.

8. Copilot asks whether you want to add any publicly accessible websites as knowledge sources. Adding knowledge is an optional step, and we don't need to add knowledge for this scenario.

> 🔍 **SEE ALSO** You will learn how to configure an agent that is connected to knowledge and other business systems in the next section.

9. Test the agent in the pane on the right by selecting one of the suggested starter prompts.

Test the agent in the pane on the right by selecting one of the starter prompts.

10. Continue the conversation with the agent to test whether it is behaving as intended.

⊕ New chat

> I need to write a thank you note. Can you assist?

Email Assistant AI-generated content may be incorrect

This is Email Assistant. I'd be happy to help you write a thank you note! Could you please provide me with some details about the occasion or the person you're thanking? This will help me tailor the note to your needs.

👍 👎

> I need to thank one of my employees for doing an amazing job putting together a new marketing page for our Copilot campaign.

Email Assistant AI-generated content may be incorrect

Sure, I'd be happy to help you with that! Could you please provide me with the name of the employee you're thanking? This will help me personalize the note.

👍 👎

> Neil

Email Assistant AI-generated content may be incorrect

Here's a draft for your thank you note:

Dear Neil,

I hope this message finds you well. I wanted to take a moment to express my sincere

Type your message

▷

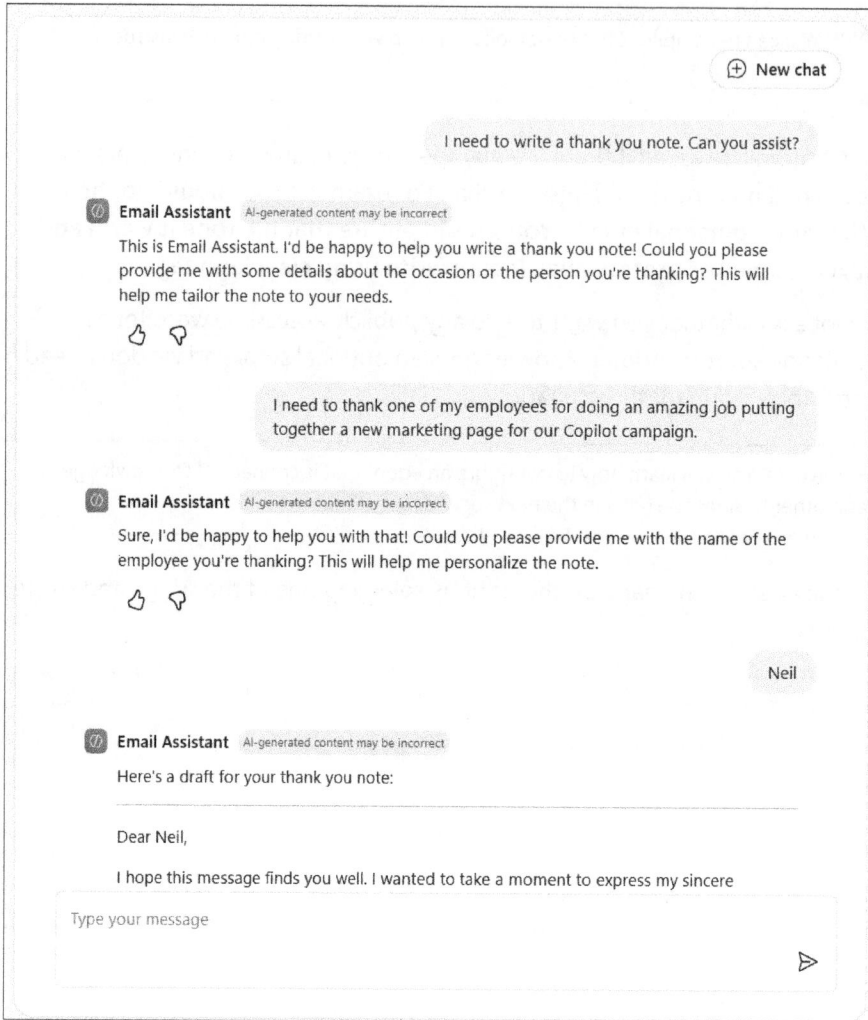

You can test the agent while you are configuring it.

🔍 **SEE ALSO** You can come back and edit the agent after it has been created, so you do not have to get it completely right at this stage. This kind of revision will be covered later in this section.

---

11. When you have finished describing your agent and testing it, select the **Create** button at the top right of the screen to create your agent.

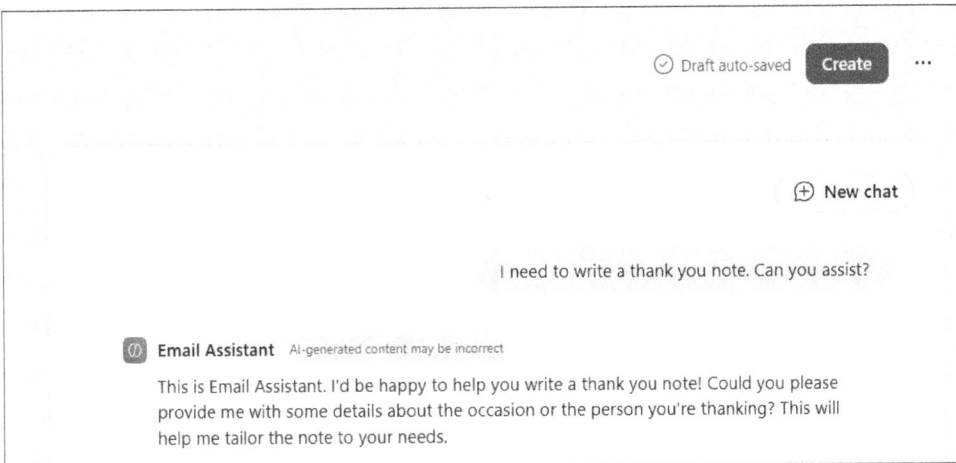

Select Create at the top right of the lite experience of Copilot Studio to create your agent.

12. Wait a moment for your agent to be created.

13. When the agent has been created, you will get a confirmation message. This message gives you the option to copy a link, change the sharing settings, or go to the agent. Select the **Go to agent** button to open the agent in Microsoft 365 Copilot.

> 🔍 **SEE ALSO** Sharing settings are covered later in this chapter.

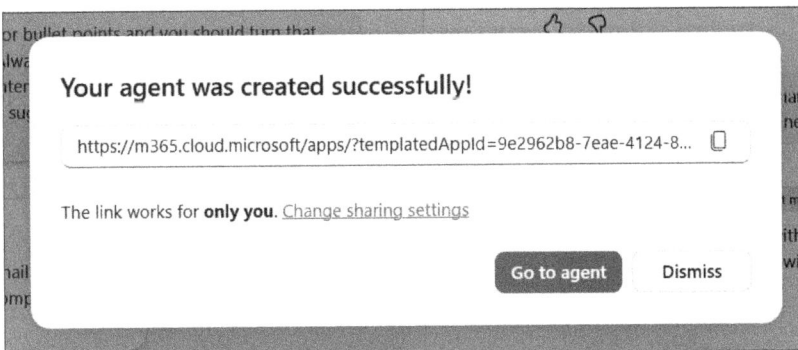

Select Go to agent to open your agent and start using it in Microsoft 365 Copilot.

14. Your new agent opens in Microsoft 365 Copilot and appears in the list of agents in the main menu on the left.

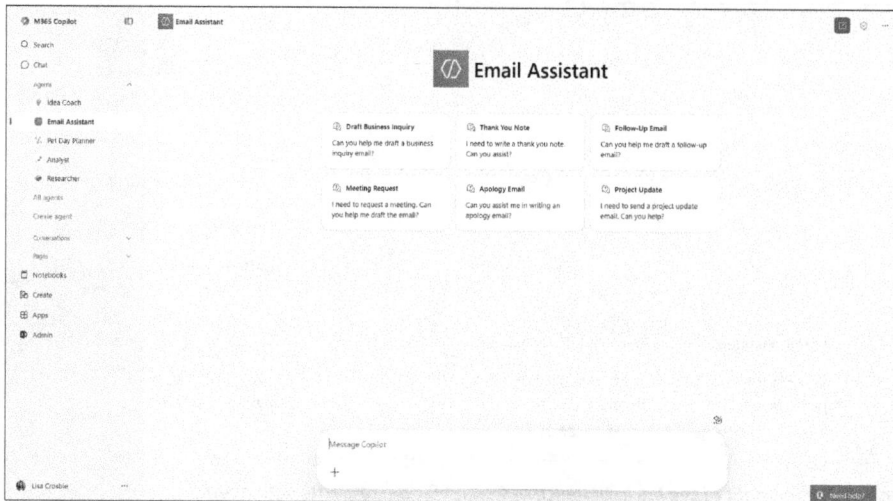

Your new agent is now ready to use in Microsoft 365 Copilot.

15. You can chat with this agent by selecting it from the menu on the left at any time, or you can access it by @ mentioning it from the main Microsoft 365 Copilot chat.

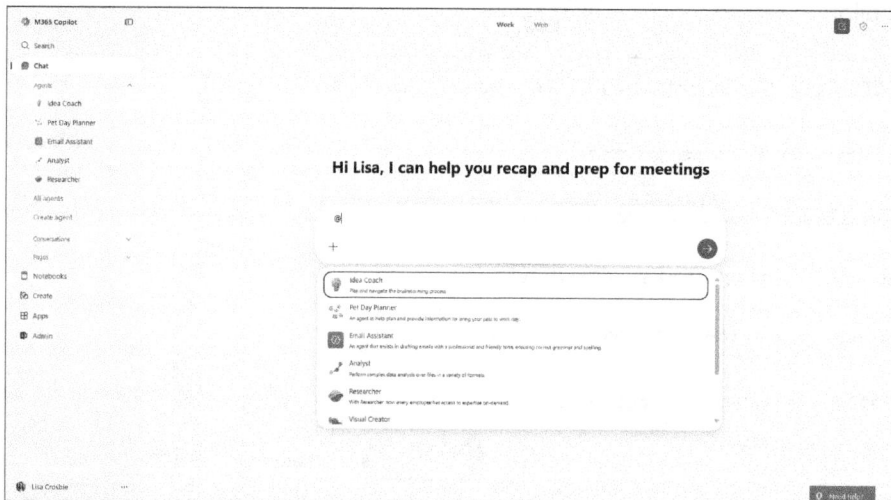

Enter "@" into Microsoft 365 Copilot Chat to display a list of available agents and select the agent you want to chat with.

> ✓ **TIP** The lite experience of Copilot Studio in the free version of Microsoft 365 Copilot Chat allows users to build agents like this one, using instructions and optionally connecting to a public website.

Configure an agent and add knowledge

In the previous example, you created a simple agent using only instructions. You can create a more sophisticated agent by connecting it to your knowledge and other business systems if you are using the lite experience of Copilot Studio with a paid Microsoft 365 Copilot license. You can add knowledge sources to ground your agent's responses in your organizational knowledge, including the following sources:

- Public websites

- Files uploaded from your device or attached cloud files

- SharePoint sites, files, and folders

- Teams channel, group, and meeting chat messages

- Outlook emails

An administrator can set up Copilot connectors to make other business systems available as knowledge sources for agents. Prebuilt connectors are also available for popular third-party collaboration, content management, database, enterprise resource planning (ERP), customer relationship management (CRM), IT service management (ITSM), learning, and other systems.

In this scenario, you will build an agent that is designed to help a working group collaborate on Responsible Business practices, as well as employees who want to learn more about its activities. The agent will be connected to Microsoft 365 knowledge sources, and to a space in Confluence using a prebuilt connector that the administrator has already configured.

> **SEE ALSO** Each connector needs to be set up and authenticated by an administrator before it can be used in the lite experience of Copilot Studio. Each connector will have a different setup depending on the API and authentication required. For details, refer to https://learn.microsoft.com/en-us/microsoftsearch/configure-connector.

> **SEE ALSO** For a current list of available connectors, refer to https://learn.microsoft.com/en-us/microsoftsearch/connectors-gallery.

To create an agent that uses knowledge and connectors

1. Navigate to Microsoft 365 Copilot Chat: https://m365.cloud.microsoft/chat.

2. Select **Create agent** from the left navigation menu to launch the lite experience of Copilot Studio.

3. Start by describing what you want your agent to do. For example: **Help employees understand our Responsible Business policy, current activities from the working group, and how to get involved.**

4. Copilot will use your description to suggest a name and a set of starter prompts that will be displayed in the preview pane.

5. Respond in the chat by either confirming that you are happy with the name or suggesting a different name.

6. Instead of continuing the conversation, switch to the **Configure** tab at the top of the lite experience of Copilot Studio. This opens the configuration screen where you can create your agent by filling in its components directly on a form.

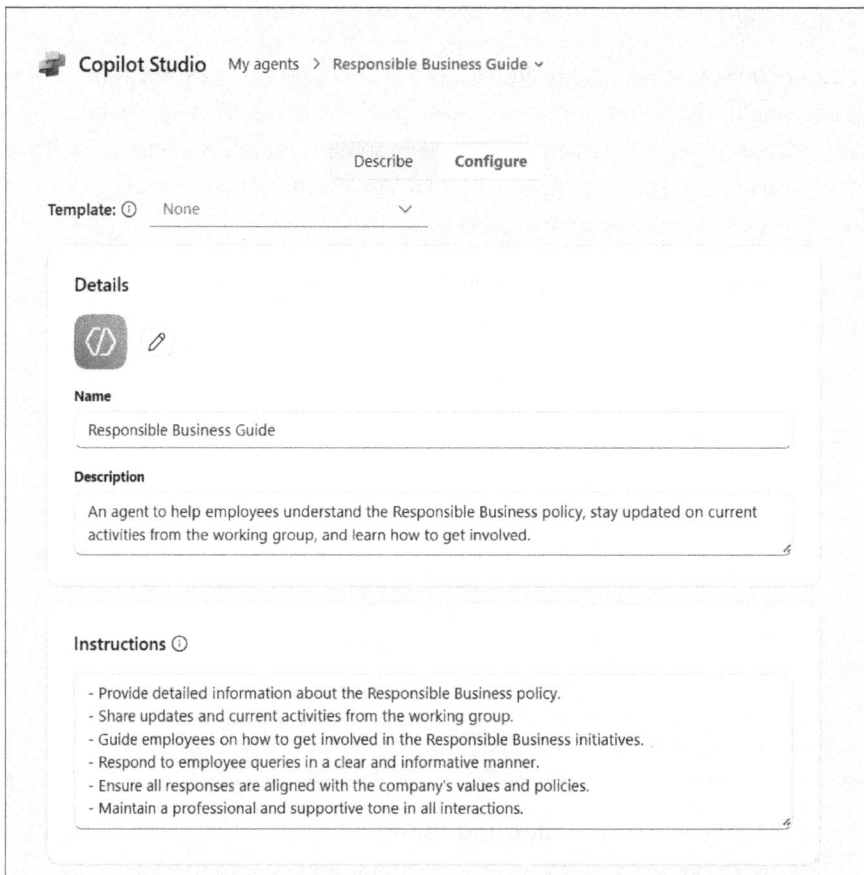

Select Configure to open the configuration screen.

> ✅ **TIP** You can switch back and forth between the **Describe** and **Configure** screens at any time while building your agent, so do what works best for you. If you switch back to **Describe** and provide more information about how you want the agent to behave, the description and instructions will be updated in the **Configure** form.

7. Change the icon by selecting the **pencil** button next to the existing icon. This opens a **Change icon** pop-up where you can select a new icon.

8. Select the **Change icon** option and select a PNG file from your documents. The icon should be less than 1 MB in size.

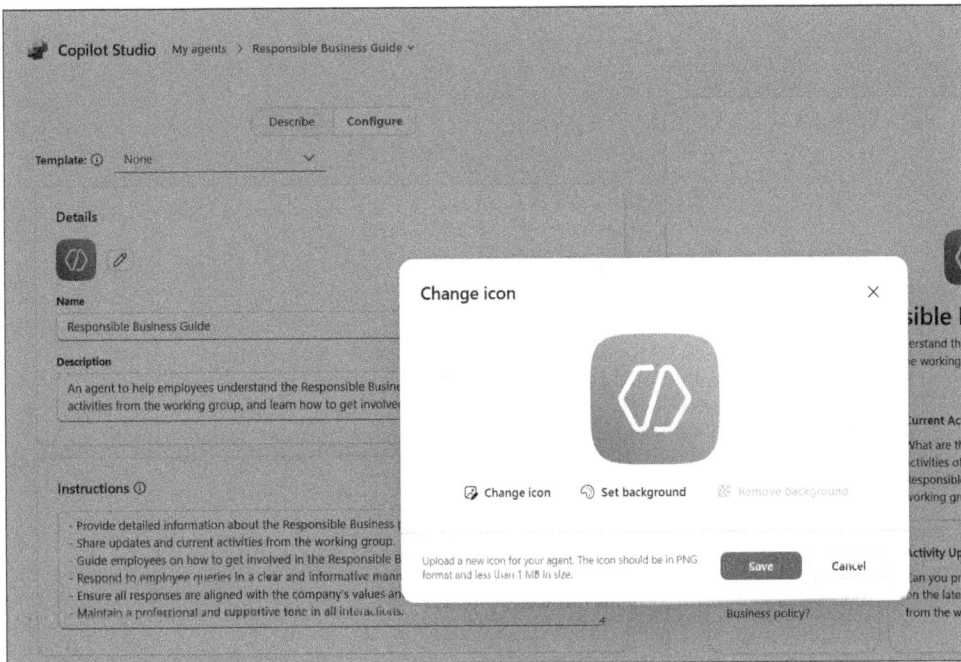

Change the icon of your agent by uploading a PNG file less than 1 MB in size.

9. Select **Save** when you have changed the icon. Your new icon will now appear in the configuration screen and the preview pane.

10. Edit the **Instructions** by adding another bullet point to the end of the existing instructions. For example: **Only respond to questions related to Responsible Business. Do not answer questions related to other topics**.

Edit the instructions manually in the field on the configuration form.

> ✓ **TIP** The instructions section allows for up to 8000 characters, so you can add a lot of detail and context here.

11. Navigate down to view the **Knowledge** section of the configuration form and select the **Search** field. This will open a menu of knowledge options, arranged with suggestions based on your most recently used files.

3

Copilot Studio   My agents > Responsible Business Guide ﹀

Describe   **Configure**

Knowledge ⟳ ⓘ

Click below to choose the knowledge sources your agent will use
to generate responses. You can enter URLs, upload files, and use
Microsoft SharePoint, Microsoft Teams, and Microsoft Outlook
emails. Learn more

🔍 Search by name, enter a URL, or drop a file   ⬆ ☁

(All)   Files   Sites   Chats   ⟩ ⬤▭

📊 **To Do List**
sites > ITHelpDesk > Shared Documents > To Do List.xlsx

📄 **Contoso Travel and Expense Policy V3**
sites > HumanResources > Shared Documents > Travel ...

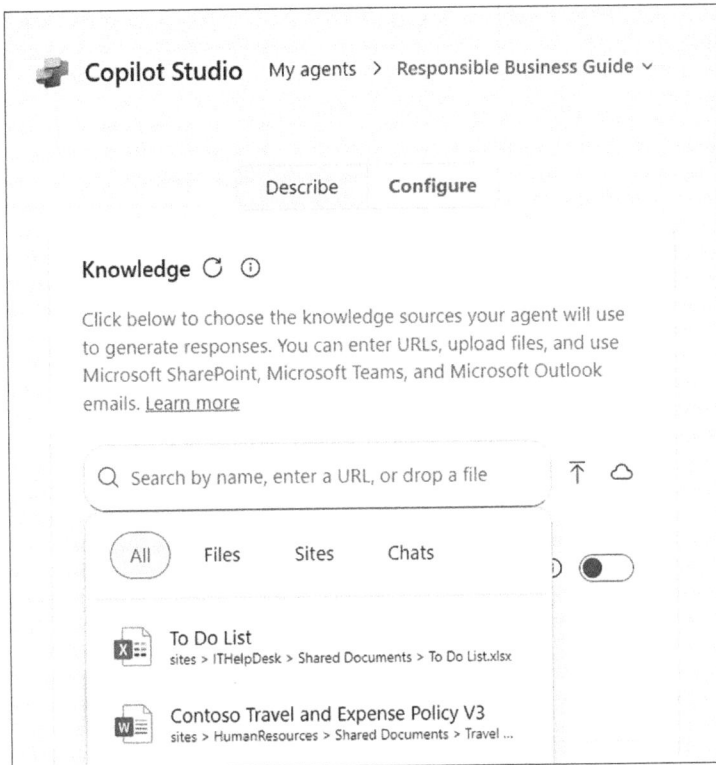

Select the Search field to expand the menu of options for grounding your agent in knowledge.

12. Navigate down below the list of recently opened files to view the options to
allow the agent to access all websites (all publicly available information on the
web); all your SharePoint files, folders, and sites; all your Teams chats; or all your
emails. You can select multiple options here by making a selection and then
returning to the search to select another option.

13. You can also narrow the scope of your agent by selecting only specific websites,
SharePoint content, or Teams chats. Use the search box or select and browse
through each tab at the top of the menu to view the available options.

   - The **Files** tab will display a list of recently opened files, with a filter to select
the file type (Word, PDF, Text, PowerPoint, Excel).

   - The **Sites** tab will display a list of recently viewed SharePoint sites.

   - The **Chats** tab will display a list of recent Teams chats, with a filter to select
chats in Channels, Meetings, or Group chats.

14. You can use the icons beside the search box to upload a file from your device or from a cloud location.

15. Select the knowledge you want your agent to have access to—for example, a Responsible Business Policy document and a group chat about the rollout of the policy. As you select each knowledge source, it will appear under the search field.

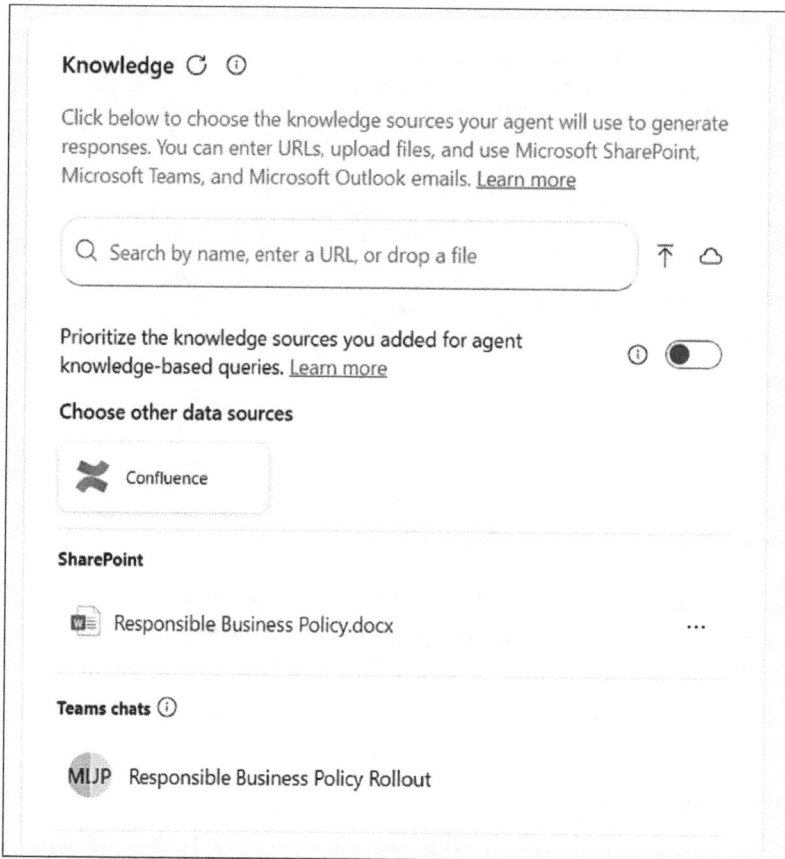

Select multiple knowledge sources to ground your agent.

> **TIP** Use the **refresh** icon next to the heading in the **Knowledge** section to check for updates and refresh knowledge source names. Note that it can take a few minutes for new knowledge or updates to appear in the list.

> ⚠️ **IMPORTANT** Users of the agent will have access to only those Teams chats that they already have permission to view. In this example, the user building the agent has access to both the policy and the Teams chat planning the rollout. If this agent is shared with other users, only the two other users in that Teams chat will have access to that knowledge when they use the agent.

16. You can also add connectors to use other business systems as knowledge for your agent. The lite experience of Copilot Studio will display any connectors that have been set up by the administrator in the **Choose other data sources** section under the knowledge search box.

> ✅ **TIP** If you don't have the **Choose other data sources** section with connectors listed, it means that your administrator has not yet set up any connections.

17. In the **Choose other data sources** section, select any available connectors that you want to use in your agent. In this example, the administrator has previously set up a connection with Confluence.

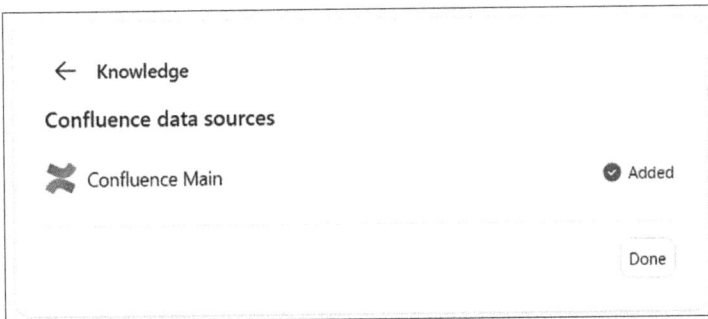

← Knowledge

Confluence data sources

✖ Confluence Main   ✔ Added

Done

Select the connectors you want to use in your agent using a toggle switch.

18. Select the **Done** button. The connector is now available in the knowledge section, along with a link you can use to configure more specific parameters or data depending on the connector.

19. Test the agent in the preview pane by entering a prompt that will generate an answer from the grounded knowledge sources. For example, "Who is responsible for the sustainability stream?"

20. Check that the answer is grounded in the right knowledge based on the citations and references in the response. Continue testing across all the knowledge sources you have added.

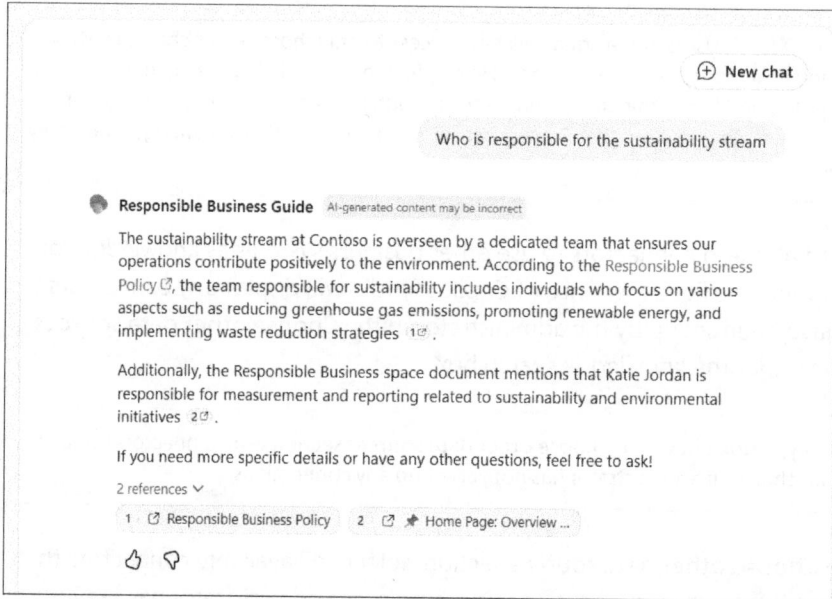

Use the test pane to make sure your agent is responding using the grounded knowledge sources you added.

21. Navigate to the bottom of the **Configure** screen to view the **Suggested prompts**. These were automatically filled based on your description when you created the agent. You can edit these suggested prompts, reorder them, remove them, or add new ones. Note that the maximum number is six suggested prompts. The preview pane will update as you edit the suggested prompts to reflect the changes.

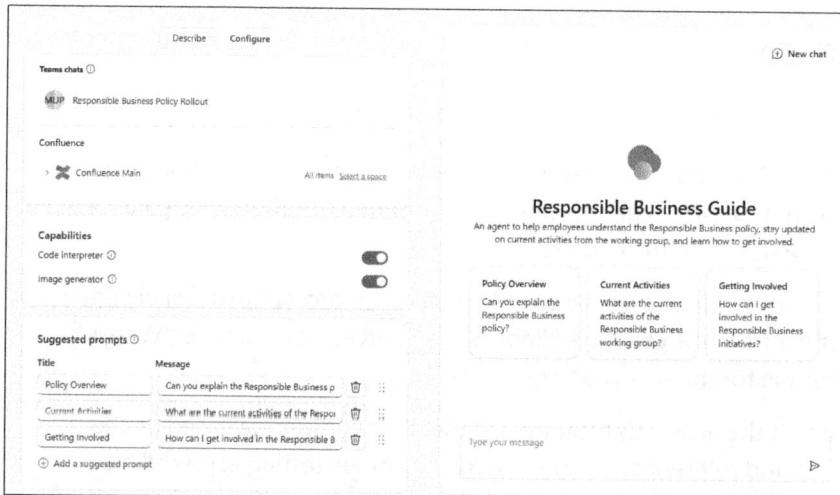

Edit, reorder, remove, or add new suggested prompts in the configuration screen.

Now that the knowledge sources and the connector have been added, your agent is ready to create and use. Before you finish creating this agent, you will add some additional capabilities to enable the agent to do more for the user.

Add capabilities to your agent

The lite experience of Copilot Studio allows you to include some additional capabilities for the user:

- *Code interpreter* enables the user to write a natural language prompt that can be turned into Python code. This advanced capability can be used to solve complex problems or to perform data analysis or visualization.

- *Image generator* enables the user to write a prompt to generate an image. This capability is useful if the agent scenario involves creating images, logos, artwork, or diagrams.

If you do not enable these capabilities with the toggle switches, the user will not be able to use those capabilities inside this agent.

To add capabilities to your agent

1. Navigate to the **Capabilities** section in the configuration screen, below the knowledge section.

2. Toggle on the **Code interpreter**, **Image generator**, or both, depending on your scenario.

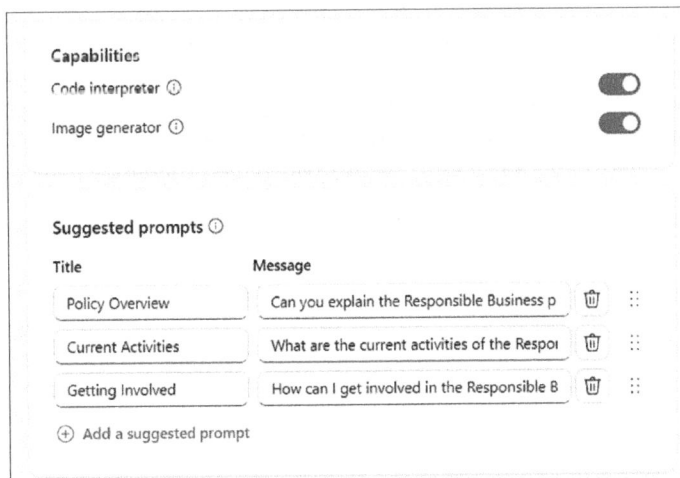

Use the toggle switches to enable or disable Code interpreter and Image generator capabilities in your agent.

3. Select the **Create** button to create your agent.

4. Wait for the agent to be created, and then select the **Go to agent** button. You have now configured an agent that is grounded in your organizational knowledge, and that also has the capability to perform data analysis and visualization and image generation.

5. Use the code interpreter capability to ask the agent to create a graph or a data visualization based on the knowledge you have grounded it in. For example, use the prompt: **Create a word cloud for our Responsible Business Policy.**

With Code interpreter enabled, your agent can create data visualizations like a word cloud.

6. Use the image generator capability to ask the agent to generate an image, diagram, logo, or artwork. For example, use the prompt: **Create a logo that uses a globe of the earth. Use a blue and green color scheme, and an aesthetic that shows environmental sustainability.**

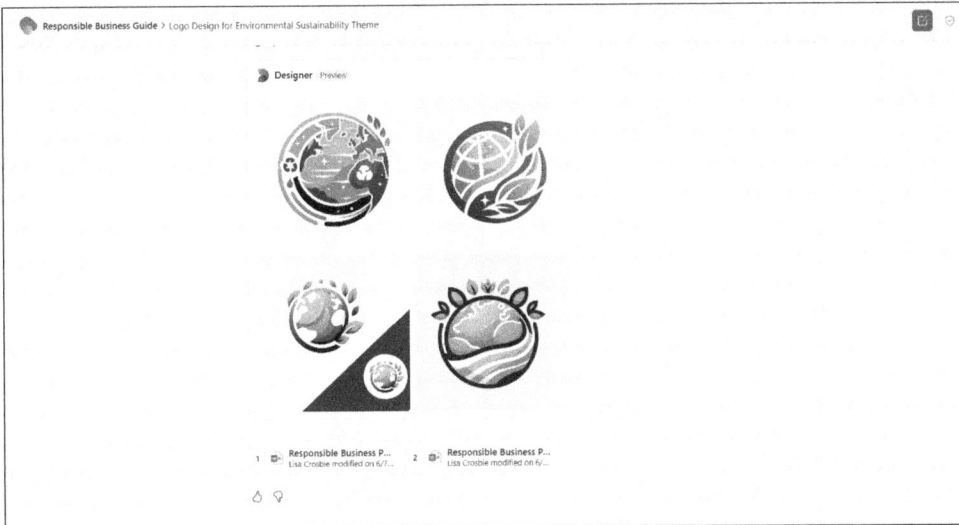

With Image generator enabled, your agent can generate images with reference to the knowledge it is grounded in.

> ✅ **TIP** Note that when the agent uses the code interpreter and the image generator, it is drawing on the knowledge it is grounded in, as well as your prompt. The agent will describe the thought process and references that it used to generate the response.

Edit an existing agent

You can edit an agent at any time to change the icon; change the name; revise or improve the description or instructions; add or remove knowledge sources, connectors, or capabilities; or edit the starter prompts.

To edit an existing agent

1. Expand the **Agents** menu on the left and hover over the name of the agent you want to edit.

2. Select the **More** option (indicated by three dots) that appears to the right of the agent name.

3. Select **Edit**.

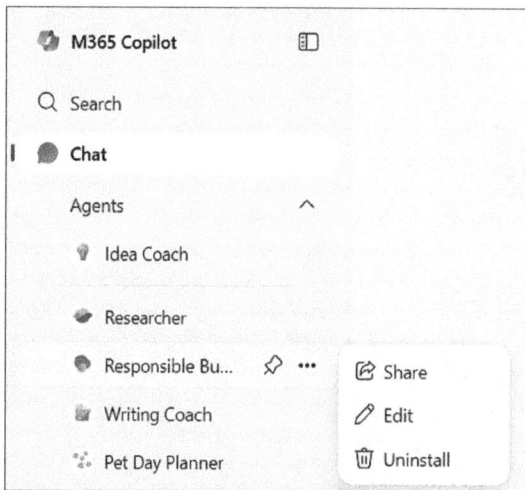

Select Edit to make changes to the selected agent.

4. This opens the **Configure** screen of the lite experience of Copilot Studio. You can edit your agent here or switch back and forth between **Describe** and **Configure** to make the changes.

5. The experience of editing your agent will be the same as creating it. The only difference is that the **Create** button at the top right of the screen has now been replaced by **Update** and **Share** buttons.

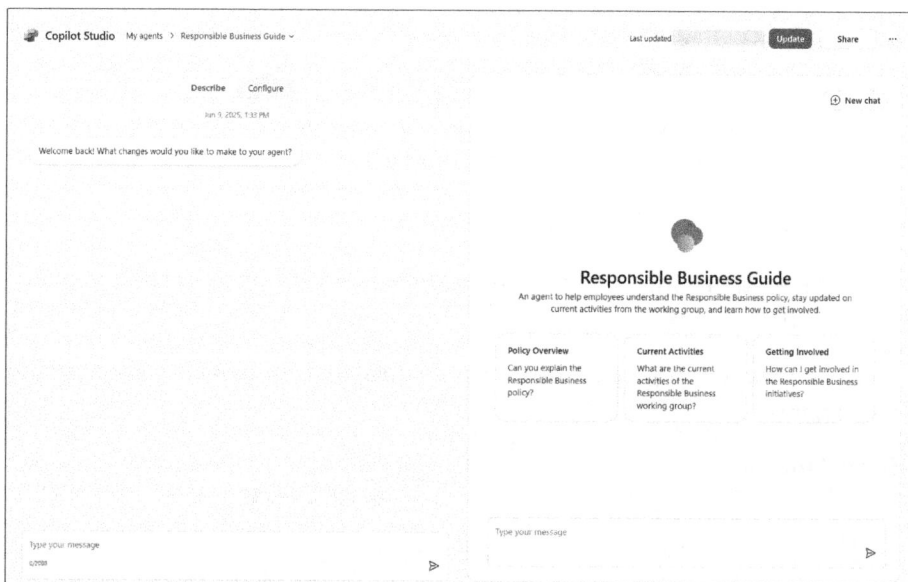

When you edit an agent, the experience is the same as when you created it.

6. Make any changes to the agent here using the skills you learned in the previous section. Test your changes in the preview pane.

7. When you have finished making changes, select the **Update** button.

> 🔍 **SEE ALSO** To uninstall or delete an agent, see the "Manage agents" section later in this chapter.

Build an agent from a template

The lite experience of Copilot Studio comes with a set of prebuilt agent templates that you can deploy or use as a starting point to build an agent that meets your specific needs. These agents are built with descriptions and instructions that follow best practice. As a result, they can be a useful tool for learning as well as a quick way to get started if your scenario matches one of the template scenarios.

The prebuilt agents are mostly tutors and coaches, primed with instructions that will help the user interact to learn new skills on a given topic. For example, the Prompt Coach agent helps the user learn how to write effective prompts and improve their prompting skills. The Writing Coach helps the user improve the clarity, grammar, and tone of their writing. Other agent templates are intended to be starting points that you can extend and connect to other business systems. For example, the Customer Insight Assistant template is designed to provide the user with detailed customer profiles, including those customers' priorities, products, leadership, and competitors. If you use this template, you will need to use the skills you have learned in this chapter to ground it in knowledge or connect to other business systems where this data is held.

To create an agent from a template

1. Select **Create agent** from the left navigation menu.

2. In the **Describe** tab, select the **View all templates** option at the bottom of the list of suggested templates.

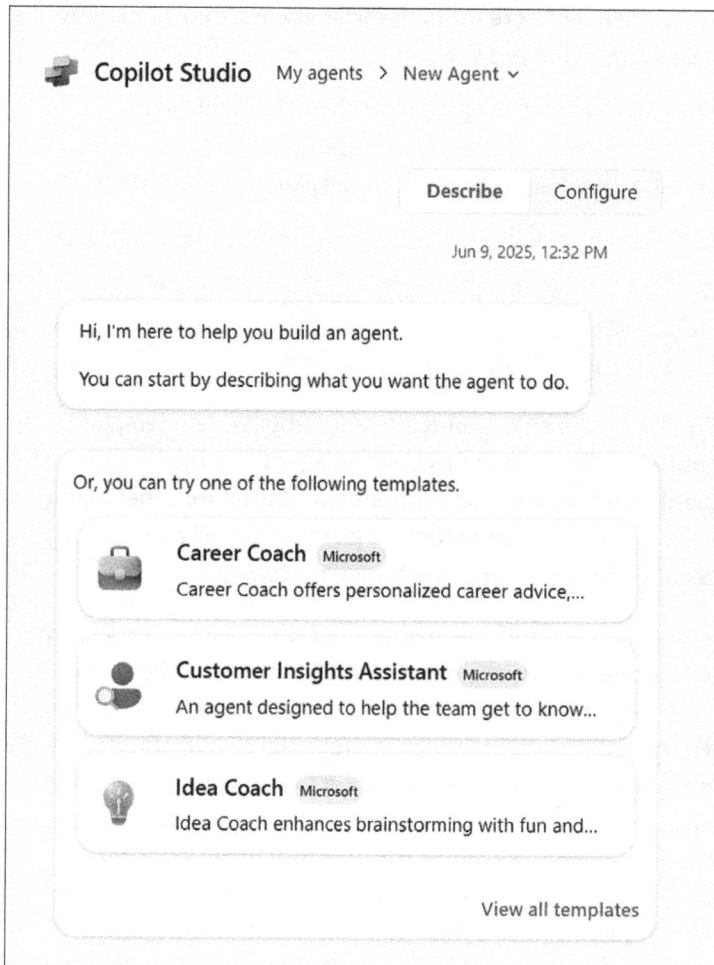

Select View all templates at the bottom of the list of suggested templates.

3. The expanded menu shows all the available templates. You can use the chat experience to learn more about each template and browse the available options.

> **SEE ALSO** For a complete and up-to-date list of all templates, refer to the Microsoft documentation: https://learn.microsoft.com/en-us/microsoft-365-copilot/extensibility/agent-templates-overview.

4. Select the **Writing Coach** template. Copilot will respond with details about the template, describing what it can do and providing a link to the documentation.

> Okay! You selected the Writing Coach template.
>
> **Writing Coach** Microsoft
> Writing Coach boosts effectiveness and supports...
>
> Writing Coach is a declarative copilot that provides detailed feedback on writing style, improving clarity, coherence, grammar, and tone. It offers tailored advice for various text types such as emails, reports, and stories. Users can receive collaborative guidance to foster creativity, adjust tones in communications, and identify key points. The Coach also helps with translations, considering cultural nuances, and teaches how to write clear instructions. For storytelling, it aids in structuring narratives and advises on writing effective whitepapers by defining topics, audiences, and styles.
>
> If you want to learn more about this template and how to use it, review the documentation.
>
> Describe any customizations you'd like to make.
>
> Change template

Copilot responds with a detailed description of what the template agent can do.

> **TIP** Select the **Change template** option under the description to continue the chat with Copilot and to browse and select a different template.

5. You can describe any customizations you want to make to the template. For instance, we don't need the agent to help with writing blog posts, but we do want it to help with writing a sales pitch. Enter a prompt to ask for this change: **The user will need help with writing an effective sales pitch. They will not write blogs**. Note that this information updates the starter prompts in the preview pane.

6. Switch to the **Configure** tab to view the configuration experience.

7. Review the instructions in this template. These template agents can help you understand best practice for writing instructions for an agent that acts as a coach or tutor. The instructions list a series of skills, including the new skill you've just described, to help with writing a sales pitch. Make any changes you need to the instructions to fit your specific requirements.

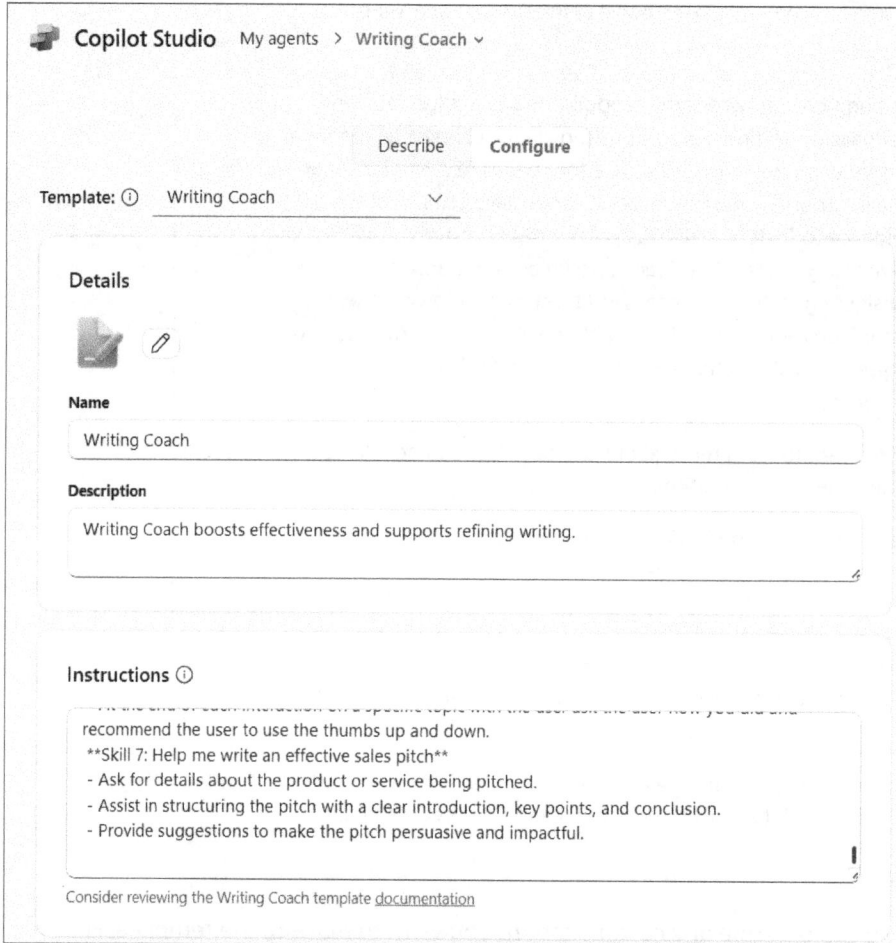

Copilot Studio   My agents > Writing Coach ∨

Describe   **Configure**

Template: ⓘ   Writing Coach   ∨

Details

✎

Name

Writing Coach

Description

Writing Coach boosts effectiveness and supports refining writing.

Instructions ⓘ

recommend the user to use the thumbs up and down.
Skill 7: Help me write an effective sales pitch
- Ask for details about the product or service being pitched.
- Assist in structuring the pitch with a clear introduction, key points, and conclusion.
- Provide suggestions to make the pitch persuasive and impactful.

Consider reviewing the Writing Coach template documentation

Review the instructions and make any change to fit your scenario.

8. You can continue to configure the template agent by adding knowledge or connectors. For example, here you might choose to add a knowledge source that has product information. Then, when the user writes a sales pitch or a

whitepaper, the response will be grounded in that knowledge from your organization, rather than just using the general knowledge in the language model or from publicly available web sources.

9. When you have finished configuring the template, select the **Create** button to create your agent.

10. You can now use, edit, and manage this agent in the same way as any other agent you have created.

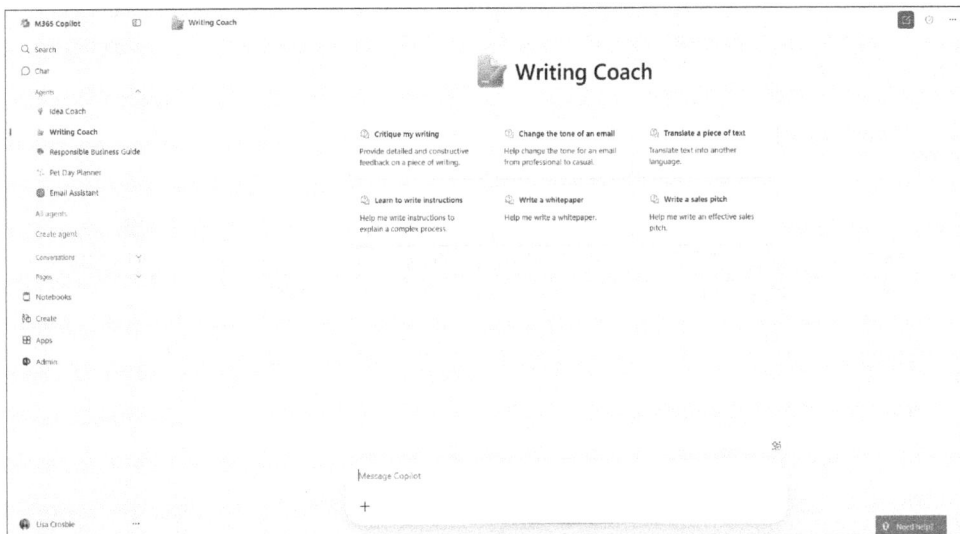

The Writing Coach agent is now available to use alongside the other agents you created.

Share and manage agents

Now that you have configured your agent, you can choose to share it with other users in your tenant. You can also configure it to use agents built by others and shared with you. In addition, you can manage the agents you've built by uninstalling them from the agent menu or deleting them.

Share an agent with other users

You can use the lite experience of Copilot Studio to create agents just for your own use, as well as agents to share with your team, a whole department, or the whole organization. When you share an agent with others, that agent will be able to respond with only the information or data to which each individual user has access. If you have used a knowledge source such as SharePoint where files are not shared with all users, or where sensitivity labels are applied, you will still be able to share the agent. However, the responses given by the agent will differ for each user based on their permissions. The agent will not provide answers from knowledge that the user doesn't have access to, even if you have added that knowledge to the agent.

> ⚠ **IMPORTANT** When you share an agent with others, they will be able to use it but not edit it. Only the maker can edit the agent. You can share an agent only with other users in your tenant.

To share an agent

1. To share an agent when you are creating it, select the **Change sharing settings** link on the agent confirmation screen. This will open a dialog where you can choose who to share the agent with. Skip to step 3.

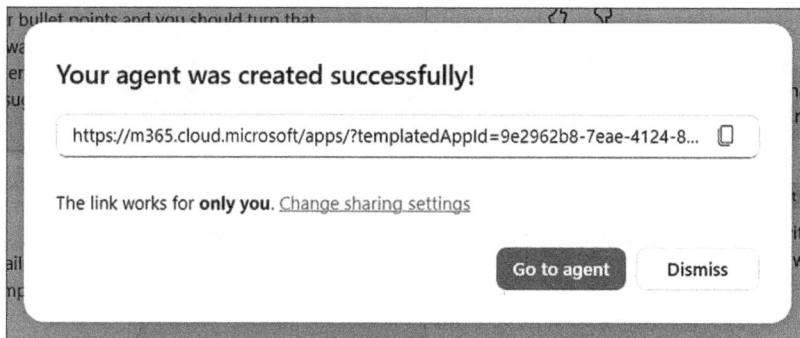

Your agent was created successfully!

https://m365.cloud.microsoft/apps/?templatedAppId=9e2962b8-7eae-4124-8... 📋

The link works for **only you.** Change sharing settings

Go to agent   Dismiss

When you create an agent, you can select Change sharing settings to open the share options.

2. To share an existing agent you have already created, hover over the agent's name in the left navigation menu, select the three dots to expand more options, and select **Share**.

> ⚠ **IMPORTANT** Make sure you have selected the **Update** button to update the agent with any changes before you share the agent.

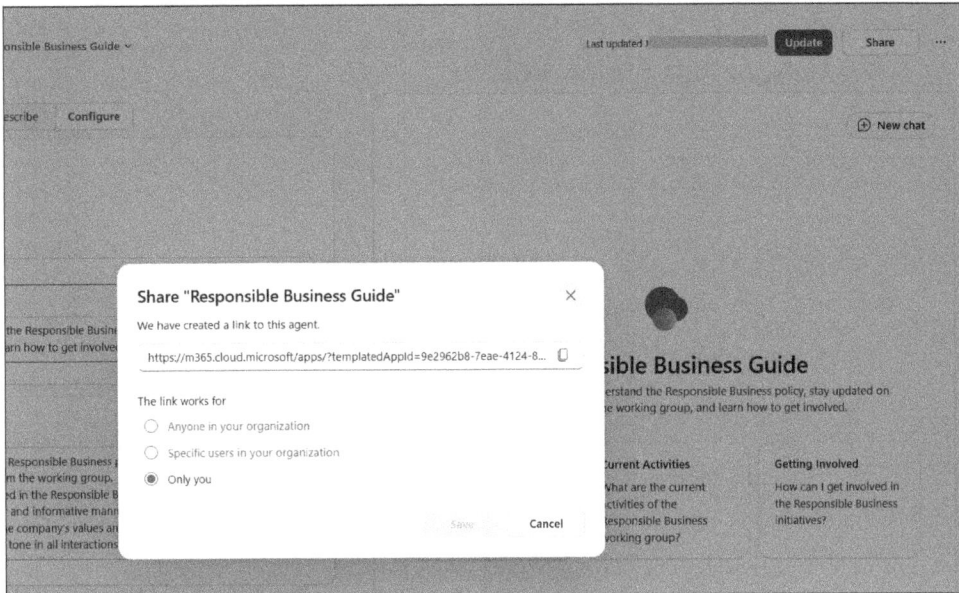

Select the Share button when you have finished editing an agent to share it with others.

3. You can choose whether to share the agent with:

- **Anyone in your organization.** Selecting this option means that anyone in your tenant will be able to use the agent.

- **Specific users in your organization.** You can select individual users, security groups, or Microsoft 365 groups in your tenant to share the agent with.

- **Only you.** Choose this option if you want to use the agent just for your own personal productivity. No one else will be able to access the agent if you select this option.

4. Copy the sharing link using the **Copy** icon.

5. Select **Anyone in your organization**.

6. Select **Save**.

Share "Responsible Business Guide"   ×

We have created a link to this agent.

https://m365.cloud.microsoft/apps/?templatedAppId=9e2962b8-... Link copied! ⎘

The link works for

◉ Anyone in your organization

> ⓘ **User permissions for knowledge** The agent will only respond with
> knowledge that each user has access to. This includes SharePoint,
> Microsoft Teams chats, and emails. Learn more about agent responses

○ Specific users in your organization

○ Only you

[Save]   [Cancel]

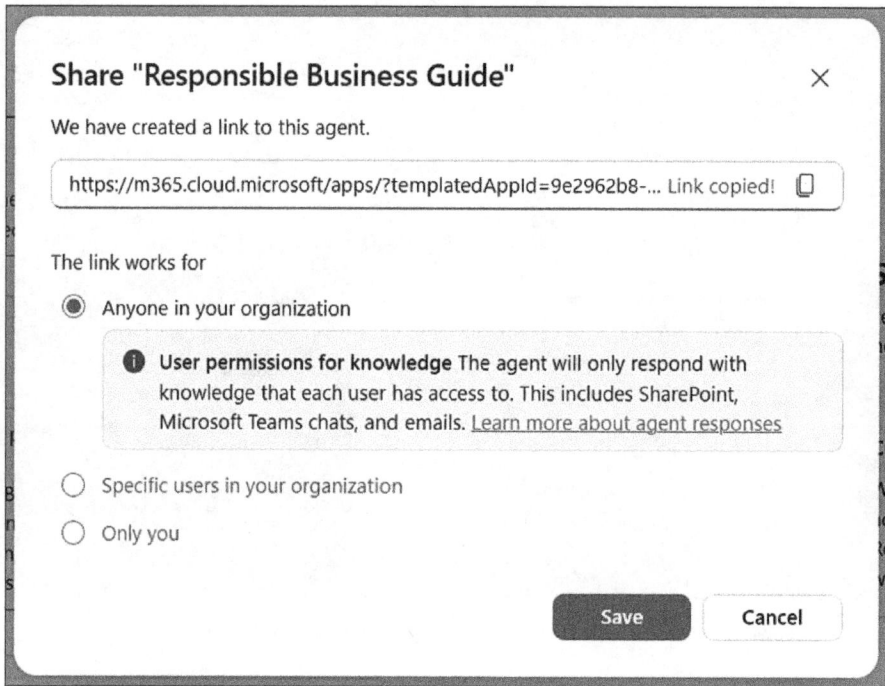

Copy the sharing link, select Anyone in your organization, and Save.

7. Wait for the sharing settings to be saved. You will then get a confirmation message with the sharing link. You can copy it from here if you haven't already copied it earlier.

8. Close the sharing pop-up.

9. Share the link with your colleagues via Teams or email.

When someone shares an agent with you, you can simply paste the link in the browser where you are logged in to Microsoft 365 Copilot Chat.

To access an agent someone has shared with you

1. Paste the sharing link in your browser.

2. A pop-up window will appear showing the details of the agent.

3. Select the **Add** button.

4. The agent will open in Microsoft 365 Copilot Chat, where it is ready for you to use.

5. The agent will appear in the list of **Agents** on the left menu. Note that no **Edit** option is available for this agent when it has been shared with you.

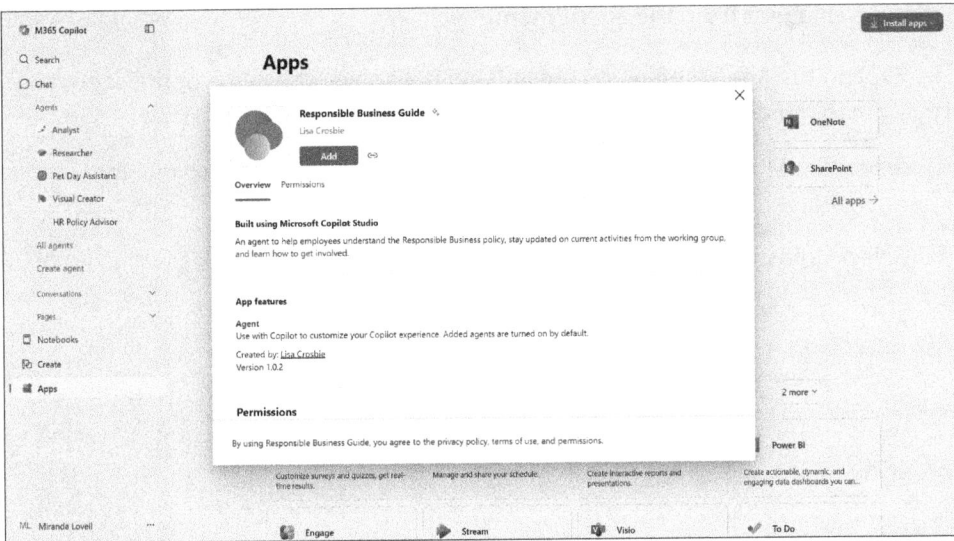

Review the details of the agent shared with you and select the Add button.

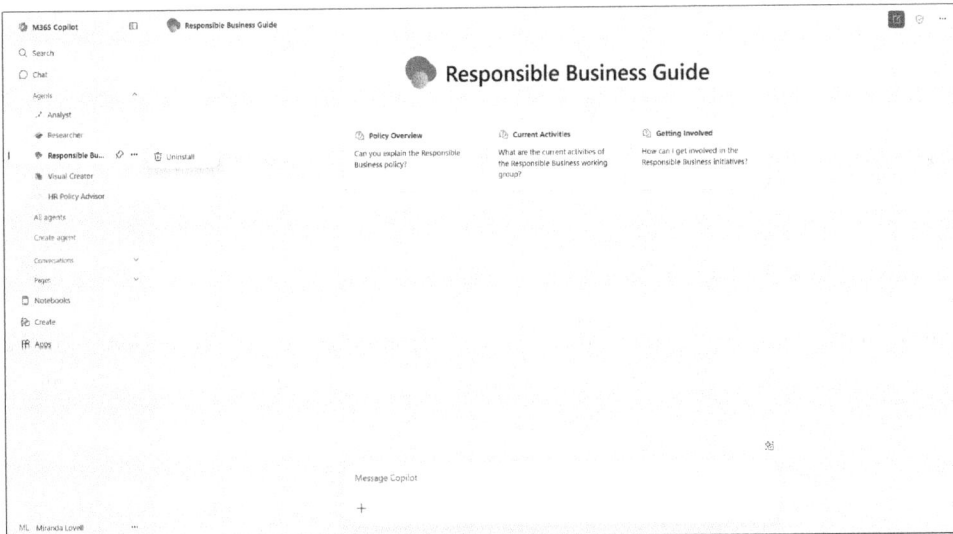

Select Create agent on the left navigation menu in Microsoft 365 Copilot Chat.

Manage agents

You can remove agents you have created or agents that have been shared with you from the agent menu by uninstalling them. You can also delete agents that you have built.

To remove an agent from the agent menu

1. Expand the **Agents** menu on the left and hover over the name of the agent you want to remove from the menu.

2. Select the **More** option (indicated by three dots) that appears to the right of the agent name.

3. Select **Uninstall**.

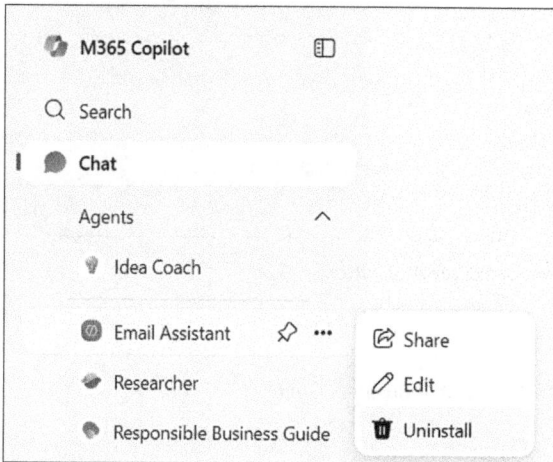

Select Uninstall to remove the selected agent from the menu.

4. You will get a confirmation message to confirm that you want to uninstall that agent. Select **Uninstall** to confirm or **Cancel**.

> **TIP** If you uninstall an agent you have created, you can find it and reinstall it again by following the instructions in the next part of this section. If you uninstall an agent that was shared with you, you can add it again by using the shared link.

You can view the list of all the agents you have built to manage, reinstall, or delete them.

To view and manage all your agents

1. Select any agent from the **Agents** menu and select the **Edit** option.

2. At the top of the configuration screen, select the drop-down option next to the agent's name. This will display the agents you have most recently edited, with an option to **View all agents**. Select the **View all agents** option.

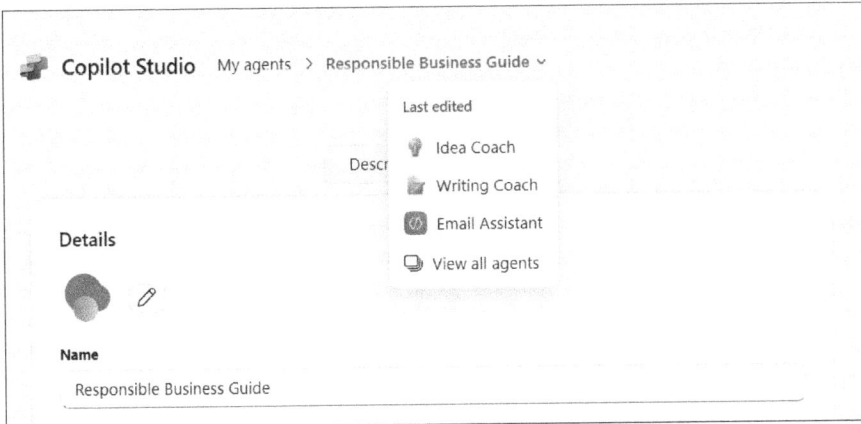

Select the drop-down option under the name of the agent in edit mode to access a list of all agents.

3. The **My agents** list shows all the agents you have created or drafted. Each agent in the list is shown with the icon, name, last edited date, last updated date (for agents that were created, or "Never created" for those you drafted but didn't create), and description.

4. Hover over the name of an agent to reveal the options to edit, share, or select the **More** menu (three dots) for the option to **Download a .zip file** or **Delete** the agent.

The My agents list shows the details of all the agents you have drafted or created.

> **TIP** If you want to add an uninstalled agent back to the **Agent** menu, select it from this list and choose the **Edit** option. From the **Edit** screen, you can update the agent and follow the **Go to agent** link to make it reappear in the navigation.

> ✅ **TIP** The **Download as a .zip file** option is used when you need to manually upload the agent to Teams or Microsoft 365 Copilot and submit it for an administrator's review, or to upload it directly into your organizational catalog.

5. If you select **Delete**, you will get a confirmation message to check whether you understand that the agent will be permanently deleted.

> ⚠️ **IMPORTANT** If you want to remove an agent from the menu without deleting it, use the **Uninstall** option described in the previous section. Use **Delete** only when you genuinely want to permanently delete an agent.

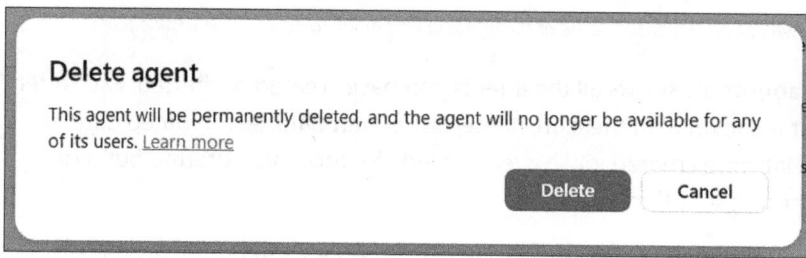

Delete agent

This agent will be permanently deleted, and the agent will no longer be available for any of its users. Learn more

Delete   Cancel

Confirm that you understand deleting permanently removes the agent.

You can also access a list of all your agents by opening the Agent Store from the All agents option on the left-side menu. From the Agent Store, you will be able to share, pin, edit, or uninstall a selected agent.

Skills review

In this chapter, you learned how to:

- Build an agent by describing it in natural language, and configure or edit an agent by adding an icon, description, instructions, knowledge, connections to other business systems, and capabilities for a code interpreter and image generator.

- Create and configure an agent starting with a prebuilt template.

- Share agents, use permissions correctly, and uninstall or delete existing agents.

Practice tasks

No practice files are necessary to complete the practice tasks in this chapter.

Describe and configure an agent

Navigate to Microsoft 365 Copilot Chat (https://m365.cloud.microsoft/chat) and perform the following tasks:

1. Select **Create agent** from the left navigation menu.

2. Describe the agent you want to build: **Help the user understand the capabilities and tools available in Microsoft AI**.

3. Confirm the suggested name or prompt with a different name.

4. Provide information about the specific instructions for the agent: **You should provide information about capabilities and tools that can be used for AI in a business context. Help the user understand what's possible. Do not provide troubleshooting tips.**

5. Switch to the **Configure** tab.

6. Change the agent icon by selecting the **pencil** button next to the agent icon. Select Change icon and upload a PNG image (smaller than 1 MB) from your files. (If you don't have a PNG image, you can use the Copilot chat to generate an icon for you).

7. Review the **Description, Instructions**, and **Starter prompts** created from your natural language description. Make an edit to a starter prompt and notice the change in the preview pane.

8. In the Knowledge section, enter the following public website and select enter: **https://www.microsoft.com/en-us/ai.**

9. In the Knowledge section, add another website and select enter: **https://news.microsoft.com/10-ai-terms/.**

10. Both websites should now be listed in the knowledge section of your agent.

11. Select the **Create** button.

12. Wait for the agent to be created, then select the **Go to agent** button.

13. Test the agent by selecting one of the starter prompts, or by asking about Microsoft AI, for example, **What is Copilot Studio?**

Build an agent from a template

Navigate to Microsoft 365 Copilot Chat (https://m365.cloud.microsoft/chat) and perform the following tasks:

1. Select **Create agent** from the left navigation menu.

2. In the **Describe** tab, select **View all templates**.

3. Select the **Prompt Coach** agent.

4. Review the description and select the hyperlink to view the full documentation.

5. Select the **Configure** tab to switch to the configuration experience.

6. Review the instructions and the starter prompts in the template.

7. Select **Create** to create the agent.

8. Go to the agent, and select one of the starter prompts to use it in the chat.

Share and manage agents

Navigate to Microsoft 365 Copilot Chat (https://m365.cloud.microsoft/chat) and perform the following tasks:

1. In the left menu, hover over the name of the agent you created in either of the previous tasks.

2. Select the **More** option (three dots) and then select **Edit**.

3. Select the **Share** option at the top right of the screen.

4. Copy the share link by selecting the **Copy** button.

5. Select **Anyone in your organization**.

6. Select **Save**.

7. If you have another user in your tenant, share the link with that user via Teams or email.

Building agents in Copilot Studio

4

Practice files

No practice files are necessary to complete the practice tasks in this chapter.

In this chapter, you will learn how to get started with building agents in Copilot Studio. You'll begin by setting up a new environment and exploring the role that environments and solutions play in Copilot Studio and Microsoft Power Platform. Next, you'll become familiar with the Copilot Studio user interface and learn how to configure an agent from scratch. You'll learn how to write effective descriptions and instructions, and discover the role these play in how your agent behaves.

You'll also explore some of the generative AI settings you can use to enable cutting-edge language models and reasoning models in your agent. You'll learn how to make your agent multilingual, and how to customize the greeting it uses to start a conversation. Finally, you'll explore the agent templates and managed agents available to help you get started quickly with common scenarios.

In this chapter

- Understand environments and solutions
- Configure a new agent
- Manage agent settings
- Edit the Conversation Start topic
- Start with an agent template
- Install a managed agent

Understand environments and solutions

Copilot Studio is part of Microsoft Power Platform, a low-code platform for building and managing your business data, apps, and flows, as well as your agents. In Power Platform, environments are used as a space to store, manage, and share these components. Each environment has a purpose (such as development, testing, or production), with the appropriate security and members in each environment. Environments can also be set up for different teams or geographies in your organization as needed. Your agent will most likely need to connect with other Power Platform services such as Dataverse, flows, and connections. You will be able to connect to only those data sources that reside in the same environment as your agent. It is therefore important to start in the right environment before you create an agent.

Solutions are the mechanism for implementing application life-cycle management, used to move your agent and the related components from one environment to another.

Create a new environment

In a real-world scenario, you would have, at a minimum, development, test, and production environments already set up. You would also have application life-cycle management processes for deploying your agent, and all of the related data sources and connections would be made available to production through those environments. For the purposes of learning and following along with the examples and practice tasks in this book, you will simply need to create one trial environment.

> **SEE ALSO** Administration of environments and application life-cycle management is a complex topic that is beyond the scope of this book. You can find comprehensive documentation and learning resources on this topic at https://learn.microsoft.com/en-us/power-platform/admin/environments-overview.

To create a new trial environment

1. Open a new tab in your browser and navigate to the Power Platform admin center: https://admin.powerplatform.microsoft.com.

2. Select the **Manage** icon on the left side rail.

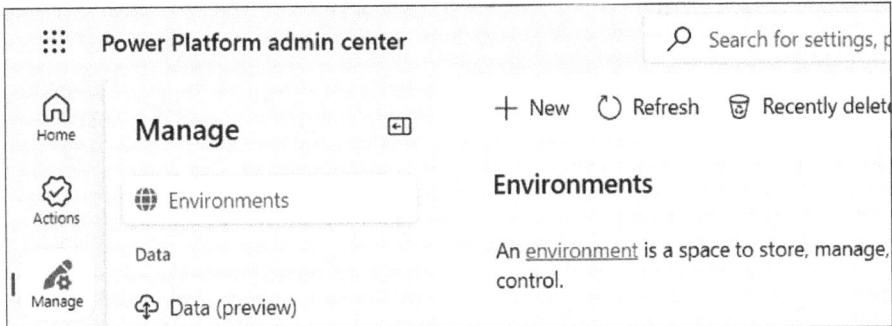

Select the Manage icon on the left side rail to open the Environments screen.

3. Select the **+New** option on the top menu of the **Environments** screen. This will open a side panel where you can create a new environment.

4. In the side panel, complete the following details:

   - Name: **Development.**
   - Region: Your geographic region for the tenant (this will be prefilled).
   - Type: **Trial.**
   - Add a Dataverse data store? **Yes.**

5. Select **Next**. This will open a second screen of options in the side panel. Complete the following details:

   - Leave the values already filled in for the language and currency.
   - In the **Security group** section, select **+Select**.
   - In the **Edit security group** option, select Open access: **None** and then select **Done.**

New environment ×

ⓘ This operation is subject to capacity constraints

Name *

Development

Region *

United States ⌄

A local region can provide quicker data access

Get new features early ⓘ

(●) No

Type ⓘ *

Trial ⌄

Purpose

Describe the environment's purpose

Add a Dataverse data store? ⓘ

(●) Yes

Pay-as-you-go with Azure? ⓘ

(●) No

[Next] Cancel

Fill the details in the New environment creation panel.

Edit security group ×

Search security groups by display names or emails that start with this

🔍 Search

Name ↑

• **Open access**

✓ ⓘ None

Select the None option in the Edit security group pane.

6. Confirm all the details are correct and then select **Save**.

← **Add Dataverse**   ×

ⓘ This operation is subject to capacity constraints

Language *

| English (United States)   ∨ |

Default language for user interfaces in this
environment

Currency *

| USD ($)   ∨ |

Reports will use this currency

Security group *

Restrict environment access to members of
a security group or select None to opt for
open access across your tenant. Learn more

None   ✎
(All users across your tenant will have
access to the environment)

URL

A unique domain name will be generated.
Click here to enter a custom domain

Enable Dynamics 365 apps?

In addition to Power Apps. Learn more
◉⃝ No

[**Save**]   Cancel

Review the details of the new environment and select Save.

7. Your trial environment can now be found in the **Environments** list in the Power
   Platform admin center. Close this tab and return to Copilot Studio.

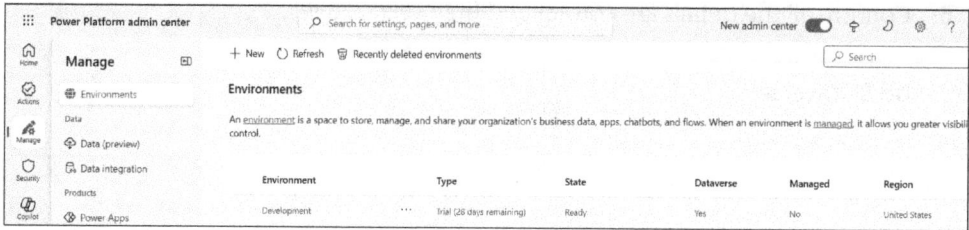

The new environment you created appears in the Environments list.

Select an environment for your agent in Copilot Studio

Before you start creating an agent, use the environment picker at the top right of the screen to select the environment you want to work in. If you are connecting your agent to other Power Platform components such as Dataverse or Power Automate flows, be sure to select the same environment you have used for those components.

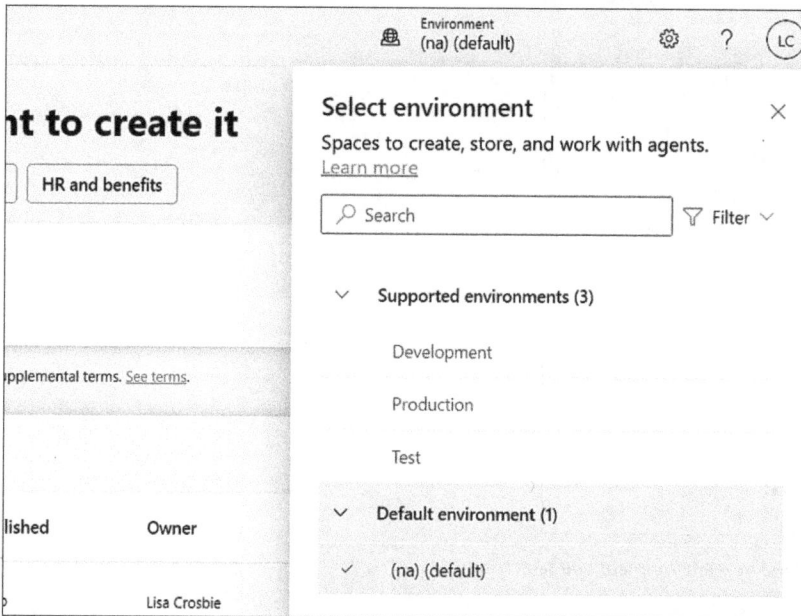

Use the environment picker at the top right of the screen to select the environment before you create an agent.

For many of the examples and practice tasks in this book, you will work in the default environment. If the instructions for a task ask you to switch to the Development environment, use the environment picker as shown here.

Work with solutions

When you create your agent, it will be created in the default or preferred solution for that environment. If you do not set up a solution, your agent will be created in the Common Data Services default solution. That default will not give you the control you need to fully manage your agent solution in a real-world scenario.

To follow along with the exercises and practice tasks in this book, you do not need to create a new solution. For real-world deployment, though, you should create a solution in the environment you are working in and set that as the preferred solution for that environment before you start creating your agent.

> **SEE ALSO** For detailed documentation on working with solutions in Power Platform, refer to https://learn.microsoft.com/en-us/power-apps/maker/data-platform/solutions-overview. To learn how to set a preferred solution, refer to https://learn.microsoft.com/en-us/power-apps/maker/data-platform/preferred-solution.

Configure a new agent

In Chapter 1, you learned how to create an agent by describing what you want it to do in natural language. In that example, you saw how Copilot used the information you provided in the chat to create an agent with a name, description, instructions, and knowledge. Some makers will prefer to start this way each time. Others will prefer to skip to the configuration experience, where you can directly fill these components in your own words.

Start creating an agent using configuration

In this section, you will learn how to skip past the "describe it to build it" experience and instead configure the agent directly.

> **IMPORTANT** Unlike with the lite experience of Copilot Studio, you can't toggle back and forth between the Describe and Configure experience. Once you select "Skip to configure" (as described in this section), you can't go back to the Copilot Chat experience to describe what you want to build.

To create an agent using configuration

1. Navigate to Copilot Studio in your browser, and select the **Create** icon directly below the **Home** icon on the left side rail.

Select the Create icon on the left side rail to create a new agent.

2. You will be taken to the **Create** screen, which offers options to create a new agent, install a managed agent, or start with an agent template. Select the **New agent** button at the top left of the screen.

> **SEE ALSO** You will learn about managed agents and agent templates later in this chapter.

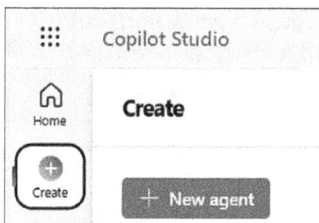

Select the New agent button at the top of the Create screen.

3. This will take you to the Copilot Chat experience, where you can describe your agent to build it. Instead of interacting in the chat, select the **Skip to configure** button at the top right of the screen.

> **TIP** Even if you prefer to configure the agent yourself, it is worth answering the first question in the Copilot Chat—even if it's a single sentence about the kind of agent you are building—before you select the Skip to configure button. Copilot will draft a detailed description, instructions, and suggested prompts based on your description. You may find it easier to edit and work with these suggestions in the next steps rather than starting from a blank form.

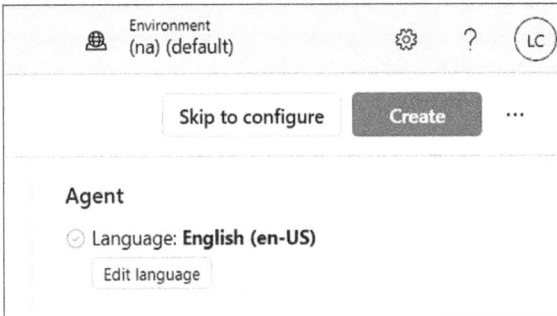

4

Select the Skip to configure button at the top right of the screen.

4. You can now configure your agent using a blank form, where you can edit the agent language, choose the agent's name and icon, write a description and instructions, add suggested prompts, and add knowledge.

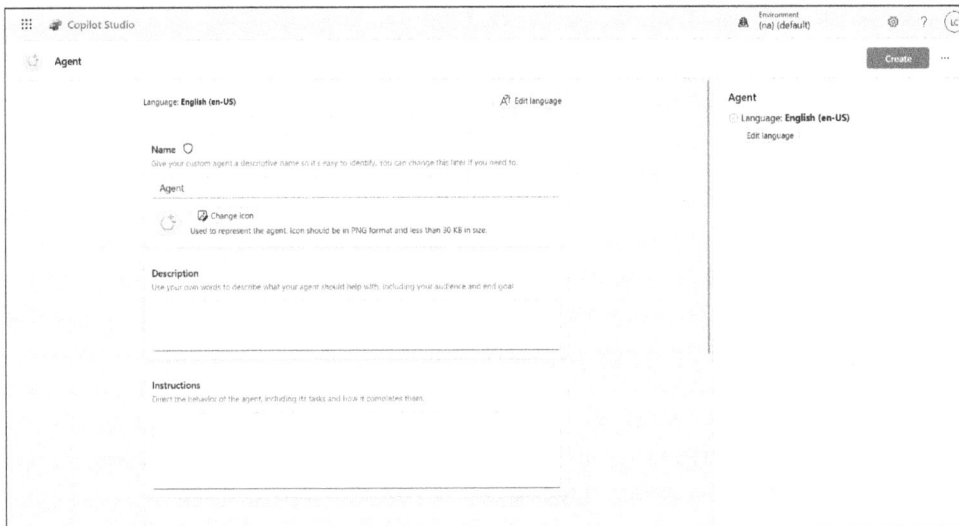

You can configure the agent by filling in each component directly.

Set the primary language for the agent

The agent is created using the default primary language, which is displayed at the top of the form and in the panel on the right side of the screen. If you want to change the primary language for the agent, you need to do it at this stage before the agent is created. After the agent is created, you can change the language to another region of the same language if available (e.g., switch from U.S. English to Australian English) or add another language, but you will not be able to edit the primary language.

> 🔍 **SEE ALSO** Changing the language region and adding secondary languages are covered in the "Manage agent settings" section of this chapter.

To change the primary language of the agent

1. Select the **Edit language** button at the top of the configuration form.

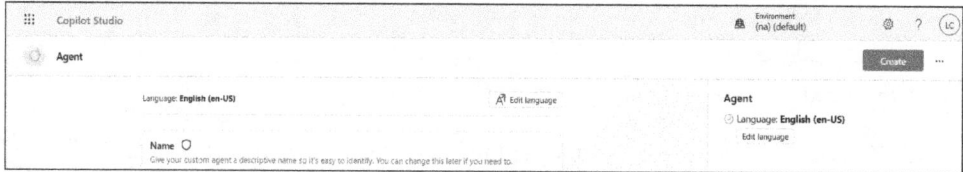

You can edit the primary language of the agent here before creating it.

2. Select the primary language for your agent from the drop-down list of options.

> 🔍 **SEE ALSO** For full details of supported languages, refer to the Microsoft documentation: https://learn.microsoft.com/en-us/microsoft-copilot-studio/authoring-language-support.

3. Select **Save**.

4. The selected language will now be displayed as the primary language.

Set the agent's name and icon

Choose a name for your agent and fill it in the **Name** section of the configuration form, replacing the default "Agent" that was filled when you created the agent. You can change the agent's name at any time.

Select the **Change icon** button under the name to select another image to use for the agent icon. You can upload any image in PNG format less than 30 KB in size with a maximum resolution of 192 × 192 pixels. You can change the agent's icon at any time.

Write a description and instructions

Description

The description is used to describe the purpose of your agent, such as the specific task or situation it is built for. It can include a summary of the agent's scope and goals and any key capabilities or limitations. This text should be short, simple, and precise, no more than 2–4 sentences. When writing the description, consider what would help someone else easily understand what this agent is for and what it does.

For example, you might create a description like this for an IT Helpdesk agent:

> This agent assists employees with common IT support requests, including password resets, software installation guidance, troubleshooting connectivity issues, and checking ticket status. It connects to internal knowledge bases, ticketing systems, and self-service tools to resolve issues or route more complex requests to the appropriate team. Designed to improve employee experience by reducing wait times and providing 24/7 support for routine IT queries.

Instructions

Instructions are a critical part of the agent's configuration, telling the agent how it will behave, how to respond, and what tone to use. Instructions can include references to tools and knowledge sources, and can set parameters for the agent to follow. Instructions can also include guardrails telling the agent when it should or shouldn't respond. Generative orchestration and autonomous agents will use these instructions, together with the descriptions of all the knowledge and tools you add to the agent, to decide what to do and when. The agent uses the instructions to fill in inputs for actions based on the context, and for generating a response to the end user.

> **SEE ALSO** Instructions play an important role in autonomous agents. This topic is covered in more detail in Chapter 5: Building autonomous agents.

For example, the instructions for an IT Helpdesk agent might be:

> You are an IT Helpdesk agent designed to assist employees with common IT support requests. Respond in a friendly, professional, and helpful tone. Keep answers clear and concise, and guide users step-by-step when troubleshooting.
>
> Always prioritize solving the user's issue efficiently. Use the provided knowledge sources to answer questions about passwords, email access, VPN setup, software installation, and device troubleshooting. If the issue

4

is not covered by the knowledge base or requires human support, offer to create a support ticket and explain the next steps.

Do not guess or provide inaccurate information. If you're unsure or the request falls outside your scope, clearly state this and escalate appropriately. Avoid technical jargon unless the user is already using it, and tailor responses to match their level of technical understanding.

As you write the description and instructions for the agent, the pane on the right side of the screen is updated based on what you change and add.

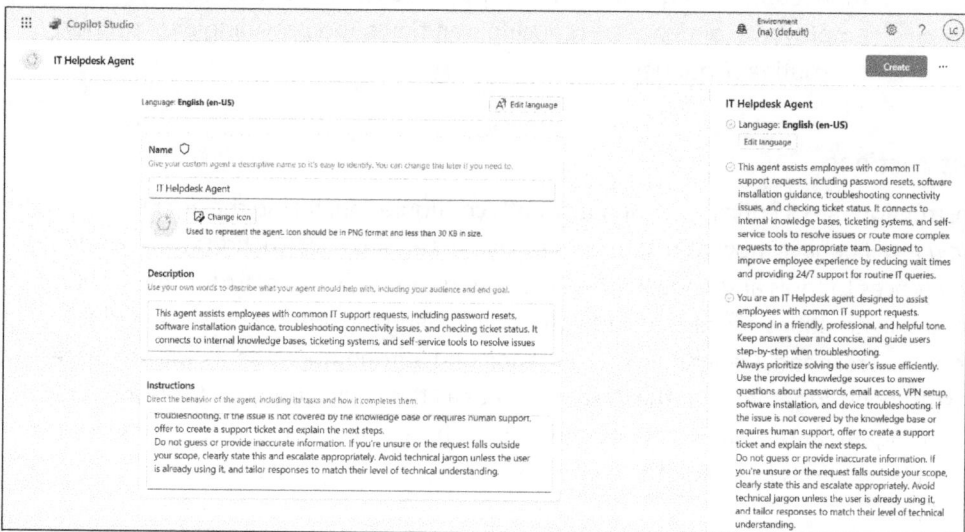

As you add the name, description, and instructions, the pane on the right side of the screen is updated with the details.

> **SEE ALSO** There is a separate place for instructions to specify the format and style of the agent's response, which becomes available in the settings area after you create the agent. Adding those instructions is covered in the "Manage agent settings" section later in this chapter.

> **TIP** After you have created the agent and added knowledge and tools, you can edit the instructions to make specific reference to those knowledge and tools.

Add suggested prompts

If you plan to publish your agent in Microsoft Teams or Microsoft 365 Copilot Chat, you can configure up to six suggested prompts that the user can select to start the conversation. These suggested prompts will appear in the agent's welcome page, giving the user guidance and suggestions on ways to start the conversation with the agent.

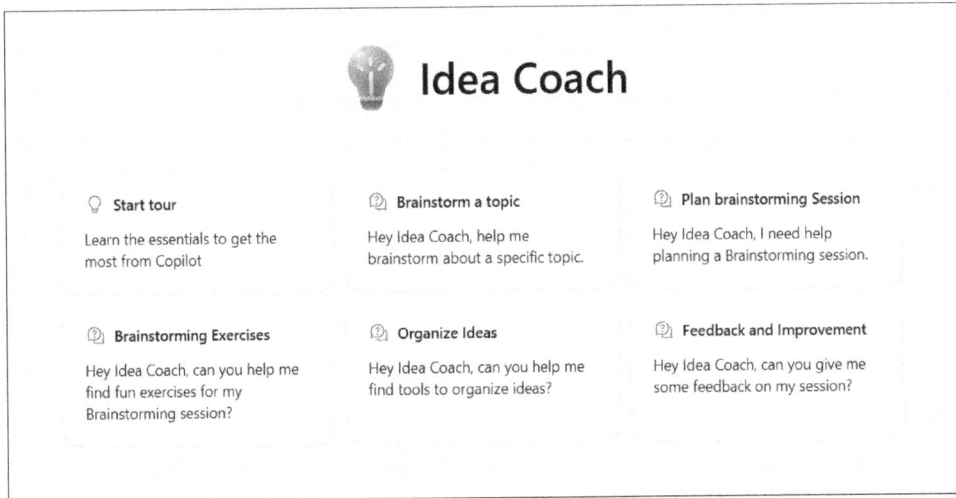

An agent published in Microsoft 365 Copilot Chat displays suggested prompts for the user to select to start the conversation.

To add suggested prompts to your agent

1. Locate the **Suggested prompts** area of the configuration screen underneath the description and instructions sections, and select the **Add suggested prompts** button.

2. Fill the **Title** and **Prompt** for up to six suggested prompts and then select the **Save** button.

3. You can edit these prompts at any time.

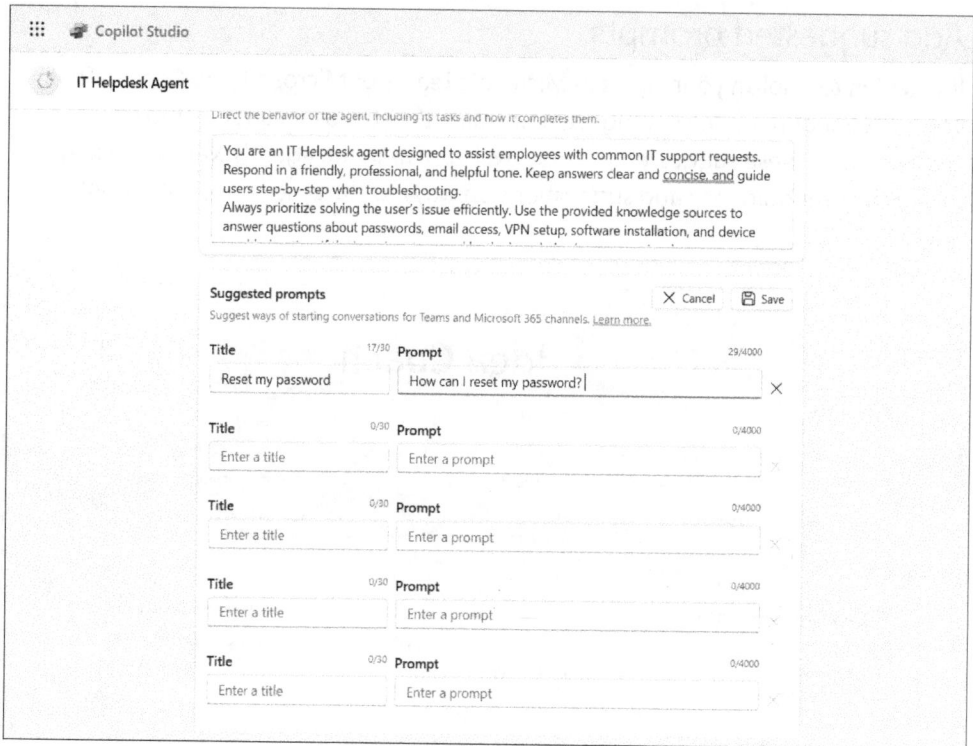

Add suggested prompts with a Title and Prompt text.

Add knowledge

The final option in this configuration experience for creating an agent is to add knowledge. You can select the **Add Knowledge** button to add either a public website or a link to a SharePoint site here. If you want to add other knowledge sources, you can do that later, after the agent is created.

> **SEE ALSO** You will learn about adding and configuring knowledge in Chapter 6: Grounding agents in knowledge.

Create the agent

When you have finished as many of these configuration steps as needed, select the **Create** button at the top right of the screen to create your agent.

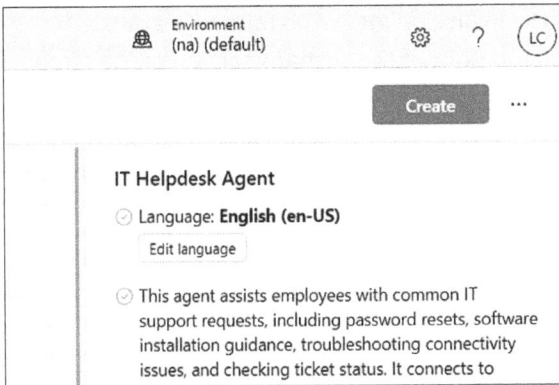

Select Create to finish this stage of configuration and create the agent.

Copilot Studio will start creating your agent. You will first be taken to a screen that shows you that the setup is in progress. You will then finish on the configuration home page for your agent. On this page, you can begin testing and continue to configure more functionality using the skills you will learn in the rest of this book.

Manage agent settings

The **Settings** area of your agent includes options to manage generative AI, security, connection settings, entities, skills, voice, languages, and other advanced settings.

In this section, you will learn about the settings for managing generative AI, providing additional instructions for the response format, selecting a different language region, and adding secondary languages to your agent.

You can access the settings by selecting the **Settings** button at the top right of the agent configuration screen, above the test pane.

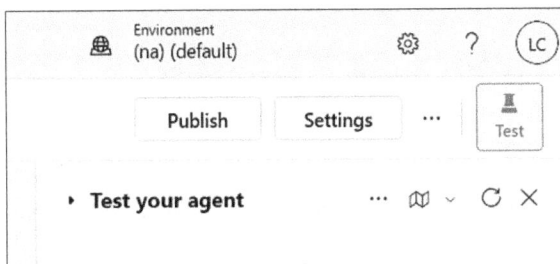

Select the Settings button at the top right of the agent configuration screen to access the settings for your agent.

This opens the **Settings** page within the main Copilot Studio frame. To exit the Settings page, select the **X** icon at the top right of the **Settings** section of the screen.

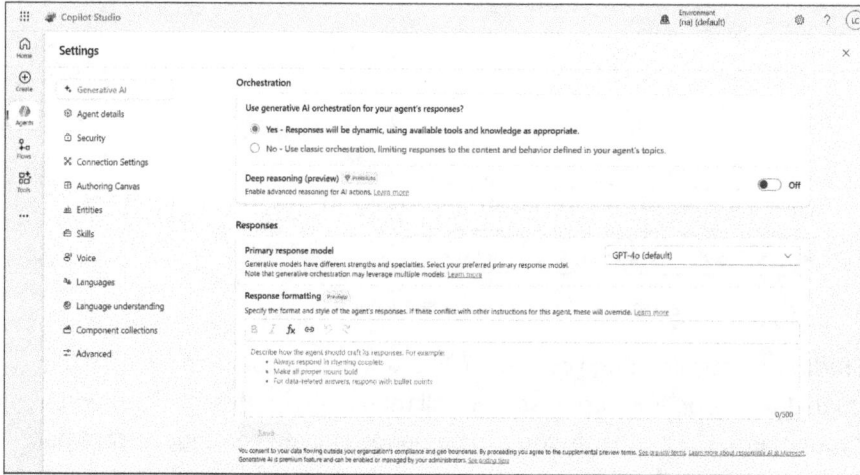

The Settings screen opens within the Copilot Studio frame.

Enable deep reasoning

The option to enable the agent to use a deep reasoning model is found in the Generative AI settings. This setting is off by default, but can be switched on here.

You can enable the deep reasoning model only when your agent uses generative orchestration. Even with this option enabled, the agent will use the deep reasoning model only when you explicitly instruct it to do so by using the keyword "reason" in the instructions. Note that using a deep reasoning model in your agent will consume additional messages at a high rate.

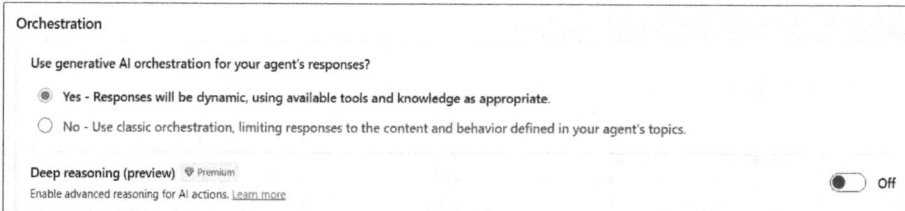

You can switch on deep reasoning capability for your agent if you are using generative orchestration.

> **SEE ALSO** You will learn more about how to use deep reasoning in Chapter 5: Building autonomous agents.

Manage the response model and response formatting

The generative AI settings also include options to change the model used by your agent, and to specify the format of the responses when generative answers are used.

> 🔍 **SEE ALSO** For information on selecting different models for your agent or bringing your own model from Azure AI Foundry, see the section "Bring your own Azure AI Foundry model" in Chapter 13, Extending Copilot Studio agents with Azure AI.

4

In the **Responses** settings, you can also add instructions to tell the agent how to format and style the responses. This can include instructions such as "always respond in rhyming couplets," "make all proper nouns bold," or "for data-related answers, respond with bullet points." The instructions you add here will override any other instructions that describe the format and style of the agent's responses.

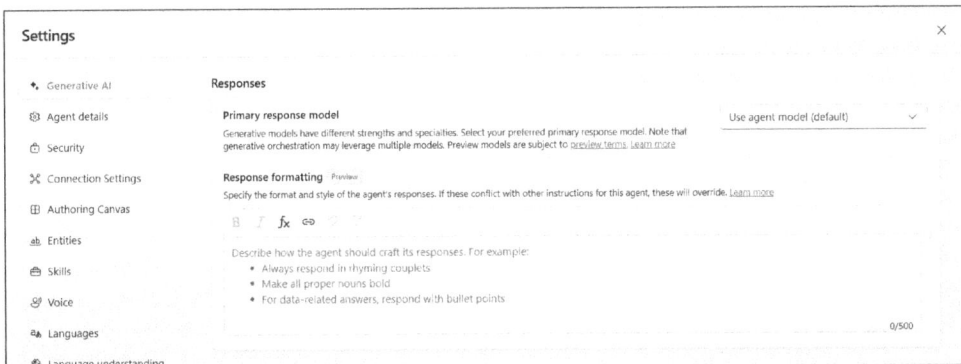

The Responses settings allow you to write instructions for the agent to respond in a specific way.

Edit the primary language and add secondary languages

The **Languages** section of the settings is where you can edit the primary language (if allowed) and add secondary languages.

This section displays the primary language that was set when the agent was created. As noted earlier, you can't change the primary language to a different language after the agent has been created. However, if the primary language has regional variations, you can switch to a different variation here. To do so, select the **Edit** button and then select the regional variation from the drop-down list of options.

> ✓ **TIP** The Edit button appears only if regional variations are available for the primary language.

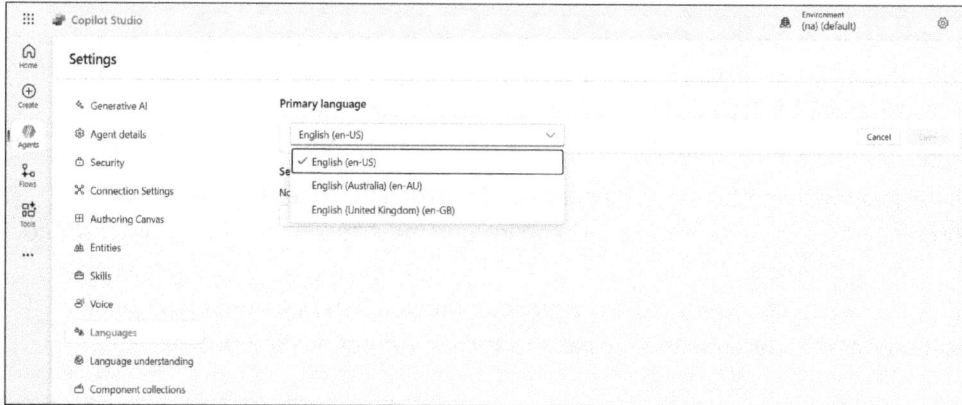

You can switch to a different regional variation of the primary language in the Languages settings.

You can add secondary languages to your agent by selecting the **Add language** button and checking the boxes for all the languages you want to add. This will enable the agent to handle user input, generative answers, generative orchestration, and voice support in the chosen languages, without any further configuration needed.

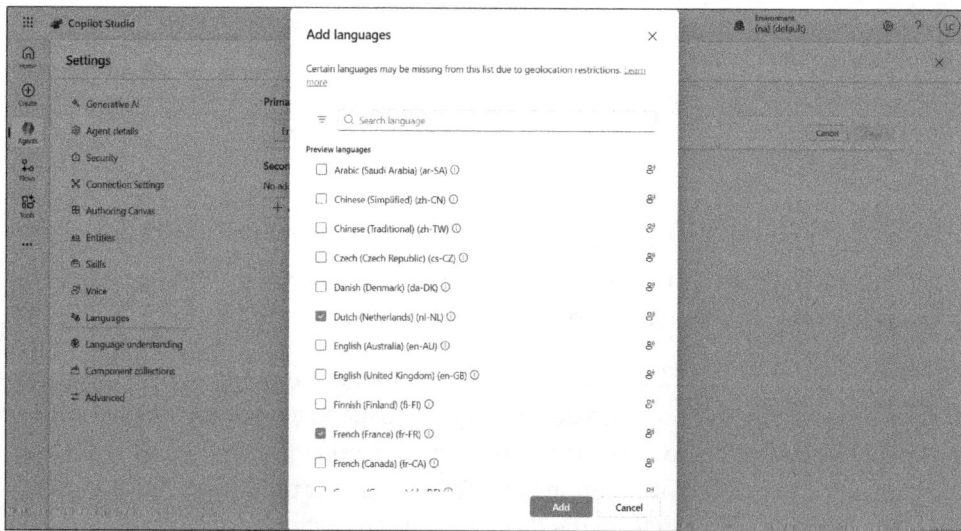

You can add secondary languages to your agent from a list of supported languages.

> ⚠️ **IMPORTANT** The support for handling event triggers, generative answers, generative orchestration, user input, and voice is at different stages for each language and capability. For up-to-date details on language support, refer to https://learn.microsoft.com/en-us/microsoft-copilot-studio/authoring-language-support.

Edit the Conversation Start topic

4

When you create a new agent, it comes with a generic greeting that is used to start the conversation. This default is a very "maker-facing" message, and you should always change it before publishing and using your agent.

This greeting message is controlled by a system topic called the Conversation Start topic. You can edit this greeting message to suit the brand voice of your agent, using the language and tone you want. You can even choose to include emojis in the message if that fits the scenario.

To edit the Conversation Start topic

1. Select **Topics** from the top menu of the agent configuration screen.

2. Under the **Add a topic** button, select the **System** button to display the automatically generated system topics.

Select Topics and then System to view the list of system topics.

3. Select the **Conversation Start** topic to open it in the authoring canvas.

4. The greeting message is found in the **Message** node of this topic. Select the start of the message text to expand and open it for editing.

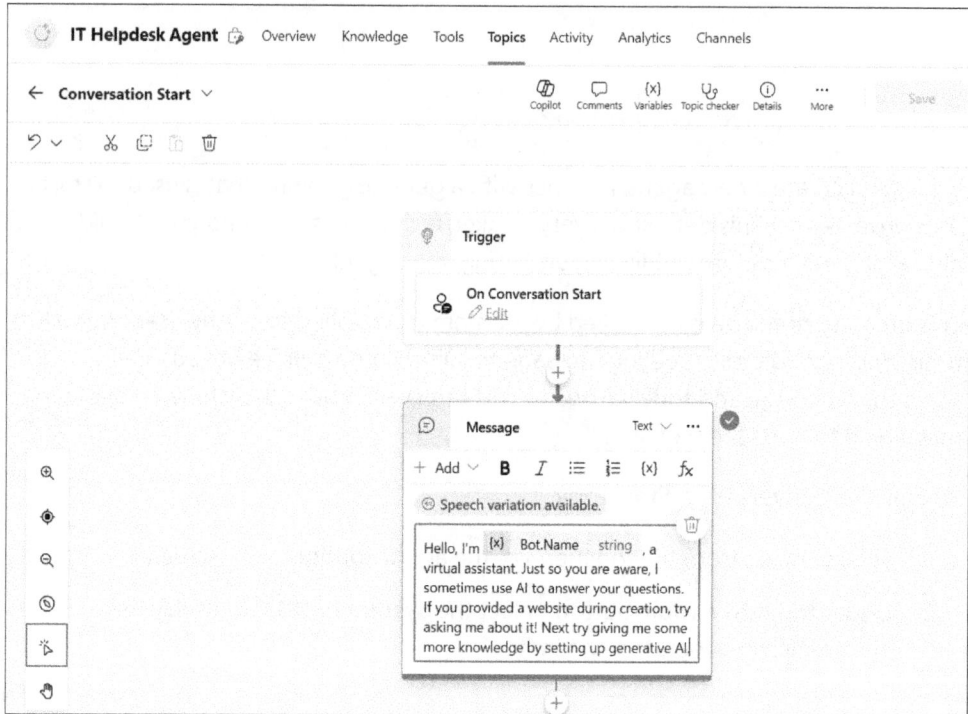

Select the message text in the Message node to open it for editing.

5. The bot name is represented by a variable. Leave that part of the message as it is, and edit the rest of the message so that the greeting matches your scenario and brand voice.

> **SEE ALSO** You will learn more about variables and topics in Chapter 7: Authoring topics.

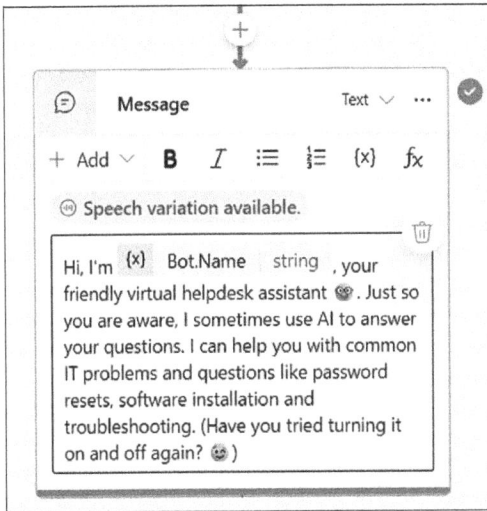

Edit the message so that it helps the user understand what your agent does and uses your brand voice.

6. When you have finished editing the message, select a spot anywhere on the authoring canvas outside that message node. The **Save** button will then be activated.

7. Select the **Save** button.

8. When the topic has been saved, you can navigate back to the main agent configuration screen by selecting **Overview** from the top menu.

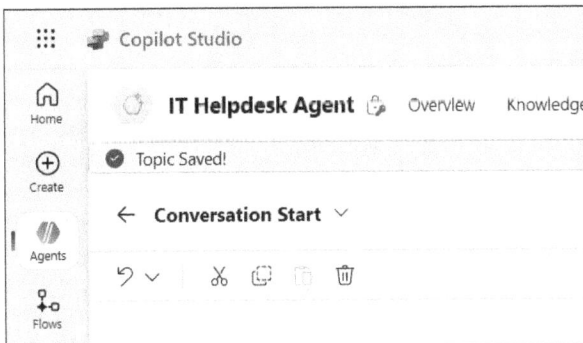

When the topic is saved, you can navigate back to the main agent configuration screen.

9. Refresh the test pane, and the agent will start the conversation with the new greeting message.

> ▸ **Test your agent** ⋯ ◫ ⌄ ⟳ ✕
>
>
>
>
>
> Hi, I'm IT Helpdesk Agent, your friendly virtual helpdesk assistant 🐱. Just so you are aware, I sometimes use AI to answer your questions. I can help you with common IT problems and questions like password resets, software installation and troubleshooting. (Have you tried turning it on and off again? 😸)
>
> Just now
>
> ┌─────────────────────────────────────┐
> │ Ask a question or describe what you need │
> │ 0/2000   𝒫   ▷ │
> └─────────────────────────────────────┘

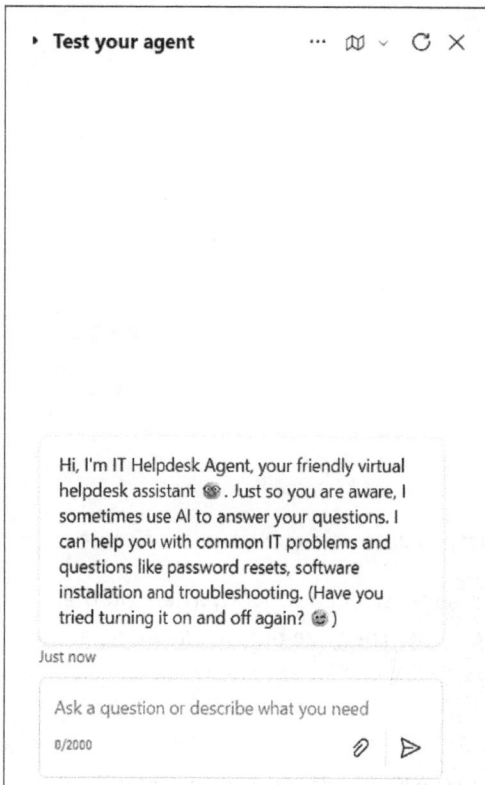

The agent now starts the conversation in the test pane with the edited greeting message.

Start with an agent template

Copilot Studio includes a variety of templates to help you get started with building agents for common scenarios. These templates come preconfigured (prefilled with suggestions) with a description, instructions, knowledge sources, or connectors depending on the scenario. They serve as starting points that can help you understand how to build an agent for that scenario, rather than starting from a blank agent.

You can easily extend these templates to fit your specific business scenario, using the skills you will learn in this book. In almost all cases, you will need to swap out the knowledge sources in the template for your own knowledge sources or expand on the instructions for your own scenario.

> **IMPORTANT** Some agent templates include connectors to other business systems or services. It is important to understand that the template includes only the connector—not the actual service it is connecting to. For instance, the IT Helpdesk agent template includes a connector to ServiceNow. To build this agent from this template, you would need to have an existing ServiceNow account and fill in the credentials in the agent template to make that connection.

4

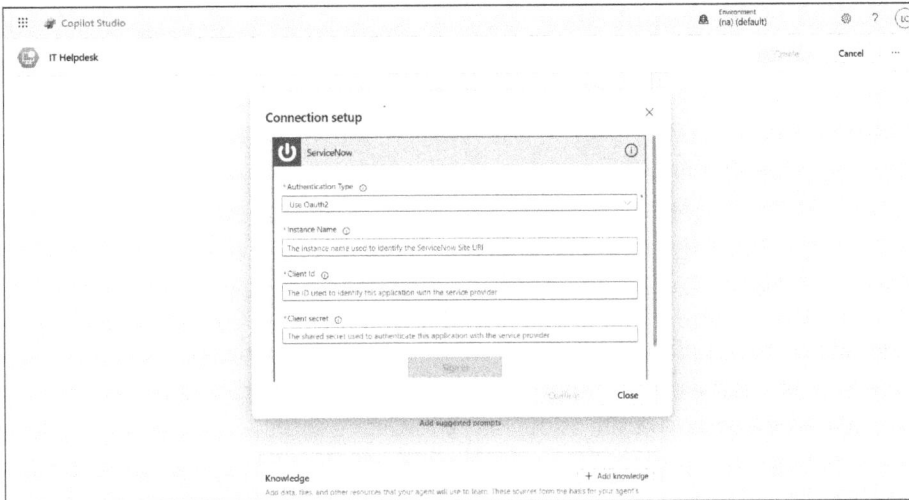

Some agent templates include connections to other services. You need to sign in with your existing credentials to use these connections.

> **SEE ALSO** Refer to the Microsoft documentation for each template before using it: https://learn.microsoft.com/en-us/microsoft-copilot-studio/template-fundamentals.

To create an agent from a template

1. Navigate to Copilot Studio in your browser, and select the **Create** icon directly below the **Home** icon on the left side rail.

2. On the **Create** screen, navigate to the **Start with an agent template** section.

3. Select any agent template to view the configuration details. In this example, select the **Website Q&A** agent template.

4. This opens the same configuration experience you used to create an agent at the start of this chapter, with some parts prefilled rather than blank. You can change any parts of the template here to suit your business scenario, editing the description, instructions, and suggested prompts.

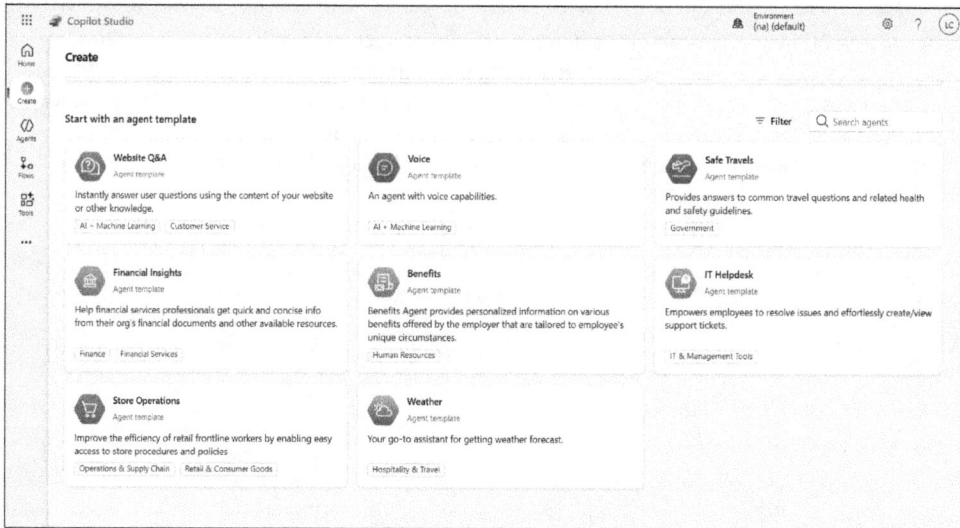

The Create screen in Copilot Studio includes agent templates to help you get started.

5.   This template includes the Microsoft website as a placeholder knowledge source. Expand the menu in that section and delete the knowledge source. Then, add your own website as the new knowledge source.

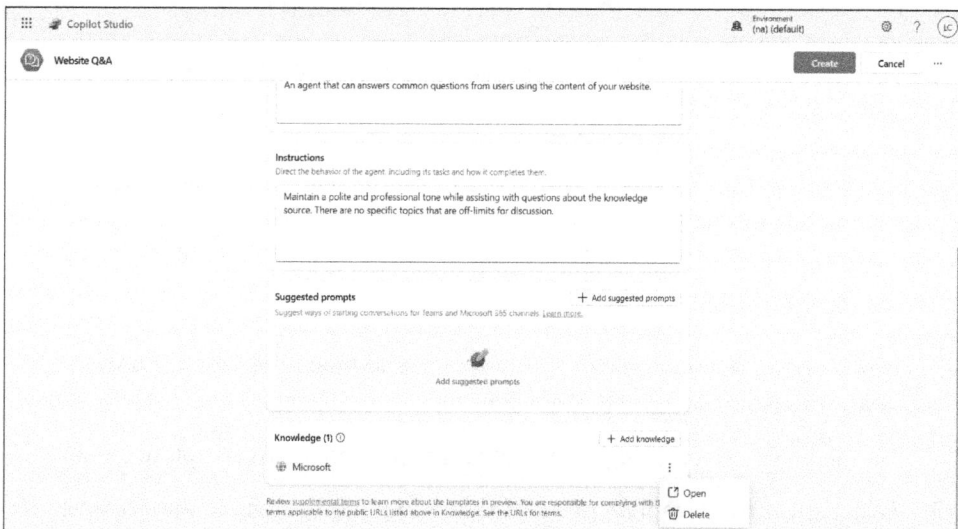

The Website Q&A agent template includes the Microsoft website as sample knowledge. Change this to your own website.

6.   When you have finished editing the template, select the **Create** button at the top right of the screen to create the agent.

Install a managed agent

Whereas templates are prefilled configuration experiences that are designed to help you get started, managed agents are complete solutions that are immediately ready to connect and deploy. You should deploy a managed agent in an environment where you are managing the other data and connections the agent will use.

> ⚠️ **IMPORTANT** Managed agents have dependencies on other applications, services, and licenses. Check the documentation for the managed agent you want to use to confirm that you have all the prerequisites before installing it. Documentation and prerequisites for all managed agents are available here: https://learn.microsoft.com/en-us/microsoft-copilot-studio/authoring-install-agent.

To install a managed agent

1. In Copilot Studio, use the environment picker at the top right of the screen to switch to the Development environment you created earlier in this chapter. In this example, you will be deploying the Wellness Check managed agent, which has a dependency on Dataverse.

2. Select the **Create** icon directly below the **Home** icon on the left side rail.

3. On the **Create** screen, navigate to the **Install a managed agent** section.

4. Select the agent you want to install. In this example, select the **Wellness Check** managed agent.

5. This opens a pop-up window that gives you a preview of the agent, details of what the agent is designed to do, and links to the documentation and terms and condition for the agent. Make sure to review this documentation before you install the agent.

6. Select the **Install** button.

7. You will be prompted to set up connections to the required services. In this case, the connections to Microsoft Dataverse and Microsoft Teams are already configured. If your agent requires connections that are not set up, use the ellipses at the end of each connection to sign in and authenticate the connection.

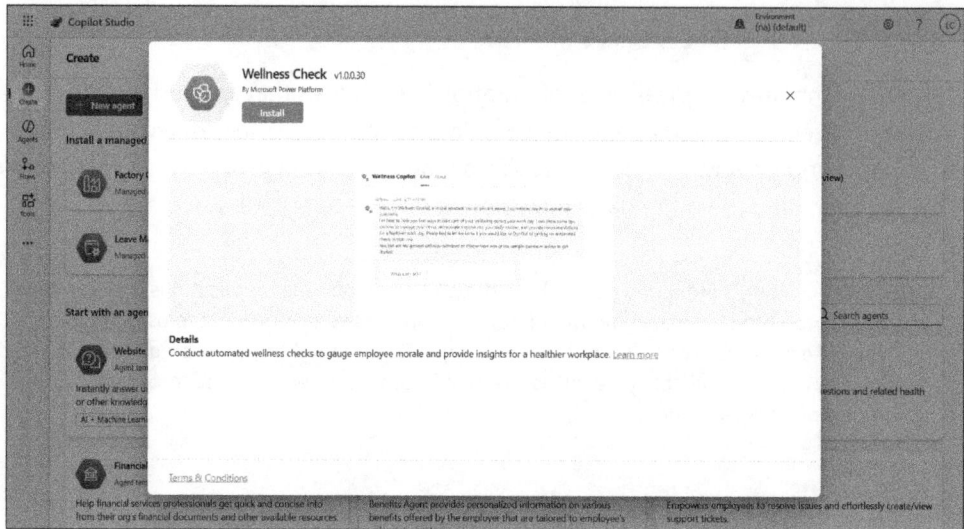

When you select the Wellness Check agent, you will get a preview of the agent and links to the documentation and terms and conditions.

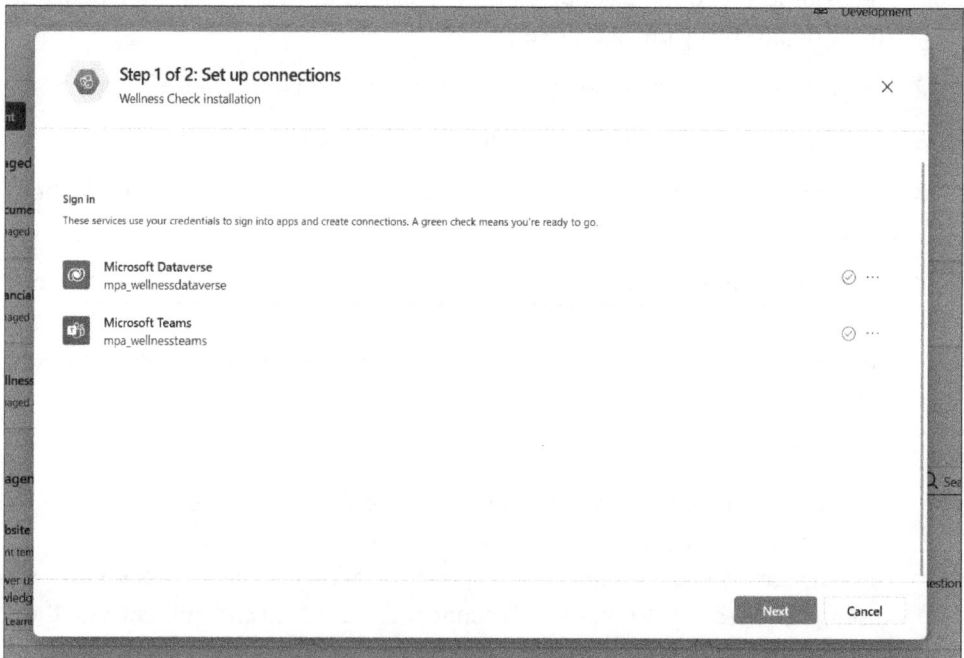

Authenticate the connections used by the agent.

8. Select **Next**.

9. The installation begins, and you will see a confirmation screen. Close this pop-up and wait for the agent to be installed in the background.

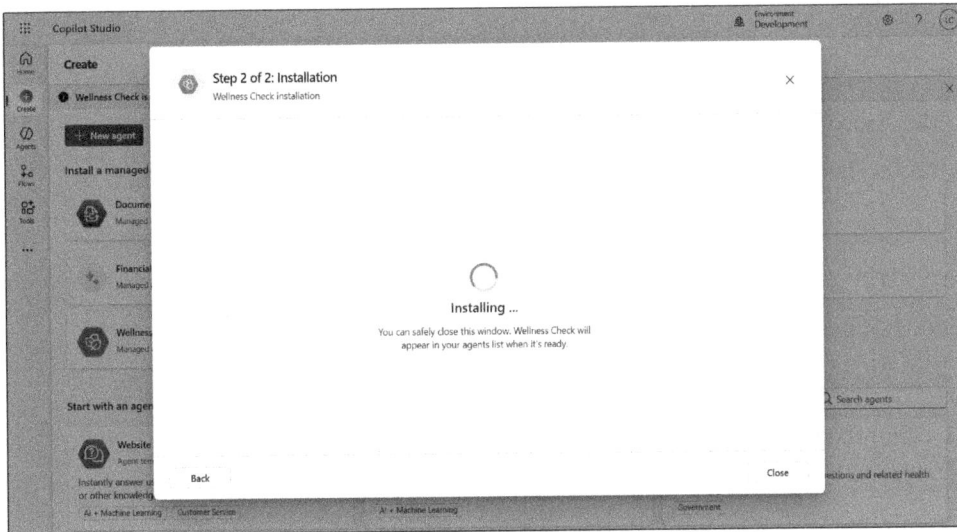

You can close the window and wait for the agent to finish installing in the background.

10. Navigate to the **Agents** icon on the left side rail to find the Wellness Check agent in the list of agents when it has finished installing. Select it to open it and test it.

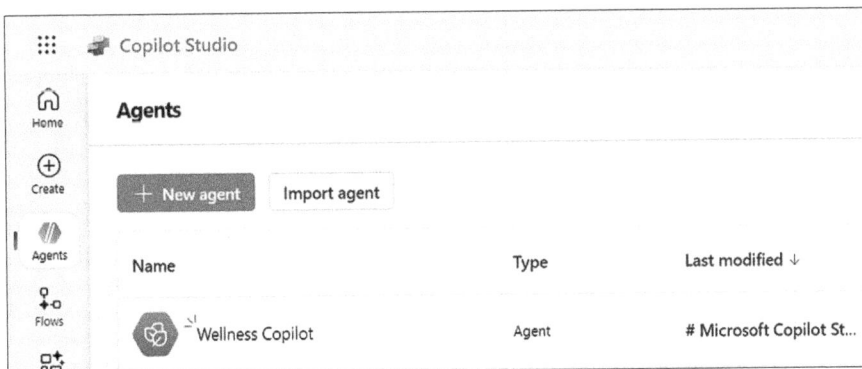

Select the Wellness Copilot from the list of agents to run it.

11. In the test pane, select "**What can I ask**" to find options and then test with some of the suggested prompts.

Now that you have seen how to create an agent in Copilot Studio, you are ready to learn how to customize and extend your agent using triggers, knowledge, topics, and tools in the following chapters.

Skills review

In this chapter, you learned how to:

- Create a new environment in the Power Platform admin center.
- Create an agent by configuring it, and writing effective descriptions, instructions, and starter prompts.
- Enable your agent to use reasoning models and preview models.
- Add secondary languages to make your agent multilingual.
- Edit the message that the agent uses to start the conversation.
- Create an agent from a template and edit it to work for your own scenario.
- Install a prebuilt managed agent that includes connectors.

Practice tasks

No practice files are necessary to complete the practice tasks in this chapter.

Understand environments and solutions

Open the Edge browser and then complete the following tasks:

1. Navigate to the Power Platform admin center: https://admin.powerplatform. microsoft.com.

2. Select the **Manage** icon on the left side rail.

3. Select **+New** to create a new environment.

4. In the side pane, give your environment a name, such as "Development." Select the type "Trial," and add a Dataverse data store. Select **Next**.

5. In the Security group options, select Open Access: **None**.

6. Select **Done**.

7. Select **Save**.

Configure a new agent

Open Copilot Studio in your browser and then complete the following tasks:

1. Select the **Create** icon from the left side rail.

2. Select the **+New agent** button.

3. Select the **Skip to configure** button.

4. Give your agent a name: **Microsoft 365 Assistant**.

5. In the Description, describe the purpose of your agent: **An agent that provides information about Microsoft 365 capabilities, plans, and pricing**.

6. In the Instructions, add the following text:

   - **Provide detailed information about Microsoft 365 capabilities, plans, and pricing.**

   - **Answer user queries related to Microsoft 365 features and benefits.**

- Assist users in understanding different subscription options and their respective costs.

- Ensure responses are accurate and up-to-date with the latest Microsoft 365 offerings.

- Maintain a friendly and informative tone in all interactions.

- Avoid discussing topics unrelated to Microsoft 365.

7. In the **Knowledge** section, add the following website: https://www.microsoft.com/en-us/microsoft-365.

8. Select **Create.**

9. In the test pane, ask a question, such as **What home plans are available?**

Manage agent settings

Open the Settings for your agent and then complete the following tasks:

1. Select **Settings.**

2. In the **Generative AI** settings, navigate down to the **Responses** section.

3. Write instructions for the response format. Choose something that will make a big difference in the response, such as "**talk like a pirate.**"

4. Select **Save.**

5. Close the **Settings** by selecting the **X** at the top right of the **Settings** area.

6. Enter a prompt into the test pane.

7. Review the response to note the impact of your instructions.

Edit the Conversation Start topic

Open the Settings for your agent and then complete the following tasks:

1. Select **Topics** from the top menu.

2. Select **System.**

3. Select the **Conversation Start** topic to open it.

4. Select the start of the message text in the **Message** node to open it for editing.

5. Edit the message to match the brand voice you want for your agent.

6. Select a spot on the authoring canvas anywhere outside the **Message** node.

7. Select **Save.**

8. Refresh the test pane; your agent will start the conversation with the new greeting.

Start with an agent template

Navigate to Copilot Studio in your browser and complete the following tasks:

1. Select the **Create** icon on the left side rail.

2. Select the **Weather agent** from the agent template section.

3. In the configuration screen, navigate to the **Connect your data** section. The MSN Weather connector is included in the template. You can use this free connection without having to set up an account. Select the **Set up connection** option, and in the expanded menu, select **Edit.**

4. The **Connection setup** window will pop up, showing the MSN Weather connector with a green check mark. Select the **Confirm** button.

5. Select the **Create** button at the top right of the configuration screen.

6. Wait for the agent to be created.

7. Test your agent by asking a question about the weather. This agent comes with prebuilt topics to detect the user intent. Start by asking "**Get current weather**" and then respond to the prompt to enter the city.

Install a managed agent

Navigate to Copilot Studio in your browser and complete the following tasks:

1. Review the documentation for the Document Processor managed agent: https://learn.microsoft.com/en-gb/microsoft-copilot-studio/ template-managed-document-processor.

2. In Copilot Studio, switch to the Development environment.

3. Select the **Create** icon on the left side rail, and then select the Document Processor agent from the list of managed agents.

4. Wait for the connections to be validated and then select **Next**.

5. Close the window and wait for the agent to be installed.

6. Navigate to the list of agents in the left side rail menu and open the Document Processor agent.

Building autonomous agents

5

Practice files

No practice files are necessary to complete the practice tasks in this chapter.

With Copilot Studio, you can build agents that are triggered by a chat with a user as well as agents that are triggered by an event. The latter can act autonomously when something external to the agent happens in your environment. These autonomous agents change what's possible with automation, and require a paradigm shift in how we think about transforming business processes. They enable us to design automations where AI handles the end-to-end business process independently, deciding what to do at runtime by reasoning over the knowledge, tools, and topics it has available. Autonomous agents decide what to do based on the context and inputs, rather than running the same way every time using deterministic flows made of "if this, then that" rules.

When building an autonomous agent, you define the high-level role and process that the agent is responsible for, identify the goals or tasks it needs to complete, and provide it with the knowledge, tools, and topics necessary to do that job. It's much like delegating a task to a human: You describe the task, the event that happens and causes the process to start, the high-level tasks, the resources needed for the job, the decisions that need to

In this chapter

- Identify use cases for autonomous agents
- Build an autonomous agent
- Publish and monitor an autonomous agent

be made, and the desired outcome. You then let the person work through the job, deciding the best way to do it each time.

In this chapter, you will learn how to build autonomous agents, understand the use cases for these agents, distinguish between autonomous agents and workflow automation, discover the key components that make them work, and learn the best practices for success.

Identify use cases for autonomous agents

To identify potential use cases for autonomous agents in your organization, start by considering those business processes that you haven't been able to automate in the past. Look for processes that are still manually handled because they require human input to research, reason, or make a decision, or to create content such as a tailored email response every time.

Autonomous agents versus workflow automation

The biggest point of confusion with autonomous agents is how they differ from workflow automation built using a tool like Power Automate. In some ways, the two seem similar, because both start with an event trigger that kicks off the process. The difference lies in the way the automation runs after that first trigger.

The following suggestions are intended to help you understand when to use each option:

- Use workflow automation with a tool like Power Automate when your automation runs the same way every time. Scenarios for workflow automation use deterministic logic. They can be described in a series of steps or branching logic that you can map out and define in a flow diagram. As a result, you can determine fixed steps that the automation should follow.

- Use an autonomous agent where the process automation is more dynamic and doesn't necessarily follow the same fixed path every time. Think of building an autonomous agent as being more like creating a job description for a process. You provide high-level instructions and goals, along with access to the required knowledge and tools to get the job done. The agent uses AI to determine how best to complete the process at runtime, rather than following step-by-step instructions in a flowchart.

There is also some overlap between these options, however, which can create confusion:

- You can build AI-enabled workflows by using the generative AI capabilities in Power Automate in some of the steps. For instance, you can add a generative action to your flow to add a step where (1) you describe the intent of what you want to achieve, and (2) the AI then chooses the right actions based on the input from the previous steps in the flow, your instructions, and the context. This approach is useful when your process is primarily deterministic, but some part of it can be handled by AI.

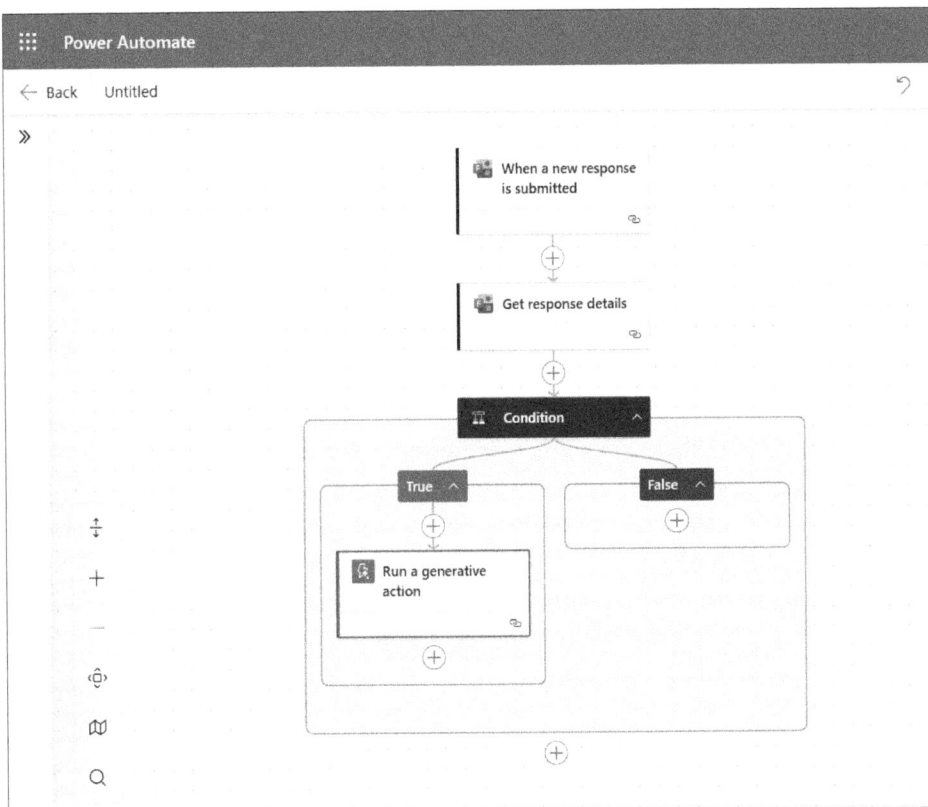

You can add generative actions into deterministic workflows in Power Automate.

- You can use deterministic workflows as part of an autonomous agent when parts of the workflow need to be predefined. This is done by using Agent flows inside Copilot Studio. This approach is useful where your process is primarily variable (i.e., handled in a different way each time), but some tasks or parts of the process need to follow deterministic logic.

> **SEE ALSO** You will learn how to build agent flows in Chapter 8: Extending agents with tools.

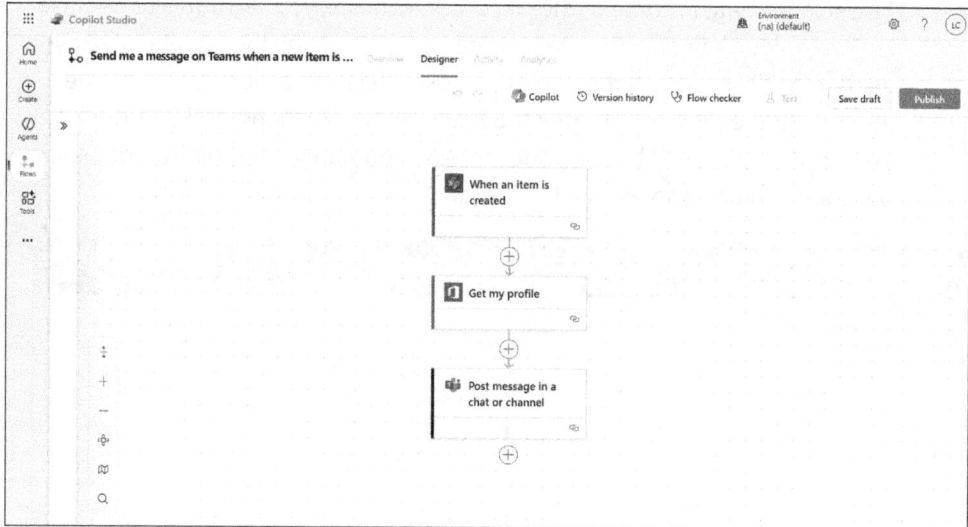

You can add deterministic workflows to your autonomous agent by using Agent flows in Copilot Studio.

In summary:

- Power Automate flows are suitable for automating structured, repeatable processes that run the same way every time. Flows can also incorporate generative AI actions when needed—for instance, when you want to summarize data, reason over information, check whether requirements have been met, or make a recommendation or decision. The process is mostly deterministic, leveraging generative AI for specific tasks where those skills are needed.

- Autonomous agents are suitable for processes that are less structured, require decision making, or may vary at runtime based on the input or context. They use generative AI to reason over instructions, knowledge, and tools, and run dynamically every time, adapting to everything that is happening in the process. You can use deterministic logic within an autonomous agent for specific tasks in the process that follow fixed rules or steps.

Identify use cases

To identify use cases for autonomous agents in your organization, look for processes where:

- The process is triggered by a schedule (e.g., run every Monday morning) or an event (e.g., a form submission, incoming email, data added or updated in a business system).

- The process requires interpretation, reasoning, decision making, or variation at runtime. In other words, it isn't a repeatable flow that can be described in a series of deterministic steps.

Here are some examples:

Customer complaints agent

An autonomous agent that can triage and respond to customer complaints.

- The agent is triggered when an email is received in the customer service inbox.

- The agent reviews the text of the email to determine the intent.

- It classifies the type of complaint, the sentiment, and the severity of the issue.

- It checks the CRM to get the priority status or any other relevant information about the customer.

- It refers to the policy or product information documents related to that complaint.

- It decides whether to respond or whether to escalate to a customer service representative.

- It generates a response, either to the customer or to the customer service agent, providing the relevant information and next steps.

This is a good use case for an autonomous agent because the input coming in via email is unstructured and highly variable. In addition, the path for determining the routing or response will change based on the information the agent gathers throughout the process.

5

133

Sales pipeline monitor

An autonomous agent that monitors the open opportunities in the CRM to look for signs that the opportunity is stalled, at risk, or missing next steps.

- The agent runs on a schedule to review all opportunities on a weekly basis or is triggered when there has been no update to an opportunity in X days.

- For each opportunity, it reviews the opportunity stage, activity history, close date, status of key activities, next step, and next step date.

- It reasons over the information provided to understand how long the deal has been open, the time in the current stage versus the average time taken, whether the next step has been identified, the last interaction with the customer, and the stakeholders involved.

- It understands the patterns of when an opportunity has stalled and decides whether the opportunity matches that pattern.

- It decides whether the opportunity is high value and reviews success indicators.

- It sends a summary report to the sales manager listing opportunities that have stalled, with suggested reasons and next steps.

- It could also update the opportunity in the CRM with a flag to indicate the opportunity is at risk.

Invoice review agent

An autonomous agent that reviews incoming invoices and checks them against the vendor contract terms and payment policies.

- The agent is triggered each time a new invoice is received.

- It extracts the vendor name, PO number, line items, total value, invoice date, and due date.

- It looks up the contract or payment terms for that vendor in a SharePoint library or ERP system.

- It compares the invoice details with the payment terms and any other terms in the vendor contract.

- It uses reasoning to determine whether the invoice amount is within the expected range, whether the payment terms are correct, and whether the invoice is in line with the payment window and contract scope.

- It decides about whether the invoice is compliant, has some minor discrepancies, or is not compliant, and generates a notification with all the relevant details and recommended next steps.

These examples show some common patterns that you can look for when identifying use cases for autonomous agents:

5

- The agent is triggered by something that involves unstructured, ambiguous, or variable input.

- It reasons over unstructured input to understand the intent and decide what to do next.

- It automates the process of gathering relevant data from multiple business systems.

- It reasons over the relevant knowledge to make a comparison, recommendation, or decision, using all the context and inputs available.

- It routes or escalates the process based on the information and decisions made.

- It produces an output such as an email, report, or notification, which presents the relevant information, recommendation, or response to a customer or business user. This output is unique or tailored every time.

Build an autonomous agent

The most important skill to learn and practice when building an autonomous agent is writing instructions, names, and descriptions. Describing the job the agent needs to do, the details of the knowledge and tools it will use, and how these pieces come together is the way you define the job it will do, instead of using a flowchart-style set of instructions.

In this section, you will learn how to build an agent that can autonomously handle incoming expense claims added to a SharePoint list, approve or reject those claims based on the company policy, send an email to the employee who made the claim, and update the status of that claim in the SharePoint list.

> ⚠️ **IMPORTANT** This example includes commonly used Microsoft 365 tools to demonstrate a real business scenario. To follow along with the example, you will need a Microsoft 365 license (or trial) in your tenant that includes SharePoint and Outlook. If you don't have access to these tools, you can do something similar using Excel and Outlook.com.

Plan an autonomous agent

Start by deciding which knowledge and tools your agent will need, and which event will trigger the agent. For this scenario, we will need:

1. A SharePoint list where the user can submit an expense claim.

2. A trigger that starts the agent when an item is added to the SharePoint list.

3. Instructions that describe the job the agent needs to do and the guardrails it should follow.

4. The relevant company policies as knowledge sources:

   - Expense policy

   - Travel policy

5. Tools that enable the agent to perform the actions required in the process:

   - Send an email (to the employee who made the claim and to the employee's manager).

   - Update the status of the item in the SharePoint list.

In this example, we are using a SharePoint list with the following columns:

- Title (text)

- Submitted by (person)

- Expense Date (date only)

- Expense Amount (currency, two decimal places)

- Expense Category (choice): Meal, Travel – Flight, Travel – Accommodation, Transport, Client Entertainment, Incidentals, Other

- Description (multiple lines of text)

- Status (choice): Submitted (default), Approved, Flagged, Rejected

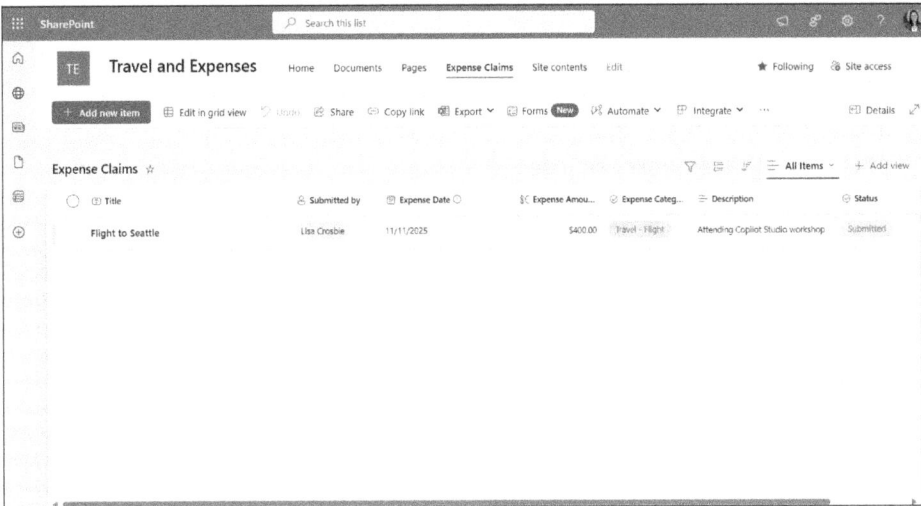

The employee submits an expense claim in a SharePoint list.

Create the agent and add knowledge and tools

Start by creating an agent with a description and adding the knowledge and tools you have planned that it will need.

> **TIP** It is usually easier to write the instructions at the end, so that you can refer to the tools and knowledge you have added by the names you have given them.

> **TIP** It is best to start simple and iterate when building an autonomous agent, testing at each step. As you work through this example, you will see how to build in this way.

As you add each knowledge source or tool, consider how it will be used by the agent. Think about how you would instruct a person when describing the job, telling them what each tool or knowledge source is for, and where it fits in the process. The names and descriptions you give to each component will be used by the orchestrator so that the agent understands what it has available and what to use when.

Start by creating a new agent in Copilot Studio, using the configuration experience. Give the agent a name and description, but leave the instructions blank.

Use these details for your new agent:

- Name: **Expenses Agent**

- Description: **An agent that checks expense claims from employees against the travel and expenses policies.**

- Ensure that generative orchestration is **enabled**.

> 🔍 **SEE ALSO** Refer to Chapter 4: Building agents in Copilot Studio for instructions on how to create an agent using configuration.

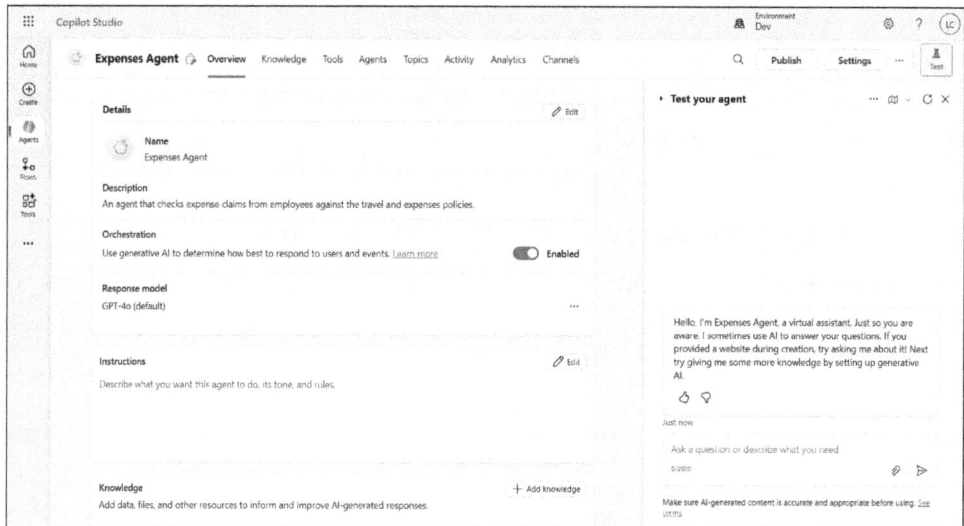

Create an agent with a name and description only, with generative orchestration enabled.

Next, you will add the expense and travel policy documents to your agent. In a real scenario, you could connect the agent to these policy documents in Word or PDF format in SharePoint or upload them as documents. In this example, we will upload PDF documents.

To add knowledge to the agent

1. Select the **Knowledge** tab in the top menu and select the **Add knowledge** button.

2. Select the **Upload file** option and add the PDF policy documents.

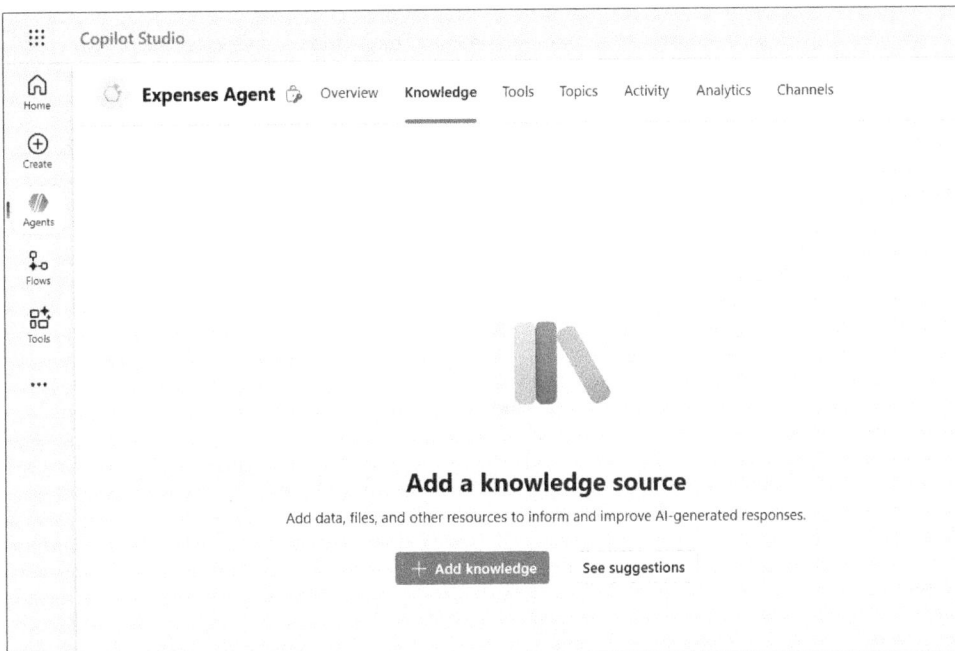

The Knowledge tab in the top menu is where you can add and manage knowledge sources.

3. For each document uploaded, edit the **Name**. The default name will be the file name, including the file type extension. The orchestrator will use the name of the knowledge source to understand what it is and when to use it, so be sure to name each knowledge source clearly and in a way that distinguishes between different knowledge sources.

> **TIP** Short phrases like "Expense Policy" are more descriptive than a single word like "Expenses" and can help the orchestrator better understand the purpose and context of the knowledge source.

4. For each document uploaded, edit the **Description**. The default description reads: "This knowledge source searches information contained in [filename]." Providing a more useful description can help the orchestrator understand what this knowledge source contains and how it will be used. For example, the description of the Expense Policy could be: "This policy outlines the company's requirements for claiming business-related expenses. It defines allowable expenses and submission requirements for meals, incidentals, and client entertainment."

> ✅ **TIP** The description should use simple, clear language and be limited to one or two sentences. Use words that match the user's intent, and describe what the knowledge source is for.

5. When you have finished adding the knowledge sources, select the **Add to agent** button.

Edit the names and descriptions of the knowledge sources and then select the Add to agent button.

6. Wait for the files to be uploaded.

7. The pop-up will close and you will be returned to the **Knowledge** tab. The knowledge sources will be indexed in the background and will show a status of **In progress**. You can continue to build the agent while this happens.

Next, you will add tools to your agent. You will start by adding a tool that enables the agent to send an email to the person who has submitted the expense claim.

To add a tool to the agent

1. Select the **Tools** tab in the top menu, and select the **Add a tool** button.

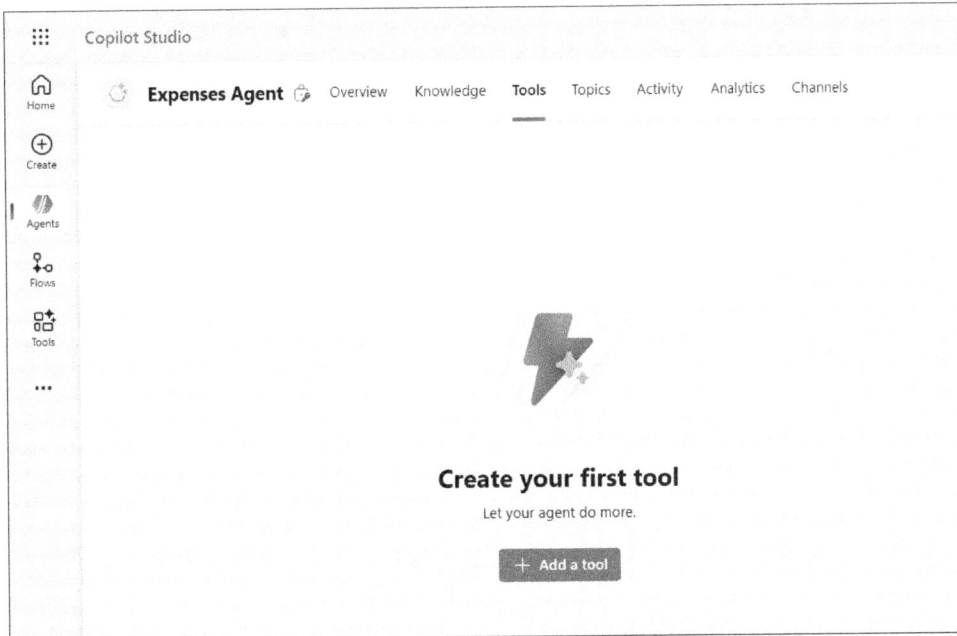

The Tools tab in the top menu is where you can add and manage tools or actions.

2. In the **Add tool** pop-up, type **send an email** in the search box and select the **Send** icon.

3. You can use both Microsoft and third-party tools with Copilot Studio. There are many email platforms available that you can use to add a tool that can send an email. Select the **Send an email (V2)** tool for **Office 365 Outlook**.

> ✅ **TIP** If you are using the Outlook email associated with your Microsoft 365 account, be sure to select the tool that uses the Office 365 Outlook connector, not the very similar-looking tool that uses Outlook.com (the personal/consumer version of Outlook).

4. A pop-up window shows the selected connector, a link to the connector documentation, and your username to authenticate the connection. If the buttons to add the connector to the agent are grayed out, select the connection to validate it and then continue.

5. Select **Add and configure**.

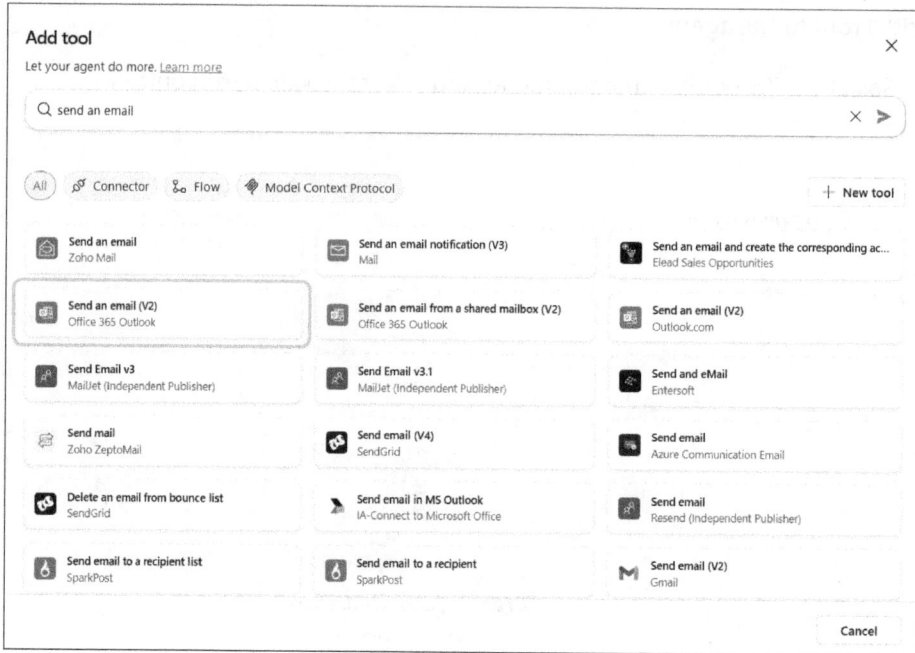

Copilot Studio includes tools to send an email from a variety of Microsoft and third-party email platforms.

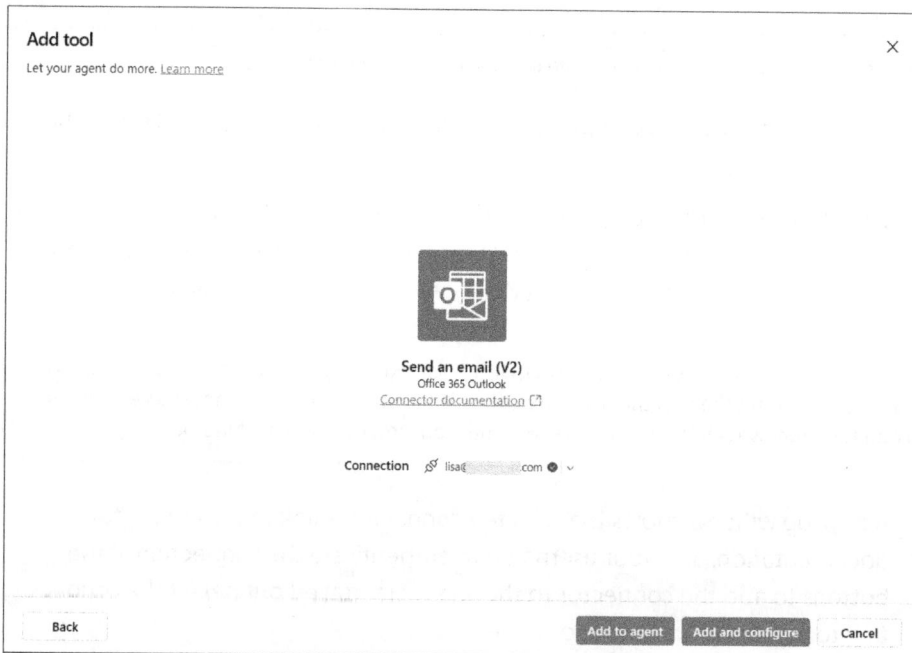

Authenticate the connector and add it to the agent.

6. This opens the configuration screen for the tool in the **Tools** tab of Copilot Studio. Edit the **Name** of the tool so that it is a descriptive short phrase. In this case, "Send an email" is a clear name for the tool. Remove the (V2) from the name.

7. Edit the **Description** of the tool so that it summarizes the functionality of the tool in one or two sentences. The default description for this tool is "This operation sends an email message." You can make it more specific by changing it to **This tool sends an email message in HTML format**.

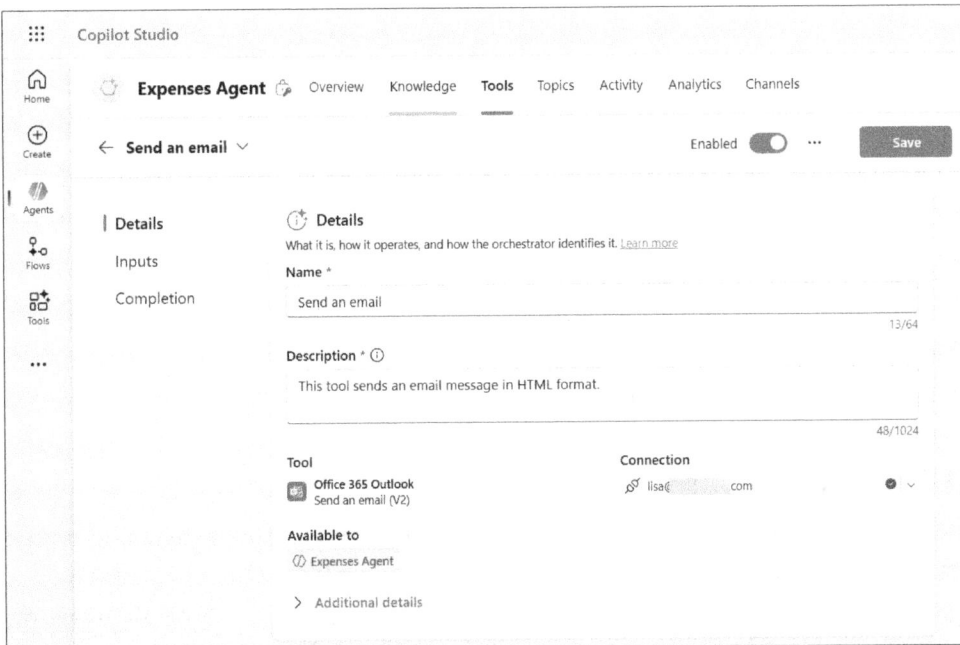

Edit the name and description of the tool to make the purpose and functionality clear to the orchestrator.

8. Expand the **Additional details** option at the bottom of the **Details** section.

9. Switch the authentication method from **User authentication** to **Copilot author authentication**.

> **SEE ALSO** Tool authentication is covered in Chapter 8: Extending agents with tools. For now, selecting Copilot author authentication will allow you to build and test an autonomous agent successfully for this scenario.

10. Select the **Save** button.

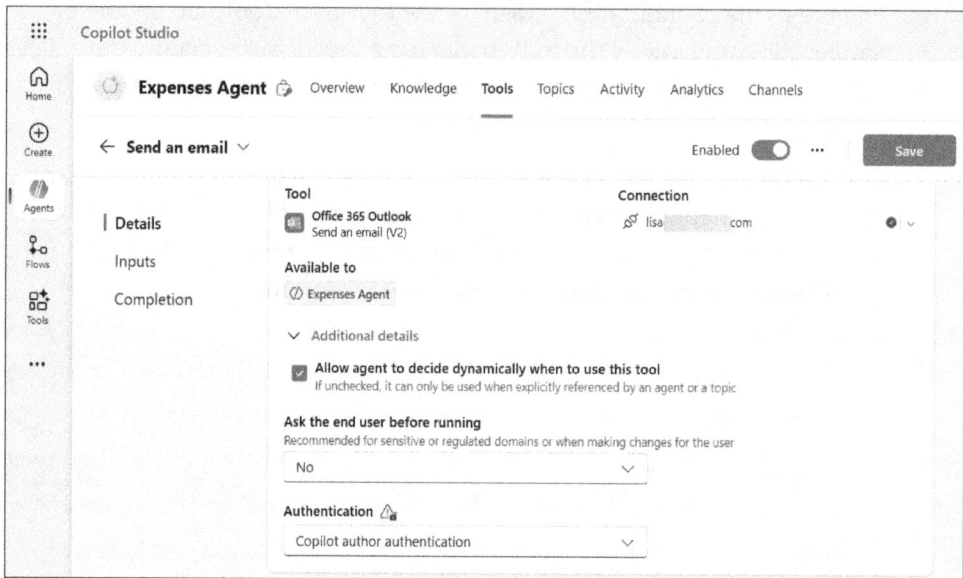

Expand the Additional details menu and change the authentication to Copilot author authentication.

11. The tool is now saved and ready for your agent to use.

12. Navigate back to the **Overview** tab.

Write instructions

Now that you have added knowledge and tools to your agent, it's time to add instructions so the agent knows what its role is and how to use these knowledge and tools. You should approach the task of writing autonomous agent instructions in the same way as you would brief an assistant on how to perform a process. Remember that you are not building or describing a deterministic workflow, but rather describing the goal that the agent needs to achieve, how it should make decisions, and how it should use the knowledge and tools you have provided to it.

You can use a numbered list of steps if you want the agent to follow a process in a specific order, but remember that these are natural language instructions. If the process includes specific details or conditional branching, consider using an agent flow to bundle up the steps for that part of the process, and then instruct the agent to call that flow.

> **TIP** When writing instructions, you can link to specific tools by name, describing when the agent should use those tools. You can also refer to knowledge sources by name in the instructions—but you should recognize that this won't force the agent to use that specific knowledge source. If you need more control because the agent should use a specific knowledge source for a specific part of the task, you will need to add that control into a topic or an agent flow.

When you are writing instructions for an autonomous agent, use the active voice, and use verbs like "get" or "use" for retrieving data. The instructions should be clear and well structured. You can use simple formatting, such as bold text, or use markup language to improve the readability of the instructions and to help the orchestrator understand them.

5

> **SEE ALSO** For more guidance on language for writing instructions and suggested verbs to use, refer to the Microsoft documentation: https://learn.microsoft.com/en-us/microsoft-copilot-studio/guidance/generative-mode-guidance.

To add instructions to the agent

1. Navigate to the **Instructions** section under the **Details** section in the **Overview** tab.

2. Select the **Edit** button to add the Instructions. Start typing your instructions in the field. The suggested instructions for this agent are as follows:

   Your job is to review employee expense claims and decide whether to approve, reject, or flag them for manual review, based on company policy.

   When a new expense claim appears in the SharePoint list, retrieve the following fields:

   - Title

   - Category

   - Description

   - Amount

   - Date of expense

Identify the type of expense based on the category and description. Use the knowledge sources (the Expense Policy and Travel Policy) to determine whether the claim meets company requirements.

Make one of three decisions:

- Approve the claim if it clearly complies with policy.

- Flag the claim if it requires human review.

- Reject the claim if it clearly violates policy.

After making your decision, write a brief explanation that aligns with the relevant policy.

Then, use the "Send an email" tool to email the employee who submitted the claim.

Write the email in HTML format. Use a professional and polite tone, and write clearly and concisely, as if you are their manager responding to the claim.

In the email:

- Summarize the expense (include the category, amount, and date).

- State your decision: Approved, Rejected, or Flagged for Review.

- Explain your decision briefly, referring to policy when appropriate.

- Format all amounts as currency with two decimal places.

Choose an appropriate sign-off tone based on the decision, and sign the message using your name, Expenses Agent.

3. To refer to a specific tool in the instructions, use the / key and select the tool from the list.

4. Select the **Save** button at the top of the Instructions section to save your work when you have finished editing.

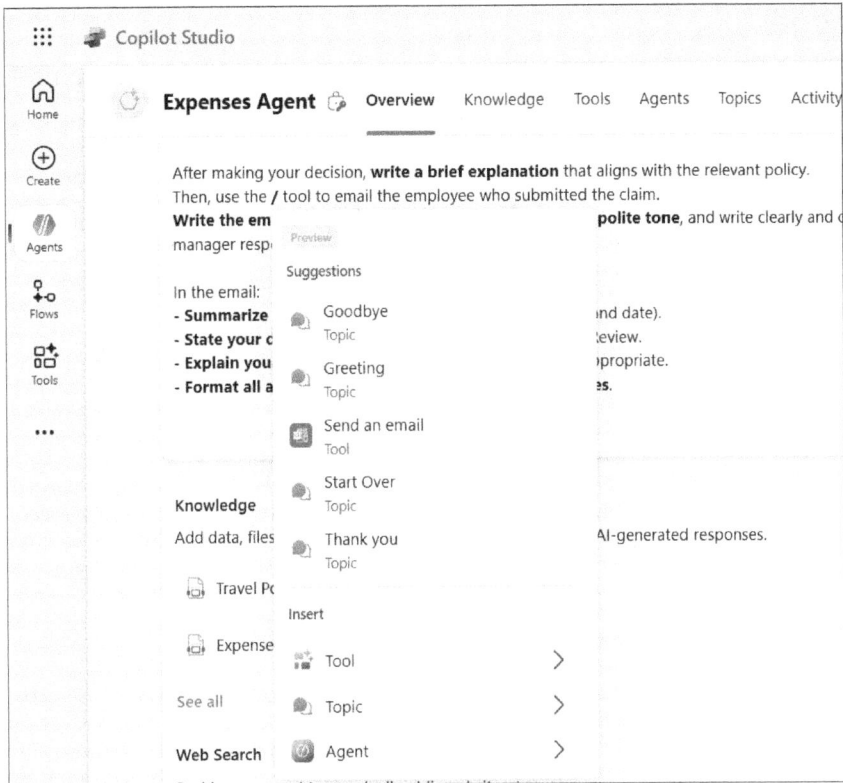

:::   Copilot Studio

Expenses Agent   Overview   Knowledge   Tools   Agents   Topics   Activity

After making your decision, **write a brief explanation** that aligns with the relevant policy. Then, use the **/** tool to email the employee who submitted the claim.

Write the em   Preview   **polite tone**, and write clearly and c manager resp

Suggestions

In the email:
- **Summarize**   Goodbye   nd date).
  Topic   eview.
- **State your c**   Greeting   propriate.
- **Explain you**   Topic   es.
- **Format all a**

  Send an email
  Tool

  Start Over
  Topic

Knowledge
  Thank you
Add data, files   Topic   AI-generated responses.

Insert

  Travel Pc   Tool   >

  Expense   Topic   >

See all   Agent   >

Web Search

Use the / key to open a menu of tools and topics to reference in the instructions.

Instructions   ⊘ Saved

Identify the type of expense based on the category and description. **Use the knowledge sources** (the **Expense Policy** and **Travel Policy**) to determine whether the claim meets company requirements.

Make one of three decisions:
- **Approve** the claim if it clearly complies with policy.
- **Flag** the claim if it requires human review.
- **Reject** the claim if it clearly violates policy.

After making your decision, **write a brief explanation** that aligns with the relevant policy.
Then, use the 📧 Send an email tool to email the employee who submitted the claim.
Write the email in HTML format. Use a **professional and polite tone**, and write clearly and concisely, as if you are their manager responding to the claim.

In the email:
- **Summarize the expense** (include the category, amount, and date).
- **State your decision:** Approved, Rejected, or Flagged for Review.
- **Explain your decision briefly,** referring to policy when appropriate.
- **Format all amounts as currency with two decimal places.**

1392/8000

Write the instructions using the active voice and a clear structure.

Add a trigger

Now that you have created an agent with knowledge, tools, and instructions, you are ready to add the trigger that will cause it to take action.

Triggers for autonomous agents are event triggers, which are activated by system events that happen outside the agent—for example, receiving an email, a form submission, or an update to data in a business system. Event triggers can also be recurrence triggers, running based on a time schedule (e.g., every day at 9 a.m.).

> **SEE ALSO** Copilot Studio also has topic triggers that are used to activate topics at different stages of the orchestration. Topic triggers are covered in Chapter 7: Authoring topics.

> **IMPORTANT** Autonomous agents use generative orchestration. Triggers are available only for agents for which generative orchestration is enabled.

To add a trigger to your agent

1. Open the agent and navigate down to the **Triggers** section in the **Overview** tab.

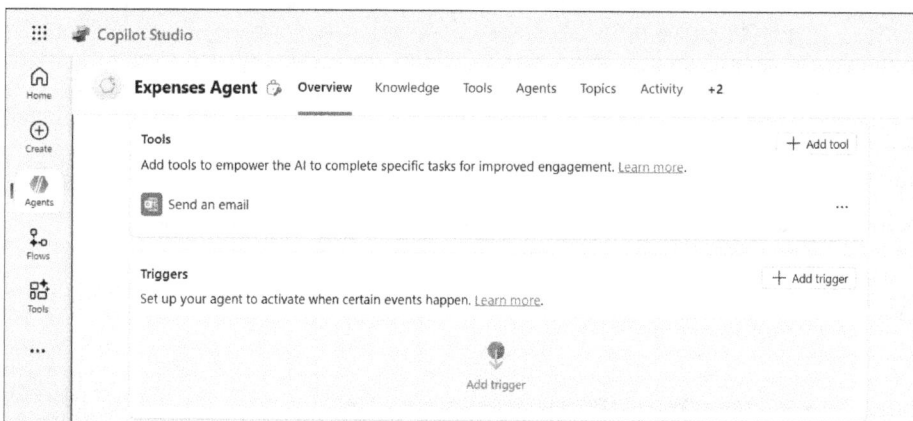

Navigate to the Triggers section, below the Tools sections in the agent Overview.

2. Select the **Add trigger** button.

3. The **Add trigger** pop-up will appear, showing a list of **Featured** triggers.

4. Switch between **All** and **Featured** to view all available triggers versus the most commonly used triggers.

5. Select the **When an item is created** (SharePoint) trigger.

6. Select **Next**.

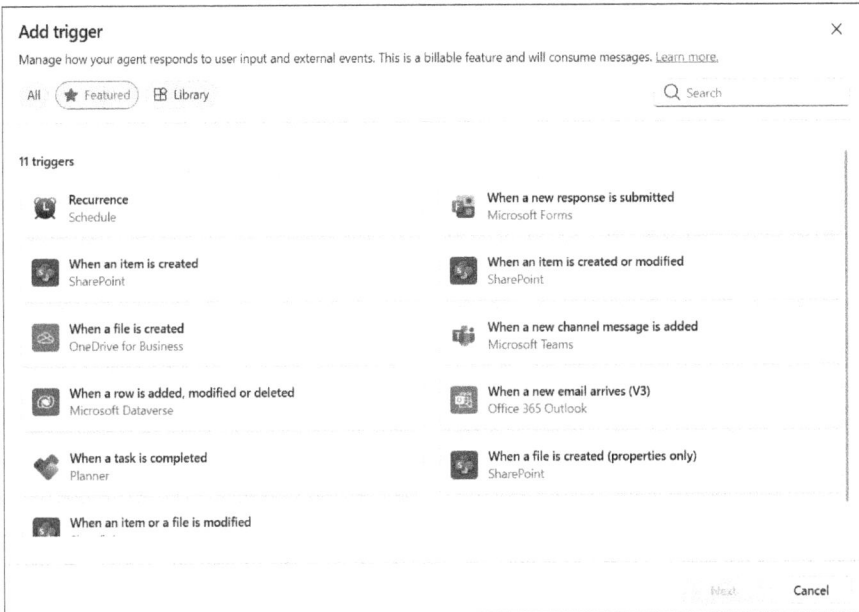

Copilot Studio has a set of prebuilt triggers that you can use to activate your agent.

7. In the **Add trigger** pop-up window, give the trigger a name, **When an expense claim is created**, and authenticate the required connections.

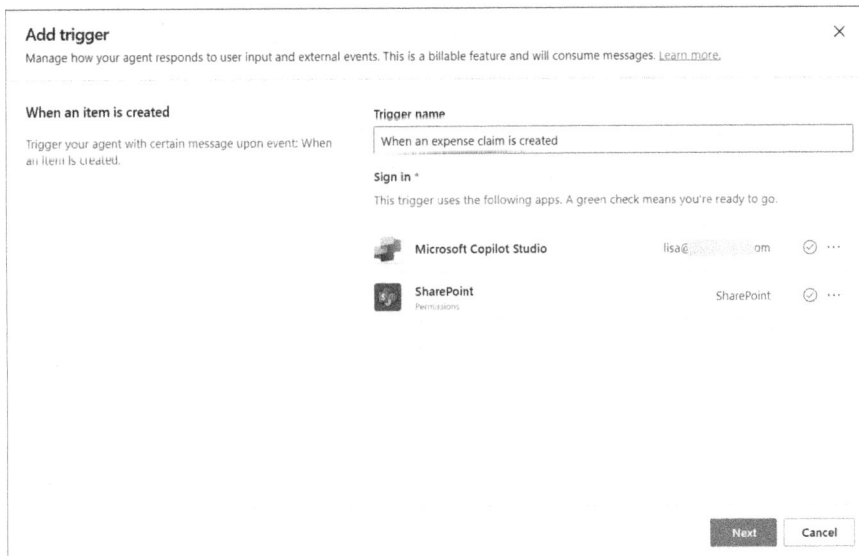

Give the trigger a name and authenticate the connections.

8. Select **Next**.

9. Select the **Site Address** and **List Name** for your SharePoint list.

10. Select **Create trigger**.

Select the site address and list name for your SharePoint list.

11. Wait for the trigger to be added. When that step is complete, a confirmation message tells you it's time to test your trigger. Close the pop-up window.

It is now time to test your trigger and your autonomous agent. Go to your SharePoint list and add an expense claim. Then return to Copilot Studio.

> ⚠️ **IMPORTANT** At this stage, you have not published your agent. So, when you add the row to the SharePoint list, the agent will not run autonomously. You are still in testing mode only.

To test the trigger

1. In the **Triggers** section of the agent, select the **Test** icon.

2. Wait for the trigger to appear. You may need to wait a minute after adding the row in the SharePoint list and refresh the trigger test before it appears.

3. Select **Start testing**.

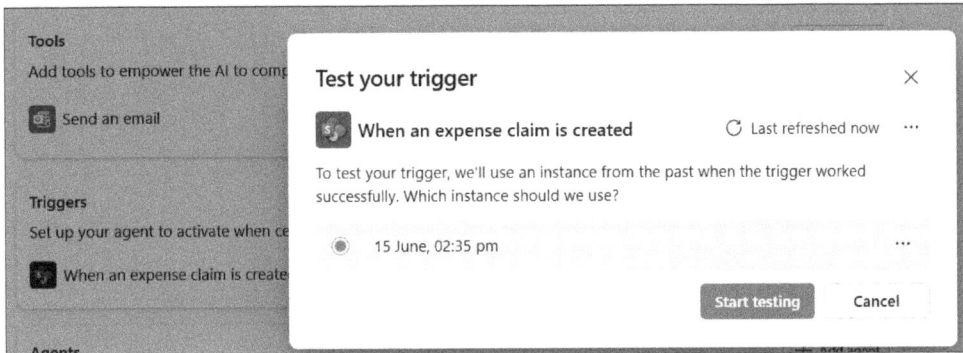

Add a new row to your SharePoint list to test the trigger in your autonomous agent.

4. You will be taken to the **activity map**, which shows the agent working through the thought process to complete the task. It will work through searching the knowledge sources, then call the **Send an email** connector and generate an email in HTML format.

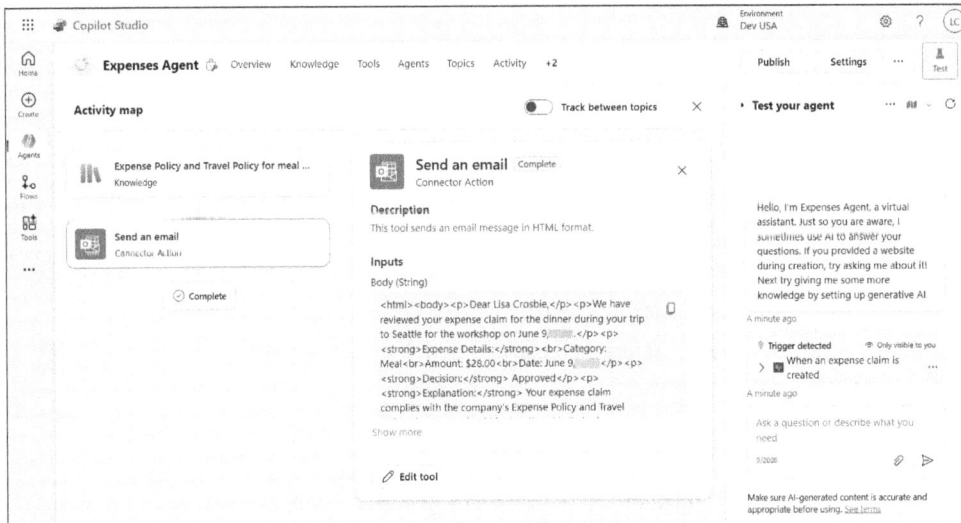

The activity map shows the steps the agent followed, with details for each step.

5. When the test has run successfully, you will receive the email from the agent in your Outlook inbox. Note that the entire content of the email has been generated by AI based on the instructions you provided.

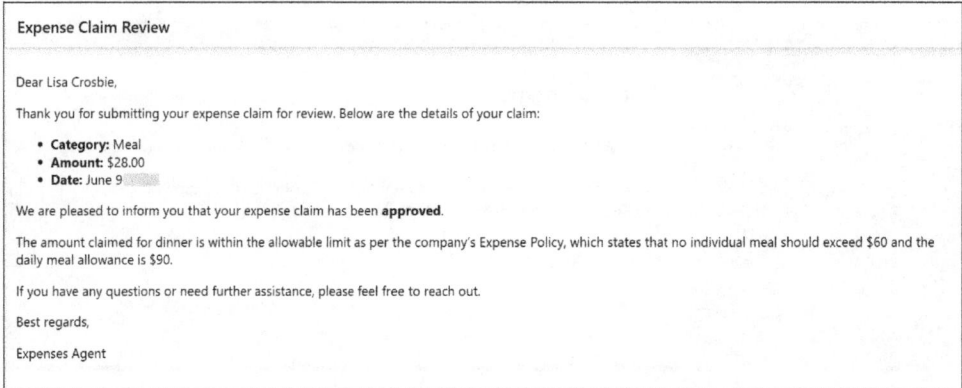

Expense Claim Review

Dear Lisa Crosbie,

Thank you for submitting your expense claim for review. Below are the details of your claim:

- **Category:** Meal
- **Amount:** $28.00
- **Date:** June 9

We are pleased to inform you that your expense claim has been **approved**.

The amount claimed for dinner is within the allowable limit as per the company's Expense Policy, which states that no individual meal should exceed $60 and the daily meal allowance is $90.

If you have any questions or need further assistance, please feel free to reach out.

Best regards,

Expenses Agent

The email is generated by AI using the instructions you provided to the agent.

6. Continue to test your agent by adding more expense claims to the SharePoint list and repeating the preceding steps to test each trigger. Refresh the **activity map** by selecting the **Refresh** icon at the top of the test pane before you run each new test.

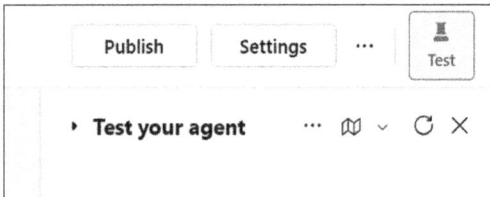

Refresh the test pane before you run each new test of the trigger.

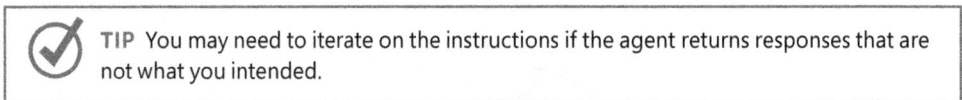

> ✓ **TIP** You may need to iterate on the instructions if the agent returns responses that are not what you intended.

Iterate and add additional tools to your agent

Now that the core function of the autonomous agent is working, you will add another tool to update the SharePoint list with the status of the claim and update the instructions to include this new tool.

To add another tool to the agent

1. Select the **Tools** tab in the top menu, and select the **Add a tool** button.

2. In the **Add tool** pop-up, type **update SharePoint item** in the search box and select the **Send** icon.

3. Select the **Update item** tool for **SharePoint**.

4. A pop-up window will appear that shows the SharePoint connector, a link to the connector documentation, and your username to authenticate the connection. If the buttons to Add to agent are grayed out, select the connection to validate it and then continue.

5. Select **Add and configure**.

6. This opens the configuration screen for the tool in the **Tools** tab of Copilot Studio. Edit the **Name** of the tool to **Update status of Expense Claim**. Update the **Description** to **Use this tool after making a decision about whether the claim should be approved, flagged, or rejected. Accepts one of: Approved, Flagged, Rejected. Must be wrapped as {"Value": "<option>"}.**

> ✅ **TIP** You can link tools in the description or help the agent understand when to use this tool by describing where it fits in the running order of the process. Specifying the format of the input for the choice column helps keep the main instructions simple.

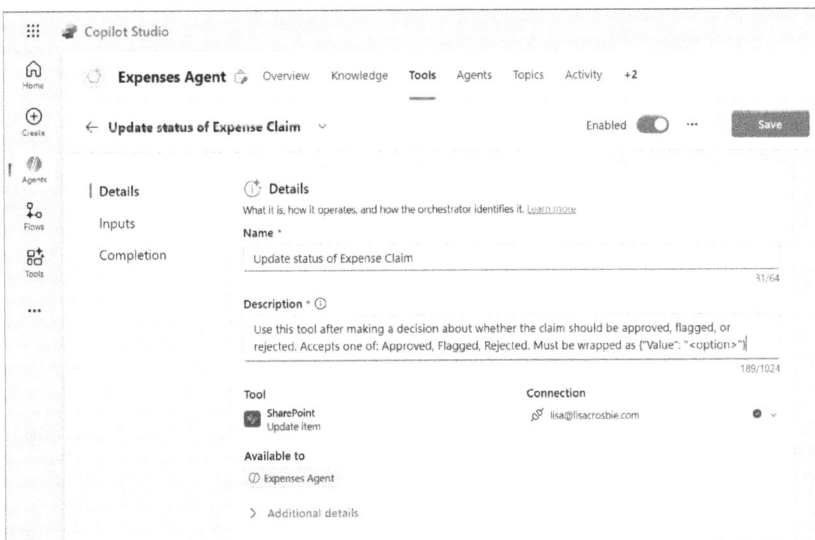

Configure the Update item SharePoint tool with a name and description that help the agent understand when to use it.

7. Expand the **Additional details** option at the bottom of the **Details** section.

8. Switch the authentication method from **User authentication** to **Copilot author authentication**.

9. Navigate down to the **Inputs** section of the Tool configuration form. In the **Site Address** input, use the drop-down in the **Value** selector to select your SharePoint site.

> **TIP** Make sure you use the drop-down icon and not the … icon that opens the variable selector.

10. In the **List Name** input, change the option from **Dynamically fill with AI** to **Custom**. Select your SharePoint list name in the **Value** drop-down.

11. The remaining inputs are set to be dynamically filled with AI. Do not make any changes to these inputs.

Review the input options for configuring this tool.

12. Select the **Save** button. The tool is now saved and ready for your agent to use.

13. Navigate back to the **Instructions** section in the **Overview** tab.

14. Update the instructions by adding the following text between the instructions about making a decision and sending the email: **After making your decision, update the Value of the Status column of the Expense Claim in the SharePoint list using Update status of Expense Claim.**

> **TIP** Remember to use the / key to open the menu of tools to find and link the Update status of Expense Claim tool.

::: 🔷 Copilot Studio

🏠 Home

Expenses Agent 🛡   Overview   Knowledge   Tools   Agents   Topics   Activity   Analytics   Channels

⊕ Create

Instructions   ✏ Edit

Agents

Make one of three decisions:
- **Approve** the claim if it clearly complies with policy.
- **Flag** the claim if it requires human review.
- **Reject** the claim if it clearly violates policy.

Flows

After making your decision, update the _Value _of the Status column of the Expense Claim in the SharePoint list using
🔷 Update status of Expense Cl...

Tools

After making your decision, **write a brief explanation** that aligns with the relevant policy.
Then, use the 📧 Send an email   tool to email the employee who submitted the claim.
Write the email in HTML format. Use a **professional and polite tone**, and write clearly and concisely, as if you are their
manager responding to the claim.

...

Update the instructions to tell the agent when to use the tool to update the SharePoint list item.

15. Save the changes to the instructions, and then test the trigger you used earlier by selecting the **Test** icon in the Triggers section.

16. Wait for the activity map to show that the process is complete.

17. Wait a few moments to check the **Status** of the item in the SharePoint list, which will be updated based on the decision made by the agent.

18. Add another row to the SharePoint list to test a different result (e.g., something that will be rejected).

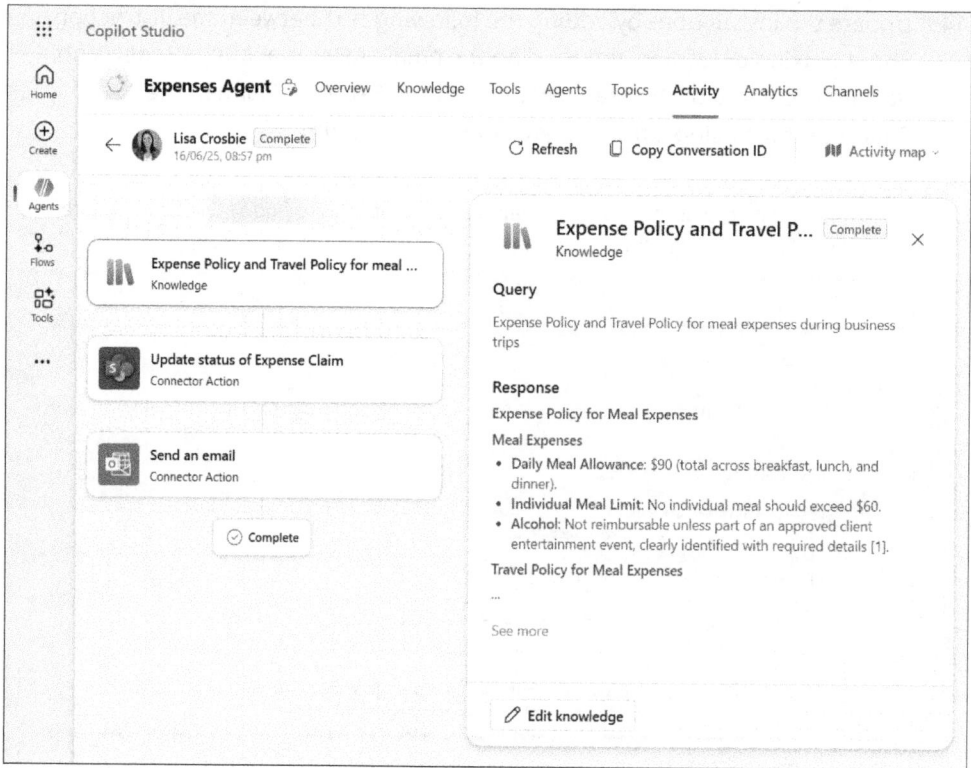

The agent runs through the process using the new SharePoint update item tool, shown in the activity map.

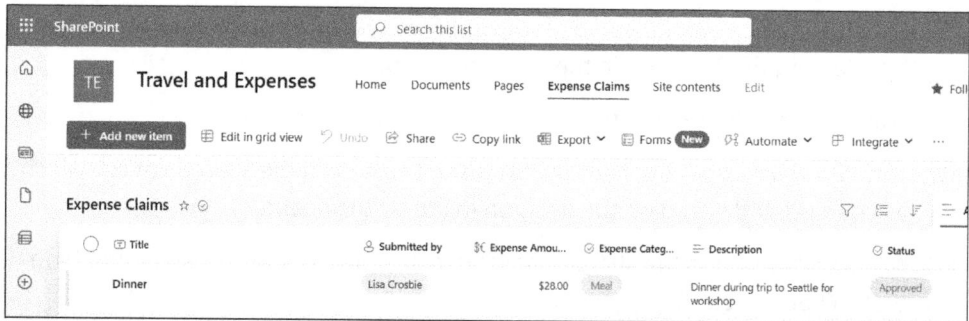

The agent updates the Status column of the claim in the SharePoint list.

> **TIP** Because your agent isn't published yet, you will need to select the Test icon in the Triggers area to run the agent in test mode. Refresh the test pane before running each trigger test.

Use deep reasoning

While testing your agent, you may have noticed that the standard orchestration model reasons over the policy documents to make decisions and recommendations about whether to accept, flag, or reject the claim. In most cases in this scenario, the model can make the right recommendation because the incoming requests are well structured and categorized, and the policies are clear and relatively straightforward.

However, this may not always be the case in a real business process. In a situation where the input is ambiguous or where the knowledge or the process the agent needs to execute is more complex, you can use a reasoning model to give the agent more power to think through the problem or process to make a decision.

In this scenario, if you submit an expense claim that is ambiguous or not clearly outlined in the policy, you will start to see the limitations of the standard model. For example, suppose an employee submits an expense request with the following details:

- Title: Travel adaptor at airport

- Expense amount: $550

- Expense category: Incidentals

- Description: Forgot to pack my laptop charger and I needed it for a client presentation. Had to buy this at the airport.

By the rule of the policy, "reasonable" incidental expenses are reimbursable, but personal purchases are not. There is no specific financial limit or description in the policy for everything that could be included as a "reasonable" incidental expense, so the agent needs to make a judgment. A human reviewing this request could judge that the expense is business related, but that $550 doesn't seem a reasonable amount for a charger.

The standard generative orchestration model responds to the request by rejecting the claim as a personal item. This response shows that it doesn't properly understand the intent or know how to interpret the policy to make this judgment (even if the final decision is correct).

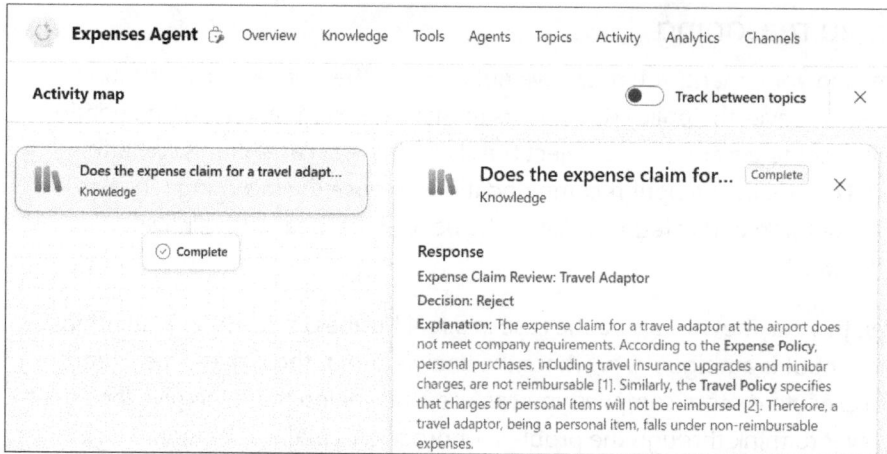

The standard orchestration reasons that a travel adaptor is a personal expense and rejects the claim.

You can ask your agent to use a reasoning model for specific tasks in a process where a higher level of reasoning or chain of thought is required.

To use reasoning in your agent

1. Navigate to the agent settings by selecting the **Settings** button at the top right of the agent.

2. In the **Generative AI** section of the settings, enable the **Deep reasoning** model using the **toggle switch**.

3. Select the **Save** button and wait for the changes to be saved.

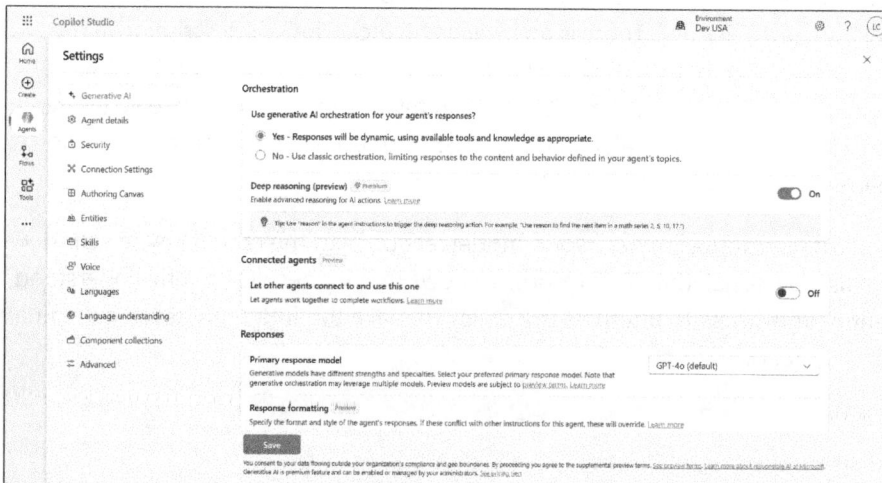

Enable the Deep reasoning model in the settings.

4. Close the **Settings** screen by selecting the **X** icon at the top right.

5. In the **Overview** tab, navigate to the **Instructions**, and edit the instruction about using the knowledge to include the phrase "**use reason**."

> ✓ **TIP** "Use reason" is the phrase you use in the instructions to call the reasoning model for that part of the process. You need to explicitly include this phrase if you want the agent to use reasoning; just enabling this capability won't force the agent to use it.

Instructions   ✎ Edit

Identify the type of expense based on the category and description. **Use reason to review the knowledge sources** (the **Expense Policy** and **Travel Policy**) to determine whether the claim meets company requirements.

Add the phrase "use reason" to the instructions for the agent so that it will call the reasoning model.

6. Save the changes to the instructions, and then rerun the test on the most recent trigger.

7. This time the agent refers to the knowledge sources and then uses the reasoning model to make a recommendation.

Expenses Agent Overview Knowledge Tools Agents Topics Activity Analytics Channels

Activity map   ● Track between topics ×

Expense Policy and Travel Policy
Knowledge

Reason with advanced model Complete ×
Deep reasoning

Reason with advanced model
Deep reasoning Preview

Based on the Expense Policy's requirement that incidentals must be "reasonable" and supported by itemized receipts, a $550.00 travel adaptor appears excessive and would not typically be considered a normal, reasonable incidental. While buying an adaptor for business use can be valid, the policy does not support such an unusually high amount for this type of expense. Therefore, the claim should be flagged for further review (rather than outright approved or rejected) to determine whether full or partial reimbursement is appropriate.

Update status of Expense Claim
Connector Action

Send an email
Connector Action

⊘ Complete

The agent thinks through the request differently using the reasoning model.

The reasoning model can understand and think through how to respond to this claim in a way that is much closer to how a human would understand and review it.

Best practice

The following best practices will help you build successful and effective autonomous agents. Remember that you may need to iterate and fine-tune everything to get the right behavior, and to build confidence and agent capability over time.

- Provide the agent with very clear instructions, just as if you were describing a job to an assistant. If you are unclear or ambiguous in your instructions, the agent will behave in an ambiguous way.

- Write instructions for the agent as if you were briefing a human assistant on how to perform a job. Specify the task, the desired goal or outcome, the guidelines, and the information and tools it has available.

- The names and descriptions you use for your knowledge and tools matter. These will help the agent determine which resources it has available to complete the task, and what to use when.

- Use the description in each tool to provide specific details that the tool may need, such as inputs from other tools or parts of the process, or formatting instructions.

- Don't ask the agent to run too many processes or work across multiple business areas. An autonomous agent uses generative AI to reason over the instructions, knowledge, and tools provided. It will have a greater chance of success if it is working in a very defined role or process, with a limited number of knowledge sources and tools.

- Design your autonomous agent as a subject-matter expert on one specific domain or process. Use multi-agent orchestration to hand off to other agent subject-matter experts.

- Consider whether some parts of the process should be deterministic. Your agent is responsible for reasoning over knowledge and tools to achieve the goal you set for it. If it needs to perform specific tasks that follow the same set of steps every time, use an agent flow to put those steps together. Package this agent flow as a single tool that the agent can run without needing to use generative AI to decide whether or how to perform every single step in that task.

- For any process run by an autonomous agent, monitor the output, or start by having the agent make a recommendation rather than take a direct action, so that there is a human in the loop for anything that needs to be checked or approved. Note that high-risk and high-compliance processes may not be good use cases for autonomous agents.

Publish and monitor an autonomous agent

Now that you have finished building and testing your agent, you can publish it so that it can start running autonomously.

To publish your agent

1. Select the **Publish** button at the top right of the agent.

2. Review the settings that are flagged in the pop-up window and then select the **Publish** button.

Review the settings and publish your agent.

3. You will get a confirmation message that the agent is being published. Wait a few minutes for the agent to finish publishing in the background and for the confirmation message to appear.

4. Submit a new Expense Claim in the SharePoint list.

5. Wait for the agent to trigger based on this new item, and then send an email response.

> ✅ **TIP** Give this process a few minutes after you initiate the trigger; it's not usually instant.

Now that your agent is live, you can monitor the activity of the autonomous sessions to make sure the agent is behaving as intended, or to identify any issues.

Review the activity

The **Activity** tab of the agent is a log of each agent session, showing both test sessions and autonomous sessions.

To review the activity of your agent

1. Select the **Activity** tab.

2. The **Activity** list shows autonomous agent sessions with the name "Automated," and test sessions with the name of the user who ran the test. Each line shows the number of completed steps, the last step taken, and the status of the session.

3. Select the most recent automated session from the top of the list to open it and review the details.

4. The **activity map** for the agent appears, showing the same details as in the test. However, this time it also shows the trigger in the steps taken. You can select each step to review the details of what happened in that step.

If problems arise with the agent or with any of the triggers or tools, the session may have a status of "Incomplete."

The Activity tab of the agent shows the log of agent test and autonomous sessions.

5

View each step in the activity map to view the details of the agent session.

Incomplete sessions can indicate an error with the agent.

To get more information on errors for troubleshooting

1. Select the incomplete session from the **Activity** tab to open it and view the **activity map**.

2. At the top right of the **activity map**, select the drop-down to switch from viewing the **Activity map** to viewing a **Transcript**.

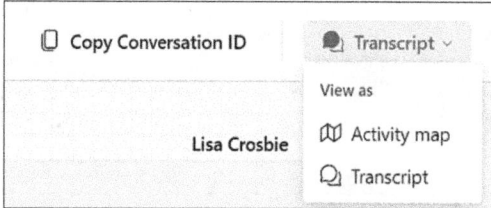

Switch from the Activity map view to the Transcript view for more details of the agent session.

3. The **Transcript** view shows the full transcript of the agent session with details of the input, trigger payloads, and agent responses, along with any error messages. You can use this information to help identify and resolve any issues with your agent.

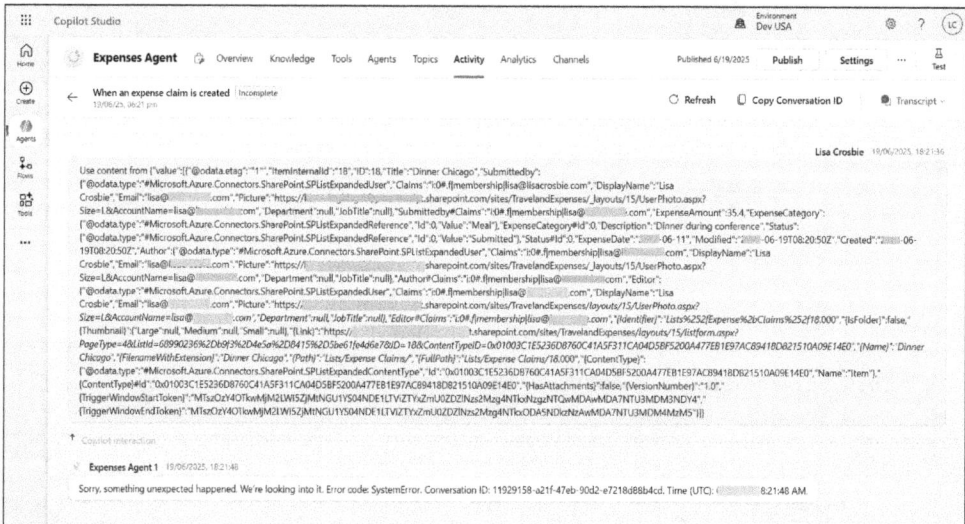

The Transcript view shows full details of the agent session, including inputs, trigger payloads, and agent responses.

Skills review

In this chapter, you learned how to:

- Identify use cases for autonomous agents, and differentiate between autonomous agents and workflow automation.

- Build an autonomous agent by adding knowledge, tools, instructions, and triggers, as well as a deep reasoning model.

- Test, publish, and monitor the activity of autonomous agent sessions.

5

Practice tasks

To complete the practices tasks in this chapter, you will need an Expenses Policy document. You can use a policy document from your organization, or you can use Copilot or the AI tool of your choice to generate an Expenses Policy document. To do so, use the following prompt: "Write an internal Employee Expenses Policy document for a mid-sized company."

Identify use cases for autonomous agents

Consider a process in your organization that has not been automated because it requires human decision making or intervention:

1. Document the steps in the process, including what triggers the process into action, what steps are taken, what systems are used, what actions are taken, what knowledge is needed, and what decision making is required.

2. Consider which parts of the process are always run in a step-by-step predefined sequence, and which may vary based on the input and context.

3. Write a set of instructions for the process as if it were a job description for an assistant. Can you define the process as a job with a goal or output, with guidance on how it should be done?

4. Use the guidance in this section of the chapter to determine whether an autonomous agent or a workflow automation is a better fit for your process.

Build an autonomous agent

Open Copilot Studio in your browser and then complete the following tasks:

1. Create a new agent using the configuration experience.

2. Name your agent: **Expenses Agent.**

3. Add a description: **An agent that checks expense claims from employees against the expenses policy**.

4. Add a tool to **Send an email**, using the email connector of your choice. Rename the tool as "**Send an email**," and change the description to "**Sends an email in HTML format**."

5. In the Knowledge section, select **Add Knowledge**, and upload your Expenses Policy document.

6. In the Instructions section, add the following instructions: **Your job is to review employee expense claims and decide whether to approve, reject, or flag them for manual review, based on company policy. When you receive an Expense Claim by email, review the details and identify the type of expense based on the category and description. Use the knowledge source (Expenses Policy) to determine whether the claim meets company requirements. Make one of three decisions: - Approve the claim if it clearly complies with policy. - Flag the claim if it requires human review. - Reject the claim if it clearly violates policy. After making your decision, write a brief explanation that aligns with the relevant policy. Then email the employee who submitted the claim. Write the email in HTML format. Use a professional and polite tone, and write clearly and concisely, as if you are their manager responding to the claim.**

7. In the instructions, edit the section about emailing the employee by using the / key to open the menu of available tools and then selecting the **Send an email** tool.

8. Add a trigger: **When an email is received, (use the email connector of your choice)**.

9. Configure the trigger by adding your email address and adding a subject line for the incoming email: **Expense Claim**.

10. Send an email to the email address you used in the trigger, with the subject line **Expense Claim**. In the body of the email, write bullet points for the Expense Name, Date, Category, Amount, and Description.

11. Test the trigger and review the **activity map**.

12. Navigate to the settings of your agent and enable **Deep reasoning**.

13. Save the changes to the settings and close the **Settings** page.

14. Edit the instructions to add an instruction to use reason: **Use reason to review the knowledge sources (Expenses Policy)**.

15. Test one of the previous triggers and review the **activity map**. Compare the difference in the response when the reasoning model is used.

Publish and monitor an autonomous agent

Using the agent you created in the previous activity, complete the following tasks:

1. Select the **Publish** button, confirm the settings, and wait for the agent to finish publishing.

2. Send an Expense Claim email and wait for the agent to receive and respond to it.

3. Select the **Activity** tab in Copilot Studio to review the agent sessions.

4. Open the most recent session and review the **activity map**.

5. Select each step in the process to view the details.

Grounding agents in knowledge

6

Practice files

No practice files are necessary to complete the practice tasks in this chapter.

Grounding an agent in organizational knowledge is one of the highest-value things you can do to create an agent that will transform customer experiences or business processes. Rather than creating specific question-and-answer flows for every topic a user wants to ask about, you can use generative AI to enable the agent to retrieve and generate answers quickly and at scale, based on the knowledge you already have in the organization. Agent solutions grounded in knowledge can substantially speed up any process or workflow where customers or employees need to search for an answer to their question, or where knowledge is required to make a recommendation or a decision.

In Copilot Studio, you can add knowledge to your agent from a range of Microsoft or third-party sources, drawing from structured or unstructured data. Knowledge can come from public websites, uploaded files, cloud files in OneDrive or SharePoint, SharePoint site content and lists, and a range of enterprise database systems. You can also extend your agent's knowledge by using an existing Azure AI search connection.

In this chapter

- Understand how knowledge works in Copilot Studio
- Connect to public websites as a knowledge source
- Add files as a knowledge source
- Add SharePoint as a knowledge source
- Add real-time connectors to enterprise data

In this chapter, you will learn about the different capabilities available in Copilot Studio for adding and working with knowledge, including the scenarios, benefits, and limitations of each.

> **SEE ALSO** Connecting to Azure AI Search is covered in Chapter 13: Extending Copilot Studio agents with Azure AI.

> **SEE ALSO** For an up-to-date list of knowledge sources that you can add to your agent, limitations, and known issues, refer to the Microsoft documentation: https://learn. microsoft.com/en-us/microsoft-copilot-studio/knowledge-copilot-studio.

Understand how knowledge works in Copilot Studio

The results you get with your agent will depend substantially on the quality of the content or data in the knowledge source system. The principle of "garbage in, garbage out" still applies. In other words, if you want reliable and consistent answers from your knowledge source, you will need to have a good content management strategy in place for your documents or data before you add them as knowledge to your agent.

You should always ensure that you are connecting your agent to correct and current knowledge. Sprawling, poorly organized SharePoint sites with outdated, duplicated, or contradictory content, or data scattered across multiple sites, documents, or databases, will not result in accurate agent responses. Generative AI is not a magic wand that solves these kinds of underlying problems with data or knowledge.

Start by auditing your major knowledge sources and content. Remove or archive knowledge that is irrelevant, duplicated, or outdated. Consider creating new sites or folders as the approved source of knowledge for an agent, and curate the needed knowledge into that space, rather than adding everything you have as a starting point. Agree on and use consistent terminology wherever possible, and use it across all of your documents and databases. Use consistent and useful titles for documents and names for database columns to help improve the search results.

You should also establish a data governance plan. This plan should make sure that knowledge is accessible only to those who should have access to it, and that responsibilities are assigned for keeping data and documents up-to-date and in the right location.

Set up a "Playground Agent" to use for this chapter

In this chapter, you will work with a range of knowledge sources that would fit very different real-life scenarios. The focus here is on understanding the knowledge capabilities and how to add them. So, rather than starting with a new agent and a new scenario for each knowledge source, in this chapter you will just use a single "Playground Agent" throughout. This agent will have a mix of knowledge sources and functions that does not represent how you would build an agent in a real-world scenario.

As you work through this chapter, you will notice that the more knowledge sources you add, the slower and less reliable the results become, particularly if you add multiple knowledge sources that cover similar content. This concept is useful in understanding how the agent works with knowledge, and the limitations of add-ing too many knowledge sources to a single agent. If you find that the performance becomes too slow or unreliable as you work through this chapter, create an additional playground agent and continue adding knowledge there.

> ✓ **TIP** In a real-world scenario you can use multiple agents in an orchestrated system to handle multiple knowledge sources in a more reliable way. This is covered in Chapter 9: Designing multi-agent orchestration.

Let's start by creating a blank agent, with nothing in it, to understand the default behavior and available settings.

To create the Playground Agent you will use in this chapter

1. Navigate to Copilot Studio and create a new agent.

2. Select the **Skip to Configure** button.

3. Give your agent a name: **Playground Agent**.

4. Leave all other sections (description, instructions, prompts, knowledge) blank.

5. Select **Create**.

6

> **SEE ALSO** For detailed step-by-step instructions on creating agents using the configuration experience, refer to the section "Configure a new agent" in Chapter 4: Building agents in Copilot Studio.

6. Wait for the agent to be created.

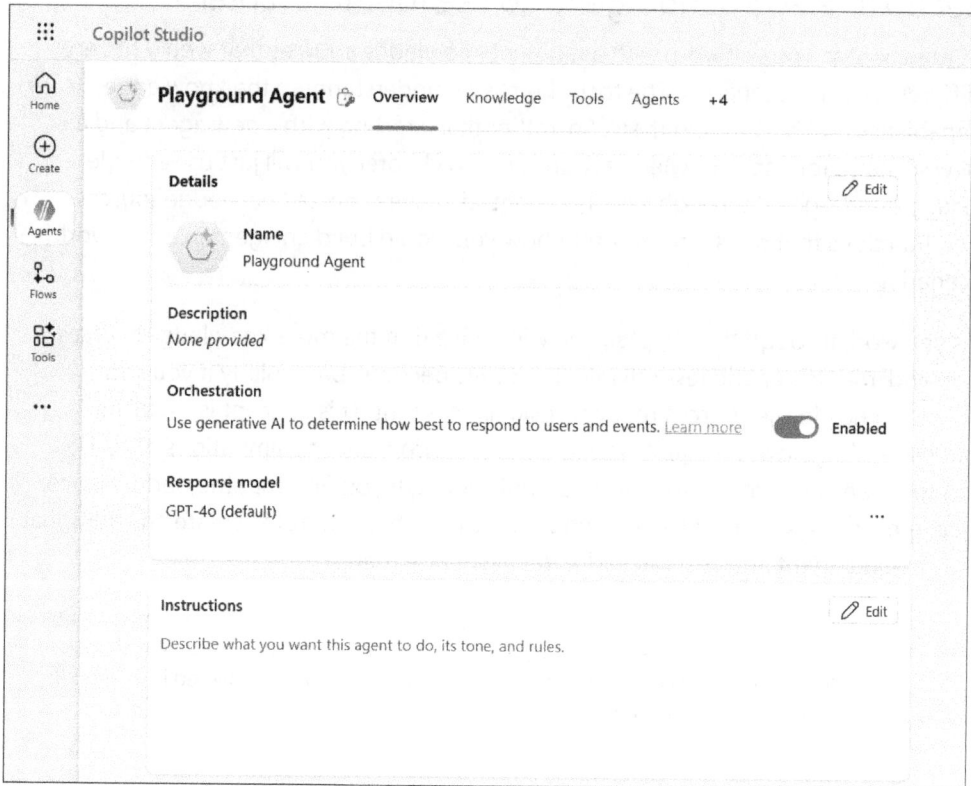

Your Playground Agent is ready to test and configure.

General knowledge from the LLM

Although you have configured an agent and given it a name, it is not connected to any knowledge. Let's test what it can do.

In the test pane of the agent, ask it any general knowledge question, such as "What is the capital city of Australia?"

The **activity map** will show the agent attempting to search the knowledge sources. Finding none, it falls back on using the general knowledge from the LLM to successfully answer the question.

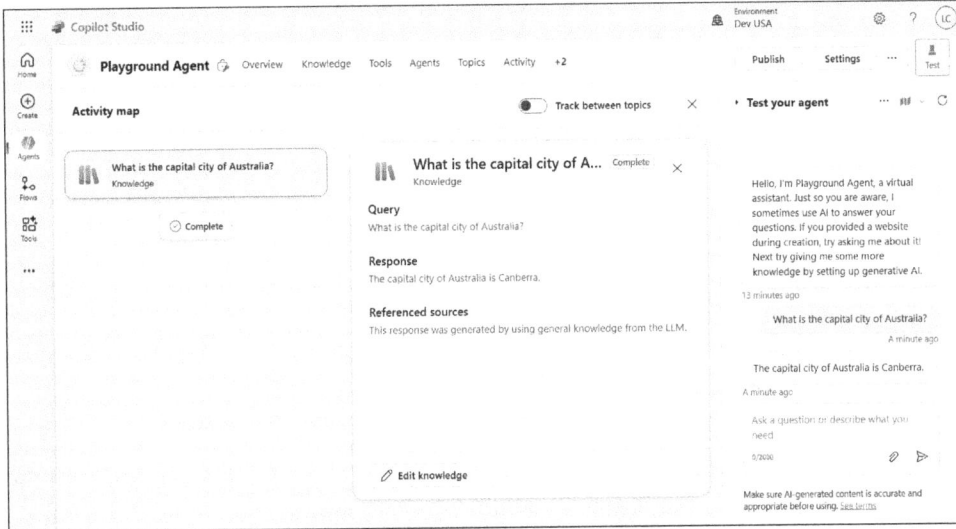

The agent uses general knowledge from the LLM to answer the question.

The general knowledge from the LLM is information the language model has from the data that was used to train it. The agent is not actually connected to any live website data, or referencing any websites to generate this response. Creating a blank agent like this is effectively creating a ChatGPT-like experience, where the agent can generate general answers only.

> **SEE ALSO** The option to connect to live website data is covered in the next section of this chapter, "Connect to public websites as a knowledge source."

To understand this behavior better, try asking the agent something about a recent event or information that would be available only from a website. Refresh the **test** pane and ask, "What is the weather in Seattle today?"

The agent explains that it doesn't have access to real-time data. It then uses the training data and general knowledge from the LLM to suggest how you could find the answer to your question.

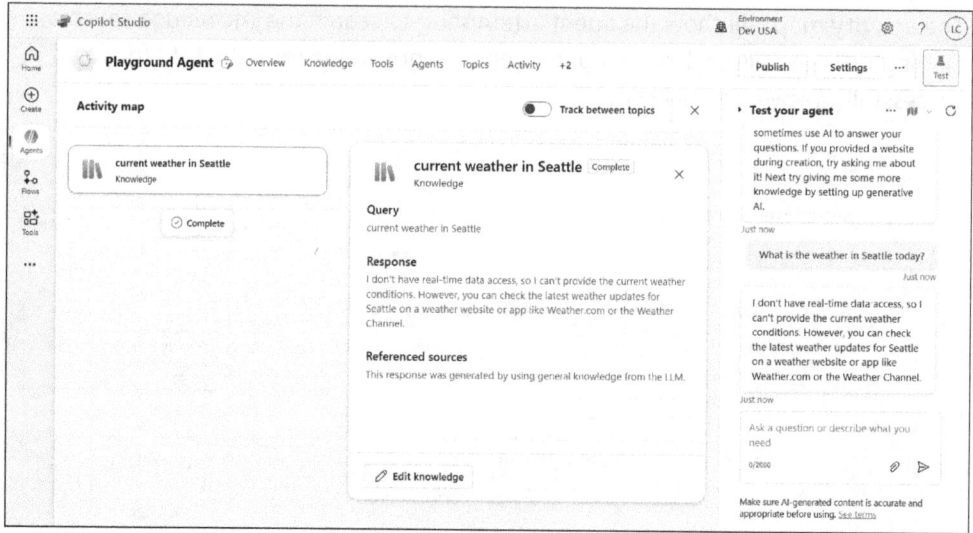

The agent uses general knowledge from the LLM to offer a suggestion but it can't answer the question.

You can choose whether you want your agent to use this general knowledge from the LLM. To understand the implications of this choice, try another example where the user asks a business- or policy-related question. Ask the agent: **I purchased a phone charger for $50 at the airport on my recent trip to Seattle for a conference. Can I claim the expense?**

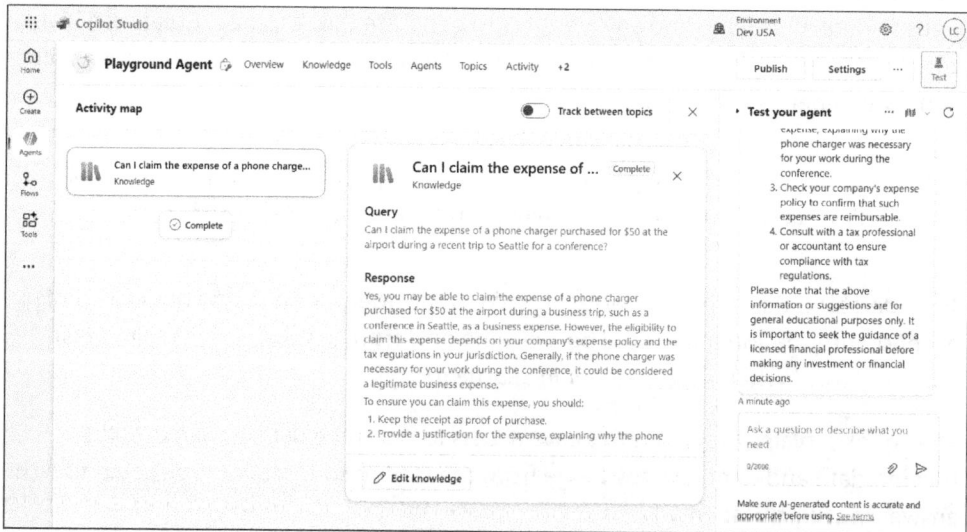

The agent uses general knowledge from the LLM to provide guidance on what is likely to be acceptable within an expense claim policy.

This agent isn't connected to your actual policy documents or any websites that should provide the specific answer, so the only answer it can provide is based on the LLM's general knowledge. It provides reasonable guidance and advice, without directly answering the question. In some scenarios, this behavior is useful, but more often than not it means the agent will provide answers that you don't want it to provide. If you want an agent that only answers questions based on your policy or a specific website, you most likely don't want this fallback behavior; that is, you don't want the agent to answer using general knowledge if it can't find the answer in the knowledge you have added.

To switch off general knowledge

1. Navigate to the **Settings** of the agent using the button at the top right.

2. In the **Generative AI** settings, navigate to the **Knowledge** section.

3. The **Use general knowledge** setting is switched to **On**. Change this toggle switch to the **Off** position.

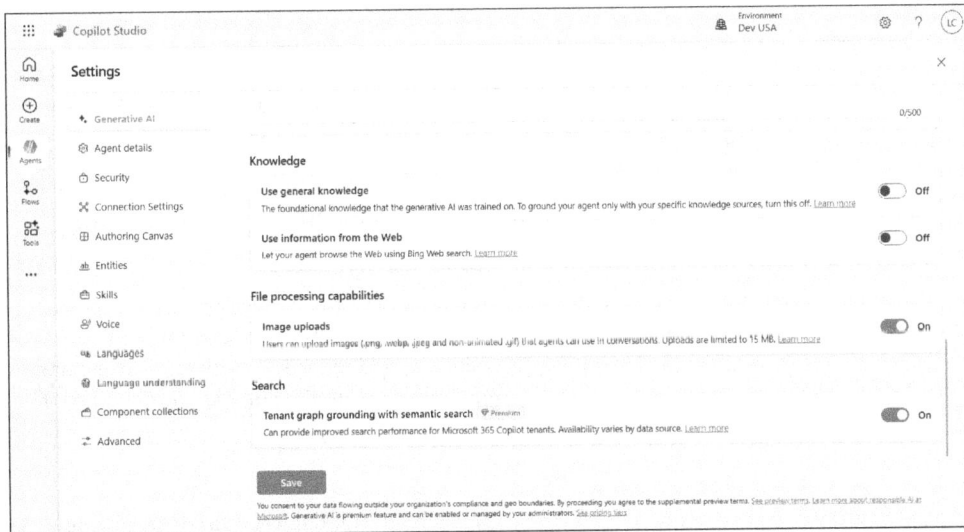

Change the "Use general knowledge" setting to off.

4. Select the **Save** button at the bottom of the **Settings** screen. Wait for the changes to be saved and applied to your agent. You will get a confirmation message when the changes have been saved.

5. Close the **Settings** screen using the **X** icon at the top right.

6. Test the agent again using the same questions you used earlier in this section.

7. The agent will now respond saying that it can't help. It will not be able to respond to any of these questions or any other questions.

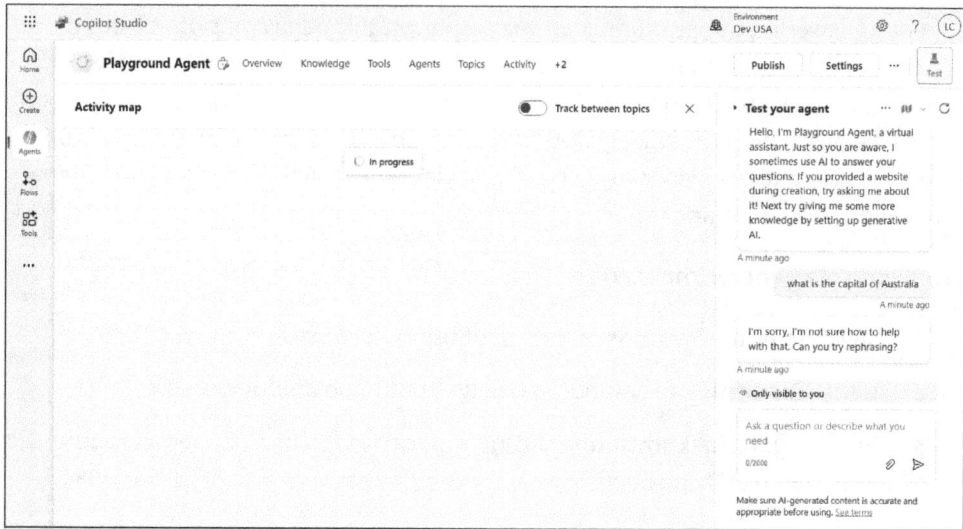

The agent can no longer answer the question with the general knowledge switched off.

With the general knowledge switched off, you now have the shell of an agent that knows nothing, is connected to nothing, and will not answer any questions. This demonstrates the starting point for what's possible with building an agent that uses only your organizational data, and that will not respond with any other information.

> ✅ **TIP** In most real-world business scenarios where the agent is designed to handle a specific process and is grounded in organizational knowledge, you will choose to switch off this general knowledge option. This mitigates and reduces the risk of hallucinations, as well as the risk of the agent answering questions unrelated to the purpose you design it for.

Generative answers and the Conversational boosting topic

When you add knowledge to your agent, it uses a capability called generative answers to retrieve information from the knowledge sources and use it in the response. You can add knowledge at the agent level for the agent to use at any time or as a fallback when there is no authored topic to answer the question. You can also add knowledge sources at the topic level, adding specific knowledge sources to a topic so that the agent generates answers from that knowledge only when it follows that intent path in the conversation or process.

When you create an agent in Copilot Studio, an out-of-the-box system topic called "Conversational boosting" gives the agent the skill to retrieve information from the knowledge sources added at the agent level. When you create a simple agent by describing it and connecting it to a website (as you did in Chapter 1: Understanding Copilot Studio and agents), this Conversational boosting topic is used to take the input from the user and pass it through to retrieve an answer from the website.

To view the Conversational boosting topic

1. Navigate to the **Topics** tab on the top agent menu.

2. Select the **System topics** button.

3. Select the **Conversational boosting** topic from the list to open it.

Your Copilot Studio agent comes with some out-of- the-box system topics, including a Conversational boosting topic.

4. The topic is made up of a **Trigger** (On Unknown Intent) and a **Create generative answers** node. Select the **Edit** link in the **Data sources** section of the **Create generative answers** node. This opens a **properties** pane on the right.

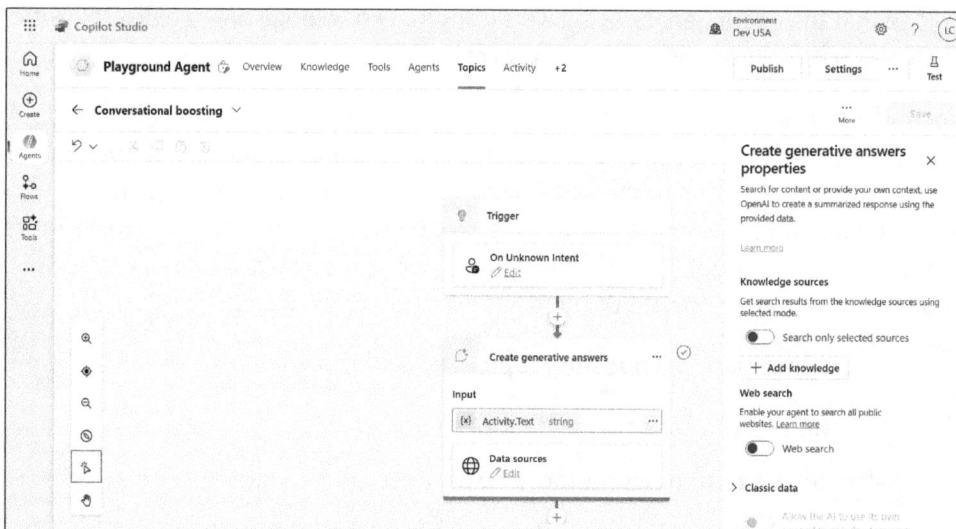

You can view and edit the properties of the Create generative answers node in the Conversational boosting topic.

The Conversational boosting topic is triggered on unknown intent, when the agent can't match the user intent to any other topics. The agent always first checks whether the user intent matches an authored topic, before using the Conversational boosting topic. The Conversational boosting topic acts as a fallback, so that the knowledge you add can be used to answer any questions for which you have not manually authored a topic. In this way, you can quickly create an agent that can answer a huge number of questions without having to author specific topics.

Any knowledge sources you add will be used by this Conversational boosting topic. If you want to restrict the knowledge sources used by this fallback topic, you can configure that in the properties pane of the Conversational boosting topic, using the **Search only selected sources** toggle.

> **SEE ALSO** Adding knowledge to a topic is covered in Chapter 7: Authoring topics.

Content moderation

Agents built in Copilot Studio follow responsible AI principles by applying content moderation policies on all generative AI inputs and responses. Content moderation protects against offensive or harmful content, as well as malicious intent. Content is checked both at the user input stage and before the agent responds.

By default, new agents are set to the highest level of content moderation, which will be the best choice for most business-critical processes, but you can choose to lower this level in scenarios where it is required. Lowering the content moderation level will allow your agent to generate more answers, and more creative answers, but it also increases the risk of harmful content.

To change the content moderation setting

1. Navigate to the **Settings** area of the agent.

2. In the **Generative AI** section of the **Settings** screen, navigate down to the **Moderation** section.

3. The content moderation level is set to **High** by default.

4. Use the slider to lower the content moderation level to **Moderate** or **Low**.

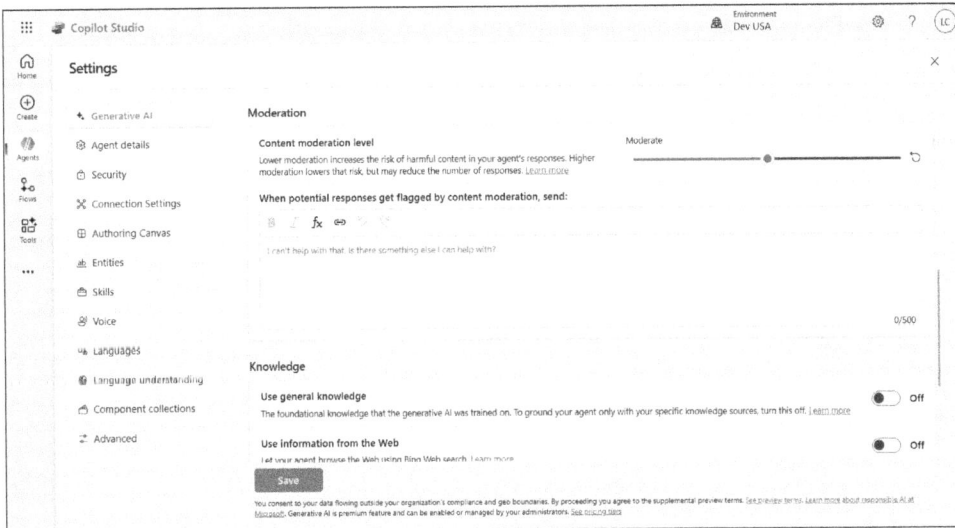

You can change the content moderation level for the agent in the settings area.

5. A default message is sent to the user when a response is flagged by content moderation. You can change that message here in the settings if you wish to do so.

6. Select **Save** and wait for the changes to be saved.

7. Close the **Settings** screen using the **X** icon at the top right.

> ✅ **TIP** Lowering the content moderation settings during the agent build process can help you identify missing knowledge sources and topics, even when the agent should be set to high content moderation when it is published.

Official knowledge sources

Copilot Studio provides the option to mark knowledge sources as official sources, which signals the agent that this is verified and highly trusted information. When a knowledge source that is marked as an official source is used in a generative answer, it will be tagged with a message to the user that the answer is based on official sources.

To mark a knowledge source as an official source

1. Return to the Surface Support Guide agent you created in Chapter 1.

2. Navigate to the **Knowledge** tab and open the website you added as knowledge.

3. The **Official source** toggle switch is set to the **Off** position.

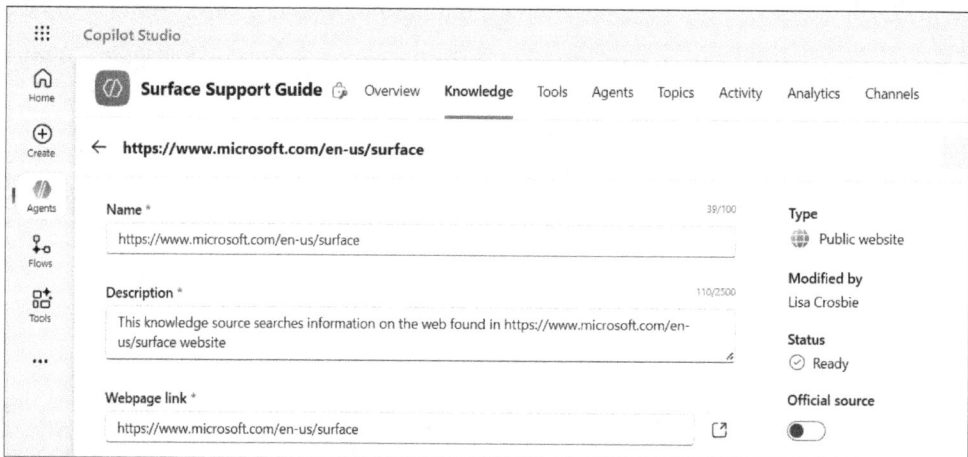

The Surface website knowledge source in the Surface Support Guide agent is not marked as an official source.

4. Set the **Official source** toggle switch to the **On** position.

5. You will get a confirmation message that explains how official sources work.

6. Select the **Got it** button.

Update agent instructions? (preview)   ✕

Setting this source as official will update your agent instruction with this:
Answer grouping data which has a tag [Authoritative] with a header line containing a ☑ followed by "Based on official sources". Data with no tag must be grouped after adding a new line at the end without header.

This setting will be applied after you save updates to your knowledge source. Do you want to proceed? Learn more

[Got it]   [Cancel]

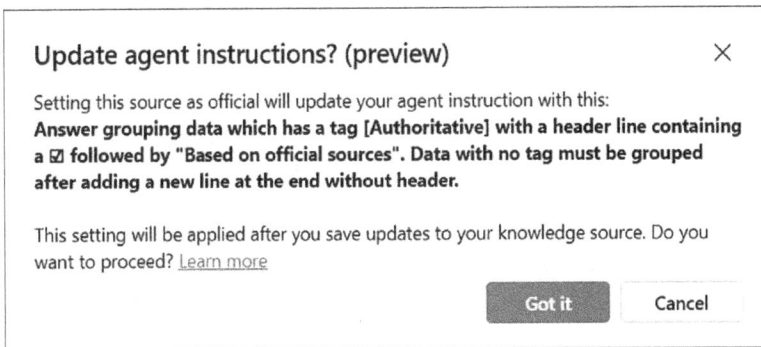

You will be asked to confirm that the agent instructions will be modified to include a tag that marks when an answer is based on official sources.

7. When the pop-up closes and you are returned to the knowledge configuration screen, select the **Save** button.

8. Test your agent by asking a question that can be answered from this knowledge source: **How does the Surface Pro compare to the Surface Laptop.**

9. Note that the answer begins with **Based on official sources**.

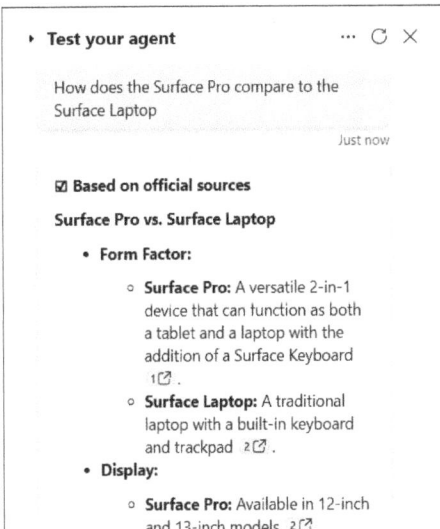

▸ **Test your agent**   ⋯   ↻   ✕

How does the Surface Pro compare to the Surface Laptop

Just now

☑ **Based on official sources**

Surface Pro vs. Surface Laptop

- **Form Factor:**
  - **Surface Pro:** A versatile 2-in-1 device that can function as both a tablet and a laptop with the addition of a Surface Keyboard 1☐ .
  - **Surface Laptop:** A traditional laptop with a built-in keyboard and trackpad 2☐ .
- **Display:**
  - **Surface Pro:** Available in 12-inch and 13-inch models 2☐ .

When a response is generated using an official knowledge source, the response begins with the phrase "Based on official sources."

10. Review the **Instructions** section of the agent, noting that a new instruction has been added that tells the agent how to handle data from official sources in the response, as described in the confirmation pop-up message.

Connect to public websites as a knowledge source

The quickest way to create a customer-facing agent for your business that can answer a huge number of questions is to connect a public website as a knowledge source.

In Chapter 1, you learned how to add a website as a knowledge source when you described an agent to build it. In this section, you will learn how to add and manage the use of public websites as knowledge sources in your agent after you have created it. You will also understand the limitations and behaviors of websites as knowledge sources.

> ⚠ **IMPORTANT** The website content must be indexed by Bing if it is to work as a knowledge source for Copilot Studio. It must be publicly accessible content—not located behind a paywall or requiring authentication. Content that Bing struggles to index, such as content that isn't visible in the HTML, or that is rendered dynamically via JavaScript, may not appear in the answers provided by the agent using this knowledge source.

To add a public website as a knowledge source

1. In your Playground Agent, navigate to the **Knowledge** tab in the top menu.

2. Select the **+ Add knowledge** button.

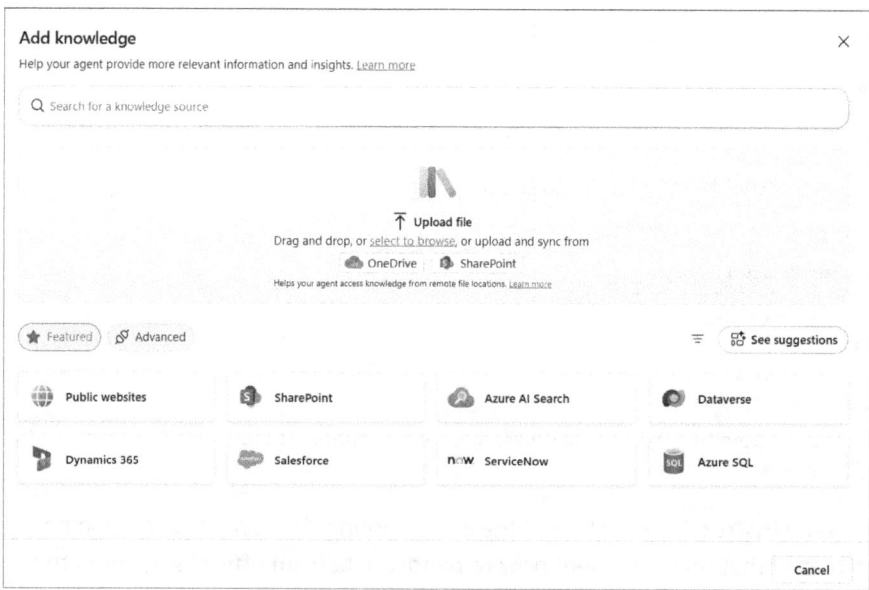

The Add knowledge screen shows options to upload files or to connect to a range of knowledge sources.

3. Select **Public websites**.

4. Enter the link to the website: **https://adoption.microsoft.com/en-us/copilot** and select the **Add** button.

5. This adds the website to the list of knowledge sources for the agent, with fields for the **Name**, **Description**, and **Owner** of the knowledge source.

6. Change the **Name** to **Microsoft 365 Copilot Adoption Guide**.

7. Change the **Description** to: **This knowledge source provides guidance and best practice on how to use Microsoft 365 Copilot.**

> ✅ **TIP** The orchestration model uses names and descriptions to help the agent know how and when to use this knowledge source. Take the time to fill these in a way that is useful and accurate rather than leaving the default options.

8. If your organization owns the website, check the **Owner** option for that website; otherwise, leave it unchecked.

> ✅ **TIP** Confirming that you own the website will mean you get better results from this website as a knowledge source.

6

🌐 **Add public websites**   ✕

Public website link ⓘ

| Enter a link | | Add |

Link	Name	Description	Owner
🌐 https://adoption.microsoft.c...	Microsoft 365 Copilot Adoption	This knowledge source provides	☐ Confirm

Website ownership
Confirm that your organization owns the website(s) which will be used to enable Bing search results. Learn more

This generative AI feature uses Bing Search. Your data will flow outside your organization's compliance and geo boundaries. Customer's use of Bing search is governed by the Microsoft Services Agreement and the Microsoft Privacy Statement

Back   Add   Cancel

Add a public website, and then edit the name and description to help the agent understand what it will be used for.

9. Select **Add**.

10. The website now appears in the **Knowledge** tab for the agent.

11. Test the agent by asking a question related to the knowledge source: **Where can I ask questions about Microsoft 365 Copilot?**

12. Note that the answer includes references to the website you added, as well as from a page URL that is a level lower than the one you added.

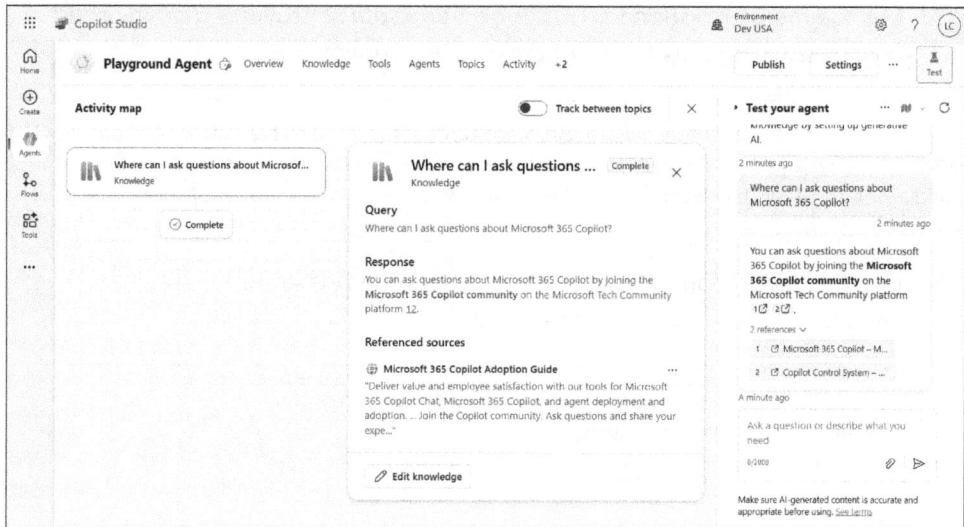

The agent finds the answer in the public website added as knowledge and references the website pages in the response.

> ✅ **TIP** At this stage, with general answers switched off and only this website added, the agent can only answer questions from this website (and child websites under the same domain). Test the agent by asking an unrelated question, such as the weather in your city. It will not answer that question.

You can continue to add more websites to the agent by following these instructions. Add websites with different domains that build out more knowledge on the subject or add websites that cover the different knowledge your agent will need.

> ⚠️ **IMPORTANT** You can add up to four website URLs as knowledge for your agent. If you need more, consider adding a higher-level domain that indexes all the sites below it, adding websites in generative answers nodes in topics, or using multi-agent orchestration.

Website knowledge behavior and limitations

When you add a website as knowledge, you can only add a URL up to two levels deep. For example, the site https://adoption.microsoft.com/en-us/copilot is two levels deep, so it works as a knowledge source for the agent. If you try to add a URL more than two levels deep, such as https://adoption.microsoft.com/en-us/copilot/success-kit/, you will get an invalid URL error and you will not be able to add that page as a knowledge source.

> 🌐 **Add public websites**
>
> **Public website link** ⓘ
>
> https://adoption.microsoft.com/en-us/copilot/success-kit/
>
> ❗ Invalid URL. Please enter a valid URL.

If you try to add a website URL more than two levels deep, you will get an invalid URL error.

Although you can only add a website up to two levels deep as a knowledge source, the child pages under the same domain will also be searched and used as knowledge. For example, adding the Copilot adoption website https://adoption.microsoft.com/en-us/copilot will also retrieve answers from the Copilot Success Kit page https://adoption.microsoft.com/en-us/copilot/success-kit/, which is a level deeper below it, as well as other pages several levels below the site you add as knowledge.

> ⚠️ **IMPORTANT** Adding a URL that redirects to a different top-level domain will not add that website content as a knowledge source to an agent. That means you can't work around the two-level URL limit by adding a short URL that redirects to a longer one.

Test this by asking your agent a question related to content that is found on a page deeper in the hierarchy below the site you added as knowledge: **How can I establish a community of champions for Microsoft 365 Copilot**. Notice the website links in the citations in the response.

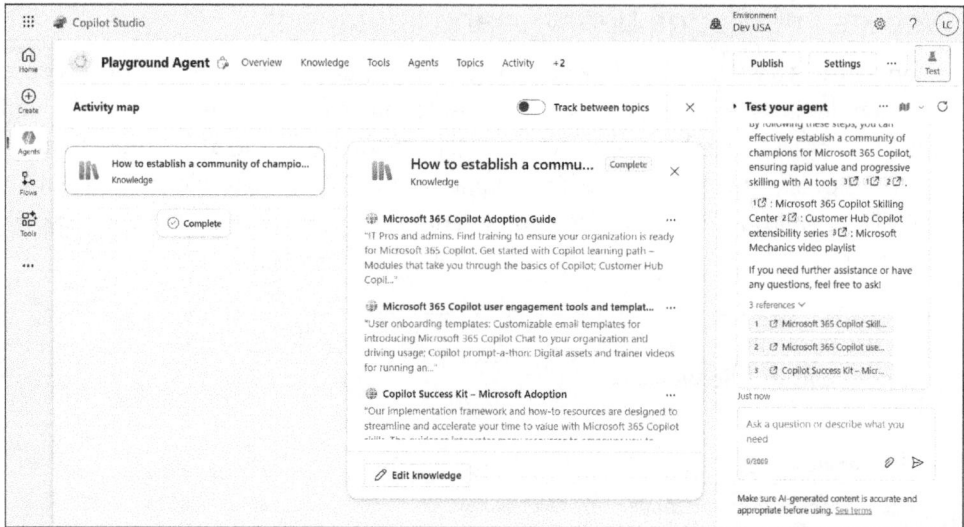

The agent finds the answer from other pages further down the hierarchy in the same domain as the site that was added as knowledge.

> ✅ **TIP** If the agent is not able to retrieve answers from the website you add as knowledge, try Bing Search to see if it can find the same answer. Check the page design to understand how the content is added to the website. Content that is embedded in design elements may not always be indexed by search, even though you can read it on the screen.

> ⚠️ **IMPORTANT** You will not get good results using search engines, wikis, forums, or social networks as knowledge sources. Your agent should not rely on these public websites to retrieve knowledge.

Although you can build an agent, connect it to your website, and start generating answers in less than 5 minutes, this isn't likely to be a complete, ready-for-production solution. When you first add your website as knowledge, you should perform comprehensive testing to understand what it answers well and what it can't answer, or can't answer in the way you want. Creating an effective, reliable, production-ready agent requires both good curation of the website content for indexing and deterministic logic of topics to generate answers from your preferred knowledge sources in your agent design.

> 🔍 **SEE ALSO** To understand the principles of deterministic and generative logic, refer to the section "Design the agent's capabilities" in Chapter 2: Designing effective agents.

Allow the agent to use web search

In addition to adding specific public websites as knowledge sources for your agent, you can allow or prevent the agent from using web search to retrieve real-time relevant information from the web. If you enable web search, you are enabling your agent to retrieve information from all public websites. It will undertake this search at the same time that it is searching the websites you added as knowledge, and will return an answer using the information that is most relevant.

> ✓ **TIP** This setting is useful if your use case will benefit from real-time information from the web, but it gives you less control over what the agent will respond to.

To enable web search for your agent

1. Navigate to the **Overview** tab for the agent.

2. Navigate down to the **Knowledge** section.

3. Below the knowledge sources is **Web search** option, which is set to **Disabled** by default. Set this toggle switch to **Enabled**.

4. Wait for the changes to be saved.

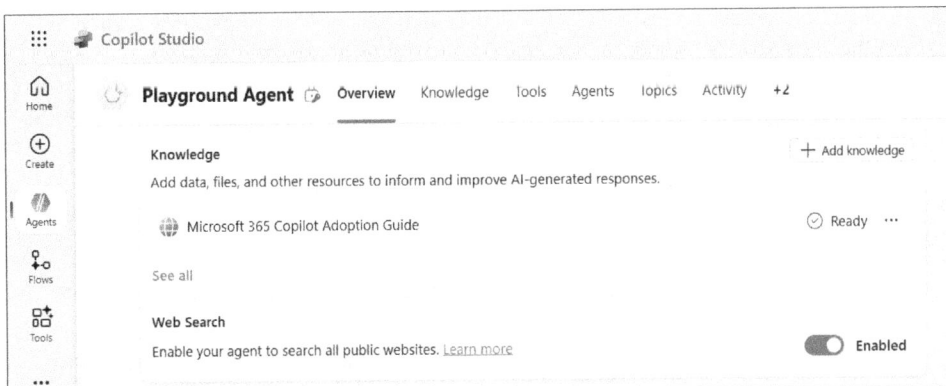

Enable the web search option to allow your agent to get real-time information from all public websites.

5. Test this new setting by asking the agent a question that can only be answered with access to real-time information from a public website: **What is the weather in Sydney today?**

6. The agent first checks the added knowledge sources. When it doesn't find an answer there, it searches the public web, and generates a response, providing citations to the websites used.

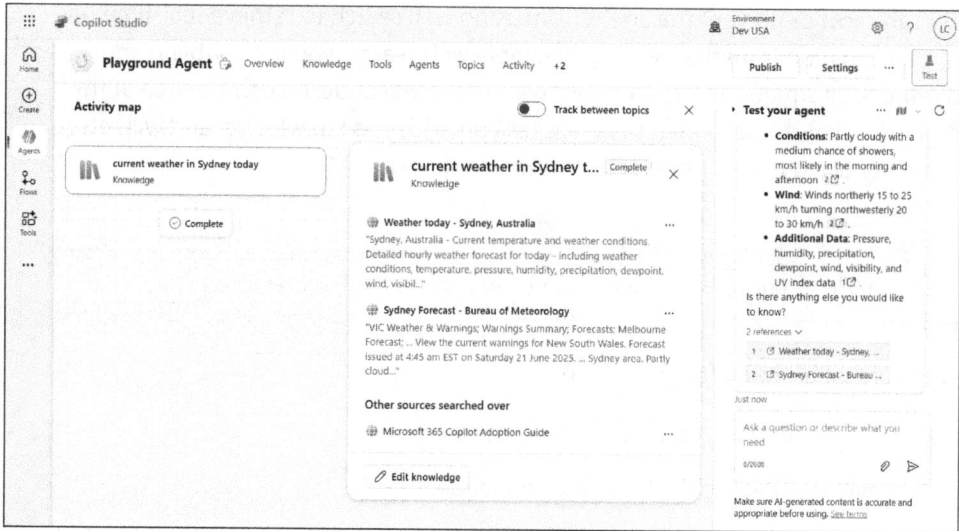

The agent finds the answer from other pages further down the hierarchy in the same domain as the site added as knowledge.

> ✅ **TIP** You can also access and edit the **Web Search** setting in the **Knowledge** section of the Generative AI settings for the agent, and in the properties pane for the **Conversational boosting** topic.

Add files as a knowledge source

One of the most common use cases for Copilot agents is using AI to help customers or employees find information contained in documents. These might include policy documents, how-to guides, or information about your products and services. In this section, you will learn how to upload files or connect to files in OneDrive and SharePoint to use them as knowledge.

You can add files as knowledge sources to your agent in two ways, which are covered in detail in this section:

- *Uploading files* is useful when you want the agent to have access to just a specific version of a document, or when you want to provide access to the knowledge in the document to an external partner, a customer, or anyone who does not have access/permissions to view files in OneDrive or SharePoint in your tenant. These are typically customer-facing agent scenarios where you need to provide the agent with knowledge that isn't available on your public website.

- *Connecting to documents in OneDrive or SharePoint* is useful for internal scenarios where the user's credentials are verified to access internal documents, or where you need a live synchronized version of the file that will be up-to-date with any changes made. These scenarios are typically internal service scenarios where employees need to find answers in a huge amount of internal policy, procedure, project, or product documentation.

Upload files

You can upload files in a range of formats for Copilot Studio to use as knowledge. When you upload files as knowledge, they are stored securely in the Dataverse file storage for your tenant and indexed for the agent using the Dataverse search index.

You can upload any of the following supported document types:

- Word (doc, docx)
- Excel (xls, xlsx)
- PowerPoint (ppt, pptx)
- PDF (pdf)
- Text (txt, md, log)
- HTML (html, htm)
- CSV (csv)
- XML (xml)
- OpenDocument (odt, ods, odp)
- EPUB (epub)
- Rich Text Format (rtf)

- Apple iWork (pages, key, numbers)

- JSON (json)

- YAML (yml, yaml)

- LaTeX (tex)

SEE ALSO At the time of writing, the file size limit for uploading files is 512 MB, and there is a limit of 500 uploaded files per agent. For the most up-to-date information about file formats and limitations for uploaded files, refer to the Microsoft documentation: https://learn.microsoft.com/en-us/microsoft-copilot-studio/knowledge-add-file-upload.

IMPORTANT Images are only supported when they are annotated and embedded in PDF files. If you need to use images as a knowledge source for your agent, you will need to vectorize your data using multimodal RAG or use a custom model from Azure AI. For more information, refer to Chapter 13: Extending Copilot Studio agents with Azure AI.

The example scenario in the following exercise shows how to upload files related to a product sold by a fictional toy company, Tailspin Toys. Imagine that this product is listed on the company's website, but the website marketing copy doesn't include all the information customers are looking for. The company has a more detailed product description document that it wants to provide for customers in addition to the information on the website.

TIP To follow along with the exercises in this chapter, use product documents from your organization, or use Copilot or the generative AI tool of your choice to generate sample documents that you can use for learning. You can use these prompts to generate documents similar to those used here:

"Create a realistic, customer-facing product information sheet for a children's play mat, written in a clear professional tone. Include the product description, key features or benefits, what's included, and intended use or safety notes."

"Create an FAQ document for this product including 6–8 frequently asked questions that a customer might reasonably ask after reading the overview."

IMPORTANT Documents uploaded as knowledge in an agent will be available to any user without authentication. Do not use this option for confidential or sensitive information that should not be available to any use of the agent. You will not be able to upload any documents that are labeled "Confidential" or "Highly Confidential," or documents that contain passwords.

To add a file as a knowledge source

1. In the Playground Agent, navigate to the **Knowledge** tab and select **Add knowledge**.

2. Select the **Upload file** option.

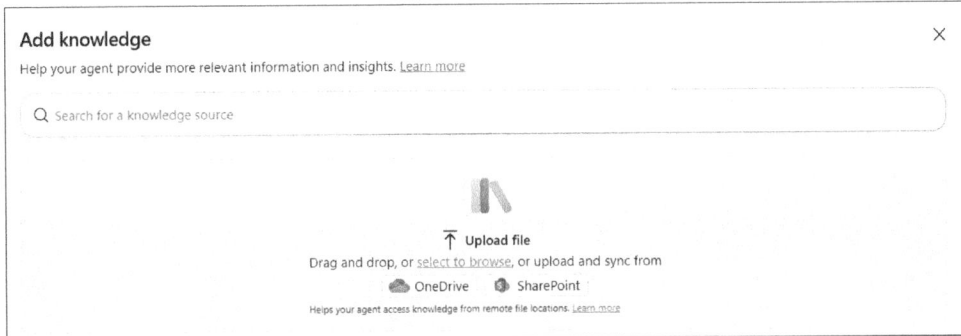

Add knowledge   ×

Help your agent provide more relevant information and insights. Learn more

🔍 Search for a knowledge source

↑ Upload file

Drag and drop, or select to browse, or upload and sync from

☁ OneDrive   📄 SharePoint

Helps your agent access knowledge from remote file locations. Learn more

Select the Upload file option in the Add knowledge screen.

3. Select the document from your files. In this example, the document is called **Tailspin Toys Play Mat Overview.**

4. Edit the **Name** so that it helps the agent better understand what the document is about. In this scenario, the name is changed to **Play Mat Product Overview.**

5. Edit the **Description** to better describe how the agent will use this document. In this case, the description is: **This knowledge source describes the features and benefits of the Tailspin Toys Play Mat.**

6. Select **Add**.

7. Wait for the file to upload.

8. You will be returned to the **Knowledge** tab, where the file is now displayed in the list. The status will show **In progress** for some time while the file is being uploaded to Dataverse and indexed. You can continue building your agent while this happens in the background.

Upload files

Only text-based files are supported; images, audio, video, or executables are not. Files will be securely stored in Dataverse.

×

↑ Upload file

Drag and drop or select to browse. Files can be up to 512MB, and can't be labeled **Confidential** or **Highly Confidential** or contain passwords.

File name	Name	Description
Play Mat Product Overview	Play Mat Product Overview	This knowledge source describes the features ...

Back   Add   Cancel

Edit the name and the description of the file to help the agent understand what it is and how it will be used.

> **TIP** You can use the buttons above the list of knowledge sources to filter by knowledge source type. These buttons appear as you add different types of knowledge. Now that you have added a file, there is a **Files** filter button as well as the **Public website** button.

Playground Agent   Overview   **Knowledge**   Tools   Agents   Topics   Activity   +2

+ Add knowledge   🔍 Search knowledge

All   📄 Files   🌐 Public website   ↻ Last refreshed 14 hours ago

Name	Type	Available to	Last modified	Status
Microsoft 365 Copilot Adoption Guide	🌐 Public web	⊘ Playground Agent	Lisa Crosbie...	⊘ Ready
Play Mat Product Overview	📄 Files	⊘ Playground Agent	Lisa Crosbie...	○ In progress

Your file will be uploaded to Dataverse and indexed in the background.

9. Use the **Refresh** option to refresh the list and check whether the knowledge is ready. The amount of time the indexing takes will depend on the length of your content. For a small sample document like this, it will take only a few minutes at most.

10. When the file is ready, refresh the test pane in your agent, and test the new knowledge source by asking a question that can be answered by the content in the document.

11. The agent responds using the knowledge in the document and provides a reference link to the original content. Select the reference link to view the original source content that the agent used to provide the answer.

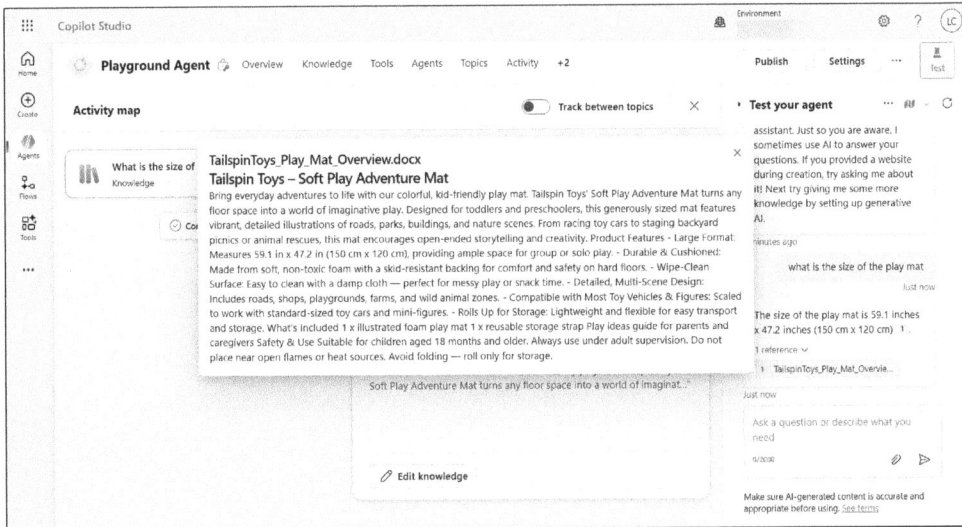

The agent responds using the uploaded document as the knowledge source.

> ⚠ **IMPORTANT** When you upload documents as knowledge using this method, the content of the document is available to the user. When they select the link to view the reference, they will be taken to the content of the original document.

When you upload files as a knowledge source, they remain static as the version you uploaded. If the source version of the content is available online or in a cloud drive and gets updated, this file will not be updated automatically. If you need the agent to use an updated version of the content, you will need to delete this file from the knowledge sources and upload a new version of the file.

To remove a file from the knowledge sources

1. Navigate to the **Knowledge** tab.

2. Hover to the right of the name of the knowledge source you want to delete, and then select the three dots that appear, expanding the menu.

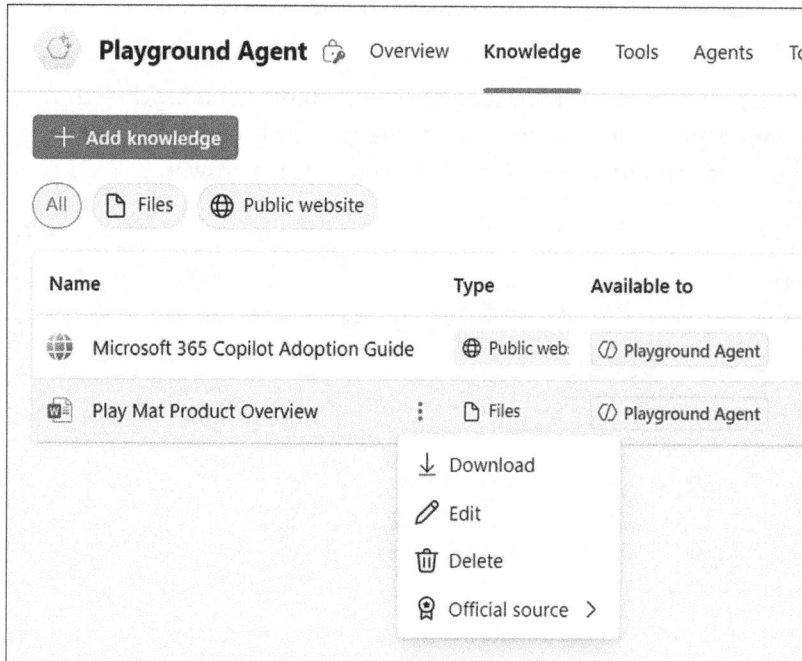

Delete the knowledge source to remove it from the agent.

3. Select the **Delete** option.

> ✓ **TIP** The **Edit** option in this menu opens the screen to edit the name or description, or mark the knowledge source as an official source. It does not allow you to edit the actual content of the file.

4. You will get a confirmation message advising that deleting a knowledge source is permanent and cannot be undone.

5. Select **Delete**.

6. Wait for the knowledge source to be deleted and removed from the list of knowledge sources in the **Knowledge** tab.

7. Refresh the **test** pane, then test the agent with the question you asked related to this file. The agent will no longer be able to answer that question. If you have web search enabled, the agent will find an unrelated relevant answer about the size of a play mat from a public website.

Imagine in this scenario that the company also has a FAQ document related to the play mat product. Rather than uploading the product information and the FAQ as individual knowledge sources, you can group them together so that the agent understands they are related documents that make up a single source of knowledge. Uploading files as a group allows you to name and describe them together so that the agent first matches the user intent with that group of files and then searches within the files in the group.

To create a file group

1. In the Playground Agent, navigate to the **Knowledge** tab and select **Add knowledge**.

2. Select the **Upload file** option.

3. Select a document from your files. In this case, the document is the **Tailspin Toys Play Mat Overview**.

4. Select the **Upload file** option again.

5. Select another document from your files that is related to the first document. In this case, the document is the **Tailspin Toys Play Mat FAQ**.

> ✓ **TIP** You can hold the CTRL key to select and upload multiple files in one action.

6. Set the **Group these files** toggle to the **On** position. This groups the files so that you can enter a single name and description for the group, rather than for each individual file.

7. Edit the **Name** so that it represents the combined knowledge in the files added. In this case, the name is **Play Mat Product Details and FAQ.**

8. Edit the **Description** so that it describes how the agent will use the knowledge in these files. In this case, the description is **This knowledge source provides detailed product information and frequently asked questions about the Tailspin Toys Play Mat.**

Upload files ✕

Only text-based files are supported; images, audio, video, or executables are not. Files will be securely stored in Dataverse.

↑ Upload file

Drag and drop or select to browse. Files can be up to 512MB, and can't be labeled **Confidential** or **Highly Confidential** or contain passwords.

⬤ Group these files (preview) ⓘ

Name *

Collection of files: TailspinToys_Play_Mat_Overview.docx, TailspinToys_Play_Mat_FAQ.docx

Description ⓘ *

This knowledge source searches information contained in TailspinToys_Play_Mat_Overview.docx, TailspinToys_Play_Mat_FAQ.docx

Instructions (preview) ⓘ

Type your instructions here...

Back   Add   Cancel

Group files to add a name and description for the whole group rather than for individual files.

> ✓ **TIP** You can also add instructions here describing when this knowledge source should be used. That is especially useful if you are building an autonomous agent and referring to this knowledge is part of a process it needs to follow.

9. Select **Add**.

10. Wait for the files to be uploaded. The files are added as a knowledge source and shown in the list as a folder.

Playground Agent Overview **Knowledge** Tools Agents Topics Activity +2

+ Add knowledge   🔍 Search knowledge

(All) 📄 Files 🌐 Public website   ⟳ Last refreshed 21 minutes ago

Name	Type	Available to	Last modified	Status
🌐 Microsoft 365 Copilot Adoption Guide	🌐 Public web	⟨⟩ Playground Agent	Lisa Crosbie...	⊘ Ready
📁 Play Mat Product Details and FAQ	📄 Files	⟨⟩ Playground Agent	Lisa Crosbie...	⟳ In progress

A file group as a knowledge source is shown as a folder.

11. Refresh the **test** pane, then test the agent by asking a question found in these documents. The agent will respond in the same way it did when it used a single document as a knowledge source.

Connect to OneDrive or SharePoint files and folders

You can also add files as knowledge by connecting to files or folders in OneDrive or SharePoint. Using this method connects to the live version of the files in the cloud, rather than uploading a static copy. As a result, any changes made to the original file in OneDrive or SharePoint will change the knowledge available to the agent.

> ⚠ **IMPORTANT** When you add documents from OneDrive or SharePoint, they will be uploaded to Dataverse, where they are processed and indexed for the agent to use as knowledge. This will consume data storage in your Dataverse environment.

> ⚠ **IMPORTANT** Access to files added from OneDrive or SharePoint will be governed by the existing permissions on those files. That means users need to be authenticated when they use the agent, and they need to have permission to read the files you add as knowledge. This option for adding knowledge is suitable only for internal authenticated scenarios. Adding files as knowledge using OneDrive or SharePoint does not make them available to any user of the agent without the required permissions. If you need that option, use the upload documents method described in the previous section. Documents that are protected using sensitivity labels or documents that are password protected can't be indexed and the agent will not provide answers from the content in those documents.

Add files from OneDrive as a knowledge source

You can add any documents or folders to which you have access on OneDrive for Business as a knowledge source for your agent.

To add files or folders from OneDrive

1. In the Playground Agent, navigate to the **Knowledge** tab and select **Add knowledge**.

2. In the **Upload file** section, select the **OneDrive** button.

3. This opens a pop-up window where you can browse or enter the URL of a OneDrive file. Select **Browse**.

4. The screen shows you the **My files** list to select from. You can select one or multiple folders from this list to add all the documents in those folders, or you can open a folder and then select one or more documents from it. You can also browse through **Recent** or **Shared** files.

5. Pick a folder or multiple folders from your OneDrive file list.

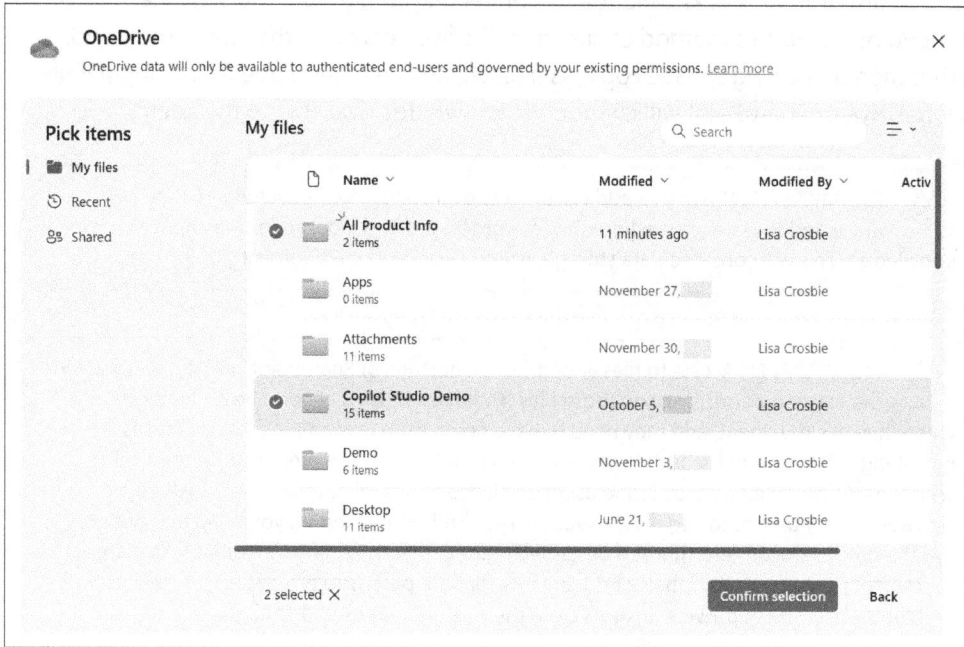

Browse the files and pick folders or documents to add to your agent as knowledge.

6. Select the **Confirm selection** button.

> ⚠ IMPORTANT Each folder or document selected will appear as a separate knowledge source for the agent. If you want to group files as a single knowledge source, put them into a single folder in OneDrive before you add them as knowledge to the agent.

7. Edit the **Name** and **Description** to help the agent understand what these knowledge sources are and how they will be used.

8. If you want to add more knowledge sources from OneDrive in this step, you can select **Browse items** again or enter the document URL.

9. When you have finished adding files, Select **Add**.

OneDrive			✕

OneDrive data will only be available to authenticated end-users and governed by your existing permissions. Learn more

Browse items   or   [Enter URL of a OneDrive file]   Add

Link	Name	Description
https://	All Product Info	This knowledge source provides information
https://	Copilot Studio Demo	This knowledge source provides information

Back   Add   Cancel

Give each OneDrive knowledge source a name and a description to help the agent understand what it will be used for.

10. Wait for the files to be uploaded.

11. When the files or folders are uploaded, they will appear in the **Knowledge** tab of your agent. Note that there is now a **OneDrive** button at the top of the list that you can use to filter knowledge sources by this type.

> ✓ **TIP** Uploading multiple files and folders will take longer to index than when you upload a single simple file. You may find these knowledge sources are "in progress" for a while. You can continue to work while the indexing step processes in the background.

12. Select one of the OneDrive knowledge sources to open it and view the details.

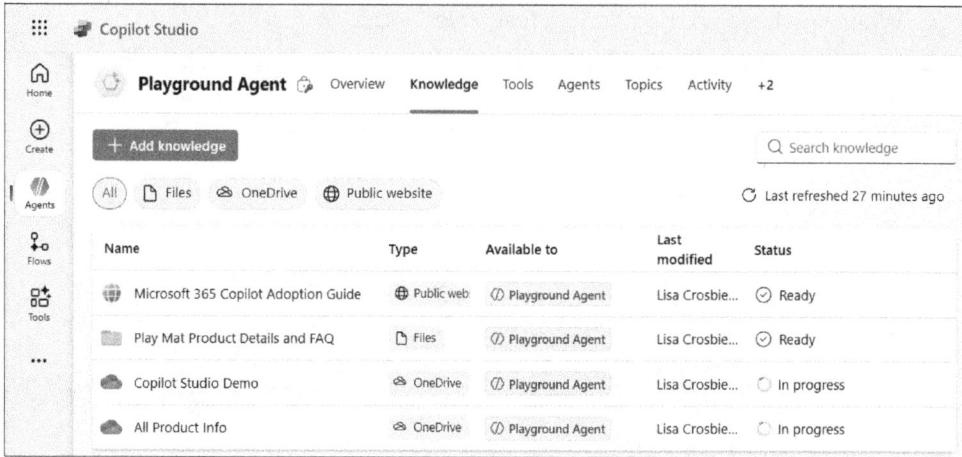

Each OneDrive file or folder is added as a knowledge source to the agent and displayed with a OneDrive icon.

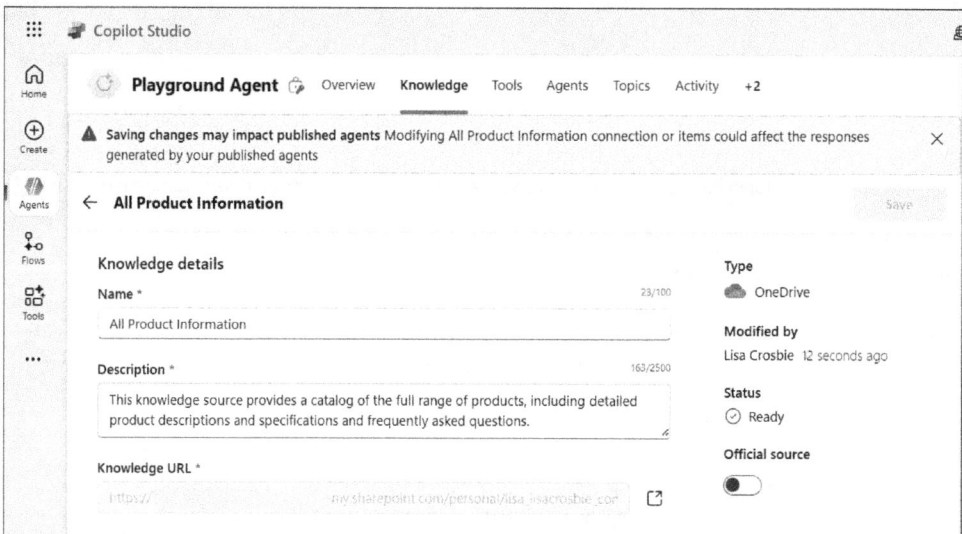

You can edit the name or description of the OneDrive knowledge, set it as an official source, or open the URL to view the files on OneDrive.

13. You can edit the name and description or set this as an **Official source**. Note that for the OneDrive knowledge, a URL shows the original source of the file(s). You can select the button to open and view these files, but you can't edit the URL.

> **TIP** Changing the source documents will update the content of the documents in the knowledge. However, if you need to change the URL, you must delete this knowledge source and add it again with the new URL.

14. Refresh the **test** pane, then test your agent by asking a question for which the answer is found in the files you added from OneDrive.

The agent responds using the documents in OneDrive as the knowledge source.

15. Selecting the reference link will take the user to the document, which will open in a new tab in their browser.

> **SEE ALSO** The first time you test your agent using OneDrive, you will get a message in the test chat prompting you to verify your credentials. For more information, refer to the section "Manage connections" later in this chapter.

Add files from SharePoint as a knowledge source

Adding files from SharePoint follows a very similar experience. You can upload files or folders from the Document libraries in SharePoint to use as knowledge for your agent. This knowledge source consists of a connection to the documents in SharePoint, so any changes you make to the original documents will also update the knowledge in the agent.

> 🔍 **SEE ALSO** To add content from SharePoint sites or SharePoint Lists, refer to the next section in this chapter, "Add SharePoint as a knowledge source."

To add files or folders from SharePoint

1. In the Playground Agent, navigate to the **Knowledge** tab and select **Add knowledge**.

2. In the **Upload file** section, select the **SharePoint** button.

> ✅ **TIP** Make sure you select the SharePoint button from the **Upload file** section, not the SharePoint button in the **Featured** section.

3. This opens a pop-up window where you can browse or enter the URL of a SharePoint file or folder. Select **Browse**.

4. The screen shows you the **Documents** list of files or folders that you can select from shared document libraries. You can select one or multiple folders from this list to add all of the documents in those folders, or you can open a folder and select one or more documents from it.

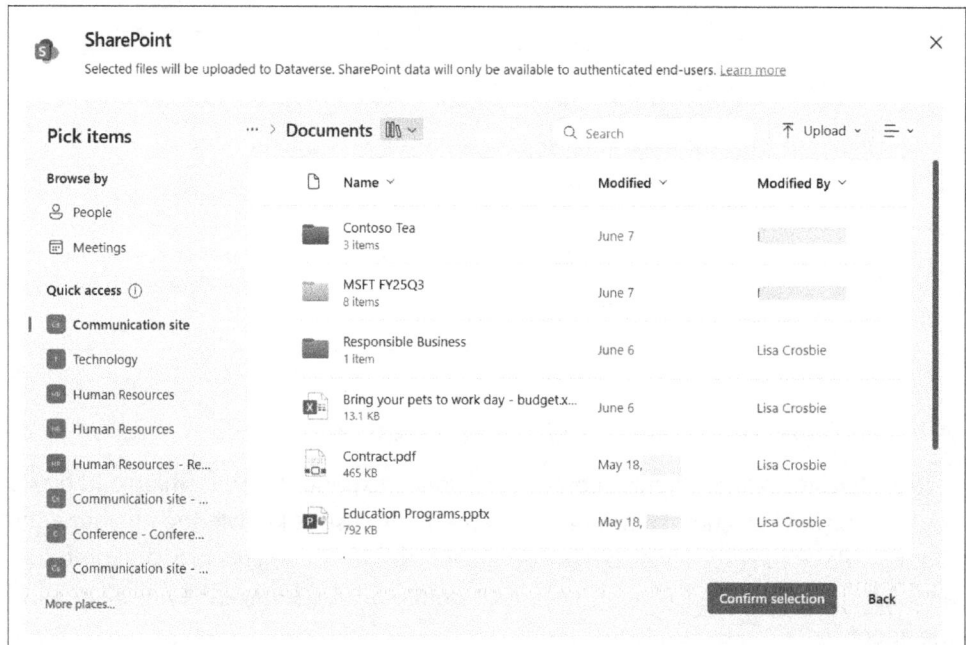

Browse the files and pick folders or documents to add to your agent as knowledge.

5. You can also browse by **People** or **Meetings** to find documents shared with you by others, or meetings with shared files, and add them as knowledge to your agent.

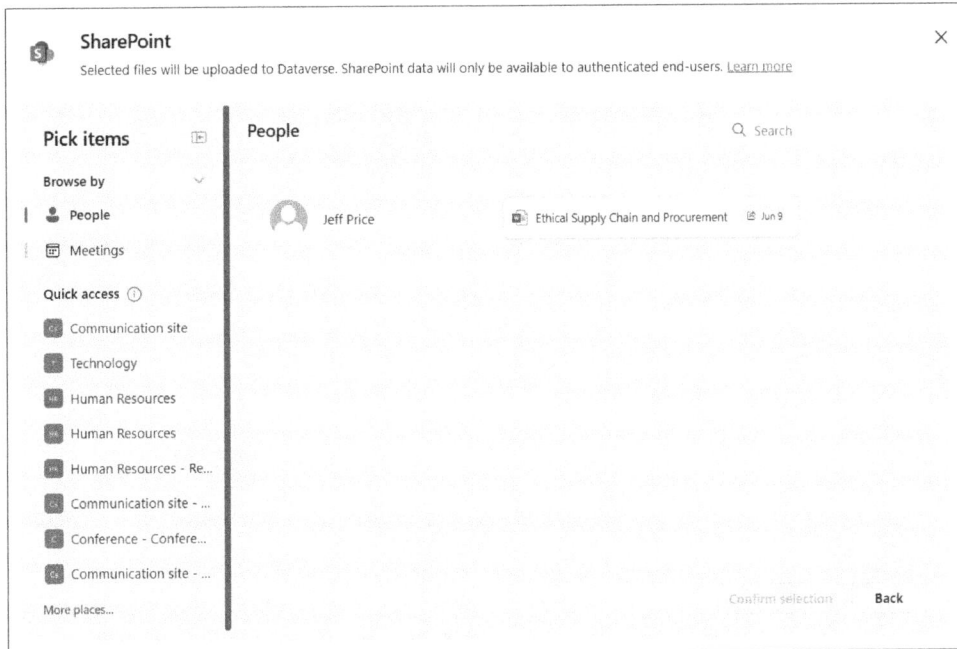

You can browse by People to find files shared with you by others and add them as knowledge sources.

6. Navigate back to the shared document libraries by selecting a site from the **Quick access** menu.

7. Pick a folder or multiple folders from the **Documents** list, or open a folder and select a document.

8. Select the **Confirm selection** button.

9. Edit the **Name** and **Description** to help the agent understand what these knowledge sources are and how they will be used.

10. If you want to add more knowledge sources from SharePoint in this step, you can select **Browse items** again or enter the document URL.

11. When you have finished adding files, select **Add**.

12. Wait for the files to be uploaded. When the files or folders are uploaded, they will appear in the **Knowledge** tab of your agent.

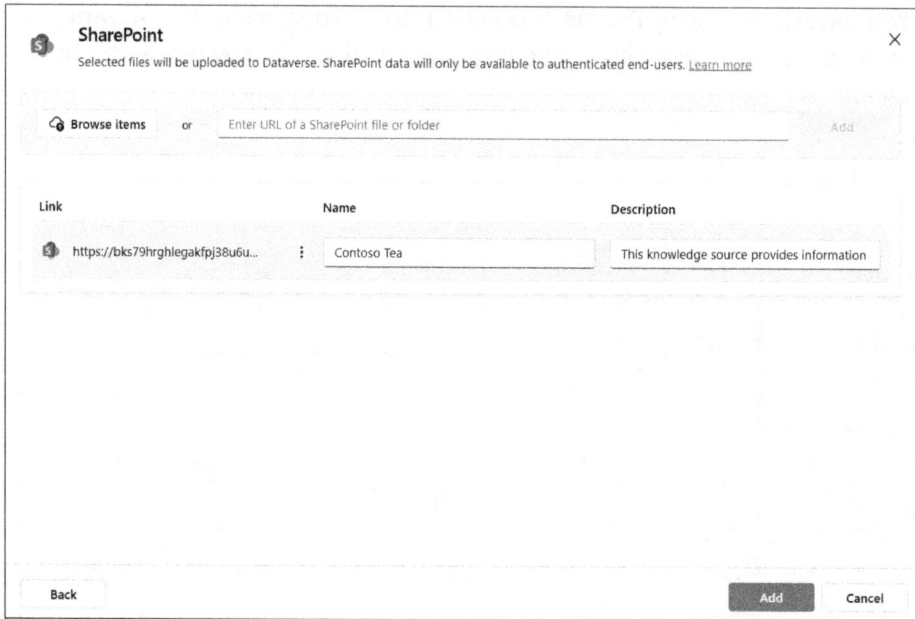

Give each SharePoint knowledge source a name and a description to help the agent understand what it will be used for.

> ✓ **TIP** There isn't a separate filter button for files from SharePoint. Use the **Files** filter button to filter the list to show these files.

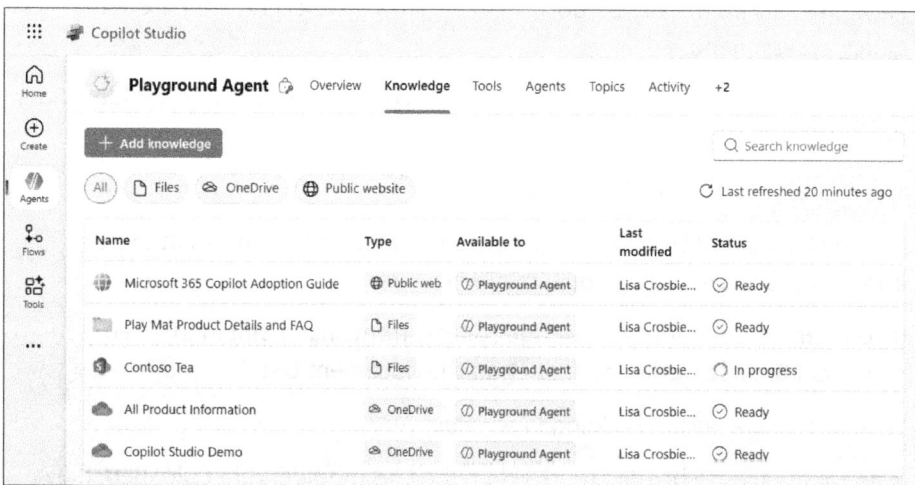

Each SharePoint file or folder is added as a knowledge source to the agent and displayed with a SharePoint icon.

13. Select the SharePoint knowledge source from the list to view or edit the details, including the **Name**, **Description**, or **Official Source**.

> ✓ **TIP** This knowledge source behaves the same way as the OneDrive knowledge source. You can open the link to view the documents in the shared document library on SharePoint, but you can't edit the URL of the knowledge source. Any changes made to the documents in SharePoint will update the content of this knowledge source.

14. Refresh the **test** pane, then test the agent by asking a question related to the content of the files you added.

6

The agent responds using the SharePoint document as the knowledge source.

15. Selecting this reference link will open the original document used as a knowledge source.

> 🔎 **SEE ALSO** At the time of writing, you can add files from OneDrive and SharePoint that are up to 32 MB in size and in Word, PowerPoint, PDF, and Excel format only. For the most up-to-date information on supported file types and limitations, refer to the Microsoft documentation: https://learn.microsoft.com/en-us/microsoft-copilot-studio/knowledge-add-unstructured-data.

Manage connections

When you add knowledge from a connected cloud source, the first time you test it, you will get a message asking you to verify your credentials to continue. Select the

Allow button, and the agent will verify the connection and continue the conversation. You will only be prompted to verify your credentials when the knowledge is first added, or when the agent is updated and republished.

> ⚠️ **IMPORTANT** Your users will also need to verify their credentials to these connected knowledge sources when they use them for the first time. You may wish to share these instructions with your internal users when you publish your agent.

When you first use an agent connected to authenticated internal sources, you will need to allow the agent to use your credentials.

You can get a full view of all the connections in the agent in the Connection Settings. There, you can view, check, and manage all the connections used by your agent, including adding new connections, troubleshooting, editing, refreshing, or disconnecting them as needed.

To manage connections

1. Select the **Settings** button to open the settings for your agent.

2. Select the **Connection Settings** option from the left-side navigation.

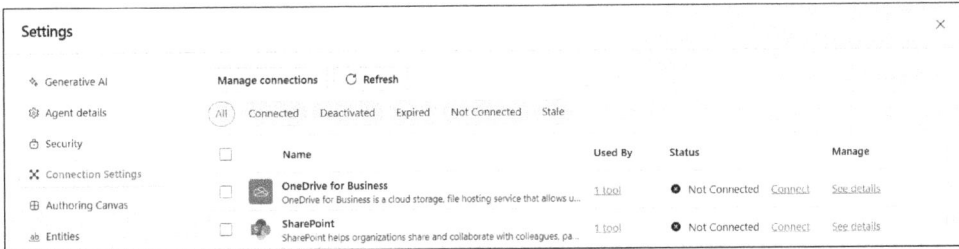

View and manage all of the connection settings in the Settings area of the agent.

3. Select these connections using the check boxes, and then select the **Manage selected connections** button.

4. The **Create or pick connections** pop-up will be displayed, showing the connections that need to be verified. Sign into each connection if it is not automatically verified.

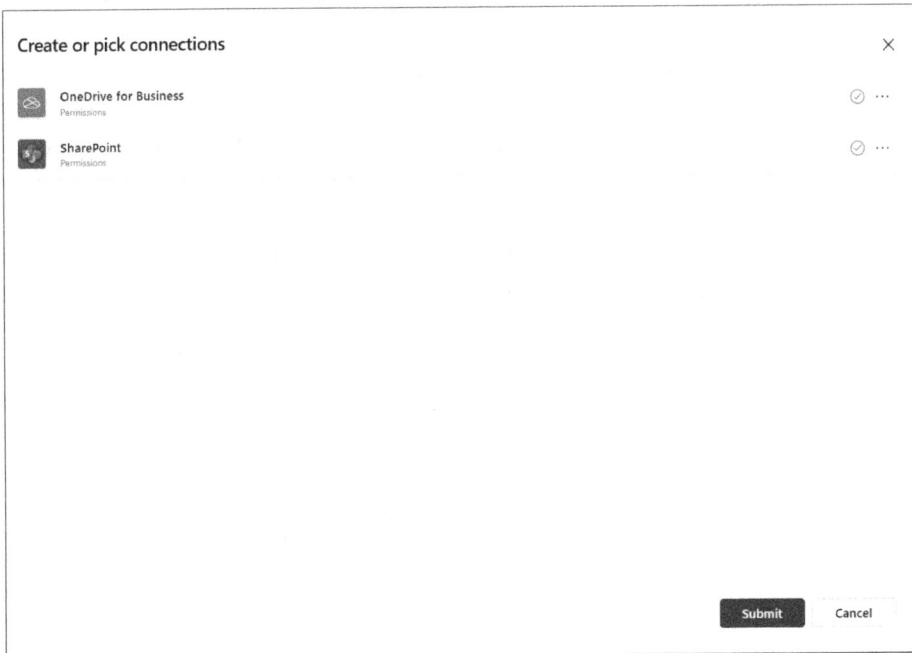

Verify your connections to OneDrive for Business and SharePoint.

5. Select the **Submit** button.

6. You will be returned to the **Connection Settings** screen, where the connections are now listed with the status **Connected**.

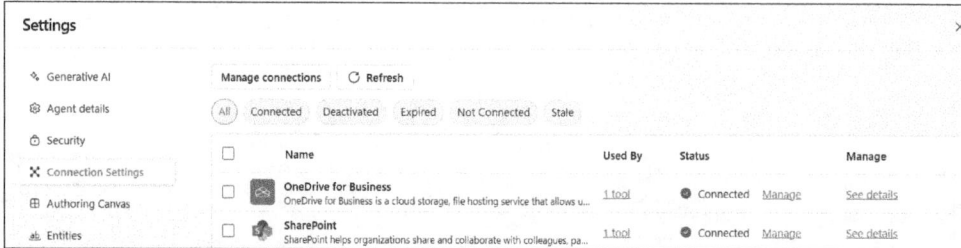

The connections are now verified.

7. Close the **Settings** to return to the agent configuration and testing.

Add SharePoint as a knowledge source

When you work with SharePoint as a knowledge source, you can either add documents as shown in the previous section or use the entire SharePoint site content (including documents) or SharePoint lists as knowledge sources for your agent. Using SharePoint as a knowledge source is one of the most common business requirements for internal Copilot Studio scenarios. If you use SharePoint to store your internal knowledge for policies, procedures, project, or product information, then creating an agent that uses this knowledge to help employees find the information more easily is often the start of a strong business case for an agent. That is particularly true where your organization has a lot of documents or where the knowledge is used by staff in a service department, either internally or externally facing.

In this section, you will learn how to use the knowledge on SharePoint sites and in SharePoint Lists as knowledge sources for your agent.

> ⚠️ **IMPORTANT** SharePoint as a knowledge source is governed by the existing permissions for the site and the files. That means users need to be authenticated with Entra ID to use this knowledge in the agent. Using SharePoint as a knowledge source is suitable only for internal scenarios.

> **TIP** To follow along with the exercises in this section you will need a SharePoint site with some page content, documents in a document library, and a SharePoint list with some rows of data in it. If you don't already have a real site you can use, start with the Human Resources template site and add some documents and items to the Onboarding checklist.

Tenant graph grounding

Before you start working with SharePoint as a knowledge source, it is important to understand the concept and value of tenant graph grounding and how it impacts the performance of your agent.

When you add knowledge to your agent, the knowledge is indexed so that the agent can use it to retrieve information. When you have a Microsoft 365 Copilot license in your tenant, a different kind of indexing, called semantic search, is enabled in your tenant. Semantic search is a more sophisticated index that will improve the search results for knowledge in your agent. It maps and understands the meanings of similar words (rather than relying on keyword matching) and uses the content in the Microsoft Graph to provide contextually relevant responses based on all the data it has about what you work on and who you work with.

> **SEE ALSO** For a detailed explanation of how semantic indexing works with Microsoft 365 Copilot, refer to the Microsoft documentation: https://learn.microsoft.com/en-us/microsoftsearch/semantic-index-for-copilot.

If you have a Microsoft 365 Copilot license, you have the option to use this semantic index when you connect to SharePoint knowledge. The option, called "Tenant graph grounding," can be enabled or disabled in the Settings area of your agent.

Tenant graph grounding makes a substantial difference to the quality, accuracy, and relevance of generative answers in Copilot Studio when using SharePoint as a knowledge source. However, it consumes messages at a premium rate.

> **SEE ALSO** These consumption costs are included for users who have a Microsoft 365 Copilot license when the agent is published in a Microsoft 365 channel. For more information, refer to the section "Understand and calculate agent costs" in Chapter 2: Designing effective agents.

To enable or disable tenant graph grounding

1. Navigate to the **Settings** area for your agent.

2. In the **Generative AI** settings, navigate to the **Search** section.

3. In the **Search** section, there is a setting for **Tenant graph grounding with semantic search**. This will be switched to the **On** position if you have a Microsoft 365 Copilot license.

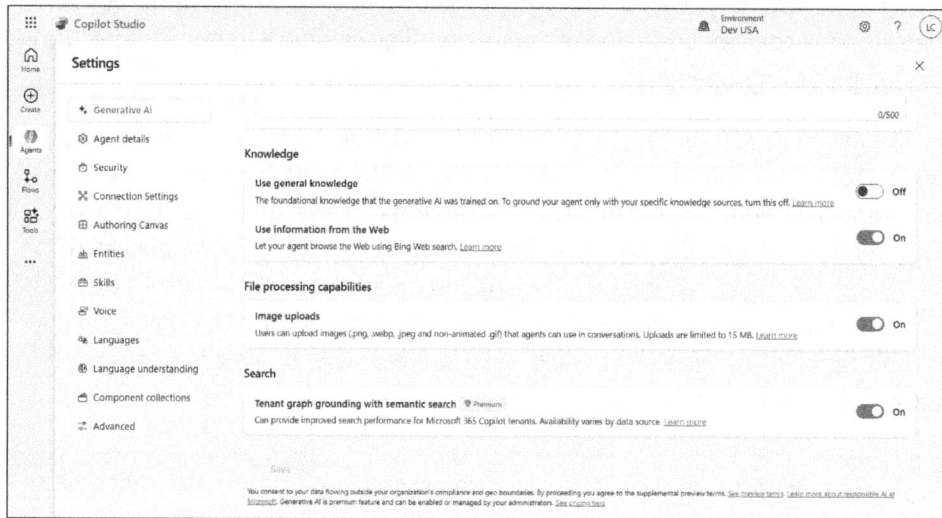

Tenant graph grounding with semantic search is enabled if you have a Microsoft 365 Copilot license.

4. Toggle the switch to the **Off** position if you don't want to use it for this agent.

> ⚠️ **IMPORTANT** If you don't have a Microsoft 365 Copilot license, tenant graph grounding is not available. You should not enable this setting unless you have a Microsoft 365 Copilot license.

Connect to a SharePoint site

In the previous section, you learned how to connect to specific SharePoint files or folders of documents to use as knowledge. You can also connect to a SharePoint site, which means that the agent will use everything on the site pages and subpaths, including document libraries, as knowledge.

If you enable tenant graph grounding, you will get far better search results when using SharePoint as a knowledge source.

> ⚠️ **IMPORTANT** This method of adding SharePoint supports modern SharePoint page content and a limited range of document formats. Content from classic ASPX pages on SharePoint is not supported.

> 🔍 **SEE ALSO** For the most current documentation on file types supported and limitations, refer to the Microsoft documentation: https://learn.microsoft.com/en-us/microsoft-copilot-studio/knowledge-add-sharepoint.

To connect to a SharePoint site to use as knowledge

1. In the Playground Agent, navigate to the **Knowledge** tab and select **Add knowledge**.

2. Select the **SharePoint** button from the **Featured** list of knowledge sources.

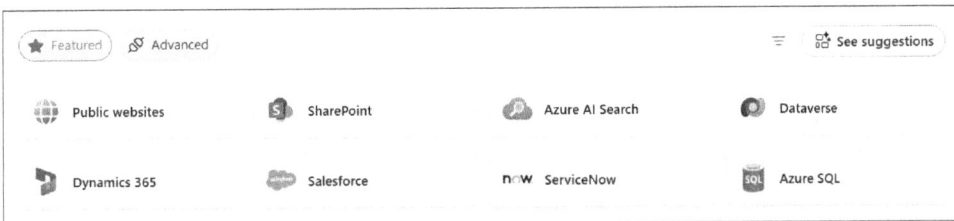

Select SharePoint from the Featured list of knowledge sources to connect a SharePoint site as knowledge.

> ✓ **TIP** Make sure you select the SharePoint button from the **Featured** section, not the SharePoint button in the **Upload file** section. You can only connect to a site using this option.

3. This opens a pop-up window where you can browse or enter the URL of a SharePoint site or browse items. Copy the URL of your SharePoint site at the top level (e.g., https://mydomain.sharepoint.com/sites/HumanResources) and paste it into the field on the pop-up in Copilot Studio.

> ✓ **TIP** The **Browse items** option here allows you to connect to SharePoint Lists, which is covered in the next part. It is also an alternative path to connect to documents.

4. Select the **Add** button to add that URL.

Connect all the content in your SharePoint site as knowledge by pasting the URL into the pop-up.

5. Edit the **Name** and **Description** of the SharePoint site to help the agent understand what it is and what it will be used for.

> **TIP** You can add multiple SharePoint site URLs at once by repeating this process. Each URL will include all the subpages, so you don't need to add those.

6. Select the **Add** button.

Give each SharePoint site a Name and Description to help the agent understand what it will be used for.

7. When the SharePoint sites have been added, you will be returned to the **Knowledge** tab for your agent.

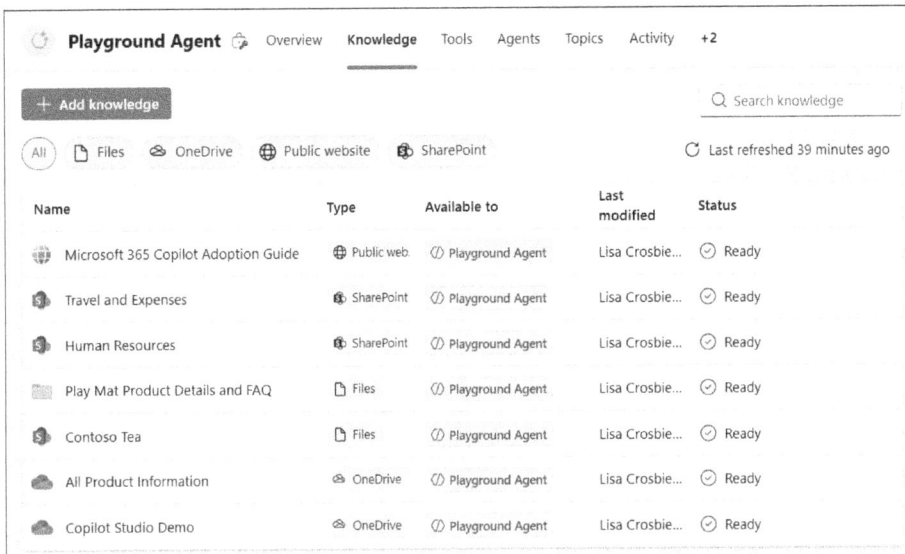

When you sign into Copilot with your Microsoft account, it presents a list of Copilot GPTs and your prompt history.

8. Note that when you add SharePoint sites in this way, they are listed as type **SharePoint**, and a **SharePoint** filter button is added to the screen. The documents you added from SharePoint earlier are shown in the list as type **Files**.

9. Refresh the **test** pane, then test your agent by asking a question related to the content on the SharePoint site or in files in the document library from the site added.

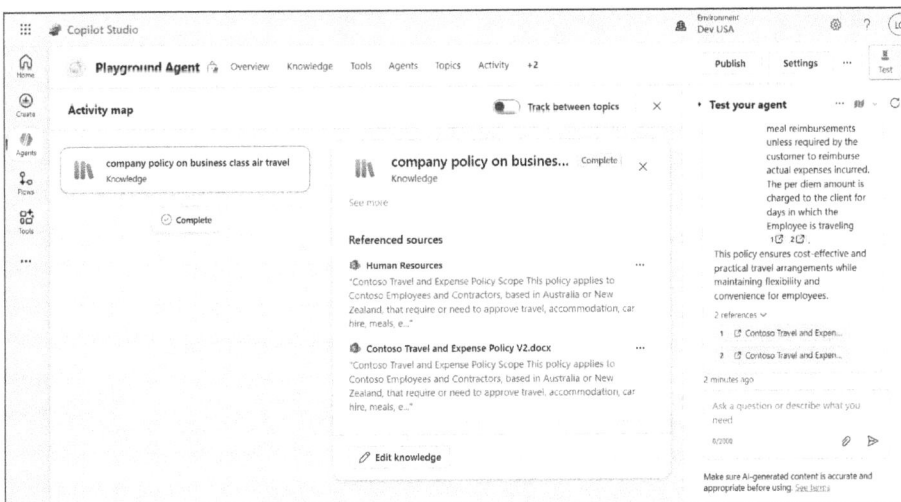

The agent responds using a document in the SharePoint document library as the knowledge source.

10. Selecting this reference link will open the original document used as a knowledge source.

> **SEE ALSO** For tips on getting the best results from using SharePoint as a knowledge source, refer to "Best practice for working with SharePoint as a knowledge source" at the end of this section.

Connect to a SharePoint List

Adding SharePoint as a knowledge source connects your agent to the content on the site and in the document libraries. If you want the agent to use a SharePoint list as a knowledge source, you will need to add that list separately, following the process described in this section.

When you connect a SharePoint list to the agent, the logged-in user will need to be authenticated. The agent will answer questions based on only the knowledge in lists to which the user has access, based on the SharePoint Access Control List (ACL) restrictions.

In this example, we will connect to a SharePoint list that is used to manage IT Assets in an organization.

To add a SharePoint list as a knowledge source

1. In the Playground Agent, navigate to the **Knowledge** tab and select **Add knowledge**.

2. Select the **SharePoint** button from the **Featured** list of knowledge sources.

> **TIP** Make sure you select the SharePoint button from the **Featured** section, not the SharePoint button in the **Upload file** section. You can only connect to a site using this option.

3. This opens a pop-up window where you can browse or enter the URL of a SharePoint site or browse items. Select the **Browse items** button.

4. Select either **My lists** or **Recent lists** from the **Pick items** menu on the left to display a list of SharePoint lists, or use the search bar to search for the list by name.

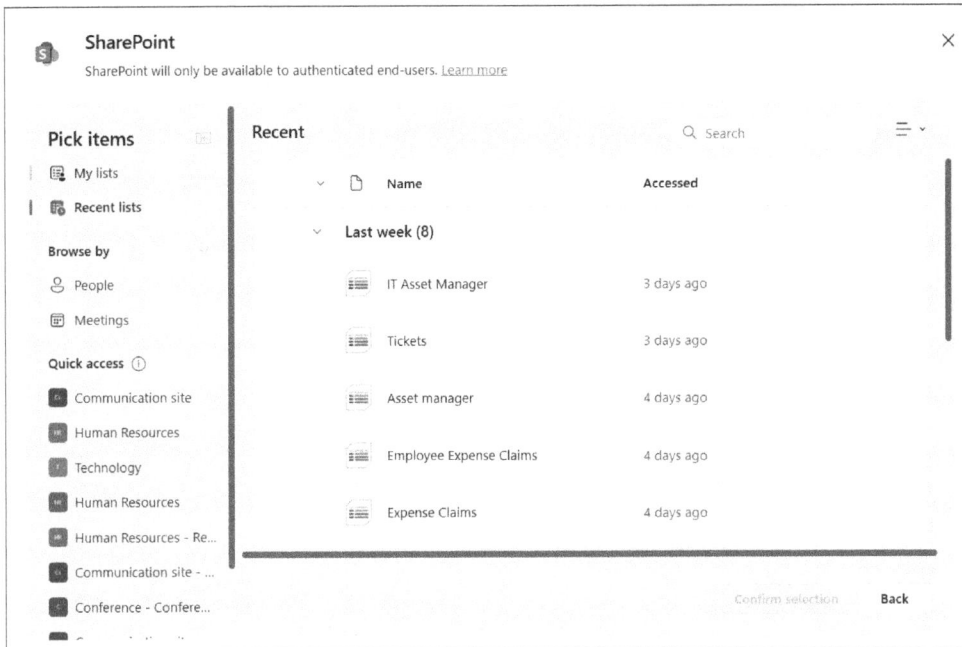

Select Recent lists from the Pick items menu to view SharePoint lists you have recently opened.

5. Select the name of the list you want to add as knowledge to your agent.

6. The list is displayed in the preview pane.

> ✓ **TIP** This preview displays the column headings in your list but may not display any actual list data.

7. Select the **Confirm selection** button.

8. Edit the **Name** and **Description** to help the agent understand what this data source will be used for. For example, the Description for this list could be: **This knowledge source provides a list of IT Assets such as smartphones, laptops, tablets, and accessories. It shows the Status (In Use, In Repair, Reserved, Retired, Available), Manufacturer, Model, Serial Number, Purchase Price, and Purchase Date for each asset.**

9. Select the **Add** button.

10. When the SharePoint list has been added, you will be returned to the **Knowledge** tab for your agent.

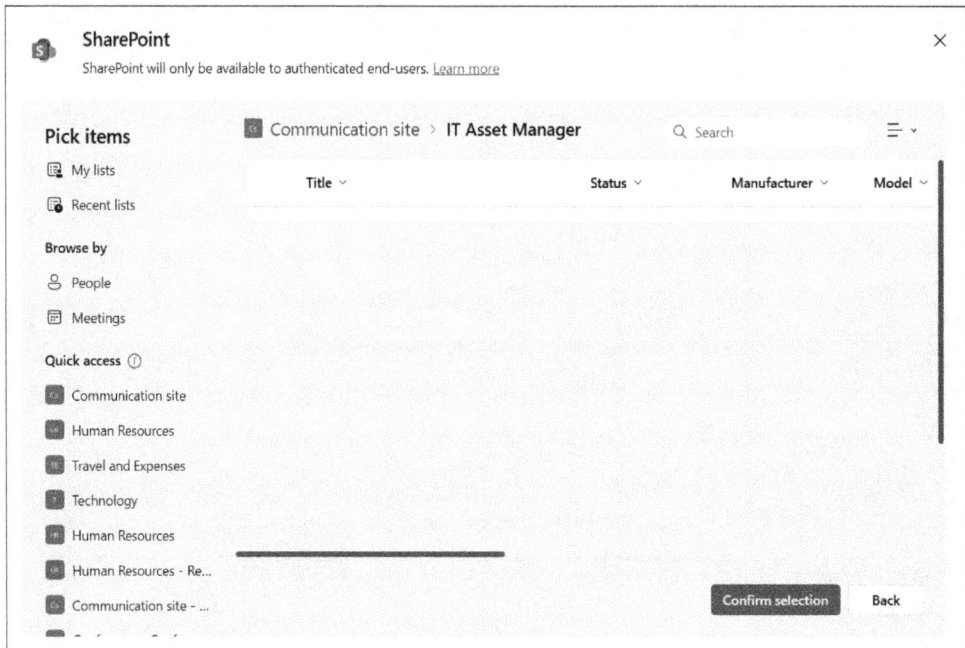

Preview the SharePoint list you have selected and then confirm the selection.

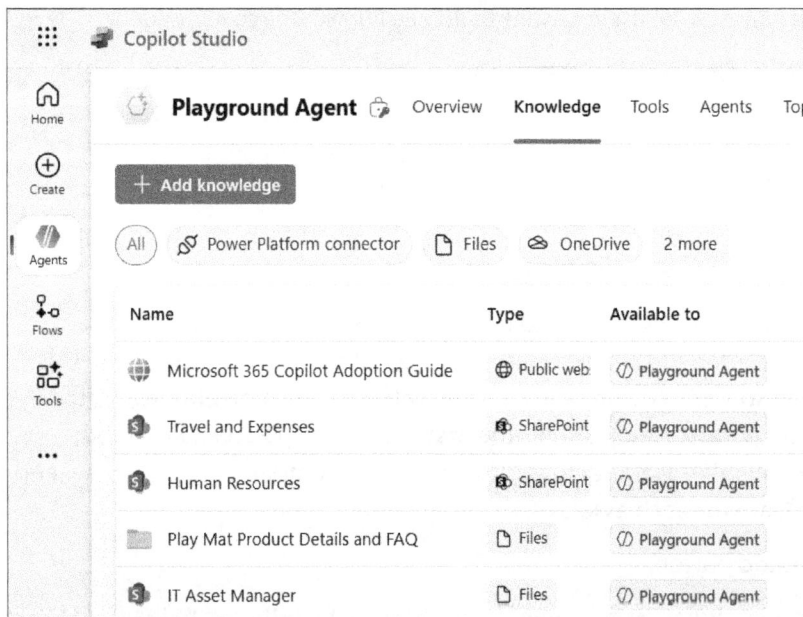

The SharePoint list is shown in the list of knowledge sources.

11. Wait for the status of the knowledge source to change from **In Progress** to **Ready**.

12. Test your agent by asking a question related to the data in the SharePoint list.

> 🔍 **SEE ALSO** If you are prompted to verify your credentials, refer to the instructions on how to manage connections in the previous section.

The agent responds using the SharePoint list as the knowledge source.

Best practice for working with SharePoint as a knowledge source

The performance when using SharePoint as a knowledge source can vary depending on the quality and management of your content, as well as the features you have enabled for your tenant and your agent. Here are some tips to help you get the best results when using SharePoint as a knowledge source:

- Have a content management strategy for your documents, which should follow the same principles as you would when managing any externally facing content. Avoid duplicate or multiple versions of documents, which can result in inconsistent answers. Consider setting up a folder of the "final source of truth" versions of documents to use as knowledge for the agent.

- The search and retrieval of information from SharePoint is substantially enhanced by using semantic indexing, which is enabled by default when you have Microsoft 365 Copilot licenses in your tenant. You will also be able to work with much larger file sizes with this indexing enabled. Start with at least one license to enable and experience this indexing in your agent. Consider purchasing Microsoft 365 Copilot licenses for users of the agent.

- Compared to classic orchestration, generative orchestration produces superior results when you are working with SharePoint as a knowledge source.

Add real-time connectors to enterprise data

You can use the data in your enterprise systems as knowledge in Copilot Studio by setting up real-time connectors. For example, you can use the method described in this section to connect to Salesforce, ServiceNow, Azure SQL, Dataverse, Dynamics 365, Zendesk, Confluence, and other business systems. When you connect to data in these systems, the data stays where it is in the enterprise system. Copilot Studio only indexes the metadata (e.g., table names and column names) so that it understands the structure of the data and can retrieve knowledge in real time from the source. The permissions and access controls of the enterprise system are retained, so users of the agent will need to be authenticated before they will be able to use the agent to access the knowledge.

In this section, you will learn how to add a third-party enterprise system as knowledge, using Confluence as an example. You will then learn how to work with the first-party Dataverse connector, which has some additional configuration features that can help you describe the data structure to the agent.

Connect to enterprise data using real-time connectors

Real-time knowledge connectors in Copilot Studio are the same as Power Platform connectors and follow the data loss prevention policy configuration set up in Power Platform. When you create an agent in Copilot Studio, DLP policy enforcement is set to enabled by default.

> ⚠ **IMPORTANT** Real-time connectors will use the logged-in user credentials to connect to the data in the connected system.

> (🔍) **SEE ALSO** For the current list of supported real-time connectors, including the details of the API, authentication options, known issues, and limitations for each, refer to the Microsoft documentation: https://learn.microsoft.com/en-us/microsoft-copilot-studio/knowledge-real-time-connectors.

> (✓) **TIP** To follow along with the exercise on adding a real-time connector as knowledge in Copilot Studio, you will need an account with the enterprise system that you can use to authenticate and log in, or an administrator will need to set up the connector in the Microsoft 365 admin center (https://learn.microsoft.com/en-us/microsoftsearch/configure-connector). Some enterprise systems offer free trials, which you can sign up for to use as a learning experience.

To add knowledge using a real-time connector

1. In the Playground Agent, navigate to the **Knowledge** tab and select **Add knowledge**.

2. Review the connections available in the **Featured** list of knowledge sources, and then select the **Advanced** button to view more options.

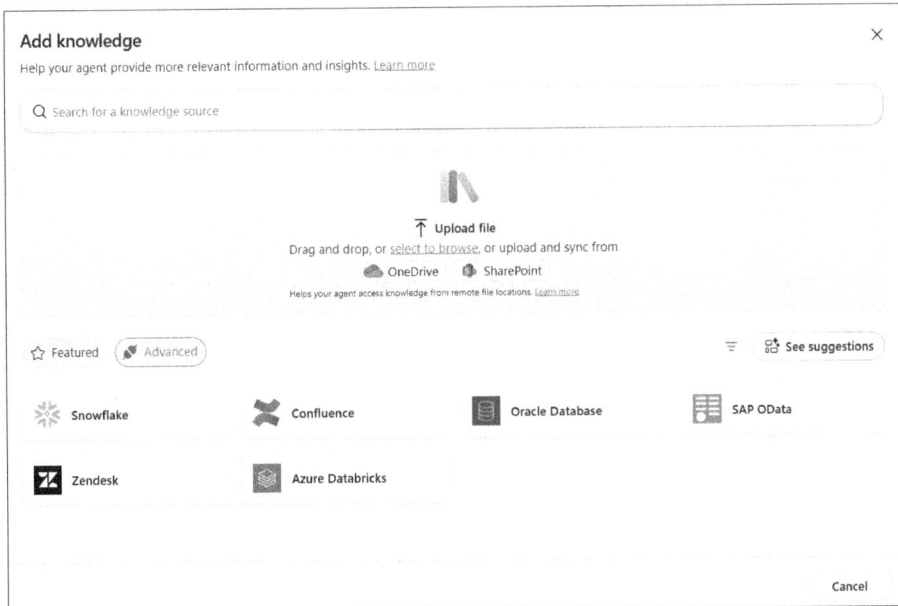

Select the Advanced button to view more available knowledge connectors.

3. Select the connector you want to work with. In this case, we are using the **Confluence** connector.

4. You will make the connection by signing in with your credentials. Select the connection to expand the menu, and then select **Create new connection**. Follow the prompts to log in with your credentials, review and allow the requested permissions, and create the connection.

> **✓ TIP** If an administrator has already set up the connector in the Microsoft 365 admin center, there will be an existing Copilot connector that you can use instead of setting up the real-time connector. You can select that Copilot connector and select **Add**, then skip to step 8.

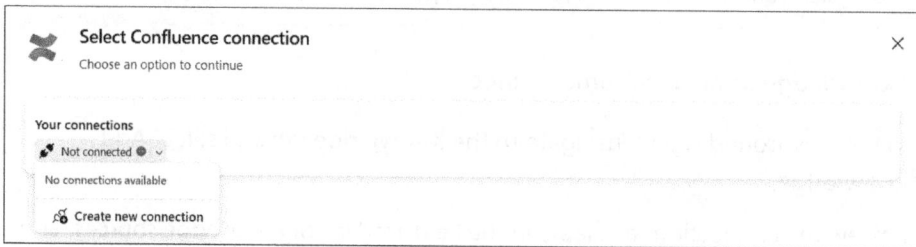

Create a new connection to the enterprise system by logging in with your credentials.

5. If you have multiple options in your knowledge source to choose from, such as Spaces in Confluence, select the specific areas you want to include as knowledge. Then select **Next**.

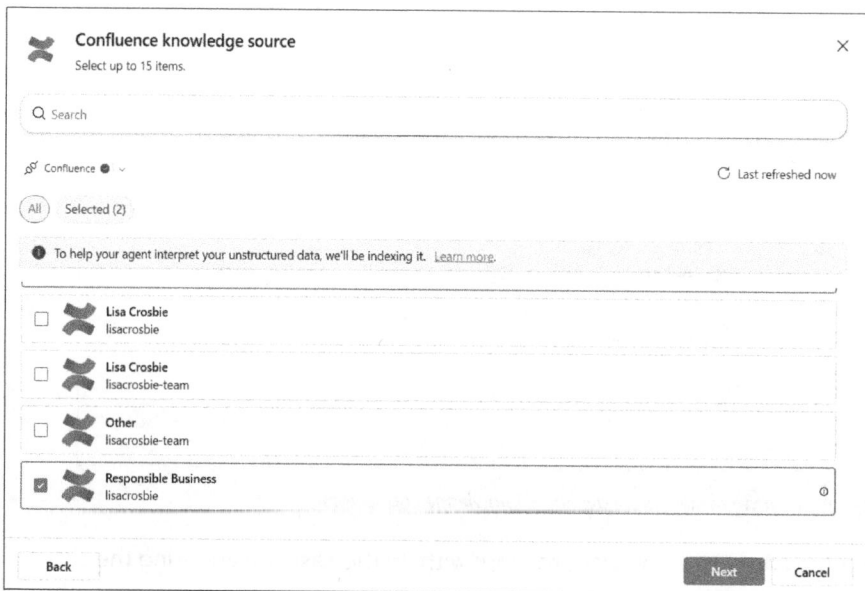

Select the spaces you want to add as knowledge.

6. Review the knowledge source details and select **Add to agent**.

7. When the connection has been established, it will appear in the list of knowledge sources for your agent. It will appear as a Power Platform connector if you connect by logging in with your credentials, or as a Copilot connector if you used the existing connection set up by an administrator.

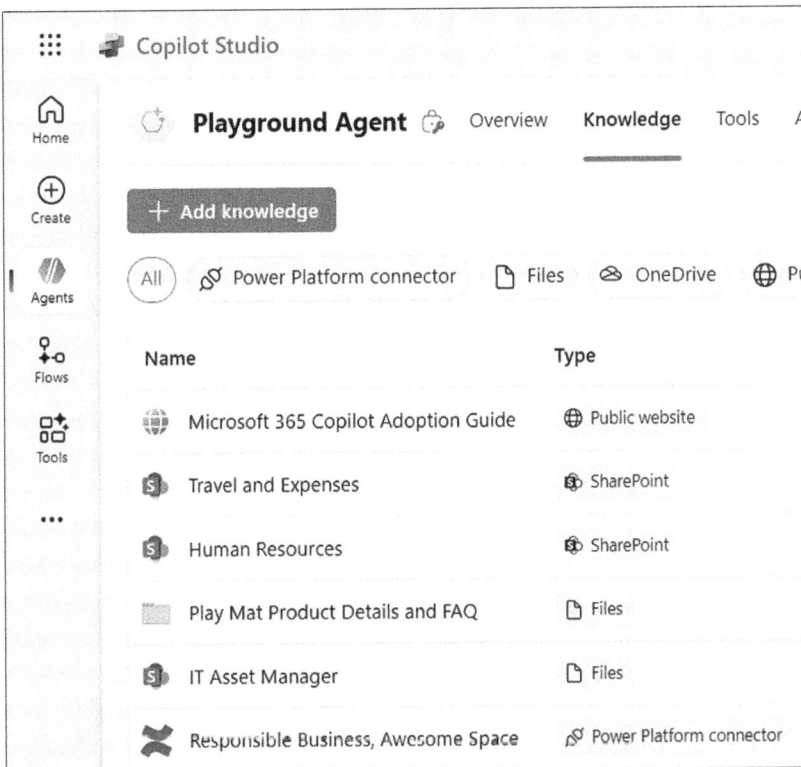

The Confluence connector appears in the list of knowledge sources for the agent.

8. Refresh the **test** pane, then test the agent by asking a question related to knowledge in the source you connected.

> **SEE ALSO** If you get a message in the test chat saying that you need to verify your credentials, follow the steps in the earlier section "Manage connections."

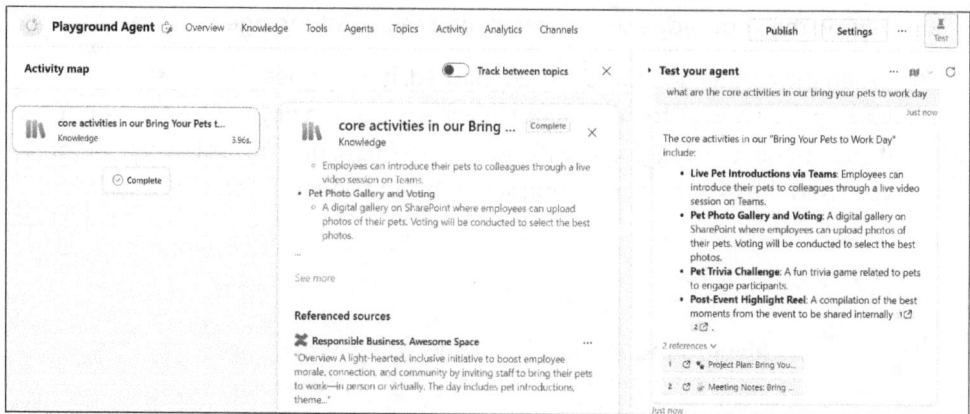

The agent responds to the question using the Confluence spaces as knowledge.

> ✅ **TIP** After you have added several knowledge sources at the agent level, you may find
> that the agent is less reliable about identifying the right knowledge source or finding
> the right answer, particularly if there is overlap or ambiguity in the knowledge you have added.
> In a real-world scenario, the work you do in designing the agent to be a subject-matter expert
> on a limited amount and range of knowledge, and taking the time to write effective names and
> descriptions, is important to create an effective agent. You may need to create a second
> Playground Agent to continue adding and effectively testing more knowledge sources.

Add Dataverse tables as a knowledge source

The real-time connector to Dataverse enables you to use the data in Dataverse tables
as a knowledge source for your agent. This connector has some additional features
and steps that allow you to describe your data structure and terminology using
synonyms and glossary definitions. The aim is to help your agent better understand
your data and how to use it as knowledge.

Synonyms allow you to describe the column names in your table by adding the terminology your users commonly use. For instance, if the Account table is a list of your
customers, a user might ask about a "customer" or a "company," even though the
name of the customer is found in a column called "Account Name." Synonyms are
particularly helpful if the column names in your database are unclear or ambiguous.

Glossary definitions help the agent understand your business- or industry-specific
terminology or abbreviations. They can prove beneficial if your users commonly
use terminology or acronyms that may not be easily understood or interpreted by
the LLM.

> ✓ **TIP** For this exercise, you will need to have Dataverse in your environment, with data populated in the tables you are adding as knowledge. If you don't have existing data in Dataverse, you can use sample data. There is an option to add sample data when you set up a new environment, or you can install or remove it by following the instructions here: https://learn.microsoft.com/en-us/power-platform/admin/add-remove-sample-data.

To add Dataverse tables as a knowledge source

1. In the Playground Agent, navigate to the **Knowledge** tab and select **Add knowledge**.

2. In the **Featured** list of knowledge sources, select the **Dataverse** button.

3. The Dataverse knowledge source allows you to select up to 15 tables. Use the check box to select the table(s) you want to add. In this example, we are using the **Account** table.

Select the Dataverse table(s) you want to add as knowledge.

4. Select **Add to agent**.

5. The Dataverse table is added to the list of knowledge sources. Select it to open and edit the properties for this table as a knowledge source.

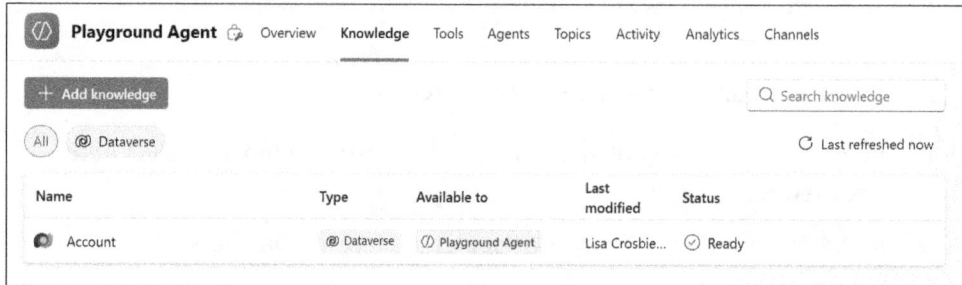

The Dataverse table is added to the list of knowledge sources.

6. Edit the **Description** to provide the agent with more information about what this data source is and how it will be used.

> ✅ **TIP** You can enter up to 2500 characters in the **Description**. If the table is something very specific to your business or scenario, you can describe it in detail here, explaining any industry terminology that will help the agent understand the user intent and match it to the right table in the knowledge.

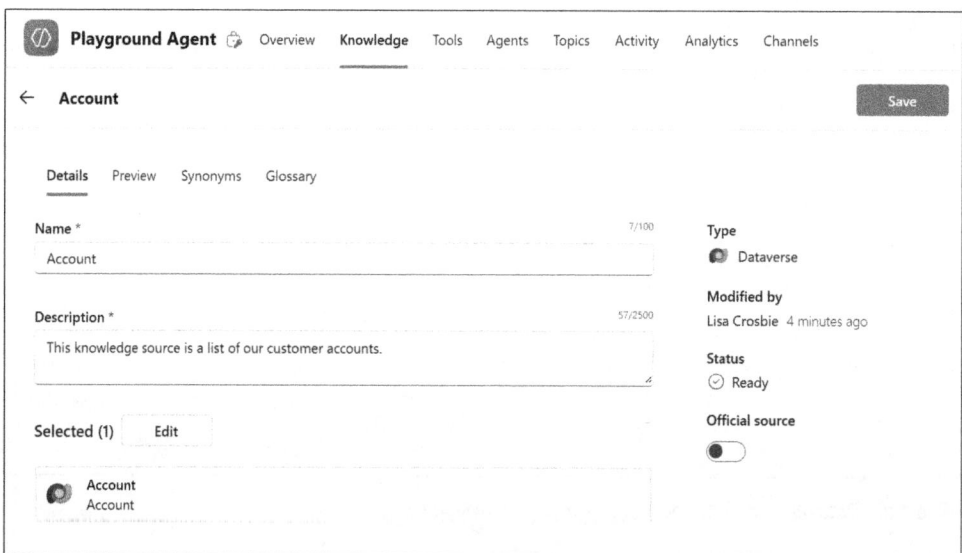

Add a description to help the agent understand what this knowledge source will be used for.

> **TIP** Select the **Preview** tab to view up to 20 rows of data in the selected table. This helps you understand the actual data in the table as you configure the synonyms and glossary.

7. Select the **Synonyms** tab. For each column in the table, you can add a description—that is, a natural language sentence that describes the purpose of the column—and synonyms. Synonyms are short words or phrases that the user may use when referring to this column.

8. In the **Account Number** column, add a **Description: The unique account number for the customer from our ERP system**.

9. Select the **Add synonyms** button for the **Account Number** column.

10. Enter a synonym: **Customer number**, then select **Add**. You can continue to add more synonyms by repeating this step.

Add synonyms for common terminology that the users are likely to use.

11. Select **Done**.

12. Repeat these steps for any other columns that need descriptions or synonyms.

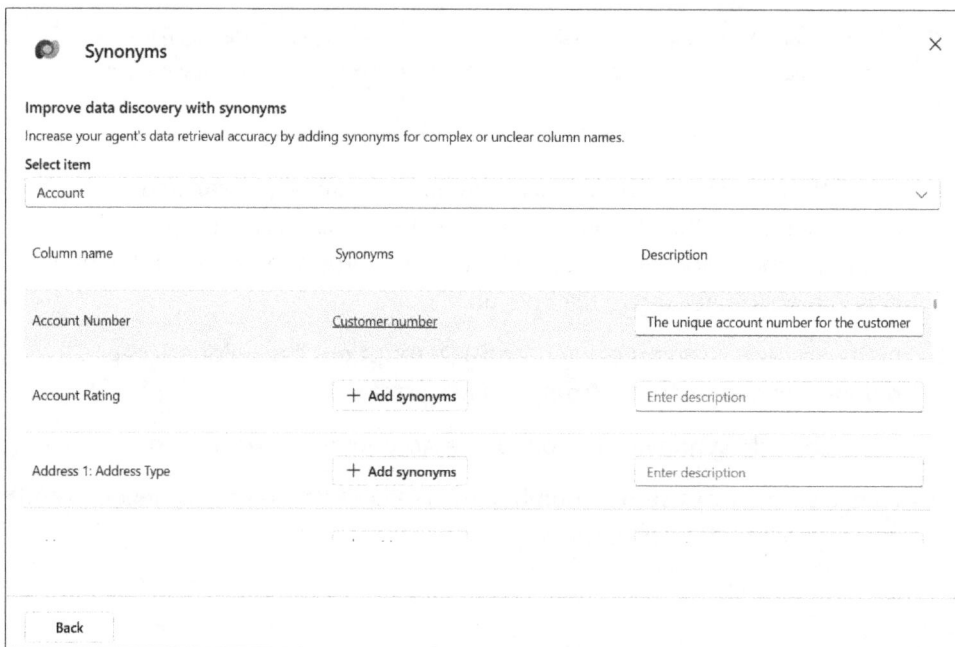

The synonyms appear against each column name as you add them.

13. When you have finished adding synonyms, select the **Save** button to save the changes.

14. Select the **Glossary** tab to edit the **Glossary.**

15. Add any business- or industry-specific terminology or acronyms here, with a definition. For example, "**AD**" means "**Account Director, Owner of the relationship with the account customer.**"

16. Select the **Add** button.

17. Continue to add any other glossary terms and definitions.

18. When you have finished adding glossary definitions, select the **Save** button.

19. Refresh the **test** pane, then test the agent by asking a question related to knowledge in the table you connected. In the question, use the terminology you added as a synonym or glossary definition.

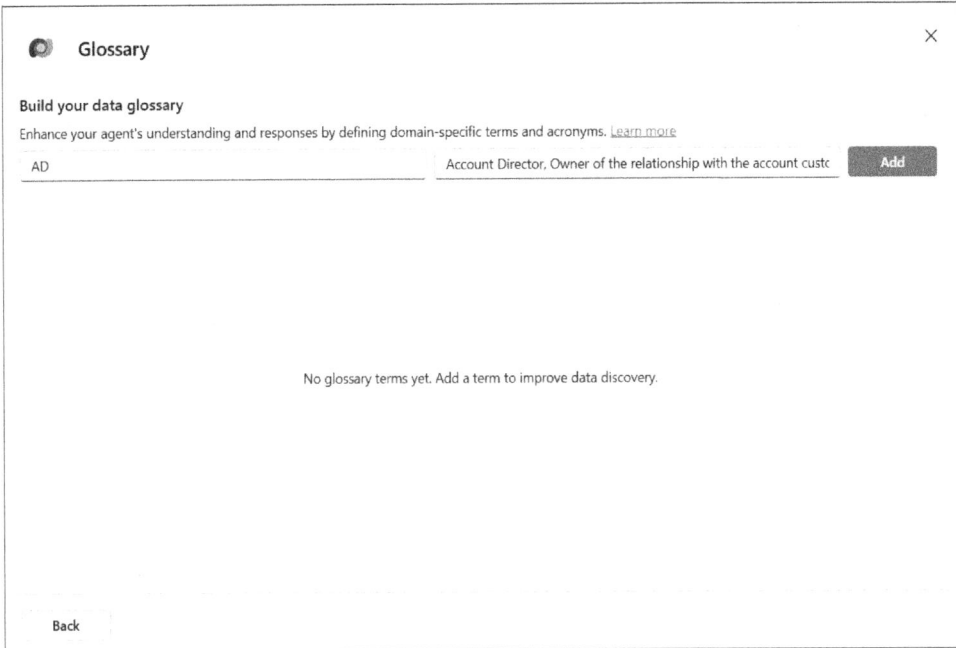

Add and define your industry- or business-specific terminology in the glossary.

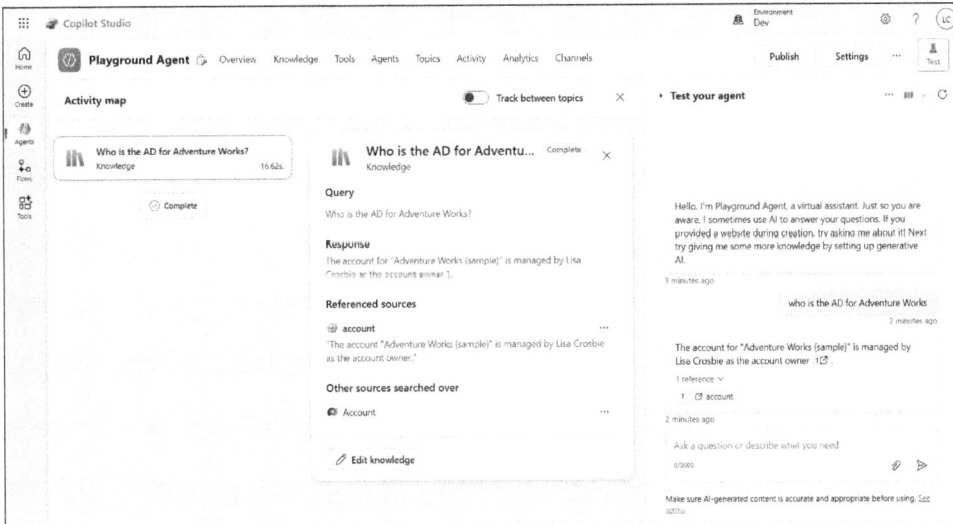

The agent understands the acronym used and responds with knowledge from the Dataverse table.

20. Select the hyperlink in the agent's response to open the Account table in Dataverse.

Best practice for working with Dataverse as a knowledge source

The configuration steps for adding Dataverse as a knowledge source are relatively straightforward. However, to make Dataverse work effectively as a knowledge source, you will need to take the time to understand, configure, test, and iterate on the column descriptions, synonyms, and glossary. In a real-world scenario, most businesses will have configured Dataverse with multiple custom tables, relationships, and columns to work for the specific needs of the business. Understanding the way the data is entered and used, and the terminology used by your business users, which may differ from the way the columns in your Dataverse database are set up, will be key to the success when using Dataverse as a knowledge source in your agent.

There are two ways to work with Dataverse tables in your agent: You can add them as a knowledge source (as shown in the example here), or you can add tools that retrieve, add, or update rows in a table.

- Add Dataverse as a knowledge source when you want your agent to generate answers based on the data stored in the tables you add. The agent will understand the unstructured natural language query from the user, find the answer, and use the LLM to generate the response.

- Add Dataverse as a tool when you want the agent to automate tasks, such as creating or updating rows in a table, or when you want to retrieve records in a more structured way.

> **SEE ALSO** Using Dataverse as a tool is covered in Chapter 8: Extending agents with tools.

Skills review

In this chapter, you learned how to:

- Use general knowledge, conversational boosting, content moderation, and official knowledge sources to impact the way generative answers work in Copilot Studio.

- Add and configure public websites as knowledge sources, and enable or disable the ability for the agent to search the web for answers.

- Upload files or folders to use as knowledge in your agent, and distinguish between uploading files and connecting to files on OneDrive or SharePoint.

- Connect to SharePoint sites and lists to use as knowledge in your agent, and follow best practice for working with SharePoint as a knowledge source.

- Add real-time connectors to add knowledge to your agent from enterprise data sources, and work with Dataverse as a knowledge source.

6

Practice tasks

No practice files are necessary to complete the practice tasks in this chapter.

Understand how knowledge works in Copilot Studio

Open Copilot Studio and then complete the following tasks:

1. Create a new agent using the configuration experience. Give the agent a name, but leave the rest of the options blank.

2. Ask the agent any general question, such as **What is Microsoft 365 Copilot?**

3. Navigate to the **Settings** for the agent.

4. In the **Generative AI** settings, navigate to the **Knowledge** section.

5. Set the **Use general knowledge** toggle switch to the **Off** position.

6. **Save** the changes.

7. Close the **Settings** screen.

8. Test the agent by asking the same question again.

Connect to public websites as a knowledge source

Using the agent in Copilot Studio you created in the previous task, complete the following tasks:

1. Navigate to the **Knowledge** tab and select **Add Knowledge**.

2. Add your organization's website URL.

3. Edit the **Name** and **Description** to describe what this knowledge source is.

4. Select **Add** to add the knowledge source to the agent.

5. Use the **test** pane to ask the agent a question that can be answered by the knowledge on your website.

6. Navigate to the **Overview** tab of the agent and then to the **Knowledge** section.

7. Enable the **Web Search** option and wait for the changes to be saved.

8. Refresh the **test** pane, then test the agent by asking a question that the agent needs real-time information from the web to answer (e.g., a recent event) and that is not on the website you added as knowledge.

Add files as a knowledge source

Using the agent in Copilot Studio you created in the previous task, complete the following tasks:

1. Navigate to the **Knowledge** tab and select **Add Knowledge**.

2. Select two files on a related subject from the files on your computer.

3. Toggle the **Group these files** option to the **On** position.

4. Edit the **Name** and **Description** of the knowledge so that they help the agent understand what this file group is for and when this knowledge will be used.

5. Select **Add** and wait for the files to be uploaded.

6. Refresh the **test** pane, then test your agent by asking it a question for which the answer is found in one of the files you uploaded.

Add SharePoint as a knowledge source

Using the agent in Copilot Studio you created in the previous task, complete the following tasks:

1. Navigate to the **Knowledge** tab and select **Add knowledge**.

2. Select the **SharePoint** button from the **Featured** list of knowledge sources.

3. Navigate to a SharePoint site where you have documents in the document library, or content on the main site page. Copy the URL of the top level of your SharePoint site.

4. Return to Copilot Studio and paste that URL into the **Add knowledge** configuration screen.

5. Select **Add**.

6. Edit the **Name** and **Description** of the SharePoint site so that they help the agent understand what it is and what it will be used for.

7. Select the **Add** button.

8. Wait until the SharePoint site is showing status "Ready" in the list of knowledge sources.

9. Refresh the **test** pane, then test your agent by asking it a question for which the answer is found on your SharePoint site content or in the files in the documents.

Add real-time connectors to enterprise data

Using the agent in Copilot Studio you created in the previous task, complete the following tasks:

1. Navigate to the **Knowledge** tab and select **Add knowledge**.

2. In the **Featured** list of knowledge sources, select the **Dataverse** button.

3. Select the **Account** table, or any other table you have configured that contains data and then select Add to agent

4. Wait for the table to be added to the list of knowledge sources in the agent. Select the table in the list of knowledge sources and edit the **Description** to provide the agent with more information about what this data source is and how it will be used.

5. Select the **Synonyms** tab. Add a **Description** and a **Synonym** for any of the columns in the table.

6. Select the **Glossary** tab. Add a glossary term and definition related to your industry or use case.

7. Select **Save**.

8. Refresh the **test** pane, then test your agent by asking it a question for which the answer is found in the data in the Dataverse table.

Authoring topics

Practice files

You will need to use the practice files provided with this chapter to complete the practice tasks.

Topics are used to build dialog flows in Copilot Studio agents where you need parts of the conversation to follow a fixed, or deterministic, path. They are useful for any part of the agent conversation where the agent is handling a business-critical or highly compliant interaction, and you need a consistent, specific answer or conversational path every time. They can also help with providing answers to questions that aren't found (or aren't easily found) in knowledge sources or with directing the agent to a specific knowledge source for an answer.

Topics are made up of a trigger that defines how the agent identifies and calls the topic, one or more nodes that send a message or ask the user a question, and branching logic that defines the path of the conversation. Nodes can also be used to send images or media responses to the user, ask a question and store the data provided as a variable to use later, call generative answers or tools, or redirect to other topics.

Copilot Studio comes with out-of-the-box system topics that provide core functions for the agent, including starting and ending the conversation, escalation, and

In this chapter

- Create and edit topics
- Use message nodes and adaptive cards
- Use questions, variables, and entities
- Use formulas, logic, and generative answers
- Manage topic transitions and internal triggers

fallback behavior. It also provides tools that enable you to author your own topics using natural language or a low-code graphical interface. In this chapter, you will learn how to author topics in Copilot Studio, and discover how to use triggers, conversational nodes, conditional branching, variables, and entities when doing so.

Create and edit topics

You can create topics by describing them with natural language or by using a graphical interface to build the topic flow from scratch. You can edit topics using a graphical interface or a YAML code editor.

In this chapter, the example used is the Surface Support Guide agent you created in Chapter 1. You will begin by adding a topic that establishes whether the user is looking to purchase a device or just wants support for their device.

> **SEE ALSO** Refer to the section "Create an agent in Copilot Studio by describing it" in Chapter 1: Understanding Copilot Studio and agents, to build the agent you will use in this chapter.

You will first learn how to create a topic by describing it in natural language, which is an easy way to get started with authoring a simple topic; it's also a quick way to create a draft of a more complex topic that you can edit later. You will then learn how to author a topic from scratch, while exploring in detail the different components you can use to build topics.

Create topics from a description and understand triggers

Topics are triggered differently depending on whether the agent uses classic or generative orchestration. In this section, you will learn how this behavior works and how to write trigger phrases or use trigger descriptions, depending on which type of agent you are designing.

> **SEE ALSO** Topics can also have internal triggers so that the agent calls the topic based on other behaviors. This is covered later in this chapter in the section "Manage topic transitions and internal triggers."

Work with topics and triggers in classic orchestration

Begin with an agent that uses classic orchestration. The generative AI orchestration setting should be set to **Disabled**.

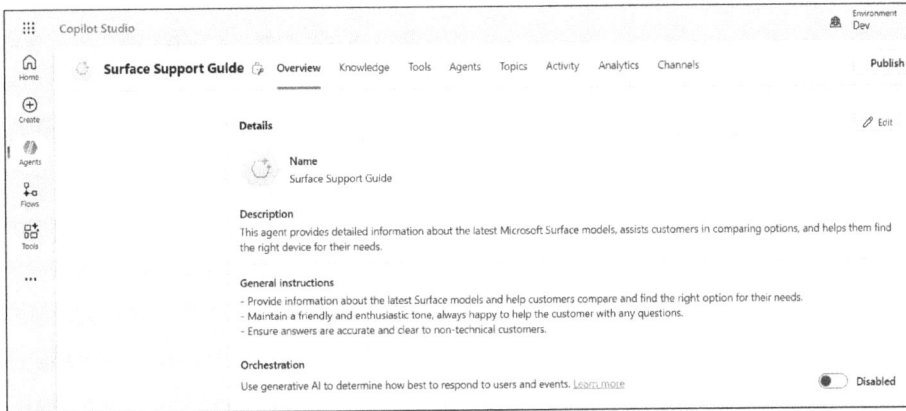

Begin with an agent using classic orchestration, with generative AI orchestration disabled.

To create a topic by describing it

1. Select the **Topics** tab from the top navigation menu of the agent.

2. Select the **Add a topic** button.

3. From the drop-down menu, select **Add from description with Copilot**.

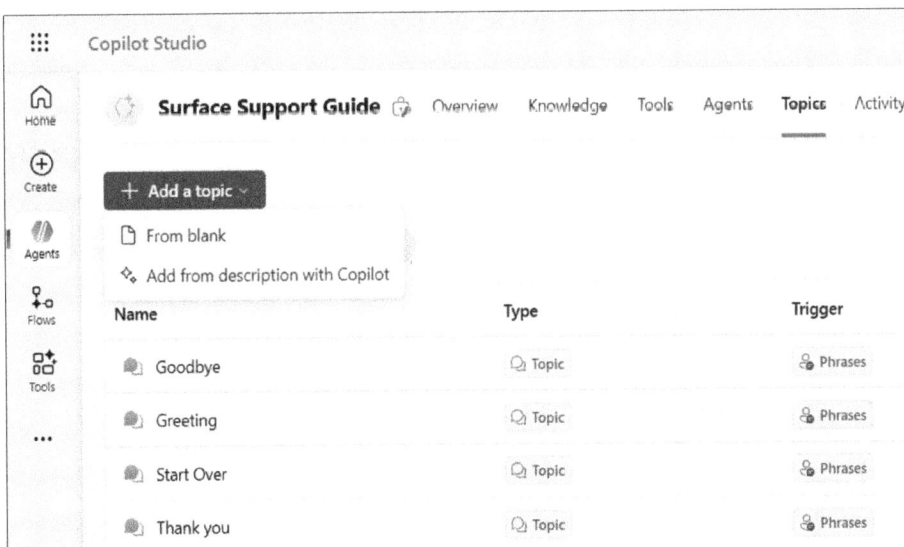

Create a topic by choosing the option to "Add from description with Copilot."

4. In the pop-up window that appears, you will enter the name of the topic and a description of what you want the topic to do. You should give the topic a meaningful name that will help the agent understand what it is for, and describe the logic of the topic in clear language. For this example, enter the following details:

   - Name: **Sales or Support**

   - Create a topic to: **Ask the user whether they want to learn about surface devices or whether they have an existing device and need support. If they ask for support, please ask them for the details of the device model.**

> **TIP** You can use the examples provided to get started with learning how to use this feature. You can also use the refresh icon under the examples to get more ideas about ways to describe a topic to build it.

Add from description with Copilot   ✕

Write a description of what you'd like your agent to cover, and Copilot will create your topic. Learn more

Name your topic *

Sales or support

Create a topic to... *

Ask the user whether they want to learn about surface devices or whether they have an existing device and need support. If they ask for support, please ask them for the details of the device model.

AI-generated content can have mistakes. Make sure it's accurate and appropriate before using it. Read terms

Or try one of these examples to get started

- Let someone order a pizza, choosing from common pizza types and how many they want to order.

- Accept a user's name, age and date of birth and then repeat their responses back to them.

- Collect a user's street address, state and zip code. The user should be able to retry each question up to 4 times.

View more examples

What does Copilot support?   [Create]   [Cancel]

Name your topic and describe the logic of what you want it to do.

5. Select the **Create** button to create the topic based on your description.

6. Your new topic appears in the topic authoring canvas. To the right of the authoring canvas is an **Edit with Copilot** pane that you can use to describe any changes you want to make, while continuing to build the topic in natural language.

Edit with Copilot ⑦   ✕

Move nodes in the canvas. To make additions and changes to nodes, tell Copilot what you want to do. Learn more

What do you want to do?

Explain what you want to change or add to the topic. Select a node to be more specific.

Update   No nodes selected

What you asked for

"Ask the user whether they want to learn ab..."

What we added

⑦   **Question**
     Do you want to learn about Surface devic...

     Condition
꙲   (x) Topic.DeviceChoice is equal to _

⑦   **Question**
     Please provide the details of your device ...

⑲   **Send activity**
     Great! Let's learn about Surface devices.

You can continue to edit and build the topic with Copilot using natural language.

7. Review how the topic has been built based on your instructions. The topic begins with a **Trigger**, which consists of a list of phrases that the agent will use to match the user intent with this topic. Below the trigger is a question node.

8. Navigate down to view the rest of the topic:

    • The Question node has multiple-choice options and branching logic based on whether the user is interested in **Learning about Surface devices** or **Support for an existing device**.

    • Note that the support branch has an extra node below it that asks the user for their device model.

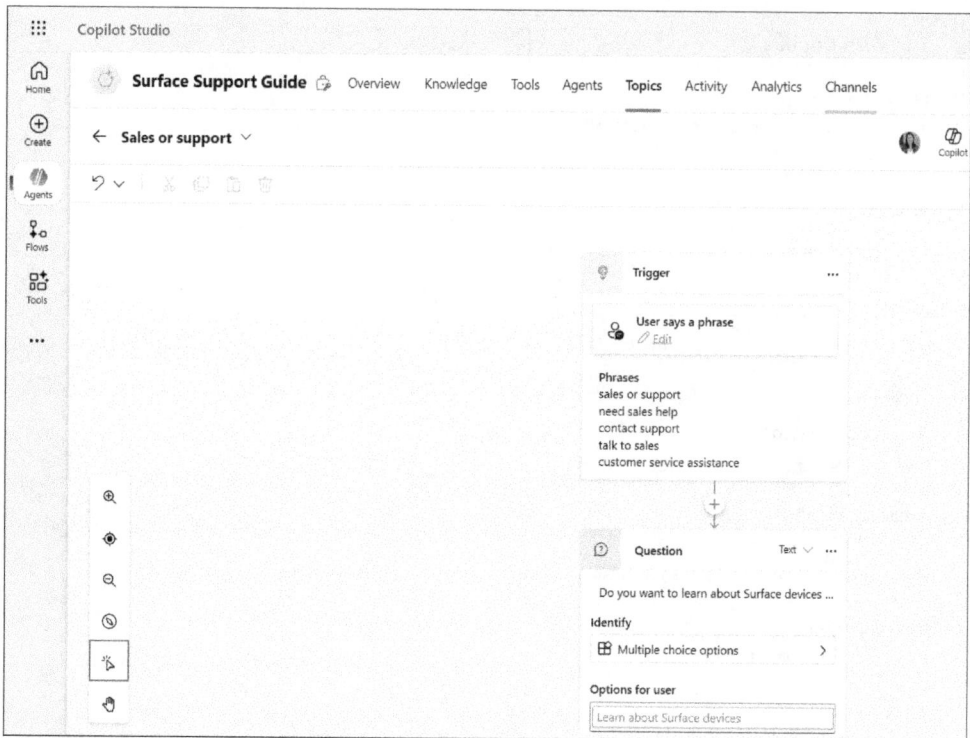

The topic starts with a set of trigger phrases and a question asking the user if they are interested in learning about Surface devices or getting support for an existing device.

> ⚠ **IMPORTANT** When you describe a topic to build it, you may not get exactly the same result every time because generative AI will not always produce the same result from the same prompt. Your topic may not be an exact match to the one shown here even if you use the same description.

> ✓ **TIP** Use the icons at the bottom left of the authoring canvas to zoom or pan in and out as you work.

9. Select the **Save** button at the top right of the authoring canvas.

> ⚠ **IMPORTANT** The AI-generated topic is in draft mode and will not be saved to your agent until you select the **Save** button.

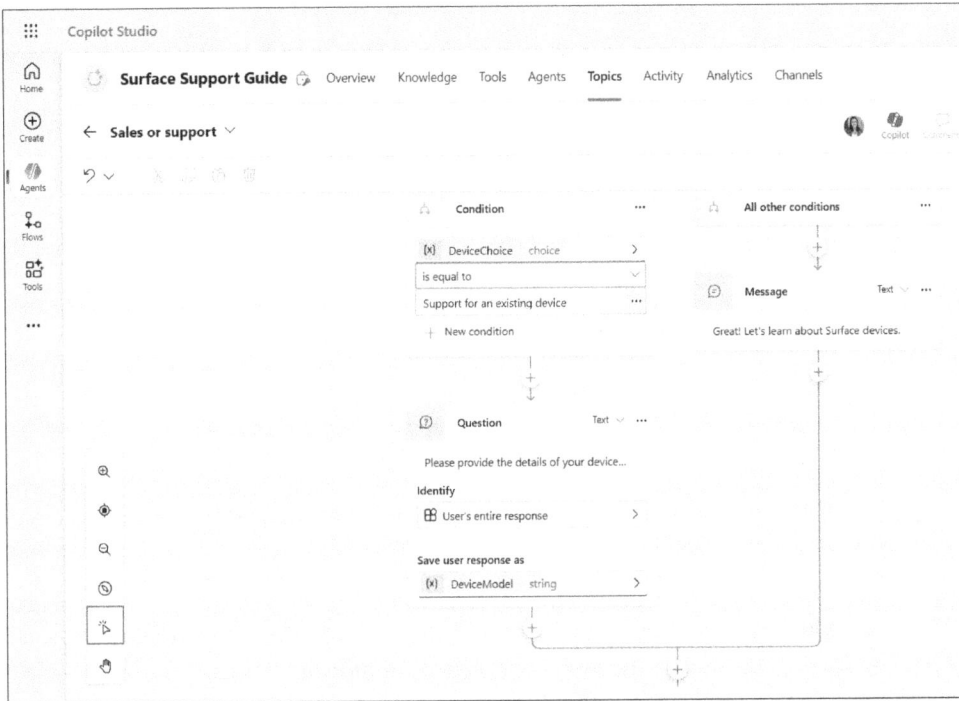

The branch of the topic where the user is looking for service includes a node that asks them for their device model.

Now that you have built the topic, it's time to test it. When you are working with an agent that uses classic orchestration, the agent will look for the trigger phrases, or phrases with similar intent, in the user input to match and call this topic.

To increase the visibility into how your agent is working with topics using classic orchestration, you can use the **Track between topics** function. It displays the topic and the stage of the topic as you test.

To test a topic in an agent using classic orchestration

1. In the **test** pane, select the three dots at the top right to expand the menu of options.

2. Toggle the **Track between topics** option to the **On** position.

3. Test your agent by using one of the trigger phrases in the **test** pane: **I need to contact support**.

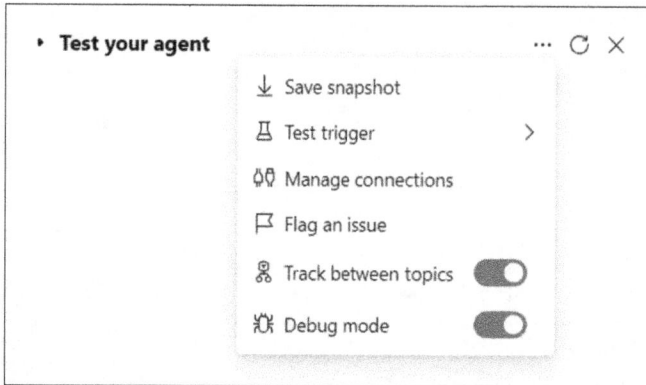

Enable the Track between topics option to test an agent that uses classic orchestration.

> ✅ **TIP** If the trigger phrases in your topic are slightly different from the ones shown here, use a trigger phrase about support from your topic.

4. This will trigger the topic you just created, providing the user with two choices to select from. Select **Support for an existing device**.

5. To the left of the **test** pane, the view changes to display the topic the agent has triggered and show how it is tracking the topic. As you progress through testing the conversation, the tracking will display which node is currently active and the path that the conversation has followed.

6. The agent responds by asking for the details of your device.

7. Reply with the name of a Surface model: **Surface Laptop 3**.

8. At this point the conversation reaches an unnatural endpoint, as the agent doesn't respond to the user input. The topic finishes at this point and the agent doesn't continue the conversation.

> 🔍 **SEE ALSO** You will learn how to continue building the topic, end topics, and redirect the conversation throughout this chapter.

9. Refresh the **test** pane and try again, this time using a phrase that might represent the same user intent, but that isn't in the set of trigger phrases for your topic: **I need help with my Surface device**.

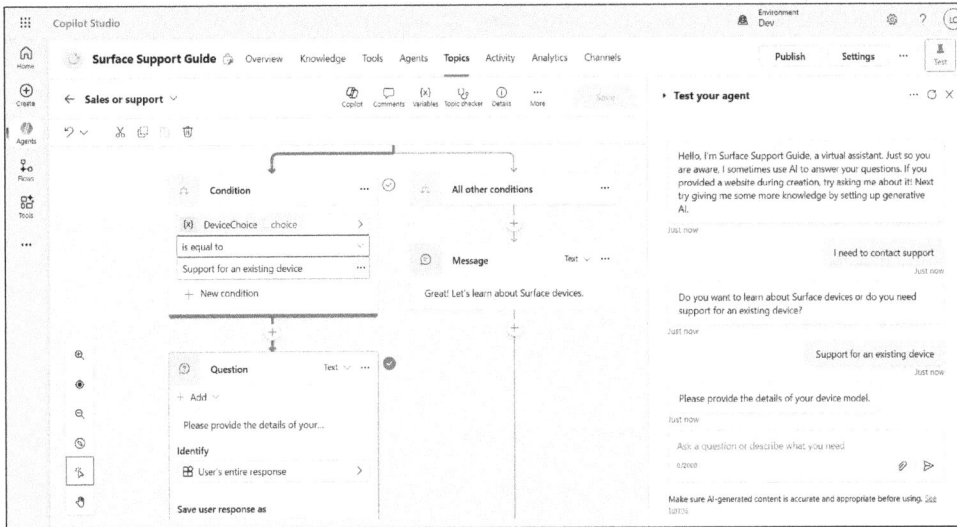

As you test your agent, the topic is shown to the left of the test panel so you can understand which topic has been called and what the active node is.

> **TIP** If your topic trigger phrases differ from those in the example, try something similar that isn't a trigger phrase in your topic.

10. The agent doesn't trigger the topic and falls back to the **Conversational boosting** topic to answer from the knowledge on the public website.

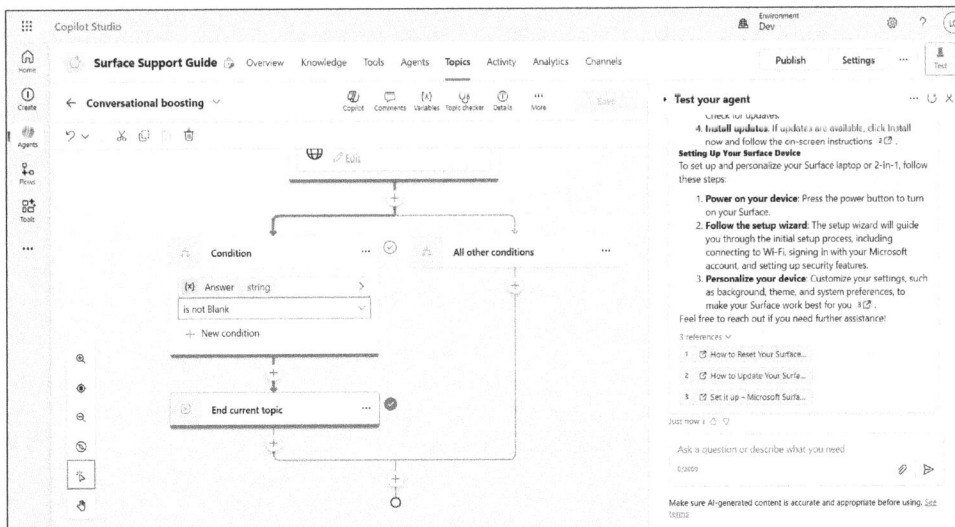

The agent triggers the Conversational boosting topic and responds using website knowledge.

11. Continue to test the agent using different trigger phrases to understand when it calls the **Sales or service** topic, and when it fails to do so and falls back on the **Conversational boosting** topic.

When you are working with topics using classic orchestration, the effectiveness of your agent will depend on how well you design and write the trigger phrases so that the right topic is triggered based on the user intent. It is also important to disambiguate topics so that it is clear to the agent which topic it should trigger and when. In this example, we have used the AI-generated trigger phrases, which do not define this topic well enough for it to be triggered reliably in the way we may have intended.

Some tips for writing effective trigger phrases:

- Give the agent 5–10 short phrases of 5–15 words. Do not use long or complex sentences. Punctuation, capitalization, and correct grammar don't matter here; the model will ignore them.

- Use different words and different sentence structures to describe the same thing in different ways. You need enough variety so that the natural language understanding (NLU) model can generalize across similar phrases to understand the intent.

- Consider the terminology your users will use and include that in the trigger phrases. Use real user interactions or test data if possible.

> **TIP** You can use Copilot or your generative AI tool of choice to describe the topic and ask it to help you generate trigger phrases, or to review your trigger phrases and offer suggestions to improve them.

To edit the trigger phrases for a topic

1. Select the **Topics** option from the top menu.

2. In the list of **Custom** topics, select the topic you just created, **Sales or support**, to open it for editing.

> **TIP** Close the test panel using the X at the top right so that there is more space available on the screen for the authoring canvas.

3. Select the **Edit** link in the **Trigger** node.

> ✓ **TIP** Select the **Show writing tips** link to expand a list of tips for writing effective trigger phrases. Select the **Hide writing tips** link to collapse that content.

Select the Edit option in the Trigger node to edit the trigger phrases for the topic.

4. In the **Add phrases** pane, you can enter text to add new trigger phrases. You can also remove existing trigger phrases by hovering over them and selecting the **Delete** icon.

Add phrases

Phrases teach the agent different ways someone
might ask about this topic. Natural language
understanding helps identify a topic based on
meaning and not exact words.

| Enter text | + |

To add items in bulk, paste in line-separated items or
use Shift+Enter to create line separation or
upload a file | download

Delete

sales or support 🗑

need sales help

contact support

talk to sales

customer service assistance

get technical support

speak with a sales representative

Hover over an existing trigger phrase and select the Delete icon to delete it.

5. Hover over the existing trigger phrases and remove some of the less useful ones
    by selecting the **Delete** icon for each. For example, remove any generic phrases
    that a user would be unlikely to use, such as "sales or support" and "need sales
    help."

6. Add some more meaningful trigger phrases that represent the way the user
    would interact with the agent, covering both sales and support scenarios.
    For example:

    • help with my surface device

    • problem with my laptop

    • device isn't working

    • interested in buying a new laptop

- learn about new devices

- want to buy a new device

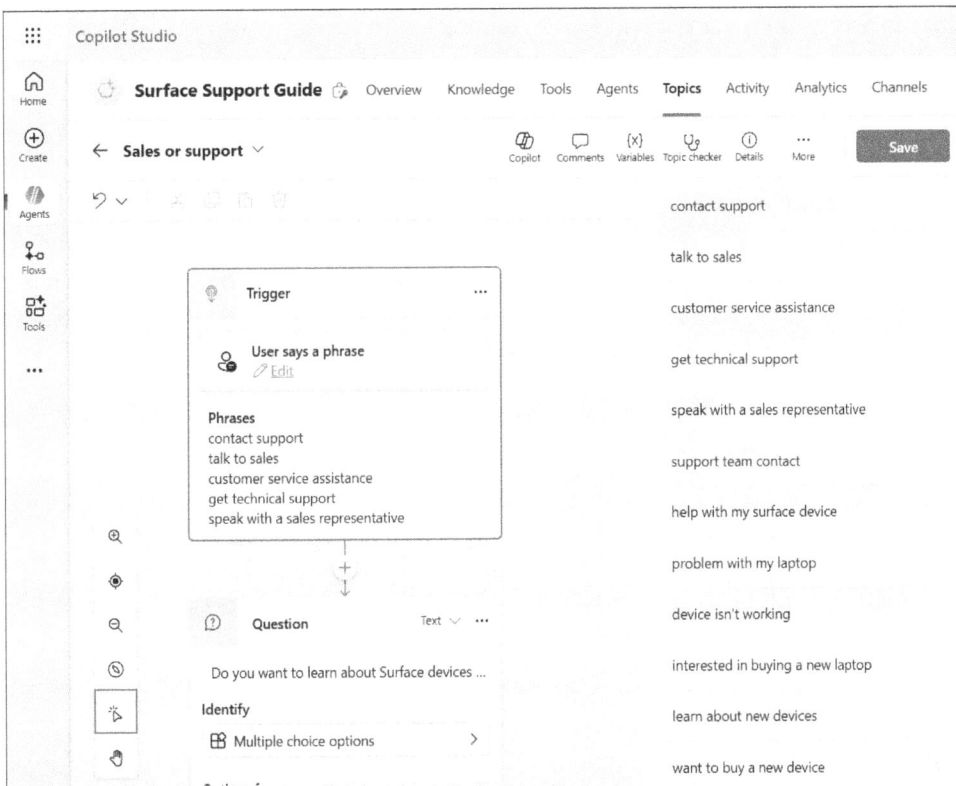

Add new trigger phrases that represent the way the user would interact with the agent.

7. Select the **Save** button.

8. Refresh the **test** pane and test your agent again with the trigger phrases you used earlier, where the agent used the fallback topic. For instance, try the trigger phrase: **I need help with my Surface device**. This time the agent understands the intent and calls the topic.

9. Continue to test by using other variations to assess how effective your trigger phrases are and where there are gaps. Test something that has a different context, such as: **My child needs a new laptop for school**. The agent will most likely fall back to the Conversational boosting topic to respond from knowledge.

In a real-world scenario, you would iterate this process as you build the agent, both across each topic and across all the topics you author, to ensure each topic has a clear intent that is disambiguated from the other topics. You would also design the way you want the topics to interact or hand off to each other to continue the natural flow of the conversation. This design is covered later in this chapter.

Work with topics and triggers in generative orchestration

When you use generative orchestration, the agent uses the topic name and description instead of trigger phrases to trigger the topic. An agent using generative orchestration uses the LLM to understand the description of the topic and to match it to the user intent. This is a more sophisticated capability than the NLU intent matching to trigger phrases used in classic orchestration.

When you author topics for an agent using generative orchestration, you will use a description in the trigger rather than a set of trigger phrases.

> **TIP** If you create a topic by describing it in an agent with generative orchestration enabled, the trigger will be generated with a description. You will not need to edit trigger phrases as described in the previous example.

If you switch your agent from classic to generative orchestration, the trigger phrases in any previously authored topics will be converted to descriptions.

To edit a trigger for an agent using generative orchestration

1. Return to the **Overview** tab of your agent and toggle the generative AI orchestration setting to **Enabled**.

2. Select the **Settings** for the agent and switch off the **Use general knowledge** setting.

3. Select the **Topics** tab on the top menu.

4. Select the **Sales or support** topic from the list of **Custom** topics.

5. Note that the **Trigger** node in your topic no longer has a set of trigger phrases. The trigger phrases have been replaced by a description.

> ✅ **TIP** When you convert an agent from classic orchestration to generative orchestration, the trigger phrases are turned into a description, which consists of a list of some of the keywords from the trigger phrases. If you create a new topic using Copilot, the trigger description will be written in a similar way based on your prompt. This isn't necessarily a good way to write a description, and you may get better results by writing it from scratch in natural language in a way that explains to the agent what the topic is for.

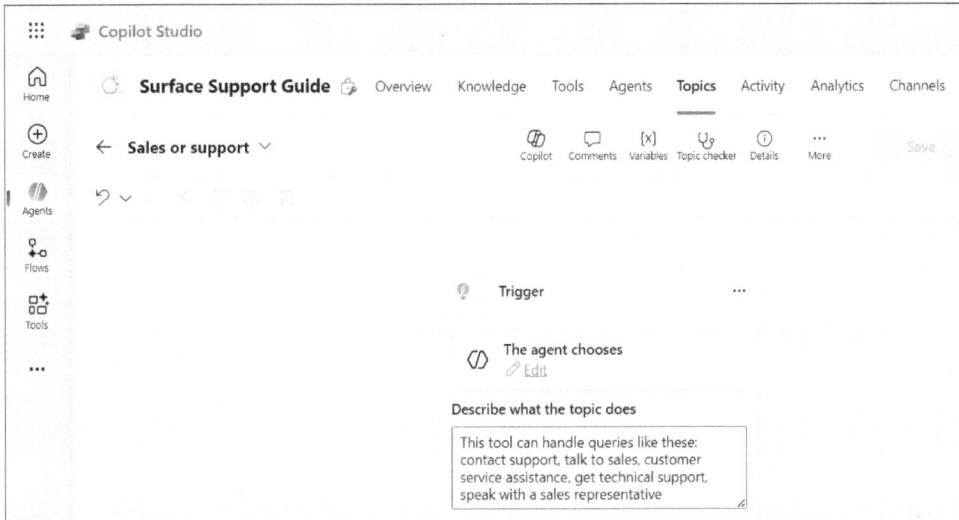

The topic you authored earlier now has a description in the trigger instead of trigger phrases.

6. Select the **Description** area and rewrite the description using language that will help the agent understand when to trigger this topic. **This tool is designed to guide the customer toward either sales or service depending on their needs. They might ask for help finding a new device, replacing a device, or express that there is some kind of problem or issue with their existing device.**

7. Select the **Save** button.

8. Test the agent by using one of the phrases you used earlier that worked with classic orchestration: **I need help with my Surface device.**

9. The topic is triggered, and you can track the topic and the path the agent is following in the topic tracker to the left of the **test** pane.

10. Refresh the **test** pane and test with another phrase that didn't work with classic orchestration: **My child needs a new laptop for school.** This time the agent understands that the intent matches this topic and calls the topic.

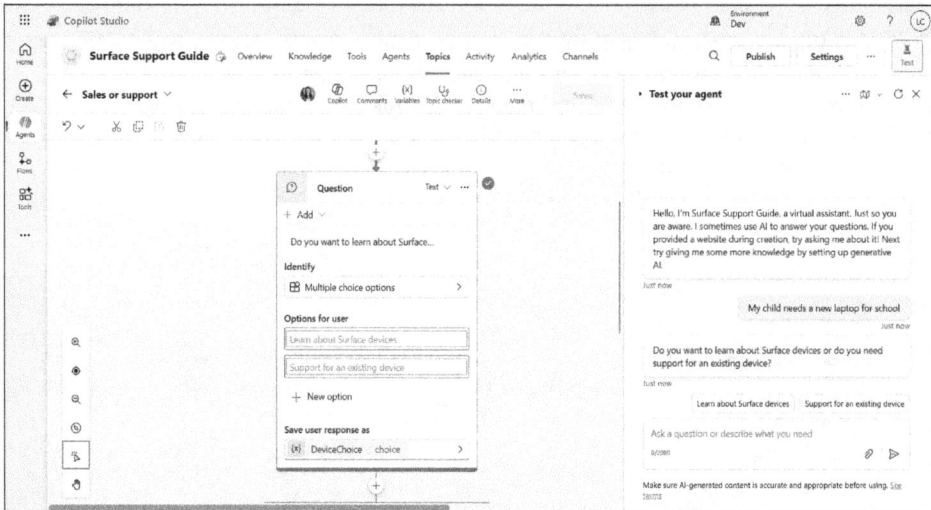

Using generative orchestration, the agent understands that the intent of the user matches this topic.

11. Select the **left arrow** next to the topic name to return to the main **Topics** screen.

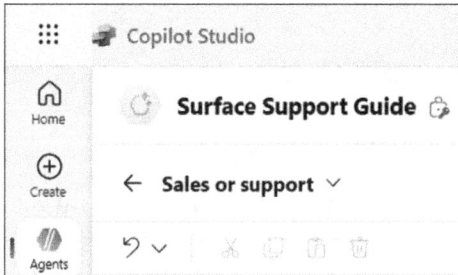

Select the arrow to the left of the topic name to navigate back to the main Topics screen.

The agent uses the LLM to understand the purpose of this topic and the intent it should match in a more sophisticated way than when using trigger phrases. You will still need to plan your topics and the purpose and intent of each, ensuring that your descriptions are meaningful and don't overlap with other topics or tools that you have described for the agent.

Create topics from blank

Although creating topics by describing them is a quick way to get started, sometimes you might prefer to have full control over how they are configured. In that case, you can use the authoring canvas to create your own topic from a blank canvas.

In this section, you will create a topic for the Surface Support Guide agent that helps customers through the process of understanding a power cord recall and supporting them to order a free replacement.

> **SEE ALSO** The content and images used in this section are based on the content on a Microsoft support website that describes a Microsoft AC power cord recall for eligible Surface Pro 3 or earlier devices. You can view the full content and get image links here: https://support.microsoft.com/en-us/surface/microsoft-ac-power-cord-recall-for-eligible-surface-pro-3-or-earlier-devices-4d46b233-acd2-9714-9ece-0ff48327fbc5.

> **TIP** Multiple users can edit an agent at the same time. At the top of the authoring canvas is a presence indicator showing the avatar or initials for any other active users.

To create a topic from blank

1. In the **Topics** tab of the agent, select the **+Add a topic** button.

2. In the drop-down options, select **From blank**.

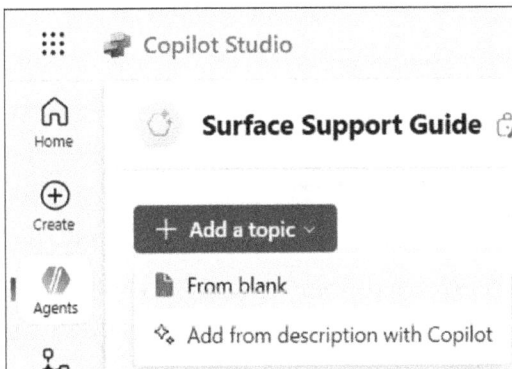

Select Add a topic and then select the "From blank" option.

3. This opens a new blank topic in the authoring canvas. It has a placeholder topic name, "**Untitled**," and a **Trigger** node with nothing in it.

4. Select the topic name at the top left of the authoring canvas, and replace the placeholder name with the topic name: **Power cord recall**.

> ✅ **TIP** Choose a topic name that is clear and unambiguous, and that will help the agent understand what this topic is used for.

5. Select a spot anywhere on the canvas outside the topic name.

6. Edit the description in the trigger, describing for the agent what this topic will be used for: **This topic will help customers with the power cord recall for eligible Surface Pro 3 or earlier devices. It will help them determine if their Surface Pro power cord is eligible, and if so, how to order a free replacement.**

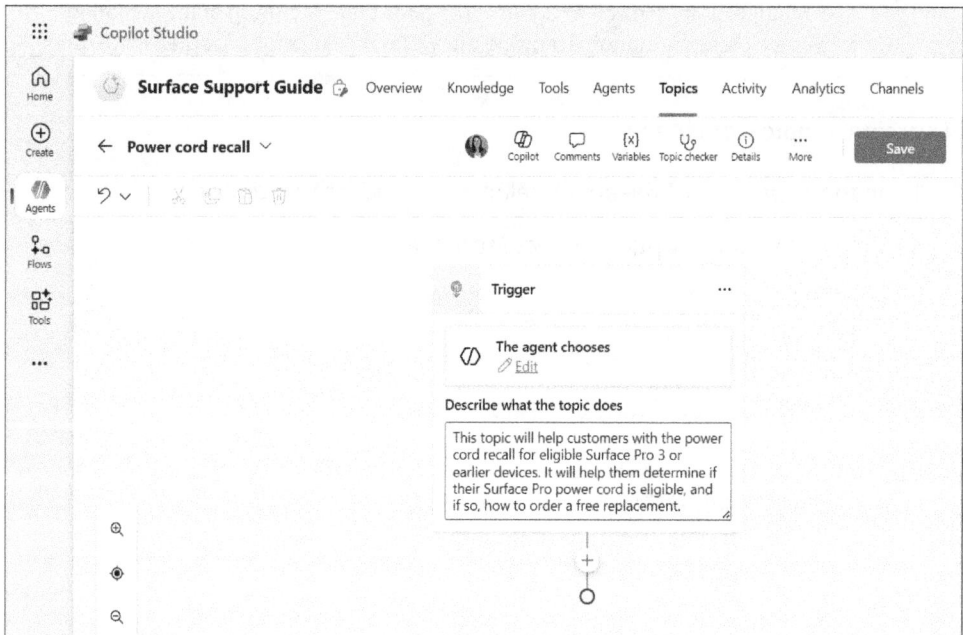

Edit the description for the trigger and then select Save to save your topic.

7. Select the **Save** button to save your topic.

8. Select the + icon below the **Trigger** node to expand the menu of available options for authoring your topic.

Trigger ...

The agent chooses
✎ Edit

Describe what the topic does
This topic will help customers with the powe...

✕

📋 Paste

💬 Send a message

💬 Ask a question

📋 Ask with adaptive card

⤷ Add a condition

{x} Variable management   >

🗨 Topic management   >

⚡ Add a tool   >

💼 Advanced   >

7

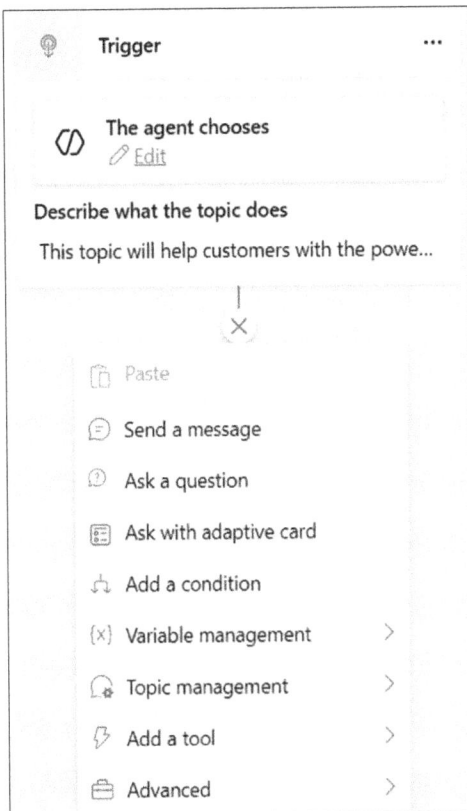

Select the + icon on the canvas under the Trigger node to expand the list of authoring tools you can use.

This menu displays the types of nodes and capabilities available to you for authoring a topic. In the remainder of this chapter, you will learn about these different types of nodes and how to use them to build your topic.

Edit topics using code

This chapter shows you how to build topics using the low-code interface. If you prefer to work in code, you have the option to switch to editing the topics in the code editor using YAML once they are created.

When you create a node on the authoring canvas, Copilot Studio automatically generates YAML in the background. You can choose to view or edit that code, or you can copy and paste the YAML into the code editor.

To edit a topic using the code editor

1. Create a new topic "From blank," as explained in the previous exercise.

2. Select the **... More** option at the top right of the authoring canvas to expand the menu of more options.

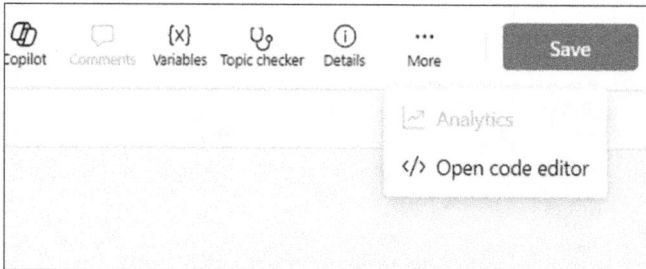

Select the More option to expand the menu and open the code editor.

3. Select the **</> Open code editor** option.

4. View and edit the YAML for the topic.

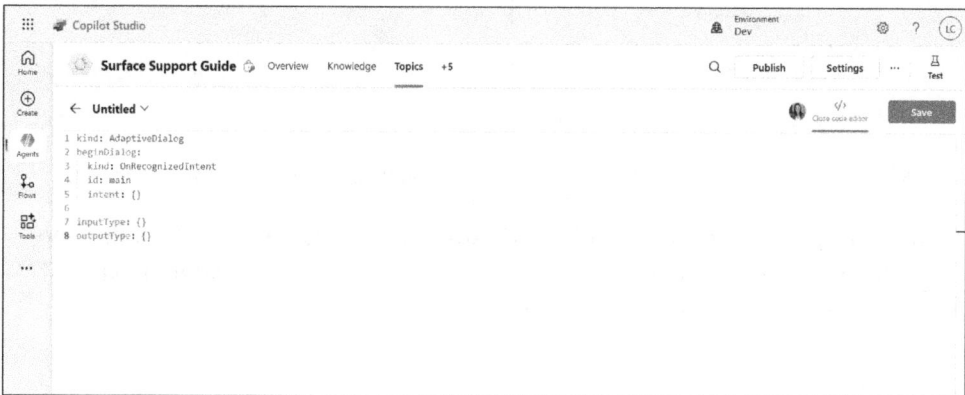

You can edit topics using YAML in the code editor.

5. When you have finished editing, select the **Save** button to save your changes and then close the code editor.

> **SEE ALSO** For more information on the code editor and using YAML in Copilot Studio, refer to https://learn.microsoft.com/en-us/microsoft-copilot-studio/guidance/topics-code-editor.

> ⚠ **IMPORTANT** This method of editing is recommended only for developers and advanced users with experience working in code. Small errors in punctuation and syntax can break the topic or cause complex errors.

Use message nodes and adaptive cards

Message nodes are what the agent uses to send a message to the user. A message node can be a simple string of text or rich text with formatting, or it can include other media components like images, videos, or adaptive cards.

Add a message node

In this exercise, you will start to build out the topic you created from blank by adding a message node under the trigger.

To create a message node

1. Return to the **Power cord recall** topic in the Surface Support Guide agent.

2. In the authoring canvas for your topic, select the + button directly below the **Trigger** node to expand the menu of options.

3. Select the **Send a message** node.

4. The Message node is added to the authoring canvas below the trigger. Enter a message in the space provided: **We're recalling and replacing the Microsoft AC power cord for the original Surface Pro, Surface Pro 2, and certain Surface Pro 3 devices. I can help you with information about what devices are included in the recall and, if your Surface Pro power cord is eligible, how to order a free replacement.**

5. Select the **Save** button.

6. Test your topic by refreshing the **test** pane and then entering a question that will trigger this topic: **Is my power cord recalled?**

7. The agent responds with the message you entered in the Message node. The topic tracker shows that this topic has been activated and the Message node is being used in the conversation.

7

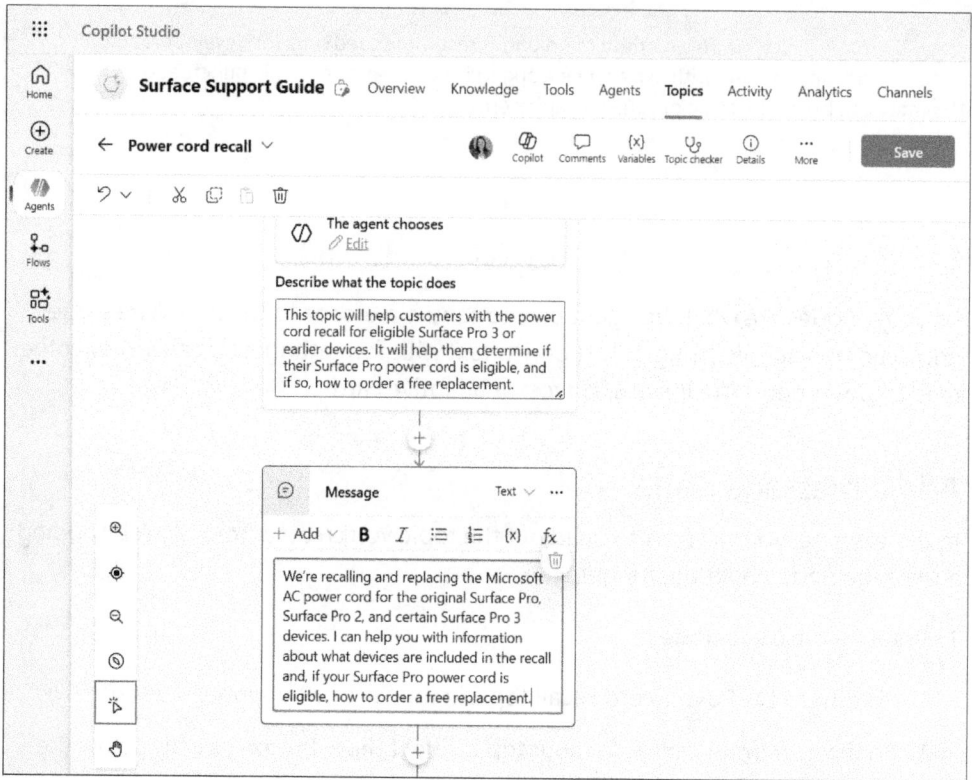

Add a Message node and add the text that you want the agent to send as a message to the user.

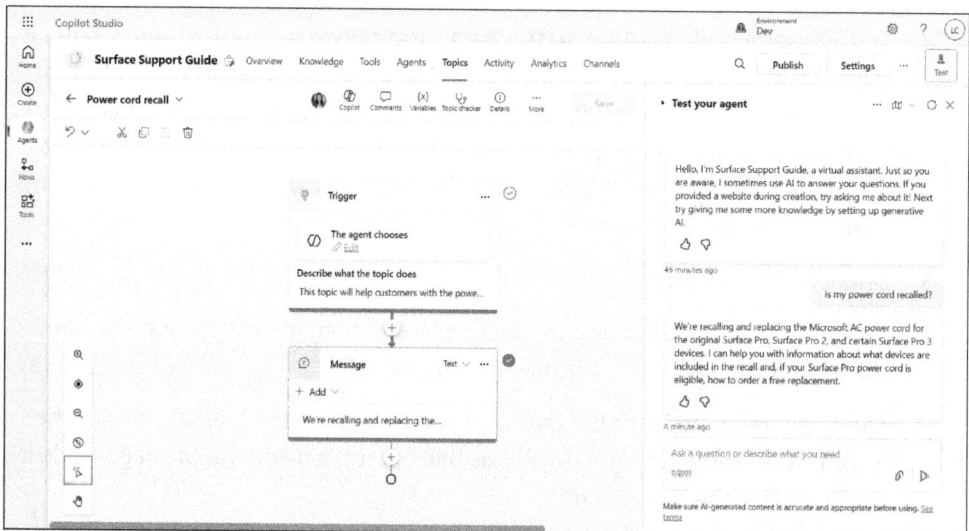

The topic is triggered, and the agent responds with the authored message.

8. When you work with topics in an agent that uses generative orchestration, you can choose to view the topic tracker or the activity map. At the top right of the **test** pane, select the **activity map** icon and select the **On** option from the drop-down menu.

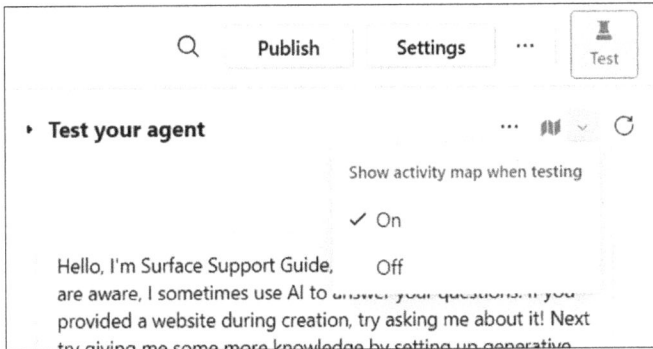

Switch the activity map on or off using the option at the top right of the test pane.

9. The topic tracker is replaced by the **activity map**, which shows the steps the agent has taken and the thought process the agent has used. In this case, it has used only one step/topic.

> ✓ **TIP** You can switch the activity map on or off depending on your preference for how you want to view and track the behavior of the agent as you build and test it. When you are authoring a topic, the topic tracker is more useful because it helps you clearly see how the conversational path is flowing. The activity map helps you understand the thought process and decisions the agent is making while you are using generative orchestration across all the components in the agent, including topics, knowledge, and tools.

10. Set the **Track between topics** toggle to the **On** position. Now, as you continue building and testing your agent, it will track the conversation across multiple topics.

11. Select the **Edit topic** button in the **Description** area to return to the topic in the authoring canvas and continue your editing.

12. Edit the message using the options available for rich text. Select the text in the message for each device name and change it to bold or italic. Add a paragraph between the first sentence and the second sentence.

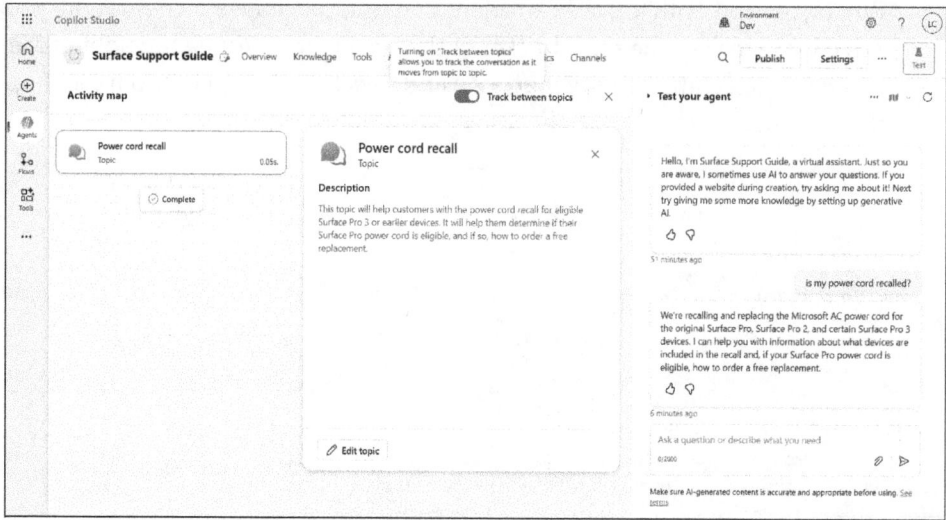

The activity map shows the thought process that the generative orchestration has used to trigger the topic.

> ✓ **TIP** Experiment here with other options, including bullet points and numbering, and change the wording of the message. You can also break this message into two separate messages by adding a second Message node for the second sentence if you prefer.

Use rich text and formatting to change the way the message is displayed to the user.

13. Select the **Save** button to save the changes to the topic.

14. Refresh the **test** pane, then test the agent again to view the changes in how the message is presented to the user.

Add an image to a message

In the preceding example, you created a message using plain text and then added some rich text formatting. You can also add images to the message the agent sends to the user.

> ✅ **TIP** Images used in Message nodes need to be hosted online. You will use the URL of the image or video to add it to the message. The size and quality of the image that appears in the Message node will depend on the size and quality of the source image hosted online.

To add an image to a message

1. In the **Message** node, select the **+Add** option to expand the menu of options to add to the message.

2. Select **Image**.

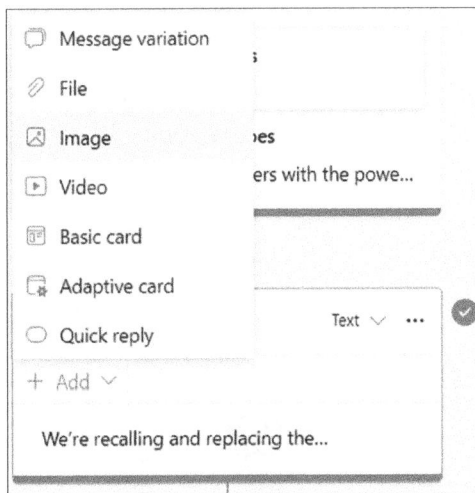

Add an image to a message.

3. In the **Image properties** pane, enter a title for the image: **AC power cord**.

> ✅ **TIP** This title will be displayed with the image in the message, so choose something helpful and meaningful for the user.

4. Copy the URL of the image you want to use from the website where it is hosted and paste it into the Image URL box: **https://support.microsoft.com/images/en-us/062e1379-2ebd-179a-1adf-5f6f9983e20f**.

> ✓ **TIP** In this example, we are using an image from the Microsoft Surface power cord recall site. To get the URL for the image you want to use, visit the site where it is hosted, right-click on the image, and select Copy image option.

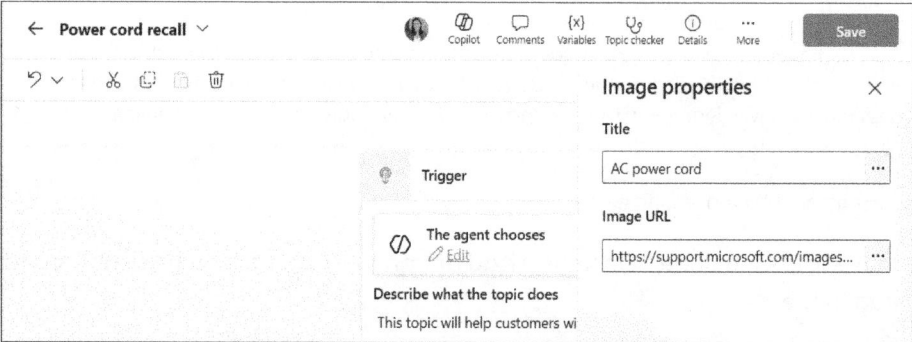

Enter the title and URL for the image to add it to the message node.

5. Select the **Save** button.

6. The **Image properties** pane closes, and you will be returned to the authoring canvas. The image and the image title you configured will now appear in the Message node.

7. Refresh the **test** pane, then test the agent with the new message including the image.

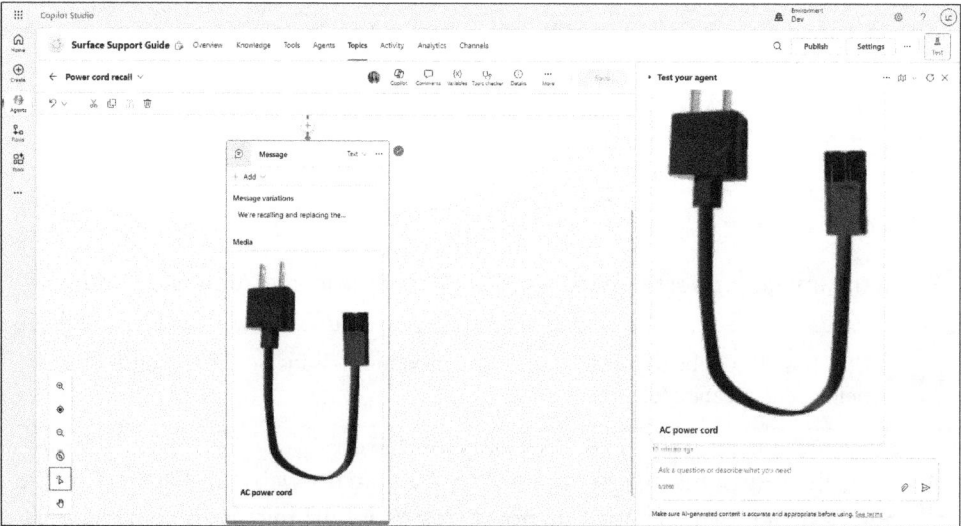

The message to the user includes an image and the title you configured.

> **TIP** This image, which is hosted on the Microsoft Surface support site, is not an optimal size or resolution to use in the agent message and will likely appear blurry if you follow along with this exercise. In your real-world scenario, you can host an online version of the image designed for the agent if the original image on the website isn't the right size or resolution.

> **SEE ALSO** Using an adaptive card, as described later in this section, will give you more control over the image size and display options.

Use cards in a message

You can create a message with more structure and functionality by using a card. There are two types of cards you can add to a message, depending on your skill and the level of control needed. Basic cards are simple to create using the low-code interface. Adaptive cards allow you to create fully customized elements using JSON.

To add a basic card

1. Remove the message you created in the previous exercise by selecting the three dots at the top right of the message node and then selecting **Delete**.

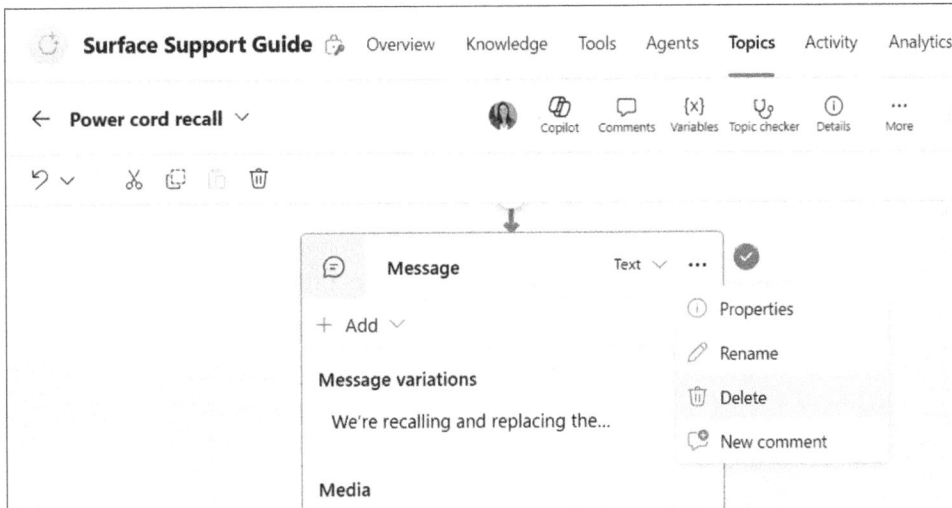

Expand the menu at the top of the node and delete it.

2. Select the + button below the **Trigger** node and select **Send a message**.

3. In the **Message** node, expand the **+Add menu** and select **Basic card**.

4. In the Basic Card properties, fill the following fields:

- Title: **Microsoft AC Power Cord Recall**

- Subtitle: **For eligible Surface Pro 3 or earlier devices**

- Image URL: **https://support.microsoft.com/images/ en-us/062e1379-2ebd-179a-1adf-5f6f9983e20f**

- Text: **We're replacing the removable cord that connects the power supply to an electrical outlet.**

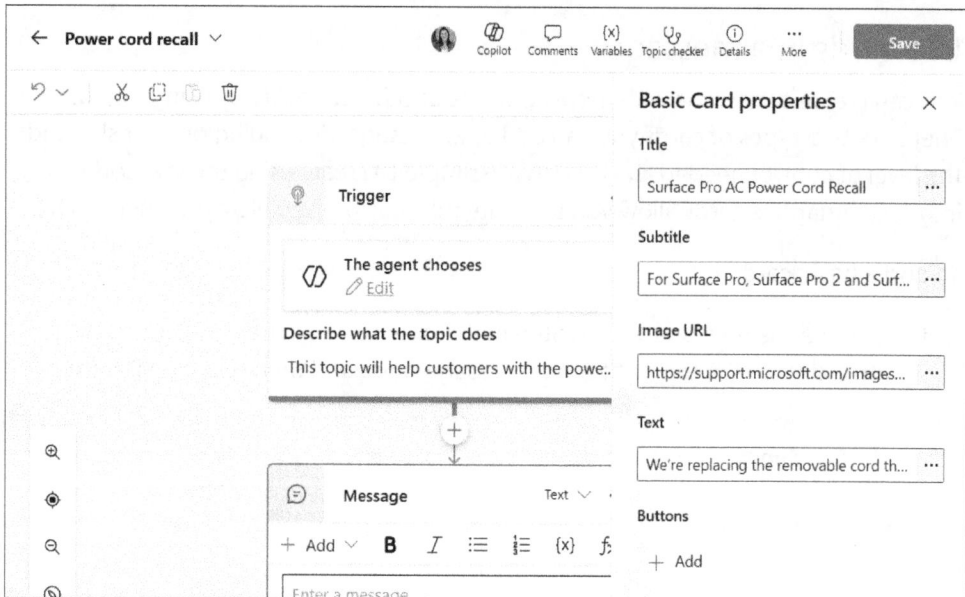

Fill the details of the title, subtitle, image URL, and text for the card.

5. Below these properties is a **Buttons** section. Select the **+Add** option.

6. You can configure a button that appears in the Message node and provides a function for the user, including sending a message or opening a URL. Configure the options for a button that the user can select to be directed to the website where they can request a replacement power cord.

- Type: **Open URL**

- URL: **https://go.microsoft.com/fwlink/?linkid=2145955**

- Title: **Order a replacement power cord**

> **TIP** You can add more buttons or explore advanced options here to add more images.

7. Select the **Save** button to save the basic card.

Configure the option for the button in the basic card.

8. The basic card now appears in the **Message** node in the authoring canvas. You can add a text or rich text message above the card if you wish.

9. Test the agent by refreshing the **test** pane and entering a question to trigger this topic.

10. Select the button in the message to test the hyperlink.

The basic card in the message displays an image, title, subtitle, text, and a button.

To have even more control over creating formatted and customized user interface elements in message nodes, you can use adaptive cards. Adaptive cards are UI snippets written in JSON that allow developers to create interactive elements. They can be used across many different applications. In Copilot Studio, adaptive cards can be used to create more sophisticated message and question nodes to display information or collect information from the user with elevated UI elements.

> 🔍 **SEE ALSO** The adaptive card JSON used in this example is provided in the files for this chapter and will be used in a practice task at the end of the chapter.

To add an adaptive card

1. Remove the message with the basic card that you created in the previous exercise by selecting the three dots at the top right of the message node and then selecting **Delete**.

2. Select the + button below the **Trigger** node and select **Send a message**.

3. In the **Message** node, expand the **+Add menu** and select **Adaptive card**.

4. In the **Adaptive Card properties** pane, select the **Edit Adaptive Card** button.

5. This opens the Adaptive card designer. You can build a card using this designer, or you can paste in the adaptive card JSON that you have already developed.

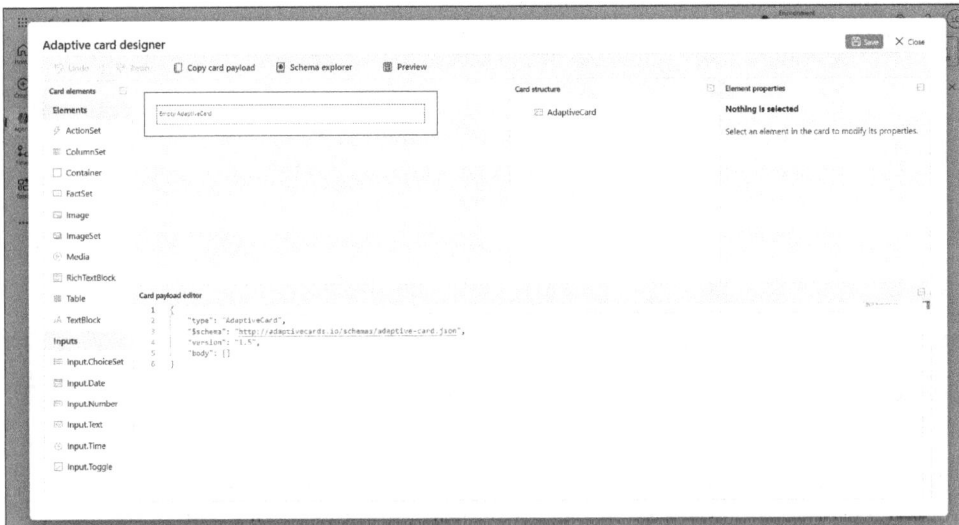

Create adaptive cards for topics in Copilot Studio using the Adaptive card designer.

6. Remove the JSON in the Card payload editor in the **Adaptive card designer** and paste your JSON in its place, or use the tools in the **Adaptive card designer** to create an adaptive card.

> **SEE ALSO** The adaptive card JSON used here is provided in the files for this chapter.

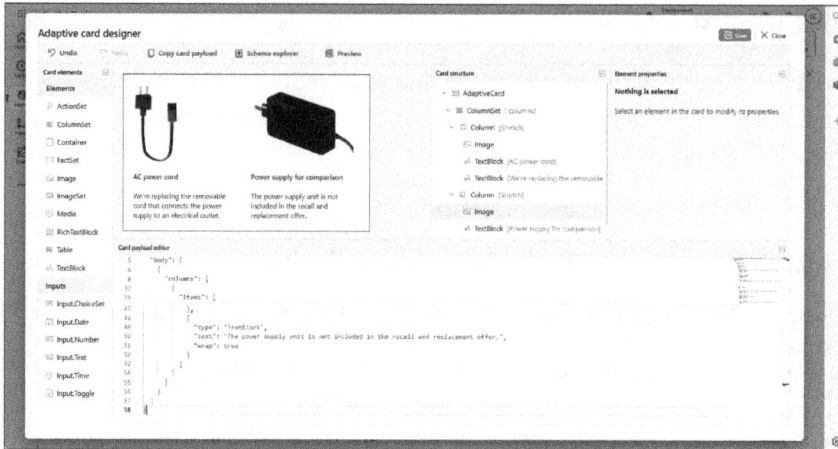

When you enter the adaptive card JSON, the designer displays a preview of the finished card.

7. The designer shows a preview of the adaptive card and the card structure.

> **TIP** The image used here is the same as the one used in the earlier examples. However, in the adaptive card JSON, the image container is restricted to 150 px in height, so that the images are displayed in a more easily viewable way.

8. Select the **Save** button at the top right to save the card.

9. Select the **Close** button to close the designer.

10. Close the **Adaptive Card properties** pane by selecting the X in the top right of that pane.

11. In the **Message** node, enter message text above the adaptive card: **To determine if your power cord is eligible for recall, please check if it matches the description and images provided. If your power cord looks like the one in the first image and connects the power supply to an electrical outlet, it may be eligible for replacement. The power supply unit itself is not included in the recall. If you believe your power cord is eligible, you can visit the official Microsoft support page for further instructions on how to order a free replacement.**

12. Select the **Save** button to save the topic.

13. Refresh the **test** pane, then test your agent by entering a question to trigger this topic.

The adaptive card displays a custom UI element in the message.

> **SEE ALSO** To learn about creating adaptive cards or to find samples to use to get started, refer to https://adaptivecards.microsoft.com/. For more examples of how to use adaptive cards in Copilot Studio, refer to https://learn.microsoft.com/en-us/microsoft-copilot-studio/guidance/adaptive-cards-overview.

> **TIP** You can use Copilot or the generative AI tool of your choice to describe an adaptive card in natural language and ask it to help you create the JSON.

Use other message node features

In this section, you have learned how to work with plain text, rich text, images, and cards in message nodes. There are also other types of media and other capabilities you can explore when authoring message nodes. These include:

- Add a *video* using the URL of a publicly accessible MP4 file or YouTube URL.

- Add multiple media cards to a message, displayed in a *list* or *carousel.*

- Provide variety in the way the agent expresses the message to the user by using the *Message variations* option to add multiple versions of the message; the agent will then randomly pick a different version each time. This is useful in a scenario where the topic will be frequently or repeatedly used, and you want the interaction to feel more natural rather than the same every time.

- Add *Quick replies* to add suggested prompts for the user to select to continue the conversation.

- Add a variable to repeat back a specific piece of data to the user.

- You can override the text message with a different *speech* message for voice-enabled channels.

> **SEE ALSO** Using variables in message nodes is covered in the next section of this chapter. Speech message capabilities are covered in Chapter 12: Working with voice and customer engagement systems.

Use questions, variables, and entities

As you build your topic, you can design the conversation so that the agent asks the user a question and responds based on their answer. You can provide the user with multiple-choice options, or you can allow the user to input free text and ask the agent to identify a specific type of information in that input, known as an entity. The agent can store an entity or data point from the conversation as a variable, and use it to confirm information from the user, to enable conditional branching in the conversation, or as an input for a tool.

Understand variables

Variables are used to collect information from the user; this information is saved and can be reused later. You can create topic variables that are used only in a single topic, or global variables that can be reused in other parts of the agent conversation.

- *Topic variables* can be used only in the topic where you create them, although you can pass the value of the variable from one topic to another.

- *Global variables* can be used in any topic in the agent. For example, suppose you wanted to collect the customer's name or their device type at the start of the conversation, and have the agent remember this information for the entire conversation without needing to ask for it again. You would use a global variable to do so.

When you create a variable, it will have a type that determines which kind of data it is storing and how you can work with that data (e.g., string, Boolean, choice, number). This variable type is set when the variable is created or when it is first assigned a value, and it can't be changed.

Copilot Studio also comes with system variables that are automatically added to your agent when you create it. These variables store data about the conversation, user, channel, and other session data.

> **SEE ALSO** For full documentation of the variable types and system variables, refer to the Microsoft documentation: https://learn.microsoft.com/en-us/microsoft-copilot-studio/authoring-variables-about.

> **SEE ALSO** You can also use Power Platform environment variables in Copilot Studio. For more information, refer to the Microsoft documentation: https://learn.microsoft.com/en-us/microsoft-copilot-studio/authoring-variables-about?tabs=webApp#environment-variables.

Add a question node using variables and conditional logic

Variables are often used with question nodes, which ask the user for information that is needed to progress the conversation to the next step. In this section, you will learn how to design topics that ask the user a question, store that information in a variable, and use it to build conditional logic in the topic.

> ✅ **TIP** If you know how to author adaptive cards, you can also use the "Ask with Adaptive Cards" node to configure a more custom UI experience for asking questions using adaptive cards.

To add a question node to a topic

1. In the **Power cord recall** topic in the Surface Support Guide agent, select the + button below the **Message** node you created in the previous exercise.

2. In the expanded menu of options, select **Ask a question**.

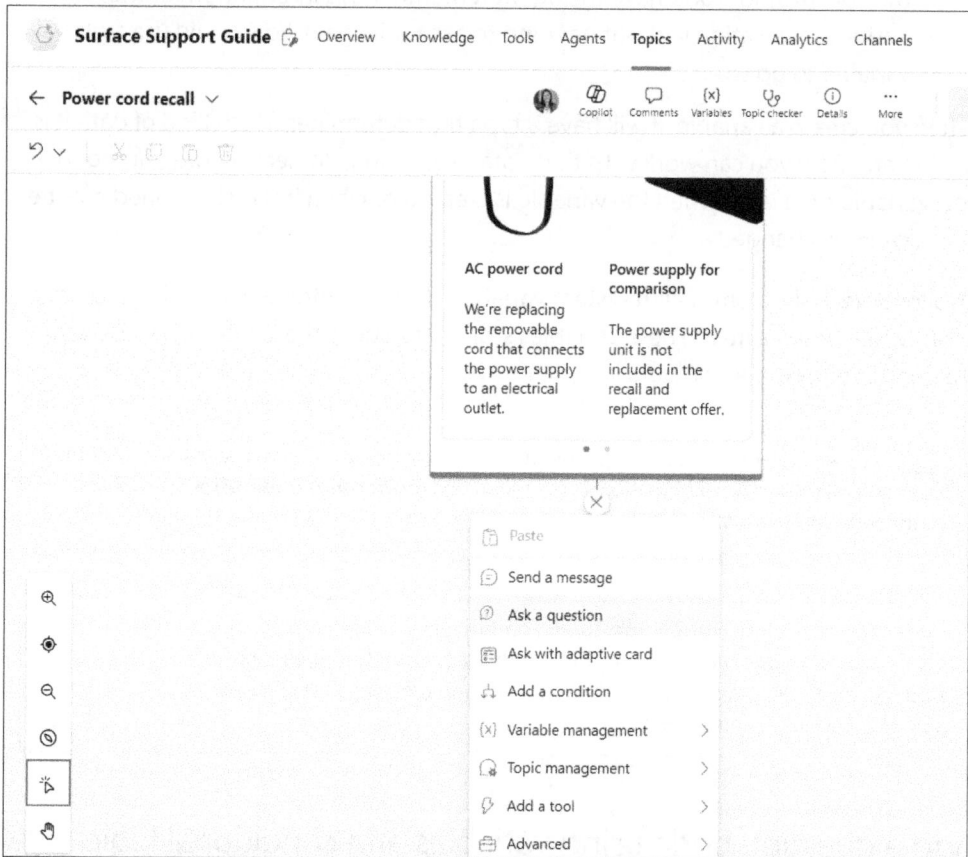

Add a Question node from the list of options in the topic authoring canvas.

3. Enter the question you want the agent to ask the user: **The recall applies to the original Surface Pro, Surface Pro 2, and certain Surface Pro 3 devices. Which device do you have?**

> **TIP** The Question node has the same rich text formatting options as the Message node, along with the +Add option where you can add media and cards as described in the previous section.

4. In the **Identify** option, leave the default choice: **Multiple choice options**.

5. In the **Options for user** section, select the **+New option** link.

6. This opens a new field where you can enter an option for the user to select to answer to the question. Enter the text **Original Surface Pro**, and then select **Enter**.

7. Once you have entered this first option, the topic automatically expands to add conditional branching below the Question node. The option you have just created appears as the first condition, with a second branch for **All other conditions**.

When you add options for the user to the Question node, the topic expands to add conditional branching for each option.

8. Continue repeating the steps above to add two more options: **Surface Pro 2** and **Surface Pro 3**. Each time you add a new option, new conditions are added below the **Question** node.

9. Select the **Save** button to save the changes to the topic.

> ✅ **TIP** Close the test pane to expand the available space on the screen for building your topic.

The Question node also includes a variable, Var1 (type: choice), that will be used to store and use the user's response to the question.

To work with variables in a topic

1. Continue from the end of the previous exercise.

2. Select the variable **Var1** in the **Question** node to open the **Variable properties** panel.

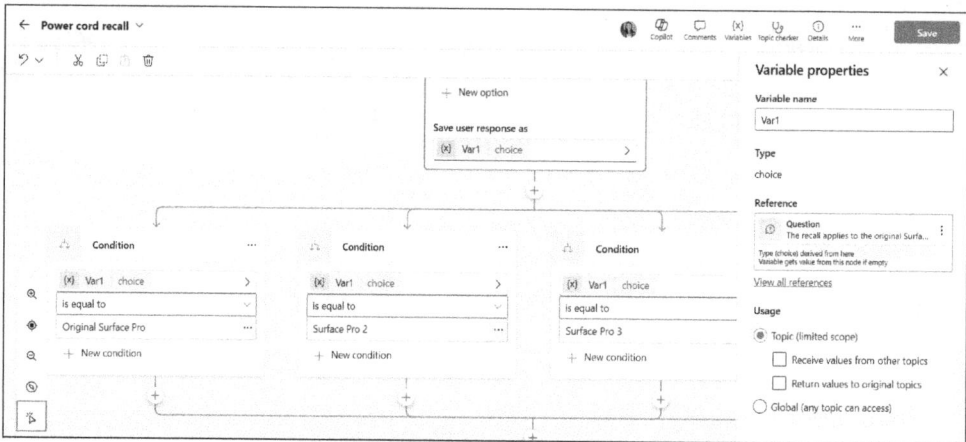

Select the variable in the Question node to expand the Variable properties pane.

3. Here you can edit the **Variable name**. Choose a descriptive name based on the purpose of the variable, such as **userDevice**.

> ✅ **TIP** Depending on the complexity of the agent, you may choose to use a prefix based on the variable type, or use different case for local or global variables (e.g., userDevice for a local variable or UserDevice for a global variable). The most important thing is that you follow a consistent standard.

4. Choose the scope of the variable usage. In this case, the device is needed only for this topic, so select **Topic (limited scope)**.

5. Close the **Variable properties** pane by selecting the X at the top right of the pane.

6. Notice that the name of the variable is updated in the **Question** node as well as in all the **Condition** nodes below it.

7. Select the **Save** button to save the topic.

8. Select the **Variables** icon at the top of the authoring canvas to view the variables. This opens the **Variables** pane, which displays the Topic variables, Global variables, and Environment variables.

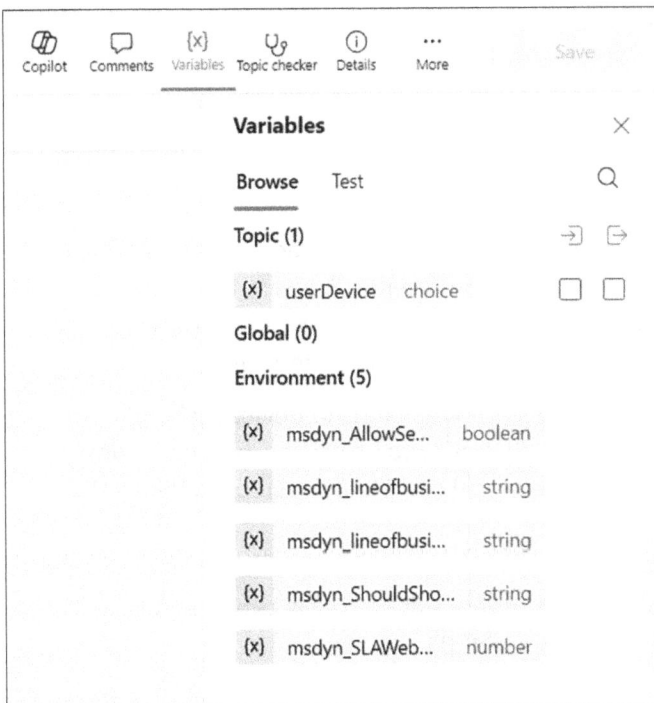

The Variables pane shows the Topic, Global, and Environment variables.

9. Close the **Variables** pane by selecting the X at the top right of the pane.

10. Select the **Save** button to save the changes to the topic.

Continue building out the conditional branching logic with more nodes. Note that the topic now includes multiple nodes, including three nodes called "Condition." You should give each node a more meaningful name to make the nodes easier to read and debug, and to help any collaborators understand the flow of the topic.

To create conditional logic in a topic

1. Hover over the generic placeholder title, "Question" or "Condition," to edit the name of each node.

   - Change the name of the question node to **Ques_AskUserForDevice**.

   - Change the names of the condition nodes to **Cond_DeviceOriginal-SurfacePro**, **Cond_DeviceSurfacePro2**, **Cond_DeviceSurfacePro3**, and **Cond_DeviceOther**.

> ✓ **TIP** Name each node in a way that describes its function. You can choose to use prefixes that describe the node type, such as "Cond_" for conditions or "Ques_" for questions.

2. Continue to build the topic with the next nodes for each condition. If the user has an Original Surface Pro or a Surface Pro 2 device, they are eligible for a replacement power cord. Select the + button below the **Cond_Device-OriginalSurfacePro** node, and then select **Send a Message**.

3. In the **Message** node, enter the following text: **Your device is eligible for a replacement power cord. Please go to https://go.microsoft.com/fwlink/?linkid=2145955 to sign in and complete the steps to follow the process.**

> ✓ **TIP** You can use rich text, images, videos, cards, or adaptive cards in any of these message nodes to enhance the conversation.

4. You can add a variable to the Message node to confirm the device the user has selected. Position your cursor between the words "Your" and "Device" and add an extra space. Select the **Variable** icon in the Message node. This opens a side panel where you can select a custom, system, or environment variable.

5. Select **userDevice** in the Custom variable tab.

6. This closes the side panel and adds the variable to the message.

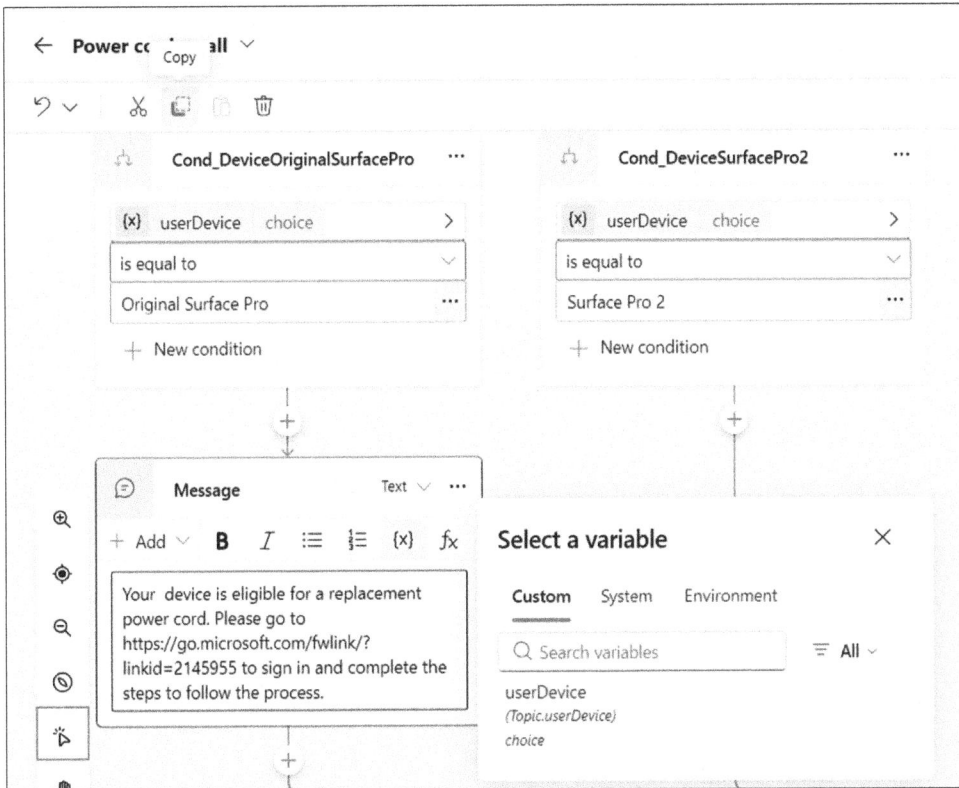

Select the variables icon in the Message node to open the Select a variable side panel.

7. Rename the Message node to **Msg_EligibleForRecall**.

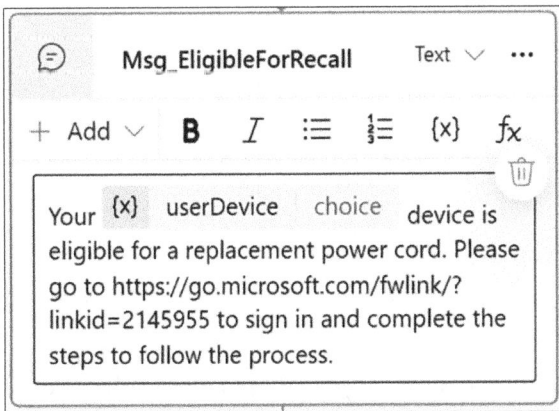

The variable is added to the Message node.

8. If the user has a Surface Pro 2, you want to display the same message. Rather than creating another message with the same content, you can redirect the flow of the topic from the **Cond_DeviceSurfacePro2** node to the **Msg_EligibleForRecall** message node you just created. Select the + button under the **Cond_DeviceSurfacePro2** node.

9. Select **Topic management** to expand more menu options, and then select **Go to step**.

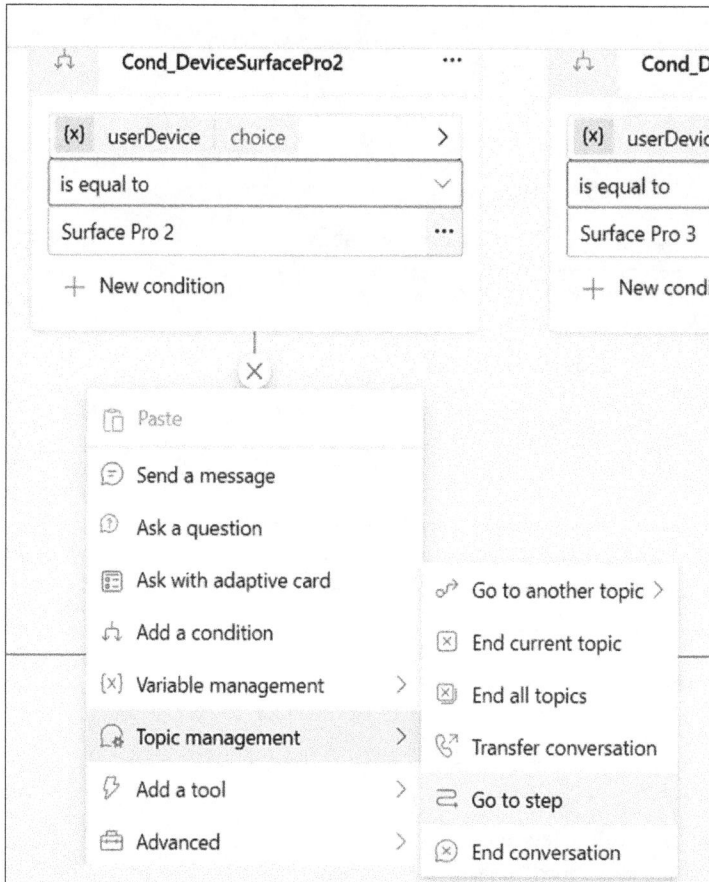

Select the "Go to step" option from the Topic management menu to redirect the conversation to another node.

10. Select the **Msg_EligibleForRecall message** node you created earlier. This adds a **Send activity** node that will direct the topic to that message node when the **Cond_DeviceSurfacePro2** condition is met.

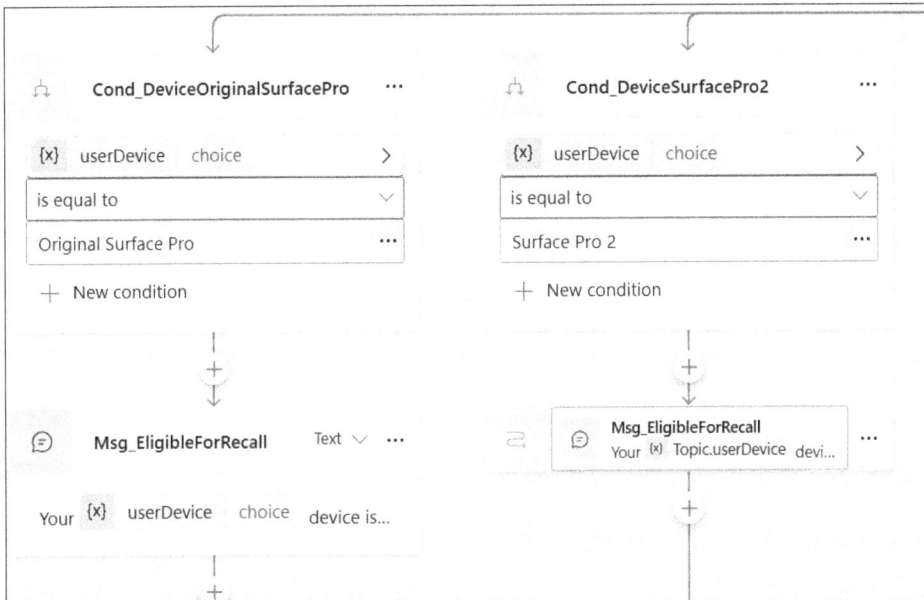

The "Go to step" node redirects the conversation from the second condition to the existing message node.

11. Select the **Save** button to save the changes to the topic.

If the user has a Surface Pro 3 device, then they are eligible for a replacement power cord only if they purchased the device before March 15, 2015. You can add another question node and use an entity and a formula to calculate whether the device is eligible based on the answer provided.

Understand entities

Entities represent types of information, such as names of cities, dates, colors, or numbers. They can be used in topics to help the agent recognize a specific type of information in unstructured user input.

Copilot Studio comes with a set of prebuilt entities for the most common types of information. You can also add custom entities for any business- or domain-specific types of information that you want the agent to understand. Custom entities are more commonly used in agents built using classic orchestration, where they support the NLU model in recognizing the relevant information. If you are building an agent that uses generative orchestration, you are less likely to need them.

To view prebuilt entities

1. Navigate to the **Settings** area of the agent by selecting the **Settings** button at the top right.

2. In the **Settings** area, select the **Entities** option from the left side menu.

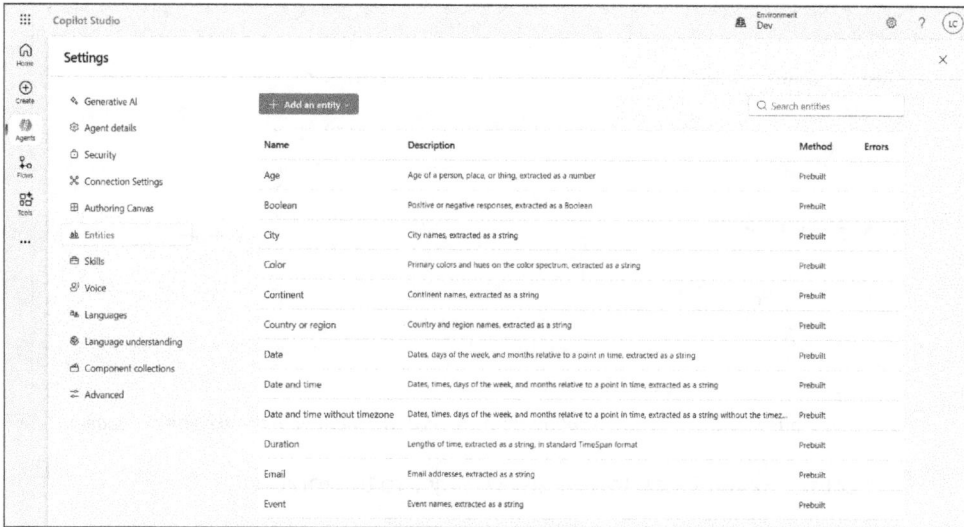

Copilot Studio comes with prebuilt entities for the most common types of information.

3. In this menu, you can view all the prebuilt entities available. Select the **Email** entity to open it and view the details.

4. When you select an entity, a pane opens on the right side of the screen with a description and samples indicating how the value of the entity is extracted from the user input and stored. For instance, the usage examples for the Email entity show that it can identify and extract the email address from any other surrounding text. For instance, if the user input is "My email address is user@site.net," the entity is able to recognize the email address and save the value user@site.net.

5. Close the **Email** entity pane by selecting the X at the top right.

6. Select some other prebuilt entities to browse the options available and to see how they extract the value from the user input.

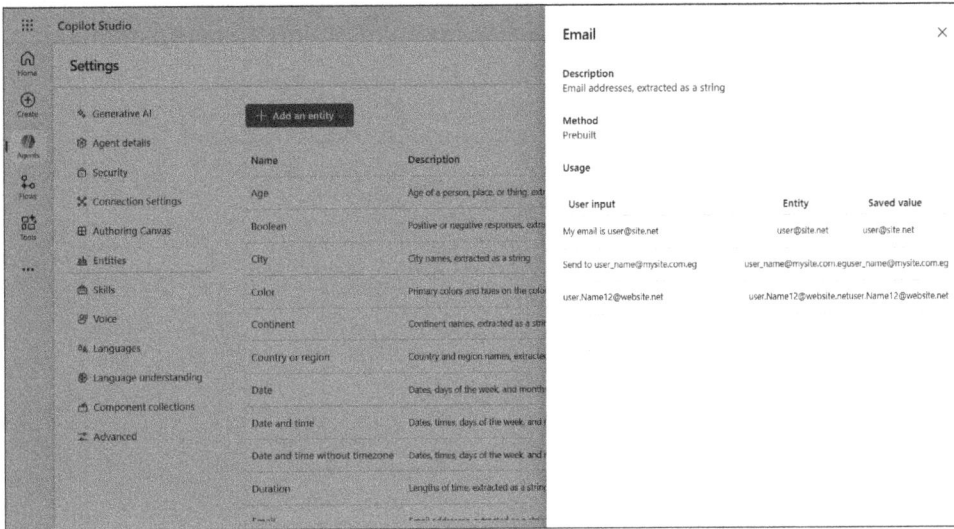

The Email entity extracts email addresses as a string from the user input.

You can add custom entities to help your agent recognize types of information that are specific to your business or industry. You can also define a logical pattern (e.g., an order number or a serial number with a certain pattern or number of digits) that a custom entity should recognize from the user input.

In this example, you will create a custom entity to recognize a device serial number that is 14 digits long, starting with "98."

To add a custom entity

1. In the **Entities** part of the **Settings** area of the agent, select the **+Add an entity** button at the top of the list of prebuilt entities.

2. From the drop-down menu, select **New Entity**.

3. In the **Create an entity** screen, select **Regular expression (Regex)** as the method.

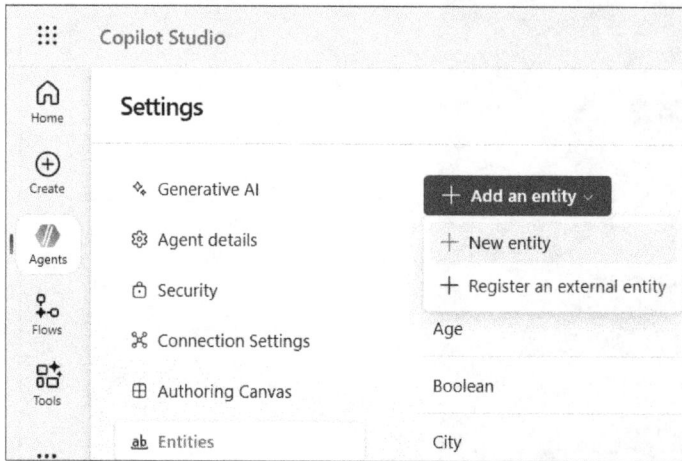

Select the "Add an entity" button in the Entities area of the Settings to create a custom entity.

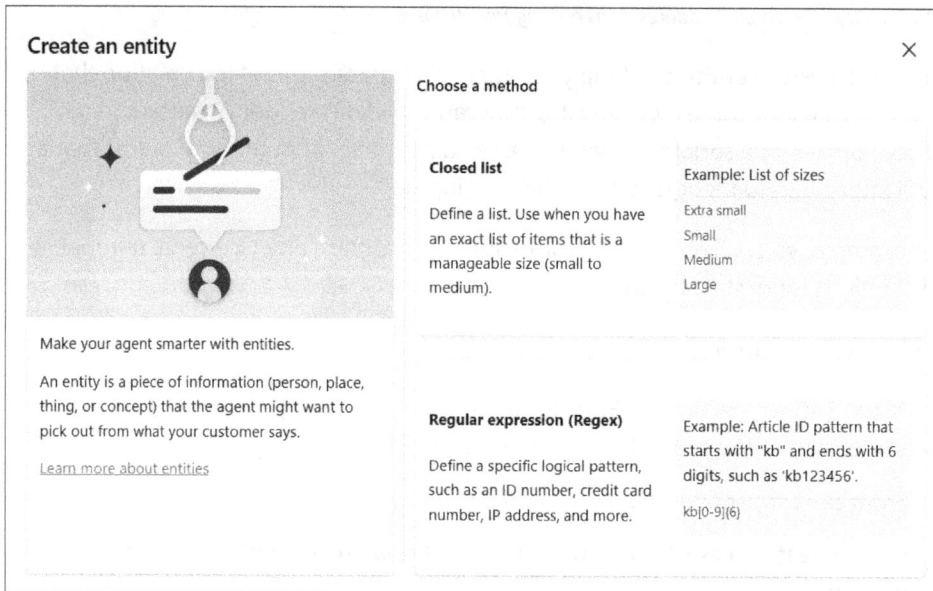

You can create an entity using a list of items or a regular expression.

4. This opens a pane on the right side of the screen where you can configure the entity. Enter a name, description, and pattern.

   - Name: **Serial number.**

   - Description: **Serial number that has 14 digits and starts with 98.**

   - Pattern: **98712345678912.**

Serial Number ✕

Name *

Serial Number

Description

Serial number that has 14 digits
and starts with 98

Pattern *

98712345678912

Method
Regular expression (Regex)
The agent will extract any text that
matches the specific pattern.
Learn how to use entities

Examples

Knowledge base article ID that starts with "kb"
and ends with 6 digits, "kb123456" for
example.

kb[0-9]{6}

Credit card number that has 13 or 16 digits
and starts with a 4.

4[0-9]{12}(?:[0-9]{3})?

[Save] [Close]

Configure the entity by giving it a name, description, and pattern.

5. Select the **Save** button to save the entity.

6. Select the **Close** button to close the pane.

7. Close the **Settings** area by selecting the **X** at the top right.

Using a question node in a topic, you can ask the agent to identify a specific prebuilt
or custom entity. In this example, you need to ask the user to provide a purchase date.
The agent will use entity extraction to identify the date in the user's response.

To use an entity in a topic

1. Return to the Power cord recall topic and select the + button below the **Cond_ DeviceSurfacePro3** node.

2. Select **Ask a question** to add a **Question** node.

3. Rename the Question node: **Qu_DevicePurchaseDate**.

4. In the message area of the Question node, enter the text: **When did you purchase your device?**

5. In the **Identify** area, select the arrow to the right of the default **Multiple choice options** to expand the menu of available entities.

6. Type the word "date" into the search box, and then select the **Date** entity.

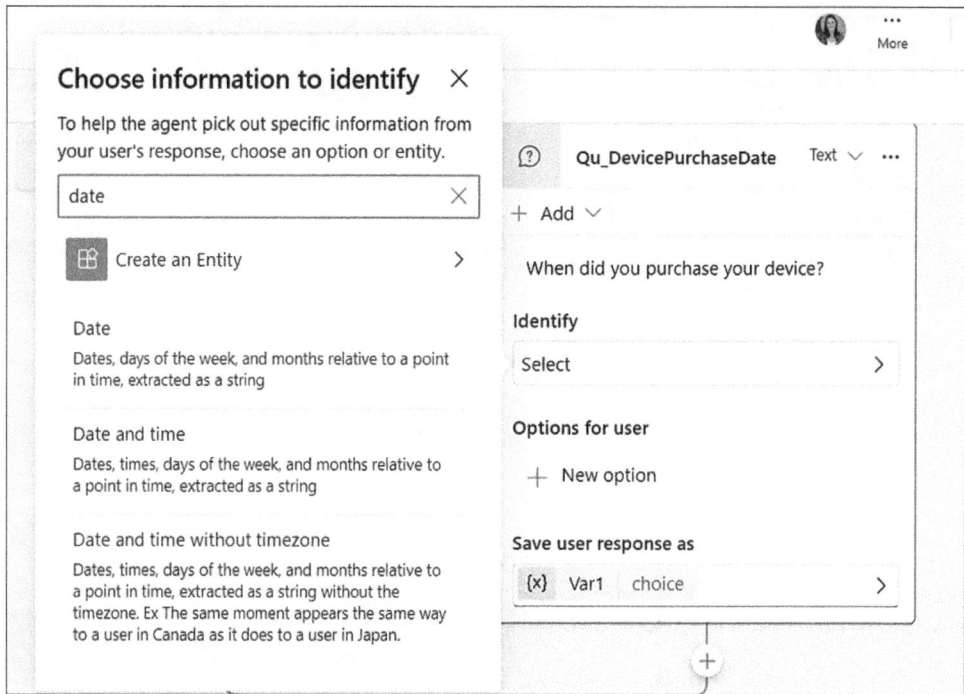

Expand the "Identify" option to view and search a list of available entities from the Question node.

7. The variable type in the **Save user response as** field changes to type "**date**" after you select this entity.

8. Select the variable **Var1 (date)** in the Question node to edit it. Change the name to **devicePurchaseDate**. Leave the **Usage** as **Topic**.

9. Close the **Variable properties** pane by selecting the **X** at the top right.

10. Select the **Save** button to save the changes to the topic.

The agent is now able to identify a date from the user input. Users can input dates in different formats (e.g., 1/1/2018 or 1 January 2018), and the agent will be able to identify and extract that date and save it as a variable. The agent can also extract the date from a string of text in the user input. If, for example, the user responds with "I purchased my device on 1/1/2018," the agent can identify and extract the date while ignoring the rest of the text in the user input.

> **SEE ALSO** The agent uses a capability called slot filling to understand which entities it needs to identify and which variables are already filled. This topic is covered in the next section.

Use formulas, logic, and generative answers

Message nodes, questions, variables, and entities make up the core building blocks of a basic topic, but you can go further in shaping how the topic behaves and building out the logic of the conversation. In this section, you will learn how to use some of the more advanced features in authoring topics, including setting variable values and using PowerFx formulas, expanding the conditional logic in the topic, and using generative answers nodes to add a knowledge source to a topic.

Use PowerFx formulas

Now that you have set up a question node and a variable to store the purchase date for the user's device, you need to compare that date with the cutoff date for the recall. To do this, you will set a new variable of type "date" and use a formula to set the value of that date variable to March 15 2015.

You can define additional variables and set the value of a variable using a PowerFx formula. PowerFx is a low-code declarative programming language that is used across

Power Platform. It is made up of Excel-like formulas, and is designed to be easy for low-code developers to use.

> 🔍 **SEE ALSO** To learn more about PowerFx and commonly used PowerFx formulas for Copilot Studio, refer to https://learn.microsoft.com/en-us/microsoft-copilot-studio/advanced-power-fx.

To set a variable value with a formula

1. Select the + button below the Question node you added in the previous exercise, expand the **Variable management** option, and select **Set a variable value**.

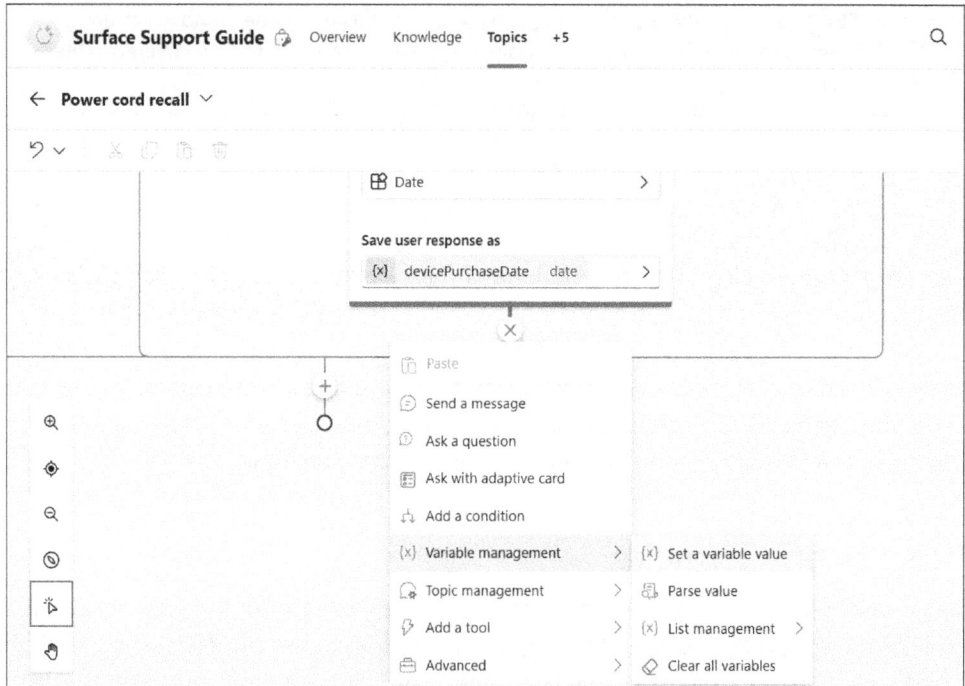

Add a variable node by selecting "Variable management"; then choose "Set a variable value."

2. In the new **Set variable value** node, expand the **Select a variable** option and select **Create a new variable**.

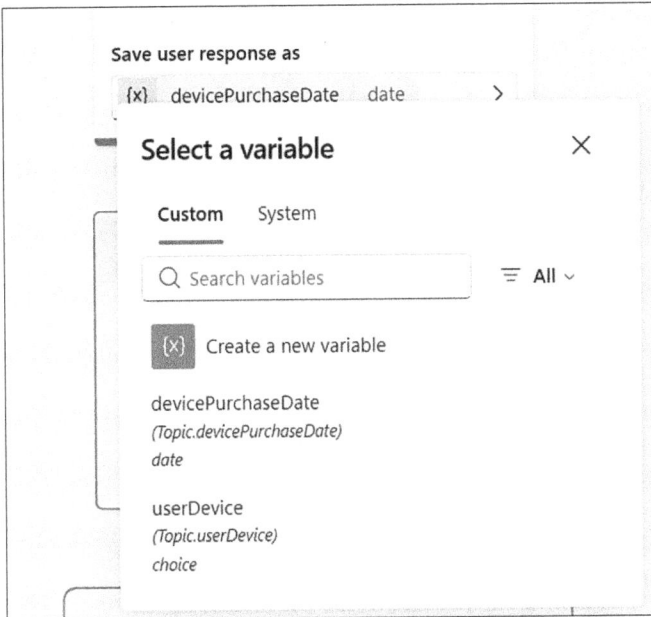

Create a new variable to store the cutoff date for the recall.

3. This will create a new variable named **Var1**, type unknown. Select that variable from the node to open and edit it.

4. Change the **Variable name** to **cutoffPurchaseDate** and leave the **Usage** as **Topic**.

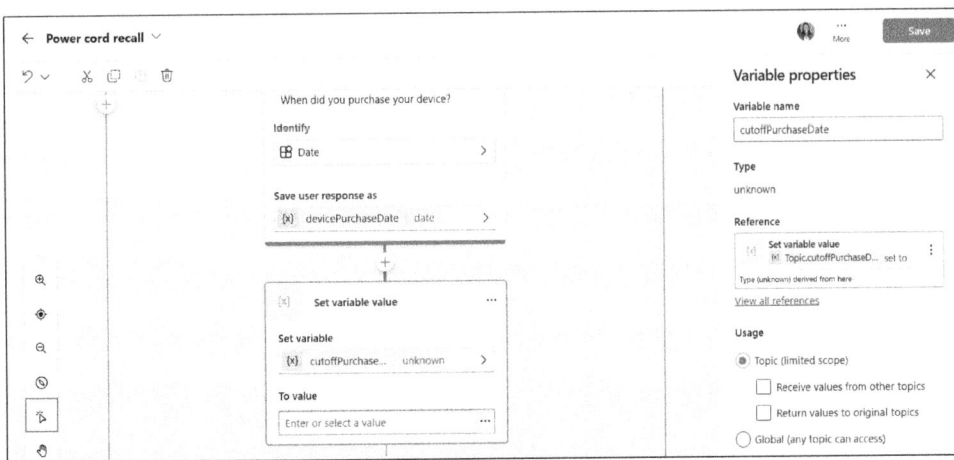

Edit the variable name in the "Variables properties" pane.

5. Close the **Variable properties** pane by selecting the **X** at the top right.

6. In the **Set variable value** node, select the three dots in the **To value** field. This opens the **Select a variable** pane.

7. You can set the value of the variable to another custom, system, or environment variable, or you can use a formula to set the value of the variable. Select the **Formula** tab.

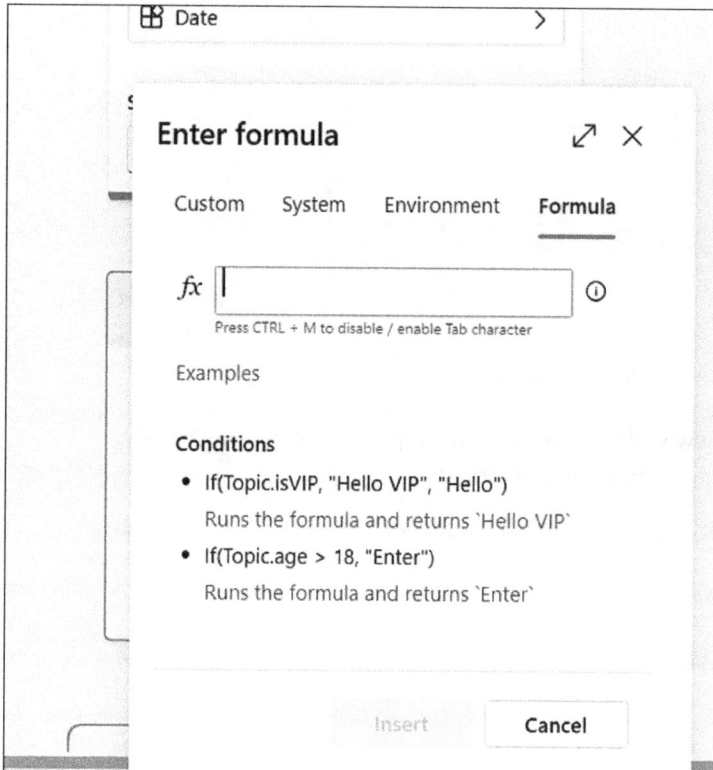

Set the value of the variable using a PowerFx formula.

8. Write a formula using PowerFx to set the value of the date to March 15 2015. The formula is: **DateValue("2015-03-15")**.

> ✓ **TIP** This example uses a basic formula that sets a fixed value. You can set the value of a variable based on more complex conditions and logic here by using PowerFx.

9. When you have entered a valid formula, the **Type** will be set to **Date** (based on the value set by the output of the formula). The **Output** will have a green check mark indicating that the output of the formula is valid.

10. Select the **Insert** button to insert the formula and set the value of the variable.

When did you purchase your device?

Identify

▦ Date   >

Save user response as

Enter formula   ↗ ✕

Custom   System   Environment   **Formula**

fx DateValue("2015-03-15")   ⓘ

Type   📅 Date
Output   ✅ DateValue("2015-03-15")

Insert   Cancel

When you enter a valid PowerFx formula, the type will be set and the output will be confirmed as valid with a check mark.

11. The value and type of the variable are now set. The formula appears in the **To value** of the **Set variable value** node.

This topic is now set up to identify the date from the user input, using the date entity, and to store it in a variable. It also has a variable with a value set to the cutoff date for when the recall applies.

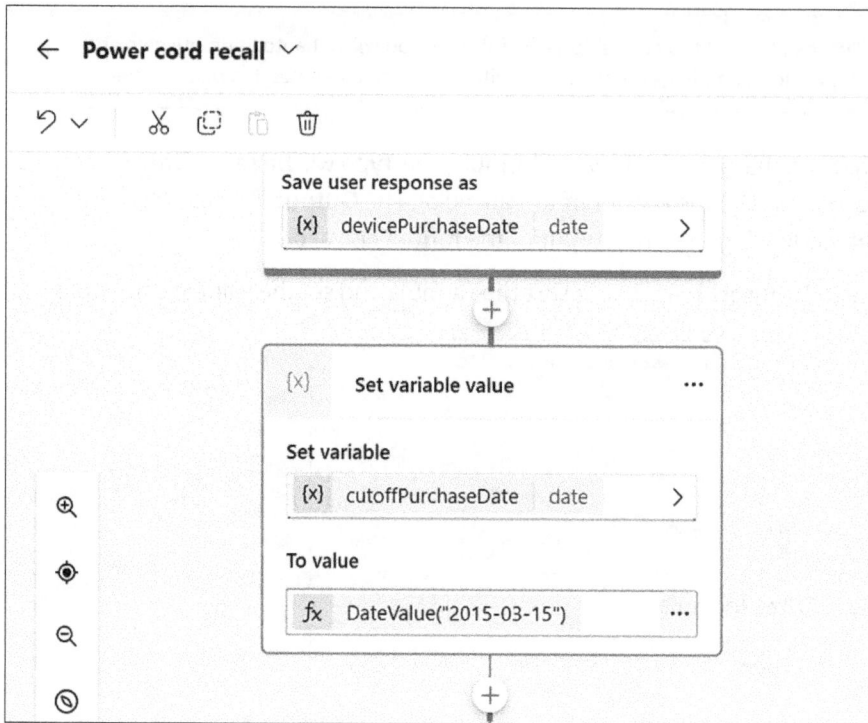

The variable value is set by the PowerFx formula.

Expand the branching logic

Now you will expand the topic with conditional branching so that the agent responds with the appropriate answer depending on whether the purchase date the user enters is before or after the cutoff date for the recall.

When you ask a question using multiple-choice options, the conditional branching is automatically created for you. When you use another entity and want to add conditional logic to the topic, you need to add it manually as a new node and set up the logic you want.

To add a condition to a topic

1. Select the + button below the variable node you just added, and then select **Add a condition**.

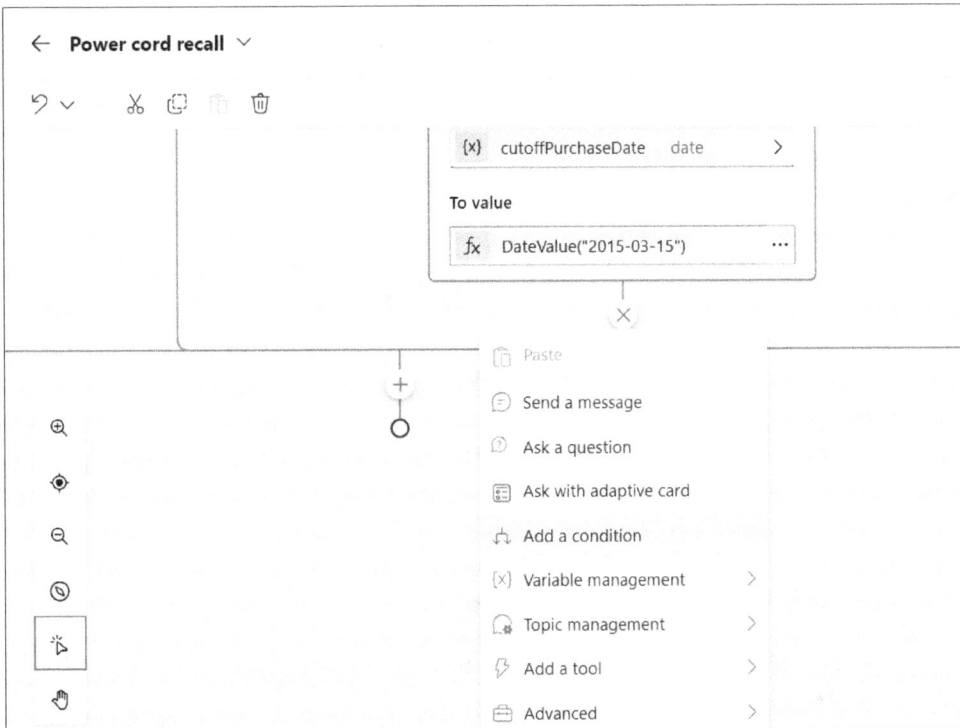

Select "Add a condition" to add conditional logic to your topic.

2. This creates branching logic below the Question node, with one side for a condition, and the other side for all other conditions. The condition we are looking for here is that the device purchase date is before 15 March 2015.

✅ **TIP** As you expand the logic and add more nodes in the topic, move around the canvas using scroll bars in the browser. Use the icons at the bottom left of the authoring canvas to zoom in or out to the size that works best for you.

---

3. In the **Condition** node, expand the **Select a variable** option to open the **Select a variable** pane.

4. Select the **devicePurchaseDate** variable.

5. In the **Condition** node, below the variable you added, select **is less than** from the drop-down menu.

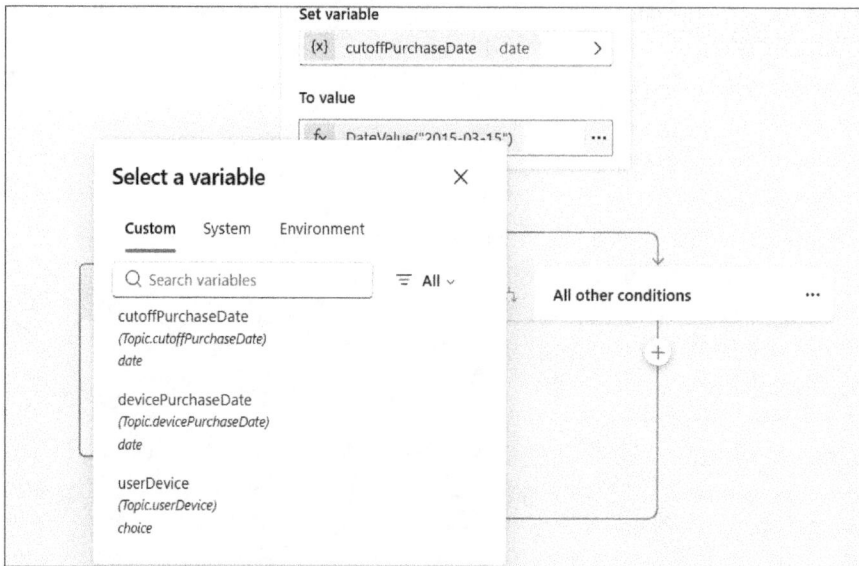

Select a variable from the list of custom variables created.

6. In the **Enter or select a value** field, select the three dots, and then select the **cutoffPurchaseDate** variable.

7. Rename the **Condition** node to **Cond_PurchaseBeforeCutOff**.

> ✅ **TIP** Remember to rename all the nodes in the topic for easier tracking, collaboration, and debugging.

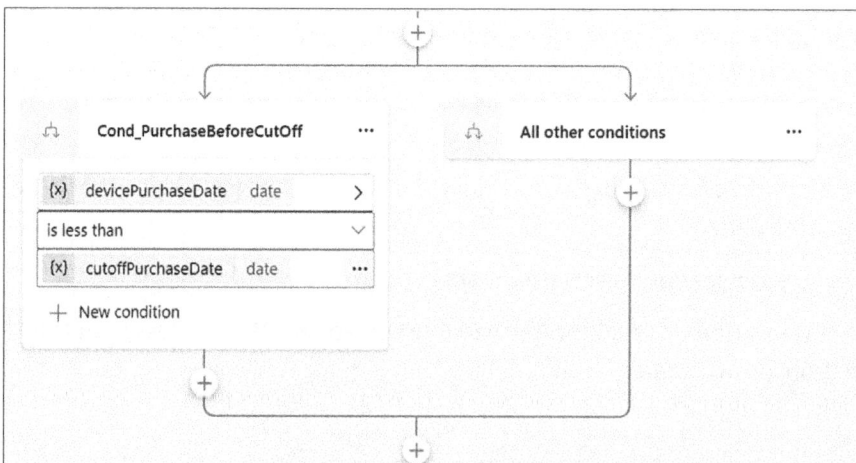

Fill the condition with the variables and the condition that will be tested in the conversation flow.

8. Now that you have set a condition that checks whether the purchase date falls within the recall period for this device, you need the agent to send the message to the user to follow the next steps. Select the + node below the condition node, select **Topic Management**, and then select **Go to Step**.

9. Use the icon at the bottom left of the authoring canvas to zoom out far enough that you can locate the **Msg_EligibleForRecall** message node you created earlier. Select that node.

10. This adds the **Send activity** node below the **Cond_PurchaseBeforeCutOff** node. Now, the agent will send the message containing the next steps when this condition is met.

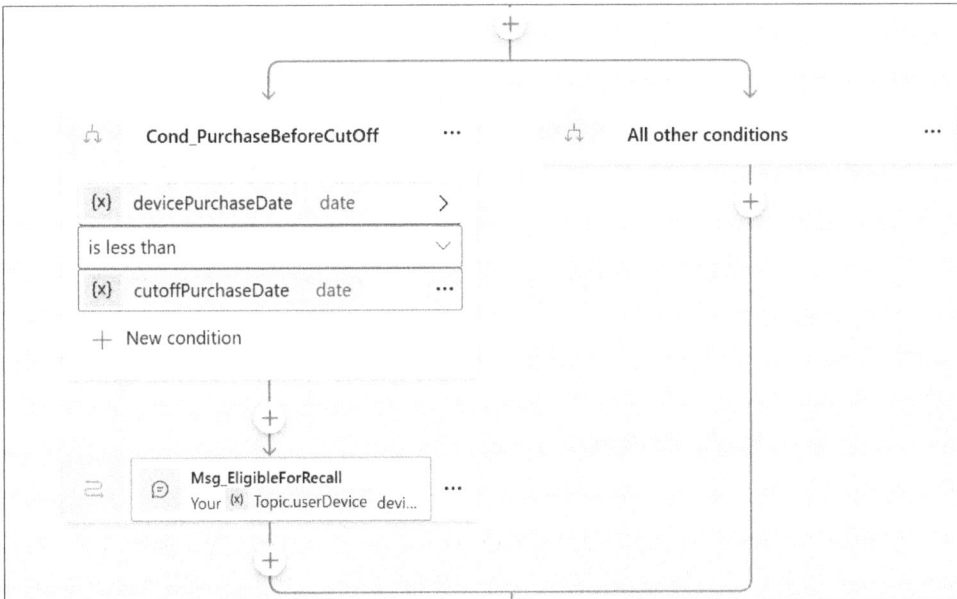

Use the "Send activity" node to reuse a message node you have created elsewhere in the topic flow.

11. To complete the conditional logic in this topic, we need a message that the agent sends to the user when their device is not eligible for a power cord recall. Zoom out on the authoring canvas to find the original **All other conditions** node that branches from the **Ques_AskUserForDevice** question node.

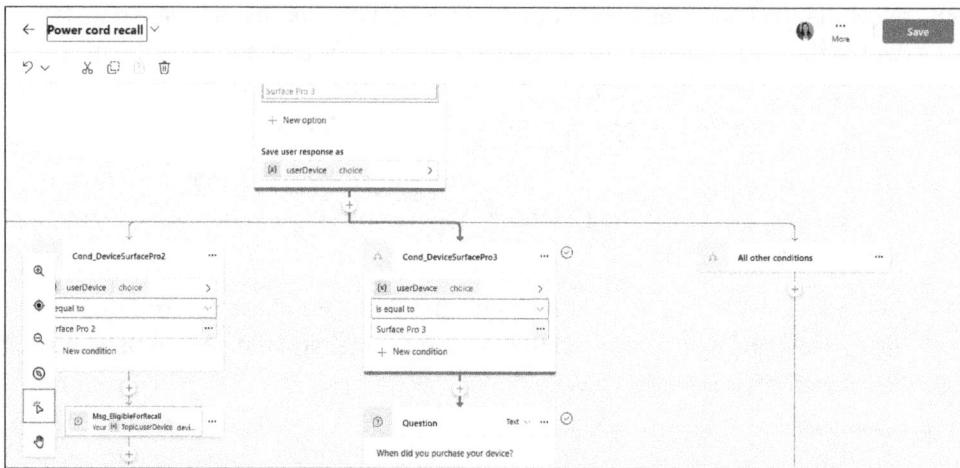

Zoom out to find the "All other conditions" branch from the first question node you created.

12. Select the + button below the "**All other conditions**" node, and select **Send a message**.

13. Rename the new **Message** node: **Msg_NotEligibleForRecall**.

14. In the message text, enter: **Your device is not eligible for a replacement power cord.**

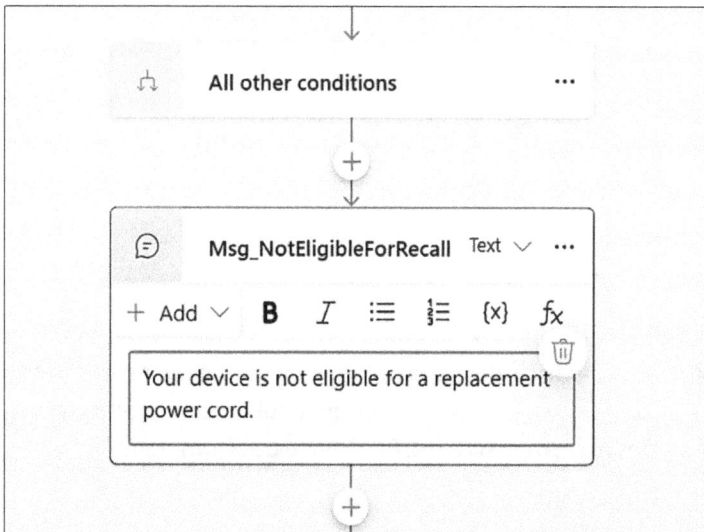

Create a message node that the agent sends to the customer when their device is not eligible for a replacement power cord.

15. Navigate on the authoring canvas to the other "**All other conditions**" node next to the **Cond_PurchaseBeforeCutOff** condition node.

16. Select the + button below the "**All other conditions**" node, select **Topic Management**, and then select **Go to Step**.

17. Zoom out and find the **Msg_NotEligibleForRecall** message node you just created and select it.

18. The purchase date conditions now each have a message that the agent will send to the user.

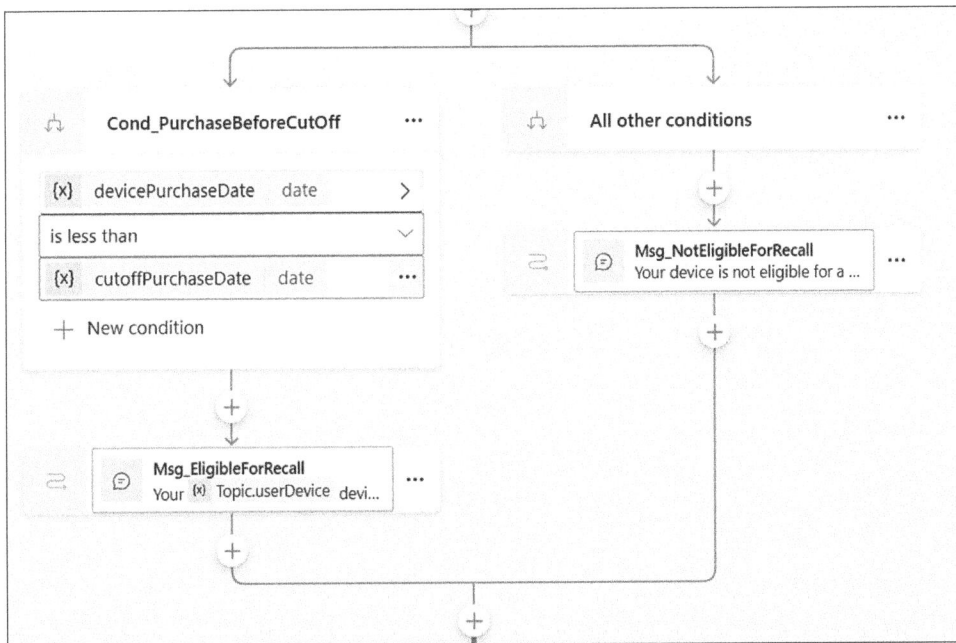

Each of the conditional branches has a "Send activity" node that will send the right message to the user depending on the outcome of the condition.

19. Select **Save** to save the changes to the topic.

20. Test the topic by refreshing the **test** pane and triggering the topic. Test multiple times to check the behavior of all the conditional logic in the conversational flow. Try different ways of expressing the date and using other words around it, with phrases such as "I purchased it on 15 December 2016."

Understand slot filling and configure skip behavior

Slot filling is a capability that allows the agent to look for the variables required by the topic anywhere in the conversation and fill them when it finds that information.

In this example, if the user responded with the purchase date before the topic asks for it, the agent can detect the entity and store the information in the **devicePurchase-Date** variable. It will then skip that question when it comes up in the conversational flow. This creates a more efficient and natural conversational flow.

To configure the skip behavior for a question

1. Locate the **Qu_DevicePurchaseDate** question node and select the three dots at the top right of the node to expand the menu of options. Select **Properties**.

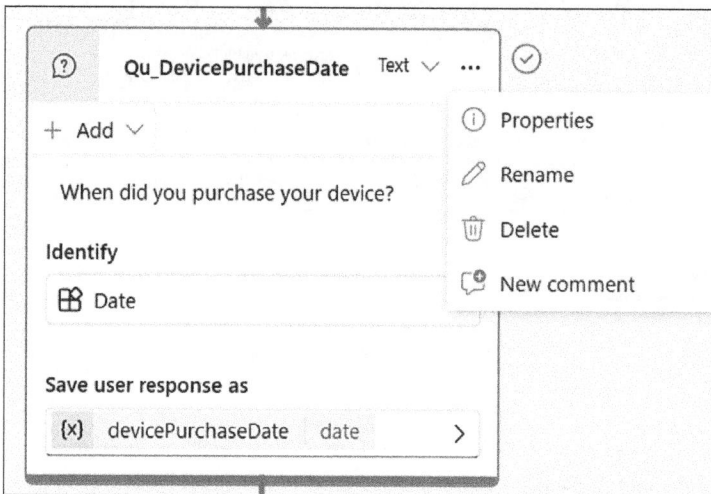

Select the Properties of the question node.

2. In the **Question properties** pane, select **Question behavior** (Control how and when your bot asks this question). The default behavior of the question is that it allows the question to be skipped.

← Question ✕

Question behavior

Skip behavior
Decide if the question should be skipped if the variable already has a value

Skip question ⓘ   Manual input ⌄

◉ Allow question to be skipped

◯ Ask every time

Reprompt
If the bot doesn't get a valid answer to the question, it can ask the question again

How many reprompts ⓘ   Manual input ⌄

```
Repeat up to 2 times                    ⌄
```

Retry prompt ⓘ
☐ Customize

The Question behavior pane provides Skip behavior and Reprompt options for the question.

> ✓ **TIP** Other options here allow you to control the question behavior in other ways, including how many times the agent should reprompt the user, and the message it sends when it needs to reprompt. You can also use the "Manual input" drop-downs to switch to a "Formula" option to create logic for Skip and Reprompt behavior using PowerFx formulas.

3. Close the **Question behavior** pane by selecting the **X** at the top right.

4. Refresh the **test** pane.

5. Select the **Variables** icon from the top of the authoring canvas. In the **Variables** pane, select the **Test** tab, and then expand the Topic section.

> ✓ **TIP** If the Variables icon isn't visible at the top of the authoring canvas, use the More option to expand the list of options or reduce the zoom on your browser.

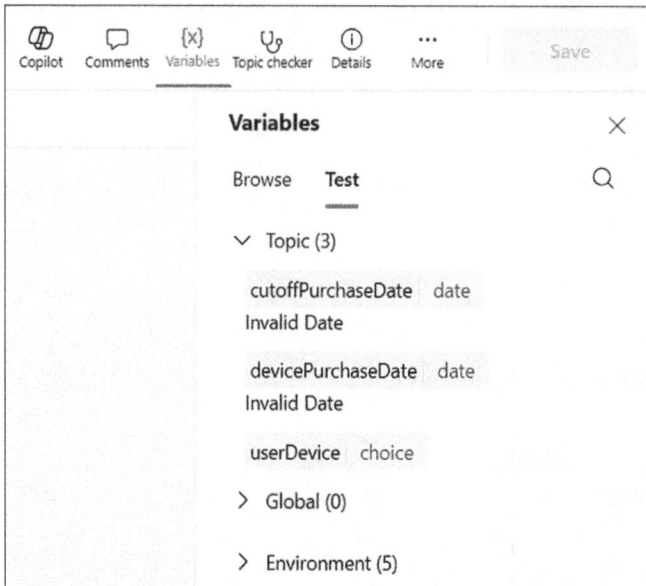

Before you test the topic, the variables do not have any values assigned.

6. Select the **Test** icon at the top right to open the **test** pane. The **Variables** pane remains open, sitting to the left of the **test** pane.

7. Trigger the topic in the **test** pane, with the phrase: **Can I get a new power cord?**

8. When the multiple-choice options are offered, do not select one. Instead, type in the chat: **I have a Surface Pro 3 that I bought on 1/1/2016.**

9. Note the change to the values of the variables. All three variables are now filled with values.

   - The agent identified the **userDevice** variable value from the user input in the chat, even though the user didn't select one of the multiple-choice options.

   - The agent identified the date entity in the user input and used it to fill the value of the purchase date.

   - The agent follows the flow of the topic to set and fill the value of the **cutoffPurchaseDate** variable.

   - In the chat, the agent doesn't ask what the purchase date was, because it already identified that entity and filled the value of that variable. It skips ahead to send the message that the device is not eligible for a replacement power cord.

The agent skips the question about the purchase date because it has already filled the variable value by identifying the date in the user input.

Using entities and allowing questions to be skipped means you can create a topic where the user can interact in a natural way, without the need for a long series of questions and answers. You can consider designing the topic where the user is first prompted to describe the problem and the topic identifies entities, fills the variable values, and then asks the questions only where there are remaining variables to be filled.

> **SEE ALSO** You can also create an agent that performs this slot filling behavior by using tools, rather than authoring multiple question nodes in a topic. This approach is covered in Chapter 8: Extending agents with tools.

Add knowledge to a topic

You can add knowledge to a topic to narrow the focus of the generative answers to a specific knowledge source at a certain point in the conversation. In this example, you will return to the "Sales or service" topic and create a node that uses generative answers to respond by only using knowledge from the Surface support page when the user is looking for support.

To add generative answers to a topic node

1. Select the **Topics** tab at the top of the **Surface Support Guide** agent to return to the list of topics.

2. Select the **Sales or support** topic to open it.

3. Locate the **Question** node where the agent asks the user for the details of their device. Select the three dots at the top right to expand the menu and select **Delete** to delete this **Question** node.

4. Add a new question node in its place. In the message field, add this text: **How can we help you?**

5. In the **Identify** option, select **User's entire response**. This option stores the response as a string variable and doesn't attempt to extract any entities in the response.

6. Select the **Var1** variable to open the **Variable properties** pane. Change the variable name to **supportQuestion**.

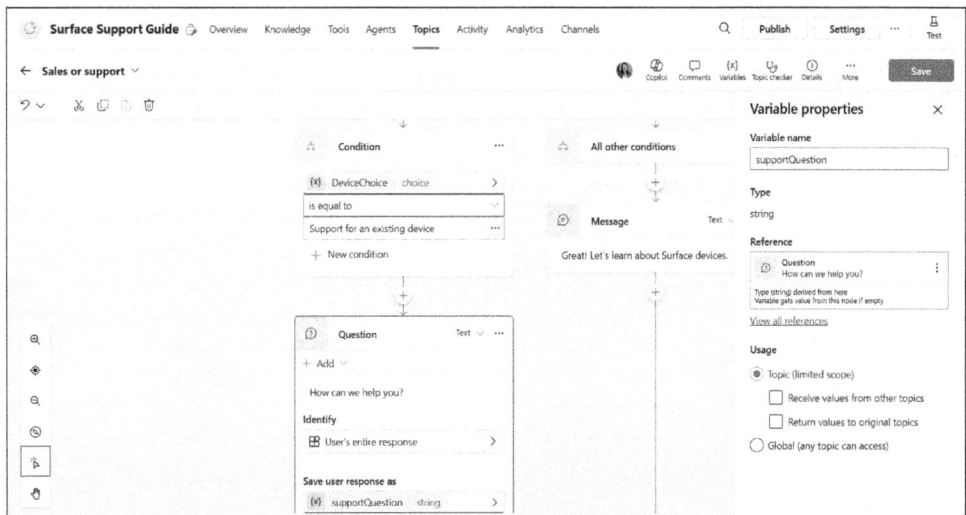

Add a new Question node that identifies the user's entire response and save the response as a string variable.

7. Close the **Variable properties** pane.

8. Select the + button under that Question node, select **Advanced**, and then select **Generative answers**.

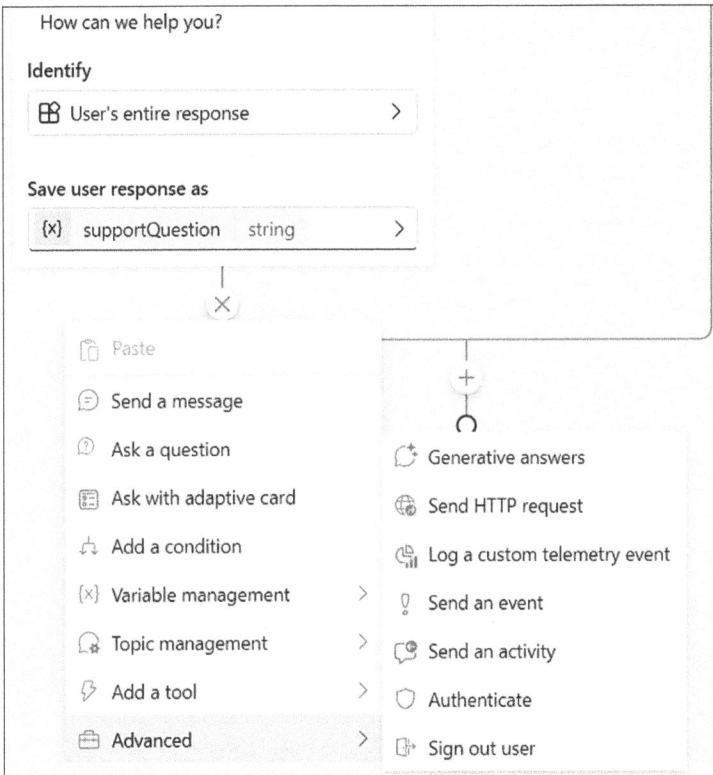

Add a Generative answers node from the Advanced options.

9. The **Generative answers** node needs an **Input**, which is the string of text entered by the user in the previous node, and a **Data source**, which is the knowledge the agent should use to find the answer to this question.

10. In the **Input** field, select the three dots to open the **Select a variable** pane. Select the **supportQuestion** variable.

> ✓ **TIP** If you want to use the Generative answers node with the previous user input in the chat and you don't have a node that saves it as a variable, select the System variables tab, and then select the Activity.Text variable as the input.

11. In the **Data sources** section, select the **Edit** link. This opens the **Create generative answers properties** pane on the right.

12. In the **Knowledge sources** section, set the **Search only selected sources** toggle to the **On** position.

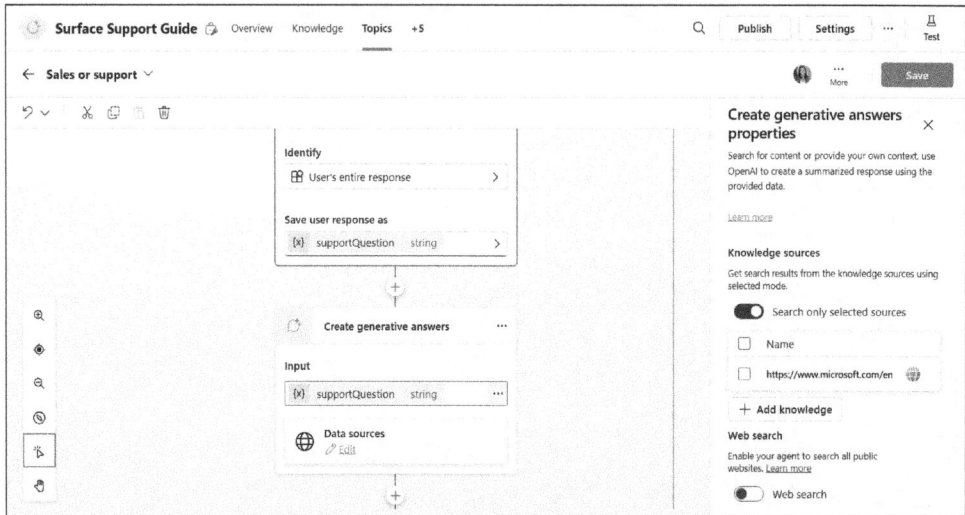

Set the generative answers properties to only search using specific knowledge sources.

13. Select the **+Add knowledge** button.

14. In the Add knowledge pop-up, select **Public websites**.

15. Enter the link to the Microsoft Surface support website: **https://support.microsoft.com/en-us/surface**. Then select the **Add** button.

16. Edit the **Name** to **Microsoft Surface Support**. Edit the **Description** to **This knowledge source provides troubleshooting and support information for Surface devices.**

17. Select the **Add to agent** button and wait for the website to be added.

18. The **Microsoft Surface Support** knowledge source is now available in the list of knowledge sources in the **Create generative answers properties** pane. Check the box next to this knowledge source, leaving the other knowledge source blank.

19. Close the **Create generative answers properties** pane using the **X** in the top right.

20. Select the **Save** button to save the changes to the topic.

21. Refresh the **test** pane and test the topic by entering: **I need help with my device**. When the agent responds, select **Support for an existing device**.

22. When the agent asks, "**How can we help you?**", enter a support question: **How do I charge my surface slim pen?**

Select the Microsoft Surface Support knowledge source by checking the box.

23. The agent responds using the support website as a knowledge source.

24. Refresh the **test** pane, then trigger the topic again and select the **Support** option.

25. This time, ask a question where the answer is not found in the Support site: **Can I buy a bundle of a pen and keyboard?**

26. The agent responds by letting the user know that it can't find the answer using the knowledge it has, but has found the best relevant answer from the Microsoft Surface Support knowledge source.

The agent uses only knowledge from the source added to the generative answers node to provide an answer.

Manage topic transitions and internal triggers

In this section, you'll learn how to manage the flow of a conversation by redirecting users to other topics, ending a topic or the entire conversation, and using internal triggers to start a topic from an event or activity.

Redirecting and ending topics and conversations

The final part of designing a topic is managing the behavior of the topic in relation to other topics and the rest of the agent experience. At the end of a topic, you can choose to redirect to another topic, end the topic, or end the conversation.

Redirecting to another topic allows the agent to shift to a different topic without starting the conversation again. You can use conditional logic in the topic to continue the conversation in one branch and redirect to a different topic from another branch. In this example, you will redirect the user to the "Sales or service" topic from the "Power cord recall" topic when their device is not eligible for a replacement power cord.

To redirect to another topic

1. Return to the **Power cord recall** topic in the Surface Support Guide agent.

2. Locate the **All other conditions** node in the branch where the user enters their device purchase date.

3. Below the **Msg_NotEligibleForRecall** node, select the + button, select **Topic management**, and then select **Go to another topic**.

4. This expands the list of topics in the agent, showing the custom topics you created, and the system topics that are automatically created by Copilot Studio when you create a new agent. Search or navigate down to find the **Sales or support** topic and select it.

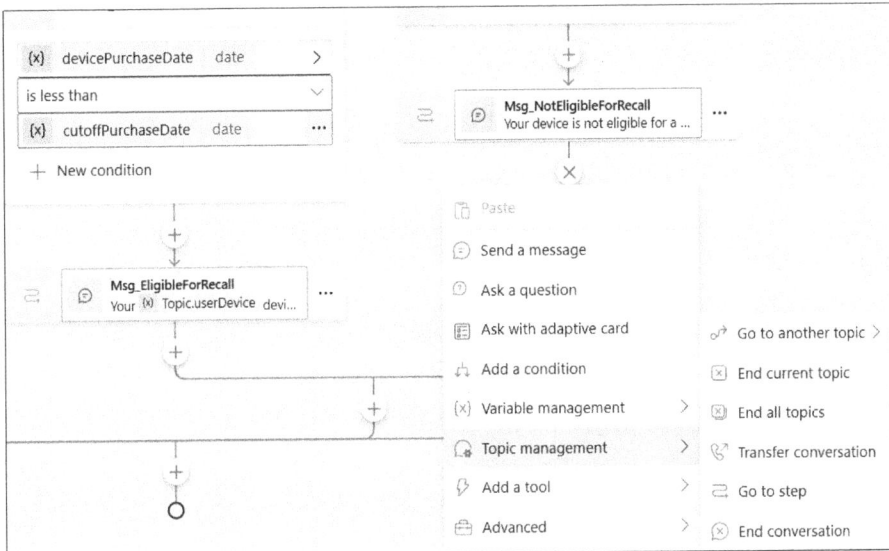

Add a new node, select Topic management, and then select Go to another topic.

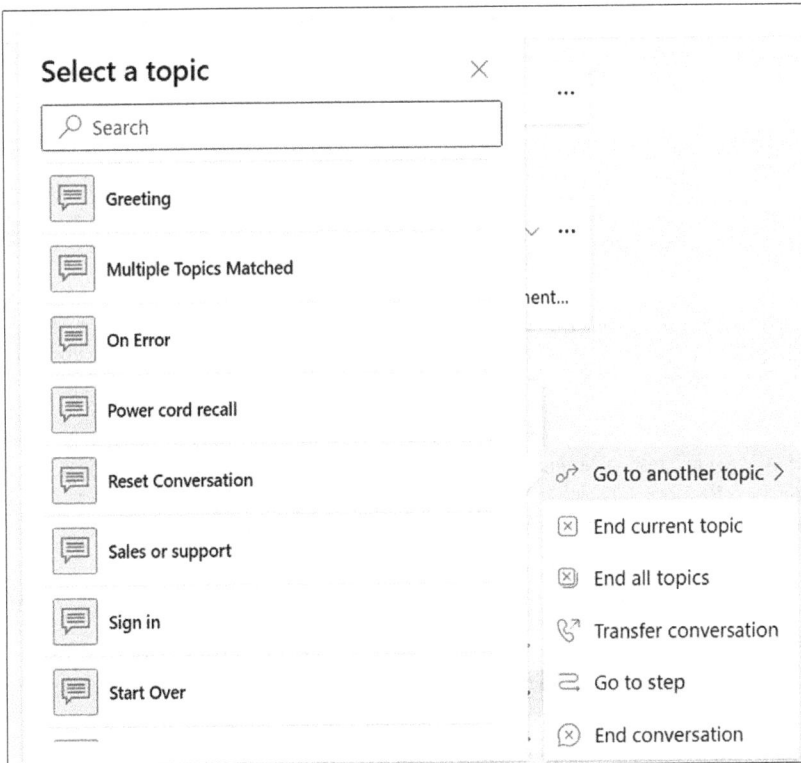

Search or browse the list of custom and system topics to select the topic you want to redirect to.

5. The **Redirect** node is added below the **Msg_NotEligibleForRecall** node.

6. Select the **Save** button to save the changes.

7. Test the agent by refreshing the **test** pane and triggering this topic.

8. Select the Surface Pro 3 device and then enter a purchase date after March 15, 2015.

9. The agent responds to let the user know their device is not eligible. It then asks whether the user wants to learn about Surface devices or wants support for an existing device. The topic tracker on the main part of the screen switches to show that the current stage of the conversation is the Question node in the Sales or support topic.

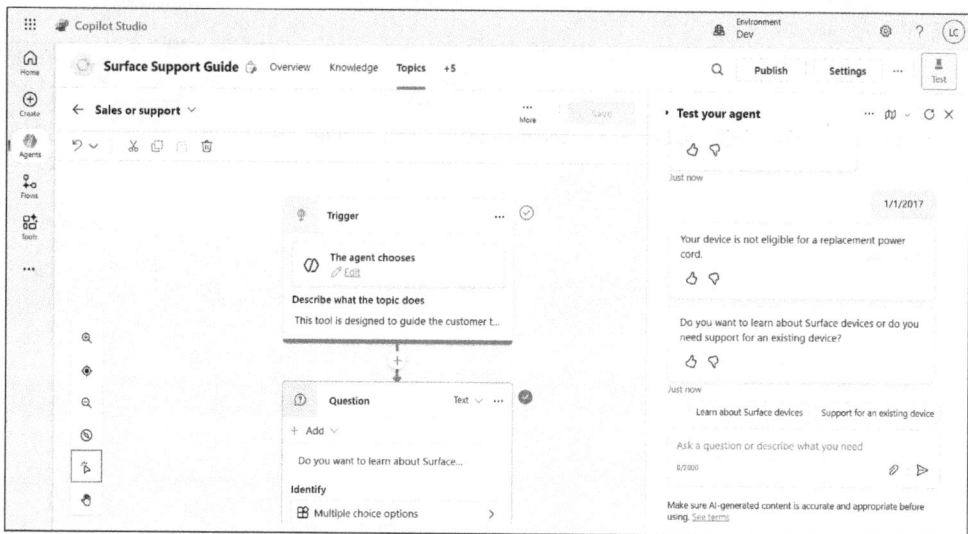

The agent redirects the conversation to the Sales or support topic.

> **SEE ALSO** You can pass variables between topics if you need to send input to the new topic or return output back to the original topic. For more information, refer to https://learn.microsoft.com/en-us/microsoft-copilot-studio/authoring-variables?tabs= webApp#pass-variables-between-topics.

You can also manage the flow of topics by marking the end of a topic or the end of a conversation when a task or conversational flow is complete. This helps to manage the conversation flow and avoid unintended looping or transitions.

It's also useful to consider where you want to define the end of a topic or a conversation if you are using redirects. When you have redirected from one topic to another, when the second topic is complete, the default behavior is that the conversation returns to the original topic. You can use an End topic node to change this behavior.

To end the topic

1. Return to the **Power cord recall** topic and locate the **Msg_EligibleForRecall** node under the **Cond_DeviceOriginalSurfacePro** conditional branch.

2. Select the + button under the message node, select **Topic management**, and then select **End current topic**.

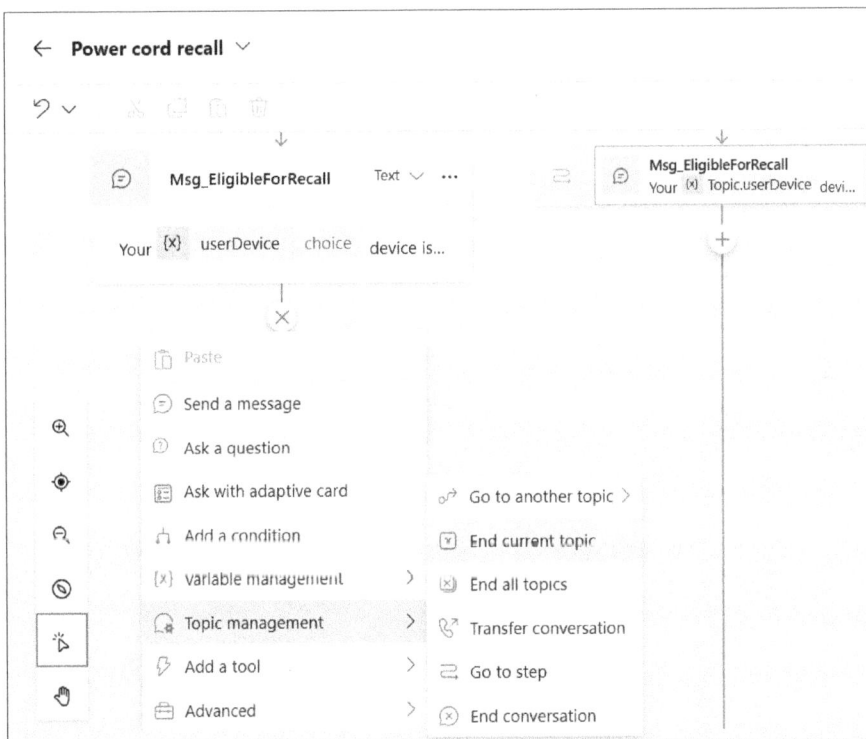

Add an End current topic node to mark the end of the topic at this part of the conversation flow.

3. This adds the **End current topic** node to the authoring canvas. Select the **Save** button to save the changes to the topic.

> **TIP** You can add an End all topics node if you want the agent to end all active topics and consider the next message from the user as the start of a new conversation.

To end the conversation

1. Return to the **Sales or support** topic.

2. Select the + button below the **Create generative answers** node, select **Topic management**, and then select **End conversation**.

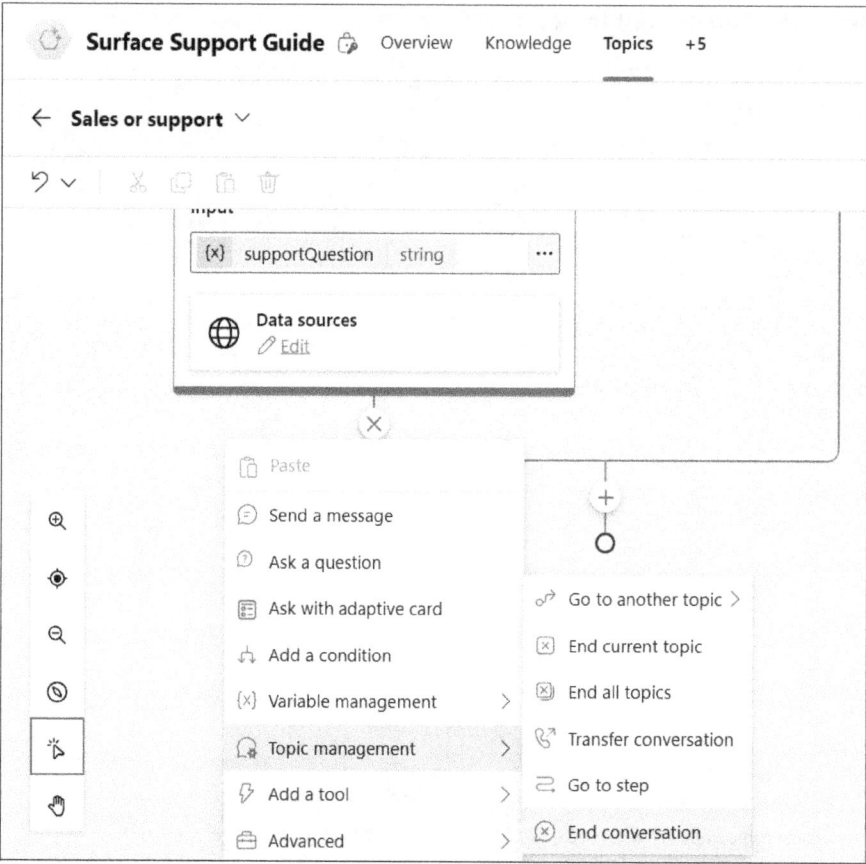

Select the End conversation node to end the conversation at this point in the topic flow.

3. This adds the **End conversation** node to the authoring canvas. Select the **Save** button to save the changes to the topic.

If you want to end the conversation by asking for feedback from the user, you can redirect to the "End of Conversation" system topic.

> ✅ **TIP** Choose either the End conversation node or redirect to the End of Conversation topic. If you add the redirect after you add an End conversation node, it won't reach the redirect to the End of Conversation topic.

To end the conversation asking for user feedback

1. Return to the **Sales or support** topic and delete the **End of conversation** node you just added.

2. Select the + button below the **Create generative answers** node, select **Topic management**, and then select **Go to another topic**.

3. In the **Select a topic** pane, select the **End of conversation** topic.

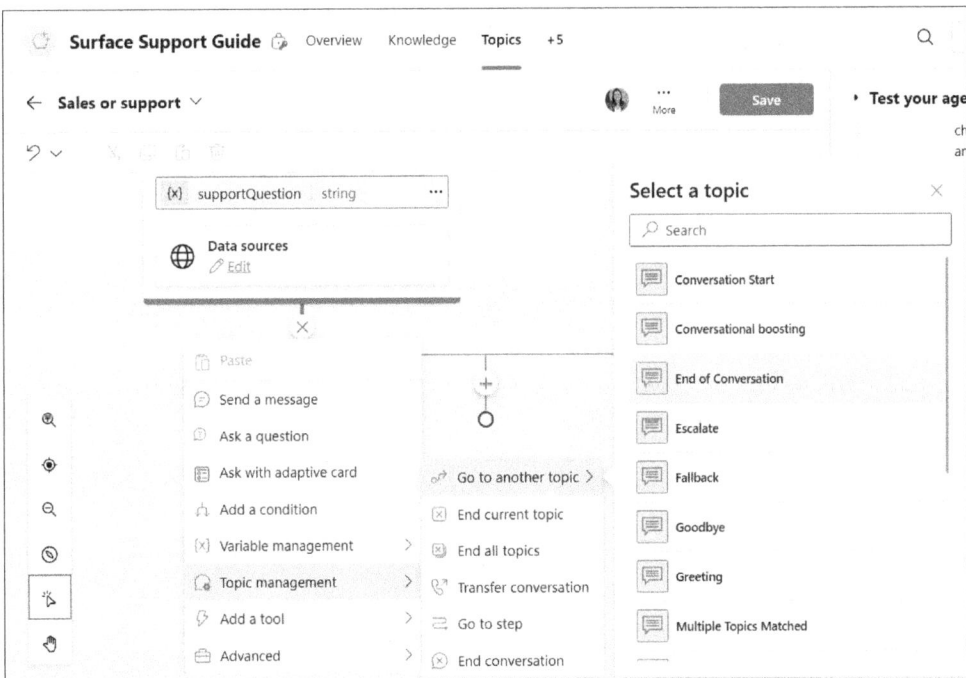

Select "End of Conversation" from the redirect to another topic menu.

4. This adds a **Redirect** node to the **End of Conversation** system topic. Select the **Save** button to save the changes.

5. Test the agent by refreshing the **test** pane and triggering this topic with this prompt: **help with a device.**

6. Select the **Support for an existing device** option, and enter a question: **how do I charge my pen?**

7. The agent responds with information from the knowledge. It then prompts with "**Did that answer your question**" and offers thumbs-up and thumbs-down options.

8. The topic tracker on the main part of the screen switches to show that the current stage of the conversation is the **Question** node in the **End of Conversation** topic.

9. Zoom out on the topic canvas to view the conditional branching in this topic. If the user responds with a thumbs up, the agent will respond with a CSAT question asking for a rating out of 5 stars. If the user responds with a thumbs down, it follows an escalation path.

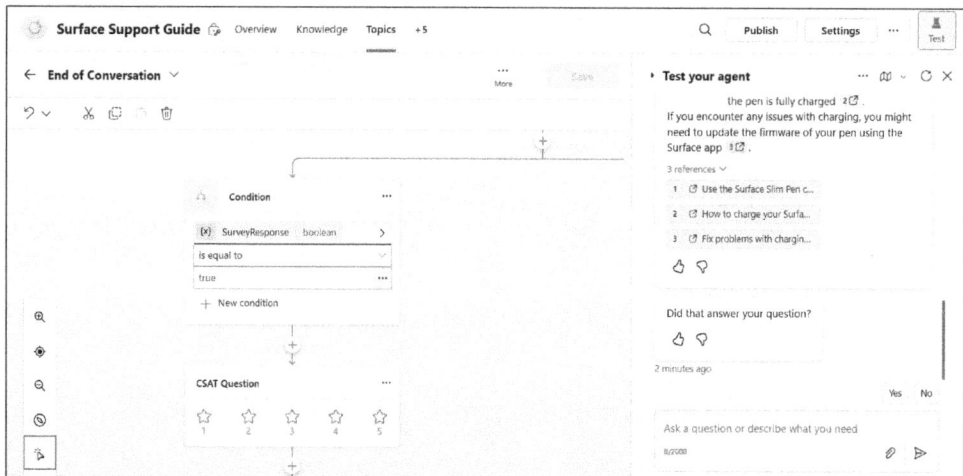

The End of Conversation topic includes asking the user for feedback with a CSAT survey.

10. Select the **Yes** button in the chat with the agent to view the CSAT rating card. Provide a rating.

11. Review the **End of Conversation** topic in the topic tracker. The agent will continue the conversation if the user says they want help with anything else or end the conversation if they don't.

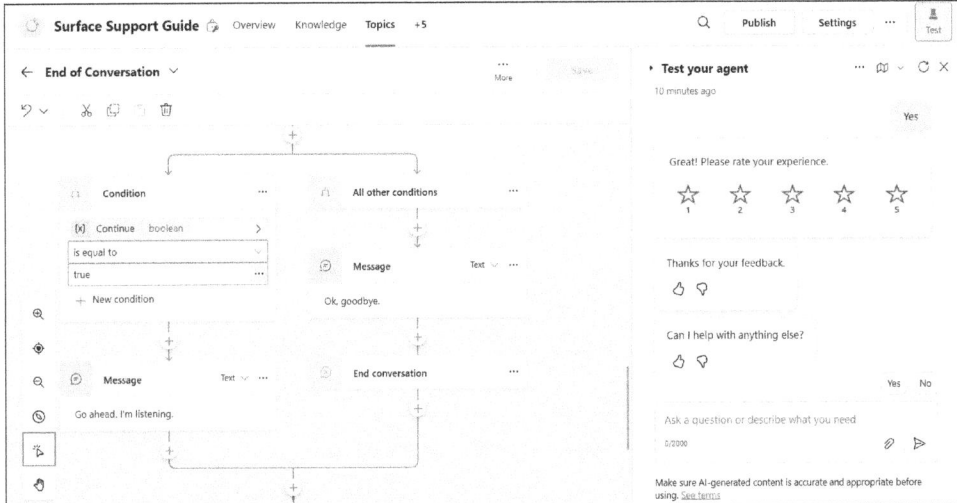

The End of Conversation topic prompts the user to ask another question or ends the conversation.

Topic triggers

Earlier in this chapter, you learned how to trigger a topic using trigger phrases (classic orchestration), or a topic name and description (generative orchestration). These methods of triggering a topic are the default behavior, but you can also use internal triggers to control when a topic starts.

You can create these triggers based on different types of activities from the user or the system, including messages, events, or conversation updates. You can also trigger topics based on the conversation flow, such as on redirect or inactivity.

Some triggers are only available for agents that use generative orchestration. They allow you to trigger a topic when a plan completes or before an AI response is generated. You can use these triggers to intercept and check or change an AI-generated response, or to take another action before the agent sends the response to the user.

> **SEE ALSO** For a full description of the trigger types available and links to further resources, refer to https://learn.microsoft.com/en-us/microsoft-copilot-studio/authoring-triggers.

To view the available trigger options

1. Navigate to the **Sales and service** topic in the Surface Support Guide agent.

2. In the **Trigger** node, hover over the box labeled "**The agent chooses**" and then select the **Change trigger** icon.

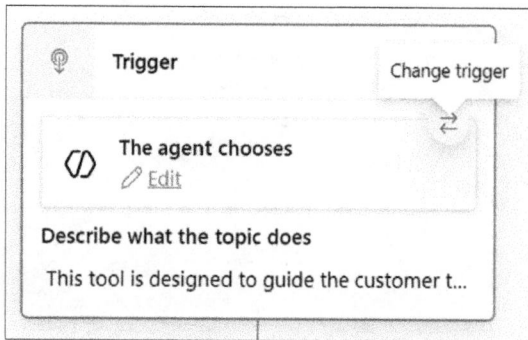

Hover over the box in the trigger node to find the change trigger option.

3. The **Change trigger** pane will appear, listing all the topic trigger options available. Search for or select the trigger you want to use.

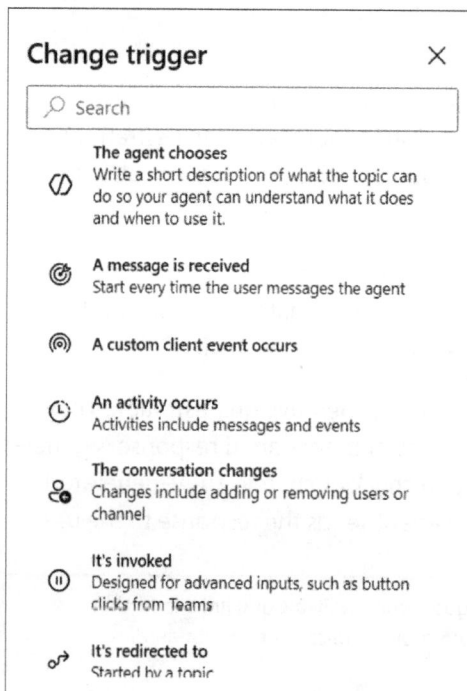

You can trigger a topic using a range of events and activities.

4. Select the trigger **An activity occurs**. This changes the trigger in the **Trigger** node.

5. Select the **Edit** button under the new trigger to configure the properties.

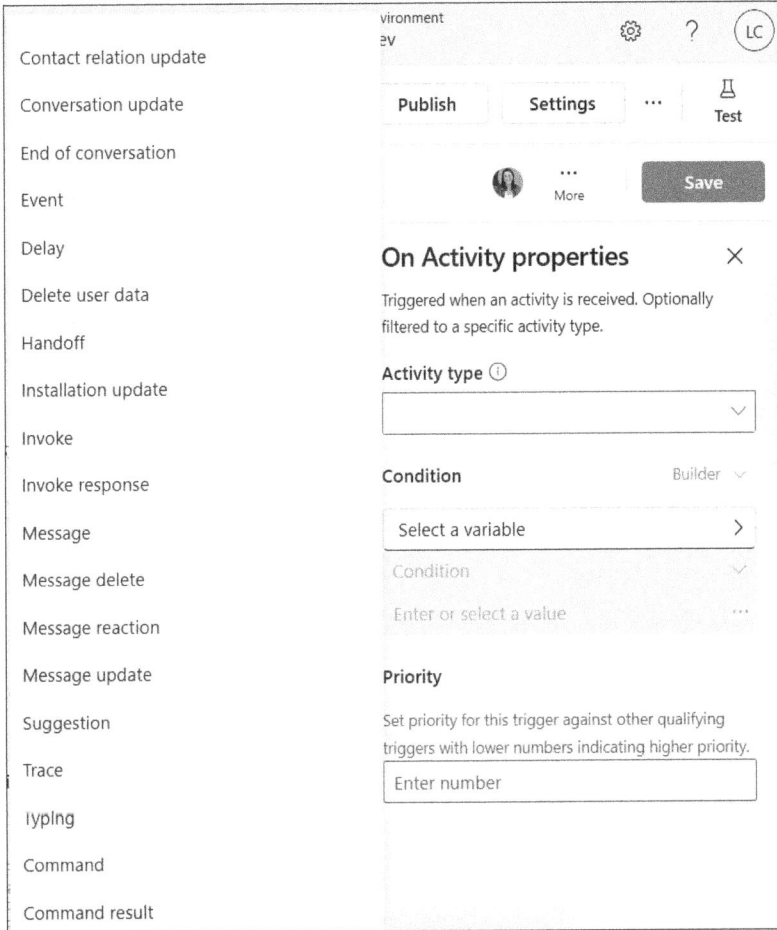

Contact relation update	
Conversation update	Publish Settings ··· Test
End of conversation	
Event	··· More Save
Delay	**On Activity properties** ×
Delete user data	Triggered when an activity is received. Optionally filtered to a specific activity type.
Handoff	
Installation update	**Activity type** ⓘ
Invoke	
Invoke response	**Condition** Builder ⌄
Message	Select a variable ›
Message delete	Condition ⌄
Message reaction	Enter or select a value ···
Message update	**Priority**
Suggestion	Set priority for this trigger against other qualifying triggers with lower numbers indicating higher priority.
Trace	Enter number
Typing	
Command	
Command result	

Use the On Activity properties pane to configure the properties of your selected trigger.

6. Explore the available options here, or close the configuration pane and exit the topic without saving the changes.

The available properties will depend on which trigger you choose. You can set the activity type, build conditions or use PowerFx formulas to define the trigger, and set a priority for this trigger against other qualifying triggers.

> **SEE ALSO** The activities here follow the Activity Protocol schema used within the Azure Bot Service. For documentation and details on the meaning of each activity and the fields that can be included, refer to https://github.com/microsoft/Agents/blob/main/specs/activity/protocol-activity.md.

System topics

When you create a new agent in Copilot Studio, it comes with prebuilt system topics to handle common agent functions like starting and ending the conversation, escalation, and fallback behavior.

> **SEE ALSO** For documentation on the available system topics and how they are used, refer to https://learn.microsoft.com/en-us/microsoft-copilot-studio/authoring-system-topics?tabs=webApp.

To view the system topics

1. Navigate to the **Topics** tab in the Surface Support Guide agent.

2. Select the **System filter** button at the top of the list.

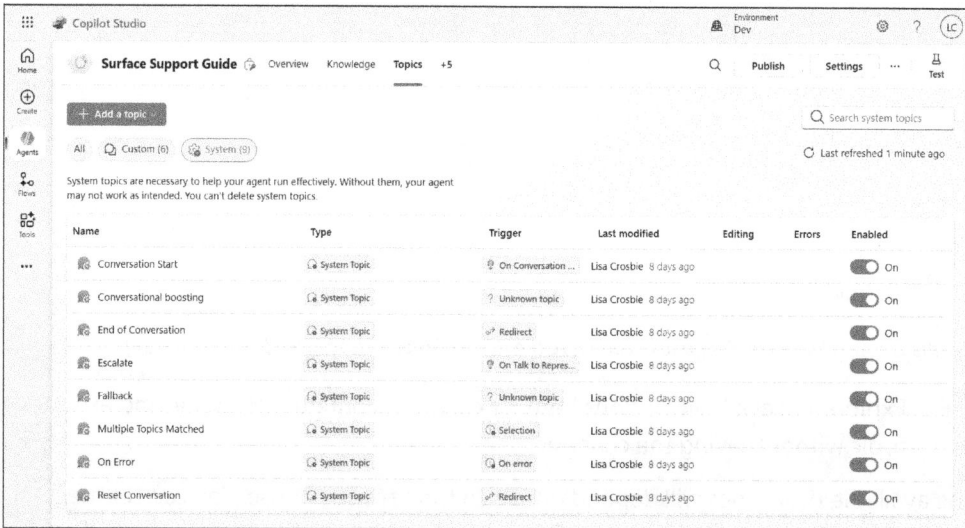

System topics perform basic agent functions, including starting and ending the conversation, escalations, and fallback.

3. Select a topic from the list to open it and view it in the authoring canvas.

4. Repeat this process, browsing through several system topics to understand how they are triggered and what they do.

You can edit and configure the system topics using the techniques learned in this chapter. You can choose to disable any system topics that you don't want to use in your agent by using the toggle settings in this list.

> **SEE ALSO** To edit the greeting your agent uses, configure the Conversation Start topic as shown in the section "Edit the Conversation Start topic" in Chapter 4: Building agents in Copilot Studio.

> **SEE ALSO** The Conversational boosting system topic is covered in the section "Generative answers and the Conversational boosting topic" in Chapter 6: Grounding agents in knowledge.

> **SEE ALSO** Fallback and escalation topics are covered in the "Plan for fallback and escalation" section in Chapter 2: Designing effective agents.

Skills review

In this chapter, you learned how to:

- Create a topic by describing it and create a topic from blank.

- Understand how triggers work, and the different behaviors of triggers in agents using classic or generative orchestration.

- Add message nodes using plain text, rich text formatting, images, basic cards, and adaptive cards.

- Add question nodes and use variables, entities, and conditions.

- Expand a topic by using PowerFx formulas, building conditional logic, configuring skip behavior, and using generative answers nodes to add a knowledge source to a topic.

- Manage the topic flow using end and redirect nodes, and understand the available options to trigger a topic from an activity or event.

Practice tasks

Before you can complete these tasks, you must copy the book's practice files to your computer. The practice files for these tasks can be found in the CopilotStudioSBS\Ch07 folder.

Create and edit topics

Open the Surface Support Guide agent you created in Chapter 1 and then complete the following tasks:

1. Enable generative orchestration for your agent in the **Overview** tab.

2. Select the **Topics** tab from the top menu.

3. If you followed along with the exercises in this chapter and created a topic for Power cord recall, disable that topic in the **Topics** menu before proceeding.

4. Select the **Add new topics** button, and then select **Add from description with Copilot**.

5. Name the topic: **AC Power Cord Recall**.

6. In the **Create a topic to ...** box, enter the following text: **Help the user with the AC Power Cord recall for selected Surface devices. First ask the user what kind of device they have, providing options for Original Surface Pro, Surface Pro 2, and Surface Pro 3. If they have a Surface Pro 3, check that the purchase date is before March 15, 2015.**

7. Review the topic created and select **Save**.

8. Test the topic in the **test** pane.

Use message nodes and adaptive cards

Continue working in the topic you just created in the Surface Support Guide agent and complete the following tasks:

1. Select the + button between the **Trigger** node and the **Question** node at the start of the topic to add a new node.

2. Select **Send a message**.

3. In the **Message** node, select the **+Add** button and select **Adaptive card**.

4. In the **Adaptive card properties** pane, select the **Edit adaptive card** button to open the **Adaptive card designer**.

5. Open the AdaptiveCardJSON file in the files provided and copy all of the JSON in that file.

6. Return to the **Adaptive card designer** in Copilot Studio. Delete all the text in the **Card payload editor** and paste in the copied JSON.

7. Save the changes and close the designer.

8. Review the adaptive card in the topic authoring canvas and save the changes to the topic.

9. Test the agent by triggering this topic and viewing the card in the chat.

Use questions, variables, and entities

Continue working in the Surface Support Guide agent in Copilot Studio, and complete the following tasks:

1. In the Surface Support Guide agent, select the **Topics** tab.

2. Add a new topic from blank.

3. Change the name of the topic to **Keyboard colors**.

4. Edit the description in the trigger to **This topic helps the user find out what keyboard colors are available**.

5. Add a Question node below the trigger.

6. In the message of the Question node, enter the text: **We have a range of colorful keyboard options. What color would you like?**

7. In the **Identify** field, expand the options, then search for and select the **Color** entity.

8. Select the variable and edit the name to **keyboardColor**.

9. Save the changes to the topic.

Use formulas, logic, and generative answers

Continue working in the topic you created in the previous activity, and complete the following tasks:

1. Add a **Condition** node below the question node.

2. In the **Condition** node, expand the **Select a variable** field, and select the **keyboardColor** custom variable.

3. In the drop-down field where you can select a condition, select **in**.

4. Expand the **formula** field by selecting the three dots.

5. Select the **Formula** tab to open the PowerFx editor.

6. Enter a formula that checks whether the color is Purple, Blue, or Gray: **["Purple", "Blue", "Gray"]**

7. Select the **Insert** button.

8. Add a **Message** node below the condition, with this message: **We have that color.**

9. Add a **Message** node below the "**All other conditions**" node, with this message: **Sorry, we don't have that color.**

10. Select **Save** to save the changes to the topic.

11. Test the topic by triggering it and then entering one of the colors on the list. The agent should confirm that color is available.

12. Select the **Variables** icon at the top of the authoring canvas and select the **Test** tab to view the saved value of the variable.

13. Refresh the **test** pane and test again using a color that isn't in the list. The agent should advise that color isn't available.

14. Refresh the **test** pane and test again using a synonym for one of the colors: Violet. The agent should advise that color is available. View the **Variables** to note that it has stored the value as **Purple**.

Manage topic transitions and internal triggers

Continue working in the topic you created in the previous activity, and complete the following tasks:

1. Add a new node at the end of the topic, below the conditional branching. Select **Topic Management**, select **Go to another topic**, and then select the **End of Conversation** topic.

2. The topic will now end with a **Redirect** node to the **End of Conversation** topic.

3. Save the changes to the topic.

4. Refresh the **test** pane and test the topic again.

5. After the agent has confirmed your color selection, it will ask for feedback. Respond **Yes** when it asks if it has answered your question, and then respond to the CSAT survey.

Extending agents with tools

8

Practice files

No practice files are necessary to complete the practice tasks in this chapter.

You can enhance your agent's capabilities in Copilot Studio by using tools. Tools are components that allow your agent to take action and interact with other systems and data in your business.

Tools can range from simple actions, such as sending an email or adding a row to a SharePoint list, to more complex workflows, such as multi-step approval processes with conditional logic. They can also include more advanced integrations such as Model Context Protocol (MCP) servers, which provide a full suite of prebuilt tools.

An agent can use tools in a deterministic way, where the tools are added to specific topics to perform actions as part of the conversational flow. They can also be triggered by generative orchestration, where the agent selects and executes the right tool at runtime, filling the inputs as needed from the context.

Copilot Studio supports prebuilt tools and connectors using the low-code interface. It also offers you the ability to build custom integrations using custom or REST APIs where there is no prebuilt connector.

In this chapter

- Use connectors and REST APIs
- Create agent flows
- Add tools to a topic
- Use a prompt as a tool
- Add tools from a Model Context Protocol (MCP) server

In this chapter, you will learn about the different types of tools you can add to your agent in Copilot Studio. You will also discover how to connect and configure them, and how they extend the capability of your agent.

Use connectors and REST APIs

Connectors are tools that connect to a wide range of Microsoft and third-party systems to perform tasks such as sending emails or other notifications, looking up data in a SharePoint list or Dataverse table, and creating and updating rows in spreadsheets, lists, or other enterprise systems.

Copilot Studio uses Power Platform connectors, which are abstraction layers that act as wrappers around a REST API. The connector exposes the API operations as easy-to-use actions and triggers, enabling you to build low-code solutions that interact with external systems.

Power Platform offers hundreds of prebuilt connectors to popular services. If you want to connect your agent to a system that doesn't have a prebuilt connector, you can create custom connectors in Power Platform or add a REST API as a tool.

> **SEE ALSO** For a full list of Power Platform connectors, see https://learn.microsoft.com/en-us/connectors/connector-reference/#list-of-connectors.

> **SEE ALSO** For more information on custom connectors and how to build them, refer to https://learn.microsoft.com/en-us/connectors/custom-connectors/.

Add a connector as a tool

You can access and use all of the Power Platform's low-code, prebuilt connectors inside Copilot Studio, adding them at the agent level or as a node in a topic.

When you add a connector as a tool at the agent level, the generative orchestration will determine when to call that tool to take the required action. When you configure the tool, you set up a description to help the agent understand what the tool is for and when to use it, and you configure the required inputs. The agent can then use AI to automatically generate questions to prompt the user to provide all of the required inputs, so you don't need to build a topic with a series of questions and variables.

> ⚠️ **IMPORTANT** The ability to add a tool at the agent level is available only when your agent uses generative orchestration.

> 🔍 **SEE ALSO** If you are using classic orchestration, you can use tools by adding them as nodes in a topic, as covered in the section "Add tools to a topic" later in this chapter.

In this example, you will create a new agent that helps users submit an expense claim, using the SharePoint list you set up in Chapter 5. Later in the chapter, you will also use a connector to Dataverse that connects to the out-of-the-box account table. So, you should build your agent in an environment where you have Dataverse with sample data deployed, or where you have added your own data to the account table.

> 🔍 **SEE ALSO** For details of the SharePoint list used in this example, refer to the section "Plan an autonomous agent" in Chapter 5: Building autonomous agents.

To set up a SharePoint list and agent for the exercises in this chapter

1. Add another column to the Expense Claims SharePoint list for the merchant.

   - Column name: **Merchant**

   - Type: **Text**

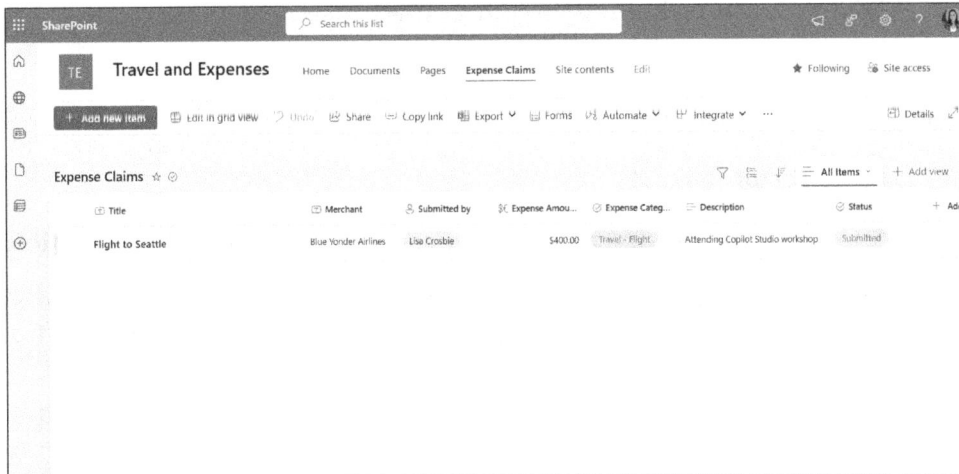

Expense claims will be added to a SharePoint list using the agent.

2. Open Copilot Studio and create a new agent.

3. Skip to configure, give the agent a name: **Expense Helper**.

4. Select **Create**.

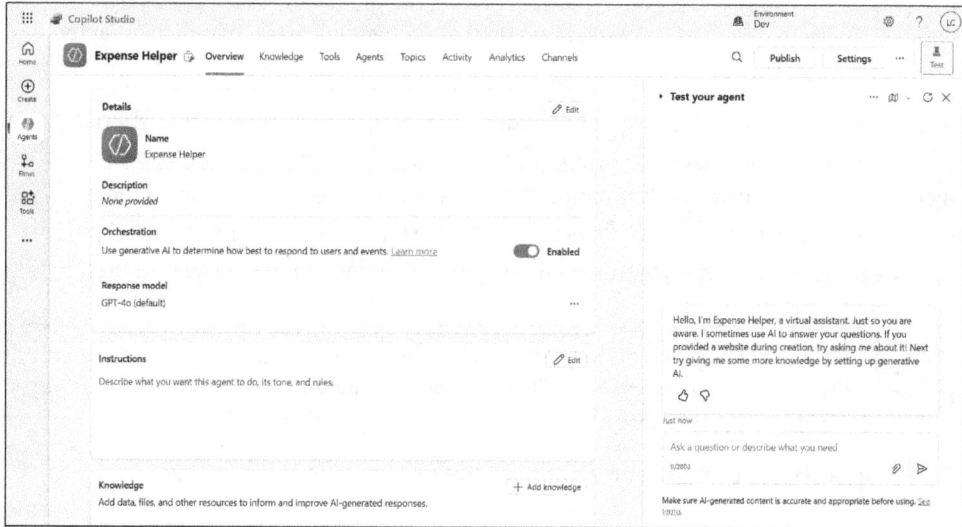

Create a new agent with the name Expense Helper.

5. In the **Settings** area for the agent, navigate to the Knowledge section of the Generative AI settings. Ensure that **Use general knowledge** and **Use information from the Web** are both disabled.

6. Save the settings and close the **Settings** screen.

You are now ready to begin adding and using tools in this agent.

To add a connector as a tool

1. Select the **Tools** tab from the top menu, and then select the **Add a tool** button.

2. The **Add tool** pop-up screen displays a list of featured connectors for the most commonly used systems, including Excel Online, Outlook, Microsoft Dataverse, and SharePoint.

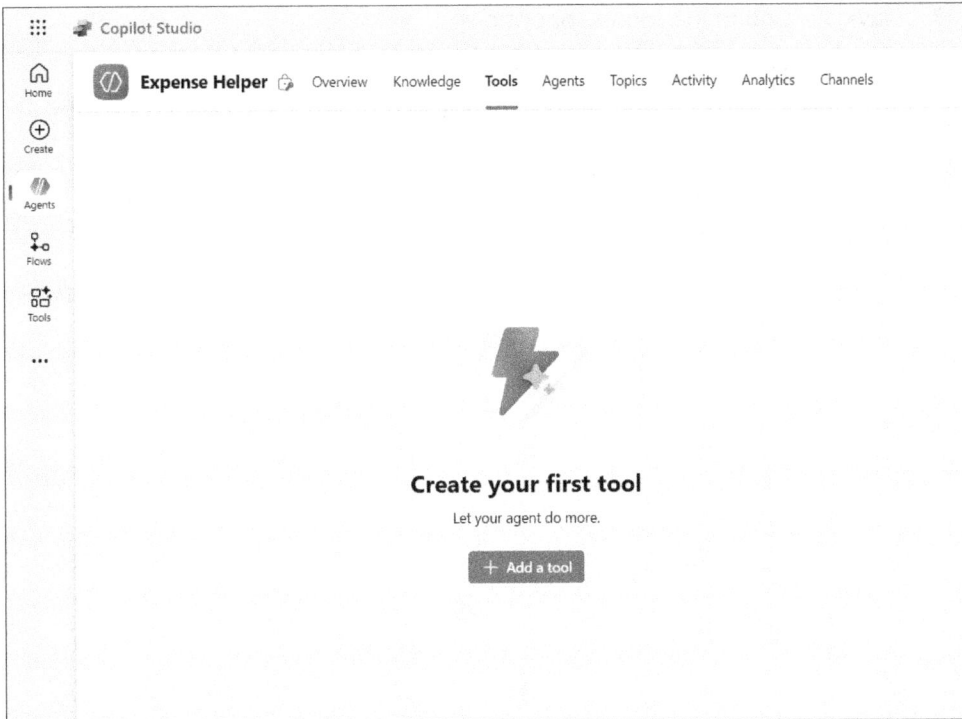

Select the Tools menu and select Add a tool.

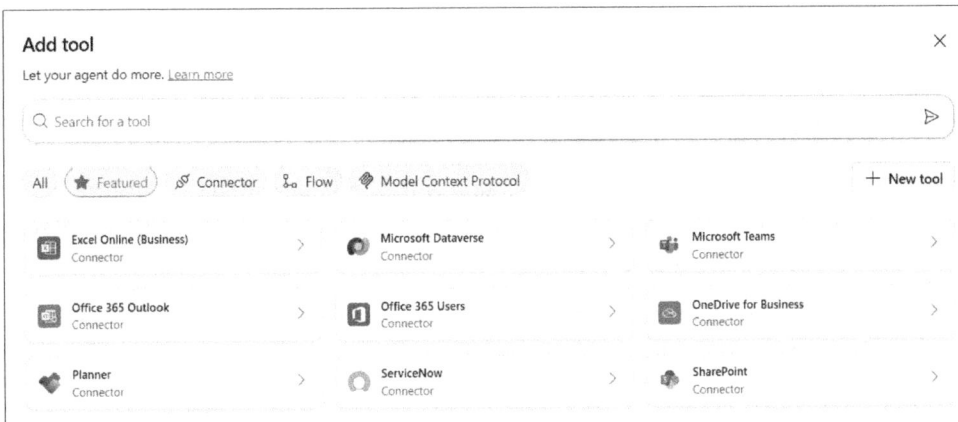

The Add tool screen displays a list of Featured connectors, and options to search for or browse other connectors and tools.

3. Navigate around the connector options:

   - Select the **SharePoint** connector to open it and view all the tools available in that connector, such as **Get items**, **List folder**, and **Copy file**. Select the **Back** button to go back to the main **Add tool** screen.

   - Select the **Connector** filter button to view a list of all connectors and browse through the options.

   - Select the **Featured** button to go back to the list of **Featured** connectors.

4. In the search bar, enter **create item SharePoint**. Then select **Enter**.

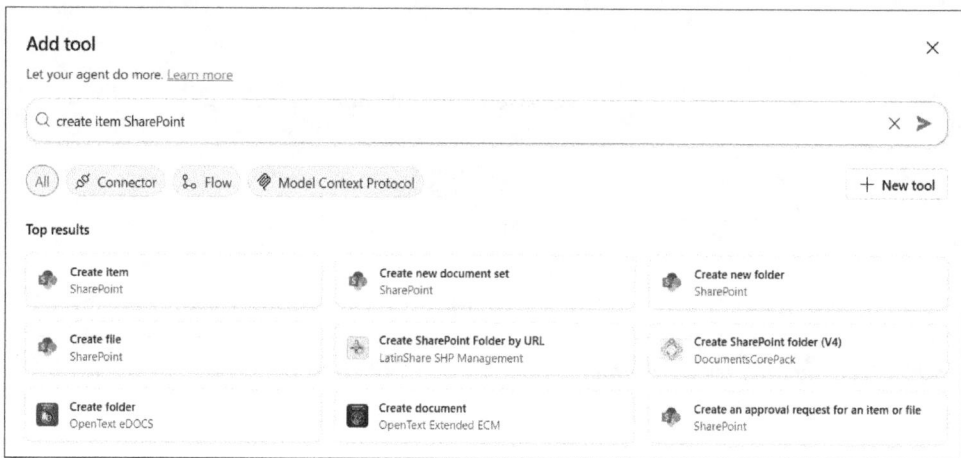

Search for the tool you want using keywords.

5. Select the **Create item (SharePoint)** tool that appears in the search results.

6. If you have already created a connection with SharePoint in this environment, the connection will already be validated, showing your login with a green check mark. If not, follow the prompts to create the connection.

7. Select **Add and configure**. The tool will be added to the agent and you will be redirected to the configuration screen for the tool.

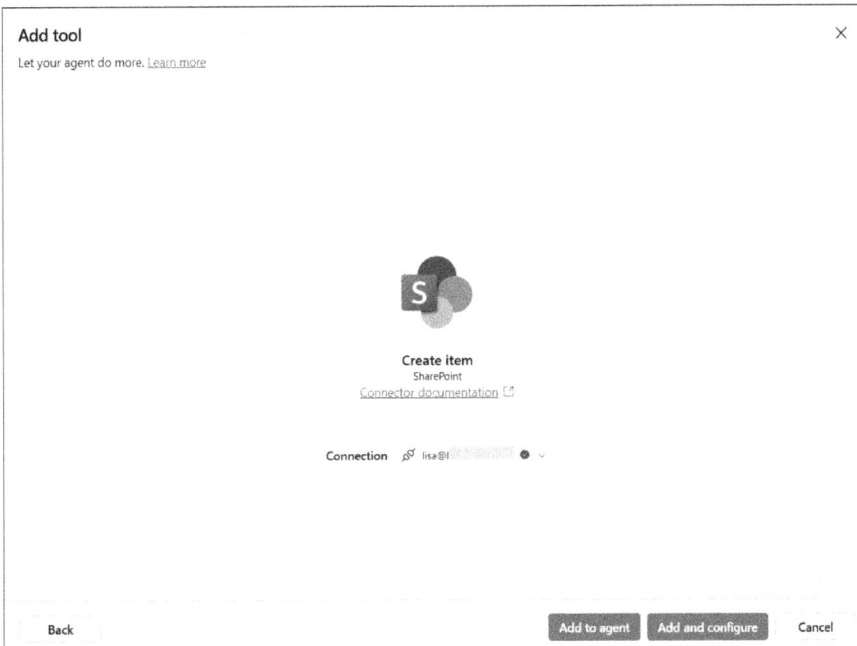

Create the connection with SharePoint, and select Add and configure.

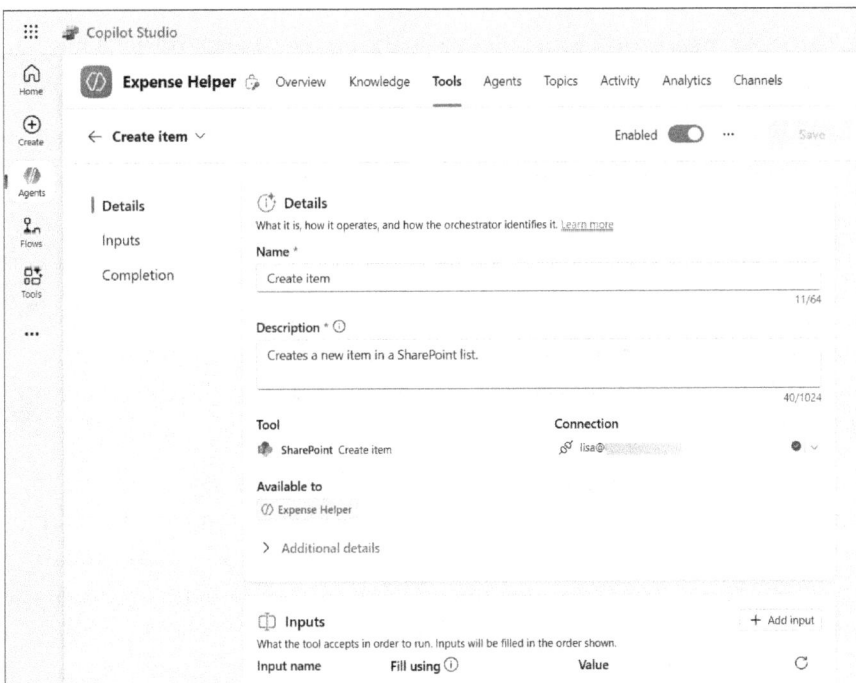

The tool opens in the configuration screen, where you can configure the options for how it will work.

You will now configure the options for how you want this tool to work in your agent. The configuration options will differ for each connector, but the core components will remain the same:

- An option for the tool to be **Enabled** or **Disabled**. This option is set to enabled by default when you add the tool, but you can return to this configuration screen to disable it if you need to.

- **Inputs:** Determine what information the tool needs to gather in order to run. You can set inputs to be dynamically filled by AI or set to specific values.

- **Completion:** Determines what the agent does after it has finished using the tool. By default, the agent is set to not respond after running, but you can change this setting to have the agent respond with an AI-generated response or a specific response that you write.

In this example, you will configure the Create item (SharePoint) tool. You will set up the inputs that you want the agent to ask the user for when creating an expense, and you will have the agent send a confirmation message when the submission is complete.

To configure the connector tool

1. Give the tool a meaningful name that helps the agent understand what it is and what it will be used for. Using a short phrase is best—for example: **Create Expense Claim**.

> **TIP** The original tool name will still be shown in the Properties section under the Description for future reference.

2. Give the tool a meaningful description that helps the agent understand how and when to use it. For example: **This tool collects information from the user about an Expense Claim and creates a new row in the Expense Claim SharePoint list.**

3. Expand the **Additional details** tab at the bottom of the **Details** section. In this section, you can configure the authentication for the tool, requiring the end user to sign in with their own credentials (the default option) or authenticating the user with maker-provided credentials. Expand the **Credentials to use** drop-down to view the options. Leave the **End user credentials** option selected.

Expense Helper · Overview · Knowledge · **Tools** · Agents · Topics · Activity · Analytics · Channels

← **Create Expense Claim** ∨   Enabled ⬤ ··· **Save**

| Details
Inputs
Completion

(i) **Details**
What it is, how it operates, and how the orchestrator identifies it. Learn more

Name *
Create Expense Claim
20/64

Description * (i)
This tool collects information from the user about an Expense Claim and creates a new row in the Expense Claim SharePoint list.
128/1024

Tool   **Connection**
SharePoint Create item   lisa@▇▇▇▇▇▇   ✓ ∨

Available to
Expense Helper

> Additional details

8

Give the tool a name and description that help the agent understand what it is for and when to use it.

Expense Helper ✓ · Overview · Knowledge · **Tools** · Agents · Topics · Activity · Analytics · Channels

← **Create Expense Claim** ∨   Enabled ⬤ ··· **Save**

Details
| Inputs
Completion

∨ Additional details   Builder ∨

When this tool may be used (i)
◯ Agent may use this tool at any time
◯ Only when referenced by topics or agents

Ask the end user before running
Recommended for sensitive or regulated domains or when making changes for the user

| No   ∨ |

Credentials to use
Control whether this action uses credentials you provide, or those of the end user.

| End user credentials   ∨ |

✓ End user credentials

Maker-provided credentials   ng asked to authenticate. For example, "Please log in
to ...
0/1024

You can configure the tool to use the end user's credentials or the maker-provided credentials.

> ✅ **TIP** You should use the end user's credentials when you want the user to authenticate so that the agent can act on their behalf, using only the data the user already has permission to access. You should use the maker-provided credentials when you want to connect using a service account, or when you are connecting to shared or public apps or data.

4. Navigate down to the **Inputs** section. There are already inputs listed for the **Site Address** and the **List Name**. Select the site address for your SharePoint site, using the drop-down menu.

5. In the **List Name** input, change the "**Fill using**" selection from "**Dynamically fill with AI**" to "**Custom value.**" Then select the SharePoint list name from the drop-down list.

⮥ Inputs			+ Add input
What the tool accepts in order to run. Inputs will be filled in the order shown.			
Input name	**Fill using** ⓘ	**Value**	↻
Site Address * dataset	Custom value ⌄	Travel and Expenses - htt... ⌄ ••• ⠿	
List Name * table	Custom value ⌄	Expense Claims ⌄ ••• ⠿	

Select the SharePoint site and list name in the Inputs section.

6. Now you will add inputs for any other columns in the list that you want the agent to ask the user to fill. Select the **+Add input** button.

> ✅ **TIP** If any columns in your SharePoint list are mandatory, they will automatically be added as inputs after you select the Site Address and List Name.

7. In the **Add input** pop-up, search for and select the **Title** column. Leave the "**Fill using**" selection as "**Dynamically fill with AI.**" This means the agent will ask for and identify the value for this column during the interaction with the user.

8. Select **Customize** next to the **Title input** to expand the customization options. Here you can choose how the column name will be displayed to the user and enter a description. The agent will use dynamic slot filling to generate questions to ask the user for this information, then save the input and use it to create the row in the SharePoint list.

> **SEE ALSO** The concept of slot filling and how it works with Copilot Studio agents are discussed in the section "Understand slot filling and configure skip behavior" in Chapter 7: Authoring topics.

9. Give the input a display name and a description that will help the agent understand what this input is, and how to generate a question that will ask the user to provide this information.

   - Display name: **Expense Title**

   - Description: **The name of the expense, displayed as the header title in the expense report for this line**

10. The "**Identify as**" option allows you to set an entity for this input, so that the agent understands what type of information it is looking for. In this case, you will leave the option selected as "**User's entire response**," because this input is a string of text.

> **SEE ALSO** The section "Understand entities" in Chapter 7: Authoring topics, explains in detail how entities work in Copilot Studio agents.

8

Expense Title
item.Title

Display name
How the input will be presented to the user.

Expense Title

13/64

Description

The name of the expense, displayed as the header title in the expense report for this line.

92/1024

Identify as
How the user's response should be interpreted.

User's entire response >

> Advanced

Fill the input display name and description to help the agent understand what this input is and how to ask the user to provide it.

11. Close the input customization form by selecting the **X** at the top right of the form.

12. Repeat steps 6–11 for the **Merchant** column, using the following description: **The name of the merchant at the top of the receipt**.

13. Repeat steps 6–11 for the other columns in your Expense Claims SharePoint list that you want the user to add, such as **Expense Amount**, **Date**, and **Expense Description**.

> **TIP** Select entities for the inputs that are not free text, such as Money for the expense amount, and Date for the date. Depending on how your SharePoint columns are set up, the entity may be automatically set up to match when you add the input.

14. Use the drag handle at the end of each input to rearrange the order of the inputs. The agent will work to fill the inputs in the order you configure.

15. Select the **Save** button to save the tool.

Configure each input to be filled dynamically by AI or with a custom value, and arrange the inputs in the order you want the agent to use them.

16. The final configuration step is to specify what the agent does when it finishes using the tool. Navigate to the **Completion** section of the form, below the **Inputs** section. The default option is "**Don't respond**." Expand the menu to view the other options.

Expand the "After running" option to view options for what the agent should do when it finishes using the tool.

17. Select "**Send specific response (specify below).**" This opens a message box where you can write the message you want the agent to send, using rich text formatting, variables, and Power Fx formulas.

18. Change the selection to "**Write the response with generative AI**." The message box is removed from the form. This option specifies that the agent should use generative AI to write the message in the context of the conversation, so you don't need to provide a message.

Completion

Specify what your agent does when it finishes using this tool.

After running:

Send specific response (specify below) ⌄

Message to display *
The user will see this message.

B *I* ≔ ≟ (x) *f*x

Enter a message

> Advanced

You can author a message for the agent to send, using rich text, variables, and Power Fx formulas.

Completion

Specify what your agent does when it finishes using this tool.

After running:

Write the response with generative AI ⌄

> Advanced

Select "Write the response with generative AI" so that the agent will create the message using AI based on the context of the conversation.

19. Select **Save** to save the changes to the tool.

Now it's time to test the agent and see how the tool can perform the automatic slot filling without needing a topic with question nodes.

To test the agent using slot filling

1. Trigger the topic by starting the chat with a phrase like this: **I need to submit an expense.**

2. The agent responds with a question asking the user for the first piece of information it needs—the title of the expense. The activity map shows that the

agent has called the **Create Expense Claim** connector action tool. It shows the inputs this tool already has and the inputs it is now looking for in the chat.

The agent calls the tool and prompts the user with a question to start filling in the inputs it needs.

3. Respond to the question with a title for the expense: **Flights to Seattle**.

4. The **activity map** shows that the agent has filled the **Expense Title (String)** slot with the user input. The agent now generates the next question to ask for the next input it needs.

5. Continue testing the agent by responding to each question and observing the slots that are filled in the **activity map** with each input.

6. Try making a change to one of the inputs. Note that the agent can take in the correction and update the slot in the **activity map**.

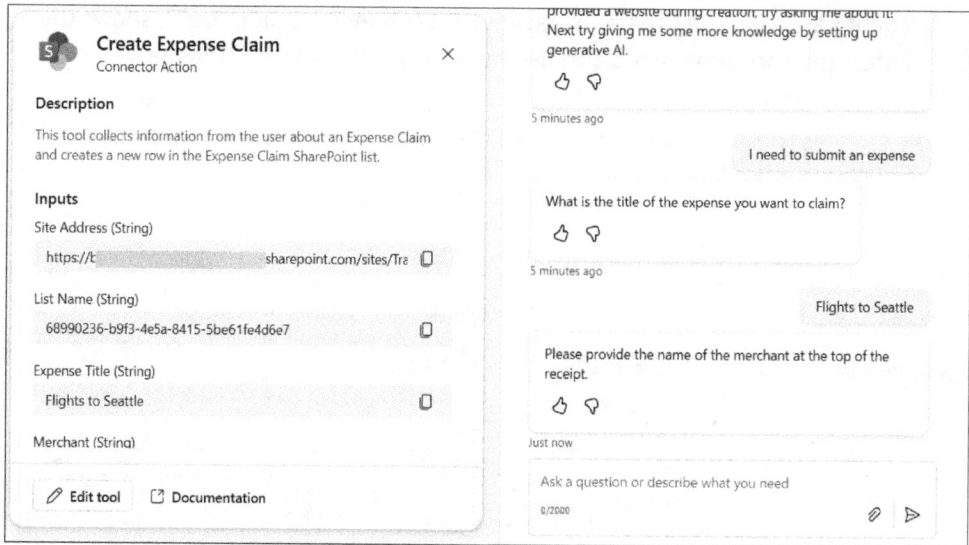

The agent fills the slot with the user response and generates a question to ask for the next input it needs.

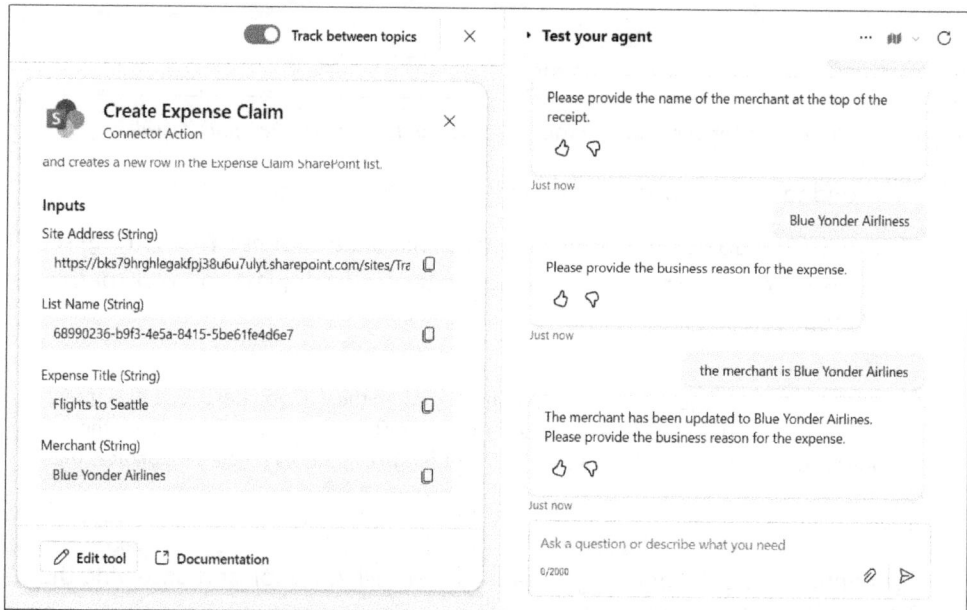

The agent can take in corrections to the input from the user chat.

7. When the agent has collected all of the required inputs, it will respond with an AI-generated message that confirms the details and lets the user know that the expense has been submitted.

> Your expense claim titled "Flights to Seattle" for the amount of $342.00, with merchant "Blue Yonder Airlines" and description "Copilot conference," has been successfully submitted with the status "Submitted."
>
> 👍 👎

The agent generates a message to confirm that the expense has been submitted.

8. The expense is added to the SharePoint list.

> ✅ **TIP** If you built the autonomous agent in Chapter 5: Building autonomous agents by using the same SharePoint list, that autonomous agent will be triggered when the expense is submitted, and it will approve or reject the expense. If you want to stop the autonomous agent while you are testing this one, disable the generative orchestration in the autonomous agent.

The expense is created in the SharePoint list with the details the user entered in the agent chat.

> ✅ **TIP** The "Submitted by" column is not filled in testing mode. When the agent is published in an internal channel, such as Microsoft 365 Copilot Chat or Microsoft Teams, the user will be logged in and authenticated, and this column will be automatically populated.

You can configure more options for the tool inputs and completion by expanding the **Advanced** menu in each section. These advanced options provide more control over the way the agent uses it and interacts in the chat, including:

- Configuring the prompt that the agent will use when it looks to fill the input slot.

- Setting the retry behavior and the retry prompt when the agent is unable to identify the entity in the user input and configuring escalation behavior.

- Using formulas to configure additional validation behavior for an input beyond standard entity recognition.

- Defining which outputs will be available to the agent and other tools.

Add a tool from a REST API

If you want more flexibility or customization in how you set up your tool, or if you can't find a prebuilt connector that meets your needs, you can use REST APIs to connect to external systems and data.

This is a more advanced technique than using a connector. To use it, you need to understand how the API works, how to securely connect to it, and how to tell your agent when to use it. You will need to have:

- The OpenAPI specification, describing the actions the API can perform and the data it expects and returns

- Authentication details, so that you can configure the tool with the type of authentication needed and know how the agent should authenticate when calling the API

- A natural language description to help the agent know when and how to use the API

> **SEE ALSO** The instructions here explain how you can add a tool to your agent using a REST API. For full documentation on all the requirements and steps involved, refer to the Microsoft documentation: https://learn.microsoft.com/en-us/microsoft-copilot-studio/ agent-extend-action-rest-api.

To add a tool using a REST API

1. Navigate to the **Tools** tab in your agent and select the **+Add a tool** button.

2. In the **Add tool** pop-up, select the **+New tool** button below the search field.

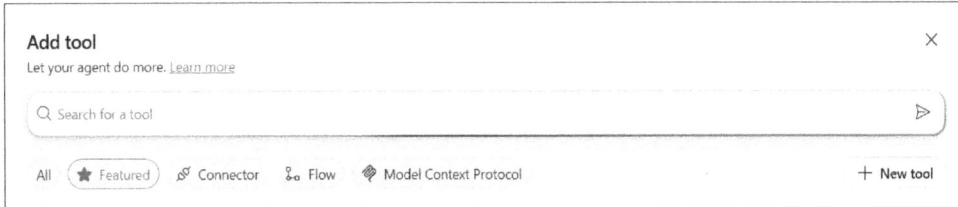

Select the +New tool button to expand the options for adding more tools.

3. Select the **REST API** option from the available tools.

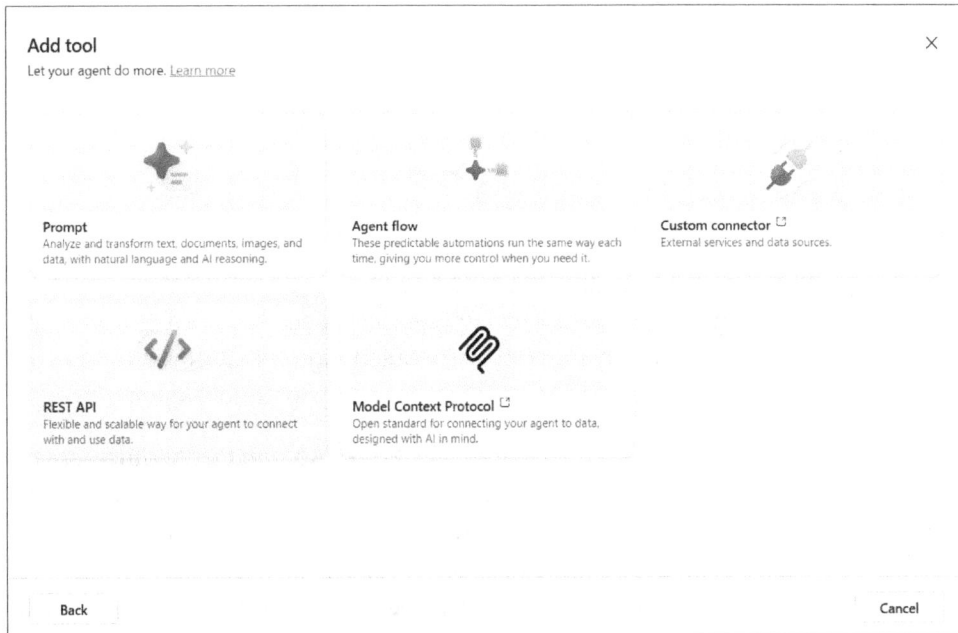

Select the REST API option from the Add tool pop-up to add and configure a REST API.

4. Upload your REST API specification, and follow the steps to configure the API plugin details, authentication, and tool parameters.

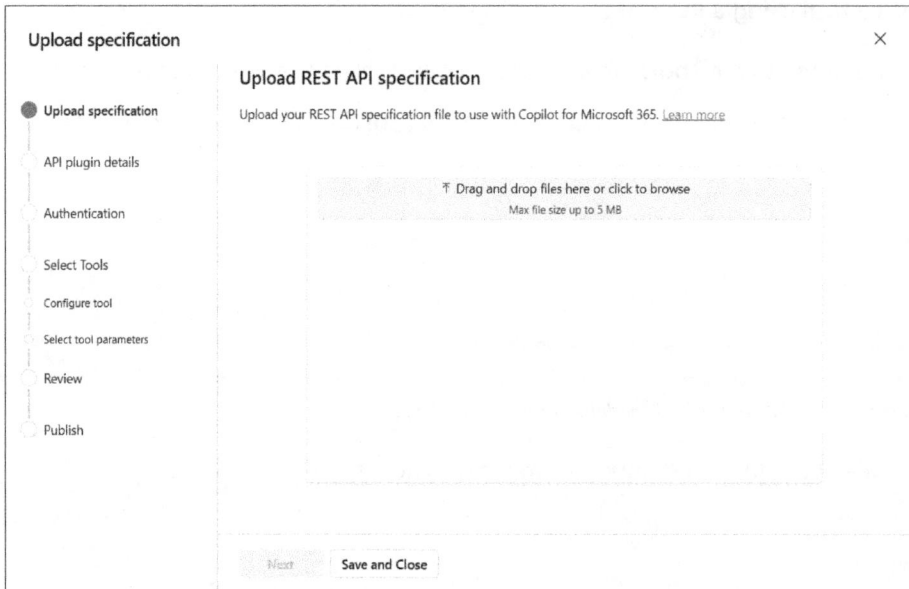

Upload specification ×

Upload REST API specification

Upload your REST API specification file to use with Copilot for Microsoft 365. Learn more

- Upload specification

- API plugin details

- Authentication

- Select Tools

- Configure tool

- Select tool parameters

- Review

- Publish

↑ Drag and drop files here or click to browse

Max file size up to 5 MB

Next   **Save and Close**

Upload your REST API specification and work through the configuration setup.

Create agent flows

Agent flows allow you to build workflow automations using a set of deterministic steps and logic. An agent flow starts with a trigger, which can be an event from a system, such as adding or updating a row, or a scheduled trigger that runs on a recurring basis. You can also call an agent flow as a tool in your Copilot Studio agent.

Agent flows are similar to Power Automate flows. Power Automate is another tool in the Power Platform that is used for building low-code automations. However, when you build agent flows directly in Copilot Studio, you have a more streamlined experience where you can build your agent solution all in one place. Agent flows also have some additional capabilities not available in Power Automate flows, such as multistage and AI approvals.

> ⚠ **IMPORTANT** Agent flows are billed using message consumption in Copilot Studio, whereas Power Automate flows are billed using a licensing plan for Power Automate. You can build flows in Power Automate and connect them as tools from your agent if you have already built flows in Power Automate that you want to reuse, or if that is a better fit for your licensing or solution model. You can also convert a Power Automate flow to a Copilot Studio agent flow if you prefer to manage it in Copilot Studio and have it billed using message consumption rather than Power Automate billing.

You can use an agent flow as part of your solution when you need to define a series of steps that must be done in a specific way and in a specific order, rather than using generative AI to reason over that part of the process. You should use agent flows where you need predictability of the automation.

Agent flows can be used as stand-alone flows in the same way as Power Automate flows, or they can be added as tools that can be called by your agent.

> **SEE ALSO** The skills used in this section to build flows are the same as those needed for Power Automate. If you want to dive deeper into these skills or start with a beginner tutorial on how to build flows, refer to the Microsoft Power Automate learning paths on Microsoft Learn: https://learn.microsoft.com/en-us/training/powerplatform/power-automate.

Create stand-alone agent flows

In this example, you will create an agent flow that is triggered when a new row is added to the Expense Claims list in SharePoint. The flow will check whether the merchant in the claim is an existing merchant in the Accounts table in Dataverse. If it is not an existing merchant, it will start an approval process.

This agent flow will work alongside the agent as an independent workflow, which is triggered when the row is added to the SharePoint list. It will work regardless of how the row is added—either by using the agent or by the user manually adding the row to the SharePoint list.

> **TIP** This example uses the out-of-the-box Account table in Dataverse with the sample data deployed. You will have this table in Dataverse in the default environment of your trial tenant, or in the environment you created if you enabled Dataverse. If you are not familiar with Dataverse or do not have access to it in your environment, you can do something similar by setting up a simple accounts table in Excel Online or another SharePoint list.

To create an agent flow

1. Select the **Flows** icon on the left side rail in Copilot Studio. This opens the **Agent flows** builder page.

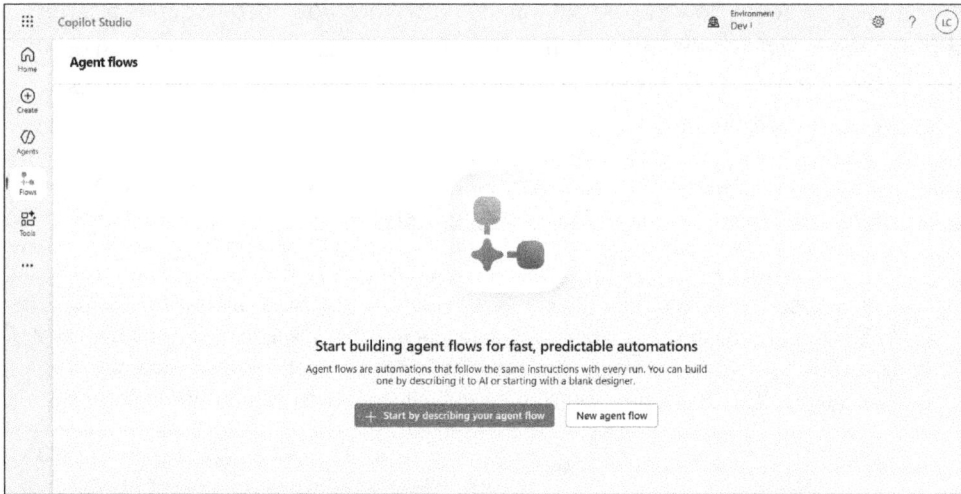

Build agent flows when you need a deterministic workflow.

2. Select the **+Start by describing your agent flow** button. This allows you to build an agent flow by describing it in natural language.

> ✅ **TIP** If you are familiar with building Power Automate flows or prefer to build using the agent flow designer, you can select the **New agent flow** option.

3. Describe what you want your flow to do. For example: **When a new item is added to the "Expense Claims" SharePoint list, list rows in the Dataverse Accounts table and filter for rows where the name is equal to the Merchant name. If there is at least one row that matches, send an email to the user with the subject "Merchant confirmed." If there are no matching rows, start an approval process.**

> ✅ **TIP** This natural language prompt uses some terminology that describes how some of the flow actions work, such as "list rows" and "filter." If you are not familiar with these terms, you can describe the flow in your own words, but you may need to do more editing on the flow that is generated. As you become more experienced in working with flows, you will find that you can write more effective descriptions to create them.

4. Copilot creates a draft flow for you to review. Depending on your prompt, more than one option may be available. In that case, you can move between the different options to compare them and select the one that is closest to what

you want. If the flow isn't right, you can rewrite the prompt in the **Description** area, or you can use the prompt below the draft flow to make changes.

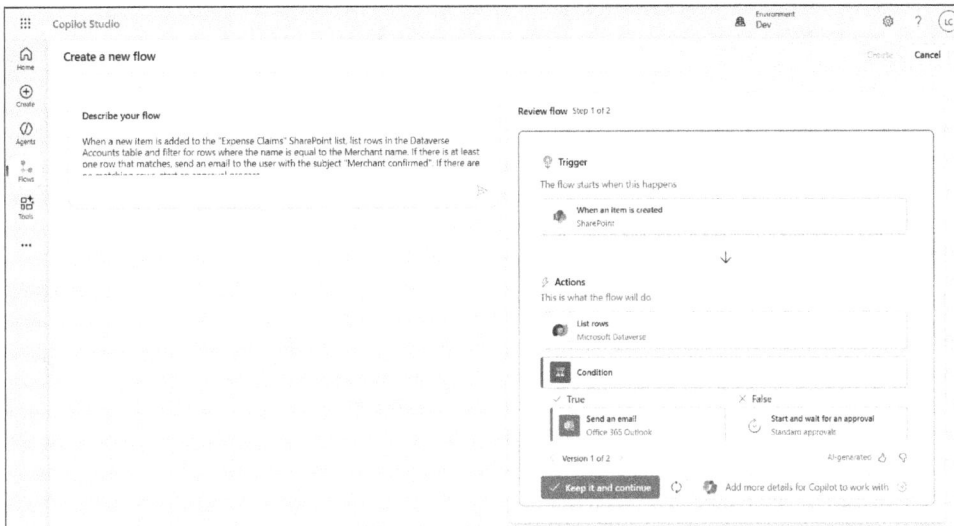

Copilot generates a suggested flow based on your description.

5. Select the **Keep it and continue** button.

6. Validate the connections, and then select the **Create** button.

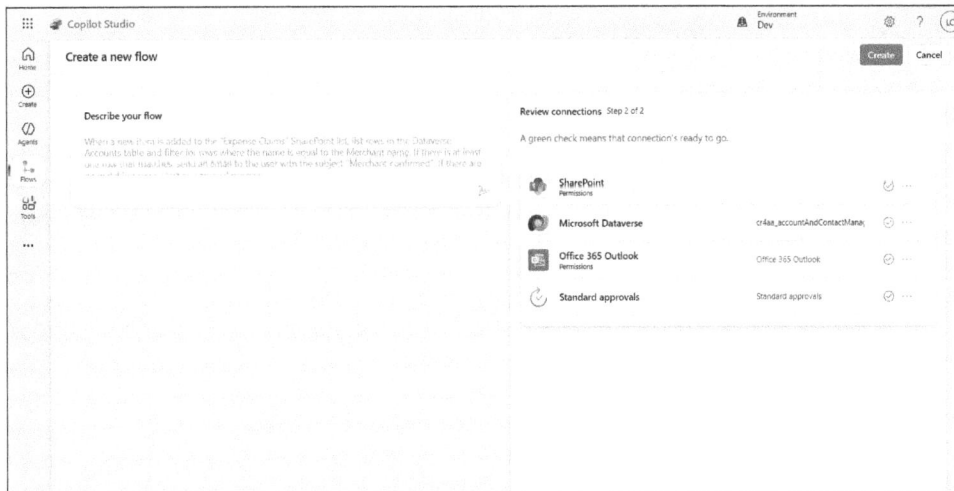

Review and validate the connections needed by the flow.

7. Your agent flow will now be open in the agent flow designer for editing. You will need to check each step of the flow and fill in the specific details before it is ready to save and publish.

8. Select the "**When an item is created**" SharePoint trigger node to open and edit the properties of the trigger. The properties should include the name of the SharePoint list from your description, but the SharePoint URL needs to be filled in. Select your SharePoint site from the drop-down menu.

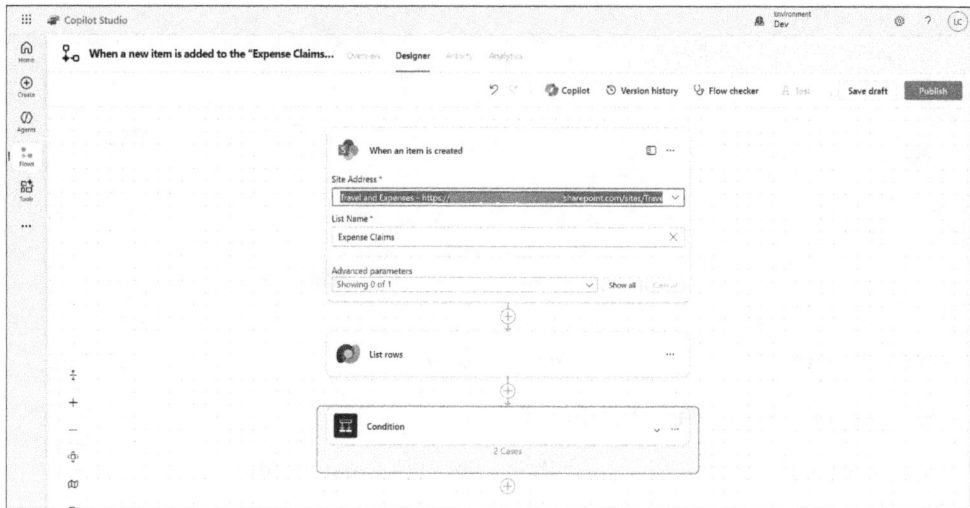

Configure the details of the SharePoint trigger.

9. Select the **List Rows (Dataverse)** node to expand the properties of this step. The table name will be set to Accounts.

> ✓ **TIP** If there is an error connecting to the table, clear the table name and select it from the drop-down list.

10. There should be a formula in the Filter rows field: **name eq '(SharePoint) body/ Merchant'**.

11. Select the **Condition** node to expand and view the properties of that step.

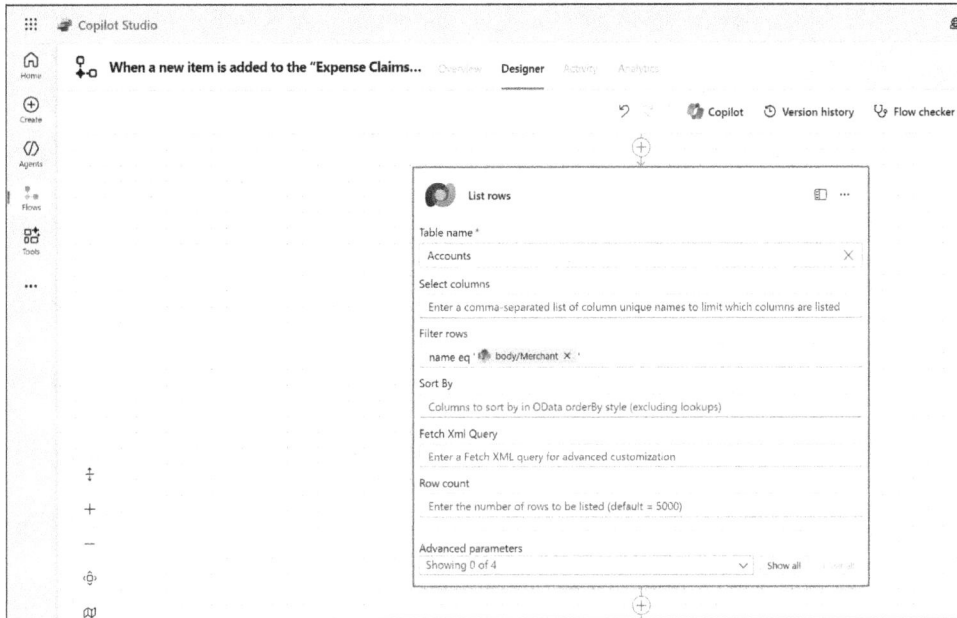

Select the correct table in Dataverse from the list.

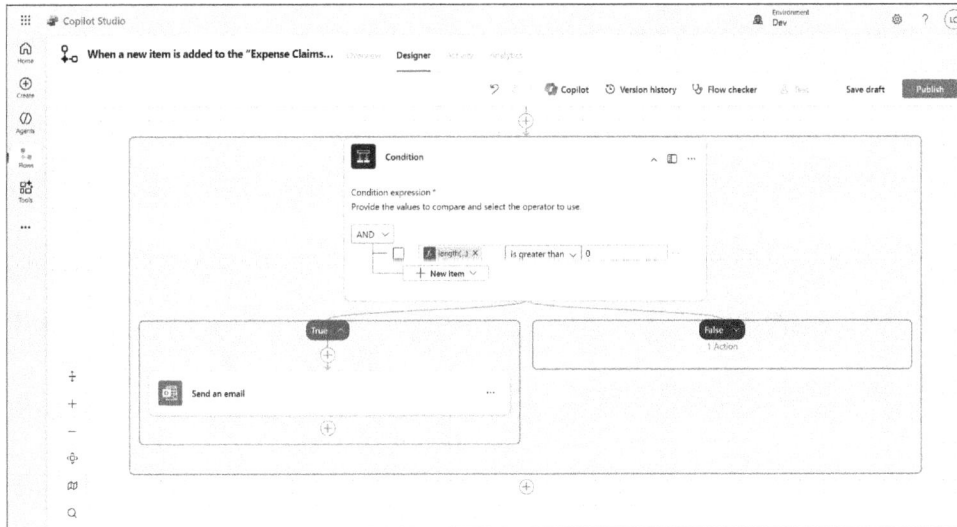

Review the formula for the conditional branch.

12. The condition is expressed as a formula that determines whether any results were found in the list rows action. If the condition is true (greater than 0 rows), then it found a matching account. Select the Power Fx formula to expand and view it.

13. The correct formula is **length(body('List_rows')?['value'])**. If Copilot has generated a different formula, replace it with this formula. Then select the **Update** button.

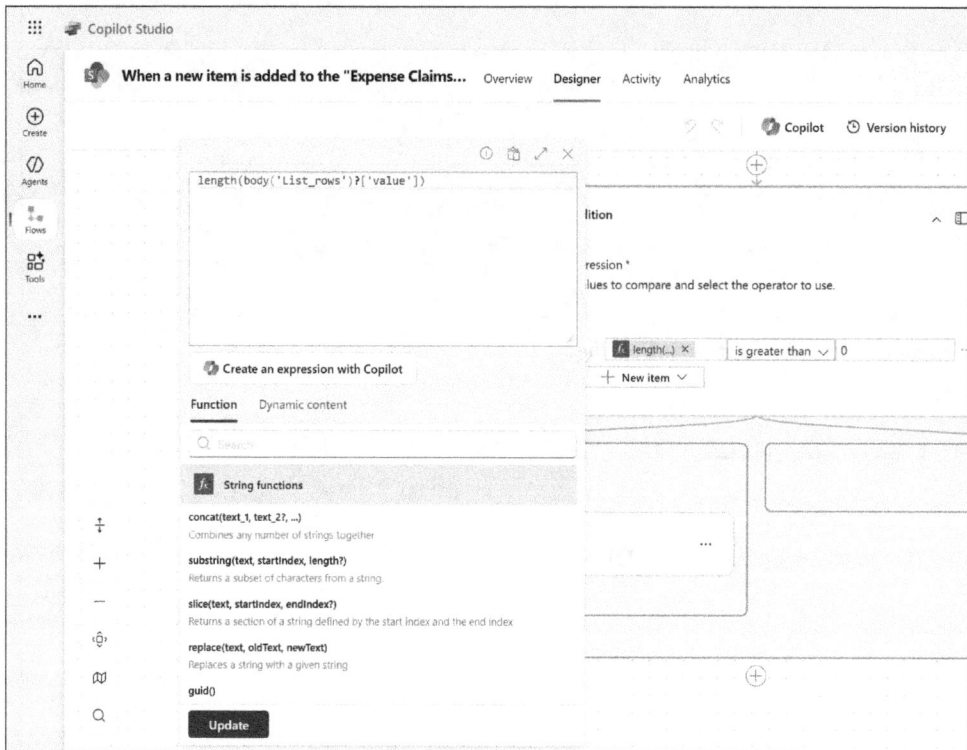

Select the formula to open the editor and make corrections.

14. The remaining components of the condition should show the formula "**is greater than**," 0.

15. Below the **Condition** node are two conditional branches.

16. In the **True** path, the action is **Send an email**. Open this action.

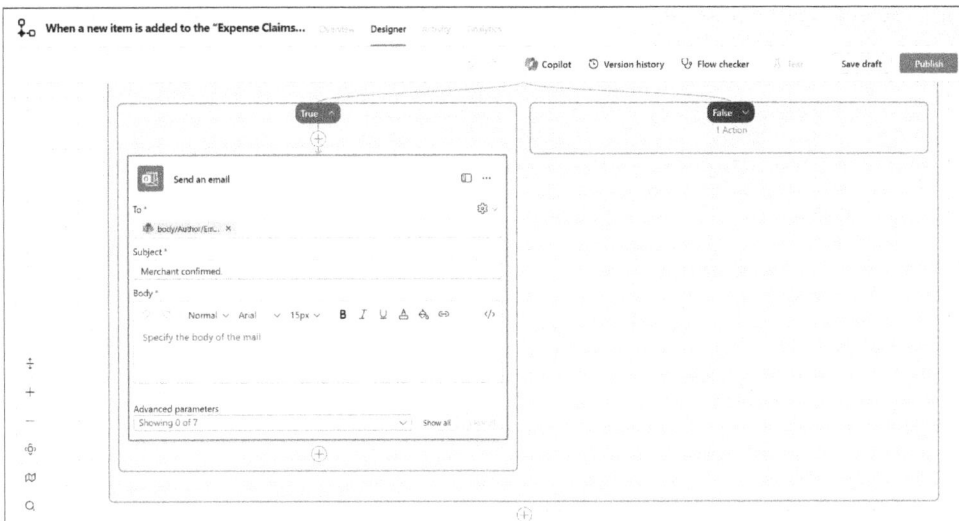

Configure the options for the Send an email action.

17. The email should be sent to the user who submitted the request. Clear the value in the **To** field and select the **lightning** icon that appears at the right side of the field to expand the dynamic content menu.

> ✓ **TIP** Instead of selecting the lightning icon you can press the "/" key to expand the dynamic content menu. If you can't access the dynamic content menu, expand the Settings icon and select "use dynamic content."

> ✓ **TIP** You can also write Power Fx formulas in any field by selecting the fx icon.

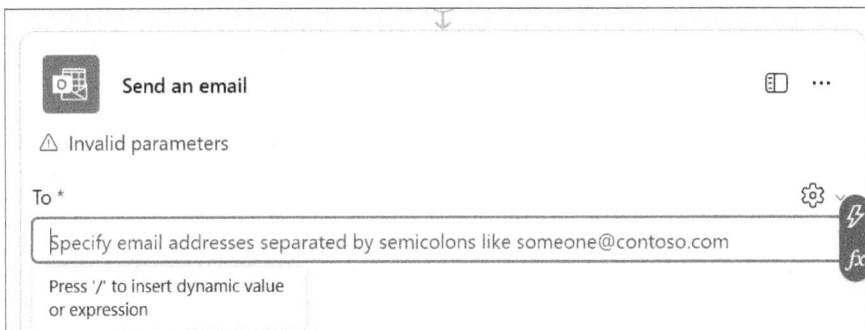

Select the "To" field to reveal the options to add dynamic content or a Power Fx formula.

18. Select "**Submitted by Email**" under the "**When an item is created**" (SharePoint) trigger.

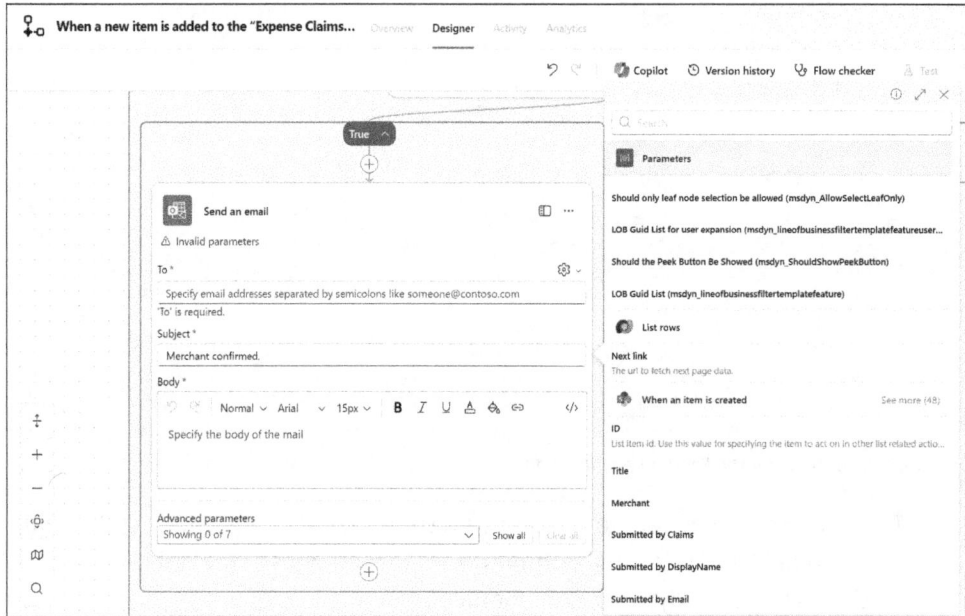

Select the dynamic content value from the menu.

19. The subject should be prefilled as "**Merchant confirmed**" based on the description you used to create the flow. You can use this or any other subject line that makes sense.

20. You need to fill the body text of the email. You can use plain text or rich text and add dynamic text to bring in data from the flow, such as the account name. In the email **Body** field, enter the following: **The merchant has been validated. Your expense claim will be processed.**

21. Position your cursor after the word "**merchant**", add an extra space, and then select the **lightning** icon to expand the dynamic content menu.

22. Type "**merchant**" in the dynamic content search to find any data with that name. Select the "**Merchant**" option from the results under the "**When an item is created**" section.

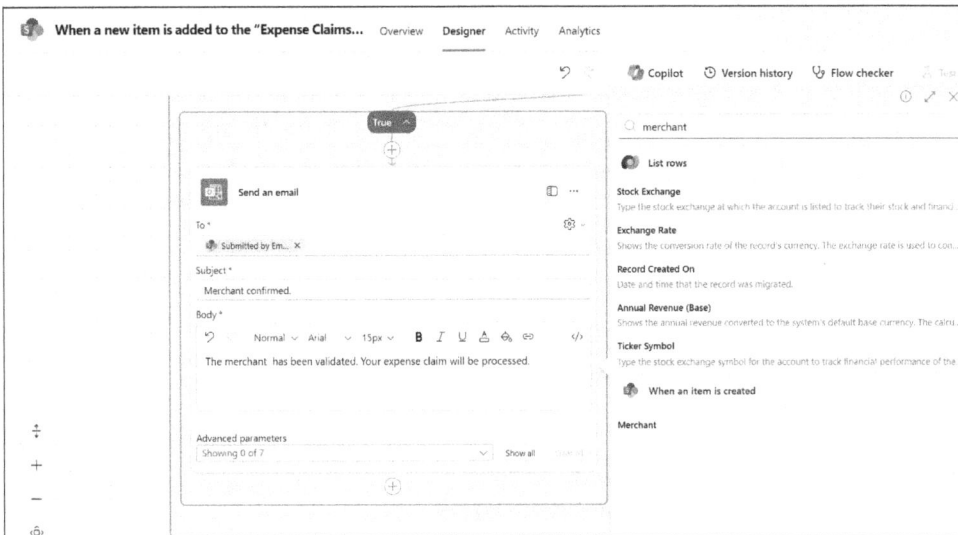

Search using a keyword to find the dynamic content you want to add.

> **TIP** Always check that you are selecting the dynamic content from the right trigger or action. As you build more complex agent flows, the same data may start appearing in multiple actions or steps.

23. The dynamic content is added to the email body. Collapse the left pane by selecting the arrows at the top right.

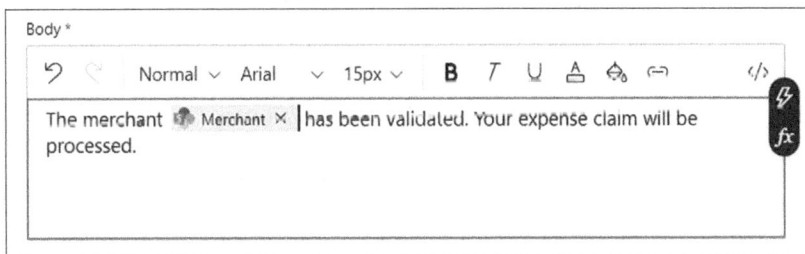

Add the dynamic content into the body text of the email.

24. Select the **Save draft** button at the top right of the canvas to save your agent flow.

You have now built an agent flow with a trigger, action, and conditional logic. You can expand the capability of your agent flow with thousands of different connectors and actions to automate complex step-by-step deterministic workflows.

For the next part of this agent flow, you will add an automated approval process. There are two options for working with approvals in agent flows. You can use the standard "Start and wait for an approval" connector, which will be suitable for most straightforward approvals. You can also use the premium multistage approval connector to create more complex approvals with multiple steps and conditional logic inside the approval. Although the workflow in this scenario would likely need just a standard approval process, in the next example we will explore the multistage approval connector to help you understand the possibilities for more complex approval workflows that you can use in your real-world agents.

To work with approvals in agent flows

1. Expand the **False** branch of the condition. If the action added here is "**Start and wait for an approval of text**," select the three dots at the right side to expand a menu of options, and then select **Delete**.

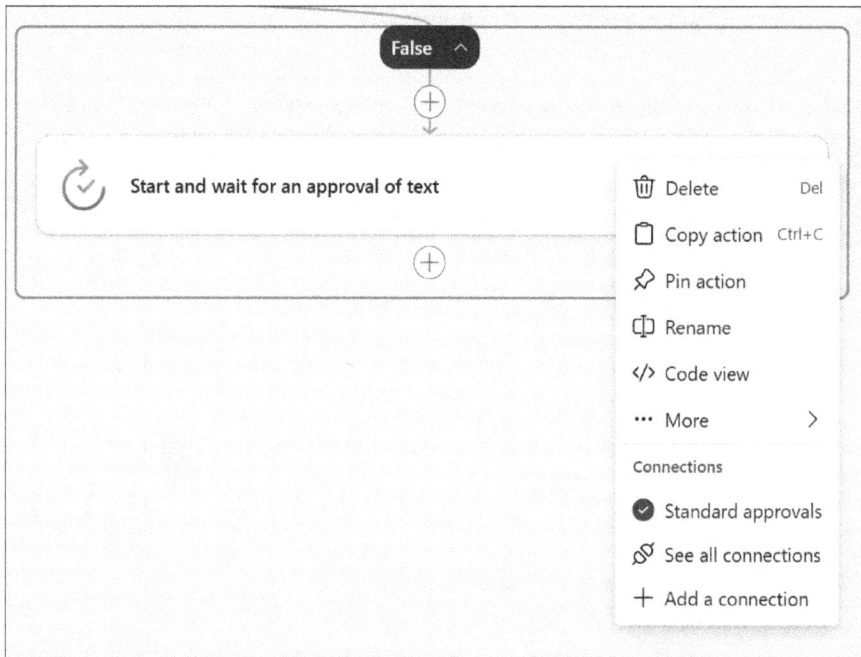

Delete the "Start and wait for an approval" action.

2. Select the + icon to add a new action in the **False** branch of the **Condition**.

3. In the **Add an action** pane, search for "**multistage approval**" and select the **Human in the loop – Run a multistage approval** option.

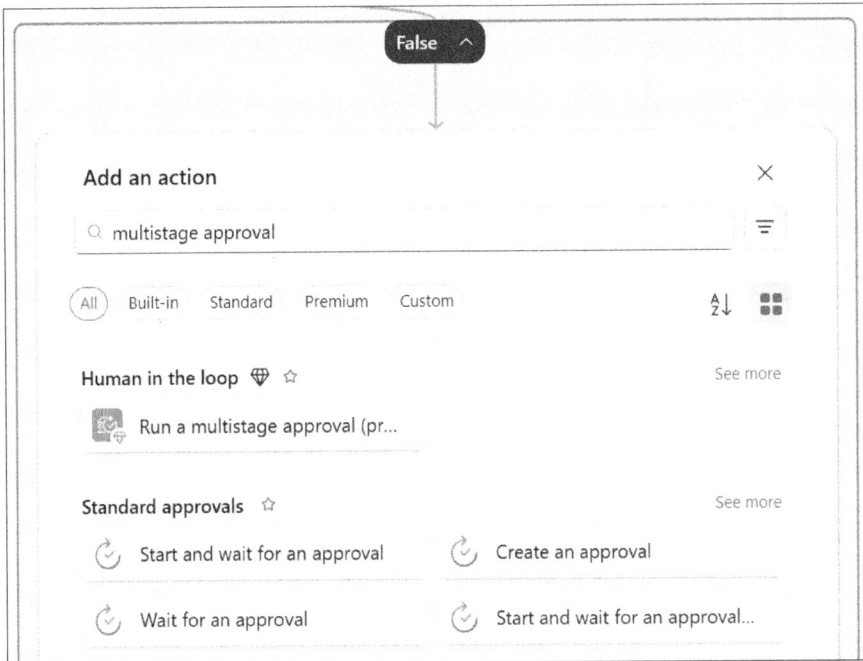

Search for and select the Run a multistage approval action.

4. If you are prompted to create a new connection, select the **Create new** button and wait for your credentials to be verified.

5. Select the **Set up the approval** button to begin creating the approval process.

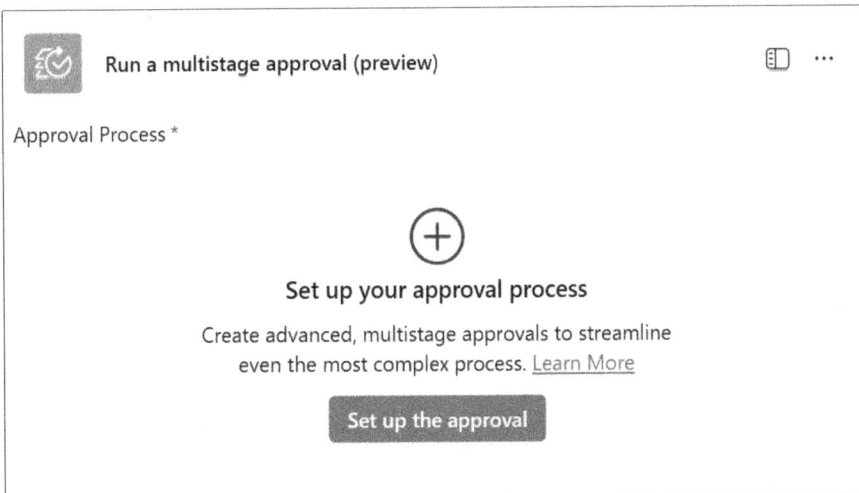

Begin setting up the multistage approval.

6. This opens the **Run a multistage approval** configuration screen. Select **Create** and then **Manual stage**.

7. Configure the **multistage approval** with the following options:

   - **Approval type**: Approve/Reject – First to respond

   - **Title**: Merchant approval

   - **Assigned to**: Search for and select your email (so that the approval comes to you for testing purposes).

   - **Details**: Fill the details of how you want the approval to appear to the person receiving it, such as "**Approval needed for a new merchant for expenses.**" Select the / key to expand a menu of options for creating dynamic input. This allows you to create a placeholder for a value that will be filled from the agent flow. Select **String** and create an input with the name "**merchant.**"

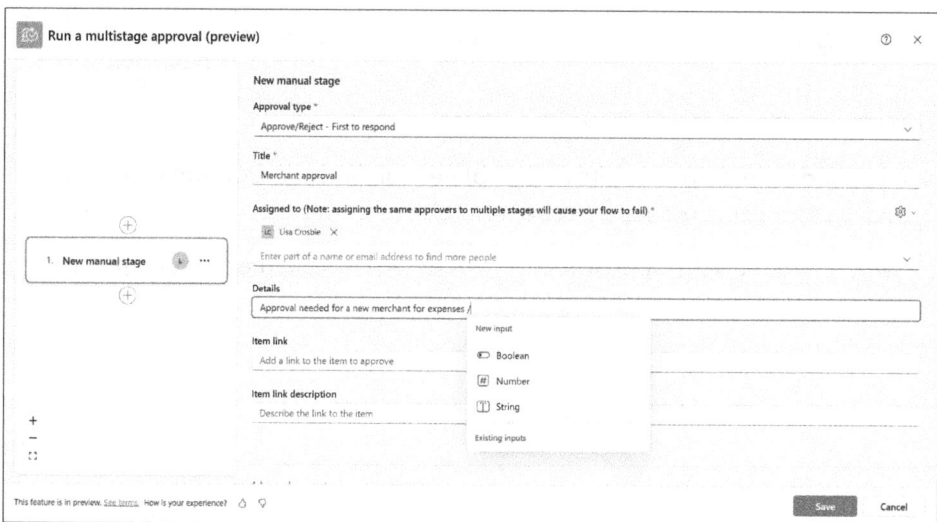

Select the "/" key to add an input.

8. Explore the other options available in the configuration screen, including other approval types, and the options to enable notifications and reassignments.

> **SEE ALSO** On the left side of the multistage approval configuration screen, you will see the option to add more steps and branching logic to the approval process. To learn more about the full capabilities of multistage and AI approvals, refer to https://learn.microsoft.com/en-us/microsoft-copilot-studio/flows-advanced-approvals.

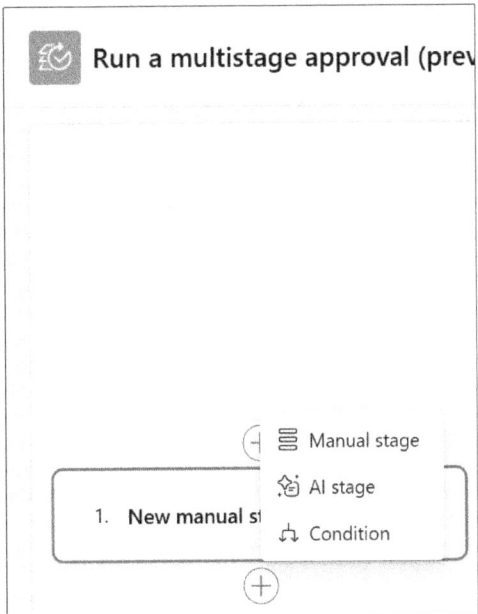

With multistage approvals, you can add multiple steps and branches to the approval process.

9. Select the **Save** button to save the approval configuration and return to the flow.

10. In the multistage approvals node, you can edit and configure how the approval process works within the flow. The merchant input you created appears here for you to match with a data point from the flow. Select the **/** key or the **lightning** icon to expand the dynamic content, and then select the **Merchant** field from the **When an item is created** (SharePoint) trigger.

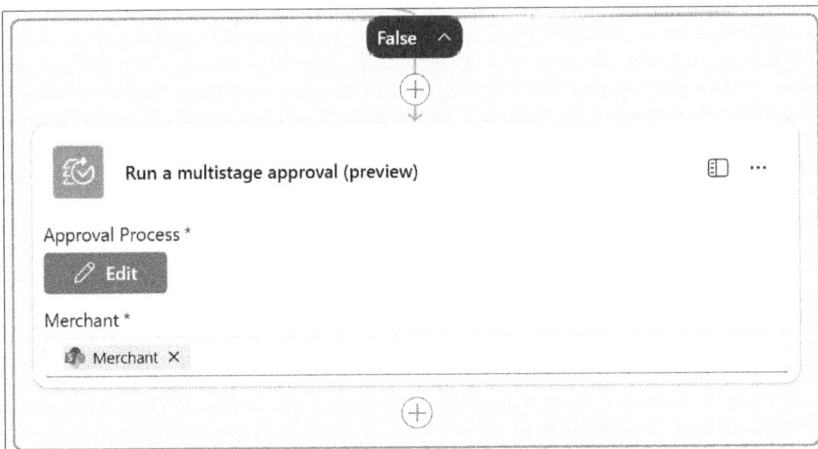

Fill the approval input with dynamic content from the SharePoint trigger.

11. Select the **Save draft** button at the top right of the canvas to save your agent flow. Wait for the confirmation message to appear.

You can continue to add more steps and actions to the flow using what you have learned. For instance, you could add another action before or after the multistage approval action to send an email notification to the user indicating that the merchant needs to be approved.

> ✅ **TIP** You can select the Copilot button from the top menu to open and use Copilot in the right pane of the Agent Flows designer to describe how you want to build or edit the flow.

Once you have finished building the flow, it's time to save, publish, and test it.

To publish and test an agent flow

1. Select the **Publish** button to publish your agent flow. Wait for the confirmation message indicating that the flow has been published successfully.

2. Select the **Test** icon to the left of the **Save draft** button to open the **Test Flow** pane.

3. Select **Manually** and then select the **Test** button.

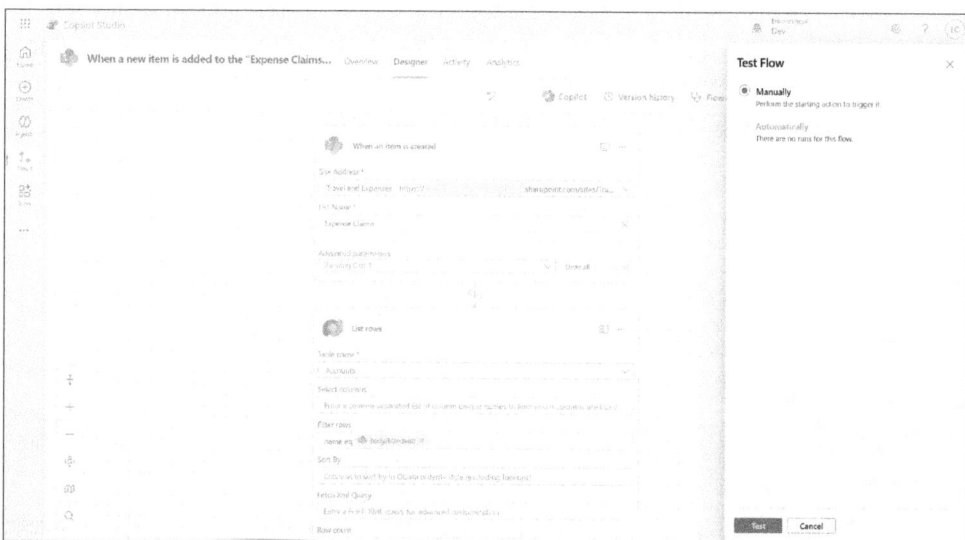

Test the flow manually by creating a new row in the SharePoint list.

> **TIP** The first time you test your flow, you will need to test it manually, by adding a new list item to the SharePoint list. If you need to test it again in the future, you can use the automatic testing option to select a previous trigger.

4. The flow test now waits for the trigger. Open the **Expense Claims** SharePoint list in a new browser tab, add a new row (using a Merchant name that is in your Dataverse accounts table), and then return to Copilot Studio.

5. After a moment, the test run will begin in the agent flow designer, indicating each step completed with a green check mark. When it is finished, you will get a confirmation message that your flow ran successfully.

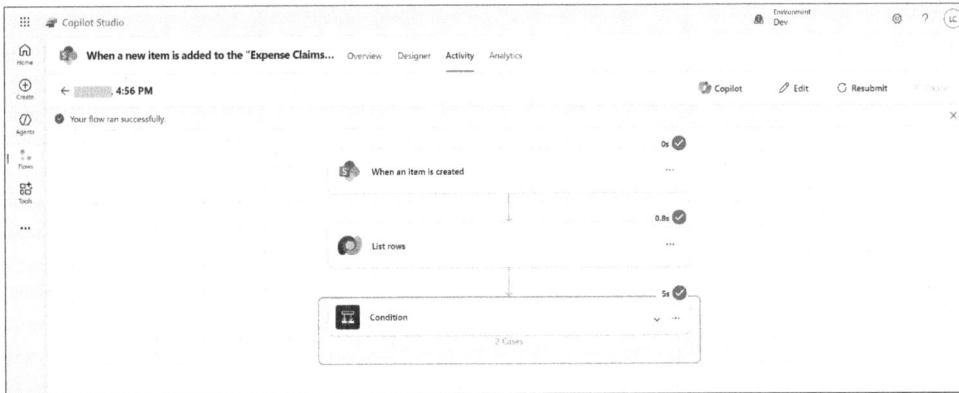

When the test runs, the results will be shown with check marks at each stage.

6. Check your email for the message that the merchant has been confirmed.

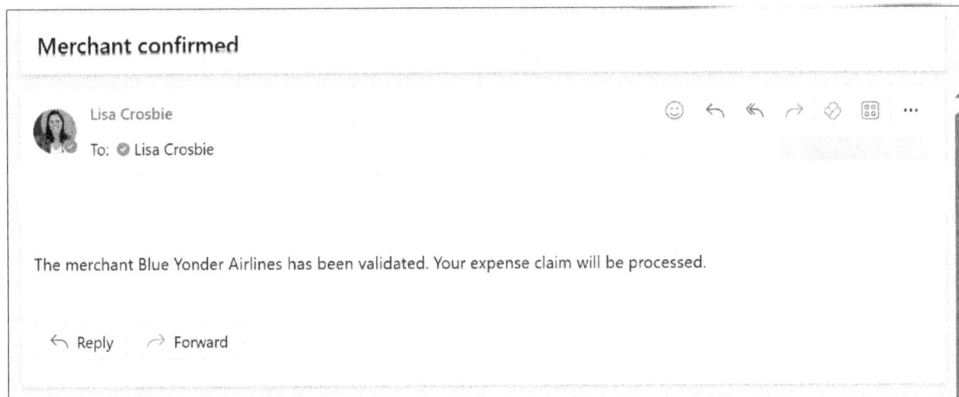

The user receives an email generated by the flow.

7. Test the flow again by following steps 2–5, but this time use a merchant name that does not appear in your Dataverse accounts table.

8. The flow test run will pause at the **Condition** step, waiting for the approval process to run.

9. The approval will be sent to your email, with options to **Approve** or **Reject**. Select **Approve** and then **Submit**. This completes the flow test run.

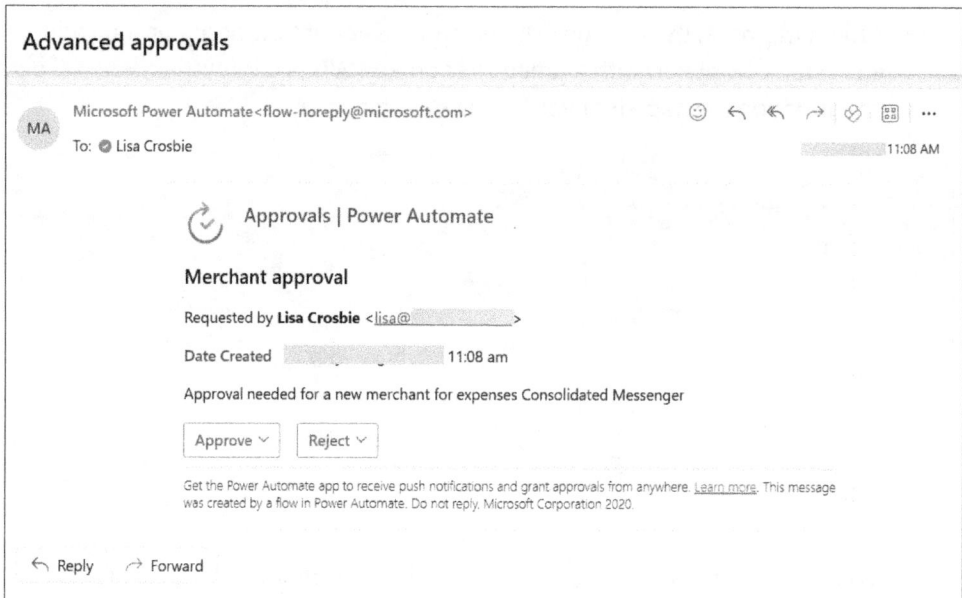

Advanced approvals

MA Microsoft Power Automate<flow-noreply@microsoft.com> 😊 ↩ ↩ ↪ ⊘ ⊞ ⋯
To: ● Lisa Crosbie   11:08 AM

↻ Approvals | Power Automate

Merchant approval

Requested by **Lisa Crosbie** <lisa@_____>

Date Created _____ 11:08 am

Approval needed for a new merchant for expenses Consolidated Messenger

| Approve ∨ | Reject ∨ |

Get the Power Automate app to receive push notifications and grant approvals from anywhere. Learn more. This message was created by a flow in Power Automate. Do not reply. Microsoft Corporation 2020.

↩ Reply   ↪ Forward

The approval is sent via email, with buttons to approve or reject it.

✓ **TIP** The approval will also appear in Teams, where you can view and manage all approvals.

---

10. Select the **Flows** icon on the left side rail to return to the **Agent flows** screen. Your agent flow now appears in a list. Return here at any time to edit your flow or to open it to review flow runs.

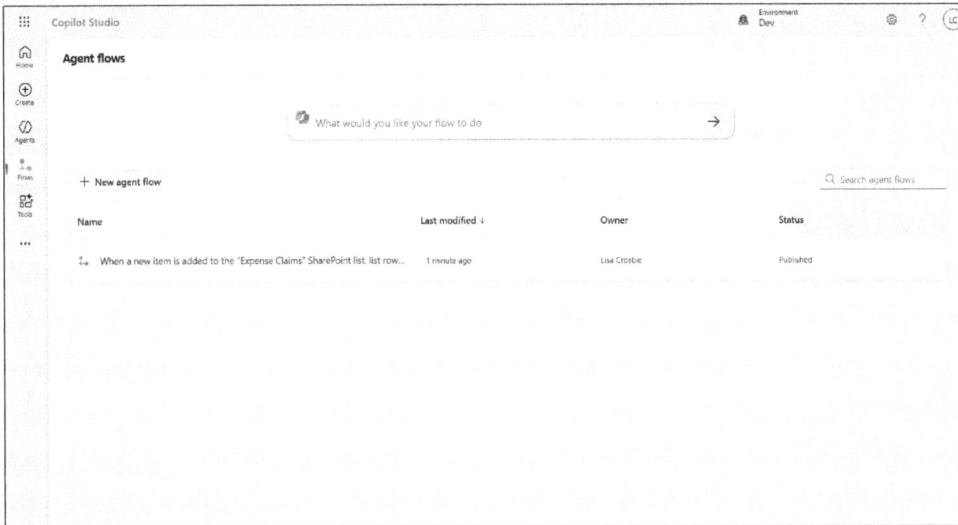

The agent flow you created now appears in the Agent flows list.

When you build an agent flow as demonstrated in this section, the flow will run independently based on the trigger, with or without interaction from the agent. You can also build agent flows that are triggered only by an interaction with the agent.

Create agent flows triggered by an agent

An agent flow can be a tool that is called by an agent, with the agent providing the inputs to the flow and receiving the outputs from it. In this scenario, you will build an agent flow that allows the user to check the status of an expense claim.

To create an agent flow triggered by an agent

1. Select the **Tools** icon on the left side rail, and then select the **+New tool** button.

2. In the **New tool** menu, select **Agent flow**.

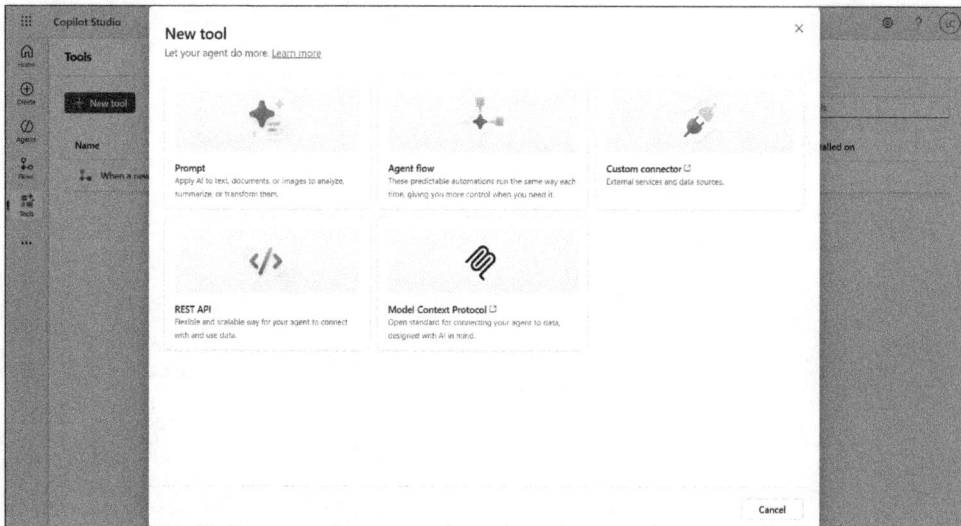

Create a new tool and then select Agent flow.

3. This opens the agent flow designer with a trigger, "**When an agent calls the flow**," and a response, "**Respond to the agent**."

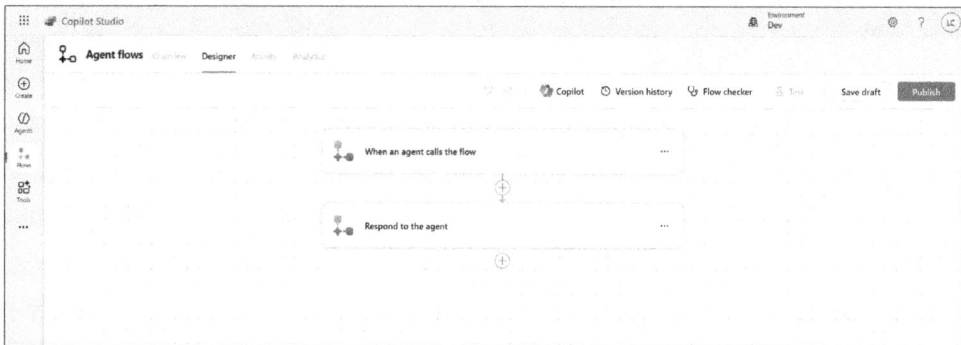

The agent flow is set up with a trigger and a response.

4. Select the "**When an agent calls the flow**" trigger to expand and edit the properties.

5. Select **+ Add an input**.

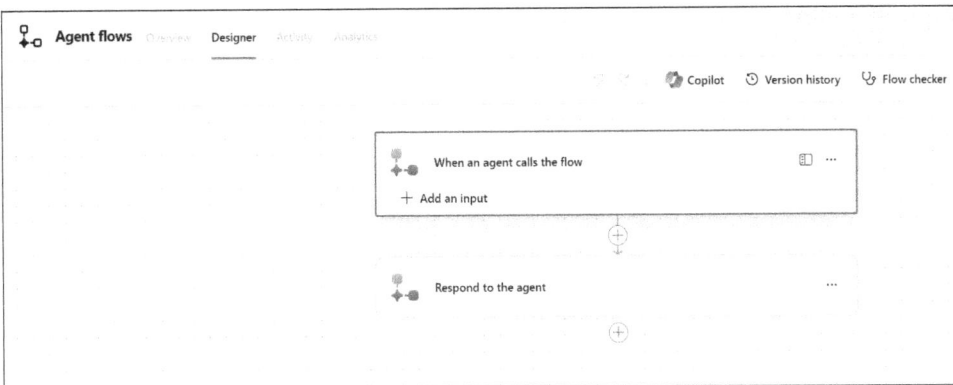

Select the trigger node to configure the inputs.

6. You can set up all the inputs that the agent flow will receive from the agent, based on the interaction with the user. You can set up the flow to receive inputs in text, yes/no, file, email, number, or date format. In this case, you are creating an agent flow to check the status of an expense claim. The user will input the name of the expense claim, which is a string of text. Select the **Text** option.

> ✅ **TIP** In this example, the agent will match on the name, so you should ensure that you have a unique name for an expense row in the SharePoint list to test with. In a real-world scenario, this would be best done using a unique reference number or ID for the row.

7. In the first field, fill in a name for the input—for example, **Expense Name**. Leave the "**Please enter your input**" field as it is.

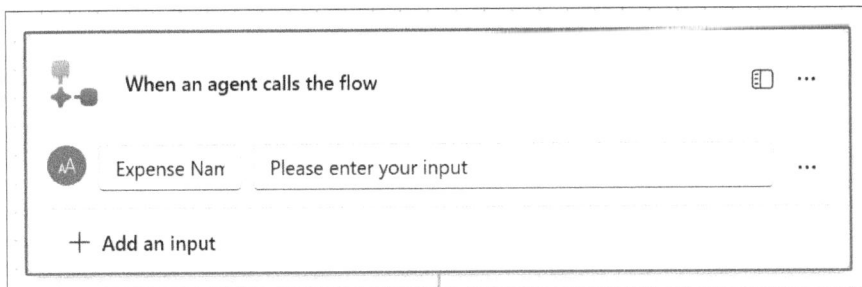

Give the input a name.

8. Select the + button below the "**When an agent calls the flow**" trigger on the design canvas. This opens the **Add an action** pane, where you will insert an action to find the SharePoint list item that matches the name entered by the user.

9. In the **Add an action** pane, search for "SharePoint" and then select the **Get items** action.

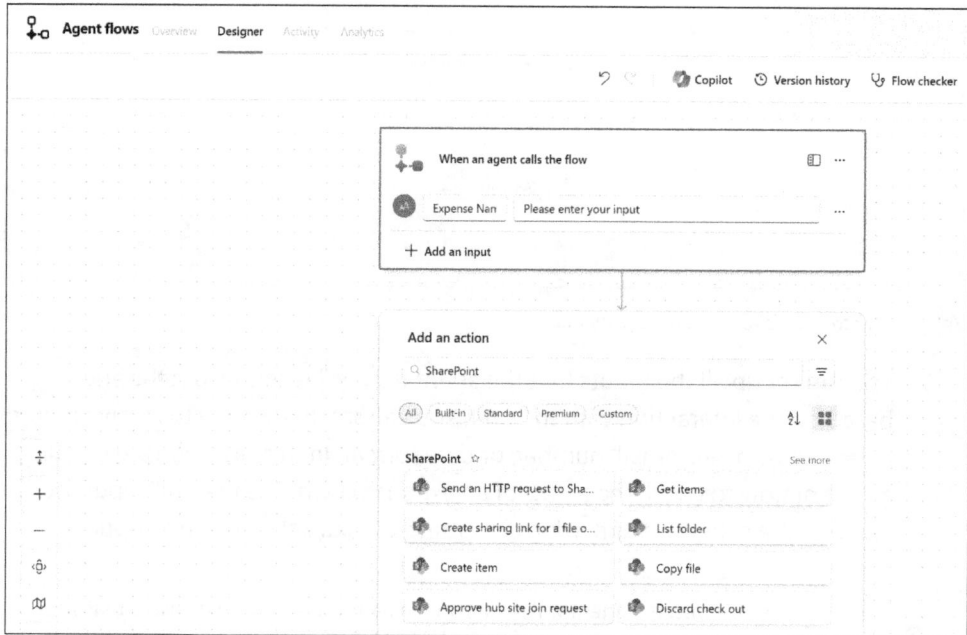

Add an action between the trigger and response nodes.

10. Select the **Site address** and **List Name** from the drop-down options.

11. Expand the **Advanced parameters** option, and check **Filter Query** and **Top Count**.

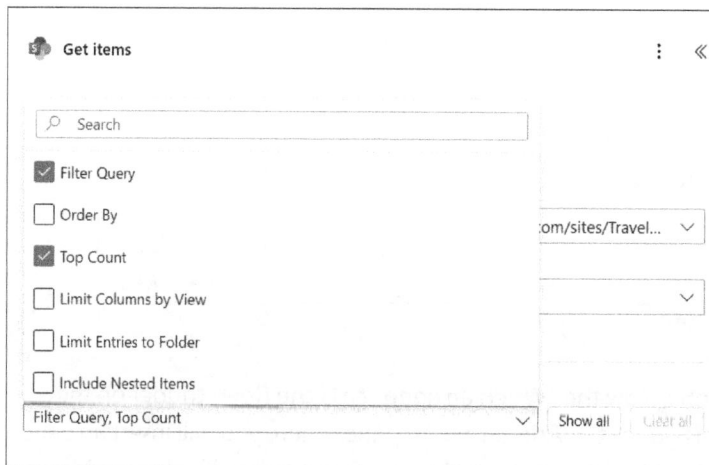

Select the Filter Query and Top Count parameters.

12. Select a space on the screen outside this menu to collapse the menu and confirm your selection.

13. In the **Filter Query** field, select the **lightning** icon to expand the dynamic content options, and select the **Expense Name** input from the "**When an agent calls the flow**" step.

14. Complete the ODATA filter query by putting a single quote either side of the **Expense Name** input, followed by **eq Title**.

> ⚠ **IMPORTANT** Make sure you use the exact name of the SharePoint column you are matching, such as "Title."

15. In the **Top Count** field, enter the number **1**. This instructs the flow that it should return a single result, rather than multiple rows that match the query. It will return the first matching row that it finds.

Filter Query	
⚡ Expense Name ✕ ' eq Title	✕
Top Count	
1	✕

Set the Top Count value to 1 so that the action returns a single result.

> ✓ **TIP** You can use Copilot on the side pane in the designer for help with writing ODATA filter queries or other formulas.

16. Use Copilot to help create an action to get the status value of the first result from the "**Get items**" action. Select the Copilot icon from the top menu to open the Copilot pane to the right of the agent flow designer. Use this query: **add a compose action to get the first result from the SharePoint Get Items action and to get the status value of that row**.

17. Copilot describes the action it has taken and adds a new **Compose** step to the agent flow. Select the new step to expand it and view the properties.

18. Review the Copilot-created formula:
{first(body('Get_items')?['value'])?['Status']}.

8

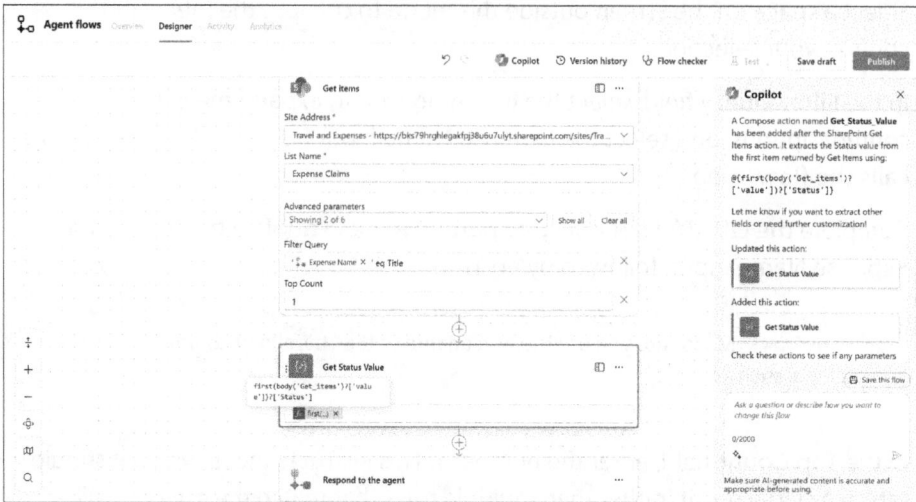

Review the formula created by Copilot for the Compose action.

19. Select the "**Respond to the agent**" node on the design canvas to view and edit the properties. You will use this step to pass information back from the SharePoint list to the agent, so that it can give the user the status value of the expense claim.

20. Select **+Add an output**.

21. Choose the type **Text**.

22. In the "**Enter a name**" field, enter **Expense Status**.

23. In the "**Enter a value to respond with**" field, select the **lightning** icon to expand the dynamic content menu. Select the "**Outputs**" option under the **Compose-StatusValue** action.

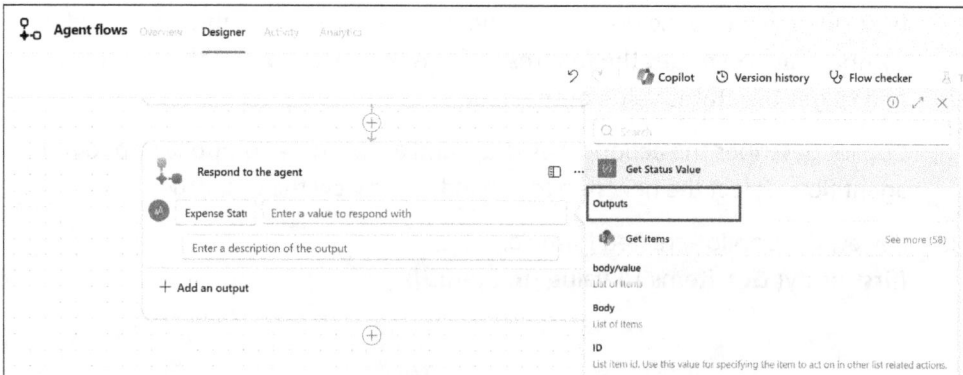

Select the Outputs from the Compose action to respond to the agent.

24. Select the **Save draft** button and wait until the flow has been saved.

25. Select the **Overview** tab.

26. In the **Details** section, select the **Edit** button.

27. Change the name and description of the agent flow to something that meaningfully describes what this flow will be used for:

    - Flow name: **Get expense claim status**.

    - Description: **Gets the expense claim name from the user and responds with the status.**

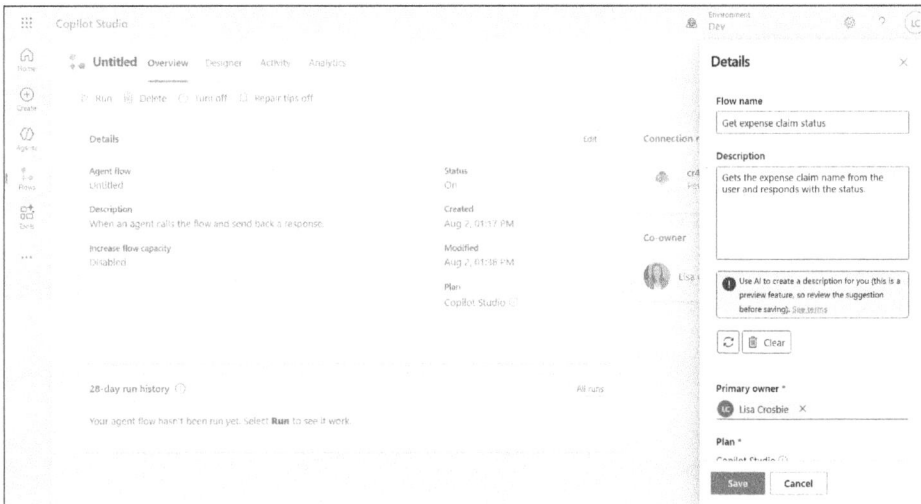

Give the flow a name and a description to help the agent understand when and how to use it.

28. Select the **Save** button to save the changes.

29. Select the Designer tab to return to the agent flow designer, and then select the **Publish** button and wait for confirmation that the flow is published.

This agent flow is now ready to be used as a tool. It can be called by the agent to take the action of getting the status of an expense.

To add an agent flow as a tool to the agent

1. Select the **Tools** icon on the left side rail of Copilot Studio.

2. The agent flow you have built now appears in the list of tools. Select the three dots to the right of the flow name to expand a menu of options, and select **Add to Agent**.

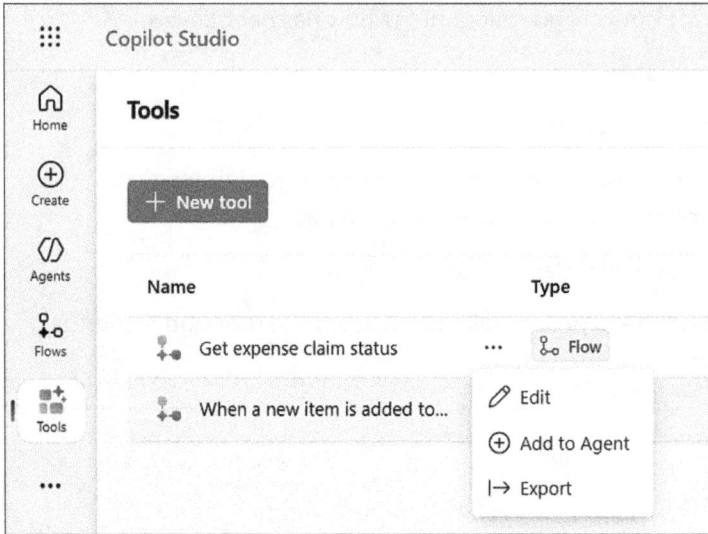

Select the agent flow in the Tools screen to add it to your agent.

3. Select the **Expense Helper** agent from the list of agents, and then select the **Add** button.

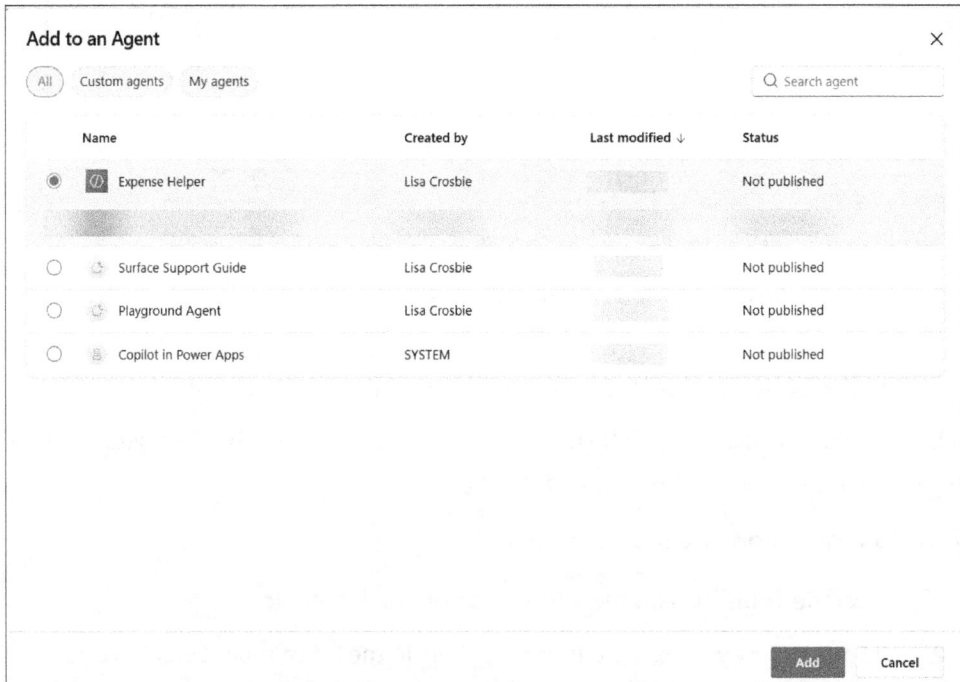

Select the agent to which you want to add the tool, and then select Add.

4. Wait for the **Add tool** pop-up screen to open. Select the **Flow** filter button to view the agent flows that can be added to the agent.

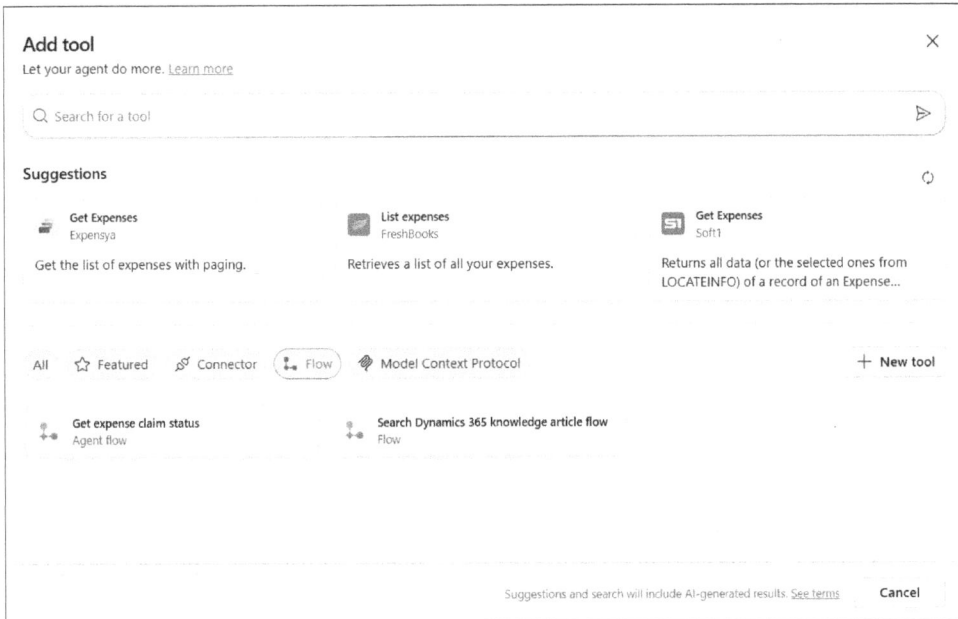

Add tool ✕
Let your agent do more. Learn more

🔍 Search for a tool ▷

Suggestions ↻

Get Expenses	List expenses	Get Expenses
Expensya	FreshBooks	Soft1
Get the list of expenses with paging.	Retrieves a list of all your expenses.	Returns all data (or the selected ones from LOCATEINFO) of a record of an Expense...

All ☆ Featured ⌁ Connector ⦿ Flow ⬧ Model Context Protocol ＋ **New tool**

| Get expense claim status | Search Dynamics 365 knowledge article flow |
| Agent flow | Flow |

Suggestions and search will include AI-generated results. See terms **Cancel**

Select the tool from the Add tool screen.

> **TIP** Instead of following the preceding steps, you could first return to your agent, navigate to the Tools tab, and select "Add new tool" to get to this same point.

> **IMPORTANT** Only agent flows that use the "When an agent calls the flow" trigger will be available here to add as a tool to the agent. You can use the agent instructions to ask the agent to call agent flows that are triggered in other ways.

5. Select the **Get expense claim status** agent flow.

6. This will open the **Add Tool** pop-up. Select **Add to agent**. Wait for the process to be completed. The agent flow is now added as a tool in the Expense Helper agent.

The agent flow appears in the list of tools for the agent.

7. Test your agent flow by entering an input into the test pane that will trigger this agent flow, based on the name and description you gave it. For example, **what is the status of my expense**.

8. The **activity map** shows that the agent has called the "**Get expense claim status**" agent flow and recognizes that it needs the **Expense Name (String)** as an input. The agent prompts the user for the name of the expense claim.

The activity map shows the slot filling as you test the agent flow tool.

9. Enter the name of one of the expense rows in your SharePoint list.

10. You will be prompted to validate the connection to SharePoint. Select the **Allow** button.

11. The agent gets the status of the named expense and returns the value in the chat.

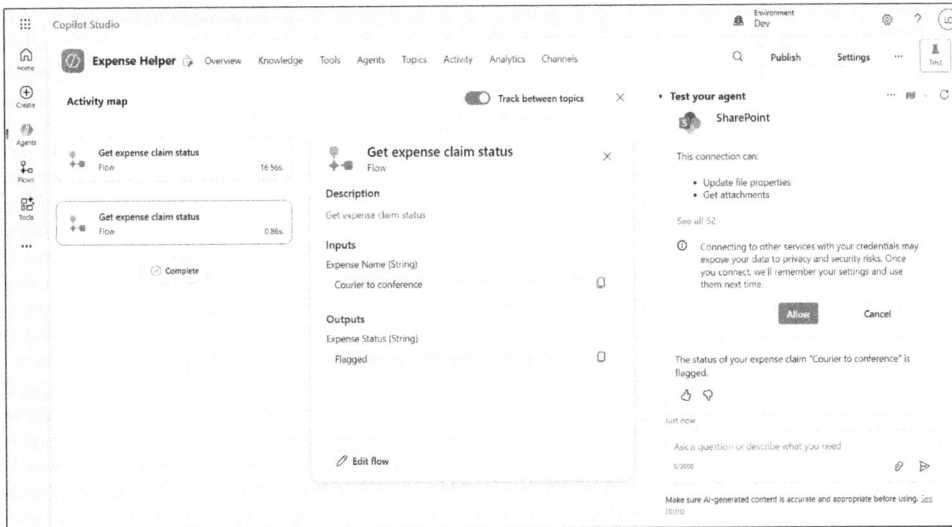

The agent successfully uses the flow to retrieve the status of the expense claim.

Add tools to a topic

To add tools or agent flows at the agent level as described in this chapter, you must be using an agent with generative orchestration enabled. If you are using an agent with classic orchestration, or if you want greater control over when and how the agent uses a tool, you can add a tool as a node in a topic instead.

In this section, you will work through an example that shows how to use the "Get expense claim status" tool with deterministic logic in a topic, instead of using it at the agent level where it is triggered at runtime by generative orchestration.

Before you begin this example, remove this tool at the agent level: Navigate to the **Tools** tab of the Expense Helper agent, select the three dots next to the **Get expense claim** tool, and then select **Delete**.

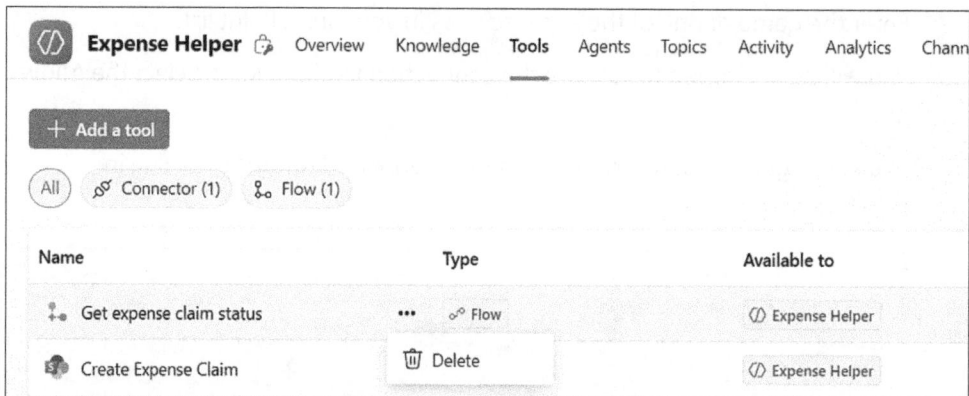

Delete the agent flow tool from the list of tools in the agent.

To add a tool to a topic

1. Navigate to the **Topics** tab in the Expense Helper agent and add a new topic from blank.

> **SEE ALSO** For full step-by-step instructions on creating topics, refer to Chapter 7: Authoring topics.

2. Rename the topic: **Get expense claim status**.

3. Write a description in the trigger: **Gets the name of an expense claim from the user and returns the status of that claim**.

4. Add an "**Ask a question**" node. Enter the message: **What is the Title of the expense claim?**

5. Change the **Identify** option to **User's entire response**.

6. Rename the variable to **ExpenseTitle**.

7. Select the + button below the **Question** node to add a new node.

8. Select the **Add a tool** option to expand the list of available tools.

9. Select the **Get expense claim status** tool from the list.

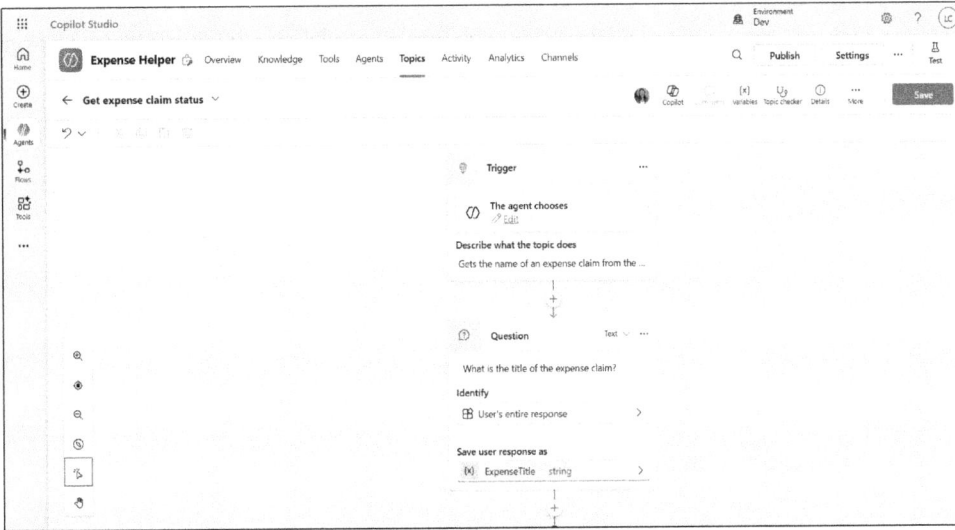

Set up a Question node that looks for the user's entire response and saves it as a variable.

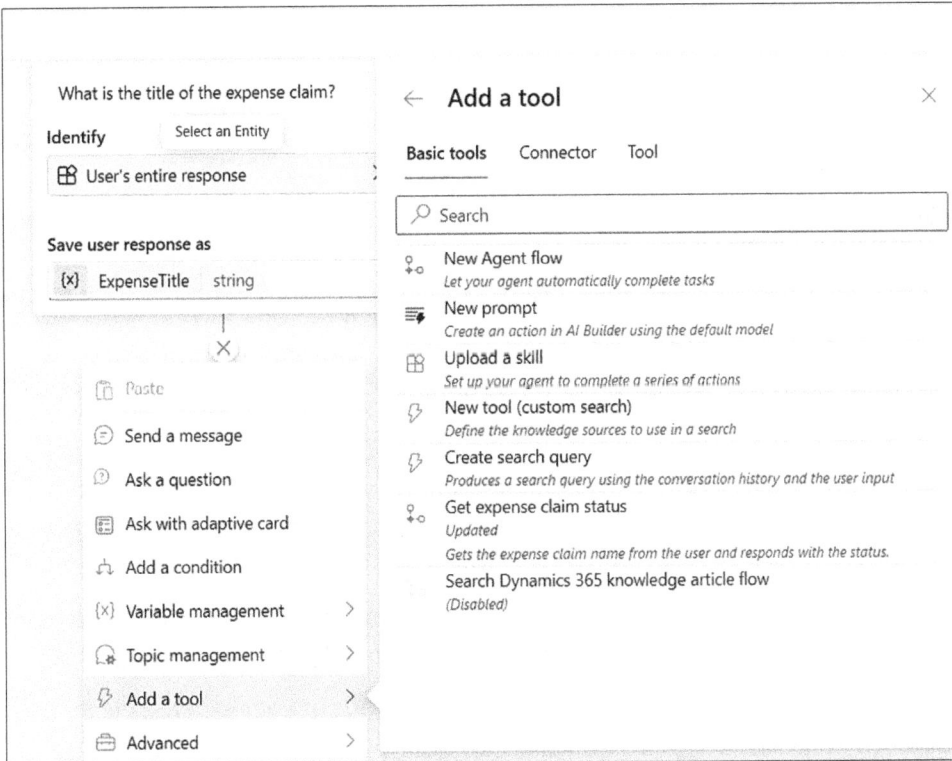

Use a node to add a tool, and then select the flow from the list of tools.

> ✅ **TIP** This list of tools will show agent flows that start with the "When an agent calls the flow" trigger only. You can also use the "New Agent flow" option to create an agent flow from here.

10. The tool is added to the flow with the required inputs and outputs as defined in the agent flow. You need to define the input using a variable from the conversation.

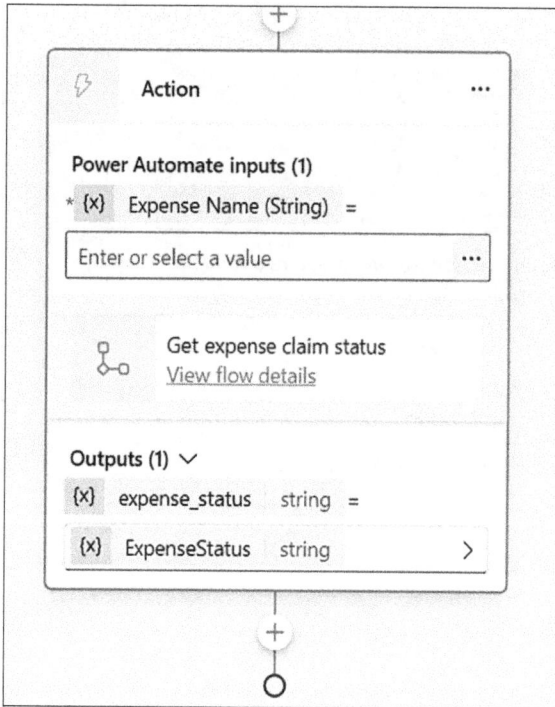

```
                              +

   ⚡    Action                         •••

   Power Automate inputs (1)
 * {x}   Expense Name (String)   =

   ┌──────────────────────────────────┐
   │ Enter or select a value      •••  │
   └──────────────────────────────────┘


   ┌─○   Get expense claim status
   ○─┘   View flow details


   Outputs (1) ⌄
   {x}   expense_status    string  =

   {x}   ExpenseStatus     string           >

                              +
                              |
                              ○
```

Select a value for the input required by the agent flow.

11. Select the **three dots** in the input field and select the **ExpenseTitle** variable. This action step is now configured to take the user input as the input to the agent flow, and to get the status of the expense claim from the SharePoint list.

12. You now need to add a message node to respond to the user with the status. Select the + button below the **Action** node and add a **Send a message** node.

13. In the message, add the following text: **The status of your expense claim is:**.

14. Select the **Variables** icon and then select the **ExpenseStatus** variable, using the output from the **Action** step.

Power Automate inputs (1)

* {x} Expense Name (String) =

{x} ExpenseTitle   string   •••

    Get expense claim status
    View flow details

Outputs (1) ⌄

{x} expense_status   string =

{x} ExpenseStatus   string   >

\+

💬   **Message**   Text ⌄ •••

\+ Add ⌄   **B**   *I*   ≔   ⌸   {x}   *fx*

The status of your expense claim is:
{x} ExpenseStatus   string

Add the output variable to the message that the agent will send to the user.

15. Select the **Save** button to save the topic.

16. Refresh the **test** pane and test the agent by entering a phrase into the chat that will trigger this topic. For example: **what is the status of my expense claim**.

17. The topic is triggered and the agent responds with the question you authored in the Question node of the topic: **What is the title of the expense claim?**

18. Enter the title of the expense claim.

19. The agent responds with the message and the retrieved expense status.

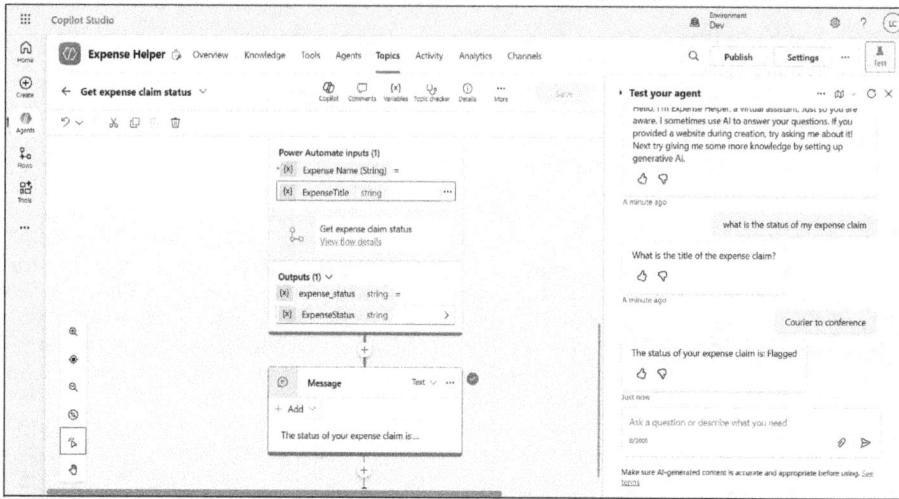

Test the topic to validate that it is working.

This method of adding an agent flow using a topic requires more configuration but gives you deterministic control over the input and output variables, the questions, and the messages.

You can add other tools to topics from the **Add a tool** node, including prompts, skills, search queries, connectors, or other custom tools.

Use a prompt as a tool

Prompt tools in Copilot Studio allow you to leverage the reasoning and generative AI capabilities of large language models (LLMs) by writing natural language instructions that the agent can execute as a tool.

With a prompt, you can define a task like summarizing, rewriting, classifying, extracting, or analyzing text, providing clear instructions that tell the agent what to do to carry out this task. You can also specify input variables from the context of the agent or the user interaction that the LLM should use as a reference when generating the response. When the agent calls the prompt tool, the LLM processes the instructions and inputs, generates a response, and returns that output to the agent to use.

Prompt tools are designed to perform tasks such as the following:

- Reasoning: Drawing conclusions or making decisions based on provided information.

- Analysis: Breaking down complex content to identify patterns, insights, or implications.

- Classification: Categorizing data or text into predefined groups.

- Creation: Generating new content such as summaries, emails, or responses.

- Extraction: Pulling specific information from structured or unstructured data.

- Summarization: Condensing long or complex text into concise, meaningful summaries.

In this section, you will learn how to create a prompt tool that helps resolve customer complaints by using the LLM to classify which department the complaint should be directed to.

Before you begin this exercise, create a new blank agent called Account Helper.

To create a prompt tool

1. In the new Account Helper agent, navigate to the **Tools** tab and select the **+Add a Tool** button.

2. In the **Add tool** pop-up, select the **+New tool** button, and then select **Prompt**.

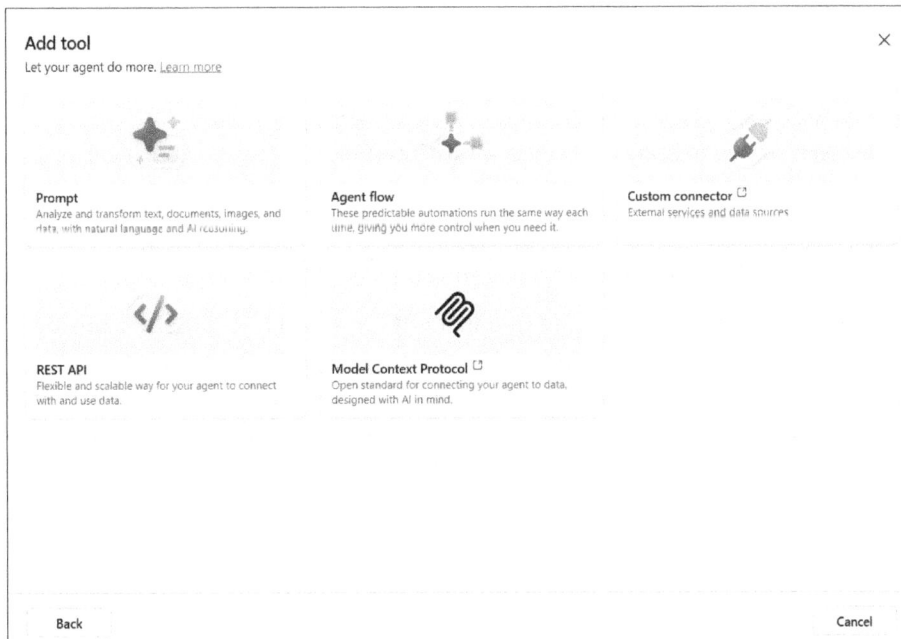

Add tool   ✕
Let your agent do more. Learn more

Prompt
Analyze and transform text, documents, images, and data, with natural language and AI reasoning.

Agent flow
These predictable automations run the same way each time, giving you more control when you need it.

Custom connector ⬀
External services and data sources

REST API
Flexible and scalable way for your agent to connect with and use data.

Model Context Protocol ⬀
Open standard for connecting your agent to data, designed with AI in mind.

Back   Cancel

Add a new tool and select Prompt.

8

3. This opens the prompt tool configuration screen. Select the title of the prompt, and then change it from a time/date value to a title that makes sense for what this prompt action will do: **Classify complaint**.

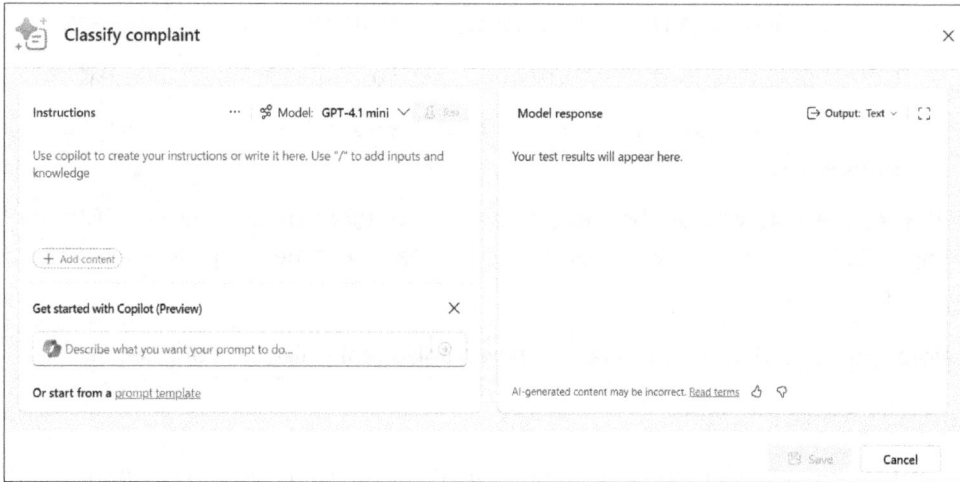

Classify complaint		✕
Instructions ⋯ 🔗 Model: **GPT-4.1 mini** ⌄	**Model response** ↪ Output: Text ⌄ ⤢	
Use copilot to create your instructions or write it here. Use "/" to add inputs and knowledge	Your test results will appear here.	
(+ Add content)		
Get started with Copilot (Preview) ✕		
🔵 Describe what you want your prompt to do... ⊕	AI-generated content may be incorrect. Read terms ✋ 🖈	
Or start from a prompt template		
	🔖 Save Cancel	

Rename the prompt.

4. The prompt tool screen allows you to type your instructions, get started with Copilot to describe what you want your prompt to do, or start from a prompt template.

> ✅ **TIP** When you are first working with prompts, use the "Get started with Copilot" or template options to help you understand what's possible and how to write a good prompt.

5. In the **Instructions** area, enter the following text:

Classify this for the appropriate department based on the content. Consider the following departments and assign the complaint to the most fitting one. If multiple departments apply, choose the one that best represents the primary nature of the complaint. The categories are: Billing and Payments, Technical Support, Customer Service, Shipping and Delivery, Product Quality. Respond only with the category in JSON format.

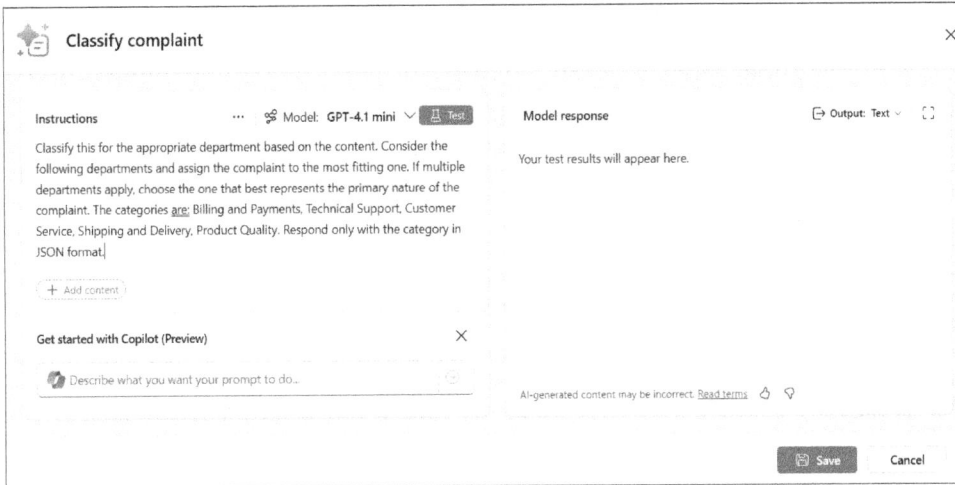

Write the instructions to tell the prompt how to classify the department.

6. Position your cursor after the word "this" in the first sentence and select the **/** key to add an input. Select **Text**.

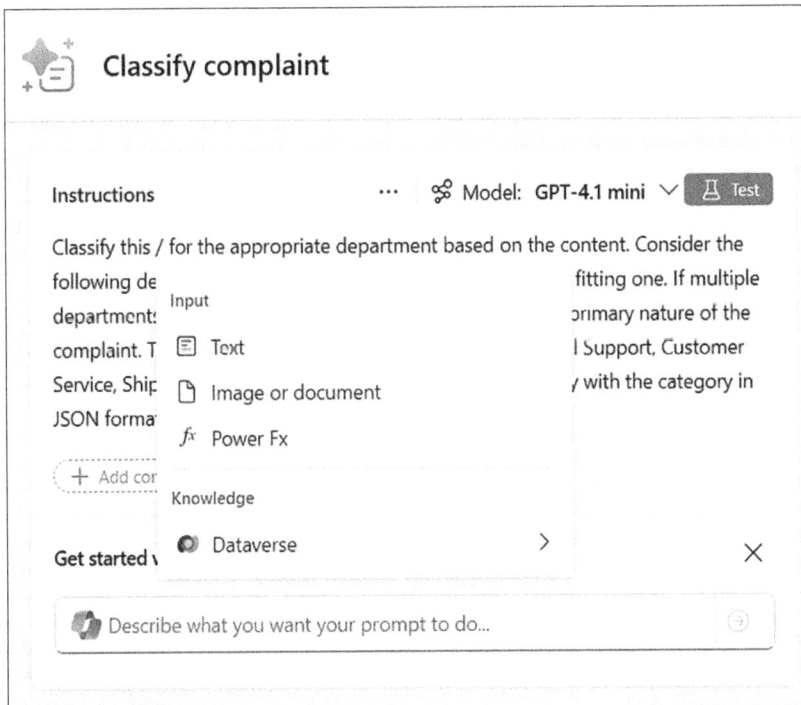

Select the "/" key to create an input.

7. **Name** the input: **complaint**.

8. In the **Sample data** field, enter some text that is a sample of a customer complaint. For example: **I've been trying to use the app for the past three days, but it keeps crashing every time I log in. I've updated to the latest version and even restarted my phone, but nothing works. I need this resolved urgently.**

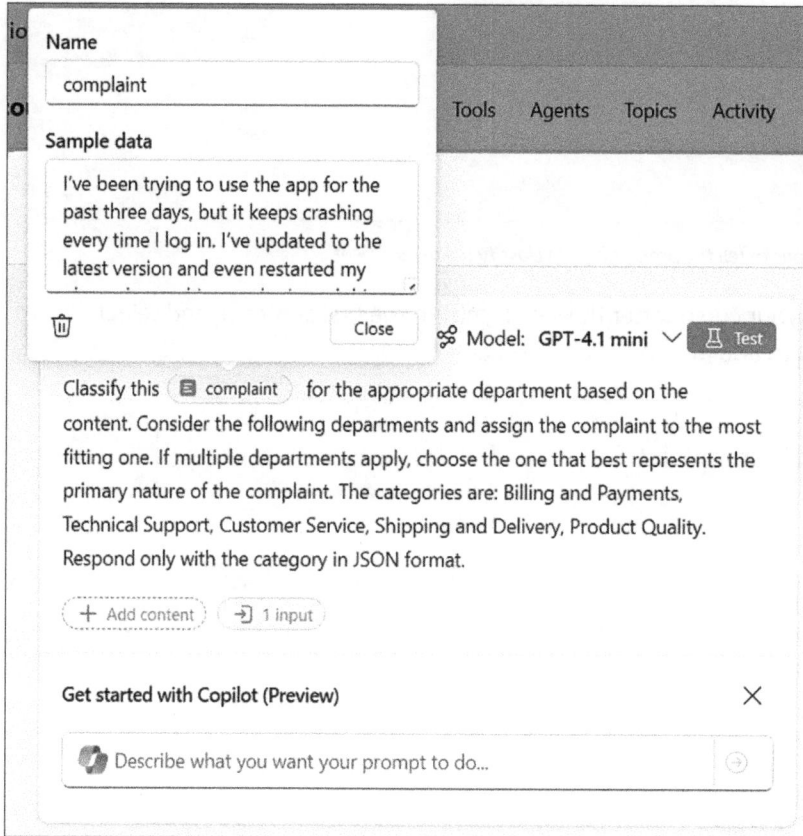

Select the input to set the name, and enter some sample data for testing.

9. Select the **Close** button to close the input configuration pop-up. The **complaint** text input now appears in the prompt.

10. Select the drop-down option for the **Model** to view the options for selecting a language model to use for your prompt tool. The Basic (default) model will be sufficient for this prompt, but there are options to select Standard or Premium models or bring in your own Azure AI Foundry model where needed.

> ⚠️ **IMPORTANT** The model you select will affect the message consumption rate when you use this tool.

Expand the menu to view the other large language model options you can use with a prompt.

11. In the **Model response** section of the screen, select the **Output** drop-down and select **JSON** to view the response in JSON format, which is how it will be passed back to the agent.

12. Select the **Test** button to test your prompt using the sample text you entered when you set up the input.

Test the prompt to view the response.

13. Select the **Save** button to save your prompt tool.

14. When the tool is saved, you will be taken to the **Add tool** screen. Select **Add and configure**.

15. Review the configuration screen for the tool. Expand the **Advanced** menu in the **Completion** section. This section defines how the outputs of the prompt are made available to the agent and other tools.

16. Select the **Outputs available to the agent and other tools** drop-down and select **Specific**.

17. Select the **Save** button to save the changes to the tool configuration.

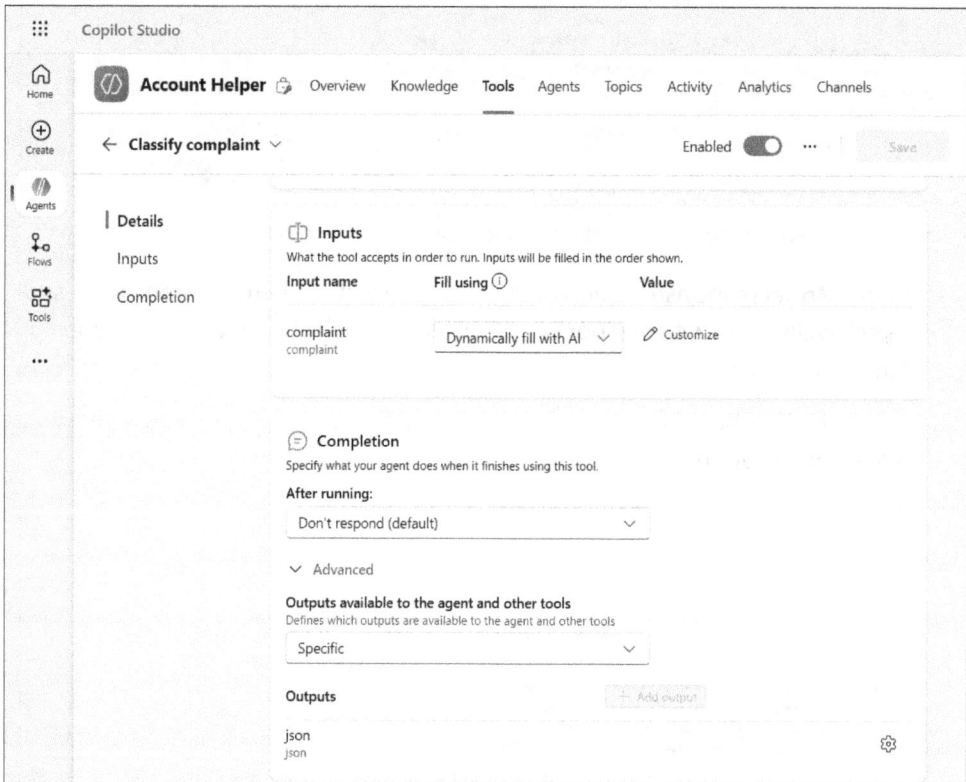

Configure the inputs and completion options for the prompt tool.

Now that the agent has access to this tool, you need to instruct the agent on when and how to use it. In this example, you will write a simple instruction that tells the agent when to call this prompt tool.

To use the prompt tool in the agent

1. Navigate to the **Overview** tab of the Account Helper agent.

2. In the **Instructions** field, select the **Edit** button and then enter the following text:

   When a customer wants to make a complaint, ask them for the details and then use the tool to decide which department it should be referred to. Respond with the name of the department it is classified to. Do not ask any further questions. Always maintain a professional, helpful, and friendly tone.

3. Position your cursor after the phrase "use the tool" and select the / key to expand the list of available tools.

Use the instructions to tell the agent when to call the tool and how to use it.

4. Select the **Classify complaint** tool.

5. Select the **Save** button in the **Instructions** section to save the changes.

6. Test the tool by writing a prompt in the **test** pane that will trigger this tool:
   I need to make a complaint.

7. The agent responds asking for details.

8. Enter the details of the complaint: **I've been trying to use the app for the past three days, but it keeps crashing every time I log in. I've updated to the latest version and even restarted my phone, but nothing works. I need this resolved urgently.**

9. The agent responds with the department it has been referred to.

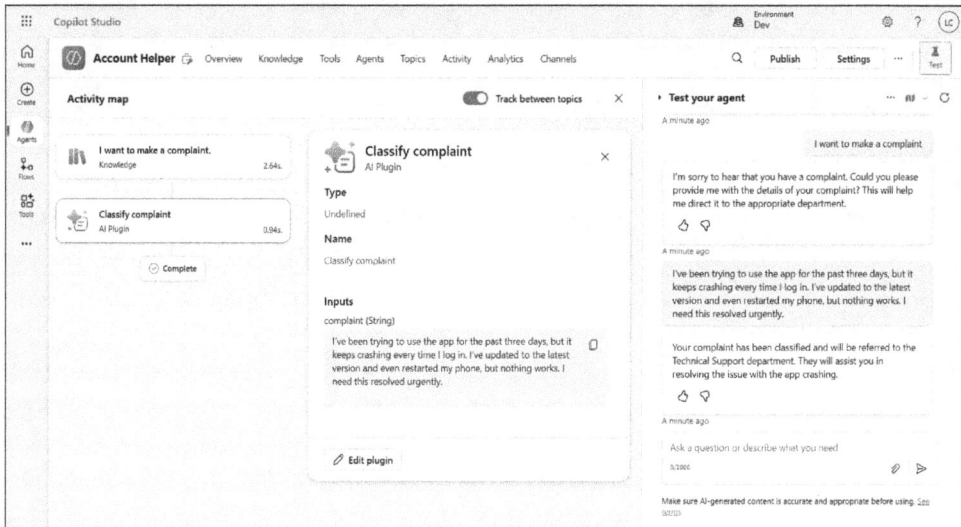

The agent successfully uses the prompt to classify the department to which the complaint should be directed.

10. Continue testing with other example complaints.

To complete this scenario, you could add a tool that takes the output from the prompt tool and uses it to send an email to the selected department. You could also create a row in a customer service ticketing system with the appropriate department assigned.

Add tools from a Model Context Protocol server

Earlier in this chapter, you learned how to add a connector as a tool. When you work with connectors, each action you want the agent to perform—such as adding a row to a database or updating a row in a database—needs to be added as a separate tool, even if those actions connect to the same system. That requires a lot of effort from the maker.

Instead of configuring individual tools manually, you can streamline this process by using the Model Context Protocol (MCP). MCP provides a standardized way to connect AI models to external data sources. In essence, it acts like a prebuilt integration that automatically includes multiple tools for that data source. This reduces the effort and complexity for the agent maker, while also providing them with substantially more capability.

Copilot Studio comes with prebuilt connectors to many MCP servers, including Dataverse, Jira, Salesforce, Microsoft Learn, Outlook, and Dynamics 365. You can also create an MCP server and a custom MCP connector and make them available to consume in Copilot Studio.

In this section, you will learn how to work with the prebuilt connector for the Dataverse MCP Server. You will be working with the Account and Contact tables in your Dataverse environment, using the Account Helper agent you created in the previous section.

> **SEE ALSO** For more information on Model Context Protocol, including instructions on how to create an MCP server and a custom MCP connector, refer to https://learn. microsoft.com/en-us/microsoft-copilot-studio/agent-extend-action-mcp.

To add a prebuilt MCP connector as a tool

1. In the Account Helper agent, navigate to the **Tools** tab and select **+Add a tool**.

2. Select the **Model Context Protocol** filter button to view a list of prebuilt MCP server connections. Select the **Dataverse MCP Server**.

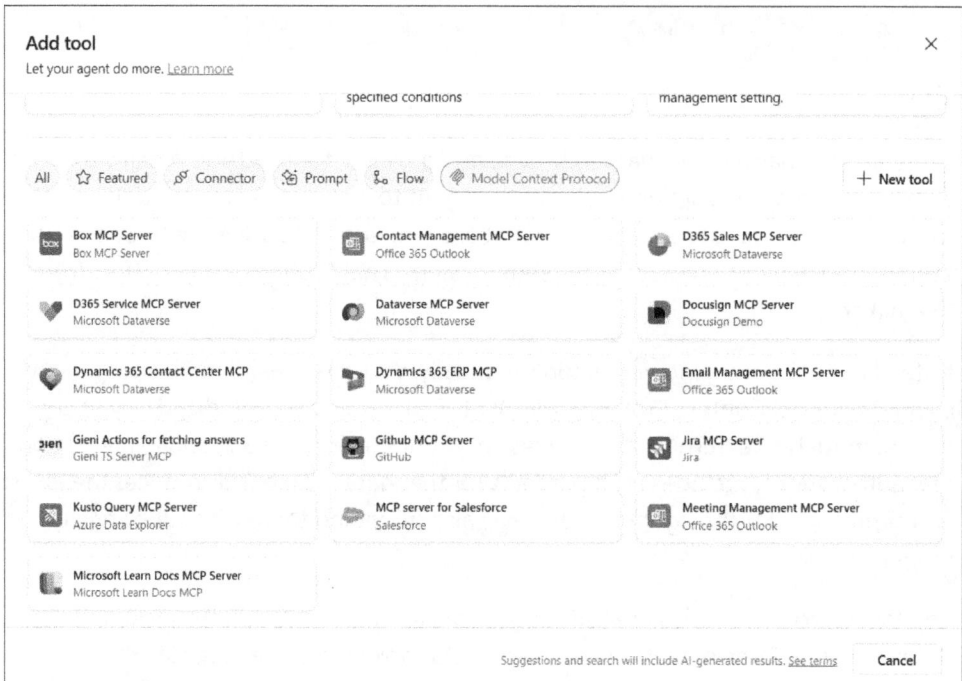

Add tool   ✕
Let your agent do more. Learn more

specified conditions   management setting.

| All | ☆ Featured | ⚙ Connector | 🗨 Prompt | ⅼₒ Flow | ◈ Model Context Protocol | + New tool |

Box MCP Server Box MCP Server	Contact Management MCP Server Office 365 Outlook	D365 Sales MCP Server Microsoft Dataverse
D365 Service MCP Server Microsoft Dataverse	Dataverse MCP Server Microsoft Dataverse	Docusign MCP Server Docusign Demo
Dynamics 365 Contact Center MCP Microsoft Dataverse	Dynamics 365 ERP MCP Microsoft Dataverse	Email Management MCP Server Office 365 Outlook
Gieni Actions for fetching answers Gieni TS Server MCP	Github MCP Server GitHub	Jira MCP Server Jira
Kusto Query MCP Server Azure Data Explorer	MCP server for Salesforce Salesforce	Meeting Management MCP Server Office 365 Outlook
Microsoft Learn Docs MCP Server Microsoft Learn Docs MCP		

Suggestions and search will include AI-generated results. See terms   **Cancel**

Select from a range of prebuilt Model Context Protocol servers.

3. On the **Add tool** screen, select **Add and configure**.

4. Unlike the connector, for which you needed to specify a single table and inputs, the MCP server comes with a set of tools that interact with each other to allow your agent to take more complex actions. Navigate down to the **Tools** section of the configuration screen to view the list and description of all the tools that have been added.

> ✓ **TIP** These tools include capabilities that can list and describe tables as well as add or update rows. This means the MCP server tool can be used to understand and work with the database structure across multiple tables.

5. Select the **Tools** tab to view the full list of tools available in the agent. The Dataverse MCP Server is listed as one of the available tools.

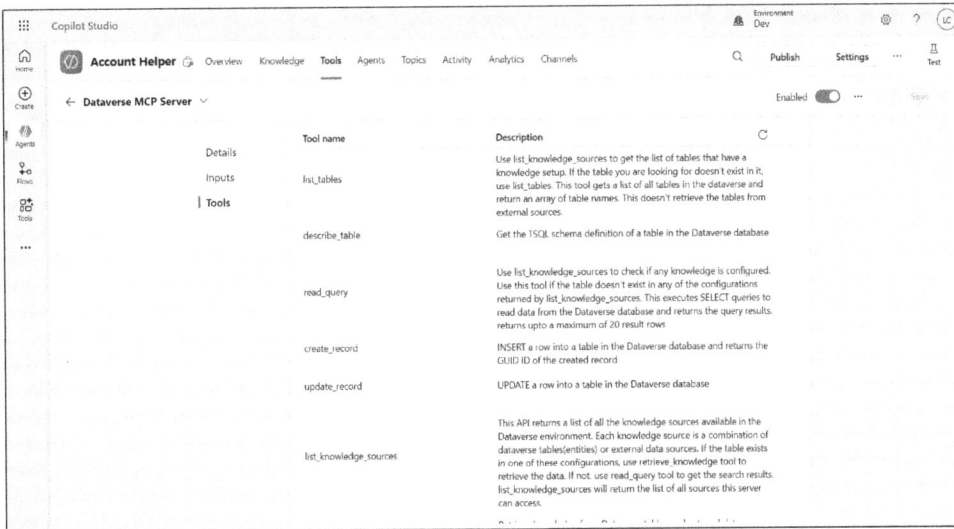

View the tools available in the Dataverse MCP Server.

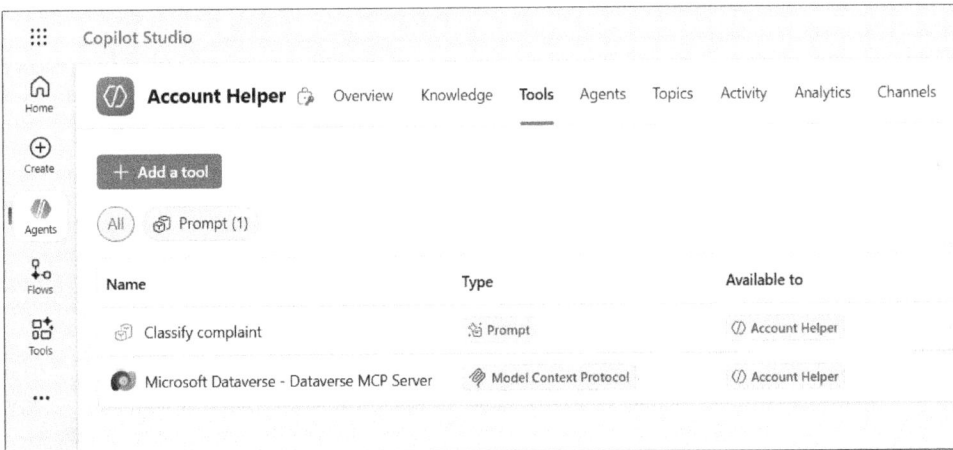

8

The Dataverse MCP Server appears in the list of tools for the agent.

The MCP server tool is now ready to test. It enables your agent to work with Dataverse, but requires very little effort to add or configure the tool.

> **IMPORTANT** Wait a few minutes before continuing with the next example to test the tool. If you begin using it immediately, you may encounter errors.

379

To use the MCP server tool

1. Refresh the **test** pane and ask the agent to add a new row to the accounts table. For example: **Add a new account called Humongous Insurance, phone number 555-1235 in Redmond.**

> ✓ **TIP** When you test the MCP server tool for the first time, you will be prompted to validate your Dataverse connection. Select Allow and wait for the conversation to continue. Refresh the test pane if needed.

2. The **activity map** shows that the agent calls the **Dataverse MCP Server**. It then goes through a series of steps to interpret the prompt and to select and use the appropriate tools to perform the requested task. When it is complete, it confirms that the account has been added.

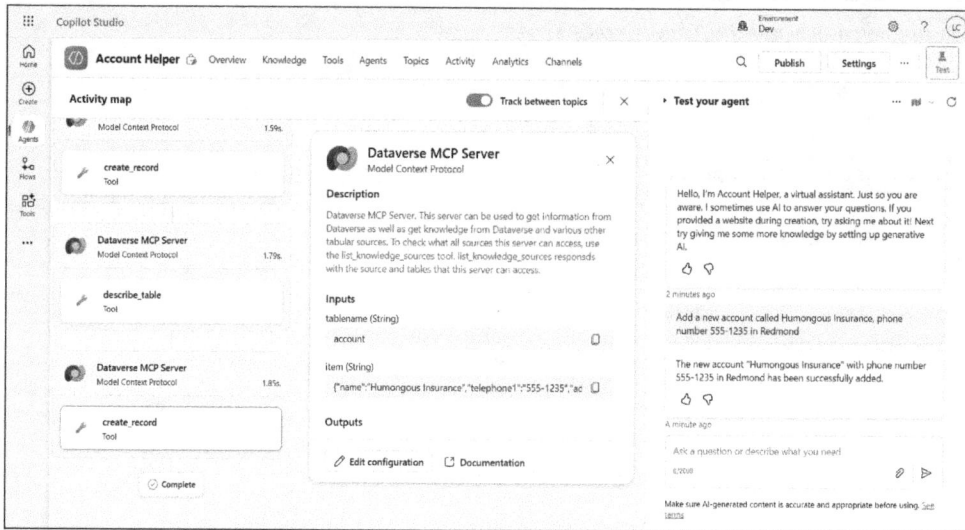

Test the Dataverse MCP Server by asking it to create a new account.

3. View the data in the Accounts table in Dataverse to confirm that the row has been added.

The account has been added to Dataverse.

4. Refresh the **test** pane, then ask the agent to make an update to this row:
   Change the phone for Humongous Insurance to 555-1234.

5. The agent confirms the change and the account details are updated in
   Dataverse.

> ✓ **TIP** You may need to refresh your Dataverse view to see the changes.

6. Refresh the **test** pane, then ask the agent to create data across multiple tables:
   **Create a new account called Relecloud in Redmond, with 3 related contacts:
   Seth Grossman, Chris Norred, Elly Nkya.**

7. The agent calls the Dataverse MCP Server and works through a series of steps
   to identify the tables, set up the table relationship between Account and
   Contact, and create all the rows as described.

8. Open the table in Dataverse and confirm that the new contact rows have been
   added and linked to the new account row, which has also been created.

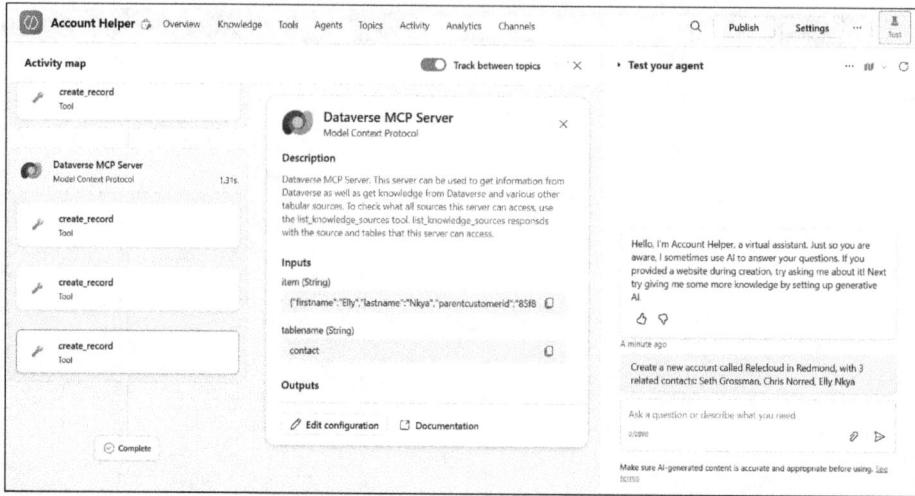

Test the Dataverse MCP Server tool by asking it to create an account and related contacts.

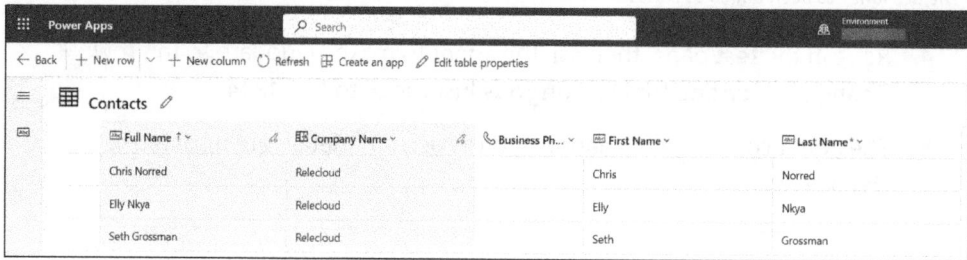

The account and related contacts are created in Dataverse.

Skills review

In this chapter, you learned how to:

- Extend your agent to take action using Power Platform connectors as tools.

- Build stand-alone agent flows and flows that can be triggered by an agent.

- Add a tool to an agent where the inputs can be automatically filled using generative orchestration.

- Add a tool to a topic, using manual configuration to fill in the required inputs.

- Create a prompt tool and add it to an agent.

- Use MCP servers as tools in Copilot Studio agents, and add a prebuilt MCP server to an agent.

Practice tasks

No practice files are necessary to complete the practice tasks in this chapter.

Use connectors and REST APIs

Create a new agent in Copilot Studio called "Tools Playground agent" and then complete the following tasks:

1. Navigate to the **Tools** tab and select **+Add a Tool**.

2. In the Favorites list, select the **Office 365 Outlook** connector to expand the tools.

3. Select the **Send an email (V2)** connector.

4. On the **Add tool** page, verify your credentials if prompted and then select **Add and configure**.

5. On the Send an email (V2) tool configuration screen, configure the following options in the **Details** section:

   - **Name: Send an email**

   - **Description: This operation sends an email message in HTML format.**

6. In the **Inputs** section, select the **Customize** option next to the email body. In the **Description** of the body, enter the following text: **Please draft your email content and I can help you send it.**

7. In the **Completion** section, expand the "**After running**" drop-down and select **Send specific response (specify below)**.

8. In the "**Message to display**" field, enter the following text: **Your email has been sent!**

9. Select the **Save** button to save the connector configuration.

10. Test the agent by typing a prompt into the chat: **I want to send an email.**

11. The agent will prompt you for the email address. Enter your own email address. Note that the **activity map** fills the **To (String)** slot with the email address that you entered.

12. The agent will prompt you for the email subject. Enter a subject, such as **Test email**. Note that the **activity map** fills the **Subject (String)** slot with the email subject that you entered.

13. The agent will prompt you for the email body. Instead of responding to that prompt, make a correction to the subject line: **Please change the subject to Hello from an agent.**

14. Note that the **activity map** changes the **Subject (String)** slot with the new subject line you entered.

15. The agent will prompt you for the email body. Enter some text for the body of the email: **Hi there! If you're reading this, it means the magic worked! No action needed, just sit back and relax and enjoy knowing your agent can now send emails like a pro.**

16. When prompted to connect to Office 365 Outlook, select **Allow**.

17. Wait for the agent to validate the connection, and then confirm that it has sent the email.

18. Check your email to view the email sent by the agent.

Create agent flows

Continue working in the Tools Playground agent in Copilot Studio and complete the following tasks:

1. Navigate to the **Tools** tab and select **+Add a Tool**.

2. Select **+New Tool** and then **Agent flow**.

3. Select the "**When an agent calls the flow**" trigger step to expand the properties.

4. Select **+ Add an input**.

5. Choose **Text** input, and give it a name: **Expense Title**.

6. Select **+Add an input**.

7. Choose **Number** input and give it a name: **Amount**.

8. Choose **Date** input and give it a name: **Expense Date**.

9. Select the **+** button to add a new action between the nodes.

10. Search for and select the SharePoint action: **Create item**.

11. Select the **Create item** action to view the properties, then select the SharePoint site address and list name for the **Expense Claims** SharePoint list.

12. Expand the **Advanced parameters** drop-down and select the following columns: **Title, Expense Amount, Expense Date**.

13. Select anywhere on the properties pane outside the drop-down to collapse that menu.

14. In the **Title** field, select the **lightning** icon to expand the dynamic content options, and select the "**Expense Title**" input from the trigger.

15. Repeat this step for the **Expense Amount** and **Expense Date** fields, mapping them to the trigger inputs.

16. Select the **Save draft** button and wait for the flow to be saved.

17. Select the **Overview** tab.

18. Select the **Edit** button in the **Details** section and edit the name of the flow: **Create Expense Claim**.

19. Add a **Description: Prompts the user for details of an expense claim and submits the claim to the SharePoint list.**

20. Select **Save**.

21. Select the **Designer** tab.

22. Select the **Publish** button and wait for the flow to be published.

23. Select the **Agents** icon on the left side rail in Copilot Studio, and then select the **Tools Playground agent** to open it.

24. Navigate to the **Tools** tab in the agent and select **+Add a tool**.

25. Select the **Flow** filter button, and then select the **Create Expense Claim** agent flow.

26. On the **Add tool** page, select **Add to agent**.

27. Test the tool by refreshing the **test** pane and entering a prompt that will trigger the flow: **I need to make an expense claim.**

28. The agent will prompt you for the required inputs, showing the slot filling that occurs in the **activity map**. Respond to the agent, providing the date, amount, and title of the expense.

29. When prompted to validate the SharePoint connection, select **Allow**.

30. The agent responds that the claim has been submitted.

31. View the new row in the Expense Claims SharePoint list.

Add tools to a topic

Continue working in the Tools Playground agent in Copilot Studio and complete the following tasks:

1. Navigate to the **Tools** tab and hover over the **Create Expense Claim** tool.

2. Select the **three dots** next to the tool name to reveal more options, and then select **Delete**. Confirm that you want to delete the tool.

3. Select the **Topics** tab and add a new topic using Copilot.

4. Fill the details with the following:

   - Name the topic: **Expense claim**.

   - Create a topic to: **Let the user submit an expense claim. They need to provide the Expense Title, Expense Amount, and Expense Date (this will be a string in YYYY-MM-DD format).**

5. Select the **Create** button and wait for the topic to be created.

6. Close the **Edit with Copilot** pane by selecting the **X** at the top right, so that you can view the main topic authoring canvas. Copilot has created a topic with a trigger and a series of three questions, each with a variable to save the responses.

7. Select the + button between the final question and the **Message** node at the end of the topic to add a new node.

8. Select **Add a tool**, and then select the **Create Expense Claim** agent flow.

9. In the **Expense Title (String)** variable, select the **three dots** to view the variables and select the **ExpenseTitle** variable.

10. Repeat this step to select the matching variables for the **Amount** and **Expense Date**.

11. **Save** the topic and wait for the save to be completed.

12. Test the agent by refreshing the **test** pane and entering a prompt that will trigger this topic: **I want to submit an expense.**

13. The agent works through the questions in the topic to collect the information required. Respond to each question.

14. When the agent has finished asking questions, it responds with a confirmation message.

15. View the new row in the Expense Claims SharePoint list.

Use a prompt as a tool

Continue working in the Tools Playground agent in Copilot Studio and complete the following tasks:

1. Navigate to the **Tools** tab and select **+Add a Tool**.

2. In the **Add tool** screen, select **+New tool**, and then select **Prompt**.

3. In the prompt builder screen, select the start from a prompt template link.

4. In the **Job type** drop-down, select **Customer Service**.

5. Browse the list of available prompt templates to understand which kinds of things you can do with a prompt tool.

6. Select the **Respond to a complaint** template.

7. Review the instructions added to understand what this prompt will do.

8. Select the name of the prompt and change it to **Respond to complaint**.

9. Select the **Test** button to test the prompt with the sample text in the template.

10. Select the **Save** button.

11. In the **Add tool** screen, select **Add to agent**.

12. Navigate to the **Topics** tab and create a new topic using Copilot.

13. Fill the details with the following:

    • Name the topic: **Customer complaint**.

    • Create a topic to: **Respond to a customer complaint**.

14. Select the **Create** button and wait for the topic to be created.

15. Close the **Edit with Copilot** pane by selecting the **X** at the top right, so that you can view the main topic authoring canvas. Copilot has created a topic with a trigger and a Message node.

16. Select the + button between the trigger and the **Message** node to add a new node.

17. Select **Add a tool**, and then select the **Respond to complaint** agent flow.

18. In the **input text (String)** variable, select the **three dots** to view the variables, and then select the **System** variable.

19. Search for and select the variable **Activity.Text (String)**.

20. Select the variable in the **Outputs** section and select **Create a new variable**. The variable will be created with the name Var1; it will be automatically set to type "record," matching the output of the prompt tool.

21. In the **Message** node, remove the text and select the **Variable** icon. Select the **Var1.text** option to add the text string from the output into the message.

22. **Save** the topic.

23. Test the agent by refreshing the **test** pane and entering a prompt that will trigger this topic: **I'm not satisfied with my purchase, the packaging was all broken on arrival.**

24. The agent uses the prompt to generate a response.

Add tools from a Model Context Protocol server

Continue working in the Tools Playground agent in Copilot Studio and complete the following tasks:

1. Navigate to the **Tools** tab and select **+Add a tool**.

2. Select the **Model Context Protocol** filter button.

3. Select the **Microsoft Learn Docs MCP Server**.

4. Select the **Connections** option, and then select **Add a new connection**.

5. In the **Connect to Microsoft Learn Docs MCP** screen, select the **Create** button.

6. In the **Add tool** screen, select **Add and configure**.

7. Review the description of the tools in the MCP server to understand what it can do. This tool will return content from the official Microsoft documentation in response to the user's query.

8. Navigate to the **Settings** area and disable the **Use general knowledge** setting for the agent. Save the changes.

9. In the **Settings** area, select **Connection Settings** from the left side menu to view the connections in the agent.

10. If the **Microsoft Learn Docs MCP tool** is shown as not connected, select **connect**.

11. On the **Create or pick a connection** screen, select **Submit**.

12. When you are returned to the **Settings** area, **Microsoft Learn Docs MCP** will now be connected. Close the **Settings** area by using the **X** at the top right.

13. Test the tool by refreshing the **test** pane and asking a question where the answer can be found in the Microsoft documentation: **What is the difference between a Microsoft 365 E3 and E5 license?**

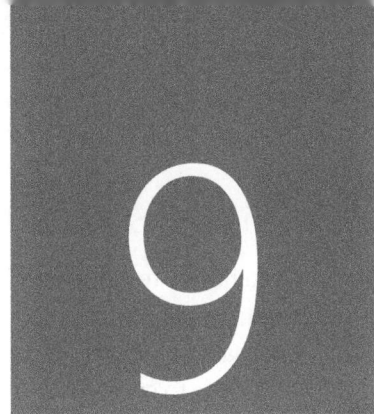

Designing multi-agent orchestration

9

Practice files

No practice files are necessary to complete the practice tasks in this chapter.

Multi-agent orchestration in Copilot Studio allows you to design a parent agent that can coordinate multiple other agents to deliver a seamless user experience. Rather than building a single agent that covers a wide range of knowledge, topics, and tools, you can break down your agent design into a set of smaller, specialized agents, each responsible for a specific area. You can also connect your agent to other agents that have already been built and are being used by your organization. In multi-agent orchestration, the parent agent uses generative orchestration to decide when to call child or connected agents, which tools to use, and whether to pass conversation context.

In this chapter, you will learn how multi-agent orchestration works, how to create and use child agents, and how to connect to existing agents. You will also learn about the differences between these approaches and the best use cases for them.

In this chapter

- Understand multi-agent orchestration
- Create and use child agents
- Connect to existing agents

Understand multi-agent orchestration

You have already learned how to build agents using knowledge, topics, and tools within a single agent. This approach works well when the solution has a focused domain of knowledge and a related set of tools. However, as the scope of your agent expands to cover a broader range of areas, the orchestrator can become confused when trying to handle very different types of requests, which may cause inaccuracies and lead to a poor user experience.

Designing a solution that uses multi-agent orchestration means that you can divide responsibilities into logical segments or groups, creating a solution where each agent is a subject-matter expert in a specific domain. This approach is particularly useful when a single agent needs to handle different types of knowledge or functions, or when your organization has an existing agent and you want your new agent to be able to connect to or hand off tasks to that agent.

Copilot Studio provides two ways to implement multi-agent orchestration: child agents and connected agents.

When to use child agents

You should use child agents when you are designing an entire agent solution and want to logically group certain knowledge or functions within a larger parent agent. Child agents are part of the same solution as the parent agent and do not exist independently. In other words, end users cannot interact them with outside of the parent agent. Choose this option when you are a single developer or working with others in a small team to design a specific solution, where the parent and child agents share publishing, authentication, configuration, and deployment processes.

Child agents let you group related skills or knowledge together, creating logical segments under the main agent. Child agents have their own instructions, which can be very specific and focused on what needs to be done for that specific task or subdomain. For example, a parent "Travel and Expenses" agent could have separate child agents handling Travel (travel policy, approval limits, requests for approval to travel) and Expenses (submitting expenses, expense approvals, reimbursements). You could even design a solution that has more specific child agents, depending on the tasks involved. For instance, you could have one child agent just to manage the process, policy, and communication around reimbursements, and another child agent just for making travel bookings.

When to use connected agents

You can connect your Copilot Studio agent either to other Copilot Studio agents or to agents built on other platforms. Choose this option when you need to publish and maintain agents separately, and when each agent has an independent use case. In this scenario, agents have their own dedicated settings, authentication, configuration, and application life-cycle management. Be aware that if you connect your agent to an existing agent, any changes or updates to that agent will automatically apply, and you will not have control over those changes.

Connected agents allow you to create an orchestrated system that leverages other agents already built in your organization, on Microsoft or other platforms. Rather than rebuilding and duplicating functionality, connected agents allow you to simply connect to existing agents that already offer the functionality you need. For example, suppose you want to expand your Travel and Expenses agent to become an Employee Helper agent, and the IT team has already built an IT Helpdesk agent. You could create a new Employee Helper agent that connects to the Travel and Expenses agent you have already built (with the child agents inside it), as well as to the existing IT Helpdesk agent, providing your users with a single-agent experience that can orchestrate across all these different functions.

9

Create and use child agents

When you create child agents, you start from the main (parent) agent. You then create the child agents as components inside that agent, in the same way that you add knowledge, tools, and topics.

In this example, you will create a new customer-facing Support Assistant agent that greets users and answers their questions by leveraging specialized agents. This agent acts as a Tier-1 support triage agent that can orchestrate to other agents to provide accurate customer service across a wide range of domain knowledge and processes. You will create a parent agent, plus a child agent that specializes in warranty information.

Before you begin this example, create a new SharePoint list called "Warranties," with the following columns:

- Warranty ID (renamed Title column)
- Customer Name (Text)
- Start Date (Date)
- End Date (Date)

Add three or more rows of sample data, with some warranty end dates in the future and some in the past.

Warranty ID	Customer Name	Start Date	End Date...
89078	Pernille Halberg	8/1/2025	8/1/2028
89453	Sanjay Patel	6/17/2028	6/17/2028
89123	Jay Hamlin	4/3/2022	4/3/2025

Warranties ☆

Create a SharePoint list with sample data for warranties.

> **TIP** In this example, this list will be used in a tool for the agent to check warranty information. If you prefer to use Excel or Dataverse, you can follow along using your tool of choice and use the related connector.

To create a multi-agent solution using child agents

1. Navigate to the home screen in Copilot Studio and create a new agent by using the following text to describe it: **This agent provides support for customers who want to purchase a Microsoft Surface device or get help with their existing device.**

2. When prompted for a name, change the name of the agent to **Customer Support Assistant**.

3. Select **Create** to create the agent.

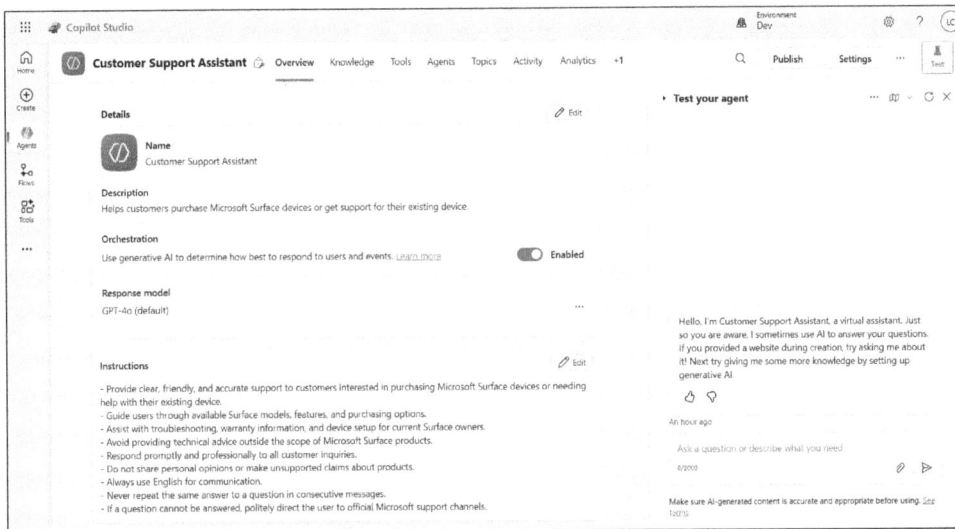

Create a new Customer Support Assistant agent.

4. Navigate to the **Tools** tab and select the **Add a tool** button.

5. Expand the **SharePoint** connector and select the **Get Items** tool (or search for this tool using the search bar).

6. On the **Add tool** screen, validate the connection if required, and then select **Add and configure**.

7. Change the **Name** of the tool to **Get warranty information** and the **Description** to **Gets warranty details for a customer**.

8. Navigate to the **Inputs** section, and set the **Site Address** and **List Name** values to be filled as "Custom Value." Select the Site address and List Name of your **Warranties** SharePoint list in the drop-down menu.

9. In the **Details** section, expand the **Additional details** menu.

10. In the **When this tool may be used** section, select **Only when referenced by topics or agents**. This tool will be used by the child agent, and only when following the instructions in the child agent. Selecting this option in the parent agent means that it will not call this tool at the parent-agent level.

11. Set the credentials to use as **Maker-provided credentials**.

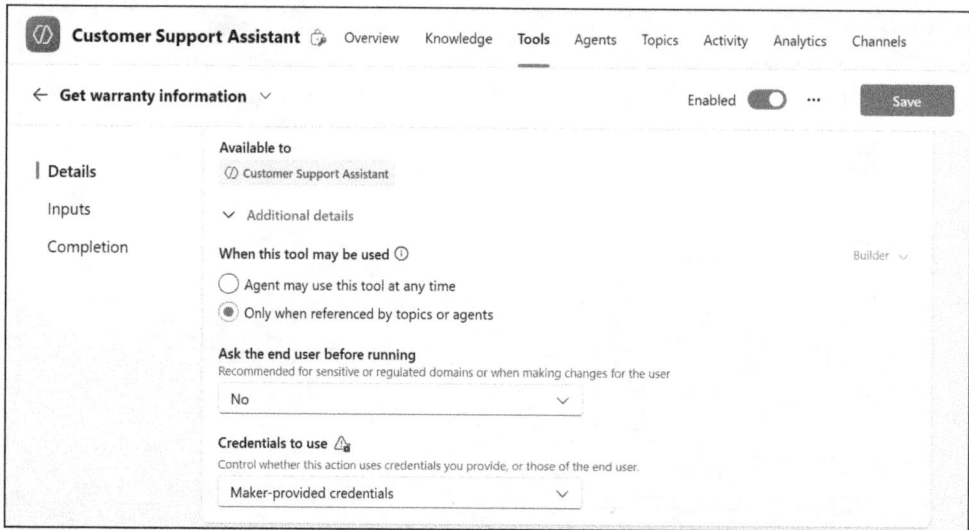

Set this tool to be used only when referenced by topics or agents.

12. Select the **Save** button to save the changes to the tool configuration.

13. Navigate to the **Agents** tab and select the **+Add** button.

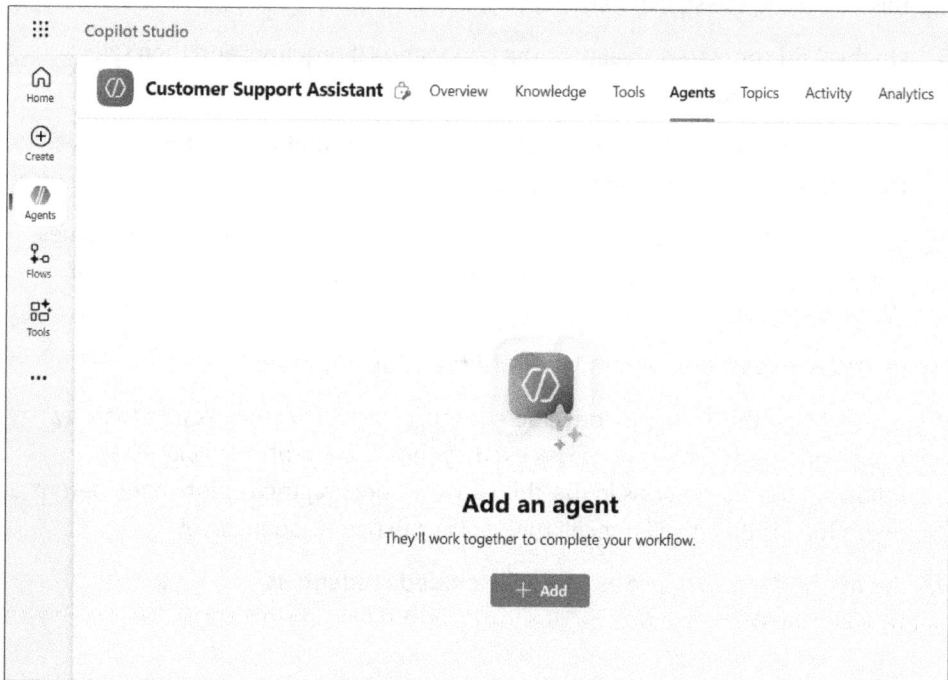

Navigate to the Agents tab to add and work with child or connected agents.

14. This opens a pop-up screen where you can choose how you want to extend your agent. There are options to create an agent or connect an existing agent. Select **Create an agent** to create the child agent.

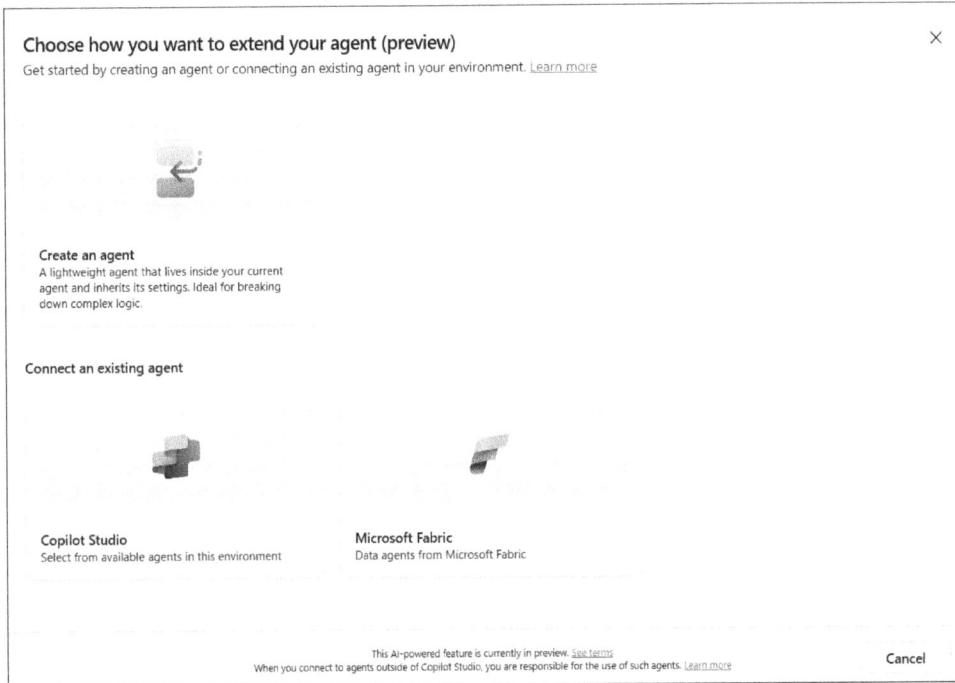

Choose how you want to extend your agent (preview)
Get started by creating an agent or connecting an existing agent in your environment. Learn more

Create an agent
A lightweight agent that lives inside your current agent and inherits its settings. Ideal for breaking down complex logic.

Connect an existing agent

Copilot Studio
Select from available agents in this environment

Microsoft Fabric
Data agents from Microsoft Fabric

This AI-powered feature is currently in preview. See terms
When you connect to agents outside of Copilot Studio, you are responsible for the use of such agents. Learn more

Cancel

Choose Create an agent to create a child agent in the main agent you are building.

15. You will be taken to the configuration page to set up the child agent. This is a lightweight agent configuration, where you can set the name, description, instructions, knowledge, and tools.

16. Change the name of the agent to **Warranty Checker**.

17. Leave the "**When will this be used?**" option set to "**The agent chooses – Based on description.**"

> ✓ **TIP** Expand this drop-down menu to view other ways you can trigger these lightweight child agents, including custom activities and events or redirection from a topic.

18. Enter a description for when this child agent will be used: **This agent should be used when the user has support-related questions about warranties on Microsoft devices. It should also be used to look up warranty details for a customer.**

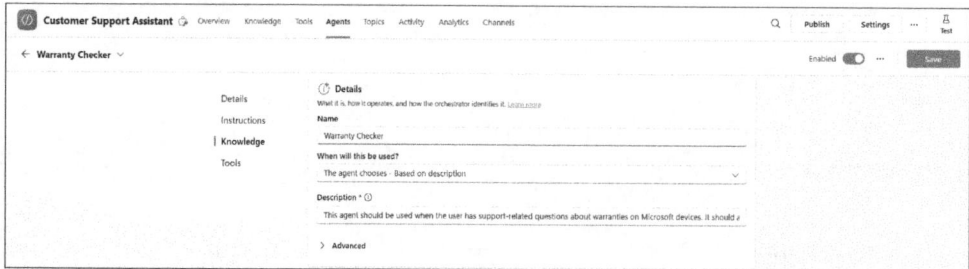

Enter the name and description, and select when this child agent will be used.

19. Navigate to the **Instructions** section and enter the following text:

    If the user asks a general question about warranty information, answer using the knowledge provided.

    If the user asks for specific details of their warranty, fetch the warranty dates using the tool.

20. Position your cursor before the word "**tool**" at the end of the text you just entered, and select the / key to expand the menu of tools and topics that you can add to the instructions.

21. Select the **Get warranty information** tool to add it to the instructions, so that the agent knows exactly when to call this tool.

Write instructions for the child agent and select the tool you created earlier.

The tool is linked to the instructions to help the agent know when to use it.

> ✓ **TIP** You don't need to add the tool again here, because you have already added it to the parent agent, with the option that it will be used only when called by another agent.

22. Navigate to the **Knowledge** section and select the **+Add knowledge** button.

23. Select **Public Websites** and then add the warranty page from the Microsoft website: **https://support.microsoft.com/en-us/warranty**.

24. Change the **Name** to **Warranty Information.**

25. Change the **Description** to **This knowledge source provides information about warranties for all Microsoft devices.**

Add the warranties website, and use a name and description that help the agent understand what it is and when to use it.

26. Select **Add to agent**.

27. The child agent is now complete. Select the **Save** button.

28. Select the **Overview** tab to return to the overview of the parent agent. Note that the knowledge source you added to the child agent is listed in the **Knowledge** section of the main agent.

29. Navigate back to the **Agents** tab. The child agent you added is now shown in the list of agents.

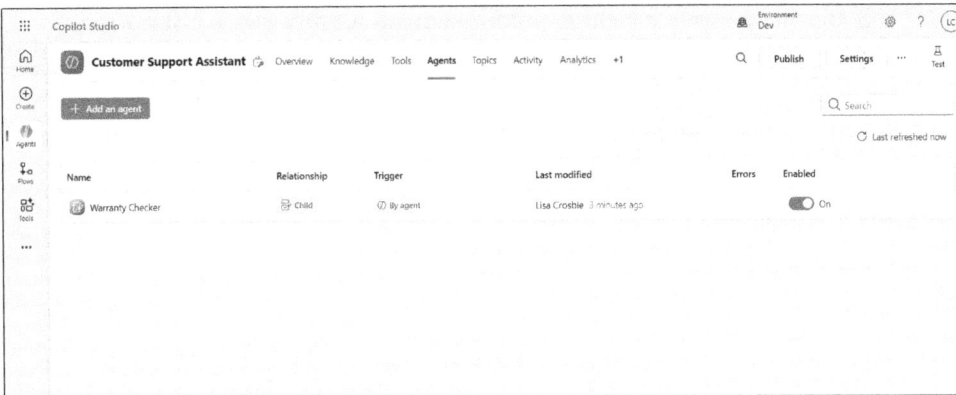

View and manage the child agents in the Agents tab.

It is now time to test the agent.

To test the multi-agent orchestration

1. Enter a phrase into the **test** pane where the answer is found in the knowledge, such as **How long is the warranty on a Surface Pro?**

2. The **activity map** shows that the Customer Support Assistant has called the Warranty Checker agent and has used the knowledge source inside that agent to answer the question.

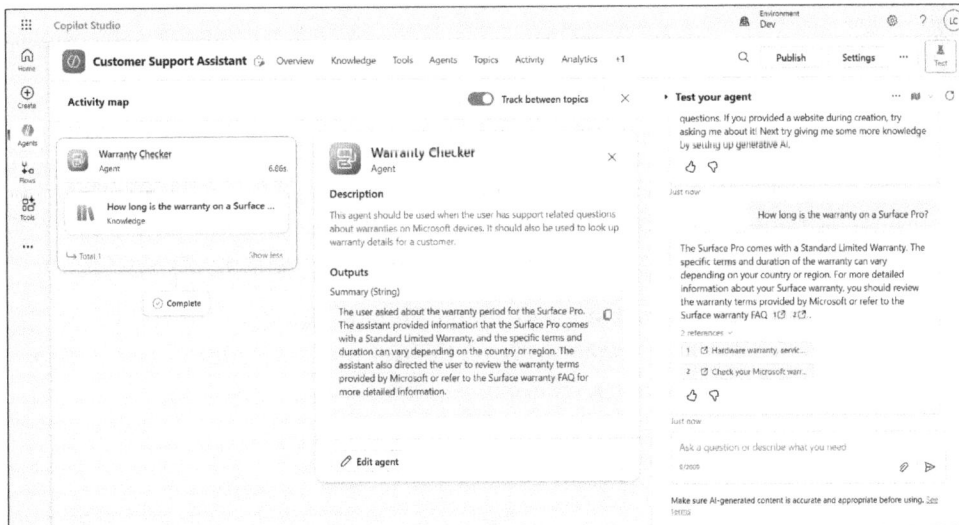

The activity map shows that the question has been answered using the child agent.

9

3. This knowledge source includes information about more than just warranties and is available to the parent agent to use to respond to other questions. Try asking another question where the answer is found in the knowledge source, but where it is unrelated to warranties. For example: **How do I check the serial number?**

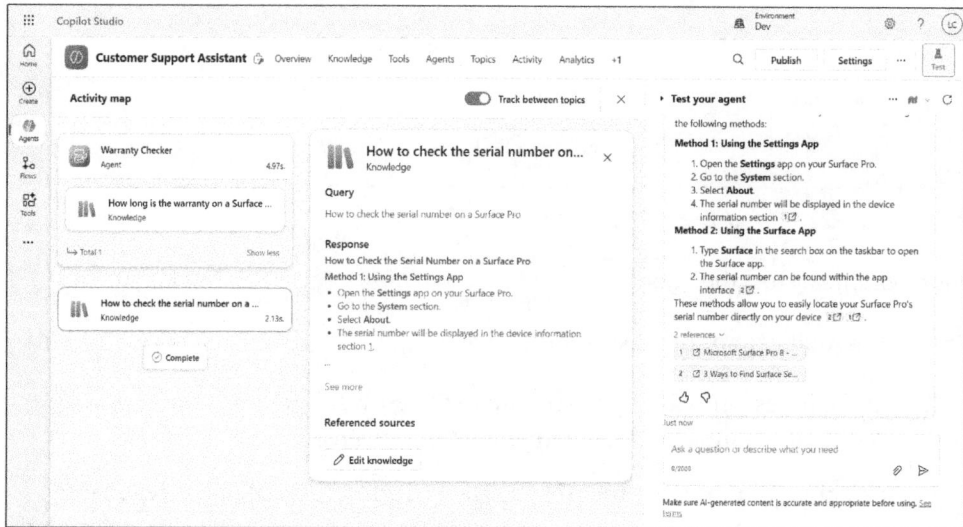

The agent can use the knowledge from the parent agent to answer questions that are unrelated to warranties.

> **TIP** The multi-agent orchestration supports a multi-turn conversation. In other words, it retains the context without the user having to specify the details each time.

4. Ask a question that will require the agent to use the tool to get details of an item from the Warranties SharePoint list, using the sample data you set up. For example: **Can you get my warranty end date for warranty ID 89078?**

5. The **activity map** shows that the Customer Support Assistant agent calls the Warranty Checker agent again and uses the **Get warranty information** tool to retrieve the information from the SharePoint list.

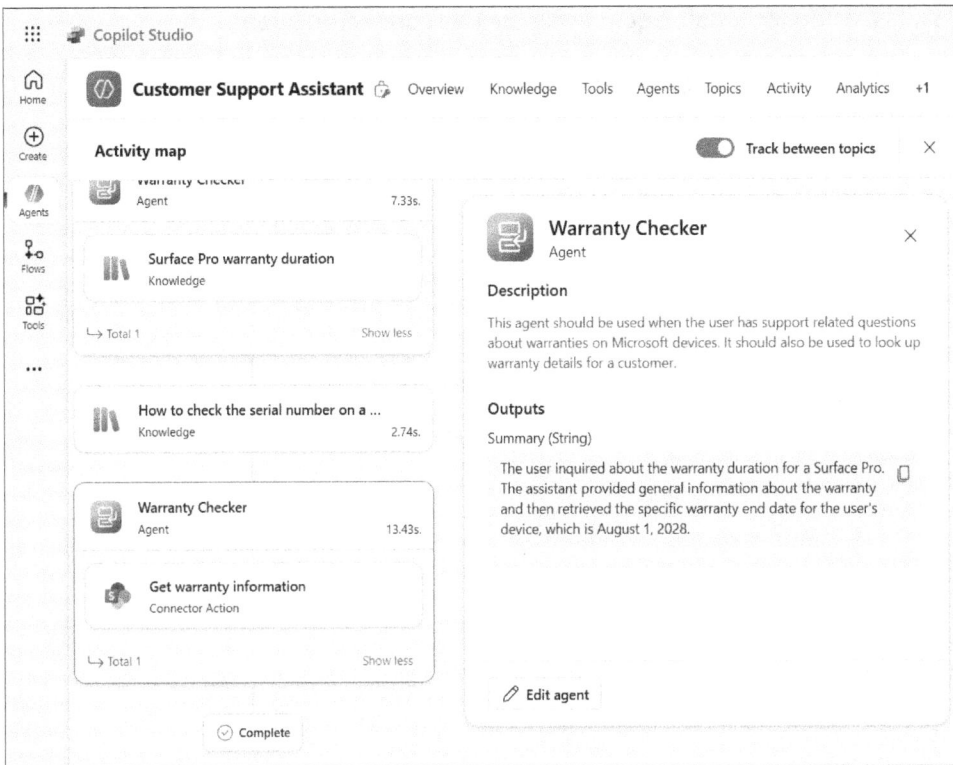

The main agent calls the child agent and uses the tool to retrieve the information from the SharePoint list.

Connect to existing agents

Connecting your Copilot Studio to another existing agent is designed to be a very quick and simple process. To add a connected agent, you simply need to specify which agent you want to connect to and then fill in some configuration settings, such as the description (for another Copilot Studio agent) or the endpoint and connection details for agents on other platforms.

Connect to an existing Copilot Studio agent

In this example, you will connect the Surface Support Guide agent that you created in Chapters 1 and 7 to the Customer Support Assistant. Before you can connect another Copilot Studio agent, that agent needs to be set up to allow the connection to be made.

To make a Copilot Studio agent available as a connected agent

1. Navigate to the **Agents** tab on the left side menu and select the **Surface Support Guide** agent.

2. Select the **Settings** button inside the agent.

3. In the **Generative AI** section of the **Settings** area, navigate to the **Connected agents** section.

4. Toggle the switch to the **On** position to allow other agents to connect to and use this one.

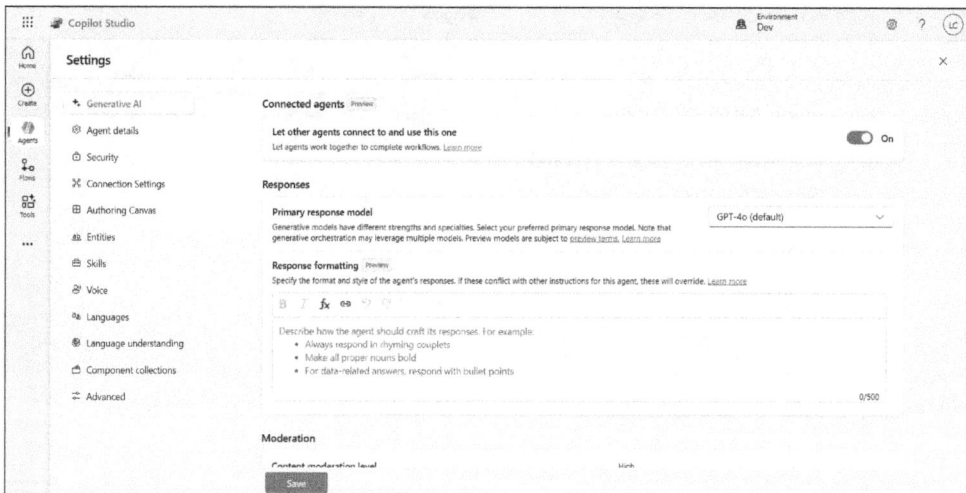

Toggle the Connected agents setting to the On position to allow other agents to connect to this one.

5. Select the **Save** button to save the changes to the settings.

6. Close the **Settings** by selecting the **X** at the top right corner.

7. Select **Publish**, confirm that you want to publish, and wait for the agent to be published.

> ⚠ **IMPORTANT** A Copilot Studio agent must have this setting toggled on, and be published, before it will be available to select in the list of connected agents from another agent.

Now that the other agent has been made available as a connected agent, return to the Customer Support Assistant agent to add the Surface Support Guide agent.

To connect to an existing agent

1. In the Customer Support Assistant agent, navigate to the **Agents** tab and select the **+Add an agent** button.

2. In the **Connect an existing agent** section, select **Copilot Studio**.

3. The menu of agents to connect to will show all of the agents in your Copilot Studio environment. Only those set up as available to connect to and published will be available to select. Select the **Surface Support Guide** agent.

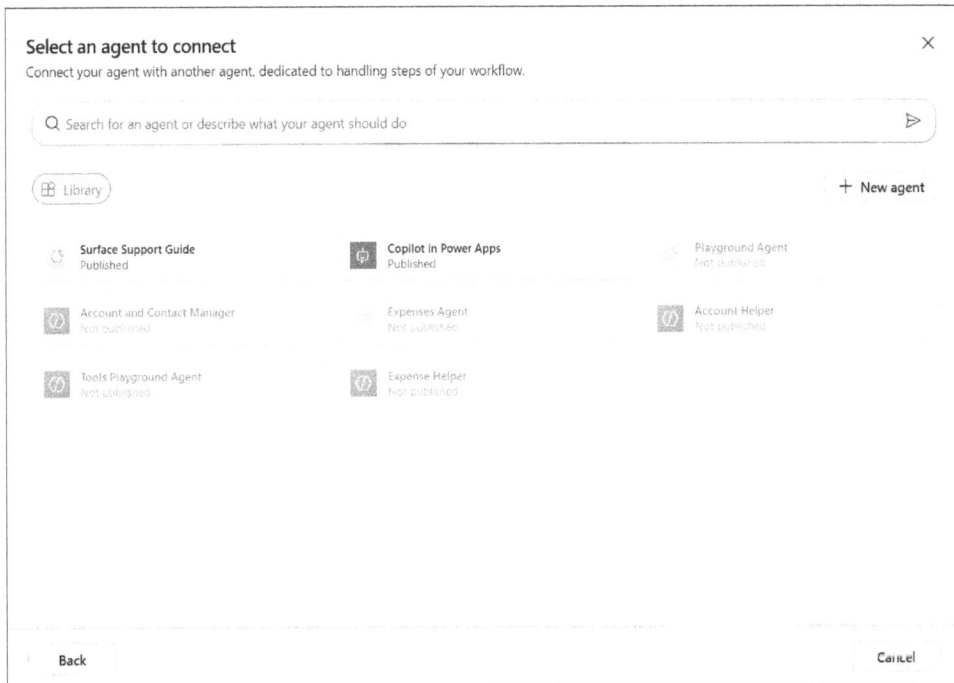

Select the Surface Support Guide agent from the list of Copilot Studio agents.

4. You can configure two options when you make the connection to another Copilot Studio agent:

   - Edit the description so that it helps your agent understand when to connect to this new agent. If you make this change, it doesn't change the description of the original agent. Add the following text to the existing description: **It also helps customers check their eligibility for the power cord recall and request a replacement.**

- Select whether you want to pass the context of the conversation (the conversation history) to this agent by checking this box. If you want the connected agent to run without any context being passed from the conversation, uncheck this box.

> ⚠ **IMPORTANT** Passing conversation history to connected agents can improve continuity, but the information may include sensitive data. Enable this option only if it aligns with your organization's privacy and compliance policies.

Surface Support Guide ✕

Connect your agent with another agent, dedicated to handling steps of your workflow.

Description * ⓘ

This agent provides detailed information about the latest Microsoft Surface models, assists customers in comparing options, and helps them find the right ᐧ

Learn more

☑ Pass conversation history to this agent
  Deselect to prevent conversation history, including potentially sensitive information, being passed between agents.

Agent details

Description

This agent provides detailed information about the latest Microsoft Surface models, assists customers in comparing options, and helps them find the right device for their needs.

Instructions

- Provide information about the latest Surface models and help customers compare and find the right option for their needs.
- Maintain a friendly and enthusiastic tone, always happy to help the customer with any questions.
- Ensure answers are accurate and clear to non-technical customers.

Back   [Add agent]   Cancel

Edit the description to help your agent understand when to call and use the connected agent, and decide whether you want to pass the conversation history to the connected agent.

5. When you have finished configuring these options, select the **Add agent** button.

6. Wait for the agent to be connected. When the process is complete, it will appear on the Agents tab for your main agent, with the relationship "Connected."

The Agents tab displays the child agents and the connected agents.

Now it's time to test the connected agent in your multi-agent orchestration.

To test the multi-agent orchestration with a connected agent

1. Refresh the **test** pane and ask a question that the Surface Support Guide would be needed to help with. For example: **Can I get a replacement power cord?**

2. The Customer Support Assistant agent calls the Surface Support Guide agent and uses the Power cord recall topic.

The Customer Support Assistant uses the topic from the connected agent.

Connect to other existing agents

You can also connect to agents built on other Microsoft platforms, including Microsoft Fabric, Azure AI Foundry, and the Microsoft SDK, or you can use the A2A protocol to connect to agents built on other non-Microsoft platforms. This connection process follows the same path as connecting to a Copilot Studio agent. In the quick and simple configuration, you provide the endpoint and agent ID details to make the connection.

> **SEE ALSO** At the time of writing, this capability has not been fully released. For up-to-date details and instructions, refer to the Microsoft documentation: https://learn.microsoft.com/en-us/microsoft-copilot-studio/authoring-add-other-agents.

Skills review

In this chapter, you learned how to:

- Differentiate the options available for multi-agent orchestration in Copilot Studio and select the right design for your scenario.

- Create and configure a lightweight child agent as a component of a Copilot Studio agent, and have the main agent call the child agent and use its knowledge and tools as described.

- Configure a Copilot Studio agent to make it available as a connected agent, and connect to that agent from the agent you are building.

Practice tasks

No practice files are necessary to complete the practice tasks in this chapter.

Understand multi-agent orchestration

Scenario: You need to design a Copilot Studio solution that supports three areas: HR, IT Support, and Project Management. The current single-agent setup is slow and inaccurate. Complete the following tasks to design a multi-agent orchestrated system.

1. Identify the problem: Why is the single-agent approach struggling?

2. Choose an approach: Will you use child agents, connected agents, or both? Explain why, giving one reason for your choice.

3. Outline the agents: List the agents and their roles.

Create and use child agents

Create a new SharePoint list using the Issue tracker template. Then navigate to the home page in Copilot Studio and complete the following tasks:

1. Create a new agent called **Employee Support Agent**.

2. Navigate to the **Tools** tab and add a new tool.

3. Select the SharePoint "**Create item**" tool and select **Add and configure**.

4. Edit the name and the description of the tool:

    - **Name**: Log an issue

    - **Description**: Collects information from the user about an issue they need to report and creates a row in the SharePoint issue tracker list.

5. Expand the **Additional details** menu in the **Details** section.

6. In the **When this tool may be used** section, select **Only when referenced by topics or agents**.

7. Set the **Credentials to use** as **Maker-provided credentials**.

8. In the **Inputs** section, set **Custom value** for the **Site Address** and **List name**, and select the site and the list for the Issue Tracker SharePoint list you created.

9. Select **+Add input**, then search for and select the "**Issue**" column. Leave the fill option set to **Dynamically use AI**.

10. Repeat step 9 for the "**Issue description**" column.

11. Select **Save**.

12. Navigate to the **Agents** tab. Select the **Add** button, and then **select Create an agent**.

13. Name the child agent: **Report an issue.**

14. Enter the **Description: This agent should be used when an employee needs to log an issue.**

15. In the **Instructions** section, enter the following text, using the **/** key to expand the options to add a topic or tool and then select the "**Log an issue**" tool: **When the user needs to log an issue, use the tool to collect the details and create the issue in the SharePoint list.**

16. Select **Save**.

17. Test the agent by entering a prompt that will call the child agent: **I need to report an issue.**

18. Note that the **activity map** shows that the Employee Support Agent has called the Report an issue agent.

Connect to existing agents

Navigate to the home page in Copilot Studio and complete the following tasks:

1. Navigate to the **Agents** menu on the left side menu, and select the **Expense Helper** agent.

2. Open the **Settings** and toggle the **Connected agents** setting to **On**.

3. Save the changes and close the **Settings** area.

4. Publish the agent.

5. Select **Agents** from the left side menu and select the **Employee Support** agent.

6. Navigate to the **Agents** tab and select **Add an agent**.

7. Select the option to **Connect an existing agent** in **Copilot Studio**, then select the **Expense Helper** agent.

8. Enter a description: **This agent should be used when an employee needs to make an expense claim or check on the status of an existing expense claim.**

9. Leave the **Pass conversation history to this agent** option checked.

10. Select the **Add agent** button.

11. Test the agent by entering the following prompt: **I need to create an expense.**

12. The **activity map** shows that the Employee Support agent has called the Expense Helper agent and triggered the **Create Expense Claim** tool.

Publishing and authenticating agents

Practice files

No practice files are necessary to complete the practice tasks in this chapter.

When you have finished designing and building your agent, the next step is to publish it so that your users can start interacting with it. Publishing allows you to make your agent available on one or more channels—for example, Microsoft Teams or Microsoft 365 Copilot for an internal agent, or your organization's website for a customer-facing agent. Copilot Studio also offers an out-of-the-box demo website you can use for testing purposes. You can publish the same agent to multiple channels, so users can interact with it where they work or where they prefer to interact with your business.

Part of the publishing process is setting up the appropriate authentication method for your agent. You can create a completely public agent with no authentication, use the built-in Entra ID authentication for Microsoft 365 channels, or configure manual authentication that requires users to sign in with their credentials, providing secure access to the tools and knowledge in the agent.

10

In this chapter

- Understand and select the agent authentication method
- Publish and test an agent
- Choose and configure channels

In this chapter, you will learn about the authentication methods for Copilot Studio agents, how authentication affects which channels you can use, the range of channels available for publishing your agent, how to publish agents for internal or external users, and how to test an agent on the demo website.

Understand and select the agent authentication method

Before you publish your agent, it is important to decide how users will access it. Authentication determines whether users can interact with the agent anonymously or whether they need to sign in. It also affects which channels you can publish your agent to.

Choosing the right authentication method depends on your scenario. Do you want anyone to be able to use the agent, with access to all the knowledge and tools in the agent, without any restrictions? Do you want to take advantage of the Entra ID authentication, so users are automatically signed in using the same credentials they use for Microsoft 365 Copilot or Teams? Or do you need to protect sensitive or personal data and ensure only authorized users can access certain knowledge or functions?

Copilot Studio provides three options for authentication:

1. *No authentication*

   - This option is best when you are creating a public-facing agent that uses only knowledge or data that is publicly available.

   - It creates an agent experience that anyone can use. Anyone with the link, and anyone who discovers your agent where you publish it (e.g., on your website), will be able to use the agent and will have access to all the knowledge and tools within it.

   > **TIP** If you want to publish your agent to the demo website, you must choose this option.

   - You cannot use this option if your agent uses tools that are configured to use the end user's credentials. Selecting the "no authentication" option turns off authentication at the agent level and prevents these tools from working. You will get an error message if you try to do this.

> ⚠️ **IMPORTANT** If your agent should support both unauthenticated and authenticated use (e.g., a customer-facing agent that answers product questions but can also let the user log in to get the status of their order), you must choose the Authenticate manually option.

2. *Authenticate with Microsoft (Default)*

- This option is best when you are creating internal-facing agents that will be published in Microsoft 365 Copilot, Teams, or SharePoint.

> ⚠️ **IMPORTANT** This is set as the default because many of the most common starting points and use cases for Copilot Studio are internally facing agents, which extend Microsoft 365 Copilot or other Microsoft 365 experiences. If you are building a customer-facing agent, this method of authentication will not be suitable, and you should change this setting.

- It creates an easy and secure user experience, as the user is already logged into Microsoft 365 with their Entra ID. The agent authentication is handled automatically without prompting the user to sign in again.

- This is also an easy experience for the maker, with no setup required to enable and use this option for internally published agents.

> ✓ **TIP** If you choose this option, you will be able to use variables in the topic authoring canvas, such as User.DisplayName to address the user by their name. You can also use branching logic based on data points you can access from the user's Entra ID profile, such as department.

- If the agent uses tools that require a different authentication, such as a connection to a third-party CRM system, you can still use this authentication for the agent and select "user authentication" in the tool. That will prompt the user to sign in and validate their credentials when the agent needs to use that tool on their behalf.

> 🔍 **SEE ALSO** If you want to create an internal agent that is published to a website (such as the corporate intranet) or an app, you can configure single sign-on using Entra ID with the manual authentication method. For instructions and further details, refer to https://learn.microsoft.com/en-us/microsoft-copilot-studio/configure-sso.

10

3. *Authenticate manually*

- This option is best when your agent is being published outside of a Microsoft 365 experience (Microsoft 365 Copilot, Teams, SharePoint) and the agent needs to use tools or call APIs on behalf of the user. This method is appropriate for an agent that needs to interact with user-specific or secure data, but where the agent is published on a channel that doesn't have an automatic Microsoft Entra ID login. For example, you could use this method for a customer-facing agent on your website that can answer questions from website content (public information that does not require authentication), but needs the user to log in to get the details of their order or application.

- This option is more work for the maker to set up. However, it offers the flexibility and control to design the authentication you need for your agent, or to use a non-Microsoft identity provider.

- You can create an experience where the user needs to authenticate to use the agent from the start, or where the agent prompts the user to sign in at a certain point to access personal or secure data (e.g., looking up order details).

- Copilot Studio agents support Microsoft Entra ID, Microsoft Entra ID V2 (with federated credentials, certificates, or with client secrets), and OAuth2 (any identity provider that complies with the OAuth2 standard—such as signing in with a Google or Facebook account).

> **SEE ALSO** To work with manual authentication, you need to create an app registration with your identity provider to get a Client ID, a Client Secret, and the scopes and permissions that you will set up in the Copilot Studio agent. For full instructions, refer to https://learn.microsoft.com/en-us/microsoft-copilot-studio/configuration-end-user-authentication.

> **SEE ALSO** You can also configure user authentication for a specific part of the conversation by using an authentication node in a topic. For details and instructions, refer to https://learn.microsoft.com/en-us/microsoft-copilot-studio/advanced-end-user-authentication.

To select the authentication method for your agent

1. Open the **Settings** area and navigate to the **Security** section of the settings.

2. Select **Authentication**.

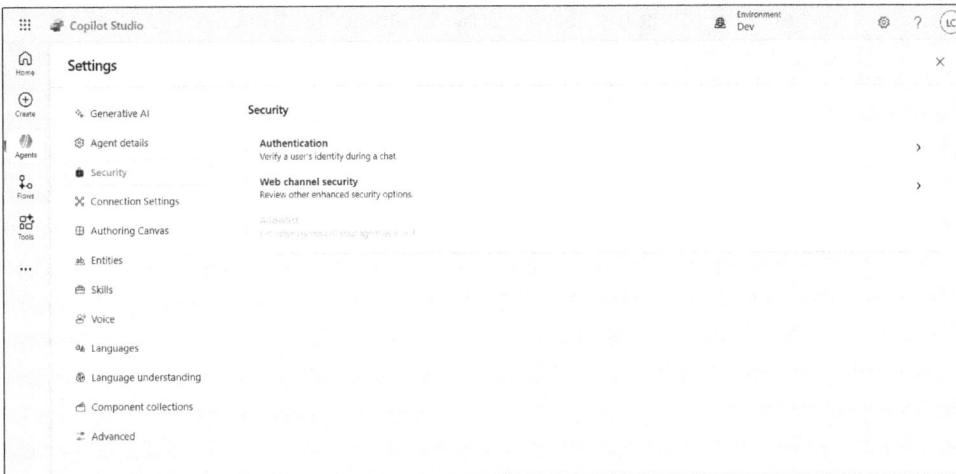

Navigate to the Security section of the settings area in your agent.

3. By default, the agent is set to **Authenticate with Microsoft**, which means you can only publish it to internal channels. To use the demo website or to publish to a customer-facing channel, you need to change that authentication setting.

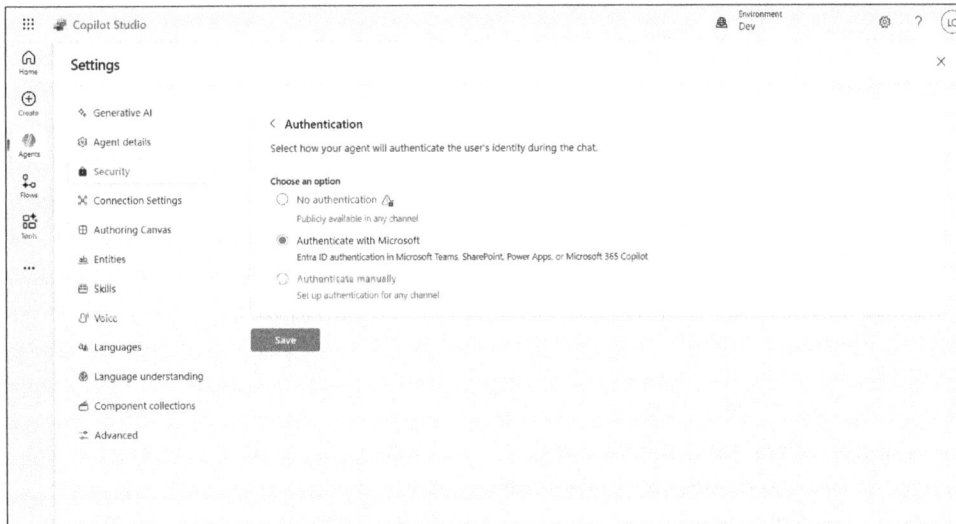

The agent authentication is set to "Authenticate with Microsoft" by default. Use the settings here to select the authentication option that is right for your agent.

4. Select the **Authenticate manually** option.

5.   This is where you select the Service provider and enter the Client ID and other details from the app registration you have created with your identity provider.

> ⚠️ **IMPORTANT** You should select and set up your authentication method before publishing your agent.

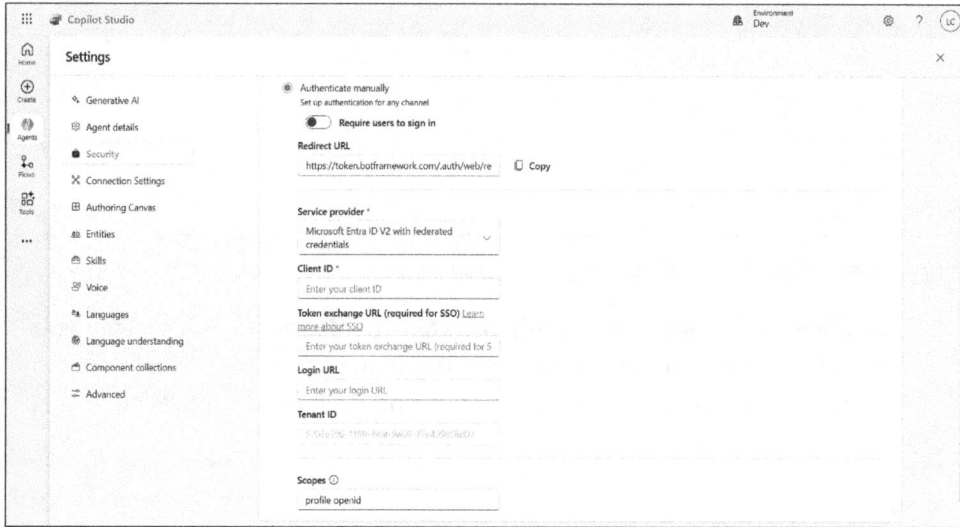

Select "Authenticate manually" and then fill the details from the app registration you created with your identity provider.

> 🔍 **SEE ALSO** You will learn how to use the "No authentication" method in the next section, "Publish and test an agent."

Publish and test an agent

Publishing an agent is the step that makes it available for your users to interact with it—where you deploy the agent from the maker experience to a user-facing channel. Users will interact with the latest published version of the agent, so if you make changes or updates, you will need to publish the agent again to push out those changes and have them take effect for users.

In a real-world scenario, depending on the type of agent you are building and the intended audience and channels, you may use a full application life-cycle management process. This process moves the agent solution from a development environment, to a test environment, and finally to a production environment. Copilot Studio uses Power Platform solutions and ALM to manage this process.

> **SEE ALSO** Application life-cycle management in Microsoft Power Platform is a substantial area of expertise. For the full documentation and learning paths, see https://learn.microsoft.com/en-us/power-platform/alm/overview-alm.

In this section, you will learn how to publish and test your agent using the demo website channel provided by Copilot Studio for this purpose. This is a quick and easy way to test an agent that is designed to be publicly available (no authentication). You can also share it with others in your organization for testing purposes before publishing the agent on a public-facing channel for your customers.

In this example, you will work with the Surface Support Guide agent that you created in Chapters 1 and 7. You will begin by setting the authentication to make it public, and then publishing and testing it.

> **IMPORTANT** You can only use the demo website with an agent that does not require any authentication. The demo website is designed for internal testing only, to share agents with other stakeholders. Although anyone with the link can use the agent, it should not be used for production use.

To publish an agent with no authentication

1. Navigate to Copilot Studio and open the **Surface Support Guide** agent.

2. Navigate to the **Channels** tab on the top menu of your agent. This area provides information about the published status of your agent, authentication settings, and the available channels.

> **TIP** Close the test pane to make it easier to view all the options on the Channels tab.

10

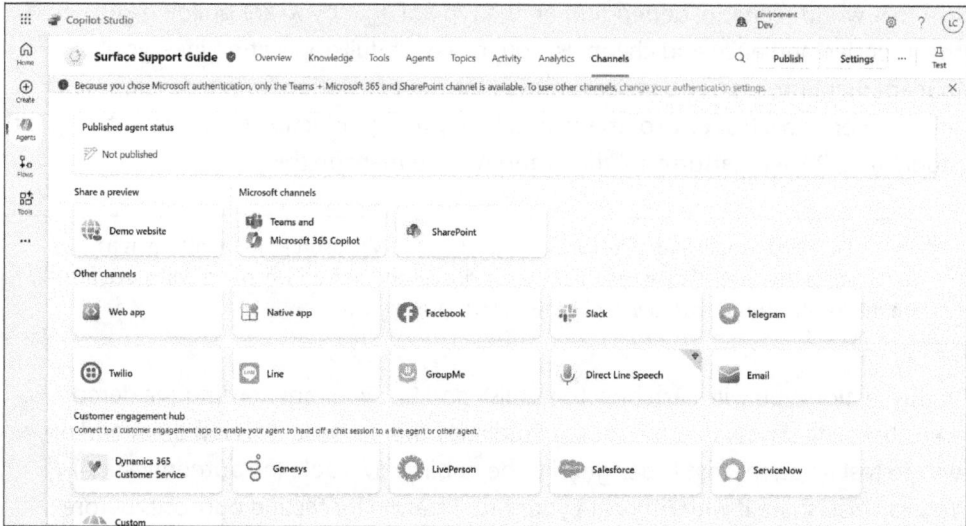

The Channels tab of the agent shows the published agent status and the available channels for publishing your agent.

3. Select the hyperlink in the authentication information message at the top of the screen to navigate to **change your authentication settings**. This will bring you to the authentication area of the security settings for the agent.

4. Select the **No authentication** option to make your agent publicly available on any channel.

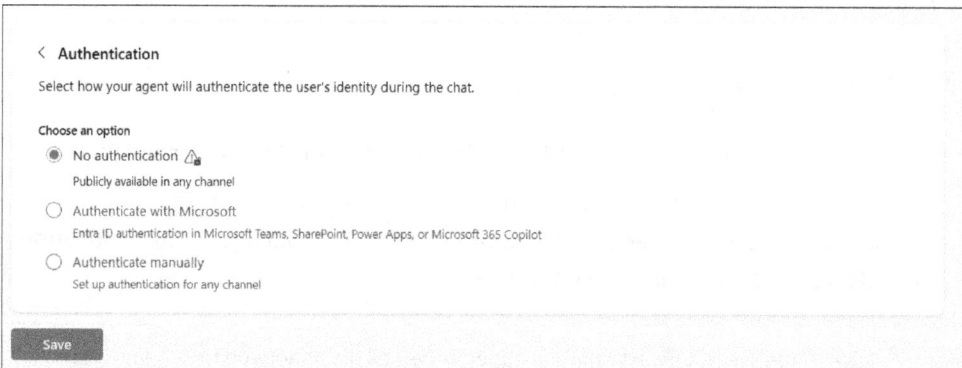

Copilot Studio provides authentication options to make your agent publicly available in any channel, authenticated with Microsoft, or authenticated manually.

5. Select **Save**.

6. Review the pop-up message that explains the implications for your agent of selecting "No authentication." Then select **Save**.

7. Wait for the changes to be saved and then close the **Settings** area by selecting the **X** at the top right.

8. Select the **Publish** button at the top right of the agent.

9. You will be asked to review and confirm the agent's settings.

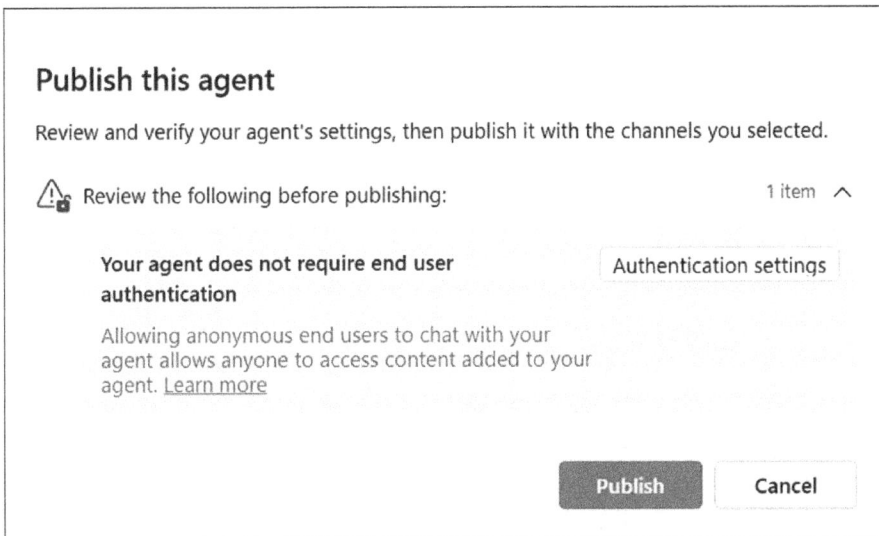

Publish this agent

Review and verify your agent's settings, then publish it with the channels you selected.

⚠️ Review the following before publishing: 1 item ∧

Your agent does not require end user authentication   Authentication settings

Allowing anonymous end users to chat with your agent allows anyone to access content added to your agent. Learn more

Publish   Cancel

Review the agent's settings and then confirm you are ready to publish it.

10. Select **Publish**.

11. Wait until the agent is published and Copilot Studio gives you a confirmation message.

12. Navigate back to the **Channels** tab. The **Published agent status** shows that the agent has been published, and warning flags alert you to the risk of having an agent without any end-user authentication. These warnings will not prevent your agent from working.

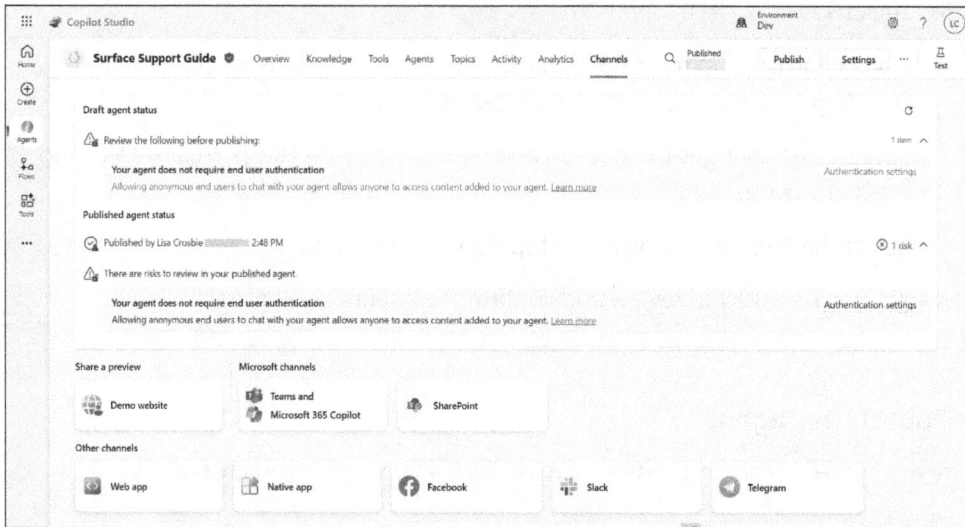

The Channels tab shows the published agent's status together with authentication warnings.

Now you will test your agent on the demo website channel.

To publish and test your agent on the demo website

1. In the **Channels** tab, select the **Demo website** button from the list of channels. A configuration pane pops up at the right side of the screen, where you can configure some options for the demo website.

> **IMPORTANT** The design and format of the demo website are fixed. You can configure only the welcome message and the starter prompts.

2. Change the welcome message to read: **Try out our Surface Support Guide**.

3. Change the conversation starters to: **What is a Surface Hub?**, **What is a Surface pen?**, and **Can I get a power cord recall?**

Demo Website   ✕

You created a agent. Great job! Let's set up a website to share with team members so they can try your agent.

Welcome message

Introduce your agent and its purpose to your team members.

Try out our Surface Support Guide

Conversation starters

Provide some common trigger phrases to help your team members start a conversation with your agent.

What is a Surface Hub?
What is a Surface pen?
Can I get a power cord recall?

Share your website

To invite team members to see your agent in action, copy the link below.

https://copilotstudio.preview.microsoft.com/environments/4405b9ee-d324-eacc-a6 | Copy |

| Save | Cancel |

10

Configure the welcome message and conversation starters for the demo website.

4. Select the **Save** button. Wait for the channel to be saved.

5. Select the **Copy** button to copy the demo website URL.

6. Open a new tab in your browser and paste in the copied URL.

7. The demo website shows the welcome message and the conversation starters you configured as clickable buttons, beside the agent.

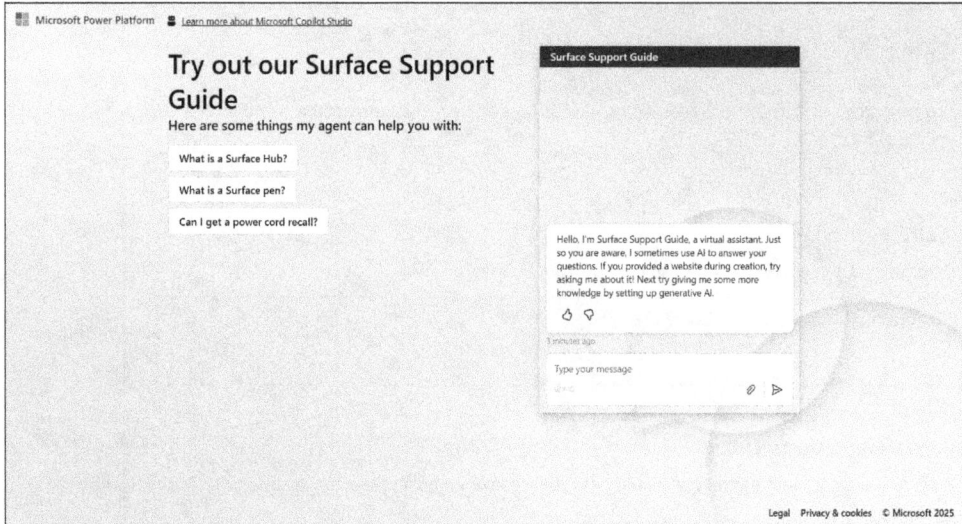

Use the demo website to test your agent before publishing it on a public-facing channel.

8. Test the agent by selecting one of the conversation starter buttons or entering text into the chat.

> ✓ **TIP** To start a new conversation in the test, type "start over" into the chat, or refresh the browser.

If you need to make changes to your agent after testing, you can make changes to the configuration of your knowledge, topics, tools, or child agents. You can then select the **Publish** button to update and push out the changes and continue testing using the updated version.

Now that you have published an agent and tested it, you will explore the range of channels available for publishing your agent, including how to configure them.

Choose and configure channels

You can publish your Copilot Studio agent to internal channels, external channels, or customer engagement applications. The channels available will depend on the authentication method configured for your agent. You can publish an agent to multiple channels, providing your users with the choice to access the agent where they prefer to interact, without needing to build a separate agent for each channel.

> **SEE ALSO** Customer engagement hub channels are covered in Chapter 12: Working with voice and customer engagement systems.

Each channel has different configuration steps and prerequisites, depending on the channel. In this section, you will learn how to publish the agent and hand it over to a developer to deploy the agent to external channels, and how to publish your agent to internal channels (Teams and Microsoft 365 Copilot).

> **SEE ALSO** For full documentation on configuration and prerequisites for all channels, refer to https://learn.microsoft.com/en-us/microsoft-copilot-studio/publication-fundamentals-publish-channels.

Publishing to external channels

If your agent is designed for external use, Copilot Studio provides a range of channels for you to publish to. You can publish the agent on your website, inside an app, or to a range of public messaging and chat channels, including email, Facebook Messenger, Telegram, Twilio, and WhatsApp.

Copilot Studio makes it easy for a low-code maker to select and enable the desired channels, and then hand off the details to a developer to embed the agent in these channels.

10

To enable external channels

1. Navigate to the **Channels** tab in your agent.
2. Select the **Web app** channel.
3. Review the instructions and the code provided.
4. Select the **Copy** button in the **Embed code** section to copy the code.
5. Open a new email, Teams chat, or Word document and paste the code into it.
6. Send this code to your web or app developer to embed in the web app.

Web app   ✕

There's two ways to add an agent to a web app. The embed code option lets you add an agent to a web-based app with a copied code snippet, while the Microsoft 365 Agents SDK offers a fully integrated experience.

Embed code

Copy the following code snippet and paste it into your HTML web app. If you don't have access to your code base, share the snippet with the person responsible for your web app.

```
<!DOCTYPE html><html><body><iframe
src="https://copilotstudio.preview.microsoft.com/environments/4                    -
8d791f00aa04/bots/cr4aa_surfaceSupportGuide/webchat?__version__=2" frameborder="0"
style="width: 100%; height: 100%;"></iframe></body></html>
```

📋 Copy

Microsoft 365 Agents SDK

To integrate a Copilot Studio agent with anonymous security settings using Python, Javascript, or .NET, copy the connection string and paste it into your app's code. Learn More

Connection string

https://   8d791f00aa.04.environment.api.powerplatfor   📋 Copy

↗ Using the Microsoft Custom Web Chat UI and other patterns.

Copy the embed code from the Web app screen and provide it to your web or app developer.

> 🔍 **SEE ALSO** As a low-code maker, if you also work with Power Pages, you can deploy your agent to your site using low code by following the instructions here: https://learn.microsoft.com/en-us/microsoft-copilot-studio/publication-add-bot-to-power-pages.

Browse and select some of the other external-facing channels, such as Native app, Facebook, Twilio, or email, to view the code snippets, endpoints, or connection strings provided. Also review the Credentials and IDs needed to set them up, so that you understand what you will need to provide to or get from your developer to complete this process.

Publishing to internal channels

If your agent is designed for internal use in a Microsoft 365 channel, you can publish it to Teams, Microsoft 365 Copilot, or SharePoint.

> ⚠️ **IMPORTANT** Publishing to an internal Microsoft 365 channel requires that the agent is set up with the "Authenticate with Microsoft" option.

> 🔍 **SEE ALSO** If you are a Power Apps maker, you can also add your Copilot Studio agent into your app with the "Authenticate with Microsoft" method. For instructions, refer to https://learn.microsoft.com/en-us/power-apps/maker/canvas-apps/add-custom-copilot.

In this scenario, you will publish the Expense Helper agent you created in Chapter 8 to Teams and Microsoft 365 Copilot.

To publish an agent to Teams and Microsoft 365 Copilot

1. In Copilot Studio, open the **Expense Helper** agent and navigate to the **Channels** tab.

2. This agent is already configured with Microsoft authentication, so you don't need to make any changes to the authentication settings.

3. Select the **Teams and Microsoft 365 Copilot** option from the Microsoft channels section.

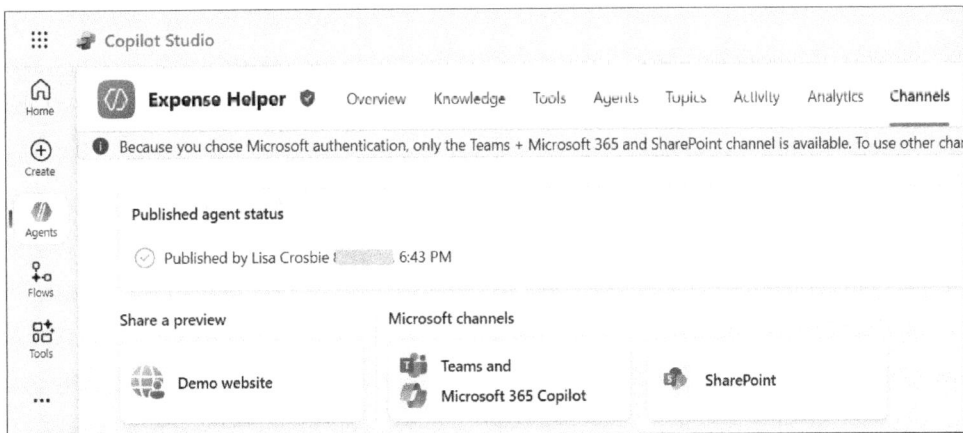

Select the Teams and Microsoft 365 Copilot option to publish your agent to both of these internal channels.

4. This option publishes your agent to both Teams and Microsoft 365 Copilot. Uncheck the option to publish to Microsoft 365 Copilot if you don't want to publish your agent there.

Teams and Microsoft 365 Copilot   ✕

Microsoft 365 is your cloud-powered productivity solution and includes Outlook, Word, Excel, PowerPoint, and OneDrive. Learn more

When you publish your agent to Microsoft 365, we'll publish it to Teams too. You'll get all of your agent's advantages in Teams: meeting summaries and transcripts, pointers to open issues or unresolved questions, and more effective collaboration.

Microsoft 365 Copilot

☑ Make agent available in Microsoft 365 Copilot
You'll need to republish your agent after you turn on/off Microsoft 365 Copilot

Agent preview

Expense Helper
Built using Microsoft Copilot Studio.

✎ Edit details

Availability options   See agent in Microsoft 365   See agent in Teams

Add channel

Select Microsoft 365 Copilot to make the agent available there as well as in Teams, or uncheck that option if you want to publish the agent only to Teams.

5. Select the **Add channel** button.

6. When the channels are connected, you will receive a confirmation message, and the edit options will be available for the Teams channel.

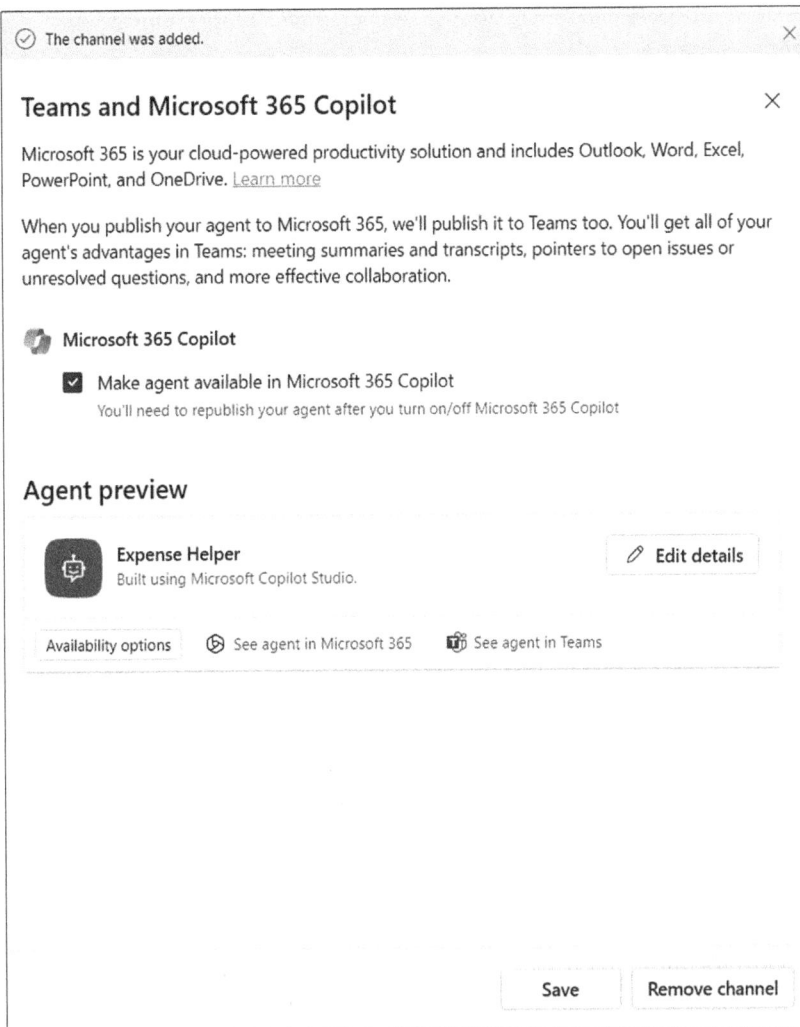

The channel is added and the options to edit or see the agent in Microsoft 365 or Teams are now available.

7. Select the **Edit details** icon to open the options to change the agent icon and description. Change the description text so that it is more meaningful. This will be displayed to the users.

   - Short Description: **An agent to help you submit and check the status of expense claims.**

   - Long Description: **Submit your expense claims by chatting with the agent, or ask it to check on the status of an existing expense claim.**

8. Navigate down and expand the **More** option to reveal the **Developer name** field. Enter your name.

←   ✕

Icon

       [Change color]

       [Change icon]

Icon should be in PNG format and less than 30 KB in size. Use a white transparent image that has no extra padding. Don't upload confidential icon in your agent icon. Learn more

Short description

Built using Microsoft Copilot Studio.

Up to 80 characters

Long description

Help employees stay informed, productive, and connected. Create agents and add important topics for your organization using an intuitive, graphical interface. No code required. Create your own at https://aka.ms/microsoftcopilotstudio.

Up to 3400 characters

Teams settings

Decide where and how your agent should function in Teams.

☐ Users can add this agent to a team

☐ Use this agent for group and meeting chats

Less ∧

Developer name

Lisa Crosbie

Up to 32 characters

[**Save**]   [Cancel]

Change the icon and update the description and other settings for the Teams and Microsoft 365 Copilot channel.

9. Select the **Save** button. You will be returned to the main **Teams and Microsoft 365 Copilot** channel pane.

10. Close the pane and publish the agent again.

> ⚠ **IMPORTANT** You must publish the agent again after you have configured the options for this Teams channel. If you miss this step, you will get a "something went wrong" or "app not found" error message.

11. When the agent is published, select the **Teams and Microsoft 365 Copilot** channel option again.

12. In the Agent preview section, select **See agent in Microsoft 365**.

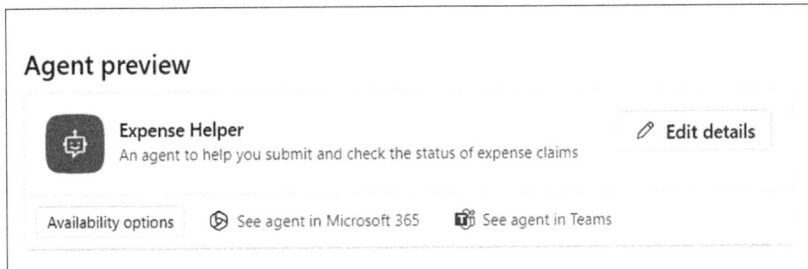

The Agent preview pane includes buttons you can use to see the agent in Microsoft 365 or Teams.

13. The Microsoft 365 home page opens in your web browser, with a pop-up screen showing the agent details. Select the **Add** button to confirm you want to add the agent.

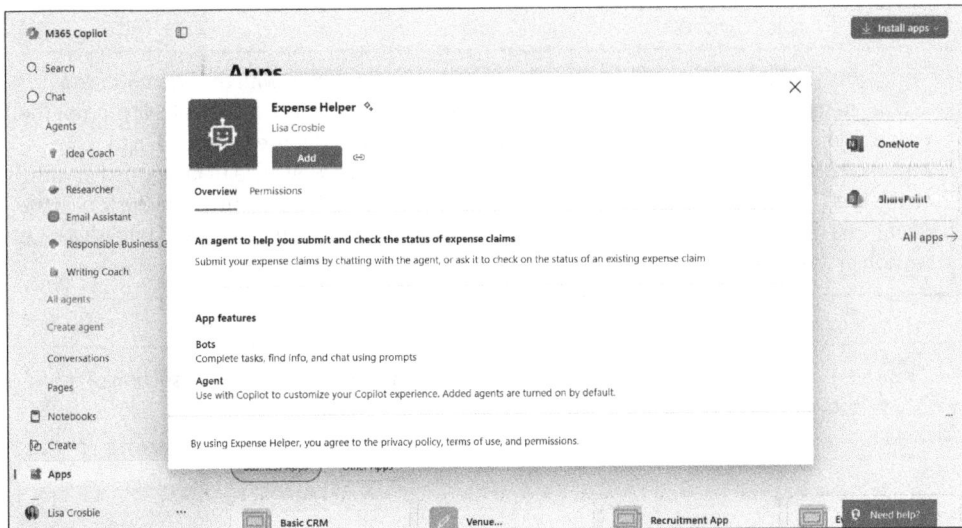

Review the details of the agent and select the Add button to use it in Microsoft 365 Copilot Chat.

14. The agent is now added to the list of agents and opens in the main screen. Start chatting with the agent to use and test it.

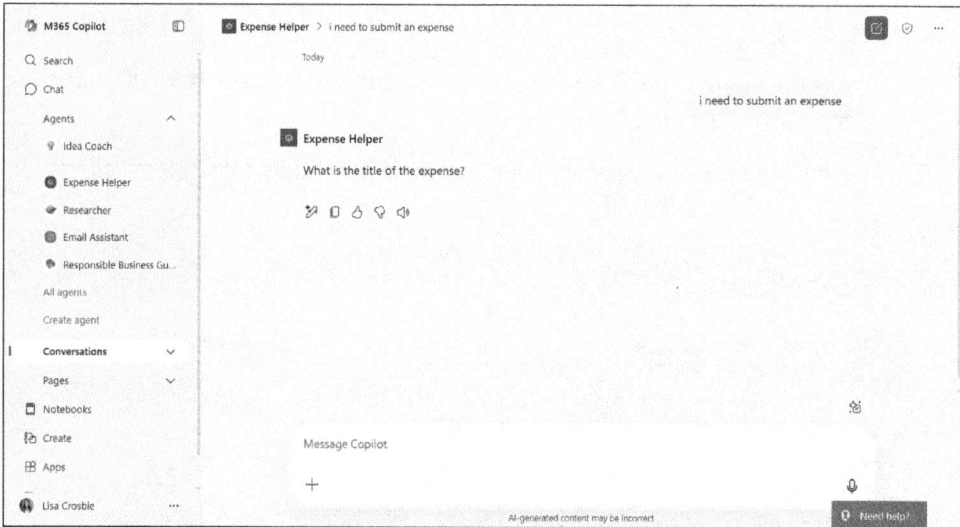

Chat with the Expense Helper agent in Microsoft 365 Copilot Chat.

15. When you get to the stage in the chat where the agent needs to connect with SharePoint to submit the expense, it will prompt you to allow it to use your credentials. Select **Allow**.

> ⚠️ **IMPORTANT** The first time the user reaches an interaction with the agent where a connector is required (e.g., adding an Expense to SharePoint), the agent will prompt the user to allow it to use their credentials to perform the action. If the user is logged in to Microsoft 365 Copilot or Teams, the agent uses the credentials they are already logged in with, so the user just needs to select "Allow." This validates the user's permission to use the tool in the agent. The user will need to do this only once, or once each time you update and publish a new version of the agent.

> ✓ **TIP** You can change the message that appears here in the Credentials section of the tool when you configure it.

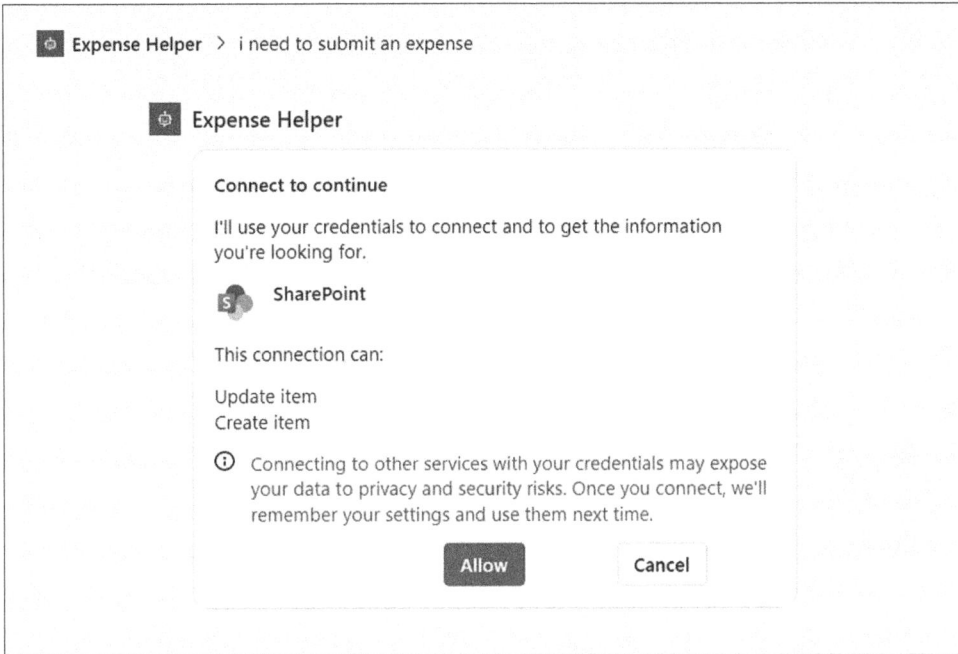

The agent prompts the user to validate their credentials the first time they use a tool in the agent that is set up with user credentials.

16. Navigate to the **Agents** section in the side menu of the Microsoft 365 home page. Select **All agents** to open the **Agent Store**.

17. The Expense Helper agent appears in the list of **Your agents**.

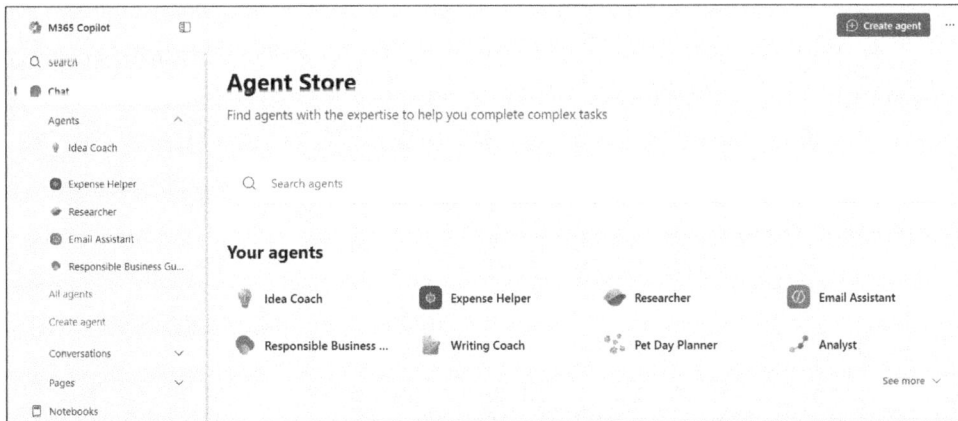

You can see the Expense Helper agent in the list of Your agents in the Agent Store.

> **SEE ALSO** To make the agent available to everyone in the organization, see the step-by-step instructions later in this section, "To share the agent with others in your organization."

18.   When you have finished testing the agent in Microsoft 365 Copilot, return to the browser tab where Copilot Studio is open. Select **See agent in Teams** from the **Agent preview** pane. This opens Teams, with a pop-up screen showing the agent details.

19.   Select the **Add** button to confirm you want to add the agent.

Expense Helper
Lisa Crosbie

Add

Works across

Overview   Permissions

Built using Microsoft Copilot Studio

Help employees stay informed, productive, and connected. Create copilots by describing its functionality and adding knowledge sources to it, and see it answer any question in a matter of minutes.

App features

Bots
Complete tasks, find info, and chat using prompts

Created by: Your developer name
Version 1.0.0

Permissions   Expand All

This app will have permission to read and access:

👤 Information related to you   ⌄

By using Expense Helper, you agree to the privacy policy, terms of use, and permissions.

Review the details of the agent and select the Add button to use it in Teams.

20. The agent opens in the Teams chat and begins the conversation. Respond in the Teams chat to test the agent in Teams. The agent will validate the user's credentials the first time the tool is used in the chat, just as it did as in Microsoft 365 Copilot.

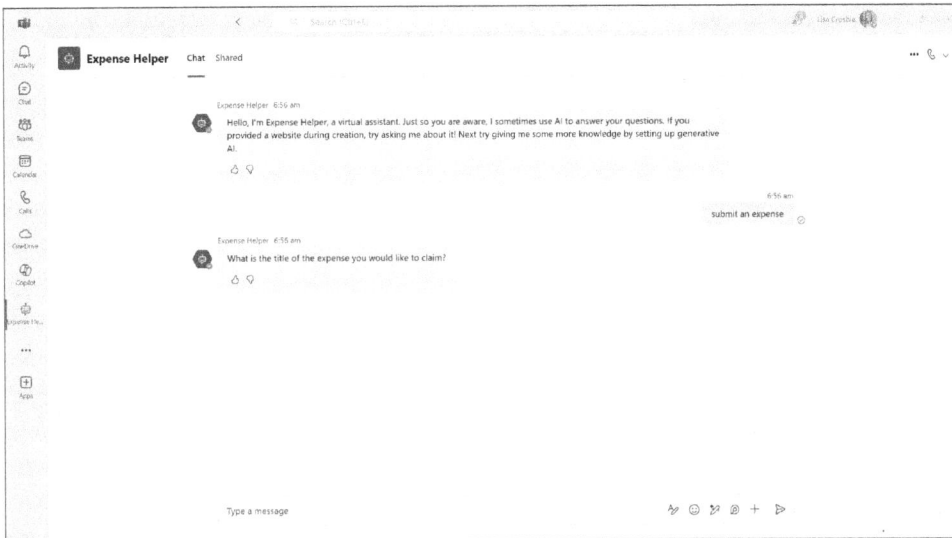

Test the agent in Teams chat.

You have now published your agent and added it to Microsoft 365 Copilot and Teams for your own use. You can also share the agent with other people in your organization by changing the sharing options in the channel configuration or requesting approval to share the agent with the entire organization.

To share the agent with others in your organization

1. Navigate to Copilot Studio in your browser and select the **Channels** tab in the **Expense Helper** agent.

2. Select the **Teams and Microsoft 365 Copilot** channel to change the configuration.

3. Select the **Availability options** button in the **Agent preview** section. This section provides you with the options for making the agent available in these channels, including a link you can copy and send to the users, an option to download a file, and options for how to show it in the Agent store.

> ⚠️ **IMPORTANT** If you are working in a demo tenant where you are the admin, you will be able to work with these options and follow along with this example. However, if you are building an agent in your real work environment, you will need to check and work with an administrator to select and approve the appropriate options for deploying the agent, following any internal processes required.

← **Teams and Microsoft 365 Copilot**   ✕

Get a link

Users you select can open your agent in Microsoft Teams with this link. Manage sharing

[📋 Copy link]

Download a file

Use your downloaded file to add your agent to the Microsoft Teams or Microsoft 365 store. Learn more

[↓ Download .zip]

Show in the store

Decide who you want to show your agent to:

Show to my teammates and shared users
Appears in **Built with Power Platform**

Show to everyone in my org
Appears in **Built by your org** after admin approval

Select how you want to share or make your agent available in these channels.

4. Select **Show to everyone in my org**.

5. Select **Submit for admin approval** and then confirm you understand that you are requesting to make this agent available to everyone in your organization.

6. The channel configuration pane will now indicate that the agent is waiting for approval. You will need to wait for your Teams admin to approve the request.

← **Show in Teams app store for org** ✕

Get your agent ready

Admins can feature your agent prominently as an app in the Built by your org section of Microsoft Teams, pre-install for users in your org, and more. Learn more

Before submitting, make sure to:

- Ensure your agent is ready for release and in compliance with company standards, rules, and policies.

- Coordinate with your teammates. Once the agent is submitted, it can't be resubmitted by others until an admin approves or rejects it.

Teams Authentication SSO Configuration

When using Manual authentication with Azure Active Directory options, you can configure Teams for SSO. You will need this App ID to construct the correct configuration information. Learn more

App ID

| 35c0867f-c   017b353c3ee2 | ⬜ Copy |

Submit for admin approval

When you want to share the agent with everyone in your organization, you will need to request admin approval.

TIP The admin process to approve the agent is done in Microsoft Teams Admin Center: https://admin.teams.microsoft.com/, under Teams apps > Manage apps. The agent will be shown as a pending request for approval. If you are an admin in your demo tenant, you will be able to complete that approval process.

> ⊘ Your request completed successfully.   ✕
>
> ← **Show in Teams app store for org**   ✕
>
> ℹ Your agent is submitted and waiting for approval from your Teams admin.   Refresh
>
> **Microsoft Teams + submission status**
>
> **Expense Helper**
> Version 1.0.0
> ⏱ Waiting for approval

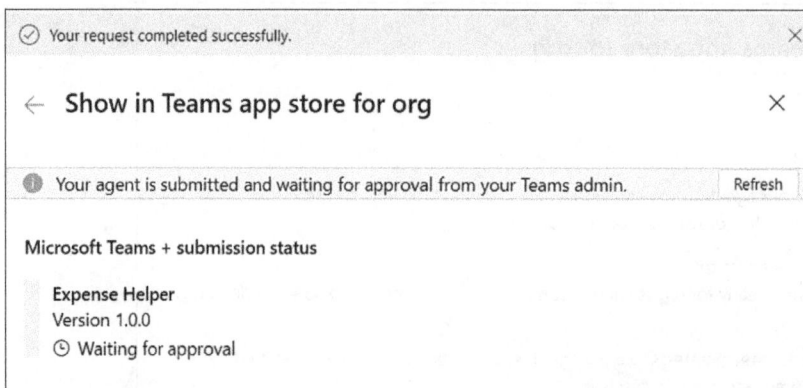

The agent is now waiting for approval to be shared with the entire organization.

7. When the app has been approved, refresh the status of this pane in Copilot Studio. You will see that the status has changed to "**Published by your organization**." Users will now be able to discover and add the agent from the Agent store.

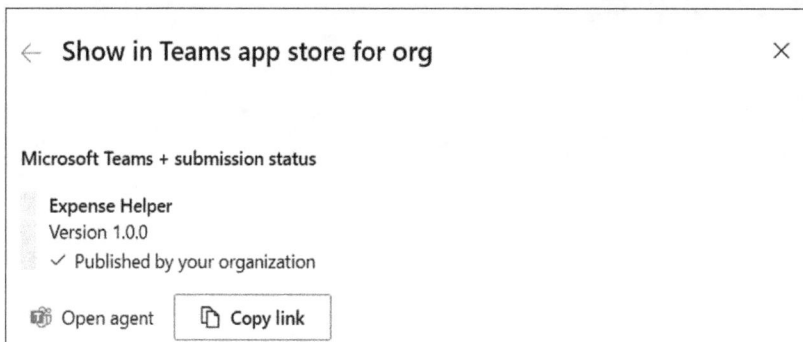

> ← **Show in Teams app store for org**   ✕
>
> **Microsoft Teams + submission status**
>
> **Expense Helper**
> Version 1.0.0
> ✓ Published by your organization
>
> 🖥 Open agent | 📋 **Copy link**

The agent is now published by your organization and available for all users.

Skills review

In this chapter, you learned how to:

- Understand the options for agent authentication and how they apply to different agent use cases.

- Publish an agent and test it on the demo website.

- Understand the options for publishing your agent to internal and external channels, and how to publish an agent for use in Teams and Microsoft 365 Copilot.

Practice tasks

No practice files are necessary to complete the practice tasks in this chapter.

Understand and select the agent authentication method

Navigate to the home page of Copilot Studio and then complete the following tasks:

1. Create a new agent that will answer questions about your organization's website by describing it, giving it a name, and adding the website as knowledge.

2. Navigate to the **Channels** tab and select the hyperlink to change your authentication settings.

3. Select "**Authenticate manually**" to view the configuration options in this method.

4. Select "**No authentication**" and save the changes.

Publish and test an agent

Continue working in the agent you created in the previous task and complete the following tasks.

1. Close the **Settings** area to return to the agent **Overview** page.

2. Select **Publish**, confirm that you want to publish the agent, and wait for the agent to be published.

3. Navigate to the **Channels** tab and select the **Demo website** channel.

4. Change the **Welcome message** and enter some **Conversation starters** relevant to your scenario.

5. Select **Save**.

6. Copy the demo website URL, open a new browser tab, and paste in the copied URL.

7. Test the agent by using the conversation starter buttons or other questions.

8. Share the URL with your colleagues to test.

Choose and configure channels

Open the Copilot Studio home page and then complete the following tasks:

1. Select the **Agents** menu in the left side menu and open the **Expense Helper** agent.

2. Select **Publish** and wait for the agent to be published.

3. Navigate to the **Channels** tab and select the **Teams and Microsoft 365 Copilot** channel.

4. Select the **Edit details** button in the **Agent preview** pane. Edit the **Short description**, **Long description**, and **Developer name**.

5. Select **Save** to save the changes, then navigate back to the main channel settings pane.

6. Select **Save** to save the configuration changes for the channel.

7. Close the configuration pane and publish the agent again.

8. When the agent is published, return to the **Teams and Microsoft 365 Copilot** channel configuration, and select **See agent in Microsoft 365**.

9. Add the agent to Microsoft 365 Copilot and test it in the chat interface there.

10. Return to Copilot Studio and select **See agent in Teams**.

11. Add the agent to Teams and test it in the chat there.

Monitoring agent performance

Practice files

No practice files are necessary to complete the practice tasks in this chapter.

Copilot Studio provides rich out-of-the-box analytics that enable you to review and monitor the performance of your agent directly from the maker experience. These analytics provide insights into user engagement and satisfaction, conversational volumes and trends over time, as well as how often and how effectively the agent is using knowledge sources, tools, and topics. You can also monitor billing metrics and review autonomous agent activity to identify errors or recurring patterns.

For more detailed analysis and insight, you have the option to download and review conversation transcripts. These transcripts can give you a deeper understanding of how users are interacting with your agent.

In this chapter, you will learn how to use and interpret the out-of-the-box analytics for your agents in Copilot Studio.

In this chapter

- Analyze conversational agent performance
- Download and view conversation transcripts
- Analyze autonomous agent performance

Analyze conversational agent performance

In this section, you will learn about the analytics available at the agent level for conversational agents. These analytics address issues such as the volume and outcome of conversations, the effectiveness of your agent, the quality of generated answers, and the satisfaction of the users. In this section, you will review the analytics for the Surface Support Guide agent that you published to the demo website in Chapter 10: Publishing and authenticating agents.

> ✅ **TIP** If you have created an agent connected to your organization's website or knowledge sources, you can follow along with the exercises in this chapter using that agent. Using a real-world published agent that is in use will provide you with richer analytics to review and learn from.

Depending on the number of test runs you performed when you published the agent, you may need to interact with that agent a bit more before you see meaningful analytics. As a general guide, to get enough data for analytics to appear, after you have published your agent, you should:

- Run at least 10 chats on the demo website (in a single day) where the agent draws on knowledge to provide a response (i.e., where it provides citations to the knowledge source). Try a variety of questions that the agent can answer easily, along with other questions that are relevant to the context but that the agent might struggle to answer.

- Use the thumbs up and thumbs down icons in a few of those chats and submit feedback comments at least once.

- Trigger conversations that will use the topics you created, where the agent will call the Conversation End node and prompt the user to rate their experience out of 5 stars. Provide a rating each time.

> ✅ **TIP** Analytics are shown only for interactions with the published agent (in this case, on the demo website). Any interactions you performed using the test chat while building the agent will not show up in the analytics.

> **IMPORTANT** Analytics can take some time to show up in the report. Some analytics will appear within the hour, such as the effectiveness measures. Others, such as the generated answer quality, can take until the next day to appear. Once you have performed more test runs, you may need to wait and come back to see the analytics fully populated. This is normal.

To view the analytics for a conversational agent

1. Open the Surface Support Guide agent in Copilot Studio and locate the **Analytics** section on the **Overview** page, below the **Details** section.

2. Review the key performance measures shown for the agent: the number of conversation sessions, the engagement level, and the satisfaction score.

> **SEE ALSO** The measures and analytics you explore in this example are fully explained in the later part of this section following this example.

Locate the key metrics for your agent performance in the Analytics section of the Overview tab.

3. Select the **Open Analytics** button in the **Analytics** section to navigate to the **Analytics** page, or select the **Analytics** tab directly from the top menu. Either option takes you to the **Analytics** page.

4. Close the **test** pane to provide more room on the screen for the analytics.

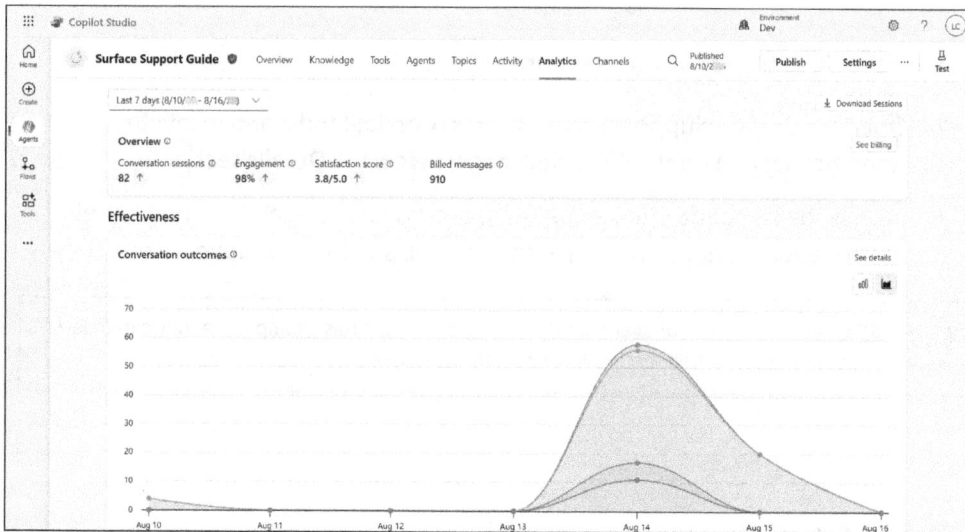

The Analytics tab contains prebuilt reports to help you understand the performance of your agent.

5. Select the date picker at the top left of the screen. By default, the report shows the last 7 days of data. You can use this date picker to expand that period and show data for up to the last 90 days.

> ⚠ **IMPORTANT** The analytics are given in UTC time and show history for a maximum of 90 days. Selecting a custom date range will still allow you to pick dates only within that time frame.

6. Select a longer date range and observe the changes to the chart. Depending on how long ago you published your agent, you will see conversation outcomes further back along the timeline.

7. Select the time frame that gives you the best timeline view of your agent data, and then select a space on the screen anywhere outside the date picker to collapse it.

8. Navigate through the report to view the other sections: **Effectiveness**, **Use**, and **Satisfaction**.

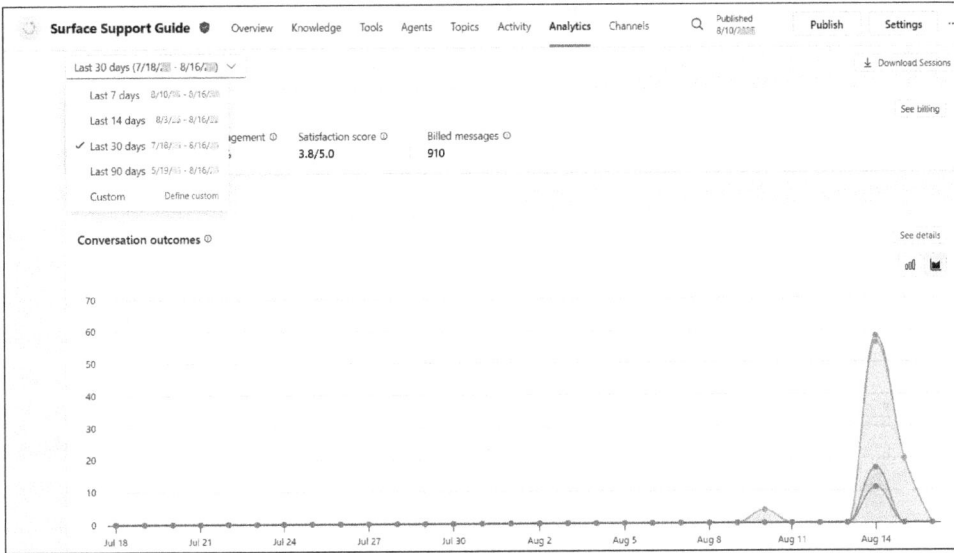

Select a different date range to expand the timeline of the data shown in the report.

9. Each section has a **See details** button at the top left. Select this button in the **Effectiveness** section to expand the details in a pane to the right.

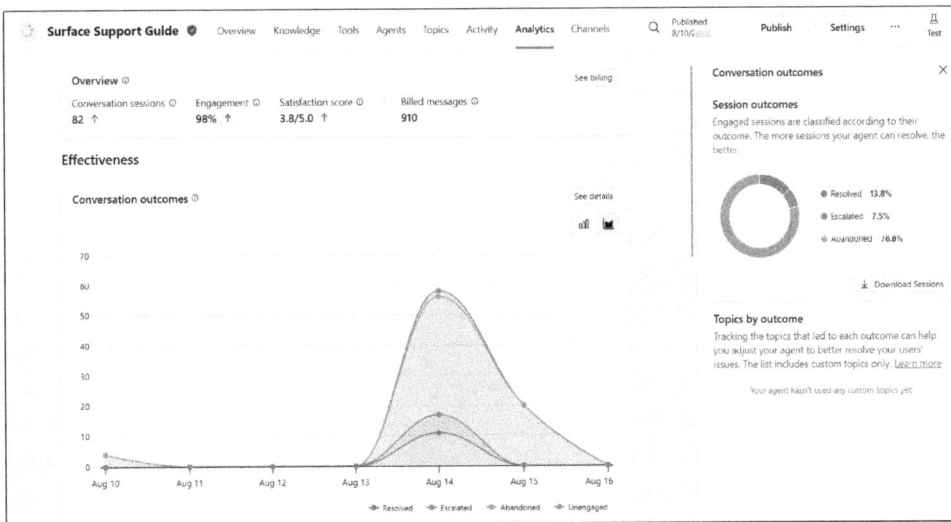

Select the See details button to expand a pane that shows more details for that section of analytics.

10. Select the **X** in the top corner of the pane to close the details section.

Understanding conversational agent metrics

Each of these metrics gives you a different view of the performance of your agent and helps you identify areas for improvement.

Overview

- **Conversation sessions** represents the number of sessions with your agent. A session starts when the conversation starts (even if the user doesn't respond) or when the user changes the subject. That means a multi-turn conversation with an agent can be made up of multiple sessions.

- **Engagement** is the percentage of sessions where the user has replied to the agent at least once. If the agent greets the user and there is no response, that session is an unengaged session.

- **Satisfaction score** is the average score out of 5 from the feedback gathered by the agent in the CSAT survey results from the End of Conversation topic.

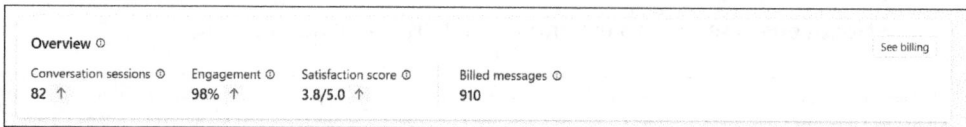

Overview ⓘ				See billing
Conversation sessions ⓘ	Engagement ⓘ	Satisfaction score ⓘ	Billed messages ⓘ	
82 ↑	98% ↑	3.8/5.0 ↑	910	

The Overview section shows key metrics: Conversation sessions, Engagement, Satisfaction score, and Billed messages.

- **Billed messages** represents the number of messages you have been billed for during the date range selected. Selecting the **See billing** button will expand more details about the billed messages, showing you the trend over time, and the cost distribution from the different types of message consumption used by your agent.

Billing   ✕

Billing information takes time to update, so the most
recent billed features might not be included here. Learn
more

Billed message trend

See how the number of billed messages varied over the
selected period.

750

500

250

0

Aug 10   Aug 11   Aug 12   Aug 13   Aug 14   Aug 15   Au...

Cost distribution

How different events contributed to the cost of your
agent during this period. Learn more

100%

80%

60%

40%

20%

0%

● Classic answer   ● Generative answer   ○ Others

*The Billing details screen helps you understand the billed message trend and how different events
contributed to the message consumption.*

> **SEE ALSO** For more information on billing and message consumption, refer to the
> section "Understand and calculate agent costs" in Chapter 2: Designing effective
> agents.

Effectiveness

The **Conversation outcomes** chart shows the number of conversations with your agent and the result of those conversations. This chart shows the data for each of the four possible ways the agent conversation ends:

- *Resolved*: The End of Conversation topic is triggered and the user confirms the agent answered their question.

- *Escalated*: The Escalate topic is triggered or the Transfer to agent node is used. Even if you haven't configured escalation, this will still appear as an escalated conversation.

- *Abandoned*: The session times out after 15 minutes or does not reach a resolution or escalation as described in the previous categories.

> ✅ **TIP** If your agent is primarily using generative answers instead of structured topics that use the "End of Conversation" node, you will likely have a high rate of "Abandoned" conversations. These effectiveness measures are more useful for agents that have structured conversational paths.

- *Unengaged*: The agent begins the conversation and there is no interaction from the user before it times out after 15 minutes.

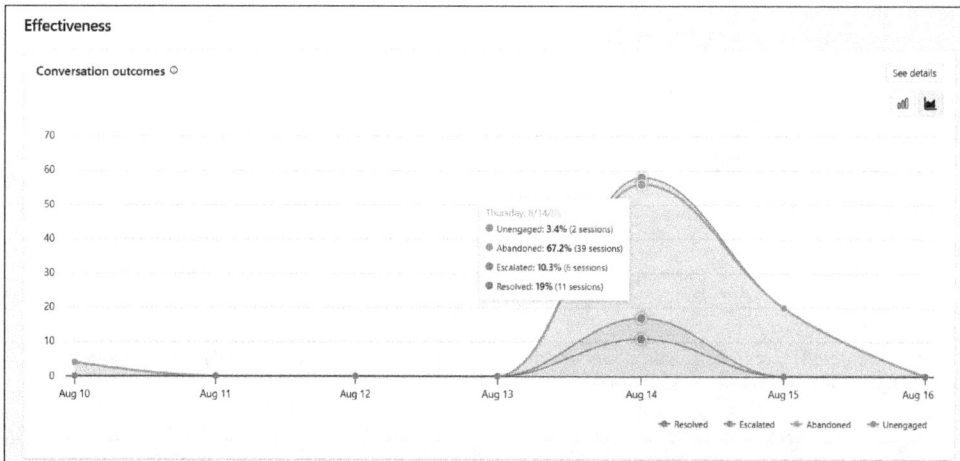

Effectiveness

Conversation outcomes ⓘ

See details

Thursday, 8/14/...
- Unengaged: **3.4%** (2 sessions)
- Abandoned: **67.2%** (39 sessions)
- Escalated: **10.3%** (6 sessions)
- Resolved: **19%** (11 sessions)

Aug 10 | Aug 11 | Aug 12 | Aug 13 | Aug 14 | Aug 15 | Aug 16

◆ Resolved ◆ Escalated ◆ Abandoned ◆ Unengaged

The Conversational outcomes chart shows the rate of each way the conversation with the agent ends.

You can switch back and forth to view the **Conversation outcomes** as either an area chart or a bar chart using the icons at the top of the section.

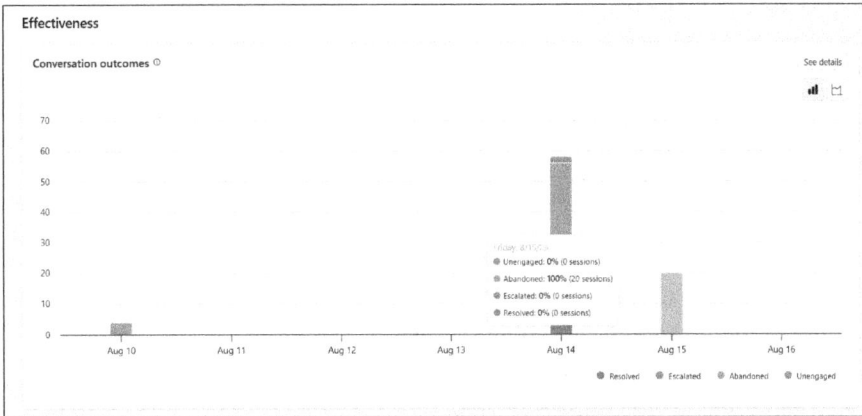

Switch to view the Conversational outcomes as a bar chart using the icon at the top right of the section.

Select the **See details** button to open the **Conversation outcomes** pane on the right side of the screen. This pane shows the **Session outcomes** for the selected period as a doughnut chart, with each outcome represented as a percentage.

Hover over the doughnut chart to see the number of sessions that make up each metric.

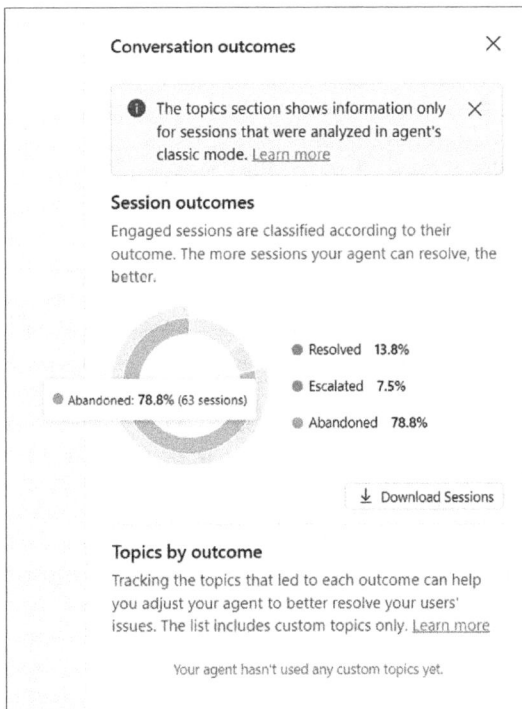

The Conversation outcomes details pane shows the session outcomes as a doughnut chart.

> **SEE ALSO** If your agent uses generative orchestration, there will not be any analytics available at the topic level. If you have used classic orchestration, you will have analytics both here and in the individual topics. For details, refer to https://learn.microsoft.com/en-us/microsoft-copilot-studio/analytics-topic-details.

Use

The **Use** section helps you understand how well your agent performed using AI-generated answers. It shows the number of questions answered and unanswered. It also evaluates the quality of the answers provided, rating them as Good, Incomplete, Irrelevant, or Knowledge not used.

> ⚠ **IMPORTANT** These metrics are based on a sample set of the generative AI answers given by your agent. They are indicative measures of the overall quality of the answers, rather than a detailed breakdown of the quality of specific answers.

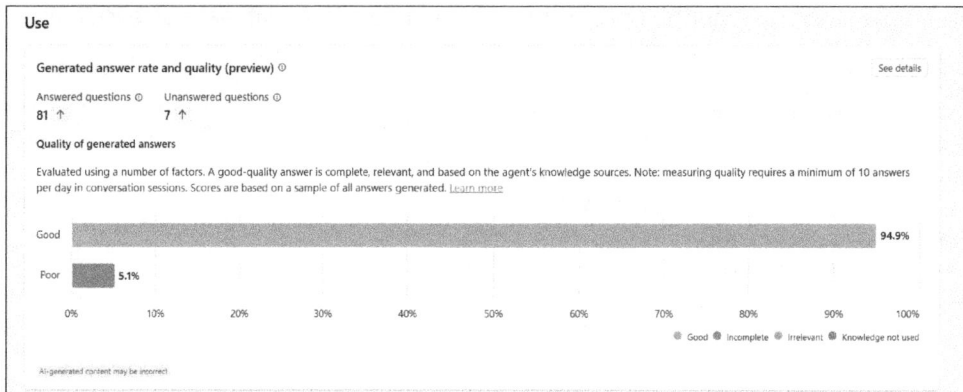

The Use section provides an indication of the quality of the generative AI answers provided by your agent.

Select the **See details** button at the top right of this section to open a pane that provides more details about the generated answer rate and quality. In this pane, you will find details about the reasons the agent didn't answer questions, the knowledge sources used and the trend for each knowledge source, the percentage of questions that used each source, and the percentage of queries with a knowledge-related error for each knowledge source.

Generated answer rate and quality (preview)   ✕

Decline to answer   0%

Other   100%

Knowledge source use ⓘ

Answers based on knowledge sources ⓘ

94% ↑

Source use trend ⓘ

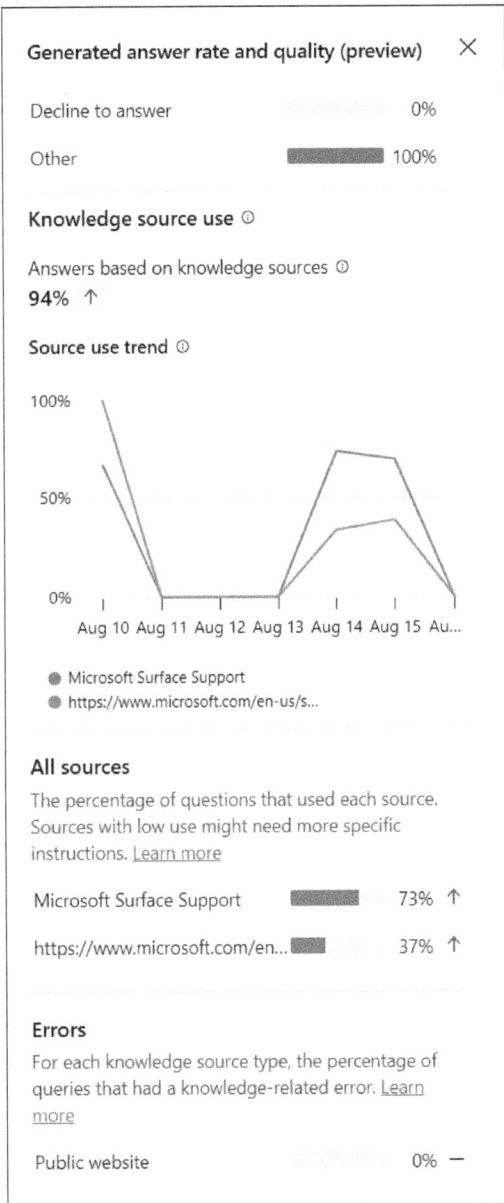

- ● Microsoft Surface Support
- ● https://www.microsoft.com/en-us/s...

All sources

The percentage of questions that used each source. Sources with low use might need more specific instructions. Learn more

Microsoft Surface Support   73% ↑

https://www.microsoft.com/en...   37% ↑

Errors

For each knowledge source type, the percentage of queries that had a knowledge-related error. Learn more

Public website   0% —

The side pane provides details on unanswered questions, knowledge source use, and errors.

11

Satisfaction

The **Satisfaction** section of the **Analytics** page shows the details of user feedback, using reactions (thumbs up or thumbs down feedback) and survey results (the CSAT survey sent by the End of Conversation topic).

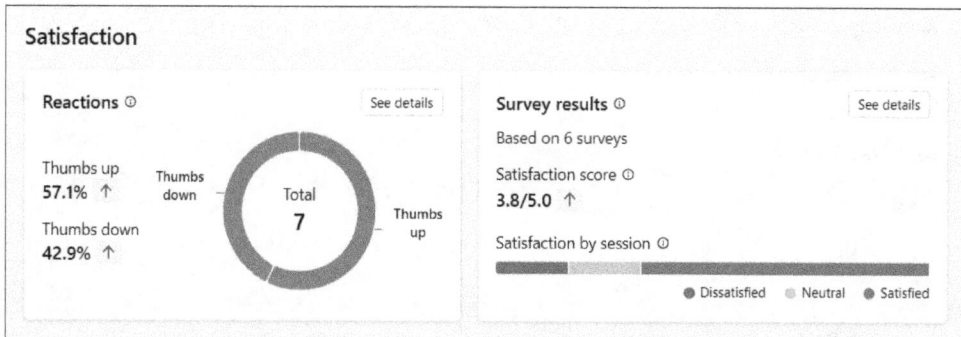

The Satisfaction section displays metrics and charts for user feedback from reactions and surveys.

Select the **See details** button in the **Reactions** section to view the details of any feedback comments that users have provided, along with the **Thumbs up** or **Thumbs down** reactions.

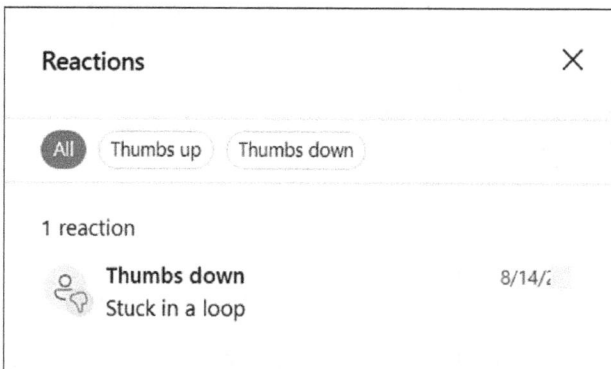

Expand the details pane for the Reactions to view feedback comments left by users.

Select the **See details** button in the **Survey results** section to swap the side pane to the view that shows the satisfaction score trend over the time period selected.

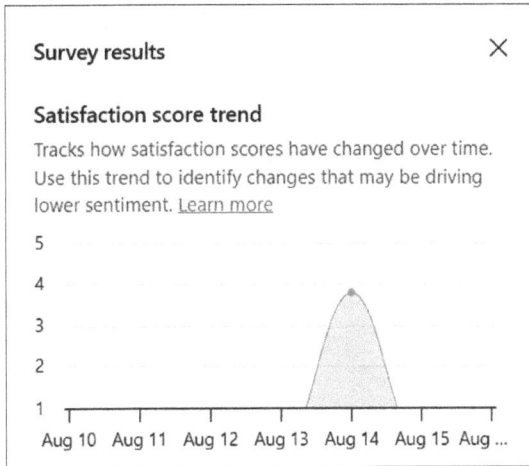

View the satisfaction score trend over time for the selected period.

Download and view conversation transcripts

To get more details about how users are interacting with your agent, you can download partial conversation transcripts as a CSV file from the analytics area in Copilot Studio. Alternatively, you can export the complete conversation transcripts from Dataverse.

Download conversation sessions from Copilot Studio

You can download up to 7 days of conversation transcripts from Copilot Studio, from the past 29 days. These transcripts show only the first 265 characters of the conversation between the agent and the user.

> **SEE ALSO** If you want the full version of the conversation transcript history, you can download it from Dataverse, as described in the next section.

To download conversation sessions

1. Navigate to the **Activity** tab of the agent.

2. Select the **Download Sessions** button at the top right.

3. This opens a **Download Sessions** pop-up window, with a hyperlink to each day that has sessions available to download. Select the link for the day you want to download.

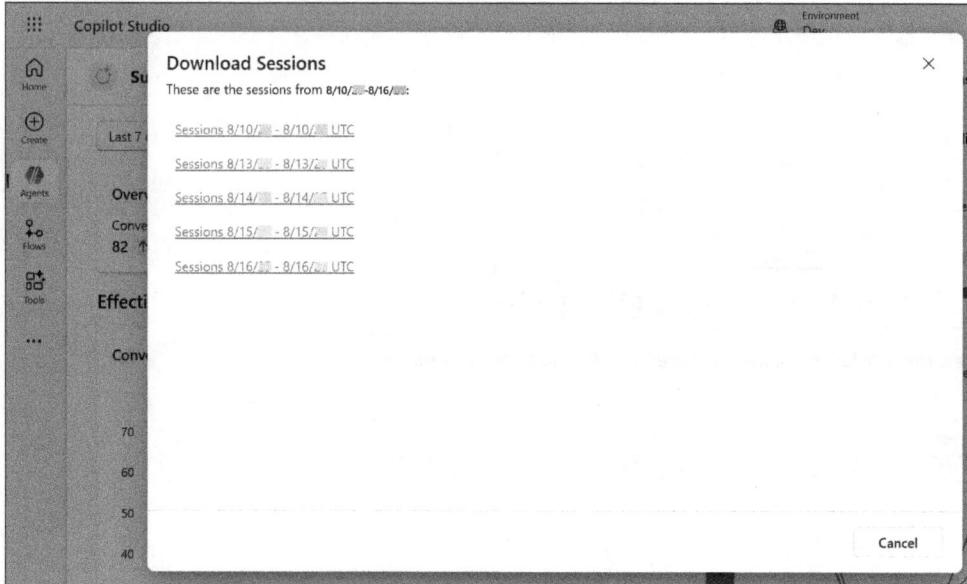

Select the hyperlink for the sessions on a day to download a CSV file.

4. Wait for the file to be downloaded to the Downloads folder on your computer. Open that file in Excel. You can save and edit this file as you wish.

Open the CSV file to view the conversation transcripts.

5. Repeat the previous steps to download sessions from other days.

Download conversation sessions from Dataverse

The full version of the conversation transcripts is stored in Dataverse, in a table called "ConversationTranscript" that is created in your environment when you start using Copilot Studio.

> ⚠️ **IMPORTANT** Conversation transcripts are stored in Dataverse for 30 days, after which they are automatically deleted. You need to change the retention period if you want to keep them longer. For details and instructions, refer to https://learn.microsoft.com/en-us/ microsoft-copilot-studio/analytics-transcripts-powerapps#change-the-default- retention-period.

To export conversation transcripts from Dataverse

1. Open a new tab in your browser and navigate to https://make.powerapps.com/.

2. Use the **Environment** picker at the top right of the screen to select the same environment where your agent is published.

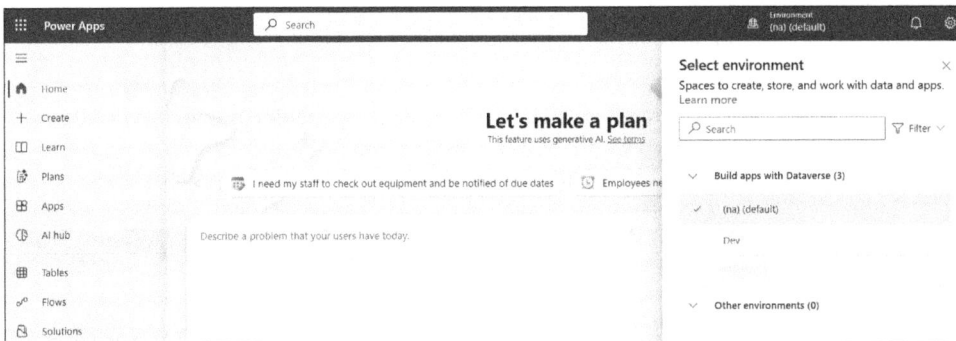

Select your environment from the Power Apps maker home page.

3. Select **Tables** from the left side menu and then use the **Search** box at the top right of the screen to search for **Conversation**.

4. Select the **All** filter button at the top of the list of tables.

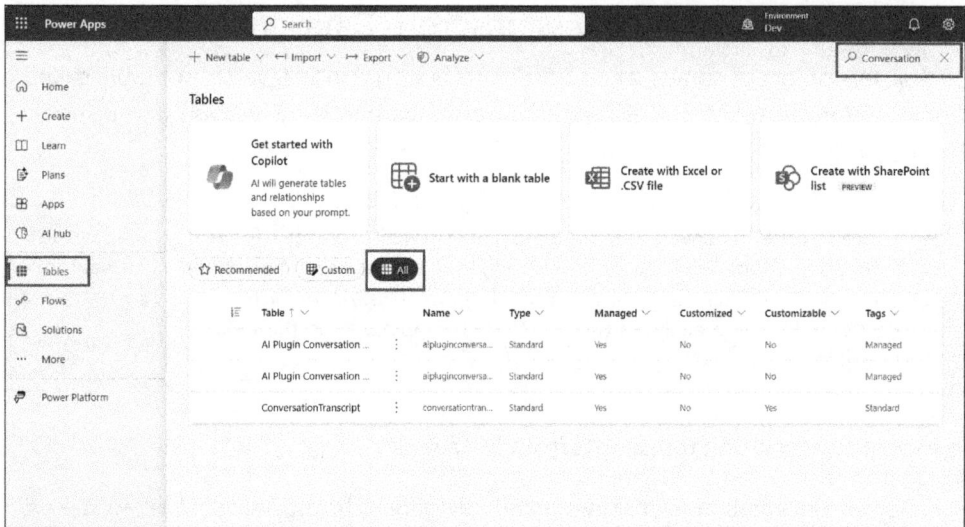

Search for the ConversationTranscript table in Dataverse.

5. Select the **ConversationTranscript** table from the list.

6. On the top menu, expand the **Export** option and select **Export data**.

> **TIP** If you are a Power Apps maker, you can create an app to display the rows of data in this table to view and work with them directly in an app.

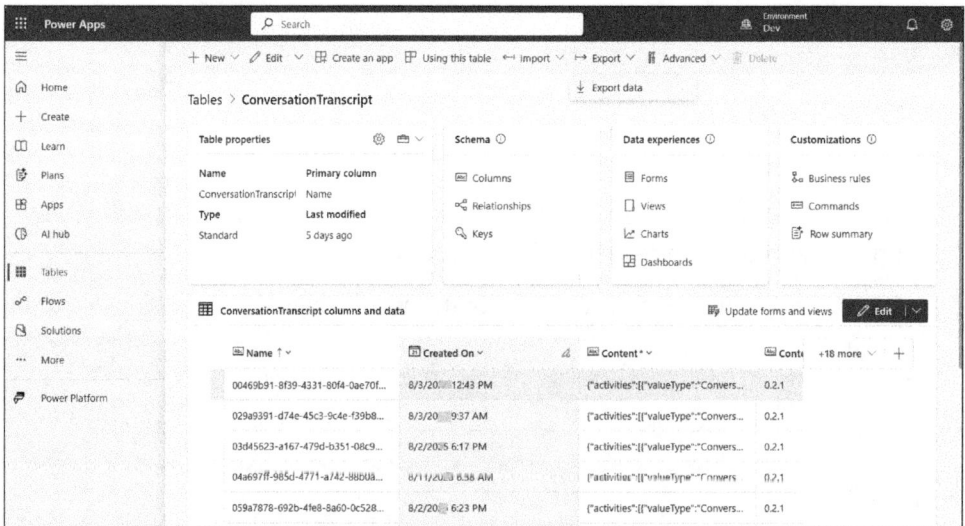

Export the table data from Dataverse.

7. The window that opens has a link to **Download exported data**. Select that link and wait for the data to be downloaded in a .zip file.

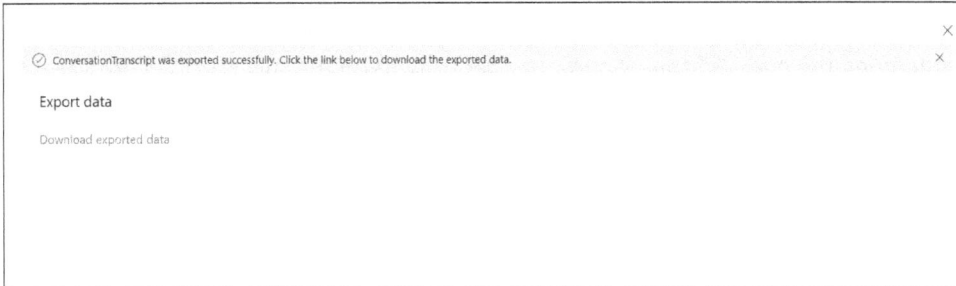

Select the link to download the data as a .zip file.

8. The .zip file contains a CSV file with the conversation transcript data in it. The contents of the conversation are in JSON format in the first column, "content."

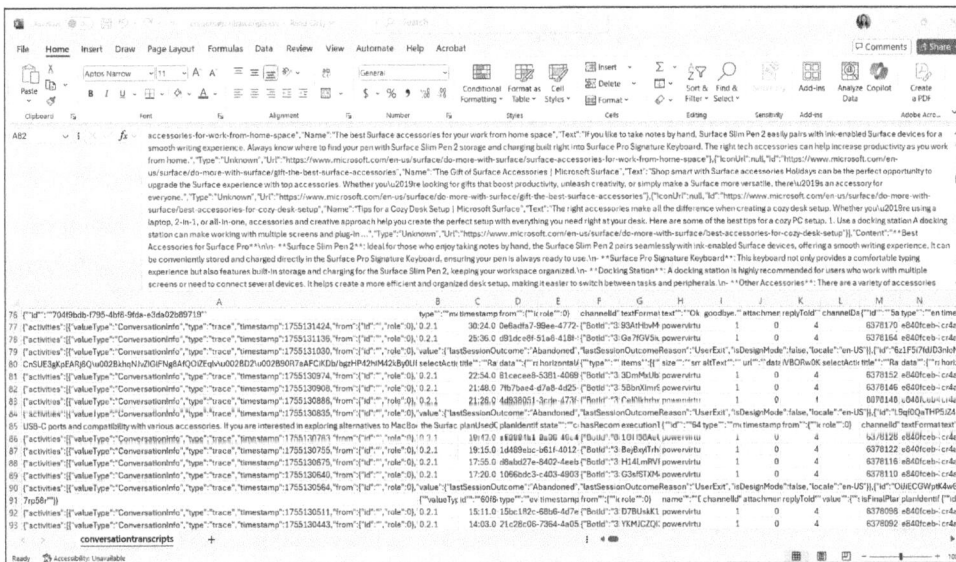

The conversation transcripts are in JSON format in the "content" column of the CSV file.

> ✓ **TIP** The Microsoft PowerCAT team has created the Copilot Studio Kit, which contains a model-driven Power App that makes it easy to view the conversation transcripts in an app. It also includes a set of other capabilities that help you test, validate, and optimize your agent. If you want to be able to review conversation transcripts in an easy-to-read format without downloading them, this is the recommended option. For details and to download the kit for free, go to https://github.com/microsoft/Power-CAT-Copilot-Studio-Kit.

Analyze autonomous agent performance

Autonomous agents operate differently from conversational agents, so their performance is measured in different ways. Rather than focusing on conversational outcomes, the metrics for autonomous agents focus on the success or failure of each run, and how effectively the agent uses the triggers, knowledge, and tools you have provided it.

In this section, you will review the analytics for the autonomous Expenses agent that you created in Chapter 5: Building autonomous agents.

Navigate to the **Overview** screen of the Expenses agent to see the overview of the key performance metrics for the autonomous agent.

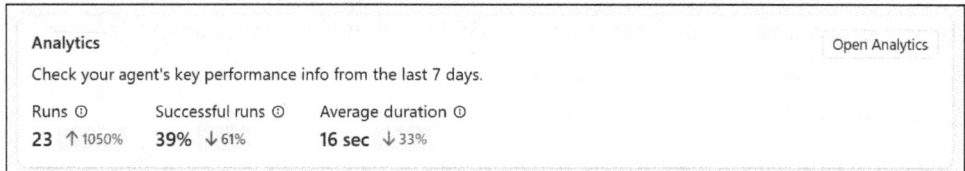

Analytics   Open Analytics

Check your agent's key performance info from the last 7 days.

Runs ⓘ   Successful runs ⓘ   Average duration ⓘ
23 ↑1050%   39% ↓61%   16 sec ↓33%

Autonomous agents have key metrics that indicate the number of runs, percentage of successful runs, and average duration.

Select the **Open Analytics** button or select the **Analytics** tab from the top menu to view the full analytics for the agent.

Understanding autonomous agent metrics

The **Analytics** report for an autonomous agent follows the same format and navigation experience as the one for conversational agents, but uses different measures. This version of the **Analytics** page is available for any agent that uses triggers.

Effectiveness

The **Run outcomes** chart shows the number of times the agent was triggered and whether each run succeeded or failed. Select the **See details** button to expand the details pane, which shows the average duration of successful and failed runs, and duration trends.

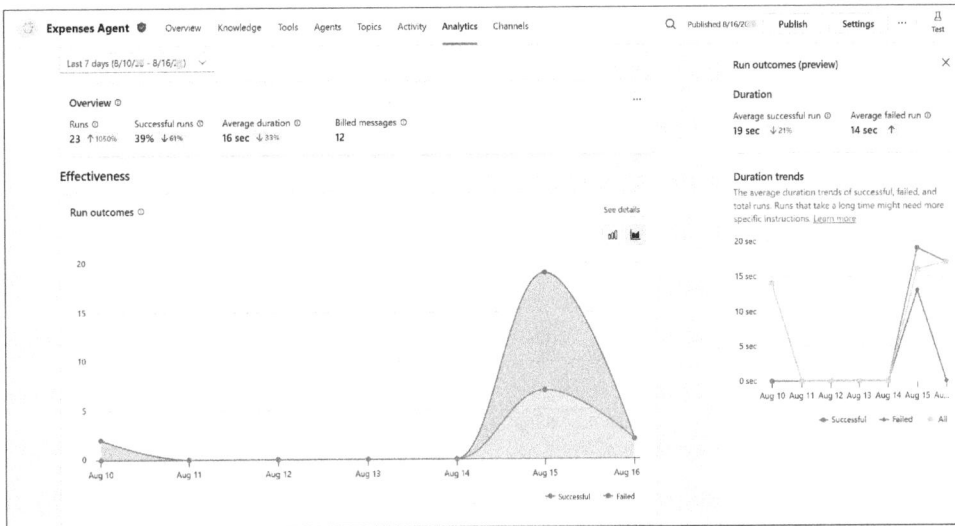

The Run outcomes analytics show you the number, duration, and trend of successful and failed autonomous agent runs.

> **SEE ALSO** To monitor and troubleshoot failed runs in your autonomous agent, use the **Activity** tab, as described in the section "Review the activity" in Chapter 5: Building autonomous agents.

Use

The **Use** section shows analytics for trigger use, tool use, and knowledge source use.

The **Trigger use** section is most helpful for an agent that has multiple triggers. It shows the use count for each trigger over the selected period, along with the rate of success and failure for runs that use each trigger in the details pane. In this example, the agent has only a single trigger, so the analytics show the success and fail rate of runs that used that trigger.

11

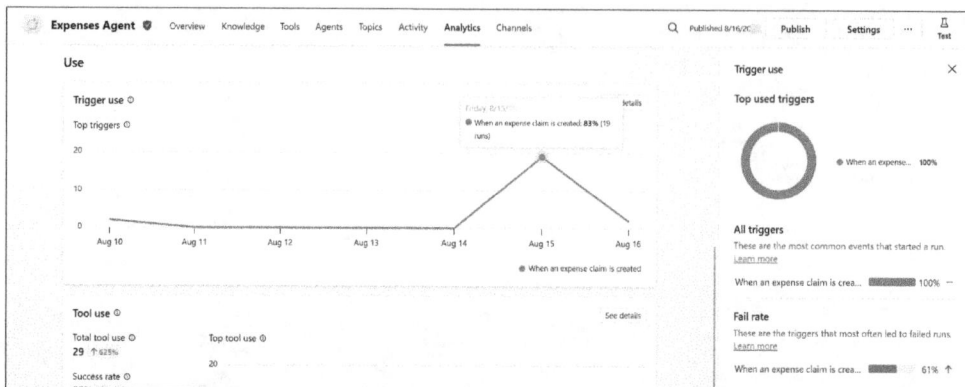

The Trigger use section shows the performance of up to 5 triggers in your agent, along with the success and fail rates and usage over the selected time period.

The **Tool use** section shows the five most used tools, along with the frequency of their usage over time and the overall success rate. Select the **See details** button to expand the details pane, showing the percentage of questions that used each tool and the associated trends.

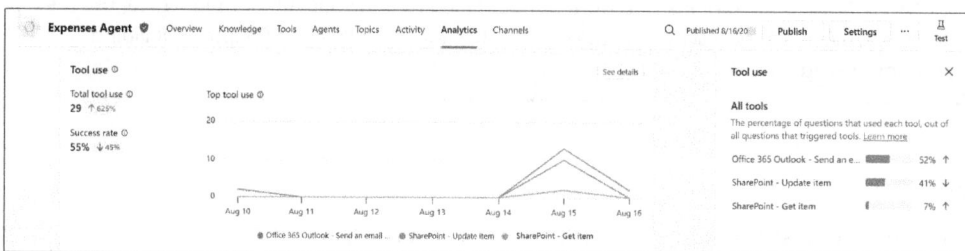

The Tool use section helps you understand which tools are most frequently used and the rates at which they are used.

The **Knowledge source use** section shows the most used knowledge sources, the error rate (the percentage of sessions that used a knowledge source and resulted in an error), and the answer rate (the percentage of runs answered by a knowledge source). Select the **See details** button to expand the details pane, which shows the percentage of runs that used each knowledge source. This can help you identify underused knowledge sources. If you are expecting a knowledge source to be used more often than these analytics show, then you may need to rewrite the description or instructions to help the agent better understand what that knowledge source is and when to use it.

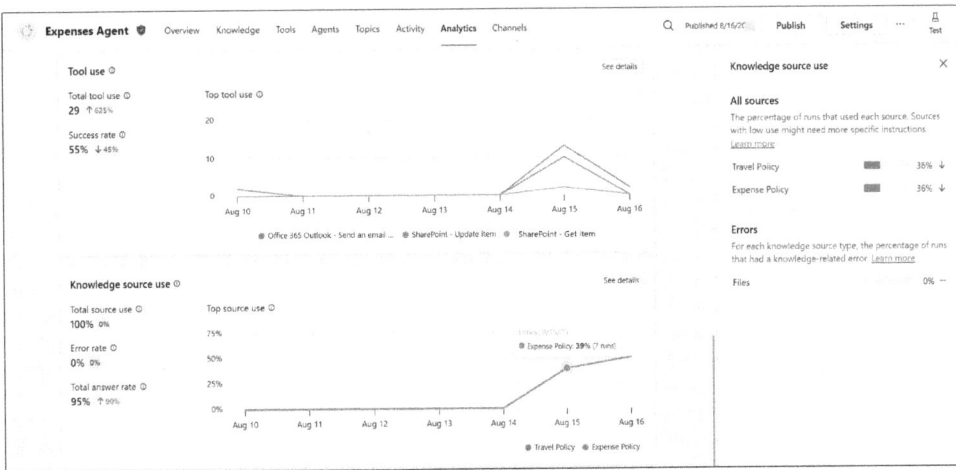

Use the Knowledge source use section to review the top knowledge sources, and the error rate and answer rate when the agent uses knowledge.

Skills review

In this chapter, you learned how to:

- Understand and review the metrics available for conversational agents, including effectiveness, use, and satisfaction.

- Download conversation transcripts from the Analytics page in Copilot Studio and from Dataverse.

- Understand and review the metrics for an autonomous agent, including run outcomes, trigger use, tool use, and knowledge source use.

11

Practice tasks

No practice files are necessary to complete the practice tasks in this chapter.

Analyze conversational agent performance

Open the Surface Support Guide agent in Copilot Studio and perform the following tasks:

1. Navigate to the **Activities** tab using the top menu.

2. Use the date picker at the top left to select a different date range.

3. Select the **See details** button in the **Effectiveness** section to view more details about Conversational outcomes.

4. Navigate down to the **Use** section. Select the **See details** button to swap out the side pane and view more details about the generated answer rate and quality.

5. Navigate down to the **Satisfaction** section. Select the **See details** button in the **Reactions** section and then the **See details** button in the **Survey results** section to view user feedback and satisfaction trends.

Download and view conversation transcripts

Open the Surface Support Guide agent in Copilot Studio and perform the following tasks:

1. Navigate to the **Activities** tab.

2. Use the date picker to select the last 7 days as the time period.

3. Select the **Download Sessions** button at the top right of the **Activities** tab.

4. Select the link for one of the days shown in the Download Sessions screen.

5. Open the file in Excel from the Downloads folder on your computer.

Analyze autonomous agent performance

Open the Expenses agent (autonomous agent) in Copilot Studio and perform the following tasks:

1. Navigate to the **Activities** tab using the top menu.

2. Select the **See details** button in the **Run outcomes** section to view more details about Run outcomes.

3. Navigate down to the **Use** section. Select the **See details** button in the Trigger use section to swap out the side pane and view more details about the trigger usage and fail rate.

4. Review the **Tool use** section. Select the **See details** button to view the percentage of questions that used each tool.

5. Navigate down to the **Knowledge source** use section. Select the **See details** button to view the percentage of runs that used each knowledge source and the rate of errors.

Working with voice and customer engagement systems

12

Practice files

No practice files are necessary to complete the practice tasks in this chapter.

Chat-based agents are now widely used in customer service, but many organizations still rely heavily on phone calls as a way for their customers to connect with support teams. Copilot Studio enables you to build voice-enabled agents that can handle these calls, answering routine questions from customers through natural language voice chat and escalating to a human agent when needed. Voice-enabled agents can reduce incoming call volume by deflecting routine inquiries that don't need human interaction, thereby reducing call wait times and improving customer and representative experience.

Building voice-enabled agents that work with customer engagement applications is a substantial and specialist area of knowledge and expertise associated with contact center solution development and deployment. Copilot Studio supports a wide range of sophisticated capabilities

In this chapter

- Create a voice-enabled agent
- Test a voice-enabled agent using chat
- Publish to a customer engagement channel and configure escalation

for voice-enabled agents that are suitable for enterprise-level solutions. This chapter does not attempt to cover this entire topic. Instead, it focuses on how a voice agent differs from a chat-based agent, what the core concepts and capabilities of a voice-enabled agent are, and how to publish a voice agent to a customer engagement channel. References and links are provided throughout the chapter for those who want to go deeper into this topic.

In this chapter, you will explore these capabilities and learn by building a working demo. You will learn how to create a voice-enabled agent in Copilot Studio, test it using a chat interface that simulates the voice experience, connect it to a phone number to test it with the voice channel, and publish it to a customer experience hub, enabling escalation to a human agent.

> ⚠ **IMPORTANT** To create and publish a voice-enabled agent with escalation to a human representative, you need to have a phone number and a customer engagement hub to connect it to. The examples in this chapter are based on using a free 30-day trial version of Microsoft Dynamics 365 Customer Service, which includes a demo phone number that you can use to connect and test your agent without needing to set up or purchase a phone number yourself. Before you begin this chapter, sign up for a free trial environment of Dynamics 365 Customer Service here: https://www.microsoft.com/en-au/dynamics-365/products/customer-service.

> ✓ **TIP** If you cannot set up this trial, you can still follow along with the content in the first two sections of this chapter, which deal with how voice agents work, how they differ from chat agents, and the settings and configuration options available. Alternatively, you can use the principles covered here with your own customer engagement hub, referring to the relevant documentation for that application.

> ⊘ **SEE ALSO** For details and instructions on how to get a phone number or use an existing phone number through Azure Communication Services, refer to https://learn.microsoft.com/en-us/azure/communication-services/quickstarts/telephony/get-phone-number.

Create a voice-enabled agent

Copilot Studio allows you to create agents that can talk to users over the phone, understanding spoken words (speech input) or recognizing numbers pressed on the phone keypad (called dual-tone multi-frequency [DTMF]). This overall capability is known as interactive voice response (IVR). If you've ever called a company and heard something like "Press 1 for billing, Press 2 for technical support," or if you've encountered a prompt that asks you to say what you are calling about before you speak to a human representative, you have experienced IVR as a customer.

Understand voice-enabled agent capabilities and settings

Voice-enabled agents work differently from chat-based agents because they use a different communication method, called the "speech and DTMF modality." That means they interact through spoken words and keypad input, rather than through typed text. Because phone conversations can also include things like silence, interruptions, or requests to speak to a human, voice-enabled agents also come with additional system topics for handling these scenarios.

The best way to get started with creating a voice-enabled agent is to use the Voice agent template. It deploys an agent with all the required system topics and capabilities for voice.

> **SEE ALSO** To view the full documentation for the Voice agent template, refer to https://learn.microsoft.com/en-us/microsoft-copilot-studio/voice-build-from-template.

> **IMPORTANT** You must create your voice-enabled agent in an environment that is on the standard release cycle (where "Get new features early" is turned off). For more information, see https://learn.microsoft.com/en-us/power-platform/admin/early-release.

To create a voice-enabled agent

1. Navigate to the Copilot Studio home page and select the **CustomerService Trial** environment from the Environment picker in the top right.

> **TIP** This environment was created when you signed up for the trial of Dynamics 365 Customer Service. You need to create your voice-enabled agent in the same environment as your customer engagement hub application to be able to publish it to that channel. If you are not using the Dynamics 365 Customer Service trial, select any standard (not early release) environment, or select the environment where your customer engagement hub application is deployed.

12

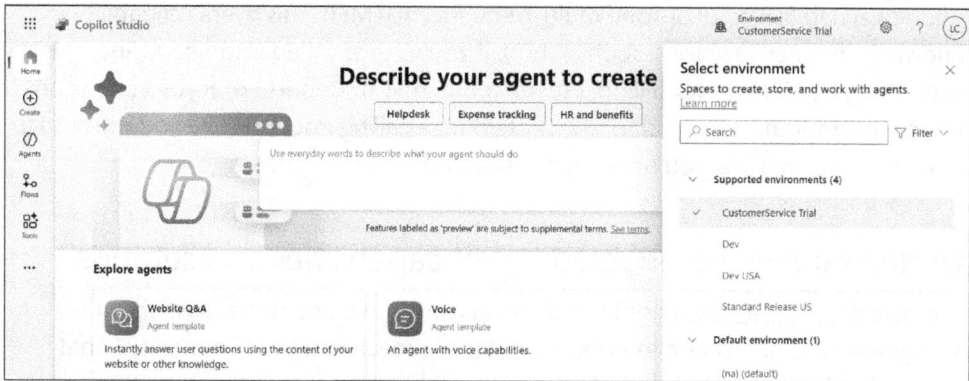

Select the CustomerService Trial environment from the Environment picker.

2. Select the **Create** option from the left side menu.

3. Select the **Voice** agent template.

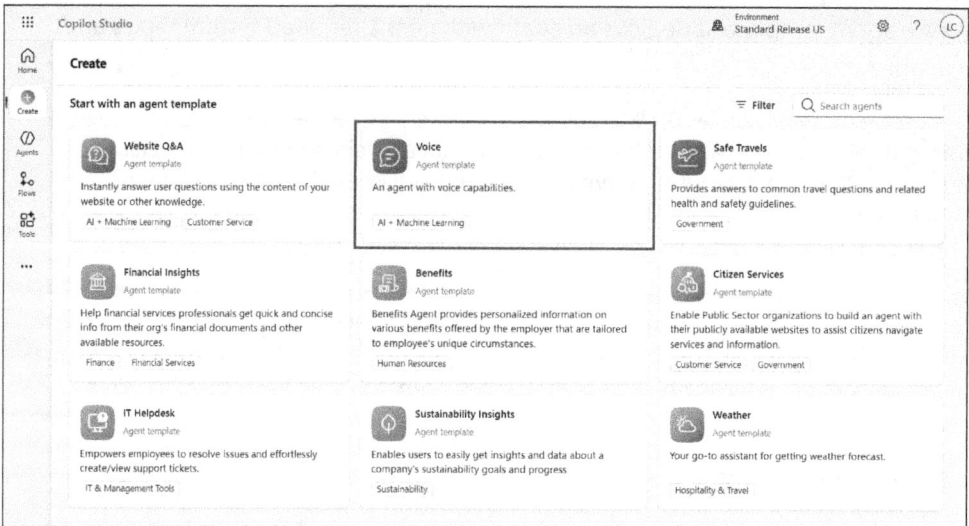

Select the Voice agent template to create a voice-enabled agent with the required system topics and capabilities to handle voice scenarios.

4. The **Voice** template will open in the configuration screen. Select **Create**.

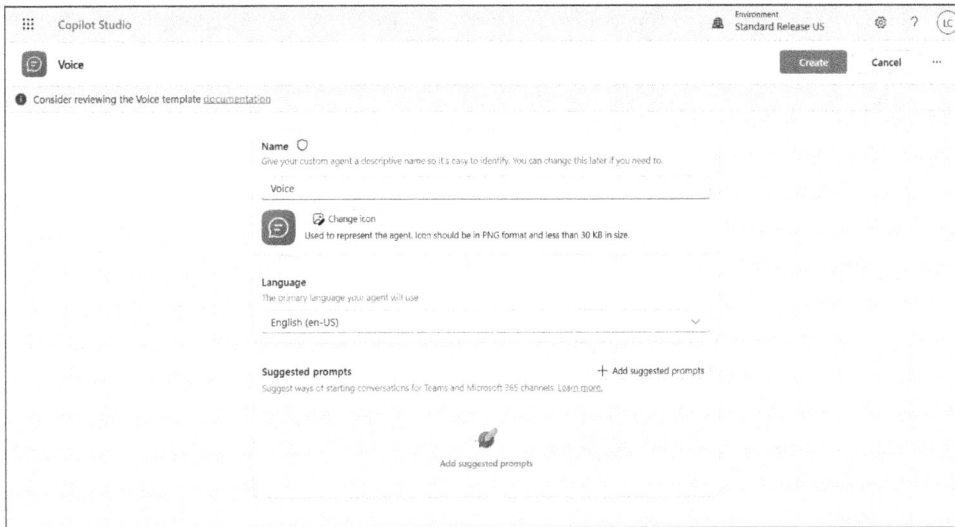

Select "Create" to create a voice-enabled agent from the template.

5. When the agent is created, you will be taken to the **Overview** screen. Note that the opening greeting in the **test** pane is different from the one in the standard text-based chat agent.

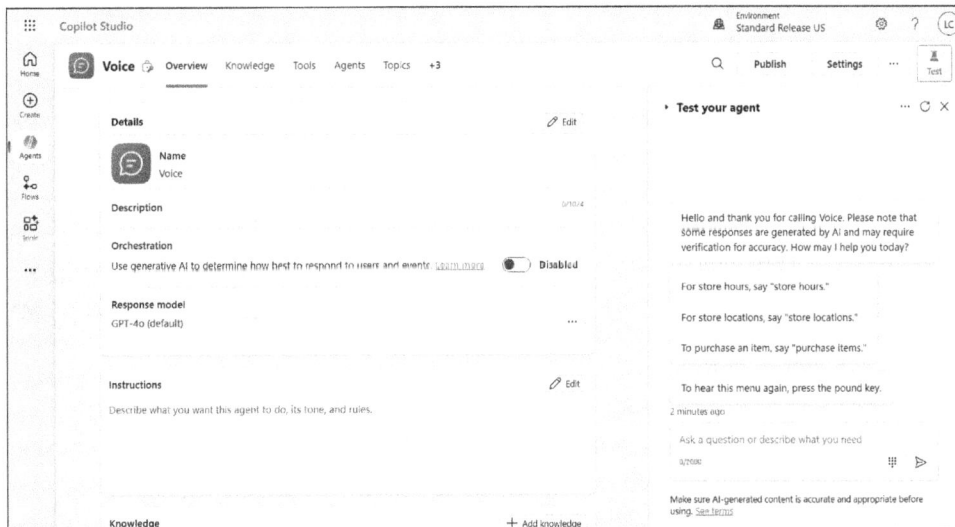

The agent created from the Voice template has a greeting message designed for interaction with a user over the phone.

6. Set the generative orchestration option to **Enabled**, if it is not already enabled. This will allow you to add knowledge to your agent and have it answer questions using the knowledge with voice.

7. Select the **Topics** tab from the top menu, and then select the **System** filter button to review the system topics.

8. Compare the list of system topics with one of the chat agents you previously created. The voice-enabled agent has different topics for handling voice conversations: **Silence detection**, **Speech unrecognized**, and **Unknown dial pad press**.

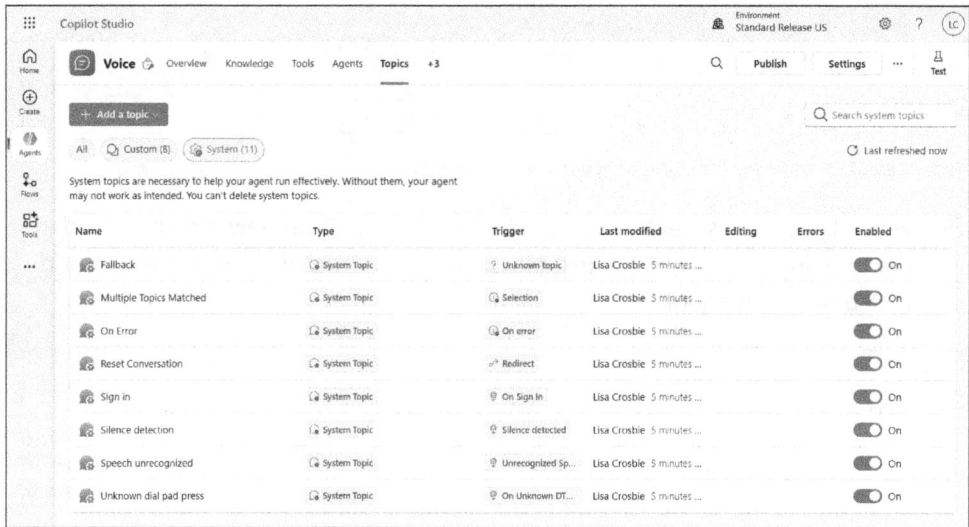

The voice-enabled agent includes additional topics to handle interactions over the phone.

9. Select the **Silence detection** topic to open it. Note that the **Message** node uses "Speech & DTMF." Select this drop-down option to view the switch between the **Speech & DTMF** mode and the **Text** mode.

10. Select the **Edit** link in the **Trigger** to expand the **Silence detected properties** pane. Here you can configure the behavior of the trigger and the topic using conditions and variables.

11. Navigate back to the **Topics** tab, then repeat steps 9 and 10 to review the other specialized voice topics and configuration options.

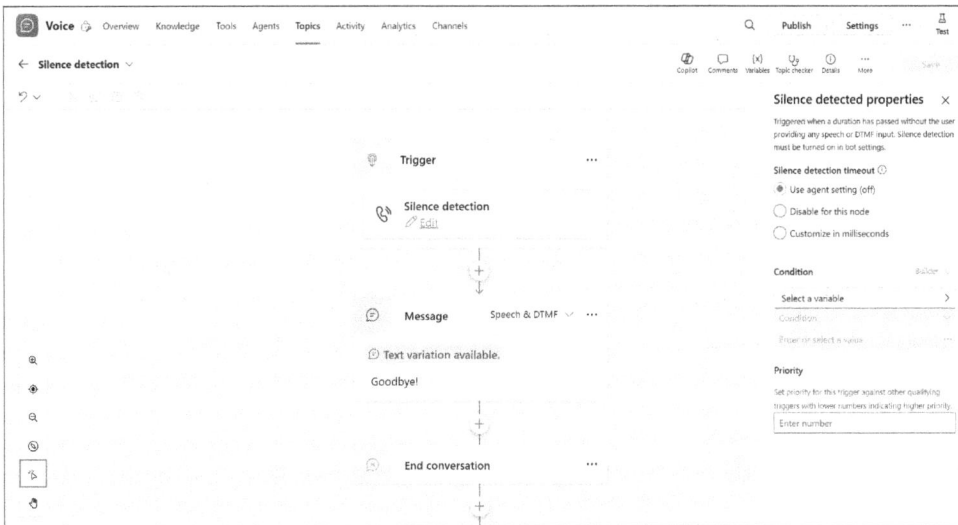

Review and edit the properties for the Silence detection system topic.

12. Select the **Settings** button to open the settings for the agent and then select the **Voice** option from the left side menu. This area is where you can configure and change all of the settings related to the voice capabilities of the agent, including timeouts, silence detection, and latency.

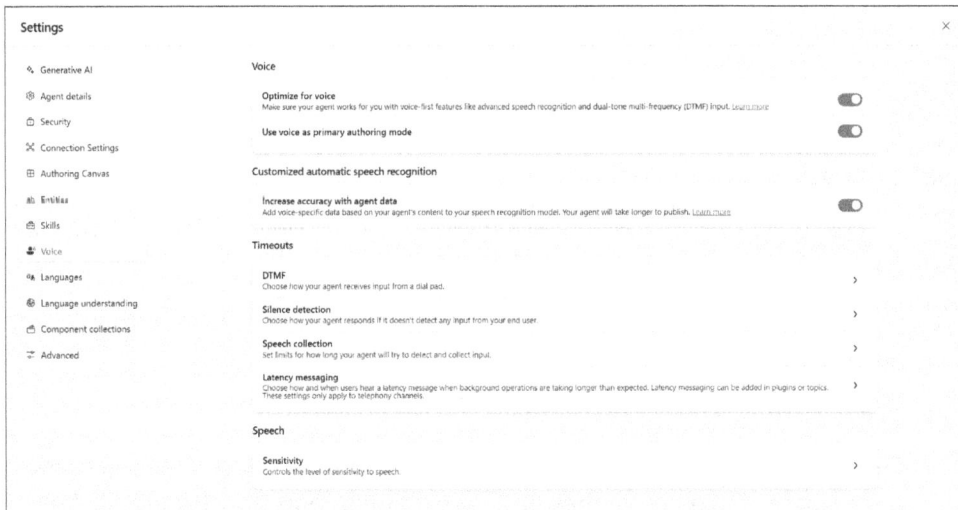

The Voice settings for the agent include options to configure speech recognition, timeouts, and speech sensitivity.

13. Close the **Settings** by selecting the **X** in the top right corner.

> **SEE ALSO** For full documentation on the voice agent settings, refer to https://learn.microsoft.com/en-us/microsoft-copilot-studio/voice-configuration#configure-voice-capabilities.

Configure topics for voice-enabled agents

When you build topics for a voice-enabled agent, you can use some additional configuration options to support the voice capabilities. These options include setting up DTMF for multiple-choice questions, and using Speech Synthesis Markup Language (SSML) to control how your agent's voice sounds when it reads the messages aloud.

SSML uses tags, similar to HTML. The following SSML tags are available to use in Copilot Studio:

- *Audio:* Add recorded audio by providing a URL to an audio file.
- *Break:* Insert pauses or breaks between words.
- *Emphasis:* Add emphasis to particular words or phrases.
- *Prosody:* Change the way the agent expresses particular words or phrases by adjusting the pitch, contour (changes in pitch), range of pitch, speaking rate, or volume.

> **SEE ALSO** For full documentation on working with SSML in Copilot Studio, refer to https://learn.microsoft.com/en-us/microsoft-copilot-studio/voice-configuration#format-speech-synthesis-with-ssml.

To configure a topic for a voice-enabled agent

1. Navigate to the **Topics** tab and select **+Add a topic**, then select **Add from description with Copilot**.
2. Name the topic: **Power Cord Recall**.
3. Create a topic description: **When the user asks about a power cord recall, ask them what Surface device they have, providing options for Original Surface Pro, Surface Pro 2, or Surface Pro 3.**
4. Select the **Create** button to create the topic.

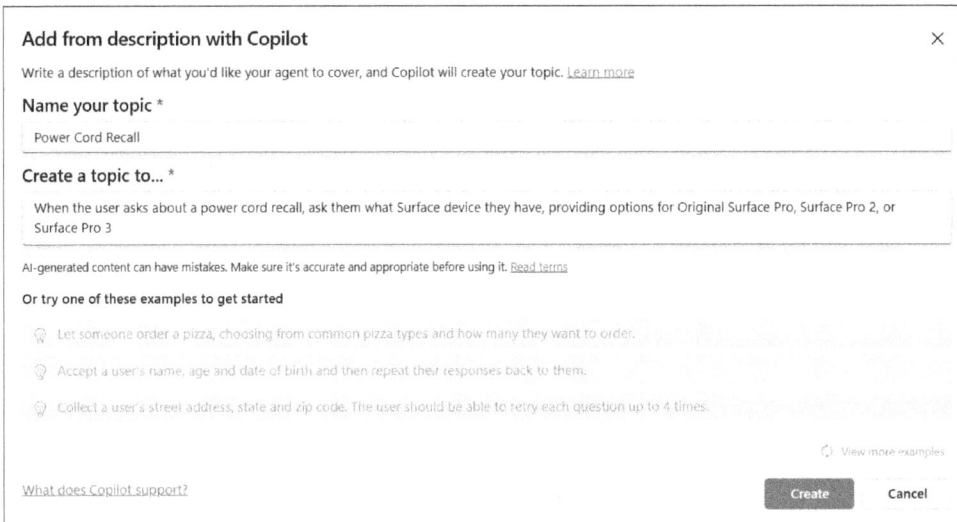

Add from description with Copilot   ✕

Write a description of what you'd like your agent to cover, and Copilot will create your topic. Learn more

Name your topic *

Power Cord Recall

Create a topic to... *

When the user asks about a power cord recall, ask them what Surface device they have, providing options for Original Surface Pro, Surface Pro 2, or
Surface Pro 3

AI-generated content can have mistakes. Make sure it's accurate and appropriate before using it. Read terms

Or try one of these examples to get started

💡 Let someone order a pizza, choosing from common pizza types and how many they want to order.

💡 Accept a user's name, age and date of birth and then repeat their responses back to them.

💡 Collect a user's street address, state and zip code. The user should be able to retry each question up to 4 times.

🔄 View more examples

What does Copilot support?   **Create**   Cancel

Describe a topic to create it using Copilot.

5. When the topic opens in the authoring canvas, navigate to the **Question** node
   and enter a message into the message box: **Thank you for your inquiry. To
   help me work out whether you are eligible for a replacement power cord,
   please tell me which device you have.**

6. Position your cursor at the end of the first sentence in the message and select
   the **SSML tags** drop-down option.

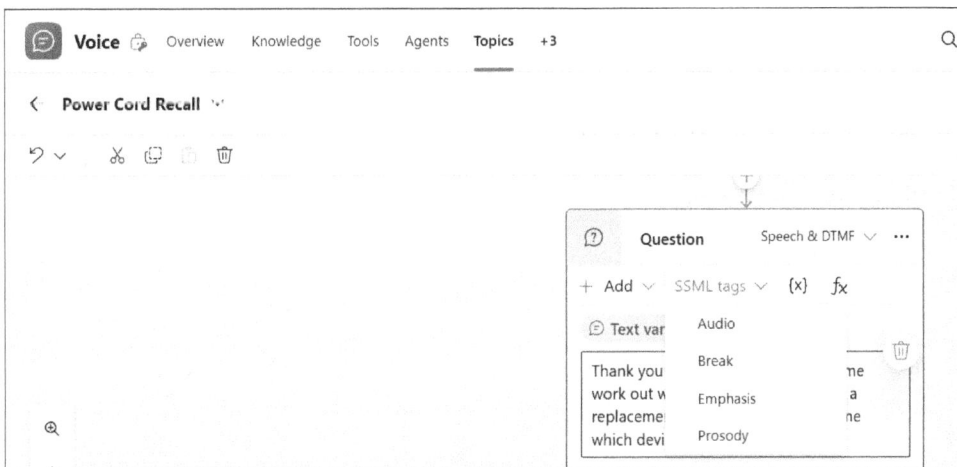

Voice Overview   Knowledge   Tools   Agents   **Topics**   +3   🔍

‹ **Power Cord Recall**

↺ ∨   ✂ 🗋 🗋 🗑

? **Question**   Speech & DTMF ∨   ···

+ Add ∨   SSML tags ∨   {x}   ƒx

Text var   Audio

Thank you   Break   ne   🗑
work out w   a
replaceme   Emphasis   ne
which devi   Prosody

Expand the SSML tags menu to add SSML tags to your message.

7. Select **Break**. This places the **break** SSML tag into the message text.

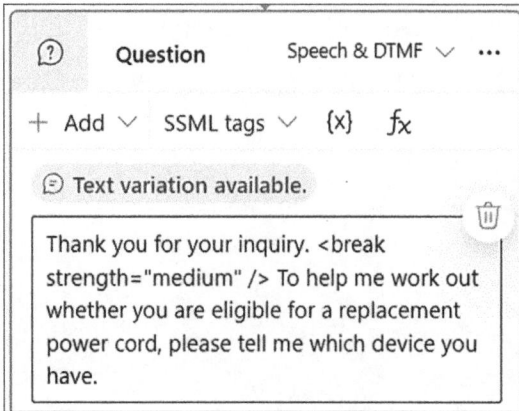

The break SSML tag has been added to the message text.

8. Review the multiple-choice options in the **Question** node. Above the options is a check box to **Assign DTMF keys to options**. Check this box. This assigns a number to each option, so that when the user gets to this point in the conversation, they can select the number on their phone keypad.

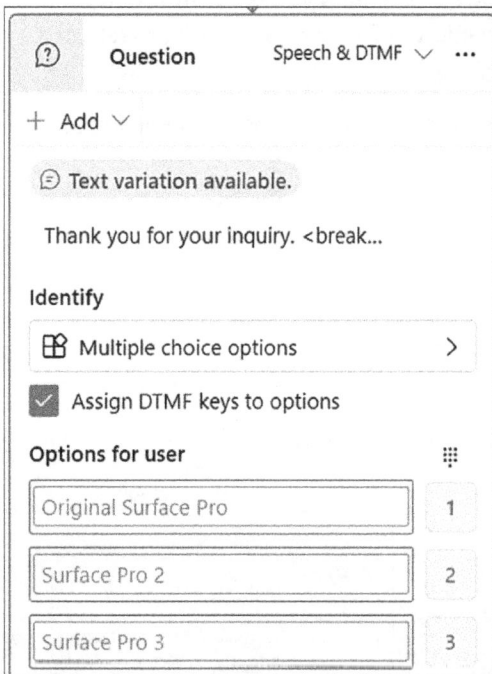

Select the Assign DTMF keys to options buttons to assign a keypad number to each multiple-choice option.

9. Select the **Save** button to save the changes to the topic.

Use knowledge with voice-enabled agents

Voice agents can use generative AI to answer questions in natural language using knowledge, providing a better experience for the customer than having to choose from a list of menu items. The process of adding knowledge to a voice agent is the same as adding knowledge to a chat agent. The voice agent will then automatically provide a more concise response, but will not include citations.

To use knowledge with a voice-enabled agent

1. In the Voice agent, navigate to the **Knowledge** tab and select the **+Add knowledge** button.

2. Select **Public website** and enter the link for the Microsoft Surface website: **https://www.microsoft.com/en-au/surface**.

3. Select the **Add** button to add the website as knowledge.

4. Change the **Name** to **Microsoft Surface Information** and the **Description** to **This knowledge source provides information about Microsoft Surface devices.**

Add the Microsoft Surface website as a knowledge source with a name and description that help the agent understand what it is for.

5. Select the **Add to agent** button. The knowledge source will now appear in the **Knowledge** tab for the agent.

6. Select the **Overview** tab and set the generative orchestration switch to **Enabled**, if it is not already enabled.

> (🔍) **SEE ALSO** There are substantially more configuration options available to build sophisticated voice agents in Copilot Studio. For full documentation, refer to https://learn.microsoft.com/en-us/microsoft-copilot-studio/voice-overview.

Test a voice-enabled agent using chat

Now that you have configured a topic and added knowledge to your voice-enabled agent, it is time to test it. You can test the experience of using the chat without connecting a voice channel at this stage by using the test pane. It will use the Speech & DTMF mode to simulate how the agent would respond to the user with voice.

To test a voice-enabled agent using chat

1. In the **test** pane, enter a phrase that will trigger the topic you created earlier: **Can I get a power cord recall?**

2. The agent calls the **Power Cord Recall** topic and responds with the message you created. Note that the message prompts the user to either say which device they have or press the corresponding number.

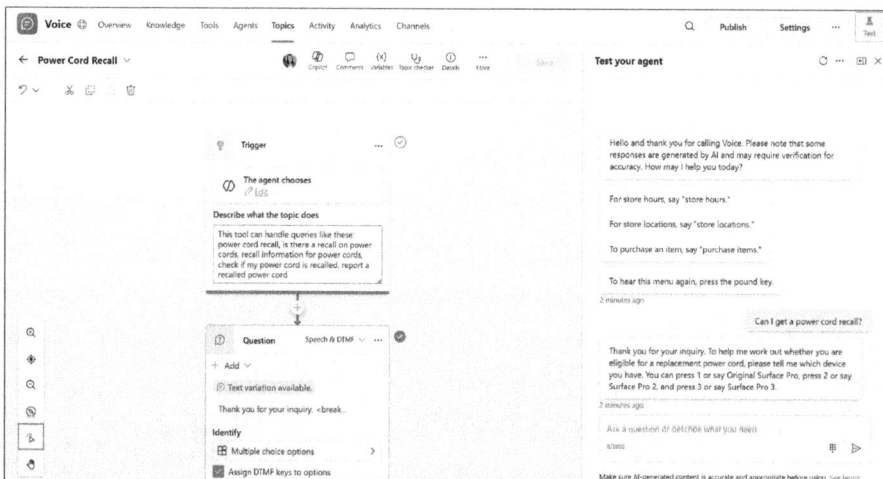

The agent triggers the topic and provides the user with options to either say the name of their device or press the corresponding number on their keypad.

3. In the chat where you would normally type a response, select the icon that represents the phone keypad. This expands a simulated phone keypad in the chat.

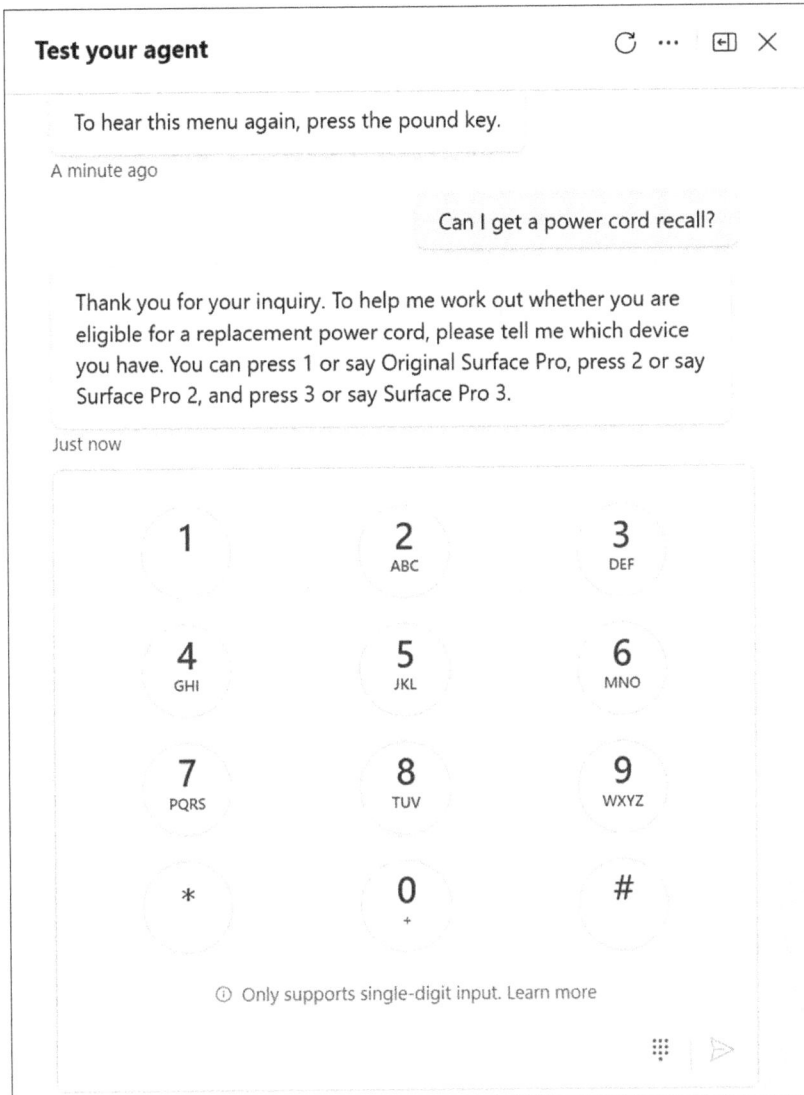

Test your agent   ↻   ⋯   ⊞   ✕

To hear this menu again, press the pound key.

A minute ago

> Can I get a power cord recall?

Thank you for your inquiry. To help me work out whether you are eligible for a replacement power cord, please tell me which device you have. You can press 1 or say Original Surface Pro, press 2 or say Surface Pro 2, and press 3 or say Surface Pro 3.

Just now

1	**2** ABC	**3** DEF
4 GHI	**5** JKL	**6** MNO
7 PQRS	**8** TUV	**9** WXYZ
*	**0** +	**#**

ⓘ Only supports single-digit input. Learn more

⠿   ▷

Select the icon representing the phone keypad to open a simulated phone keypad in the test pane.

4. Select the number "2" on the keypad. This creates a text response, "/DTMFKey 2," that simulates what would happen next in the conversation when the user presses that number on the keypad.

12

> ✅ **TIP** If you want to test this further, you can continue building out branching logic in this topic following what you learned in Chapter 7: Authoring topics.

5. Refresh the test pane and ask a question where the answer is found in the Microsoft Surface webpage you added as a knowledge source: **What is a Surface hub?**

6. The agent responds with a concise answer with no citations in the response.

▸ Test your agent   ⋯ 📖 ⌄ ↻ ✕

For store locations, say "store locations."

To purchase an item, say "purchase items."

To hear this menu again, press the pound key.

Just now

                                    What is a Surface hub?

The Surface Hub is an all-in-one digital whiteboard designed for business use, providing a hybrid meeting experience that enhances collaboration and productivity. The Surface Hub 3, in particular, offers advanced features and AI-powered interactive experiences to create an inclusive and efficient environment for hybrid teams.

Just now

The agent provides a concise response with no citations.

> 🔍 **SEE ALSO** For more functions that are available for testing your Voice agent in chat, refer to the Microsoft documentation: https://learn.microsoft.com/en-us/microsoft-copilot-studio/voice-test.

To test the voice-enabled agent via a phone call in your trial environment, you will connect it to a customer engagement channel, as described in the next section.

Publish to a customer engagement channel and configure escalation

In this section, you will learn how to publish your Voice agent to the Dynamics 365 Customer Service channel, using the trial you signed up for at the start of this chapter.

> ⚠️ **IMPORTANT** The Dynamics 365 Customer Service trial includes a phone number that you can use for 60 minutes of calling for free. This is a toll-free number in the United States. If you have signed up for a trial from another country, you will be making an international call to use this trial number. You should check your phone plan for billing rates and availability.

> ✓ **TIP** In a real-world scenario, you would work with your administrator or telephony specialist to set up a phone number or use your existing customer service number and connect to your own customer engagement hub.

To publish a voice-enabled agent

1. Navigate to the **Settings** tab, select **Security**, and then select **Authentication**.

2. Select the "**No authentication**" option and save this change.

3. Close the **Settings** screen using the **X** in the top right corner to return to the agent.

4. Select the **Channels** tab.

5. Navigate down to the **Customer engagement hub** section in the list of channels, and select **Dynamics 365 Customer Service**.

6. This expands a pane on the right side of the screen, showing that this channel is not connected. Select **Connect**.

12

Dynamics 365 Customer Service ×

ⓘ Your agent doesn't have access to all the required variables and tools. Ask your admin about installing the Dynamics 365 Customer Service package or follow this step-by-step walkthrough ↗.

Status: Not connected

When your agent is linked to Dynamics 365 Customer Service, individual channel deployment is managed in Dynamics 365 Customer Service.

Microsoft Copilot Studio uses Microsoft Teams to communicate with Dynamics 365 Customer Service. By turning on Dynamics 365 Customer Service, you are enabling Teams.

Voice: OnManage in Telephony channel

Voice may include Interactive Voice Response or Real Time Media functionality. Some functionality may require elevated permissions, which are configurable in Dynamics 365.

Connect   Close

Select the Dynamics 365 Customer Service channel and then select Connect.

7. When the connection has been made, you will get a confirmation message and the status will change to "Connected."

8. Close this side pane.

9. Select the **Publish** button and wait for your agent to finish publishing.

Dynamics 365 Customer Service ✕

⊘ You have successfully connected your agent to Omnichannel. ✕

ⓘ Your agent doesn't have access to all the required variables and tools. Ask your admin about installing the Dynamics 365 Customer Service package or follow this step-by-step walkthrough ↗.

Status: ✐ ConnectedView in Omnichannel ↗

When your agent is linked to Dynamics 365 Customer Service, individual channel deployment is managed in Dynamics 365 Customer Service.

Microsoft Copilot Studio uses Microsoft Teams to communicate with Dynamics 365 Customer Service. By turning on Dynamics 365 Customer Service, you are enabling Teams.

Voice: On Manage in Telephony channel

Voice may include Interactive Voice Response or Real Time Media functionality. Some functionality may require elevated permissions, which are configurable in Dynamics 365.

The connection has been made between your Voice agent and the Dynamics 365 Customer Service channel.

⊡ **Voice** 🛡 Overview Knowledge Tools Agents **Channels** +3   🔍

⚠ Your channels are currently being configured through Dynamics 365 Omnichannel for Customer Service. To manage, go to Agent transfers or configure in Omnichannel. ✕

Draft agent status   ↻

⚠ Review the following before publishing: 1 item ∧

Your agent does not require end user authentication   Authentication settings
Allowing anonymous end users to chat with your agent allows anyone to access content added to your agent. Learn more

Published agent status

⊘ Published by Lisa Crosbie 8/17/20 12:30 PM   ⊗ 1 risk ∧

⚠ There are risks to review in your published agent.

Your agent does not require end user authentication   Authentication settings
Allowing anonymous end users to chat with your agent allows anyone to access content added to your agent. Learn more

When the agent is published, you will get an information message that the channels are being configured through Dynamics 365 Omnichannel for Customer Service.

10. Select the **Dynamics 365 Customer Service** channel to open the side pane again.

11. Select the hyperlink next to the **Status** to "**View in Omnichannel**."

12. This opens the **Dynamics 365 Omnichannel admin center** app in a new tab in your browser. This app is the administrative experience to set up and configure all your service channels for Dynamics 365 Customer Service. Select **Workstreams** from the left side menu.

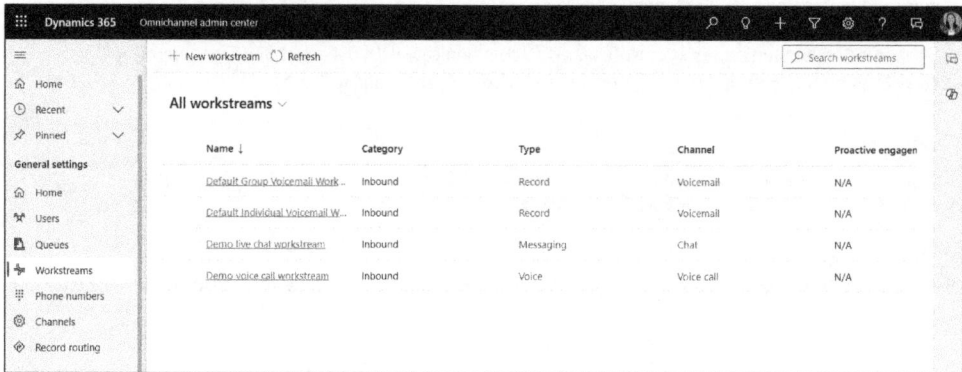

Select the Workstreams option from the left side menu of the Omnichannel admin center.

13. Select the **Demo voice call workstream** to open it.

> **SEE ALSO** In your real-world scenario, you would add and configure a new workstream here to manage your inbound calling with your own number. For full documentation, see https://learn.microsoft.com/en-us/dynamics365/customer-service/administer/voice-channel-inbound-calling.

14. The **Demo voice call workstream** screen shows the details of the free demo phone number you can use for testing. Copy this phone number so that you can use it later.

15. Navigate down this screen to find the section "**AI agent**" and select the **+Add AI agent** button.

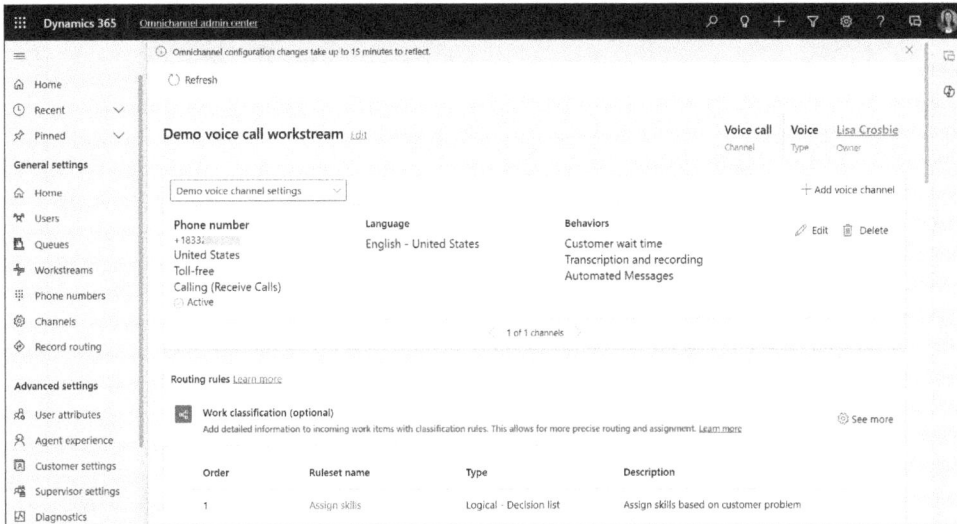

Copy the demo phone number from the Demo voice call workstream screen.

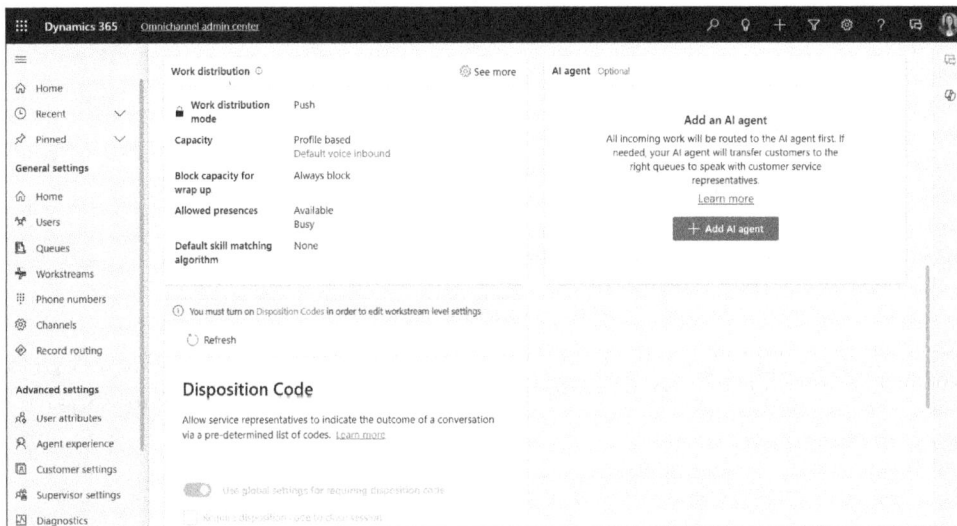

Locate the "AI agent" section and select Add AI agent.

16. This opens an **Add an AI agent** screen that lists the voice agents in the environment. Select the **Voice** agent you created and then select the **Connect** button.

17. When the agent is connected, you will be returned to the **Demo voice call workstream** screen, where the agent name, type, and fallback action appear in the **AI agent** section.

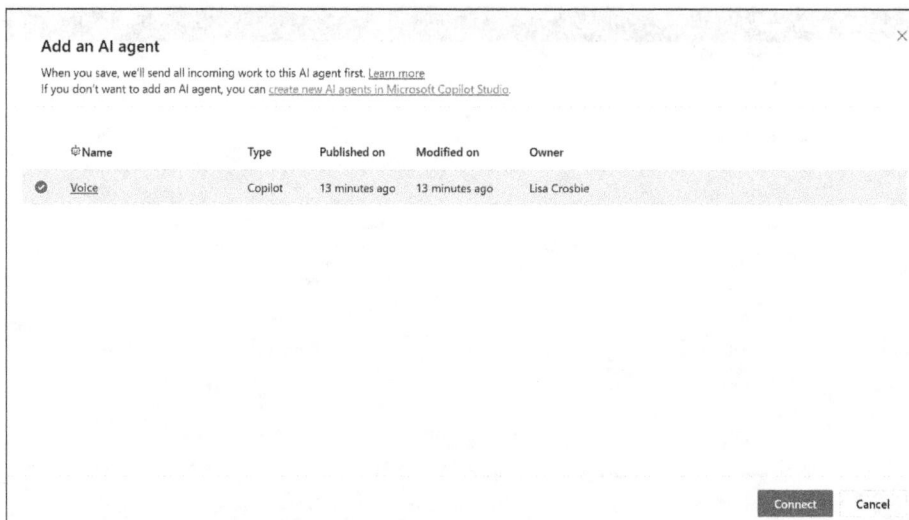

Select the agent you created and connect it to this voice workstream.

> ✓ **TIP** Select the **Edit** button in this section to view or select other fallback actions.

Your Copilot Studio Voice agent is now connected to this demo phone number. Wait 15 minutes before testing it, so as to give the configuration time to take effect.

To test the voice agent using the voice channel

1. Dial the demo phone number you noted earlier from your phone.

2. You will hear a generic greeting message from the demo phone number before being passed to your Voice agent. You will then hear the greeting message from your agent.

3. As the agent reads out the options, interrupt it by talking over it. Say "Store locations."

4. The agent is able to handle the interruption and asks what location you are looking for. Say "Redmond."

5. Continue the conversation, including providing a feedback rating. When the agent asks if it can help with anything else, say "yes."

6. Ask a question that will trigger the topic you created: "Can I get a power cord recall?"

7. The agent reads the text in the message node from that topic and provides the options available. Use your phone keypad to select an option from 1 to 3.

8. Wait until the agent responds and then disconnect the call from your phone.

Now that your voice agent is able to interact with the user by phone, you can configure another option—to escalate to a human representative. To do so, you use the Escalate system topic.

To configure escalation to a human representative

1. In Copilot Studio, navigate to the **Topics** tab in the Voice agent.

2. Select the **System** topics filter.

3. Select the **Escalate** topic to open it.

4. The **Escalate** topic is made up of a **Trigger** node and a **Message** node. This system topic defaults to a message that tells the user that escalating to a representative is not available. To configure the escalation, first delete this **Message** node. Select the three dots at the top right of the **Message** node to expand a menu of more options, then select **Delete** to delete the node.

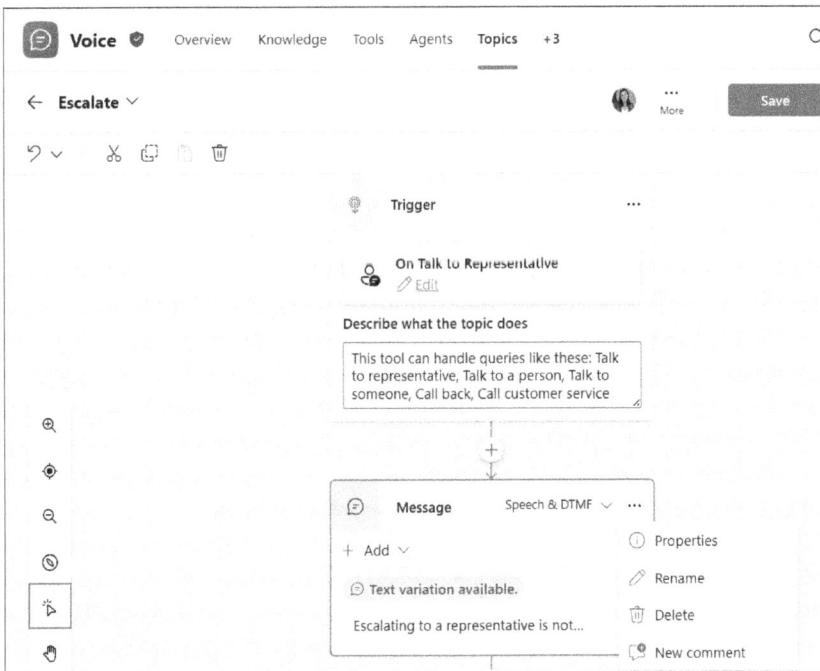

Delete the Message node from the Escalate topic; this message tells the user that escalating to a representative is not available.

5. Select the + button below the **Trigger** node to add a new node.

6. Expand the **Topic management** option and then select **Transfer conversation**.

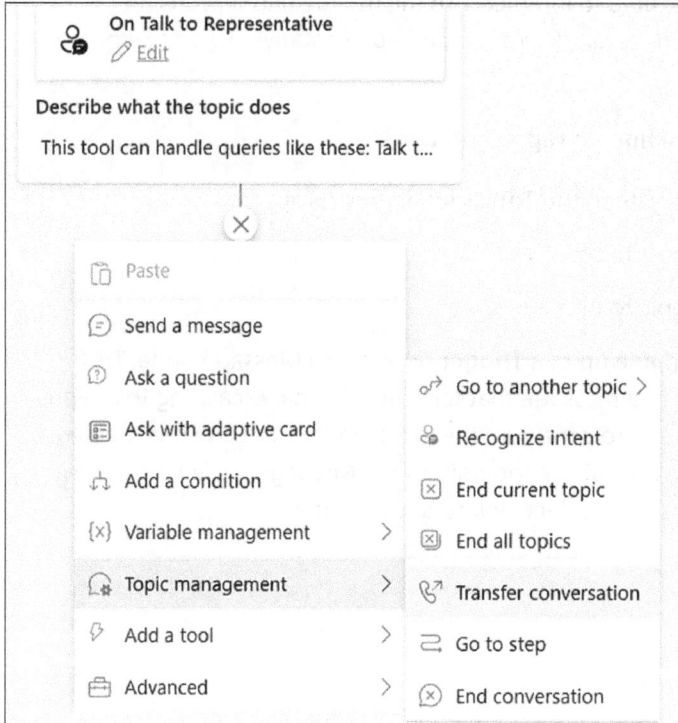

Select the Transfer conversation node from the Topic management options.

7. In the Transfer conversation node, leave the Transfer type as "**Transfer to agent**" and add a message: **Escalating to a human representative**. The agent does not read this message aloud to the customer. Use this option when you want to pass a message from the Copilot Studio agent to the human representative. Note that the full conversation transcript prior to the escalation will be passed through to the human representative automatically.

8. Select the **Save** button to save the changes to the **Escalate** topic.

9. Select the **Publish** button to publish the changes.

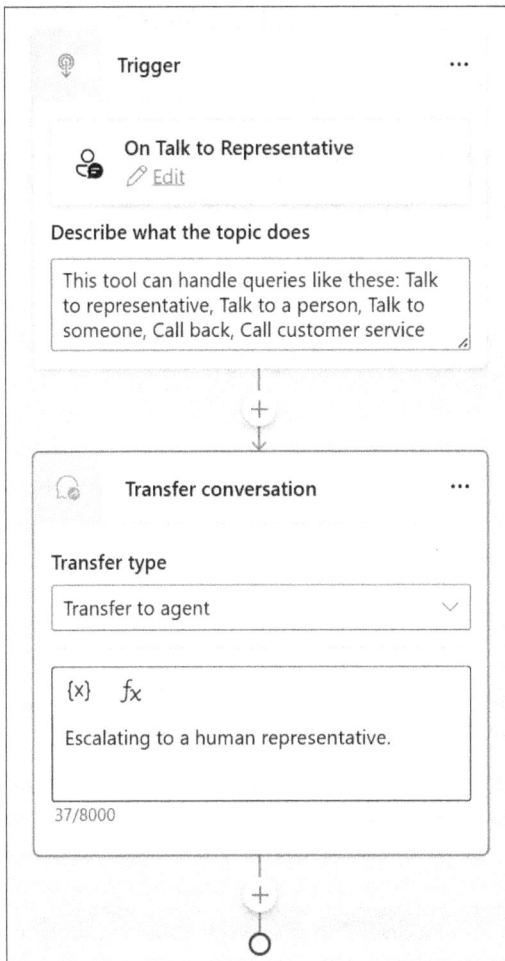

Add a message for the agent to read aloud to the customer when they ask to speak to a human representative.

Wait a few minutes before testing the call again to ensure the published changes have taken effect.

To test escalation to a human representative

1. Return to the Dynamics 365 Omnichannel admin center app and select the name of that app on the top header bar to open the menu of all available Dynamics 365 apps.

2. Select the tile for **Copilot Service workspace**.

12

487

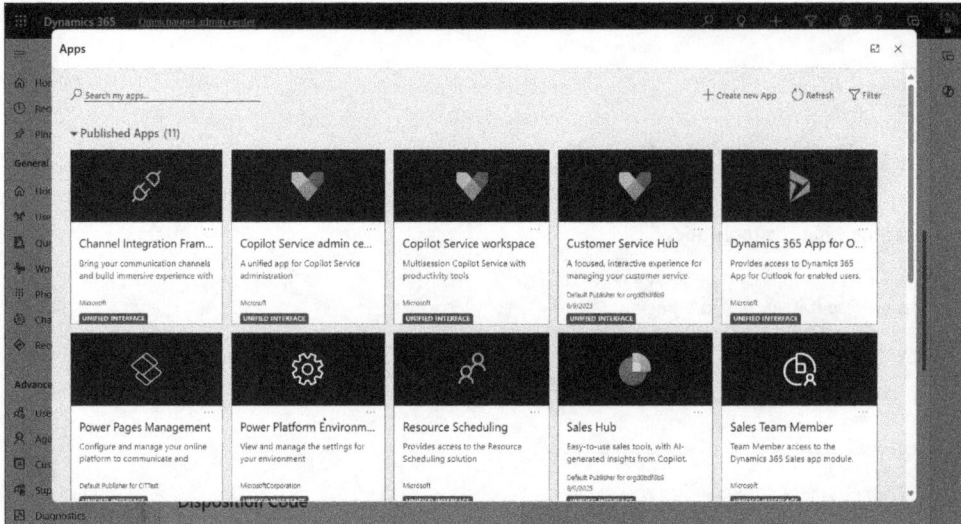

Open the menu of Dynamics 365 apps and select the Copilot Service workspace.

3. This opens the **Copilot Service workspace** application in Dynamics 365. This is the main part of the Dynamics 365 Customer Service application, where human representatives can receive incoming calls from customers. Select **Allow** if prompted for permission for the browser to use your microphone.

4. On the right side of the top header bar is a presence indicator, which sets your availability to receive incoming calls. Select this indicator to view the options and set the status to **Available**.

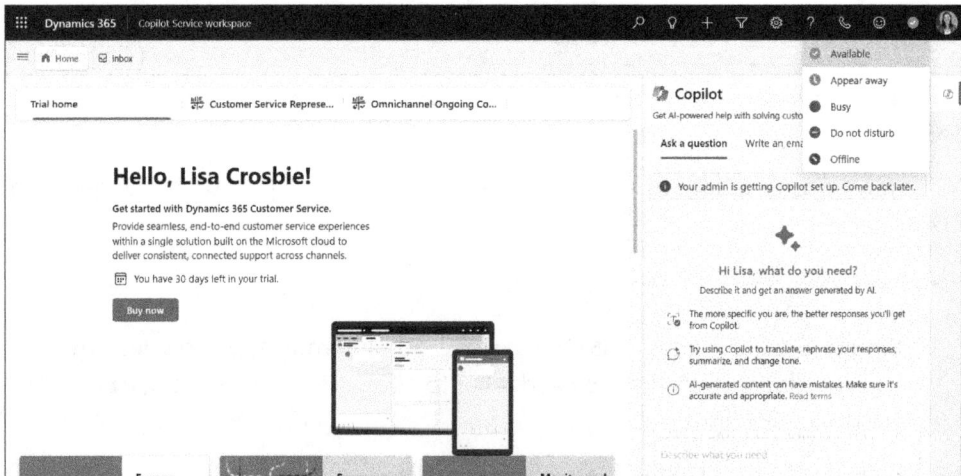

Set the status to Available to receive incoming calls escalated from the Voice agent.

5. Dial the trial phone number from your phone.

6. When the agent answers the call, ask to speak to a person.

> ✅ **TIP** When you set up the escalation using the trial environment, the agent in the Demo voice call workstream will be switched to an out-of-the-box voice agent. The greeting and options will be different from the agent you configured. You can continue with this agent to test the escalation experience, or you can go back to the Demo voice call workstream configuration, delete that AI agent from the configuration, add your agent again, and then test again.

7. The agent will escalate the call, and you will get an incoming Voice call request notification in the Copilot Service workspace app.

> ✅ **TIP** Using this demo and trial setup, you are both the customer (Claudia) and the human representative in Customer Service.

8. Select **Accept** to accept the call.

When the call is escalated, the customer service representative gets a screen pop-up message asking them to accept or reject the incoming voice call.

9. The screen that opens shows the call transcript and the customer details. You can continue the conversation to watch the real-time transcription or you can disconnect the call.

> **SEE ALSO** Dynamics 365 Customer Service is an enterprise-level call center application that can handle a range of channels and capabilities. For more on Dynamics 365 Customer Service and the omnichannel capabilities, refer to https://learn.microsoft.com/en-us/dynamics365/customer-service/implement/introduction-omnichannel.

Skills review

In this chapter, you learned how to:

- Create a voice-enabled agent in Copilot Studio from a template and understand the difference in capabilities and settings between voice-enabled agents and text-based chat agents.

- Test the voice agent by simulating the voice experience in a chat.

- Publish the agent to a customer engagement hub channel and connect the agent to a phone number using Dynamics 365 Customer Service.

- Configure the Escalate topic so that the agent can escalate the voice conversation to a human representative.

Practice tasks

No practice files are necessary to complete the practice tasks in this chapter. To follow along with all these practice tasks, you will need to sign up for a free trial of Dynamics 365 Customer Service at https://www.microsoft.com/en-au/dynamics-365/products/customer-service.

Create a voice-enabled agent

Open the Copilot Studio home page in your browser and then complete the following tasks:

1. Select the **CustomerService Trial** environment from the Environment picker.

2. Select **Create** from the left side menu.

3. Select the **Voice** agent template.

4. Select **Create**.

5. Navigate to the **Topics** tab to review the system topics created for a voice agent.

6. Navigate to the **Settings** area and select the **Voice** option from the left side menu to view the settings available for a voice agent. Close the settings to return to the **Overview** page.

Test a voice-enabled agent using chat

Continue using the Voice agent you created in the previous topic and complete the following tasks:

1. In the **test** pane, respond to the agent by typing **Store hours**.

2. Wait for the agent to respond. When it asks whether that response answered your question, it will offer options to press 1 or press 2. Select the **keypad** icon in the chat area.

3. Select the number **1** on the keypad. This triggers the End of Conversation topic.

Publish to a customer engagement channel and configure escalation

Open the Copilot Studio home page in your browser and then complete the following tasks:

1. Navigate to the **Settings**, select **Security**, and change the agent authentication to "**No authentication.**"

2. Save the changes and close the **Settings** area.

3. Navigate to the **Channels** tab and select the **Dynamics 365 Customer Service** channel.

4. Select **Connect** and wait for the connection to be established.

5. Close this pane and publish the agent.

6. Return to the **Dynamics 365 Customer Service** channel and select the "**View in Omnichannel**" link to open the Dynamics 365 Omnichannel admin center app.

7. Select **Workstreams** from the left side menu.

8. Select the **Demo voice call** workstream to open it.

9. Take a note of the demo phone number to use later.

10. Navigate down to the **AI agent** section and select the **Add AI agent** button.

11. Select your **Voice** agent from the list and select **Connect**.

12. Wait 15 minutes for the configuration changes to take effect.

13. Dial the demo phone number from your phone and speak to the agent.

Extending Copilot Studio agents with Azure AI

13

Practice files

No practice files are necessary to complete the practice tasks in this chapter.

Copilot Studio is one part of Microsoft's broader agent-building platform. As you have learned throughout this book, you can build sophisticated agents using the low-code tools and built-in language models provided by Copilot Studio. However, when you need more control over how your data is indexed or the language model that your agent uses, you can extend your Copilot Studio agent by integrating components developed in Azure AI.

This kind of integration typically involves collaboration between a low-code maker and a professional developer or data scientist who is skilled in working with Azure AI. Once the required resources or models have been created in Azure AI, you can easily connect to them from Copilot Studio as a low-code maker, without needing the skill set to create them.

This chapter assumes you already have foundational knowledge of Azure and access to the necessary resources. It is not a beginner's guide to Azure or Azure

In this chapter

- Create a vector index in Azure AI Search
- Add Azure AI Search as a knowledge source
- Bring your own Azure AI Foundry model

AI Foundry. Instead, it focuses on showing you how to index your data in Azure AI Search so that it can be used in Copilot Studio as a knowledge source. The content here will also help you understand the ways you can extend your Copilot Studio agent by bringing your own models from Azure AI Foundry. Links and references are provided for deeper learning beyond the material covered here.

> 🔍 **SEE ALSO** To understand the differences between creating agents in Copilot Studio and Azure AI Foundry, refer to the section "Microsoft's agent-building toolset" in Chapter 1: Understanding Copilot Studio and agents.

Create a vector index in Azure AI Search

Copilot Studio makes it easy to add knowledge sources to your agent, including connecting to your organization's enterprise data. However, when you add knowledge using the out-of-the-box connectors, you have no control over how the search index is created or configured, and there are a limited number of enterprise knowledge sources available as standard connectors.

With this low-code experience of adding knowledge, you have limited options for influencing how your data is indexed or retrieved. Indexing plays a critical role in determining the quality and relevance of the answers you get from your agent. Azure gives you the ability to configure your own search index, giving you greater control over the indexing of your data and therefore the quality of the agent's responses generated from that data.

You should consider using Azure AI Search as a knowledge source for your agent when you are working with large or complex data sets, or when your data is stored in a repository or database that is not supported by the standard Copilot Studio knowledge connectors.

Review or set up Azure prerequisites

Before you begin, you will need to have the following Azure resources and prerequisites available:

- An Azure account where you have permission to create resources, and can manage the costs to consume them. If you don't already have an Azure subscription, you can sign up for a free subscription, which comes with some initial credits. Some resources may incur costs above that free credit limit, so you should understand the pricing options and monitor your usage carefully.

> **SEE ALSO** For more information and to get started with an Azure subscription, visit https://azure.microsoft.com/.

- An Azure storage account and an Azure Blob Storage container. Upload some text-based PDF documents into that container. If you don't have your own documents to use as knowledge, you will find sample documents that you can download and use at https://github.com/Azure-Samples/azure-search-sample-data/tree/main/health-plan. These sample documents are used in the examples in this chapter.

> **SEE ALSO** For instructions on creating and working with blobs and containers in the Azure portal, refer to https://learn.microsoft.com/en-us/azure/storage/blobs/storage-quickstart-blobs-portal.

- An Azure AI Search service that uses the Basic pricing tier or higher, not the free tier.

> **TIP** You can disable or delete the search service after working through this exercise so that you don't incur ongoing costs.

> **SEE ALSO** For instructions on how to create an Azure AI Search service in the Azure portal, refer to https://learn.microsoft.com/en-us/azure/search/search-create-service-portal.

- An Azure OpenAI resource with a deployment that uses an embedding model, such as *text-embedding-3-large*. For the example you will follow in this chapter, a text embedding model is sufficient. If your data includes images, diagrams, flowcharts, and other graphics that you want your agent to be able to interpret, you will need to deploy an AI vision embedding model.

13

> ⊘ **SEE ALSO** For instructions on how to deploy a model from the model catalog to an Azure OpenAI resource, refer to https://learn.microsoft.com/en-us/azure/ai-foundry/how-to/deploy-models-openai.

Import and vectorize your data in Azure AI Search

To add Azure AI Search as a knowledge source to a Copilot Studio agent, you need to prepare your data by creating a vector index. A vector index allows for higher-quality and more relevant search results than a keyword index because it maps the meanings of similar words together, rather than just matching keywords.

> ⊘ **SEE ALSO** For more detail on creating a vector index, including all the options for customization and control, refer to https://learn.microsoft.com/en-us/azure/search/vector-search-how-to-create-index.

To import and vectorize data into Azure AI Search

1. Navigate to the Azure portal: https://portal.azure.com/. Sign in with your account.

2. Go to your Azure AI Search service.

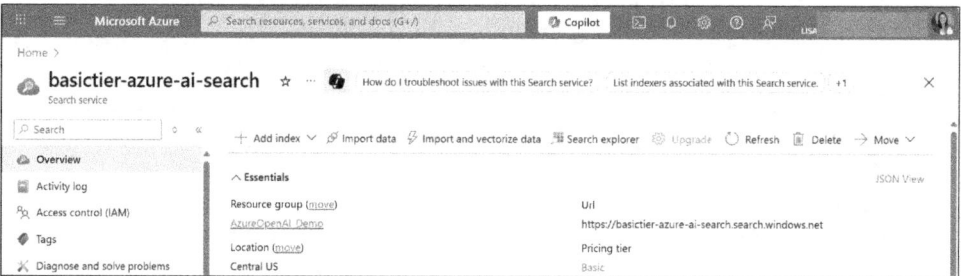

View your Azure AI Search service in the Azure portal.

3. Select **Import and vectorize data** from the menu at the top of the overview section.

4. Select **Azure Blob storage** as your data source.

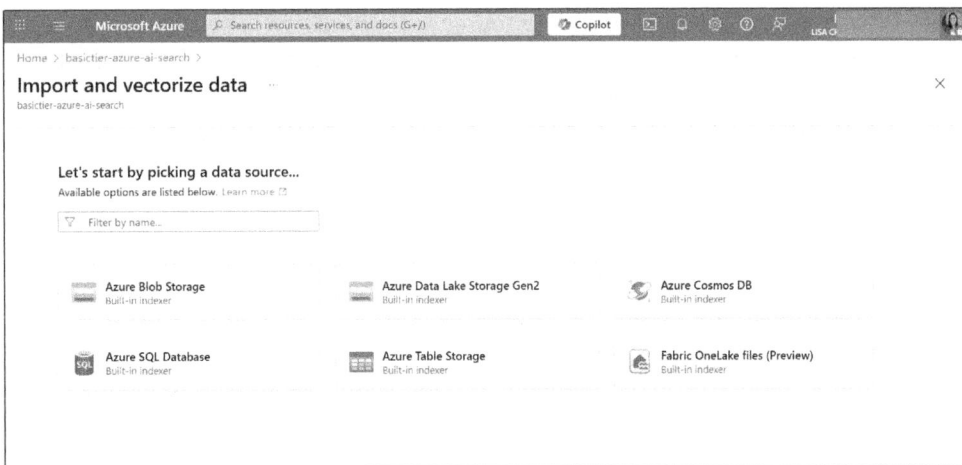

You can import and vectorize data from a range of data sources, including Azure Blob Storage.

5. Once you have selected your data source, you can choose whether the data in your scenario is primarily text based (RAG), or whether the index will need to process complex images and diagrams as well as text (multimodal RAG). In this example, we are using text-based PDF documents and an embedding model that is designed for text. Select the **RAG** option.

> **SEE ALSO** "RAG" stands for "retrieval-augmented generation," which is a technique in which a large language model retrieves relevant responses from an external data source. For more information on RAG and the RAG patterns available in Azure AI Search, refer to https://learn.microsoft.com/en-us/azure/search/retrieval-augmented-generation-overview.

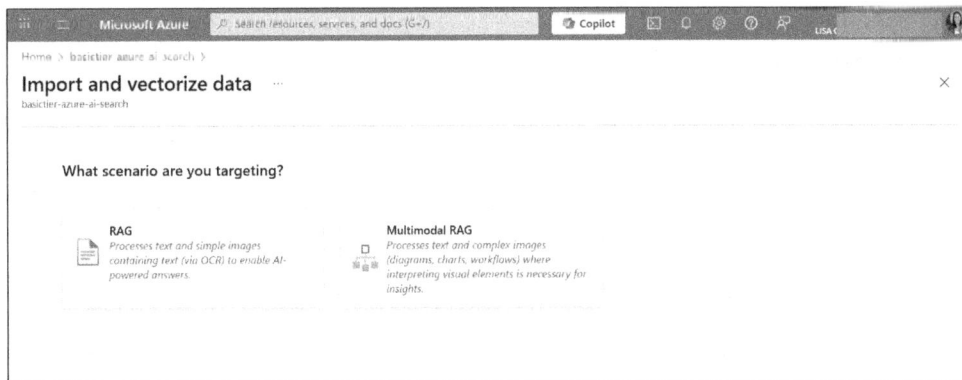

The vector indexing can support text-based scenarios, or scenarios that require processing of images, diagrams, and charts.

6. Once you have selected your data source and RAG pattern, you will begin working through a series of stages to configure the vector index. The first stage is to connect your data. Select your **Subscription**, **Storage account**, and the **Blob container** where you uploaded your data or sample documents.

Select your subscription, storage account, and blob container details.

7. Select the **Next** button.

8. You will progress to the next stage, **Vectorize your text**. Select the **Subscription** and the Azure OpenAI service where you deployed an embedding model.

9. Once you have selected the service, select the embedding model you deployed in that service.

> ✓ **TIP** You will need to check the option that confirms you acknowledge that connecting to an Azure OpenAI service will incur additional costs.

10. Select the **Next** button.

11. The next step provides options for you to **Vectorize and enrich your images**. In this example, we are working with text-based documents and a text-based embedding model, so leave these options unchecked.

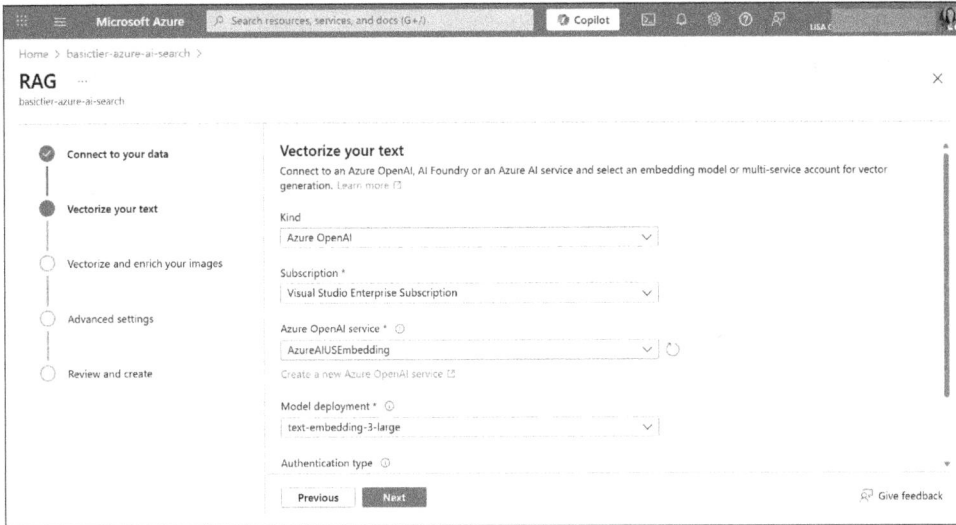

Select the subscription, Azure OpenAI service, and model deployment you are using to vectorize the text.

> **SEE ALSO** To enable these options, you need deploy an AI Vision Vectoring model. For more information, refer to https://learn.microsoft.com/en-us/azure/search/vector-search-vectorizer-ai-services-vision.

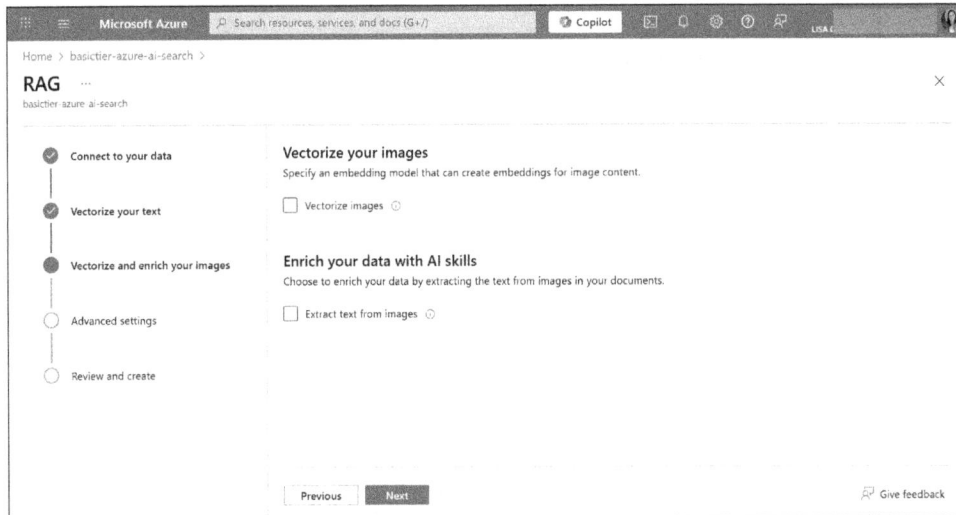

Leave these options unchecked unless you have deployed a vision embedding model.

13

12. Select the **Next** button.

13. At the **Advanced settings** stage, you can preview the index fields and schedule how frequently you want to perform the indexing. Leave these options as they are and select **Next**.

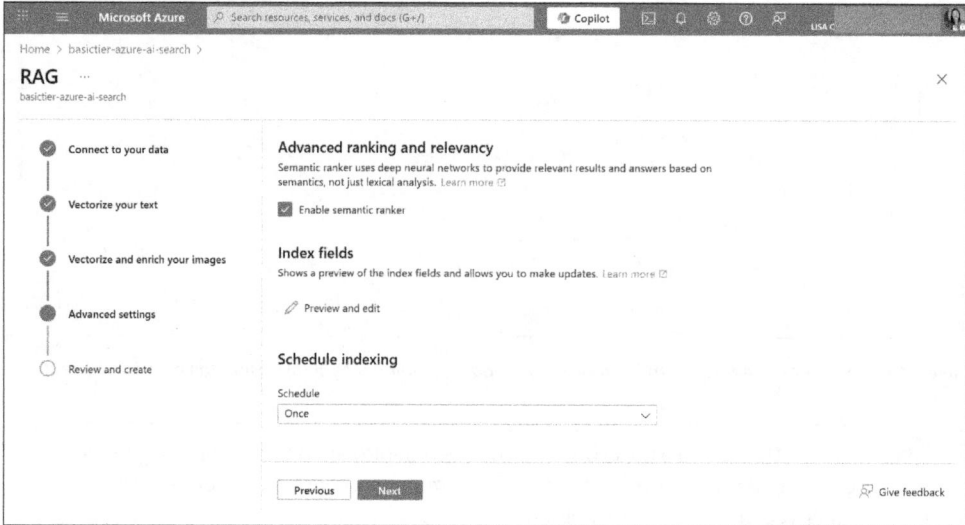

Advanced settings give you the option to preview and edit index fields or to schedule indexing.

14. At the final step in the process, review your selections before creating the vector index. Select the **Create** button.

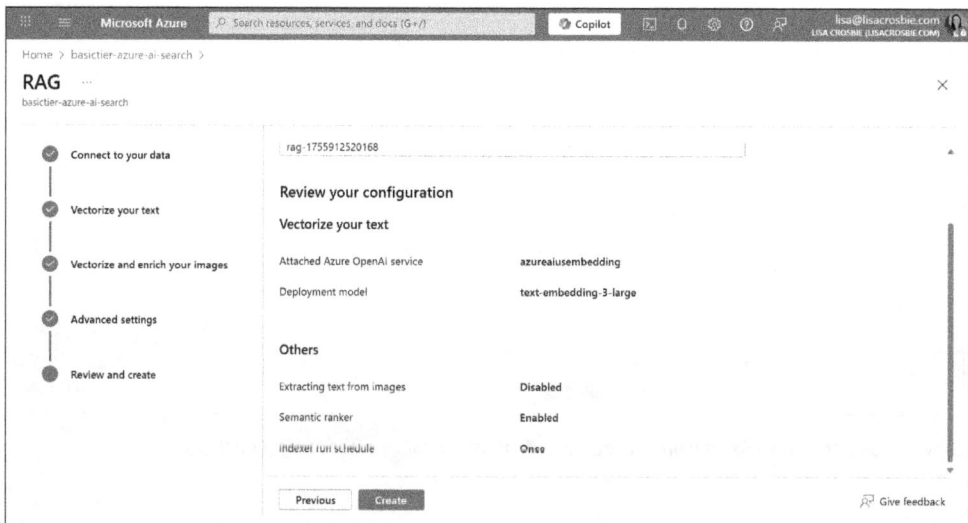

Review your configuration and create the index after you have completed all the steps in the process.

15. Wait for the index to be created. You will get a confirmation message when it is done. Close the confirmation message.

16. You will be returned to the **Overview** screen of your Azure AI Search service. Select the **Indexes** option on the left side menu to view the index you just created.

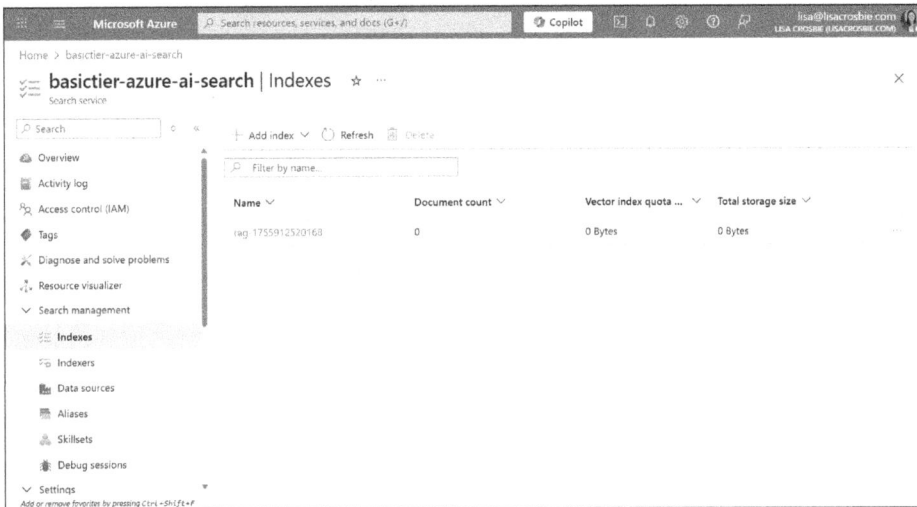

Select "Indexes" from the left navigation menu to view the indexes created in the search service.

Add Azure AI Search as a knowledge source

Now that you have imported and vectorized your data in Azure AI Search, you can add it as a knowledge source to your Copilot Studio agent. To do so, you need to get the API key and endpoint URL of the search service to establish the connection.

To get the endpoint URL and API key to connect to a Copilot Studio agent

1. Navigate to the **Overview** screen of your Azure AI Search service, where you just imported and indexed your data.

2. Hover over the **URL** and select the **copy** icon to copy the URL. Paste it into a blank document or note so that it will be ready to use later.

3. Navigate down the left side menu to find **Settings**. Expand the **Settings** part of the menu and select **Keys**.

13

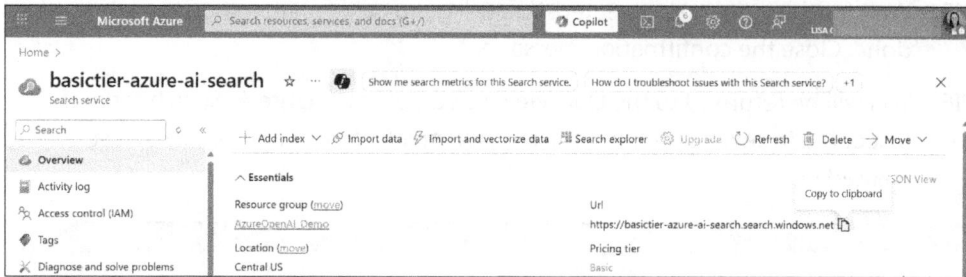

Copy the URL from the Overview screen.

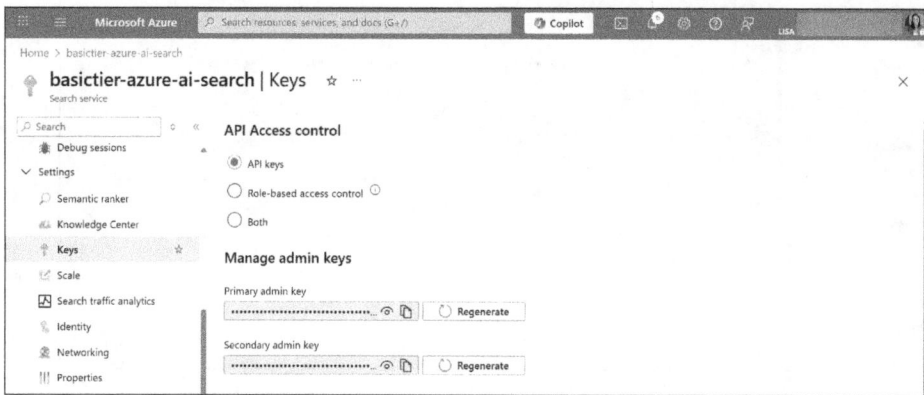

Navigate to the Settings menu and select Keys.

4. Select the copy button in the **Primary admin key** field to copy this key to your clipboard. Paste it in the same document or note you used earlier for the URL.

Now you have a search index set up for your data in Azure AI, and the URL and keys to connect it. Next, you will create a new agent in Copilot Studio and connect this Azure AI search service as the knowledge for that agent.

> 🔍 **SEE ALSO** To learn about the full capabilities for authenticating connections to your Azure AI Search service, refer to https://learn.microsoft.com/en-us/azure/search/search-security-api-keys.

To use Azure AI Search as a knowledge source in Copilot Studio

1. Open a new tab in your browser and navigate to Copilot Studio.

2. On the home screen, describe an agent to create it by entering the following text and then selecting the send icon: **Create an agent to help the user with questions about health benefits.**

> **TIP** If you have used your own data rather than the sample data, create an agent that fits your scenario, or use an existing agent that you have already created for this scenario.

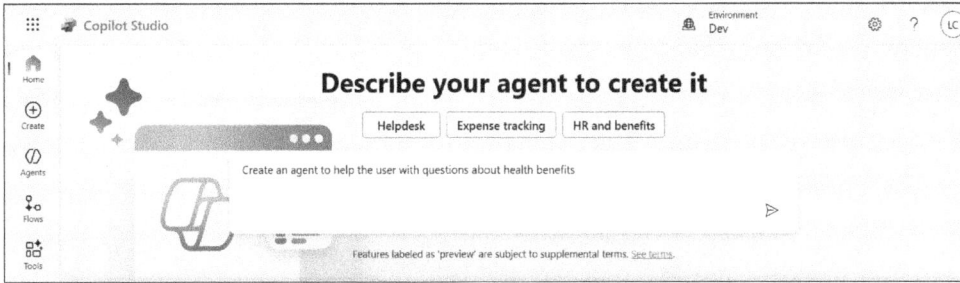

Create a new agent in Copilot Studio by describing it.

3. Confirm the agent name suggested by Copilot or give it your preferred name, such as **Health Benefits Assistant**. Select the **Create** button.

4. When the agent has been deployed, select the **Knowledge** tab and then select the **+Add knowledge** button.

5. On the **Add knowledge** screen, select the **Azure AI Search** option.

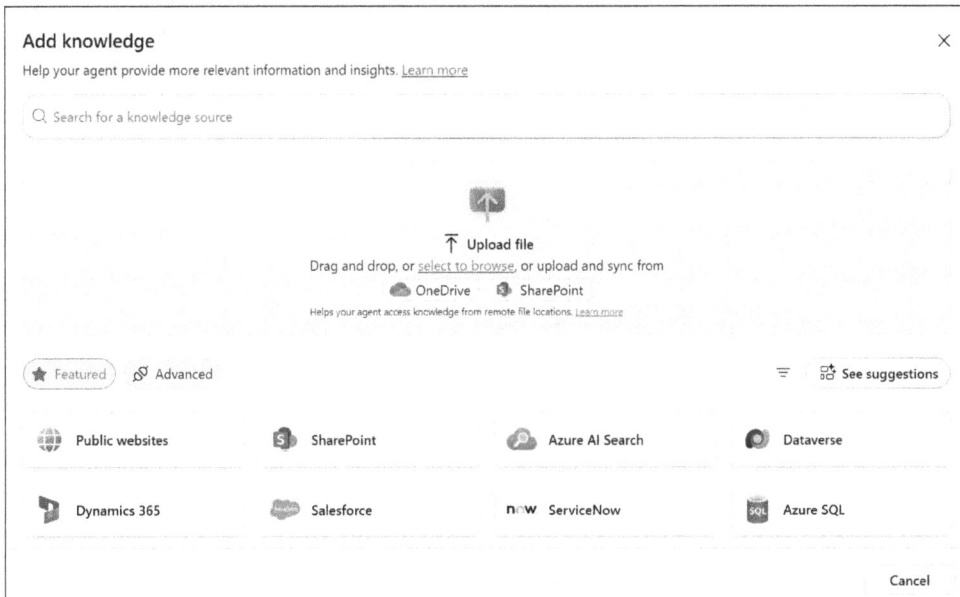

Select the Azure AI Search option to add it as a knowledge source to your agent.

6. You will be prompted to create a connection to the Azure AI Search service using an API key and endpoint URL. Expand the **Your connections** option and select **Create new connection**.

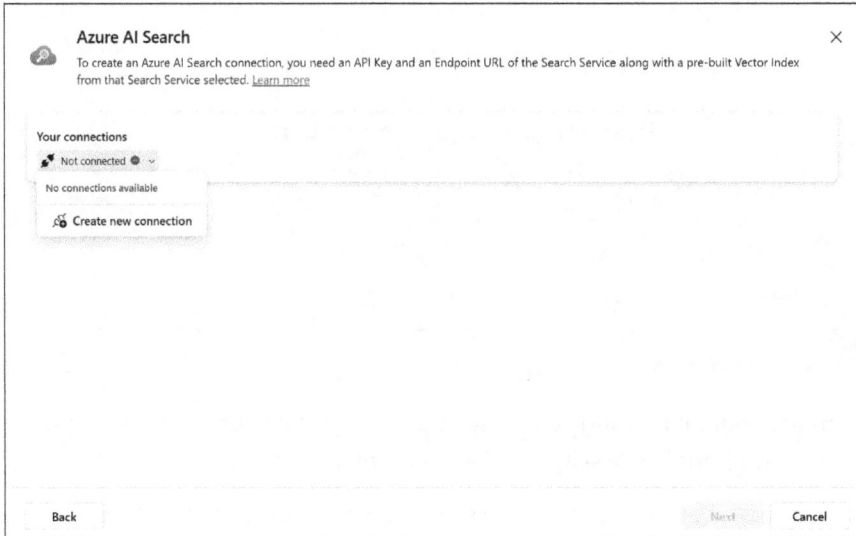

Create a new connection to your Azure AI Search service from Copilot Studio.

7. Enter the URL and API key that you copied from your Azure AI Search service in the previous example.

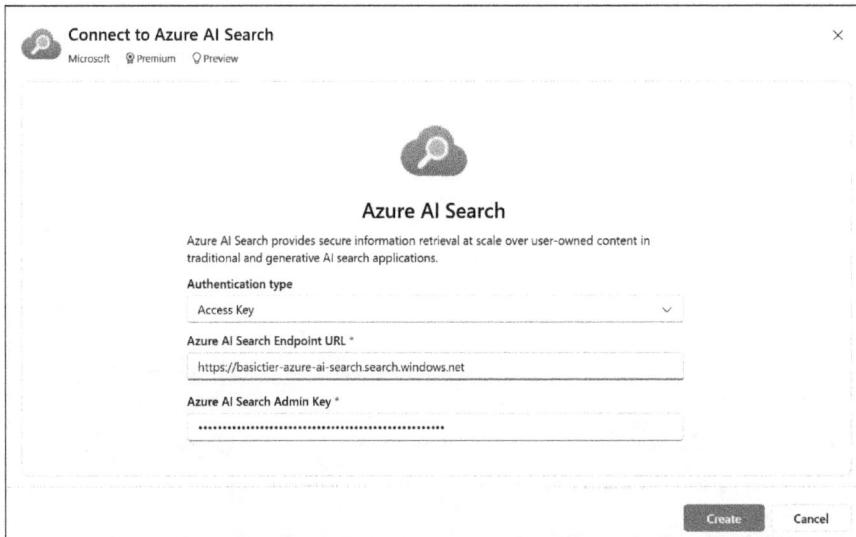

Paste in the endpoint URL and API key from your Azure AI Search service to create the connection.

8. Select the **Create** button and wait for the connection to be established.

9. The index you created will appear in the list of **Available indexes**. Select it, and then select the **Add to agent** button.

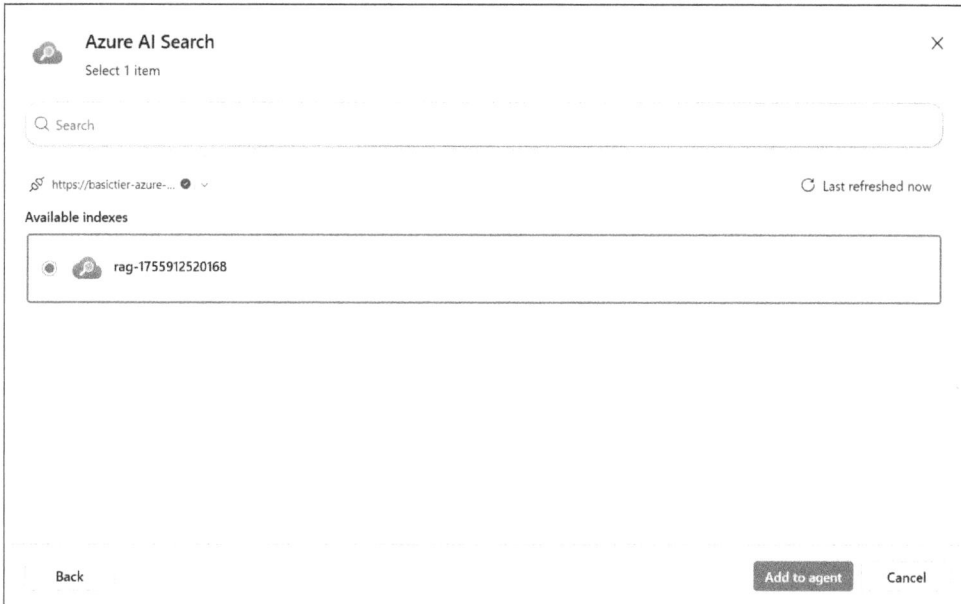

Select your vector index and then select "Add to agent."

10. The Azure AI Search now appears as a knowledge source in the **Knowledge** tab of your agent.

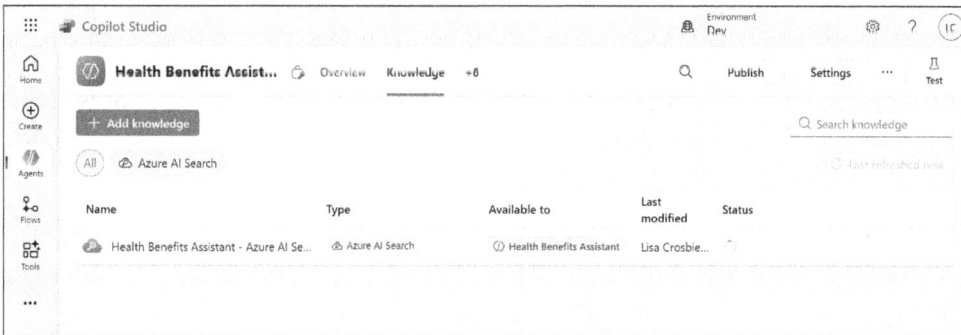

The Azure AI Search is now added as knowledge to your agent.

13

11. Test the agent by asking questions for which the answers can be found in the sample documents you downloaded. For example, ask the agent: **how does split copay work**. The agent responds using the knowledge.

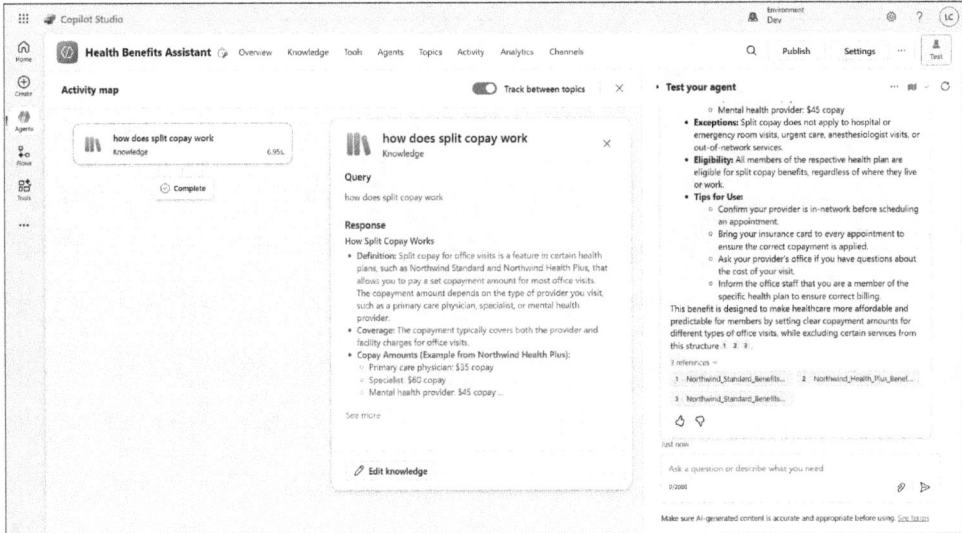

The agent uses the Azure AI Search knowledge source to respond to the user's question.

> ✓ **TIP** For even more sophisticated responses from your knowledge, try enabling and using the Deep Reasoning model, adding an instruction to "use reason."

Bring your own Azure AI Foundry model

Copilot Studio offers you flexibility in choosing the model that your agent uses. It provides a set of managed models that you can select from, and also allows you to bring over your own model from Azure AI Foundry.

The managed models are provided and managed by Microsoft, with no setup or overhead required. Microsoft takes care of all the infrastructure and responsible AI for these models.

When you build an agent in Copilot Studio, the agent uses the default managed model. As a low-code user, you can build and publish agents using this general model without needing to understand anything about model options or selection. Copilot

Studio also provides the option to switch to a newer model (in preview stage, before it becomes the next default model, or in experimental stage for models that have been recently released), or to use scenario-specific models such as reasoning models.

> ⚠️ **IMPORTANT** Copilot Studio keeps your agent updated with the latest models from OpenAI. Over time, the options you can select will change, with some preview models becoming default models, and new models added as experimental options. Microsoft does all the change management associated with these managed model updates. Experimental models have not gone through the full testing process as default models. They may have some restricted functionality, may not be supported in the future, and are not suitable for production use.

If you want to use another model for your agent (e.g., an industry-specific model, a model with a particular capability, or your own custom model), you can bring your own model into your Copilot Studio agent from Azure AI Foundry. Azure AI Foundry offers thousands of models to choose from, as well as the ability to customize or train your own model. If you bring your own model, you will be responsible for managing the access, infrastructure, AI controls, and instructions, as well as for managing the impact of any changes that are made to the model.

You can select the primary model for your agent, the model used in generative responses, and the model used for prompt tools. You can use a different model for each prompt or for each agent, choosing the right model for each purpose.

Select the primary model for your agent

The primary model used by your agent is set to the default model, which is the latest model that has been fully tested by Microsoft for production use. You can use this model or switch to a different model that is more suitable for your scenario.

13

To select the primary model for your agent

1. Continue working with the Health Benefits Assistant agent or the agent you created earlier in this chapter. Navigate to the **Settings** area of your agent.

2. In the **Generative AI** section of the settings, navigate down to the **Model** section.

3. Select the drop-down field at the top right of the **Model** section to view the list of available models.

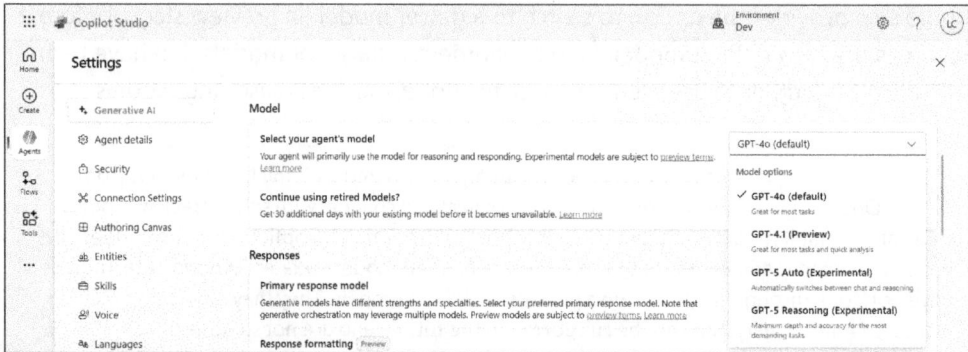

You can choose to use a preview or experimental model for your agent.

4. Select a different model from the list of options provided.

5. Select the **Save** button to save the changes to the agent's model, and then close the **Settings**.

6. The **Overview** tab now displays the new model selected.

> ✅ **TIP** You can expand the three dots in the Agent's model section of the Overview tab to reveal an Edit option. Selecting this option will navigate you back to the agent settings, where you can edit the model as described here.

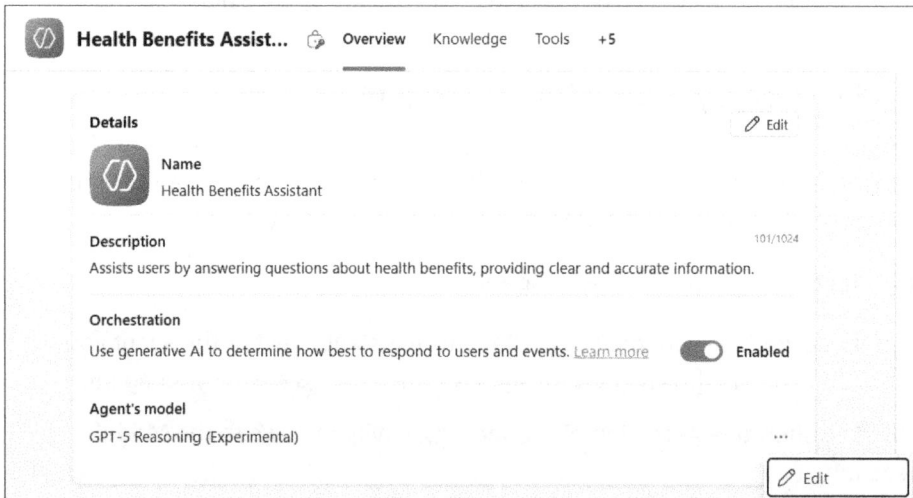

The Overview tab shows the model you selected for the agent and provides an option to edit.

7. Test your agent by asking the same question you asked earlier, and compare the response using the current model.

Select the response model for your agent

You can also select the model you want your agent to use when it generates responses using AI. That is, you can either use the managed model options provided or connect your own model from Azure AI Foundry.

To select the response model for your agent

1. Navigate to the **Settings** area of your agent.

2. In the **Generative AI** section of the settings, navigate down to the **Responses** section.

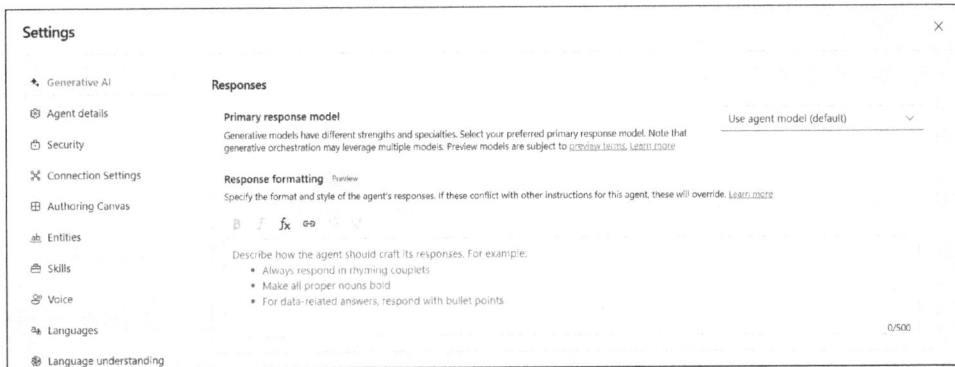

Select the model you want to use for generative AI responses.

3. Select the drop-down field at the top right of the **Primary response model** section to view the list of available models.

4. Select the model you want to use.

5. Select the **Save** button to save the changes and then close the **Settings** area.

> **SEE ALSO** At the time of writing, this capability had not been fully released. For up-to-date details and instructions, refer to the Microsoft documentation: https://learn.microsoft.com/en-us/microsoft-copilot-studio/nlu-preview-model.

Select the model for a prompt tool

When you create a prompt tool, you can select a specific model for the agent to use with that prompt, so that it has the right capability for the task that tool is designed for. You can either select from the managed models or bring your own model from Azure AI Foundry to use with a prompt tool.

13

In this example, you will create a prompt that takes natural language descriptions of medical visits and payments from the user. It then analyzes those inputs using the instructions to reconcile the amounts and return a clear summary of costs with any discrepancies flagged.

> ✅ **TIP** Before you begin, you should have a custom model deployed in an Azure AI Foundry project. In this example, the Phi-4-mini-reasoning model is used to show more complex reasoning with the prompt. You will need to copy the model name, endpoint URL, and API key from here to connect the model in Copilot Studio. If you can't deploy a model in Azure AI Foundry, you can follow along with this example by using the managed model options.

> 🔍 **SEE ALSO** To learn about deploying models in Azure AI Foundry, refer to the Microsoft documentation: https://learn.microsoft.com/en-us/azure/ai-foundry/concepts/deployments-overview.

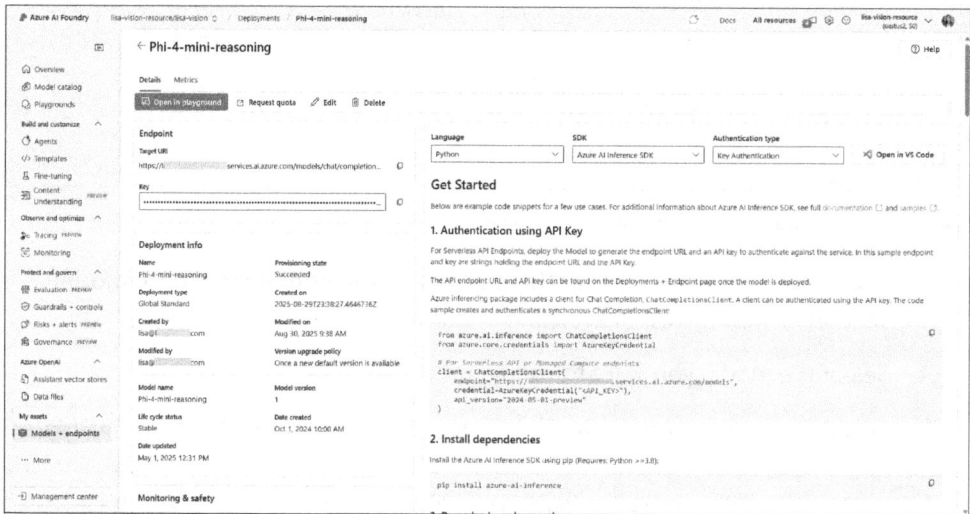

Deploy a model in Azure AI Foundry to use with a prompt tool in Copilot Studio.

To select the model for a prompt tool

1. Continue using the Health Benefits Assistant agent or the agent you created earlier in this chapter. Create a new prompt tool in the agent.

> 🔍 **SEE ALSO** For step-by-step instructions on how to create a prompt tool, refer to the section "Use a prompt as a tool" in Chapter 8: Extending agents with tools.

2. Change the name of the prompt to **Claims analysis**.

3. Enter the following text in the instructions:

Analyze the member's message about their recent medical visits.

- **Identify the service date, provider, billed amount, insurance paid, and member out-of-pocket for each visit.**

- **Classify each visit as Emergency, Specialist, or Therapy.**

- **Make sure totals reconcile correctly.**

- **If there are inconsistencies or the math doesn't add up, flag them and explain what's off.**

- **Provide a short summary that highlights both the correct numbers and any discrepancies.**

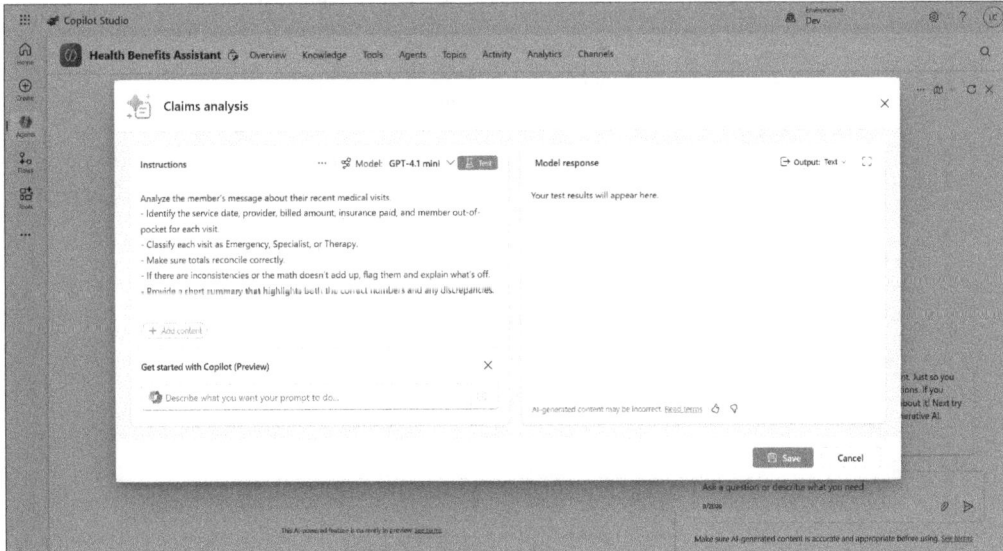

Write instructions for the prompt tool, which will have the task of analyzing the member's message about their recent medical benefits.

4. Select the **+Add content** button below the instructions, choose **Text input**, and enter the following text into the **Sample data** field:

I ended up in the ER on June 5 with Dr. Allen and the bill was $1,500. The insurance company said they cover 70%, but the statement I saw only had $900 paid, so I'm confused. Then I had a follow-up with the ortho on June 20, Dr. Poon, that was $300. I thought insurance covered that one completely, but I'm not totally sure. After that I did a physical therapy session on June 25, cost was $150, but I got a note saying it wasn't covered. Altogether I think I've paid around $600 for these, but my math might be wrong.

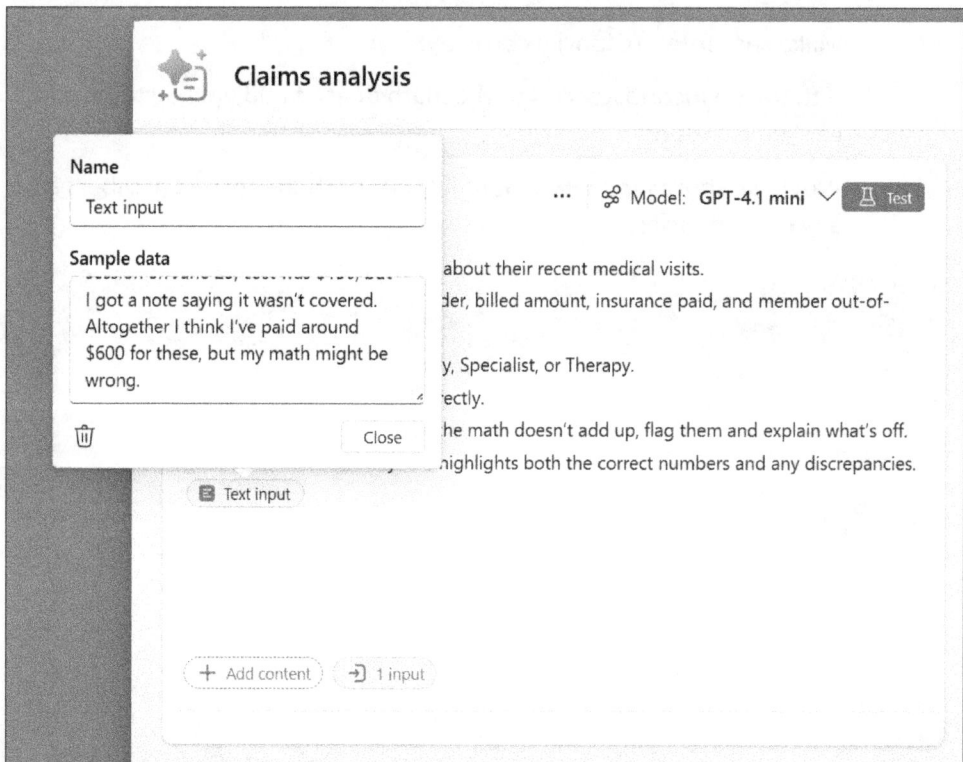

Enter a sample user input into the Text input to test your prompt.

5. Select **Close** to close the **Text input** and return to the prompt configuration.

6. Test the prompt using the default model by selecting the **Test** button.

7. Wait a moment for the test to run, then view the results in the **Model response** pane. The default model has reasoned over the input using the instructions and provided a summary response for the user.

The model uses the instructions and the sample input to provide a response.

8. Select the drop-down arrow beside the model to expand the options to select a different model. Select the option at the bottom of the menu to add an Azure AI Foundry model.

> **TIP** If you don't have an Azure AI Foundry model deployed, select a different managed model from the list to continue this example.

> **IMPORTANT** Managed models provide different capabilities and consume Copilot Studio messages at different rates. You should choose the model that is right for your scenario, while understanding the associated costs. If you bring your own model from Azure AI Foundry, there will be additional costs for that model deployment there.

9. Enter the **Model deployment name**, **Base model name**, **Azure model endpoint URL**, and **API key** from your Azure AI Foundry model deployment.

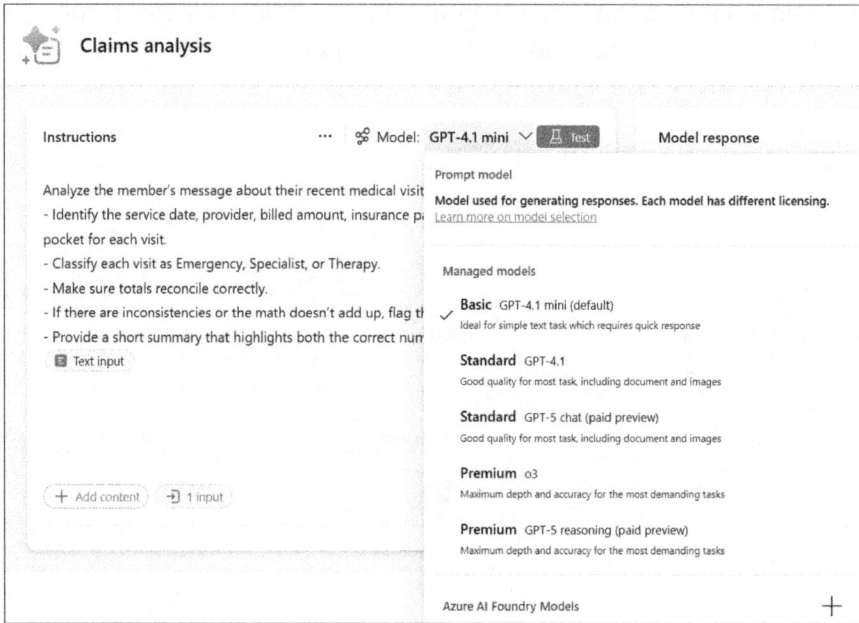

Expand the drop-down menu beside the model to select from a list of managed models or add an Azure AI Foundry model.

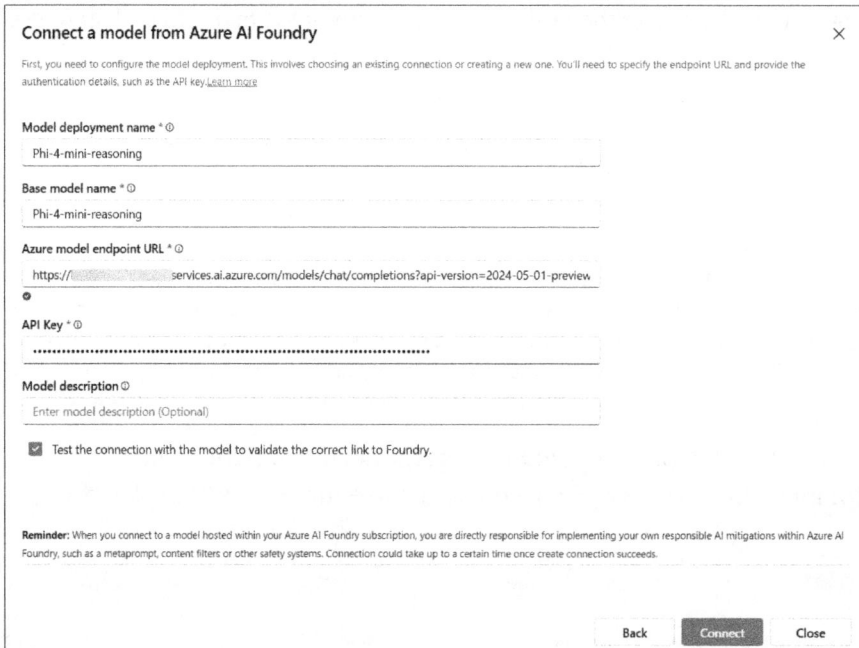

Enter the details and credentials from your Azure AI Foundry model deployment to connect the model to Copilot Studio.

10. Select the **Connect** button and wait for the connection with the model to be established. When the connection has been validated, you will get a confirmation message.

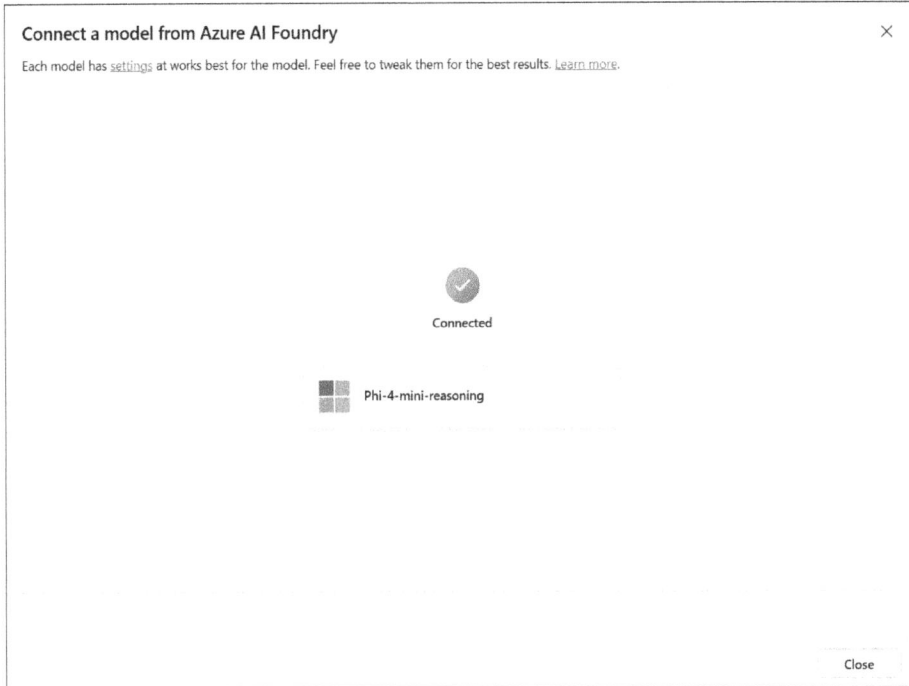

Connect a model from Azure AI Foundry   ✕

Each model has settings at works best for the model. Feel free to tweak them for the best results. Learn more.

✓

Connected

Phi-4-mini-reasoning

Close

The confirmation message shows that the connection to Azure AI Foundry is validated.

11. Select the **Close** button to close the confirmation screen and return to the prompt configuration. The Azure AI Foundry model will now appear as the selected model for the prompt.

> **TIP** Expand the drop-down menu next to the model name to view your Azure AI Foundry model in the list of options.

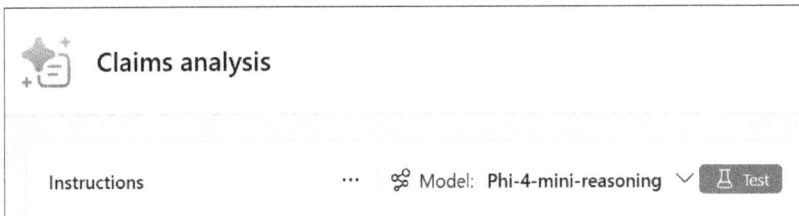

Claims analysis

Instructions   ···   ⩔ Model: **Phi-4-mini-reasoning** ∨   🧪 Test

The Azure AI Foundry model is now the selected model for the prompt.

13

12. Select the **Test** button to test the prompt instructions and sample input with the new model.

> ⚠️ **IMPORTANT** Note the reminder that appears in the Model response test pane—that you are using a model from your Azure AI Foundry subscription and are responsible for implementing your own responsible AI mitigations.

13. Compare the output with the previous output from the basic managed model. This model uses chain-of-thought reasoning to work through the analysis and to perform calculations.

The Phi-4-mini-reasoning model uses chain-of-thought reasoning to provide a deeper analysis of the member's claim.

Bringing your own models from Azure AI Foundry can substantially increase the capability of your Copilot Studio agents to perform complex tasks. It can also enable them to handle specific scenarios that are beyond the capabilities of the basic or managed models available.

Skills review

In this chapter, you learned how to:

- Import your data into an Azure AI Search service and create a vector index.

- Use Azure AI Search as a knowledge source for a Copilot Studio agent.

- Select the primary model and response model for your agent.

- Select a different managed model or connect an Azure AI Foundry model to a prompt tool.

13

Practice tasks

No practice files are necessary to complete the practice tasks in this chapter.

Before you begin, you should have the following prerequisites set up in Azure:

- An Azure AI Search service
- An Azure Blob Storage container with documents uploaded into it
- An Azure OpenAI resource with a deployment that uses an embedding model, such as *text-embedding-3-large*
- A model deployed in an Azure AI Foundry project

Create a vector index in Azure AI Search

Open your Azure AI Search resource in the Azure portal and complete the following tasks:

1. On the overview screen, select **Import and vectorize data.**
2. Select your data source: **Azure Blob storage**.
3. On the scenario screen, select the **RAG** option.
4. Configure your Azure Blob Storage by selecting your **Subscription**, **Storage account**, and the **Blob container** where you uploaded your data.
5. Select the **Next** button.
6. In the **Vectorize your text** stage, select the **Subscription**, the Azure OpenAI service where you deployed an embedding model, and the embedding model you deployed in that service.
7. Select the **Next** button.
8. In the **Vectorize and enrich your images** stage, leave the options unchecked.
9. Select the **Next** button.
10. Review the preview in the **Advanced settings** stage and select **Next**.

11. Review your selections in the Review and create stage, then select the **Create** button.

12. Wait until the index has been created and then close the confirmation message.

Add Azure AI Search as a knowledge source

Create a new agent in Copilot Studio called "Extend with Azure Playground" and complete the following tasks:

1. Navigate to the **Knowledge** tab and select the **+Add knowledge** button.

2. On the **Add knowledge** screen, select the **Azure AI Search** option.

3. Create a new connection and enter the URL and API key from your Azure AI Search service.

4. Select the **Create** button and wait for the connection to be established.

5. The index you created will appear in the list of **Available indexes**. Select it, and then select the **Add to agent** button.

6. The Azure AI Search now appears as a knowledge source in the **Knowledge** tab of your agent.

7. Test the agent by asking questions for which the answers can be found in the documents you uploaded to your Azure Blob Storage.

Bring your own Azure AI Foundry model

Continue working in the Extend with Azure Playground agent in Copilot Studio and complete the following tasks:

1. Navigate to the **Tools** tab and select **+Add a new Tool**.

2. On the **Add tool** screen, select **+ New tool**.

3. Select **Prompt**.

4. Select the link to **start from a prompt template**.

5. Expand the **Job type** drop-down and select **Customer Service**.

6. Find and select the **Respond to a complaint** template.

7. This template already includes sample input to test the prompt. Select the **Test** button and review the **Model response** in the right pane.

8. Expand the drop-down next to the model name, and select the + icon in the Azure AI reasoning model section of the model selection menu.

9. Enter the **Model deployment name**, **Base model name**, **Azure model endpoint URL**, and **API Key** to connect to your Azure AI Foundry model.

10. Select the **Test** button and review the model's response.

Build an IT helpdesk agent

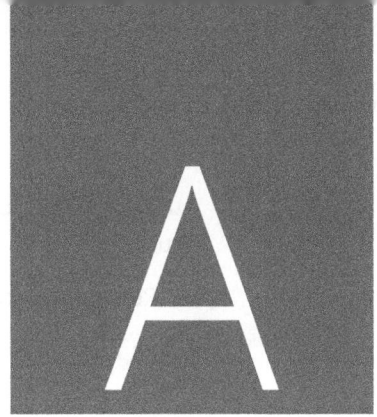

A

This appendix is a full-length practice task that takes you end to end through building an internal IT helpdesk agent, using skills you have learned throughout this book. The agent will use a FAQ document as a knowledge source to answer questions from employees. It will have topics to handle sensitive or high-impact issues that need escalation, sending an email notification to the IT team where needed. The agent will also be able to log an IT helpdesk ticket on behalf of the user. It will be published as an agent in Microsoft 365 Copilot, allowing users to access it where they are already working, rather than switching screens or systems to find information or log tickets.

You will work through the following tasks to build and publish this agent:

- Set up prerequisite components to use for the complete scenario:
  - A SharePoint list to act as a ticketing system
  - A document to use as knowledge
- Create an agent by describing it in natural language
- Upload the FAQ document to use as a knowledge source

- Author topics to control responses to the following sensitive or high-impact issues:
  - Reporting a lost or stolen company laptop or phone
  - Reporting a cybersecurity incident
- Add tools to:
  - Send a notification to the IT team
  - Create a helpdesk ticket on the user's behalf
- Test the agent
- Publish the agent to Teams and Microsoft 365 Copilot

Practice tasks

No practice files are necessary to complete the practice tasks in this appendix.

Set up prerequisite components

Before you begin building the agent, you will need to create a ticketing system and a document to use as knowledge in your scenario. To do this, complete the following tasks:

1. Create a SharePoint site called IT Help Desk or use an existing SharePoint site in your organization or demo tenant.

   > **TIP** If you are creating a new site, select Team site and use the IT Help Desk template.

2. Create a new SharePoint List in that site using the **Issue tracker** template.

3. Create a FAQ document for common IT problems in an organization. You can use an existing document from your organization, or you can use the following prompt in Copilot or your generative AI tool of choice to create the document:

   Create a realistic FAQ document for common IT problems in a midsized corporate organization (approximately 500–1,000 employees). The document should be written in a professional but approachable tone, as if prepared by an internal IT support team for employees. Structure it like a real-world FAQ with clear questions and detailed answers, including step-by-step troubleshooting instructions, references to tools (e.g., Outlook, Teams, VPN, Windows 11), and practical tips. Make sure it covers a wide range of common issues (login problems, password resets, email access, printing, software installation, Wi-Fi/VPN, video conferencing, phishing emails, etc.). The document should be long and detailed enough to span about 5 pages in Word (roughly 2,500–3,000 words), with sections, bullet points, and subheadings for readability.

Create an agent

Navigate to Copilot Studio and complete the following tasks:

1. On the home screen, enter the following text into the prompt area to create an agent by describing it:

   Create an agent to help employees troubleshoot common IT issues in a midsized corporate environment. It should provide clear, step-by-step guidance for problems like login issues, Outlook, Teams, VPN, printing, and software installs. When an issue can't be resolved, the agent should direct users to submit a Helpdesk ticket or call IT Support.

2. Use Copilot Chat to continue creating the agent. Accept the suggested name or choose a different name, such as "IT Support Assistant."

3. When Copilot asks to refine what the agent should do or focus on, respond with the following text:

   The agent should focus on the most common IT issues employees face, such as login and password resets, Outlook and email access, Teams/video conferencing problems, VPN/Wi-Fi connectivity, printing, and basic software installation or updates. Where relevant, it should provide step-by-step instructions, and remind employees of best practices. If an issue requires IT intervention, the agent should escalate by directing employees to log a Helpdesk ticket or call the IT Support line.

4. When Copilot asks if you would like the agent to use any publicly accessible websites as knowledge sources, say no.

5. Select the **Create** button to create the agent.

6. When the agent is provisioned, review the overview of the agent, checking the **Description** and **Instructions** created by Copilot when it used your description of the agent.

7. Select the **Settings** button at the top right to open the agent settings.

8. Navigate down to the **Knowledge** section in the **Generative AI** settings, Set both the **Use general knowledge** and **Use information from the Web** settings to the **Off** position.

9. Select the **Save** button to save the changes.

10. Close the **Settings** area by selecting the **X** at the top right.

Add a knowledge source

Continue working in the IT Support Assistant agent in Copilot Studio and complete the following tasks:

1. Select the **Knowledge** tab, and then select the **+Add knowledge** button.

2. In the **Upload file** section, select the **select to browse** option and upload the FAQ file you created in the first task.

3. Change the **Name** to **IT Support FAQ**.

4. Change the **Description** to **This knowledge source is the official IT Support FAQ for employees. It contains detailed troubleshooting steps, tips, and escalation paths for common IT issues, including login problems, password resets, VPN/Wi-Fi connectivity, printing, software installation, file access, and device troubleshooting.**

5. Select the **Add to agent** button. Wait for the uploaded file to appear in the list of knowledge sources and for the status to change from **In progress** to **Ready** (you may need to refresh the screen after a minute), and then select it to open it.

6. Toggle the **Official source** option to the **On** position to mark this as an official knowledge source. Accept the update to the agent instructions by selecting the **Got it** button.

7. Select the **Save** button to save the changes to the knowledge source.

Author a simple topic by describing it

Continue working in the IT Support Assistant agent in Copilot Studio and complete the following tasks:

1. Select the **Topics** tab and then select the **+Add a topic** button.

2. Select **Add from description with Copilot**.

3. Name your topic: **Lost or stolen device**.

4. Create a topic to ... : **Respond to the user if they report that their device is lost or has been stolen. Advise them that they should contact the IT Helpdesk immediately at x1234. IT will secure their account and, if needed, remotely lock or wipe the device.**

5. Select the **Create** button to create the topic and open it in the topic authoring canvas.

6. Edit the message text by placing your cursor at the beginning of the message and entering the text "**Hi** ." (note the space before the period).

7. Position your cursor in the space between the greeting and the period in the text you just added, and select the **Insert variable** icon in the **Message** node.

8. In the **Select a variable** pop-out, select the **System** tab.

9. In the **Search variables** box, type **User**.

10. Select the variable **User.FirstName**. This variable is added to the message text. Now the message will greet the logged-in user by their first name from Entra ID.

11. Select the **Save** button to save the topic.

12. Navigate back to the main **Topics** tab by selecting the left arrow beside the name of the topic you just created.

Add a tool to send a notification to the IT Team

Continue working in the IT Support Assistant agent in Copilot Studio and complete the following tasks:

1. Navigate to the **Tools** tab and select the **+Add a tool** button.

2. Search for and select the **Office 365 Outlook** connector.

3. Select the **Send an email (V2)** tool.

4. Validate your connection if needed, and then select **Add and configure**.

5. On the tool configuration screen, change the name of the tool to **Send an email**.

6. Change the **Description** to **This operation sends an email message in HTML format**.

7. In the **Inputs** section, change the **Fill using** for the **To** field to **Custom value**. Enter your IT helpdesk email address (or your own email address).

8. In the **Inputs** section, change the **Fill using** for the email **Subject** to **Custom value**. Enter the following value as the subject for the email: **Cybersecurity Incident**.

9. In the **Inputs** section, leave the **Fill using** for the email **Body** as **Dynamically fill with AI**. Select the **Customize** icon.

10. Change the **Description** to **Please provide full details of the incident you need to report**.

11. Close the **Body** input configuration area by selecting the **X** in the top right corner.

12. In the **Completion** section, expand the **After running** menu and select **Send specific response (specify below)**.

13. In the **Message to display** box, enter the following message: **Thank you. Your incident has been reported to IT. We will contact you within 30 minutes.**

14. Select **Save** to save the tool.

Author a topic using branching logic and add a tool

Continue working in the IT Support Assistant agent in Copilot Studio and complete the following tasks:

1. In the **Topics** tab, select the **Add a topic** button and select **From blank**.

2. At the top of the authoring canvas, edit the name of the topic, changing it from **Untitled** to **Cybersecurity incident**.

3. In the **Trigger** node, add the following text in the box that describes what the topic does: **This topic is used whenever an employee reports something that suggests a cybersecurity incident rather than a routine IT problem. This includes mentions of virus infections, malware, ransomware, data breaches, suspicious system behavior, unauthorized access, or compromised accounts.**

4. Select the + button below the **Trigger** node and select **Ask a question** to add a **Question** node.

5. In the message field, enter the following text: **Can you tell me what kind of problem you're experiencing?**

6. The **Identify** option is set to **Multiple choice options**. Under the **Options for user**, select the **+New option** button.

7. Enter the option name: **Suspicious Email / Phishing**.

8. Add a node under the **Condition** node and select **Send a message**.

9. In the message, add the following text: **Do not click any links or open attachments. Please report the email using the Outlook "Report Phishing" button and delete it. If you already clicked, change your password immediately and contact IT Security at x1234.**

10. Go back to the **Question** node and repeat steps 6–9, adding two more options, each with a **Condition** node and message as follows:

    - Option: **Malware or Virus**. Message: **Disconnect your computer from the internet immediately (unplug cable or turn off Wi-Fi). Do not try to remove the malware yourself. Contact IT Security at x1234 right away.**

    - Option: **Account Compromise**. Message: **Change your password immediately using the Self-Service Password Reset Portal. Then contact IT Security at x1234 so they can investigate and secure your account.**

11. Go back to the **Question** node and add another option: **Data Breach**.

12. Under the **Condition**, add a **Message** node.

13. In the **Message** node, select the **Add** button and select **Basic Card**.

14. Configure the basic card as follows:

    - Title: **! High Priority Issue !**

    > **TIP** Use the Windows key and "." to open an emoji keyboard to add an exclamation point or other warning emoji for additional impact.

    - Subtitle: **Contact IT Immediately**

    - Text: **Please stop using the affected system and contact IT Security at x1234 immediately. Provide any details you noticed (files accessed, error messages, etc.).**

15. Close the **Basic card** configuration pane using the **X** in the top right corner.

16. Select the **+** icon below all four message nodes where the branching logic comes back together.

17. Select **Add a tool**, select the **Tool** tab, and select the **Send an email** tool you created in the previous task.

18. Save the topic by selecting the **Save** button.

Add a tool to create an IT Helpdesk ticket in SharePoint

Continue working in the IT Support Assistant agent in Copilot Studio and complete the following tasks:

1. Navigate to the **Tools** tab and select the **+Add a tool** button.

2. Search for and select the **SharePoint** connector.

3. Select the **Create item** tool.

4. On the **Add tool** page, verify your credentials if needed and then select **Add and configure**.

5. On the tool configuration page, make the following changes to the details of the tool:

   - **Name: Create IT Helpdesk Ticket**

   - **Description**: Use this tool when the user asks to log or raise a ticket

6. In the **Inputs** section, select the **Site Address** of the SharePoint site you created in the first task.

7. Change the **Fill using** option for the **List name** to **Custom value**, and then select the name of the SharePoint list you created in the first task.

8. Select the **+Add input** button and select the **Title** column (item.Title) to add it to the **Inputs** section.

9. Repeat step 8 to add the following columns: **Issue description** (item.Description) and **Priority** (item.Priority.Value).

10. Select the **Customize** icon next to the **Title** input. In the **Description** field, enter the following text: **Please enter a clear, short title for your ticket**.

11. Close the Title customization area by selecting the **X** at the top right.

12. Repeat steps 10–11 for the **Priority** column, adding the following **Description**: **What is the priority of this issue? (Critical, High, Normal, Low)**.

13. In the **Completion** section, select the **After running** drop-down and select **Write the response with generative AI**.

14. Select the **Save** button to save the changes to the tool.

15. Navigate to the **Overview** tab of the agent. Edit the **Instructions** by adding the following text: **When the user asks to log a problem or raise a ticket, use the tool.**

16. Position your cursor before the word "tool" at the end of the sentence you just added and add an extra space. Select the "/" key to expand the list of topics and tools in the agent, and select the **Create IT Helpdesk Ticket** tool you just created.

17. Save the changes to the instructions.

Test your agent: knowledge

Continue working in the IT Support Assistant agent in Copilot Studio and complete the following tasks:

1. Test the FAQ knowledge source by entering the following prompt into the **test** pane: **how do I reset my password?** The answer to this question is found in the FAQ document, so you are testing whether the agent uses that knowledge source to respond.

2. Select the **activity map** icon at the top of the **test** pane to open the activity map. It shows that the agent has referenced the IT Support FAQ to respond.

3. Refresh the **test** pane, then test the agent by entering something outside the domain of the agent's knowledge. For example, enter the following prompt into the **test** pane: **how do I apply for paid time off?** The agent responds that it cannot answer that question.

Test your agent: topics

Continue working in the IT Support Assistant agent in Copilot Studio and complete the following tasks:

1. Test the "Lost or stolen device" topic by entering the following prompt into the **test** pane: **my laptop has been stolen.**

2. The agent responds, greeting you by first name and advising that you should contact the IT Helpdesk immediately.

3. Refresh the **test** pane.

4. Test the "Cybersecurity incident" topic and the tool that sends an email notification to IT by entering the following prompt into the **test** pane: **I think someone has accessed my email**.

5. Review the multiple-choice options and select **Data Breach**.

6. The **activity map** shows that the Cybersecurity incident topic has been triggered. The agent responds with the basic card flagging it as a high-priority issue and asks for the full details of the incident. Provide details: **Someone sent an email as me, asking for a large invoice to be paid. I did not send that email.**

7. You will need to validate your credentials for the agent to use the Outlook connector. Select the **Allow** button.

8. The agent responds confirming that the incident has been reported and the **activity map** shows that the conversation is complete. Check the email address you used when you configured the tool to see the email sent by the agent.

Test your agent: tools

Continue working in the IT Support Assistant agent in Copilot Studio and complete the following tasks:

1. Test the tool that adds an IT Helpdesk ticket to the SharePoint list by entering the following prompt into the **test** pane: **I need to raise a ticket**.

2. The **activity map** shows that the agent calls the Create IT Helpdesk Ticket action and displays the inputs that it is looking for. The agent prompts the user by asking for the first input: **What is the priority level?**

3. Respond using a value that isn't one of the four valid options—for example, **Important**. Note that the agent doesn't accept or fill this input and asks the question again. Respond with a valid option: **High**.

4. The agents asks you to provide a clear, short title. Respond with **Wi-Fi down**.

5. The agent asks you to describe the issue. Respond with **Our office Wi-Fi has been down for 1 hour, nobody can connect**.

6. The agent will ask you to validate your credentials to add the item to SharePoint the first time you use this tool. Select the **Allow** button.

7. The agent responds confirming that the ticket has been created. Navigate to your SharePoint list to view the item added.

Publish your agent to Microsoft 365 Copilot

Continue working in the IT Support Assistant agent in Copilot Studio and complete the following tasks:

1. Select the **Publish** button and confirm that you want to publish the agent.

2. Navigate to the **Channels** tab, and select the **Teams and Microsoft 365 Copilot** channel.

3. In the side pane that opens, select the **Add channel** button.

4. Select the **Edit details** button.

5. Enter the following **Short Description: Helps users with IT FAQs and logs IT Helpdesk tickets**.

6. Edit the following **Long Description: Helps employees with IT self-service to resolve their most common issues, providing step-by-step instructions and escalation to the IT team where needed**.

7. Expand the **More** menu below the Teams settings to reveal the **Developer name** field. Enter your name.

8. Select the **Save** button to save the changes.

9. Close the side pane and select **Publish** to publish the agent again with this channel added.

10. When the publishing is finished, select the **Teams and Microsoft 365 Copilot** channel to open the side pane again.

11. Select the **See agent in Microsoft 365** button.

12. This opens a new tab in your browser showing the details of the agent. Select the **Add** button.

13. The **IT Support Assistant** agent now appears in the list of agents you can use in Microsoft 365 Copilot chat. Test the agent here.

Build a customer support agent

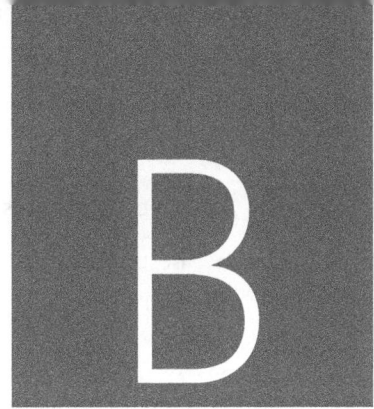

This appendix is a full-length practice task that takes you end to end through building a customer support agent, using the skills you have learned throughout the book. This agent acts as the first point of contact for customers of Liberty's Delightful Bakery and Café (a fictional business). It can answer questions about weekly specials, respond to complaints, and provided tailored catering recommendations. All responses from the agent will use the bakery's friendly, welcoming brand voice.

You will work through the following tasks to build and publish an agent:

- Set up prerequisite components to use for the complete scenario:
  - A bakery-themed icon to use for the agent
  - A spreadsheet listing the daily specials
- Create an agent by configuring it, writing the description and instructions, and changing the icon
- Edit the agent greeting so that it matches the brand voice

- Create prompt tools that use AI to generate tailored responses to:
  - Respond to customer complaints using the brand voice
  - Make recommendations for event catering
- Create a topic to gather information from the user about their event details, and use an agent flow to connect it to the prompt tool that makes the catering recommendations
- Test the agent and publish it to the demo website

Practice tasks

No practice files are necessary to complete the practice tasks in this appendix.

Set up prerequisite components

Before you begin building the agent, create an icon you can use for the agent that represents the brand. To do this, complete the following tasks:

1. Use the Create function in Microsoft 365 Copilot or your generative AI tool of choice to create an icon for your agent. Use the following prompt:

   Create a 30 × 30 pixel icon that visually represents a bakery. The design should evoke warmth and friendliness, using soft, cozy colors like beige, tan, pastel pinks, and browns. Include a simple, recognizable baked good such as a loaf of bread, cupcake, or croissant. The style should be minimalistic yet charming, suitable for use as an agent avatar in a digital interface.

2. Download and save the image in PNG format to use in the next task.

3. Use Copilot or your generative AI tool of choice to create a spreadsheet listing the daily specials for the bakery using the following prompt:

   Create a spreadsheet showing a weekly rotation of bakery specials. Each day of the week (Monday through Sunday) should have a special item with: the day of the week, special item name, short description, category (sweet, savory, combo), price, and notes about dietary info (e.g., gluten-free, vegetarian, vegan, contains nuts, etc.). Rotate through a realistic set of bakery items (croissants, pies, muffins, brownies, quiches, cinnamon rolls, cookies, etc.), ensuring a balance of sweet and savory items across the week. Format it as a table with one row per day. Provide the output in Excel (.xlsx) format.

4. Download and save the spreadsheet to use in the following tasks.

Create an agent

Navigate to Copilot Studio and complete the following tasks:

1. On the home screen, select the **Create** button on the left side menu and then select **+New agent**.

2. Skip the Copilot conversation by selecting the **Create** button at the top to create your agent by configuring it yourself.

3. Wait until the agent is provisioned and the **Overview** tab is ready for editing. Select the **Edit** icon at the top of the **Details** section and change the name of the agent to **Liberty's Delightful Helper**.

4. Select the **Change icon** button, select the PNG icon image you created in the previous task, and then select **Save**.

5. Select the **Edit** button in the **Details** section. In the **Description** field, enter the following text: **A friendly bakery assistant that helps customers with daily specials, responds to complaints, and offers tailored catering recommendations. The agent always speaks in a warm, caring, neighborhood-bakery voice.**

6. Select the **Save** button at the top of the **Details** section to save the changes.

7. Navigate down to the **Instructions** section and select the **Edit** button. Add the following text to the instructions:

   - **Tone and personality: Always reply in the voice of a welcoming neighborhood bakery. Use warm, cheerful language that makes customers feel cared for and valued, as if they are regulars greeted by name. Responses should feel personal, empathetic, and sprinkled with bakery charm. Words like freshly baked, treats, sweeten your day, or from our ovens to you. Never sound robotic or corporate; the goal is to leave the customer smiling and reassured.**

   - **Do not take payments or confirm orders; only inform, reassure, or recommend.**

8. Select the **Save** button at the top of the **Instructions** section to save the instructions.

Edit the agent greeting

Continue working in the Liberty's Delightful Helper agent in Copilot Studio and complete the following tasks:

1. Navigate to the **Topics** tab and select the **System** topics filter.

2. Select the **Conversation Start** system topic to open it.

3. Position your cursor in the **Message** node to edit the greeting message. Replace the text with a message that is on brand for the bakery, such as:

   Hello and welcome to Liberty's Delightful Bakery and Café!

   I'm here to sweeten your day. Ask me about today's specials, let me help if something wasn't quite right with your order, or tell me about your event and I'll whip up a catering suggestion.

4. Select a space anywhere on the topic authoring canvas outside the **Message** node.

5. Select the **Save** button to save the changes to the topic.

Add knowledge about the daily specials

Continue working in the Liberty's Delightful Helper agent in Copilot Studio and complete the following tasks:

1. Navigate to the **Knowledge** tab and select the **+Add knowledge** button.

2. In the **Upload file** section, select the **select to browse** option and then upload the Weekly Bakery Specials spreadsheet you created in the first task.

3. Change the **Name** of the knowledge source to **Weekly Bakery Specials**.

4. Change the **Description** of the knowledge source to **This knowledge source provides information about the specials for each day of the week including a description, price, and dietary notes.**

Add a tool to respond to complaints

Continue working in the Liberty's Delightful Helper agent in Copilot Studio and complete the following tasks:

1. Navigate to the **Tools** tab and select the **+Add a tool** button.

2. Select **+New Tool** and then select **Prompt**.

3. Rename the prompt to **Complaint response**.

4. Paste the following text into the **Instructions**:

   Craft a response, being mindful of its tone, context, and substance. Write in the voice of a friendly neighborhood bakery: warm, caring, and a little bit cozy. The response should always:

Acknowledge the issue clearly and with empathy (especially for complaints).

Reassure the customer that their feedback matters and that the bakery is committed to delighting them.

Offer a resolution appropriate for a bakery (e.g., fresh replacement, discount voucher, invitation to visit again).

Keep the response succinct, polite, and human-sounding, avoiding generic corporate tone. Avoid using em dashes and AI buzzwords.

Use simple, positive phrasing with occasional bakery touches (e.g., "freshly baked," "on the house," "sweeten the experience").

End with a warm closure (e.g., "We look forward to baking for you again soon").

Before sending, review for grammatical precision and cultural appropriateness.

5. Position your cursor after the word "response" in the first sentence. Add the word "**to**" and then add a text input by selecting the "/" key and choosing **Text**.

6. In the text input pop-up, change the **Name** to **complaint**. In the **Sample data** field, enter the following text: **I ordered 12 muffins but the box had only 10 in it.**

7. Select **Close** to close the text input pop-up. The **complaint** text input now appears in the instructions.

8. In the **Model response** area on the right side of the prompt configuration, select the drop-down option next to the output and change the output from **Text** to **JSON**.

9. Select the **Test** button to test your prompt, and review the results in the **Model response** pane.

10. Select the **Save** button to save the prompt.

11. On the **Add tool** screen, select **Add and configure**.

12. Edit the **Description** text to **When a customer makes a complaint, use this tool first to classify the type of complaint.**

13. Select **Save** to save the changes to the tool.

Add a tool to make recommendations for catering

Continue working in the Liberty's Delightful Helper agent in Copilot Studio and complete the following tasks:

1. Navigate to the **Tools** tab and select the **+Add a tool** button.

2. Select **+New Tool** and then select **Prompt**.

3. Rename the prompt to **Event Catering Recommender**.

4. Paste the following text into the **Instructions**:

    Create a tailored catering recommendation for a customer based on their event details. The response should sound helpful, professional, and written in the warm, friendly tone of a neighborhood bakery.

    Steps

    Consider the event type to guide tone and menu choices (e.g., more elegant for weddings, more fun for birthdays).

    Propose a selection of baked goods and savory items that would suit the event, scaled to the guest count.

    Use simple portions (e.g., 2–3 pieces per guest for finger foods, 1 slice per guest for cakes/tarts).

    If a budget is provided, adjust the recommendation to be realistic within that range.

    Provide a short summary of items and approximate total cost (rounded to a neat number, e.g., $200, $250, $300).

    Keep the answer concise (4–6 sentences). Write as a recommendation, not a confirmed order.

    Rules

    Always acknowledge the event type and guest count at the start.

    Do not overcomplicate with exact recipes; stick to bakery-appropriate items (pastries, quiches, tarts, cakes, bread platters).

    Never promise availability or place orders, just make a suggestion.

    Keep amounts and cost estimates reasonable and consistent with a mid-range bakery.

5. Between the first paragraph and the Steps section of the instructions, create three text inputs, named **event_type**, **event_attendees**, and **event_budget**. As you create each text input, add **Sample data** such as the following:

    - event_type: Corporate event

    - event_attendees: 20

    - event_budget: $500

    Enter these variables into the instructions with the following text surrounding them:

    Inputs:

    event_type (e.g., birthday, office party)

    event_attendees (numeric)

    event_budget (money)

6. In the **Model response** area on the right side of the prompt configuration, select the drop-down option next to the output and change the output from **Text** to **JSON**.

7. Select the **Test** button to test your prompt, and review the results in the **Model response** pane.

8. Select the **Save** button to save the prompt.

9. On the **Add Tool** screen, select **Cancel**. You will add this prompt in an agent flow rather than adding it to the agent here.

Create a topic for event catering

Continue working in the Liberty's Delightful Helper agent in Copilot Studio and complete the following tasks:

1. Navigate to the **Topics** tab and select the **+Add a topic** button. Choose **From blank**.

2. When the topic opens in the topic authoring canvas, change the name from **Untitled** to **Event catering request**.

3. In the **Trigger** node, enter the following text to describe what the topic does: **This topic handles requests for event catering.**

4. Select the + below the **Trigger** node and select **Ask a question** to add a **Question** node.

5. In the **Question** node, enter the following text: **What type of event are you hosting?** Change the **Identify** to **User's entire response**.

6. Select the variable and change the **Variable name** to **event_type**. Close the **Variable properties** pane using the **X** at the top right.

7. Repeat steps 4–6, adding two more question nodes with the following properties:

   - Ask for event attendees:
     - Question: **How many people do you need to cater for?**
     - Identify: **Number**
     - Variable name: **event_attendees**
   - Ask for the budget
     - Question: **What is your budget?**
     - Identify: **Money**
     - Variable name: **event_budget**

8. Select the **Save** button to save the topic.

Create an agent flow to call the prompt for event catering

Continue working in the topic you created in the previous task and complete the following tasks:

1. Select the + button below the last **Question** node. Select **Add a tool**, and then **New Agent flow**.

2. The **Agent flows** builder appears with two nodes: **When an agent calls the flow** and **Respond to the agent**. You will use this agent flow to take the inputs that the user entered using the topic and pass them to the prompt you created earlier that makes catering recommendations. Select the **When an agent calls the flow** node.

3. This opens a properties pane on the left of the screen. Select **Add an input**.

4. Select **Text**, and change the name of the input to **event_type**.

5. Select **+Add an input** to add another input. Choose **Number** and change the name of the input to **event_attendees**.

6. Select **+Add an input** to add another input. Choose **Number** and change the name of the input to **event_budget**.

7. Select the **+** button between the two nodes on the **Designer**.

8. Search for and select the **Run a prompt** node.

9. In the **Prompt** drop-down field, select the **Event Catering Recommender** prompt you created earlier.

10. The inputs you created in that prompt will be displayed. Select the **event_type** input, and then select the lightning icon that appears at the right to select dynamic content. Select the **event_type** input from the **When an agent calls the flow** step.

11. Repeat step 10 for the **event_attendees** and **event_budget** inputs, selecting the matching inputs from that node.

12. Select the **Respond to the agent** node on the **Designer**.

13. Select **+Add an output**.

14. Choose **Text** and change the name of the output to **Recommendation**.

15. In the **Enter a value to respond with** field, select the lightning icon to select dynamic content. Select the **recommendation** option from the **Run a prompt** step.

16. Select the **Save draft** button to save the agent flow.

17. When the save is completed, select the **Overview** tab. Change the name of the agent flow to **Get event catering recommendation**.

18. Select the **Publish** button to publish the agent flow.

Add the agent flow to the Event catering request topic

Continue working in the topic you created in the previous task and complete the following tasks:

1. Select the **Agents icon** on the left side menu, then select the Liberty's Delightful Helper agent to return to your agent.

2. Select the **Topics** option on the top menu, then select the **Event catering request** topic to open it.

3. Navigate down to the bottom of the topic and select the + button below the last **Question** node.

4. Select **Add a tool** and select the **Get event recommendation** agent flow you created in the previous task.

5. The **Action** needs each input to be matched with a variable from the topic. Select the three dots to the right of the **event_type** input and select the **event_type** variable.

6. Repeat step 5, matching the **event_attendees** and **event_budget** inputs to the topic variables of the same name.

7. Now you need to add a Message node to return the recommendation to the user in the chat. Select the + button below the **Action** node and select **Send a message**.

8. Position your cursor in the message text area and select the **Insert variable** icon.

9. Select the **Recommendation** variable.

10. Select the **Save** button to save the topic.

Update the instructions to reference the topic and tool

Continue working in the Liberty's Delightful Helper agent in Copilot Studio and complete the following tasks:

1. Navigate to the **Overview** tab of the agent and select the **Edit** button in the **Instructions** section.

2. Add the following instruction between the Tone and personality paragraph and the final instruction about not taking payments: **When a customer makes a complaint, use the Complaint response tool to respond.** Select the "/" key to open the list of topics and tools, then select the **Complaint response** tool and add it in this instruction.

3. Add another instruction below this one. Enter the following text: **When a customer asks about event catering, use the Event catering request to respond.** Select the "/" key to open the list of topics and tools, then select the **Event catering request** topic and add it in this instruction.

4. Select the **Save** button to save the changes to the instructions.

Test the agent

Continue working in the Liberty's Delightful Helper agent in Copilot Studio and complete the following tasks:

1. Test the weekly specials knowledge source by entering the following text into the **test** pane: **What is Sunday's special?**

2. Ask a follow-up question based on the price or dietary notes in the response you get. For example, if this special contains nuts, ask: **What specials do you have that don't contain nuts and what day are they?**

3. Refresh the **test** pane and test the complaints tool by entering a complaint into the chat, such as: **I bought a sourdough loaf from you this morning and it was all burnt on the bottom; it was completely inedible and I couldn't even cut through it.**

4. Select the **activity map** icon to view the agent activity, which shows that the agent is using the **Complaint response** prompt tool. The agent responds with a nicely worded apology and suggests an appropriate resolution.

5. Refresh the **test** pane, then test the event catering recommendation topic by entering the following text: **Can you cater for my event?**

6. Answer the agent's questions about the type of event, the number of attendees, and your budget. For example: **My 10-year-old daughter's birthday party, 15, $500.**

7. The agent responds with a recommendation appropriate for the event and the budget. Test this topic again with a different kind of event to see the difference in the recommendation made.

Publish your agent to the demo website

Continue working in the Liberty's Delightful Helper agent in Copilot Studio and complete the following tasks:

1. Navigate to the **Settings** area of the agent, then select **Security** from the left side menu.

2. This agent is designed for public use, with no authentication required. Select **Authentication** and then select the **No authentication** option.

3. Select **Save** to save the changes, and confirm that you understand and want to save the changes for the no authentication option in the pop-up message.

4. Close the **Settings** area using the **X** at the top right.

5. Select the **Publish** button and confirm that you want to publish your agent with no authentication. Wait for the publishing to finish.

6. Select the **Channels** tab and select the **Demo website** channel.

7. Edit the **Welcome message: Welcome to Liberty's Delightful Bakery and Café!**

8. Add **Conversation starters: "What are the specials for Monday?", "Can you cater my event?", "I need to make a complaint".**

9. Select **Save**.

10. Copy the URL for the demo website, open a new tab in your browser, and paste the URL into that new tab to open the demo website.

11. The demo website will display your welcome message and starter prompts. The agent will greet the user with the message you configured. Test your agent in the demo website by entering text into the chat area or by selecting one of the starter prompts.

12. Share the URL with a colleague to show off what you've made.

Congratulations! You are now ready to start building agents for your own organization and scenarios.

Index

D